Studies in Economic History

Series Editor

Tetsuji Okazaki, Faculty of Economics, The University of Tokyo, Bunkyo-ku, Tokyo, Japan

Aims and Scope

This series from Springer provides a platform for works in economic history that truly integrate economics and history. Books on a wide range of related topics are welcomed and encouraged, including those in macro-economic history, financial history, labor history, industrial history, agricultural history, the history of institutions and organizations, spatial economic history, law and economic history, political economic history, historical demography, and environmental history.

Economic history studies have greatly developed over the past several decades through application of economics and econometrics. Particularly in recent years, a variety of new economic theories and sophisticated econometric techniques—including game theory, spatial economics, and generalized method of moment (GMM)—have been introduced for the great benefit of economic historians and the research community.

At the same time, a good economic history study should contribute more than just an application of economics and econometrics to past data. It raises novel research questions, proposes a new view of history, and/or provides rich documentation. This series is intended to integrate data analysis, close examination of archival works, and application of theoretical frameworks to offer new insights and even provide opportunities to rethink theories.

The purview of this new Springer series is truly global, encompassing all nations and areas of the world as well as all eras from ancient times to the present. The editorial board, who are internationally renowned leaders among economic historians, carefully evaluate and judge each manuscript, referring to reports from expert reviewers. The series publishes contributions by university professors and others well established in the academic community, as well as work deemed to be of equivalent merit.

All books and chapters in the Studies in Economic History book series are indexed in Scopus.

More information about this series at http://www.springer.com/series/13279

Juro Teranishi

Culture and Institutions in the Economic Growth of Japan

Springer

Juro Teranishi
Professor Emeritus
Hitotsubashi University
Kunitachi, Tokyo, Japan

ISSN 2364-1797 ISSN 2364-1800 (electronic)
Studies in Economic History
ISBN 978-4-431-55626-8 ISBN 978-4-431-55627-5 (eBook)
https://doi.org/10.1007/978-4-431-55627-5

This Springer imprint is published by the registered company Springer Japan KK part of Springer Nature.
The registered company address is: Shiroyama Trust Tower, 4-3-1 Toranomon, Minato-ku, Tokyo 105-6005, Japan

To the late professors Fujino Shozaburo, Nakamura Takafusa and Uzawa Hirofumi.

To my friends Fukuda Shin'ichi, Inoki Takenori, Hugh Patrick and the late Royama Shoichi.

Preface

As globalization proceeds, the institutions of countries have increased similarity with each other, partly owing to the modernization led by Occidental capitalism and partly to the institutional competition thereafter. Reflecting the homogenization of institutions, culture related to economic behavior has also shown significant convergence in order to facilitate international transactions and interactions. In view of the recent difficulties in policy coordination related to global issues, however, it seems that the internalized part of culture, both beliefs and values, remains substantially different between countries in various geographical, ethnic and religious conditions and with diverse historical backgrounds.

Claiming that economic variables that have been regarded as causes of economic growth, such as technological progress, the accumulation of physical and human capital and economy of scale, are not real causes but only phenomena of economic growth, Douglas North has maintained that the fundamental determinants of economic performance and growth are institutions and that culture plays only a secondary and subsidiary role. Institutions, defined as human-devised rules of the game, such as regulations and laws, are major and fundamental actors that cause growth through structuring and ordering the market mechanisms and coordinating the incentives of economic agents. If we follow North's assertion, the aforementioned diversity in internalized culture does not matter for economic performance. This book claims, however, that not only institutions but also the internalized culture, defined as the historically transmitted beliefs and values specific to each country, is also indispensable as a fundamental determinant of economic performance. Culture was the main factor in some countries for structuring and ordering the markets and coordinating incentives, through bringing about conventions and establishing the norms of behavior of individuals. Japan, before the Meiji Restoration in the mid-nineteenth century, is a typical case. It seems that North's emphasis on institutions is not a balanced view. Both internalized culture and institutions could evolve autonomously and be responsible for bringing about workable and efficient market order: institutions mainly by way of providing constraints on individual behavior and culture mainly through giving rise to conventions and the standards of conduct followed by individuals. This book contends, further, that, through influencing the cost of developing institutions and culture, the internalized part of culture is closely related to the choice by which a country chooses among the alternatives of institutions, culture, or some mix of both to structure and order markets. We will try to construct a coherent model to explain the dynamics of the evolution of culture and its interaction with institutions covering the thirteenth to twentieth-century Japan.

In our model, culture is composed of two parts, both of which are composed of beliefs and values: the behavioral part and the internalized part. The behavioral part of culture, behavioral beliefs and values, is in charge of daily interactions between individuals and social groups in the coordination of market behavior. Game theoretic interactions of individuals are a typical representation of the working of the behavioral part of culture. Internalized beliefs are related to the structures and details of the world that individuals experience, and internalized values are related to the criteria of rational behavior such as cognitive, ethical and aesthetic values. The basic mode of the working of the behavioral part of culture is dependent on the internalized part of culture. In addition, the relative costs of establishing culture and institutions in a country are mainly influenced by the internalized culture. Each individual is assumed to develop a mental model to decipher and evaluate his environment, the world he experiences, and to express his opinion about the desirable method of structuring and ordering markets and shaping incentives. We believe the relative costs are dependent on the easiness of summarizing the opinions of individuals and, hence, on the content of internalized beliefs. The costs of establishing institutions were low in the Occident, where the internalized belief about the experienced world was based on the notion of the public, which was more or less homogeneous among individuals; while in Japan, where the internalized belief was composed of others nearby, the membership of which differs significantly among individuals, the cost was high.

In Japan before the Meiji Restoration in the mid-nineteenth century, individuals were mainly interested in the interaction with others nearby, and there was scarcely any notion of the public and society as a whole in the internalized beliefs of individuals, partly owing to the strong concerns with the accumulation of karma through interaction with others nearby in the imaginary concept of transmigration in Buddhism. Moreover, concerns with others nearby was especially strong in Japan owing to historical experience. Religious reform in Japan took place in the midst of the acceleration of the marketization of the economy when the ancient centralized economic system began to decline, so practice simplification promoted by the reform induced the behavior to seek religious merits for enlightenment in occupational activities. Individuals were motivated to be distinguished in their occupational activities, so that occupational specialization and the social division of labor were accelerated further. Owing to this sanctification of occupational behavior, interaction with others nearby came to have a significant influence on the internalized view of individuals.

Because the membership of the group of others nearby differs significantly among individuals, the establishment of efficient institutions for ordering and coordinating market conduct through summarizing the diverse opinions in society was very costly, so that structuring and ordering the market economy was mainly carried out by culture, especially ethics, in pre-Meiji Restoration Japan through establishing conventions of conduct and standardization of conduct. Ethics were purposefully developed and disseminated by the government and elites, such as private intellectuals and the samurai, during the Tokugawa era in the seventeenth to mid-nineteenth centuries. Conventions of conduct were agreed upon within a small group, the norms of group interaction were established among groups and, further, the chain relationships between groups expanded gradually onto the macro level. In the Occident, where there was the religion-related notion of the public and of humans created by the omnipotent God as well as collective intentionality among individuals in the form of participation and cooperation in societal activities in the internalized culture of individuals, it was less costly to establish institutions that could bind constituents. Individuals were ready to gather, or ready to imagine getting together in one place as in the models of the social contract theory and could agree upon rules all at once at the macro level.

It is important to note that the difference of costs is caused by the easiness of the convergence of mental models, the representation of internalized culture at the individual level, through interaction among individuals. In the Occident, the mental model is mainly composed of the concept of the public, which was commonly held among individuals by and large, while in Japan the mental model was mainly composed of others nearby in the imaginary process of transmigration, the membership of which differed considerably among individuals. The difference in the content of mental models explains the degree of easiness of sharing of mental models, hence level of collective intentionality at individual level, giving rise to differences in costs to establish institutions between Japan and the Occident. In Japan, where content of the mental models among individuals differ significantly, the sharing of mental models is not easy, so that cost of establishing institution is high, compared with the Occident.

While the economic development of the Occident was due largely to the development of industrial technology nurtured under the development of various institutional devices to coordinate activities, the economic growth of Japan during the Tokugawa era was caused by the decrease in transaction costs in commercial activities owing to the standardization of conduct nurtured through the purposive development of culture and to the effort levels of small producers enhanced by religious motivation. The development of industrial technology in the Occident and the transaction-cost effect of ethics in Japan was also related to the pattern of the internalized value of culture. In the Occident, cognitive values have gained importance over time, and in Japan ethical values became dominant toward the early modern period. This explains the importance of ethical development in Japanese history and of the development of cognitive sciences in the Occident. High respect for ethical values explains the importance of the role of culture in ordering transactions in Japan, and high respect for cognitive values seems to be responsible for the importance of institutions related to the development of industrial technology. While internalized beliefs play a pivotal role in the determination of costs of establishing institutions, internalized value affects the pattern of growth through the choice between cognitive and ethnic values.

This book is a preliminary attempt to give a coherent explanation of the socio-economic dynamics of Japan from the thirteenth to the twentieth century by means of the evolution of internalized culture and the role of culture in ordering the markets.

North denied the active role of culture in ordering the markets on the ground that culture is too persistent to be changed operationally and that change in culture is difficult to be managed purposefully. Both conditions do not apply to Japan before the Meiji Restoration. During the Tokugawa era, the government led the process of working on culture for the purpose of ordering society and established new ethical codes suitable for the stability of the socio-economy. On the other hand, institutions in Japan before the Meiji Restoration were substantially inefficient operationally owing to the conflicts in the value system between the two governments, the aristocratic government based on the imperial court and the samurai governments, as well as to the conflicts between feudalistic rules and Buddhist-related behavioral conventions and values. Moreover, institutions were seriously persistent despite their inefficiency due to the interest group activities of governments. The samurai government of the Tokugawa era did not care about any economic inefficiency caused by the institutional devises to defend itself from antagonistic powers.

After the Meiji Restoration, Occidental institutions and industrial technology rapidly entered Japan, and the Japanese energetically absorbed the Occidental cultural system crystalized in enlightenment culture. The struggle of the Meiji leaders to establish national integrity and spirit was an attempt to adapt imported Occidental institutions to the traditional internalized culture and to maintain the merits of historical tradition as far as possible. While their policies were generally successful, the policy to establish a surrogate or substitute for the concept of the public, *kokutai* (national polity), was not—the concept of the *kokutai* was one of the reasons for the rise of militarism during the 1930s. It was a policy to change the historically inherited internalized culture by establishing a surrogate of the Occidental concept of the public by means of institutional devices. In view of the persistence of culture, such a policy was destined to fail. It is difficult to believe that the Meiji leaders were so ignorant that they were unable to understand the persistence of the internalized part of the mental models, so we must conclude that, since international tensions in early Meiji Japan were so serious, they adopted the policy as a second-best policy based on bounded rationality. We believe that, despite the attempt by the Meiji leaders, the internalized culture nurtured historically is still living deeply in the mindset of the Japanese. It is not easy to implement the fusion or substitution of the traditional internalized culture with any 'advanced' culture of foreign countries. We must be more cautious and serious in this regard in view of the failure of the Meiji leaders. It seems most important to find a way for the cooperation and coexistence of both cultures on the basis of deep understanding and mutual respect. Competition and the eventual convergence of institutions and technology as well as the behavioral part of culture are essential for the efficiency of the global economy, while the diversity of and respect for the internalized culture of countries seems to be indispensable for the harmonious development of global cooperation and the maintenance of the creativity of humans in the long run.

Not only institutions but also culture matters in the ordering of the markets and economic behavior. Under the condition of the homogenization of institutions in the globalized economy and the persistence of cultural factors indigenous in each country, it is the institutional–cultural mix that must be investigated. The convergence of institutions in the global economy does not necessarily mean the homogenization of the method of structuring and ordering markets. Differences in culture influence the economic performance of countries either through directly affecting the working of the markets or through changing the importance of given institutions in ordering the markets. The degree of mixture between historically inherited culture and globalized institutions is determined by the internalized part of culture of each country.

It seems that various phenomena of disharmony in the global economy nowadays are rooted in the differences in the institutional–cultural mix between countries. To cope with urgent issues related to global economic coordination and the provision of international public goods, we need to face the difficult problem of how to harmonize the diverse institutional–cultural mix of countries. It is necessary to incorporate the structure of the internalized part of culture into the study of globalization. This book, concerned with an investigation of the long-term evolution of the internalized part of culture in Japan, was partly motivated to deliberate on the meaning of the Japanese institutional–cultural mix in the global economy.

Kunitachi, Japan Juro Teranishi

Contents

About the Author

Juro Teranishi is a professor emeritus of Hitotsubashi University. From 1970 through 2006, he was a professor at the Institute of Economic Research of Hitotsubashi University and a visiting professor at Yale University from 1976 to 1978, and at the Australian National University in 1985 and 1986. He also served as an adviser to the Institute of Monetary and Economic Studies of the Bank of Japan, as a counselor of the Association of Economics of The University of Tokyo, and as an adviser to the Bureau of High-Level Education of the Ministry of Education and Science. He was on the editorial board of the *Pacific-Basin Finance Journal*, of *Oxford Development Studies*, and of *The Developing Economies*. Among the books he has edited are *The Japanese Experience of Economic Reforms* (St. Martin's and Macmillan Press, 1993) and *Designing Financial Systems in East Asia and Japan* (Routledge Curzon, 2004).

Glossary[1]

bakufu	Samurai government
***bakuhan* system**	Polity composed of the Tokugawa *bakufu* and *han*
bonnō	Earthly desire and passion, attachment to life
bunkoku-hō	**Daimyo domain law**
bushi	**Samurai**
chingo-kokka	Religious protection of the state
chōnin	**City dwellers** (merchants and artisans)
daimyo	Regional feudal lord
daisen-nō	**Payment of tax by farmers in cash**
dogō	**Indigenous samurai lords (leaders)**
ekō	**Merit transfer**
en	Interpersonal relationship (largely determined by *engi* in the concept of *kū*)
engi	Arising from causation and relationship
fudai	**Hereditary vassal**
gekokujyō	Social upheaval where those below overcome those above
gō	**Karma**
gokenin	**Housemen**
gyōkai-dantai	**Industrial association**
han	*Daimyo* domain (in the Tokugawa era)
hanbatsu	Oligarchy in the Meiji government in which political power was monopolized by the winning coalition, the Satsuma and Chōshū
hansatsu	Local paper currency (issued by *han*)
honjyo-ryōke	Owners of manor (usually aristocrats or big temples and shrines)

[1]Words in **bold** are used in the main text. Interpretation are given at least for the first appearance in each chapter, either in English or Japanese. Part of the interpretation (Japanese into English) is adapted from the glossary in Totman C (1981) *Japan before Perry; a short history*. University of California Press, Berkeley, Los Angeles and London.

ichien-shihai	**Integrated control of territory**
ie	House
igyō	**Practice simplification, easy practice principle**
ikki	Uprising
jitō	Estate steward
kabu-nakama	**Trade association** (the Tokugawa era)
keibiishi	**Judicial and policing office**
kendan	**Maintenance of social security**
kokuga	**Provincial governor's office**
kokujin	Indigenous lords
kokutai	National polity
kōryō	**government-owned land**
kū	Relativity (of the relationship among constituents of the world)
***kyūdō* principle (behavior)**	(Behavior based on) the true-way pursuing principle
mappō-shisō	Theory on the end of Buddhism
meibōka	Men of repute
mikkyō	Esoteric theory of Buddhism
mujyō	Mutability
nangyō	**Hard practice**
ōhō-buppō-isō *theory*	Theory of mutual dependence between the law of the emperor and the law of Buddhism
rinne	**Transmigration**
ryōshu	**Lord of the manor**
***ritsuryō* system**	Law-and-order system, centralized and nationalized system
sankin-kōtai	Alternate attendance in Edo
satori	**Enlightenment** (attainment of Buddhahood)
sengoku *daimyo*	Warring States period *daimyo*
shiki	Official position (a set of income rights and official positions associated with bureaucratic roles)
shitaji-chūbun	Dividing the rights to land half-and-half between competing parties
shōen	**Manor**
***shōen-kōryo* system**	Coexistence of manor and government-owned land system
shōkan	**Manor (*shōen*) official**
***shokubun* regulation**	Occupation and role regulation
shugo	Military governor
sōson	**Village**
toimaru	**Guild merchant**
***tokubun-ken* (right)**	Manor income right
***tokusei-rei* (order)**	Debt cancelation order
tozama daimyo	**Outside*daimyo*, non-hereditary*daimyo***
ujyō	Living things

za	**Trade association** (*kabu-nakama* in the Tokugawa era)
zazen	**Seated meditation** in the Zen sect

Chapter 1
The Culture and Institutions of Japan

It has become well known that Japan experienced sustained economic growth before the Meiji Restoration in 1868. During the early modern Tokugawa era, the Japanese economy grew at an annual rate of 0.51% from 1600 to 1721 and 0.33% from 1721 to 1874 (Takashima 2017), comparable to the rate of growth of 0.41% of 12 Western Europe countries during the period 1500–1820 (Maddison 2007). It is important to note that Japan's growth was attained under conditions of self-imposed isolation. In other words, Japan's growth was purely domestic and hence an endogenous phenomenon, whereas the growth of the Occident owed much to the exogenous impacts on the expansion of foreign trade as a result of geographical discoveries and the development of new trade routes after around 1500.

This book investigates the mechanism of the endogenous growth of Tokugawa Japan from socio-economic history since the thirteenth century and deliberates about its impacts on the economy after the Meiji Restoration. It will be shown that the moderate but sustained growth for more than two centuries during the Tokugawa era was caused by the development of domestic commerce owing to the alleviation of information asymmetry and, hence, as a result of a decline in transaction costs. Behind the changes in transaction costs were dynamic changes in trust levels in society during the fourteenth through the eighteenth century and its interactions with another major cultural trait based on Buddhism activism, the *kyūdō* (true-way pursuing) principle, and the stabilizing influence of Shintoism. Although the influence of religions had already significantly weakened in the modern Japan, the cultural traits of religious origin had been embedded deeply in the socio-economic system of Japan. The evolution of the socio-economic and political system after the Meiji Restoration was subject to the strong influence of cultural traits nurtured during the thirteenth century through the Tokugawa era.

The level of trust in society as well as the role played by the *kyūdō* principle underwent dynamic changes in the long-term history of Japan. Trust that had been nurtured in the homogeneous society during the ancient era deteriorated as the centralized and nationalized economic system, the *ritsuryō* (law and order) system, declined,

J. Teranishi, *Culture and Institutions in the Economic Growth of Japan*,
Studies in Economic History,
https://doi.org/10.1007/978-4-431-55627-5_1

and conflicts between aristocrats and the newly born samurai class intensified. The *kyūdō* principle, in the sense of the attitude to the accumulation of religious merits in daily occupational activities, and *kyūdō* behavior based on the *kyūdō* principle, which emerged under the strong influence of new Buddhism sects, Kamakura new Buddhism, accelerated specialization in occupational activities by individuals and hence the social division of labor, enhancing the heterogeneity of the society. Coupled with the decline of the centralized system as well as conflicts between aristocrats and samurai due to difference in value system, this gave rise to serious informational asymmetry and brought about a society full of moral hazards and adverse selection. The deterioration of trust culminated in turmoil, with ubiquitous internal wars, slaughter and looting during the Warring States period in the final part of the medieval era. The rehabilitation of peace by the Tokugawa *bakufu* (samurai government) in early modern Japan was accompanied by the reestablishment of trust as well as the renewed role of *kyūdō* behavior. The alleviation of information asymmetry owing to standardization of conduct through the development of new ethic codes by *bakufu* and private intellectuals brought about a significant reduction of transaction costs, giving rise to commerce-based economic growth. *Kyūdō* behavior came to play an important role in enhancing productivity through the accumulation of organization-specific skills and human capital under the condition of restricted labor mobility during the Tokugawa era.

Behind the important role in economic growth played by cultural traits such as trust and *kyūdō* behavior were characteristics of the internalized beliefs and value in the mindset of individuals in Japan. We contend that the worldview that related the structure of society to the internalized part of culture nurtured by Buddhist thinking, which respected interpersonal relationships with others nearby, was responsible for the high social costs to establish institutions, so that culture, instead of institutions, was chosen as a mechanism to structure and order the market and coordinate socio-economic incentives. This characteristic of the internalized part of culture in Japan stands in salient contrast with the Occident, where institutions have been chosen as a mechanism for ordering socio-economic activities. It is contended that, in the Occident, the social cost of establishing institutions was low owing to the worldview of the internalized culture, in which the abstract concept of the public and participation in collective activities have been respected.

1.1 Two Perspectives

The endogenous economic growth of Tokugawa Japan was carried out in a capitalism mechanism through profit-maximizing behavior by private economic units composed of peasants and merchants. It is worthy of investigation partly because it was not caused by industrialization based on factory production, and partly because cultural factors rather than institutions played a central role in ordering socio-economic activities. It is evidence for the diversity of cultural origins of capitalism in global economic history.

The investigation in this book is conducted from two perspectives. First is the perspective of the relative importance of culture and institutions. The mechanism of interaction and relative importance between culture and institutions in the Occident is still controversial between those who advocate the leading role of formal institutions or human-devised rules as determinants of the framework of human conduct regarding economic growth and those who emphasize the fundamental role of culture in ordering the market mechanism and shaping socio-economic incentives conducive to higher effort level and economic growth. In the history up to the Tokugawa era in Japan, in general culture took the initiative regarding the changes in the development of the socio-political framework of economic activities, and institutions largely played secondary and subsidiary roles to cultural changes and even frequently failed to catch up with the changes caused by culture.

Second is the perspective of efficiency as a cause of economic growth. Economic efficiency takes the form either of a decline of production costs regarding firm activities or of transaction costs in the markets regarding commercial activities. In the long run, the rapid growth of a capitalist economy is brought about by the exploitation of economies of scale either in production that reduces the long-term average costs as a function of scale of production of firms or in commerce and distribution that reduces the average transaction costs per commodity. While the rapid growth of the Occident after the mid-eighteenth century occurred as a result of economies of scale of production owing to innovation in production technology, in Tokugawa Japan, the scale economy was brought about by a drastic reduction in transaction costs owing to standardization of conduct and alleviation of information asymmetry in market transactions.

It is suggested that, while the difference in the first perspective between Japan and the Occident is concerned with different views of the world with respect to the structure of society in the internalized beliefs of culture, the difference in the second perspective is related to the different views of the world with respect to the relationship between humans and nature. The structure of society in the Japanese worldview is mainly composed of others nearby, whereas in the Occident the structure of society in the worldview is composed of abstract individuals, typically seen in the concept of the public. The relationship with nature in Japan is characterized by the coexistence and harmony between humans and nature, whereas in the Occident the relationship is one of control and domination of nature by humans.

In the Occident, the worldview regarding the relationship between humans and nature had significant bearings on the pattern of economic growth based on innovation in industrial technology, partly through the notion of anthropocentrism that motivated the utilization of nature for the sake of human welfare and partly through the synergy effect with the worldview related to the structure of the society, inducing the development of institutions that enabled to mobilize resources and knowledge toward development of mass production technology for the sake of the public. In Japan, the relationship between growth based on the reduction of transaction costs and a worldview regarding the relationship between human and nature was not significant. Harmony with nature did not allow the exploitation of nature for the sake of humans. Instead, the changes in transaction costs occurred owing to the evolution of a worldview related to the structure of the society. Purposive efforts to develop ethical codes and standards of conduct by the government and intellectuals to rehabilitate the trust levels, which had been seriously diminished during the period before the establishment of the Tokugawa regime, resulted in the standardization of conduct and the reduction of information asymmetry, almost unintendedly leading to the reduction in transaction costs. Let us give a brief explanation of these points and show the relationship between our investigation and existing literatures.

1.1.1 Culture and Institutions

It is our basic contention that both culture and institutions enhance the efficiency and fairness of markets by ordering and structuring market mechanisms and coordinating the incentives and behavior of participants. Owing to the significant influence of Douglas North, modern economics have devoted considerable efforts to analyzing the role of institutions in market ordering and economic performance. Starting from the challenging assertion in North and Thomas (1973) that the 'factors we have listed (innovation, economy of scale, education, capital accumulation, etc.) are not causes of growth; they *are* growth. This book focuses on what causes economic growth', North maintained not only the fundamental role of institutions in determining economic growth but also contended that institutions play a leading role over culture. The seminal study (North 1990) on institution and economic performance contends that institutions, defined as human-devised rules of the game, such as rules, laws and constitutions, comprise fundamental determinants of long-term economic performance, while 'informal institutions' in his terminology,[1] such as conventions, norms of behavior and self-imposed codes of conduct, are so deep-seated in cultural inheritance that they change mainly in response to institutions and play only secondary, although persistent, roles in economic growth. Needless to say, a plethora of literature has appeared to support the North theorem during the last couple of decades.

In particular, Acemoglu, Johnson and Robinson (2005), using cross-country data as well as historical evidence, contend that institutions matter in giving rise to differences of economic performance, emphasizing the role of political power and political institutions in the equilibrium structure of economic institutions. They deny the role of culture from the viewpoint of the endogeneity of culture[2]. It is claimed that, since

[1] Alesina and Guliano (2015) opposed this definition of culture on the ground that 'labelling "everything"—from, say, the level of reciprocal trust in a society to constitutional rules about voting systems—as institutions' is confusing. Moreover, they contend that the label of 'informal institution' has a connotation that formal institutions determine informal ones, and that the latter, culture, are by definition of secondary importance.

[2] They start their argument with criticisms of Weber (1905) from the viewpoint of endogeneity of the effect of religion. Quoting Tawney (1926) and Hill (1964), it is claimed that Weber's assertion of a causal effect from religious beliefs to economic outcome suffers from the endogeneity problem in the sense that, while religion might have influenced economic outcome, the religious change

culture is one of the factors that influence economic outcome, it has an innate tendency to suffer from the endogeneity problem, and that the institution in general is a more powerful and direct factor that affects economic performance than culture. It is difficult to accept their assertion, at least in the context of economic history of Japan. In this book, we will assert the autonomous role of culture in structuring and ordering the market in the historical context of Japan. Moreover, they make a stronger assertion that institutions are the fundamental cause of difference in economic development in international comparison. Their assertion regarding the effect of institutions on economic performance, is seriously marred, however, by the lack of consideration of the difference in the cost of establishing institutions among countries. Because this is a common feature of the studies following the North theory, we will discuss it shortly below.

Tabellini (2008) is a pioneering study that incorporate cultural factors explicitly, but it is developed on the assumption of the predominant power of institutions. He contends that well-functioning institutions are observed in countries where individual values are conscious with generalized (as opposed to limited) morality and were ruled by non-despotic political institutions in the past. This work is also construed as an assertion of the endogeneity of culture since it is asserted that culture related to the quality of modern institutions is determined by the degree of despotic or feudalistic nature of institutions in the past. The concept of generalized and limited morality, however, is highly inspiring since it is related to the issue of sharing of internalized culture in a country, which comprises one of the key topics of this book. We will examine the concept in more detail in the next chapter.

The relative importance of culture and institutions in ordering markets and socio-economic incentives, and in the long-term process of economic growth, has recently become a controversial issue. Alesina and Giuliano (2015) present substantial evidence for the interaction between and mutual dependence of changes in institutions and culture by means of an extensive survey of the literature, raising doubts about the assertion of the autonomous working of institutions. There has appeared literature that emphasizes a more positive and active role for culture. Greif (1993,

could have been a result of economic outcome. If the authors intend to mean by the term 'economic outcome' the rise of capitalism, their criticism seems to be a little bit off the mark, since Weber did not assert that Puritanism caused capitalism. His article pointed out only that Puritanism was effective in rejecting the traditional lifestyle that had comprised an internal obstacle to the formation of capitalism (Weber 1905, p. 15). Weber even said that 'we have no intention of defending any such foolishly doctrinaire thesis as that the 'capitalistic spirit' (as always in the provisional sense of the word in which we are using it), let alone capitalism itself, could only arise as a result of the certain influence of the Reformation' (Weber 1905, p. 36). Incidentally, Tawney (1926) criticized Weber on the grounds of his neglect of the social conditions in which the Reformation was born as a result of the economic revolution caused by geographical discovery and the like, and claimed that, while Puritanism was helpful in organizing social order, religious reform itself was an outgrowth of changes in social order (introduction to the 1937 version). Hill (1964) emphasized the influence of the decline of local society during the Sixteenth and seventeenth centuries on religious reform, such as the progress of enclosure, the development of the national market, changes in the manor system, the deterioration of the parish and so on. It must be noted that all of these assertions do not contradict with Weber's theory. However, this book will show that the Weber theory in his essay (Weber 1905)is more effective in explaining the capitalism in the Oriental countries like Japan.

1994, 2006) are pioneer works on the effects of 'cultural beliefs' (beliefs in the behavioral part of mental models in our terminology) on institutional arrangements. Guiso et al. (2003, 2006) present abundant evidence for the effects on economic outcome of cultural factors such as religion and ethnicity by use of international comparative data as well as in inter-state data in the United States. Moreover, Landes (2000) and McCloskey (2006) assert the importance of culture in terms of motivation in capitalistic economies. Landes (2000) refers to the positive relationship between culture and growth, pointing out that high Weberian values that emphasized goodness resulted in the making of a new man with high levels of individualism, literacy and a rigorous concept of time. McCloskey (2006) also contends that bourgeois virtues or ethics inherited from the Age of Commerce, such as prudence, courage and hope, and the like, gave rise to capitalistic development after the mid-nineteenth century, eventually realizing not only material but also spiritual progress.

Through an examination of the roles of culture in Japan, this book will show that North's assertion regarding the predominance of institutions as compared to culture, which seems to be derived mainly from the experience in the Occident, is not necessarily applicable to the experience of Japan before the Meiji Restoration, and will present a hypothesis that, in Japan, culture was a fundamental determinant of the framework of economic performance. The reason for the difference between the Occident and Japan lies in the difference in costs for structuring and ordering economic behavior among individuals. In the Occident the establishment of institutions was less costly than in Japan, while in Japan cultural ordering was available at a lower cost than institutions.

We believe that there are two ways to establish a workable order in the market and in society for effective economic performance—one based on institutional constraints on economic conduct and another based on the sharing of conventions and the standardizing of economic conduct. The choice between the two ways is dependent on the costs for society. The costs of the former seem to be lower in the Occident and the latter to be lower in Japan.[3] It seems that North's assertion regarding the predominance of institutions as compared to culture is rooted in the neglect of the social cost of ordering the market.

Why do the costs of establishing a workable structure and order in the market and society differ? This can be explained by the differences between the Occident and Japan in the worldview with respect to the structure of society in the internalized beliefs. In the Occident, partly owing to the influence of Christianity, individuals have an abstract notion of the whole human being and the public in the internalized beliefs of culture, while in Japan, under the strong influence of Buddhism, there was no notion of abstract society and the public, and internalized beliefs and values were mainly composed of detailed information and concerns about others nearby,

[3]This is no doubt a somewhat generalized statement. North (1990) contends that formal institutions define the structure of rights in a specific exchange, and informal institutions based on culture play a major role in actual agreements (p. 61). In Japan before the Meiji Restoration, too, there is no doubt that institutions provided overall structure in the interaction of individuals. However, it is contended that the institutions were highly inefficient, and culture fulfilled a more important role both in the definition of the structure of exchange and in the actual outcome of exchanges.

with whom individuals interact in the imaginary process of transmigration and the accumulation of karma. We assume that each individual develops a mental model to decipher and evaluate his environment, the world he experiences, and form his opinion about the desirable method of structuring and ordering markets. The relative costs of ordering the market and society are dependent on the easiness of summarizing the opinions of the constituents of society through the sharing of mental models. The sharing of mental models is easier when the content of the mental models of individuals is more homogeneous. There is a fundamental difference in the degree of homogeneousness of the content of the mental models. While the concept of the public in the Occident is more or less the same among individuals, so that the mental models of individuals have a shared content, in Japan the membership of the concept of others nearby differs considerably among individuals, because each group of others nearby is made up of different individuals, so it is quite difficult to have a shared content of mental models among individuals. This explains the fundamental difficulty in the sharing of mental models and hence the convergence of opinions about agreeable institutions in Japan. It follows that in the Occident it is less costly to reach consensus about agreeable systems of institutions, whereas in Japan such consensus is costly, and it is not easy to establish institutions that impose constraints on individual behavior.

Moreover, since institutions are mechanisms to regulate the behavior of individuals in society and they are socially stipulated, for institutions as rules to retain effectiveness, the prevention of opportunistic behavior is indispensable. While opportunistic behavior is a ubiquitous phenomenon in any country, in Japan where there is a tendency for individuals to behave in relationship with others nearby, there exists the possibility of rampant opportunistic behavior, consequently making not only establishing but also enforcement of institutions costly. This is because interaction with others nearby in the imaginary conception of transmigration has value for individuals that encompass their past as well as future lives, overriding the value of agreement about institutions that is based on contracts in the present life. Discretionary sanctions as well as free rider behavior caused by consideration of others nearby frequently raise the cost of the effective enforcement of institutions even higher.[4]

It follows that, in Japan, instead of establishing and enforcing institutions, social order was more effectively maintained through the process of intimate coordination among others nearby. A small group of individuals develop standards of conduct and conventions that bind members within the group. Among such small groups are developed standards of conduct and conventions related to group interactions, and a decentralized chain relationship of groups develops horizontally into macro-level standards of conduct and conventions. This is the cultural mechanism to establish

[4]North and Thomas (1973) claim that, since private enforcement is costly due to externality, enforcement costs are lowered usually by assigning the role to the government. We are contending that, even if the government is assigned the role, costs would have been comparatively higher in Japan owing to behavior based on others nearby.

social order in Japan. We will further explain this mechanism in Chapter 2 in relationship with the autonomy of cultural change and the cost of sharing mental models in establishing institutions and culture.

Returning to Acemoglu et al. (2005), it seems that the influence on economic performance needs to be evaluated not only by the magnitude of estimated coefficients of the institution on economic performance (benefits) but also by taking into consideration the cost of establishing institutions and culture. The authors contend that the role of institutions in the economic outcome lies in the effect on shaping economic incentives. One must notice, however, that the role of culture on economic outcome lies also in its effect on the cost of establishing incentive system in society. Assuming that there is not much difference in the estimated coefficients of comparative statics between institutions and culture, in which the endogeneity issue is adequately controlled by means of instrumental variables and the like, what counts in the decision of people who try to reorganize their society should be the benefits, net of costs of institutional and cultural changes, for society. We believe that there is a significant difference in the costs to work on the incentive system among societies.

Moreover, we consider that the reason for the lack of the general applicability of North's proposition is rooted not only in the failure to take into account the costs for establishing market order but also in his preconception of the basic nature of culture. North (1990) characterizes cultural factors ('informal institutions' in his terminology) in comparison with institutions (formal institutions) with respect to the role related to economic performance by two traits—non-operationality in the sense of the difficulty to be targeted by purposive policy and persistence compared with institutions that can be changed overnight. In some circumstances outside of the Occident, or at least with respect to pre-Meiji Restoration Japan, neither characterizations apply. In Japan, people have actively worked upon the establishment and improvement of ethical systems related to individual behavior and, consequently, intentionally changed culture. Culture could be changed by purposive activity. It is contended that even the internalized part of culture could change radically over the long run. On the other hand, while we do not deny culture is sometimes very persistent, institutions have also been extremely persistent, quite often because of interest group politics aimed at the survival of the existing system and have been inefficient, not to say exploitive, continuing to exist despite their misfunctioning. During the medieval period, this was due partly to the dual character of the government—the aristocratic government based on the imperial court and the samurai governments. Institutions were seriously persistent despite their inefficiency due to the interest group activities of the aristocratic and samurai classes. The inefficiency of the Tokugawa *bakufu* in economic policy was another example, which survived more than two centuries despite seriously inefficient economic institutions owing to a delicate political balance between the *bakufu* (samurai government) and antagonistic *daimyos*.

Incidentally, removing the cover of Calvinism and interpreting in the terminology of modern economic theory, Weber's 'spirit' could be construed to be composed of standards of conduct or conventions conducive to enhance effort level and coordination. In other words, the 'spirit' of capitalism is nothing but a culture of capitalism in the terminology of this book. However, it is important to note that Weber (1905) never asserted that culture was a cause of the emergence of Occidental capitalism based on factory production and industrial technology. Instead, his assertion is perfectly congruent with the institutional origin of capitalism. As is already well recognized, Weber's emphasis on the 'spirit' of capitalism is marred by his methodology in the sense of narrowness of issue-setting regarding the emergence of modern capitalism. Although he had conducted extensive research into the religious background of economic behavior in world religions, covering Confucianism, Buddhism, Hinduism, Taoism and so on, the conclusion he obtained was that, in any religion other than Protestantism, he was unable to find clear religious teachings suitable for the development of modern capitalism. This assertion reflects the fact that what he sought was a religious background for the attitude suitable for Western-type factory-based development. It was beyond his imagination that small family-owned peasant farming motivated by profit could supply a large number of commodities to markets with the help of innovative merchants. This was actually what happened in the economic development of Tokugawa Japan as well as in Sung dynasty of China (Teranishi 2018, Ch. 5). Furthermore, the purpose of his study lay in the clarification of why the cultural phenomena, including the development of science and arts as well as the birth of capitalism that have universal value, occurred only in the Occident. The limitation of this purpose does not lie in the flavor of eurocentrism and modernization theory from the present day viewpoint, but rather reflects the fact that his motivation for the study was formed at the beginning of the twentieth century, when most of Asian and non-Occidental countries were deeply asleep and oriental study in the Occident as well as religious study within each Asian country were still at a nascent stage.[5]

1.1.2 Transaction Costs vs Production Costs

In terms of the nature of innovation and the consequent efficiency of the economic system, the characteristic of economic growth of Tokugawa Japan lies in the fact that innovation that triggered growth was concerned with transaction and distribution of commodities, and that consequent efficiency was brought about through the decline in transaction costs.

---

[5]In Japan, the study of the Kamakura new Buddhism, a main theme in the study of this book, started from contributions such as Ienaga (1940) or Inoue (1956) as is discussed in Chapter 4, although casual reference appeared before the World War II by such researchers as Shimaji Mokurai (1838–1911) and his son-in-law Shimaji Daitō (1875–1927). Full-scale study occurred after the 1970s when voluminous historical documents came to be published in the *Nihon-Shisou-Taikei* series of Iwanami Shoten.

In the Occident, innovation occurred in production technology, and growth was triggered by a secular decline in production costs. Innovation of production technology was due to the development of natural science as well as the environment that applied the science to the production technology. According to Mokyr (2017), the development of natural science in the Occident was due to the rise of the competitive market for useful knowledge that grew up in the transnational community of the Republic of Letters and to cultural breakthrough in the belief that the human lot can be continually improved by bettering the understanding of natural phenomena and applying the knowledge to production technology. Moreover, there were engineering skills accumulated in a group of mechanics in England, in particular, and their capability in implementing incremental micro-inventions realized the application of scientific knowledge to engineering (Mokyr 1999). The synergy between scientific discovery brought about in the transnational community of researchers and a thick layer of engineers embodying applied technology resulted in a 'self-generating cascade' of technological innovation that realized sustained growth based on innovation in production technology.

Development based on innovation in production technology is not the only way to growth, however. Schumpeter (1926) points out five patterns of innovation as causes for economic development: invention of new products, introduction of new methods of production including new methods of commerce, development of new markets, attainment of new materials and achievement of new organization. The innovation in the Occident depicted by Mokyr was mainly concerned with the first and the second pattern of innovation in manufacturing. We will claim that the economic development of Tokugawa Japan was concerned with the innovation of the second pattern regarding commerce.

The Tokugawa growth was triggered by the infrastructure investment of the Tokugawa *bakufu* in marine transportation for the purpose of transporting tax revenue obtained in the form of rice to the rice markets in Osaka and Edo (Tokyo). The effect of this innovation, however, is once-and-for-all and unable to give rise to sustained growth. The sustained growth of Tokugawa Japan that continued for more than two centuries was mainly caused by the continuous decline in transaction costs due to the alleviation of information asymmetry among economic agents in various regions and classes over the entire country. The reduction in transaction costs occurred for many reasons. The rehabilitation of trust in society with reestablished peace as a result of compromise among antagonistic *daimyos* was a fundamental factor. The institutional innovation of *shokubun* (occupation and role) regulation that classified all citizens into four classes distinguished by occupation had been effective in establishing homogeneous social groups within common occupations. The standardization of conduct owing to the development and diffusion of moral codes brought about by the purposive effort by the *bakufu* (samurai government) and private intellectuals was the most persistent factor for alleviating mistrust among economic agents and offsetting the scarcity of open information. Because of standardization of conduct through the development of moral codes, individuals came to be able to forecast the reaction of agents in transactions with higher subjective probability, and the sense of sharing the same moral codes nurtured a convention of reciprocity in society, reducing the room for moral hazard considerably. In Chapter 6, it is shown that these effects on information asymmetry resulted in a reduction of transaction costs in commerce, represented by a drastic reduction of risk premiums in the interest rates of financial markets during the eighteenth century.

Mokyr contends that growth caused by a decline in transaction costs, Smithian growth by his terminology, cannot explain modern economic growth because growth exclusively based on a cooperative ethic will eventually peter out unless accompanied by innovation and productivity growth (Mokyr 2017, p. 122). The experience of Tokugawa Japan that continued more than two centuries seems to cast doubt on the general applicability of this assertion, although the rate of growth was low compared with the growth of Europe after the mid-eighteenth century.

It is also claimed that the Tokugawa growth was due to the effect of the positive role of *kyūdō* behavior that enhanced the effort level of small producers drastically.[6] *Kyūdō* behavior in the Tokugawa era was a powerful engine to enhance the effort level and improve the quality of products. Moreover, popular ethics, in which such standards of conduct as diligence, frugality and thrift comprised major recommended items of values, emerged as precepts for harmonizing individual behavior with social order and scarcity of resources.

It is worth noting that, behind the difference in the sources of economy of scale between the Occident and Japan lies the different worldviews with respect to the relationship between humans and nature. In the Occident, nature is considered to be under the control of humans on the basis of the Christian notion of anthropocentrism—a belief in the creator God who has designed the universe and nature for the use of humans. In Japan, coexistence with nature is the basic notion regarding the relationship with nature nurtured in the Buddhism tradition. The Japanese notion of coexistence with nature is rooted in the worldview we experience during transmigration. Since the souls of humans were obliged to experience lives as animals and insects in the process of transmigration, they inevitably become friendly with the nature in which animals and insects live. The notion of coexistence was intensified due to the awe and respect of nature nurtured in indigenous Shintoism tradition. Chapter 4 discusses this point further.

The anthropological view of the Occident has its origin in Christianity during the medieval period. Oakley (1961) claims that, while there had been coexistence between the two views about nature during the medieval age, the theory of law of nature as immanent nurtured in Greek philosophical thinking and the Christian view

[6]Puritan ascetism emphasized by Weber (1905) could be regarded as a standard of conduct conducive to enhance the effort level in capitalistic society. It is interesting to note that the standard of conduct related to effort levels in the Buddhist tradition of Japan is substantially different from the 'spirit' of capitalism in the Christian world. Buddhism never emphasized ascetism as the rule of conduct recommended as religious practice. Instead, Buddhism allowed the free play of avarice and desire, and the emphasis on the necessity to overcome those profane motivations was the essence of Buddhist teaching. However, *kyūdō*—behavior brought about by religious reform in Japan in the thirteenth century became a powerful engine of Tokugawa growth by enhancing the effort level and improving the quality of products.

that the law of nature was imposed upon the world by the decree of the omnipotent God who created it, the latter established its predominance in the seventeenth century, and that virtuosi of science such as Rene Descartes and Isaac Newton, ardent followers of the anthropocentric view, rejected compromise between the two views. White (1978) analyzes the emergence of anthropocentrism in the medieval Occident. It is contended that the development of modern technology after the thirteenth century was due not to necessity or social conditions but mainly to the 'borrowing culture' of technology from abroad, and that, after experiencing change in the attitude to manual labor and mechanical technology, around the 1450s European intellectuals came to regard technical progress not as a project of invention but as an historic and happy fact. It came to be axiomatic that man is serving God by serving himself in the technological mastery of nature, and technological aggression, rather than reverent coexistence, is man's posture toward nature (pp. 250–251).

Mokyr (2017) claims that anthropocentricism was the ultimate trigger for the growth of the Occident. Based on scientific and engineering innovation in the two centuries between Columbus and Newton, European culture underwent radical changes, giving rise to a new belief shared by elites that the 'human lot can be continually improved by bettering understanding of natural phenomenon and applying the understanding to production' (Mokyr 2017, p. xiiv). In other words, he contends that industrial development based on the factory production system in the Occident has two roots of origin in the internalized belief in the mindset of individuals. First is the concern with the lot of humans that brought about the mass production system for the supply of goods to the public, and another was the accumulation of scientific knowledge obtained through research including the 'interrogation' of nature by experimentation. In terms of the worldview in the internalized part of culture the former root is concerned with the structure of society and the latter root with the relationship between humans and nature. It is interesting to note that, while the view about human–nature relationship played a significantly positive role in reducing production costs in the Occident, according to Mokyr, in the case of Japan the view composed by the concept of coexistence and harmony with nature did not play such a significant role. Certainly, it explains the reason that Japan did not develop industrial technology to utilize nature for the sake of human welfare, just as the organic view of the universe in China deterred the development of industrial technology (Needham 1969). It seems, however, that the harmonic view of nature seems to be unable to explain directly the development of ethics that caused the reduction of transaction costs in Japan. In other words, while the worldview with respect to the relationship between nature and humans had an important bearing on the economic development of the Occident, such an effect was not significant in Japan. The growth of Japan based on the reduction of transaction costs was mainly rooted in the worldview with respect to the structure of society, and probably very little in the worldview related to the human–nature relationship. Incidentally, the argument by Needham is discussed in the Appendix to Chapter 3 and the relationship between humans and nature is dealt with in the Appendix 2 to Chapter 4.

It is necessary to point out that, while the assertion of Mokyr about the effect of the anthropocentric view is important in highlighting the role of culture in the

Occident, it is regrettable that he refers very little to the development of institutions by the support of states, such as the financial system, joint-stock corporations and judicial institutions that enabled the conversion of scientific discovery into industrial and engineering technology. Moreover, his emphasis on the role of the establishment of the transnational community of the Republic of Letters seems to be largely a phenomenon related to the institutional arrangements for the evolution of culture, in which, given the political fragmentation of Europe, kings and lords provided institutions that protected the development of useful knowledge. Further, another factor, which is claimed to be responsible for cultural change, the openness and willingness to absorb foreign ideas, was also due largely to institutional conditions that necessitated competitive import of foreign useful knowledge by states under the political condition of a fragmented Europe. In order to judge whether the culture of anthropocentricism was a fundamental cause of the growth of the Occident based on innovation in industrial technology, we need to implement more serious comparative research between the effects of institutional arrangements provided mainly by states and the impacts of the evolution and diffusion of the culture of anthropocentricism on the motivation of individuals including the masses. In other words, it is difficult to disregard the possibility that, in a regression equation, in which economic growth is used as dependent variable, the coefficient of the variable representing the effect of the anthropocentric worldview could be significant and with the correct sign, but the magnitude of the coefficient might be very small compared with other explanatory variables representing the effect of institutions. Although the argument of Mokyr is highly insightful, we are still not persuaded by the claim that emphasizes the role of culture against institutions with respect to the Occident.

1.2 Culture and Socio-Economic Performance

We will define culture as simply as possible. Culture is a set of customary beliefs and values that are transmitted fairly unchanged from generation to generation among individuals and by social groups. This definition is almost the same as the one in Guiso et al. (2006).[7] While they also refer to ethnic groups, we do not incorporate ethnic groups into our definition because differences in ethnic groups was not of much importance in the Japanese growth process under consideration.[8] Moreover, we do not touch upon the issue of conflicts among religious groups. Although the evolution of religions had a significant influence on cultural change, hence on socio-economic performance in Japan, there were no conflicts between religious groups.

[7] They define culture as 'those customary beliefs and values that ethnic, religious and social groups transmit fairly unchanged from generation to generation'.

[8] The Japanese archipelago was originally inhabited by indigenous hunting people, part of whom was considered to be the ancestor of the Ainu now, before the arrival of new Mongoloid people around the third century BC. The indigenous hunting people were conquered by the immigrants by the end of Heian era, who brought agriculture to the archipelago, but both melt into each other shortly thereafter, and the ethnic origin of the Japanese was established.

While there did occur conflicts among different sects in each religion, two major religions, Buddhism and Shintoism, coexisted with interactions and division of labor by and large before the Meiji Restoration. Sometimes there occurred severe controversies in terms of theoretical issues as well as political implications between Buddhism and Shintoism.[9] Such controversies and conflicts, however, were mainly carried out at the level of academics and politics, and there never occurred serious social conflict that divided the nation into different religious groups. Let us sketch the changes overtime in the values and beliefs related to the main religions, Buddhism and Shintoism, and the value systems of two important social groups, aristocrats and samurai.

Beliefs and Values Related to Religions

It is important to identify the reasons why Buddhism had a significant influence in medieval Japan and left persistent effects on the behavioral pattern of the Japanese thereafter. We believe that there are both direct and indirect influences. The direct influence was related to the introduction of the concept that denied the preexisting ancient view of affirmation of the present world.[10] The denial of the present world was caused by two reasons. First is the graveness of karma. Under the influence of Buddhism, individuals were motivated to lead their lives in consideration of accumulated amounts of karma. Karma is accumulated through deeds in daily life vis-à-vis others nearby. Good deeds accumulate good karma and bad deeds bad karma. There is no cancellation of good karma by bad karma and bad karma by good karma. Accumulated karma cannot be reduced unless individuals accept retribution; for bad karma, bad retribution is given, and for good karma, good retribution.[11] The graveness of

---

[9]During the Tokugawa period, some *daimyos* repressed Buddhist temples for the purpose of keeping the masses of their domain from the influence of 'evil and demoralized' teachings and, at the beginning of the Meiji era, there occurred governmental repression of Buddhism for the purpose of establishing national Shintoism. For the sake of simplicity, we will not touch upon Christianity, which was transferred to Japan at the end of the Warring States period, or the movements of new religions that emerged after the end of the Tokugawa era.

[10]Bellah (1964) contends that the major difference between primitive and archaic religion and historic religion lies in the introduction of the concept of world rejection and that the historic religion introduced to the Occident, Christianity, introduced the notion of human beings to be salvaged. Buddhism as transferred to Japan also introduced the concept of the denial of the present life as well as the notion of the destination of humans to be salvaged, both of which were absent in pre-existing Shintoism. While Christianity, that assumes an omnipotent God, brought about the concept of individualism that respects the dignity of each individual who faces one-to-one with God, Buddhism in Japan did not bring individualism but rather the notion of the close relationship with others nearby with whom one might have a relationship through the process of transmigration and the sense of coexistence with animals and plants with which one might also meet in the process of transmigration. The latter notion of coexistence with all the living things in the world is thought to have been nurtured through the interaction of the newly arrived Buddhism with the indigenous Shintoism. The complementary relationship between Shintoism and Buddhism played an important role in the changing mentality of the Japanese. The behavior of Buddhists to seek salvation could quite often be too radical and aggressive, and the tendency toward preestablished harmony in Shintoism worked to mitigate the offensiveness of Buddhism radicalism.

[11]Under the rules of early Buddhism, there was no interpersonal transfer of karma; retribution of one's karma must be borne by oneself. This rule, however, was substantially relaxed in Mahayana Buddhism. See Chapter 4.

these properties of karma induced individuals to live ethically, not only because the present life of individuals is under the persistent influence of the retribution of karma accumulated in the past lives, but also because the accumulated amount of karma at the end of life in this world determines the state of the world in the future life. The second reason for the negation of the present life is the mutability of human life under the transmigration process. Even if one can enjoy this life owing to accumulated good karma, there is no assurance to be able to get out transmigration and obtain Buddhahood. There exists always the possibility to be reborn another less comfortable state in transmigration and even the possibility of going to hell again and again in one's future lives. Ienaga (1940) claims that the mutability of human life or the discontinuity of this world and future world was the ultimate factor that induced individuals to have a negative worldview.

Even more important than the direct impact was indirect impact of Buddhism on the internalized part of culture. The mental model about the structure and details of the world we experience, which we call internalized belief, is composed of beliefs about social structure and about the relationship between humans and nature and is largely formulated by the worldviews described by Buddhism. Since the influence of karma accumulated in the process of transmigration is so serious, in the sense that karma determines destiny in the present life as well as future lives, individuals in medieval Japan led their daily lives always evaluating the accumulated amount of karma. This inevitably led them to be concerned with their relationship with others nearby, because karma is produced by deeds vis-à-vis others nearby. As a result, the internalized belief of the mental model of Buddhists are composed of relationships with others nearby. In this mechanism of formulation of the internalized part of culture, there is no room for the operation of the concept of the public or society, which comprise the content of the internalized belief in the Occident. Moreover, since it was possible for individuals to live lives as insects and animals in the process of transmigration, they were led to have a sense of harmony and coexistence with nature, and this sense was intensified by the theory of Buddhahood of animals and plants developed in medieval period Japan (Appendix 2 to Chapter 4).This characteristic of the internalized belief, related to the concept of society composed of others nearby, in particular, is crucially important in formulating the socio-economic system in Japan.

In the following, our analysis is mainly concerned with Buddhism, especially with respect to the cultural traits regarding the ordinary life of the masses. This does not imply, however, that it is sufficient to analyze the role of Buddhism in the religious aspect of Japan. Buddhism, that conceives that the essence of human beings lies in excessive attachment and desire or avarice, is a religion that provoke passion in human activities. The negation of this world gave people a strong incentive to seek salvation, and this quite often induced the paradoxical result of a destabilizing effect on the society. Although the teaching of Buddhism was aimed at overcoming the innate urge of avarice, it is undeniable that Buddhism tended to approve the behavior impelled by excessive desire and avarice as a temporal and exceptional phenomenon, partly because leaders of the Buddhism circle were liable to take a generous stance to such behaviors in order to emphasize the benefits and effects of final salvation, especially during the times of severe distress of society. Moreover, the concept of universal Buddhahood that was crystalized as *hongaku* theory—that everyone is qualified to attain Buddhahood without any serious practice—was liable to allow self-indulgent behavior. Believers tended to consider that they were allowed to do whatever their avarice dictates, since, at the final moment, they were destined to be salvaged. *Hongaku* theory is discussed in detail in Chapter 4.

It is important to note that negation of this world by Buddhism did not replace the affirmative and harmonious view of the world nor retarded the development of preexisting Shintoism. As will be explained in the following chapters, Buddhism teaching coexisted with Shintoism at least after the eighth century formally in the form of syncretic fusion of Shintoism and Buddhism, although Buddhism was long considered to be of a higher status. The influence of Shintoism was significant whenever destabilizing thought arising from the negation of this world became excessive. With a theory based on affirmation of this world and teachings that recommended discipline and harmony with natural order, Shintoism fulfilled an indispensable stabilizing role on the mentality of the Japanese and society, that was liable to be destabilized due to the approval of self-indulgent behavior by Buddhism. Chapter 5 shows that the turmoil during the Warring States period was caused, at least partly, by the influence of Buddhism.

Buddhism may have introduced dynamism into Japanese society, but the dynamic and innovating effects of Buddhism were possible because of the existence of the stabilizing influence of Shintoism. It will be argued that the reason that the turmoil in the Warring States period did not result in catastrophe lay in the role of Shintoism. A bicycle can travel fast because it is equipped with brakes. Shintoism inherited an indigenous concept of an affirmative view of this world. It is often pointed out that the affirmative view prevailed during the medieval age when individuals were under the strong influence of Buddhism. Although this paradoxical phenomenon seems to reflect the partly positive attitude of individuals in socio-economic activity owing to economic growth that began gradually after the fourteenth century, the main reason seems to lie in the influence of Shintoism that emphasized affirmation of this world.[12] We will discuss this point more in Chapter 4.

Furthermore, it is worth pointing out that, although Shintoism had fulfilled a stabilizing role in Japanese society, its influence on the internalized part of culture was not necessarily far reaching. Shintoism did not have a social model related to human interactions. Although Shintoism emphasized the importance of the sense of being nestled in the bosom of nature for individuals so as to obtain the benefits of the fertility of nature and secure safety from natural calamities and other external source of damage, it never articulated the relationship of the structure of society,

[12] Ienaga (1940) claims that medieval Japan was a world of absolute affirmation built on the thought of absolute negation but considers that the paradoxical result is due to the emergence of the concept of *sesshu-husha* (ingesting living things with thankfulness of lives). See Chapter 4 on this point.

either composed of others nearby or the public, with nature. The internalized part of culture of the Japanese seems to be formulated following mainly Buddhism theory.

Beliefs and Values of Social Groups

Among social groups, our analysis is mainly concerned with the cultural interaction between the value systems of samurai and aristocrats, while, during the Tokugawa period, we will also talk about conflicts between samurai and merchants in relation to the physiocracy policy of the Tokugawa *bakufu*. Our analysis starts with the radical changes in the economic system and culture in thirteenth-century Japan, when the existing system of centralized and nationalized economy, that comprised the basis of the reign by aristocracy, the *ritsuryō* system, began to decline, and the emergence of new classes of merchants and samurai heralded the new era of market economy and heterogeneous society accompanied by the progress of the social division of labor. The samurai class established its own government, Kamakura *bakufu*, at the end of the twelfth century, creating serious conflicts with aristocrats over landholding and value systems.

A plethora of literature has been written about conflicts regarding landholding, which we will discuss in the following chapters. The victory of the samurai class over the aristocracy in the landholding conflicts brought about the decline and downfall of aristocrats toward the sixteenth century. More fundamental conflicts with deep social impacts, however, were the struggle regarding the value systems of the two classes. While aristocrats in charge of administrative roles were a class with expertise in knowledge and ritual orders, the samurai in charge of the military and policing role of the government was a class with action and spiritual orders. Unlike the aristocracy in the Occidental countries,[13] aristocrats in Japan were not concerned with military matters by themselves, and the samurai were long despised as a class in charge of the bloody businesses disliked by the aristocracy and the Shintoism tradition (Yoshie 1986, pp. 174–175). Probably for this reason,[14] Minamoto Yoritomo, the founder of the Kamakura *bakufu*, established his *bakufu* office in Kamakura, a city about 400 km east of the capital city Kyoto, at the end of the twelfth century. In Kamakura, Yoritomo developed original samurai ethics based on martial arts and the feudal relation of master and vassals. Shoguns of the Muromachi *bakufu* opened an office in Kyoto after the collapse of the Kamakura *bakufu* during the first half of the fourteenth century, however, and tried to merge samurai ethic with aristocratic ethic, with consequent serious confusion and confrontation with the aristocracy.

Partly because aristocrats manipulated their right to allocate official rankings in the imperial court as political instruments and partly because the samurai tried to catch up with aristocratic ethics and status at the court, class conflicts regarding value systems between samurai and aristocrats had a significant influence on socio-political

[13]In the Occident, aristocrats were engaged in military actions by themselves. Tawney (1941) refers to the transformation of the 'gentry addicted to war' into the landowning established class, traditionally occupied by the aristocrats, during the mid-sixteenth century through mid-seventeenth century England.

[14]Another reason for the opening of the *bakufu* in Kamakura was that eastern Japan was the main base on which the Minamoto family had traditionally exercised influence.

performance through the impacts on the working of institutions. Important institutions fell into disfunction due to the impacts of the conflicts. The samurai government of the Muromachi era, Muromachi *bakufu*, declined largely due to the inability to harmonize the value systems of samurai and aristocrats. Feudalism as a basic institution within samurai society lost efficiency in such matters as providing an efficient judicial system and the integrity in collective behavior of samurai organizations. This was because quite often religious motivation comprised a higher dimension value than feudal contract, leading to the proliferation of self-salvation behavior, whereby conflicts among samurai groups were resolved without ruling by masters.

Furthermore, under the strong predilection for aristocratic culture by samurai, the cultural struggle within the samurai class between samurai groups that respected military capability and samurai ethics and other groups that valued family status in line with aristocratic ranking was one of the main reasons that aggravated the confusion during the Warring States period, characterized by the social upheaval called *gekokujyō* (social upheaval where those below overcome those above). *Gekokujyō* could be construed as a phenomenon of adverse selection in the hiring market of vassals *a la* Akerlof (1970) under the condition of information asymmetry about the capability of applicants. When the family status of applicants was adopted as the criterion for hiring rather than capability in military technique, the samurai who were competent in martial arts tended to leave the hiring market, causing a deterioration of the military quality of applicants. In Chapter 5 it is discussed that, given the presence of information asymmetry about the capability of applicants for vassals, those *daimyos* who respected family status more than military capability tended to hire less capable vassals, so they were defeated in battle by those *daimyos* who respected military capability more than family status. This was the basic reason for the unprecedented upheaval of social order during the Warring States period.

1.2.1 Mental Models and Cultural Traits

Let us have a preliminary discussion of the conceptual framework of mental models. A more detailed discussion is given in Chapter 2.

In this book culture is considered to be composed of two parts: the behavioral and the internalized part. The behavioral part is in charge of interactions among individuals in various contingencies and comprises behavioral beliefs and values. Behavioral beliefs are beliefs about the behavior of others in the interaction of individuals in various contingencies, and behavioral values reflect utility and profits arising from interactions with others, quite often game theoretic. The internalized part of culture represents deep cognitive and evaluation systems and is composed of internalized beliefs and values. Internalized beliefs are concerned with the cognitive view of the structures and details of the environment, the world individuals experience. There are two aspects to the worldview, one related to the structure of society and the other related to the relationship between humans and nature. Internalized values refer to the value system behind the criteria of rational behavior based on internalized belief, and is usually composed of cognitive, ethical and aesthetic values.

With respect to internalized culture we use a special concept, the mental model representing internalized culture at the individual level. Each individual is assumed to develop a mental model to decipher and evaluate his environment, the world he experiences, and form his opinion about the desirable method of ordering and structuring markets and society. The deciphering of the environment is concerned with internal beliefs, and the evaluation with internalized value. With respect to the issue of the choice of method of ordering and structuring markets, we believe that individuals take an active stance and form their opinions about the environment of their economic activities through development of mental models. In other words, they fulfil a sort of political role either implicitly or explicitly. Although this image of individuals might recall for readers the notion of political entrepreneurs in North (1990), referred to below, we are not referring to special occupational politicians but more generally to constituents of society. In other words, we assume that *every* individual in society has his mental model and forms some opinion about the environment of his economic activities.

With respect to behavioral culture, we consider that individuals are quite passive. Individuals are assumed to follow maximizing behavior on the basis of the behavioral part of the culture of society, which is formed under the significant influence of the internalized part of culture.[15] The influence of the internalized part of culture on the behavioral part of culture occurs through two routes. First are the changes in the relative importance of three basic values in the internalized values. It is often claimed that cognitive value has enhanced importance in modern Occidental thinking, probably reflecting the rapid development of the sciences and pushing aside both ethical and aesthetic values. In Japan, as will be discussed below, the samurai governments pursued ethical values in the governance of the socio-economy. Second is through changes in the mental models to decipher the world that individuals experience. Historically, religions have exerted significant influence on the formation and evolution of the model. The perceived effectiveness of the internalized beliefs in the mental models is quite often an engine that drives the evolution of the mental models. When socio-economic phenomena increase complexity beyond the capacity of the existing models, individuals seek better models. The rapid rise in the complexity of socio-economic phenomena owing to the development of the social division of labor or new production methods seems to have necessitated changes in models.[16]

---

[15] In an attempt to explain how 'institution' is established as a social equilibrium of game-theoretic interaction among individuals, Aoki (2011) presents a model in which the behavioral part of the mental model changes flexibly like various government regulations and laws in the real world. In order to judge the relevance of the Aoki model to reality, we need to conduct more investigation into how the behavioral part of the mental model, such as individualistic or collective tendency in behavioral patterns, discussed in Greif (2006), changes over time. At least, Greif seems to suggest the significant persistence in the behavioral part of the mental models. It seems to be more pertinent to believe that the changes in the behavioral part of culture is basically incurred by changes in the internalized part of culture.

[16] In terms of modern science, Quine (1995) points out that the volume and complexity of scientific knowledge have 'outpaced knowledge about knowledge', and Hands (2001) considers that economic

The internalized worldview of individuals, internalized beliefs, changed gradually but radically during the period from the medieval to early modern period in Japan. The religious model of the worldview seems gradually to have lost effectiveness to decipher the world, changing rapidly due to the acceleration of the social division of labor. Individuals tried to develop new internalized belief models that could analyze the social division of labor more effectively, while at the same time they sought new value systems in the internalized part of culture to accommodate the phenomenon. The Japanese experience suggests that the internalized part of culture, and hence mental models, changes radically over a very long period. Changes in internal beliefs and values had a significant influence on the behavioral part of culture in the long term. Moreover, differences in the internalized part of culture matters significantly in a comparison between social groups or in international comparisons of socio-economic systems.

The term 'cultural changes' is a summary concept of factors that affect the internalized systems of the beliefs and values of social groups. Cultural changes affect the performance of the socio-economy through changes in the mental models of individuals. Changes in the mental models affect socio-economic performance through socio-economic interactions among individuals by way of influencing the behavioral part of culture. The mechanism whereby the interaction between individuals affects socio-economic performance could be effectively summarized by changes in phenomenal representation called cultural traits. It follows that it is convenient to focus on cultural traits to analyze the effect of the internalized part of culture on the socio-economic system. Changes in the pattern of socio-economic performance could be described by cultural traits since individuals can manage and adapt to the traits through their behavior in the socio-economy. While, partly owing to the constraints on the availability of data, existing studies have focused on the direct statistical relationship between such cultural variables related to religion and ethnicity and variables describing socio-economic performance, this methodology, probably based on the assumption that religion and ethnicity are representations of the internalized part of culture, is liable to fail to capture the actual mechanism that works through the mental models. By focusing on cultural traits, we can more adequately analyze the mechanism, in which cultural changes embodied in mental models influence socio-economic performance by way of the behavior of individuals and social groups, which is under the strong influence of the internalized part of culture over the long term. In the following, our analysis focuses on two cultural traits, the *kyūdō* (true-way pursuing) principle and trust, and tries to examine how cultural changes or changes in the internalized part of culture affect human behavior and how cultural changes affect socio-economic performance through the behavior of individuals and social groups.

In summary, the relationship between cultural variables, such as religion and ethnicity, and variables related to socio-economic performance in this book is as follows. Exogenous shocks, such as the evolution of religions and the change in the

---

methodology has been forced to move away from rule-based methodology to the increased role of naturalistic and sociological approaches in order to cope with the increased complexity of the world.

ethnic structure of society, impact on the socio-economic environment of individuals. Individuals are induced to decipher and evaluate their environment by use of their mental models, and seek desirable methods of structuring and ordering the markets as well as incentive systems in the new environment. The interaction and convergence of the mental models of individuals result in the establishment of new institutions and the new development of standards of conduct in the socio-economy. Although we do not have data on the mental models, the analysis of cultural traits, such as trust and *kyūdō* behavior, enables us to trace the mechanism by which changes in mental models results in changes in institutions and culture, which, in turn, influences socio-economic performance, and hence the environment of individuals.

1.2.2 The Kyūdō *(True-Way Pursuing) Principle*

Cultural changes related to religion comprise the main theme of our analysis. In particular, a cultural trait related to religious change, the *kyūdō* (true-way pursuing) principle, played a leading role in the history of socio-economic dynamics. The *Kyūdō* principle was born during the thirteenth through fourteenth century, when the reform of Mahayana Buddhism to ease and simplify religious practice was implemented and disseminated. The reform was undertaken so as to be suitable for the salvation of the masses, who were unable to afford enough time and probably enough energy to implement hard practice (*nangyō*), traditional since the era of early Buddhism. The new doctrine of easy practice (*igyō*) introduced by new Buddhism sects was accepted widely, and, since it enabled individuals to practice religious training during occupational activities, individuals were induced to seek religious meaning in occupational activity, sometimes in hobby and artistic activity in the case of rich aristocrats,[17] giving rise to the *kyūdō* principle. The *kyūdō* principle had a significant influence on the socio-economy of Japan before the Meiji Restoration. The specialization of occupational activities owing to the diffusion of *kyūdō* behavior brought about the diversity and heterogeneity of society. While the heterogeneity of society in the sense of the social division of labor is beneficial for the development of the economy, the heterogenization of society quite often aggravates informational symmetry under the condition of underdevelopment of informationery infrastructures, consequently leading to the deterioration of trust in society. During the fifteenth and sixteenth centuries, the latter aspect of heterogenization, intensified by *kyūdō* behavior including by the samurai class, damaged society through rampant moral hazard and adverse selection, causing a serious prevalence of mistrust, distrust and hence the violence of the Warring State period. During the seventeenth through mid-nineteenth century, under the reign of Tokugawa *bakufu*, the latter aspect of heterogenization of society owing to *kyūdō* behavior was effectively coped with by the development of ethical codes and the standardization of conduct within and among various classes, leading to the

[17] See Teranishi (2014, pp. 242–245) for discussion of the Muromachi shoguns in the protection of the development of *nō*-play and the hobby activity of singing by the retired emperor Go-Shirakawa.

amelioration of informational asymmetry and the reduction of transaction costs of the economy. The economic growth based on the coordination of small producers by the commerce sector during the period was due significantly to the enhanced effort level by the *kyūdō* principle in production as well as reduction of transaction costs.

Let us discuss in more detail the process of evolution of the *kyūdō* principle. As the centralized and nationalized economic system, the *ritsuryō* system, declined during the twelfth and thirteenth centuries, Japanese Buddhism was obliged to face severe social turmoil and unrest in society, and the new sects, Kamakura new Buddhism, was born. While the traditional old Buddhism maintained their stance to pray for the safety of the state and probably for the elite class, the new Buddhism tried to change the stance of religious salvation drastically to one aimed at the salvation of the masses in poverty and distress.

Over a couple of centuries, alongside theoretical and political conflicts with the old Buddhism, the influence of the new Buddhism diffused among the masses in various sections in the country. The consequent change in the teaching from hard training in the monasteries to easy practicing (*igyō*) in the place of secular daily life induced a radical change in the behavioral pattern of individuals. Individuals were encouraged to practice easy assignments but, at the same time, to pursue attainment of enlightenment through sincere effort to understand the structure of the world, clarified by the Buddha. The workplace or job spot became the place of religious practice, and activities related to occupations came to be regarded as having instrumental value to be used to reach enlightenment. The theory behind the instrumental value, merit transfer (*ekō*) theory, was developed by the Mahayana Buddhism from the first century AD. Chapter 4 gives a detailed explanation of the development of the theory, especially about the importance of merit transfer of quality transformation.

The attitude toward occupational activities to seek religious merit to reach enlightenment was called *kyūdō*; *kyū* means seeking, and *dō* means way of doing. In other words, *kyūdō* means pursuit of the true way. In the *kyūdō* principle, people tried to find the truth of the world, understood by the Buddha, in their daily occupational activities in order to arrive at enlightenment, and to accumulate good karma (*gō*) in occupational activity in order to be reborn in better states in the process of transmigration. The term *kyūdō* behavior is used to express behavior based on the *kyūdō* principle. *Kyūdō* behavior by increasingly large numbers of people changed the social scenery radically in the sense that everyone in society during the medieval period aspired to specialization and distinction in his occupational activities through an effort to find truth clarified by the Buddha or to accumulate good karma. During the period from the thirteenth through fifteenth century, increased specialization in occupational activity was seen in every area including handicraft manufacturing, performing arts, paintings, construction of Japanese-style buildings and gardening, and martial skills in the case of the samurai. Many new kinds of artisans emerged, and, in order to coordinate various occupations and production stages for the production of refined goods, the merchant class raised its social importance.

The *kyūdō* principle had significant effects on the economic behavior of individuals in two respects. Individuals were motivated to produce refined and sophisticated products so as to be distinguished in their occupation. There is no doubt that such behavior raised the effort level in production, and the degree of specialization of technology and social development of labor, contributing to the growth of economy. At the same time, however, the accelerated degree of specialization in occupations and hence the accelerated social division of labor through *kyūdō* behavior resulted in an aggravation of informational asymmetry. The once homogenous society, where everyone made everything, was converted into a heterogeneous society, where everyone was in charge of a specialized and different role. Because the development of informational system lagged behind the acceleration of the social division of labor and heterogenization of society, the increased diversity of behavioral patterns made it difficult to forecast the behavior of others, leading to the aggravation of information asymmetry and, hence, a decline in the level of trust in society. Together with the development of the market economy owing to the privatization of the centralized and nationalized economic system, the *ritsuryō* system, it was inevitable that various phenomena related to informational asymmetry emerged and spread in society. In sum, religious reform in Japan came to have significant impacts on the socio-economic dynamics by way of two cultural traits; through the direct effect of the *kyūdō* principle on the effort level and the specialization of technology, and through its indirect influence on the level of trust by way of information asymmetry.

Incidentally, one may notice that there are many activities with the term *dō* in Japanese—sa-*dō* (tea ceremony), ka-*dō* (flower arrangement), sho-*dō* (calligraphy), jyu-*dō* (judo), ken-*dō* (Japanese fencing) and so on. Furthermore, bushi-*dō* is a general term that implies involvement as *kyūdō* behavior in various activities related to the daily life and occupation of *bushi* (samurai). Although these activities do not now have the original meaning related to Buddhism salvation, participants in these activities seem to be requested to seek something spiritual beyond mere skill and technique.

Samurai is a broader term than the term *bushi* because it included such people as clerks at high-ranking temples and indigenous warriors in rural areas, whereas the term *bushi* was confined to the warriors who were specialists in martial skills in charge of military jobs during the medieval and early modern period.[18] In this book we use the term samurai also for professional warriors in Japan, partly because the broader definition is suitable in this book that covers a long period, and partly because the word samurai is already used in English.

It is interesting to note that there occurred a sort of dialectic changes in *kyūdō* behavior. During the first part of the medieval era, the social division of labor and the emergence of heterogeneity in the socio-economy were accelerated by the peculiar lifestyle to pursue Buddhism truth in profane occupational lives. The desire to be distinguished in one's occupational specialty brought about the blossoming of cultural activities in many areas during the South–North Dynasty era (mid-fourteenth century), which, under the protection of Muromachi *bakufu*, culminated in the development of so-called Japanese culture such as the tea-ceremony, *nō*-play and

[18]The definition of the *bushi* class was rigorously established during the reign of the third Tokugawa shogun Iemitsu, who promulgated *Shoshi-shohatto* in 1632. A detailed definition of *bushi* and the other classes is given in Takigawa (1985, pp. 168–182, vol. 2).

Japanese-style gardens, through merging samurai spirits with aristocratic elegancy and refinement as well as with the esthetics nurtured in Buddhist artistic traditions.

The *kyūdō* principle, however, in the style developed among samurai, became a disturbing factor in the Warring States period when the trust system considerably deteriorated. Self-salvation behavior that required to seek resolution in territorial disputes through private battles was an expression of the *kyūdō* principle in the samurai style. This, together with the inadequateness of Buddhist moral codes originally prepared for the quiet and isolated monastery environment, comprised a major factor that amplified confusion in the feudal system, and the deterioration and dysfunction of political order in the Warring States period.

After the recovery of peace by the Tokugawa *bakufu*, the *kyūdō* principle came to play a positive and constructive role once again. Tokugawa *bakufu* introduced the *shokubun* regulation (occupation and role regulation), a class system based on occupational division suitable for the enhanced social division of labor and, at the same time, endowed the samurai class with the monopoly right of violence and assigned them the role of the ethical leadership of society. As a result, not only samurai but also private individuals were encouraged to devote themselves to *kyūdō* behavior in occupational activity, eventually realizing sustained production efficiency. The incentive effects of *kyōdō* behavior seem to have been converted into socially accepted conviction in the Tokugawa era.

The conversion of the religion-based attitude into social conviction in the social evolution seems to be a typical case of a process characterized by Hegelian dialectic development. In other words, *kyōdō* behavior was converted into social conviction after society recovered from the turmoil caused by the *kyūdō* principle and by the inadequacy of existing Buddhist moral codes with respect to the human relationship under the developed social division of labor. Faced with the enormous social turmoil during the Warring States period, serious skepticism toward *kyōdō* behavior grew in society. This skepticism was finally overcome in the Tokugawa era when a new workable system of ethical codes as social standards of conduct was established. The leadership of the samurai and private intellectuals in the establishment of new ethical codes transformed private devotion in *kyūdō* behavior into an engine for social prosperity. Through this process, beliefs and motivation based on religion were converted into social beliefs and values. The largely unintended economic growth during the Tokugawa era was realized as a cultural phenomenon.

1.2.3 Trust and Information

We define the term 'trust' as the degree of easiness regarding forecasting of the behavior of others under the condition of imperfect information.[19] This definition

[19]The methodology for analyzing imperfect information and imperfect markets developed in Greenwald and Stiglitz (1986, 1988) are still of crucial importance in understanding the dynamics in cultural changes from the viewpoint of information.

is synonymous with the definition in Knack and Zack (2001) of trust as 'subjective probability with which an agent assesses that another agent or group of agents will perform a particular action'.[20] While occasionally we use the term 'trust' in a somewhat broader sense of subjective probability held by society as a whole, using the expression social level of trust, this concept is still strictly used in relationship with the cognitive model of individuals in society.

Guiso, Sapienza and Zigalus (2003) define the term 'trust' following the World Value Survey database, which defines trust as an affirmative response to the question of 'Generally speaking, would you say that most people can be trusted or that you can't be too careful in dealing with people?'. This definition treats trust as a social aspect through defining it by way of expected utility arising from interaction among individuals. While their definition seems to be useful in the analysis utilizing the concept of social capital *a la* Putnam, we refrain from using the concept of social capital in this book, so that we will define trust from a purely informational aspect.

Putnam (1993) considers that trust is one of the components of social capital along with such factors as cooperation, participation and social instruction. In other words, Putnam, who is mainly interested in the influence of 'civic culture' on the quality of political institutions, treats trust as a property of society, social capital, that enables collective behaviors. However, collective behavior in society is not a precisely examined concept although there exists a useful analysis of the relationship of easiness of collective action and size of groups provided in Olson (1965)[21] and we will present a preliminary analysis of the collectivism of the Japanese related to stakeholder society in Chapter 8. Moreover, although we do not deny the role of trust as an aspect of culture that enhance social capital in Japan, we do not use the concept of social capital in our analysis, which is too general to describe interactions with institutions and other cultural traits. So, we define the term trust in relation to a strictly behavioral viewpoint of individuals under the condition of imperfect information.

Trust as a higher forecastability of behavior of others is synonymous to the lower level of information asymmetry among individuals. Asymmetric information plays a crucial role in the commerce-based economic growth of Japan, because asymmetric information determines the cost of information and hence transaction costs in the economy. The level of trust or the degree of information asymmetry is dependent on the availability of information infrastructure as well as the degree of forecastability owing to standardization of behavioral patterns among individuals. The former is related to information facility in society, including printing, publication

---

[20]The concept of trust in Akerlof (1970) is used with a similar meaning.

[21]Olson (1965) explains the under-provision of public goods by means of group behavior, arguing that the group provision of public goods encounters special difficulties since individuals can benefit without incurring the costs of provision owing to non-excludability. Individual incentives will work against the formation of groups aimed at the provision of public goods. Moreover, Olson emphasizes that the extent of the free-rider problem would be a function of group size, so that small groups would be more likely to perform better than large groups. This is because as the group size becomes large, the benefits for a single member of the group from collective action get smaller, while the costs of organizing the group increase.

and other communication instruments, while the latter is related to the degree of homogeneousness of values and behavioral patterns by the constituents of the society.

Let us give a preliminary picture of the evolution of trust overtime. Japan started from a homogeneous society in which the social division of labor was still underdeveloped, so that the behavioral pattern of individuals was more or less forecastable. Under the centralized and nationalized *ritsuryō* system, Japanese society was highly homogeneous. Everyone except for the aristocracy cultivated farmland, caught fish in the sea and rivers, manufactured tools for daily use and sold surplus product at roadside markets. Since the behavioral pattern of individuals was similar among individuals, there was not so much necessity for information production. Everyone could forecast the reaction of others from past conduct and conventions. The homogeneity of society underwent drastic deterioration due to the decline of the *ritsuryō* system and the consequent emergence of the market economy and new classes, merchants and the samurai. As the heterogeneity of activities increased, the difficulties in forecasting and understanding of the behavior of others became significant.

The necessity for information was amplified further as individuals began to adopt *kyudō* behavior in order to become specialists in various activities. Due to the combined effects of accelerated heterogenization of society caused by the decline in the *ritsuryō* economic system that accompanied the privatization of state factories of consumption goods, and the accelerated occupational specialization owing to the diffusion of *kyūdō* principle, there occurred serious shortages of information. After the thirteenth century the accelerated progress of social division of labor converted the previously homogeneous society into a highly heterogeneous society with a high degree of informational asymmetry.

Under the reign of Muromachi *bakufu* established in the mid-fourteenth century, relationship-based politics adopted by the *bakufu* triggered a further reduction of trust in society. The prevalence of cheating and shirking or various moral hazards in general in central government politics resulted in a significant deterioration of trust, which was already in jeopardy due to information asymmetry in society. Confusion within the socio-political system and the deterioration of trust in society due to information asymmetry, aggravated by conflicts between the samurai and aristocrats over the acquisition of land as well as cultural leadership, reached a peak during the Warring State period.

The degraded trust finally collapsed altogether when adverse selection in the hiring market of vassals by *daimyos* caused a phenomenon called *gekokujyō*, a social upheaval, where those below overcame those above, leading to a desperate era, full of violence and internal battles. The Warring States period that continued for more than one and half centuries emerged. Radical changes in the internalized mentality of society, with an emphasis on the necessity of peace and the recovery of social order in every strata of society, resulted in the establishment of the Tokugawa *bakufu*, as a compromise between the Tokugawa clan and antagonistic *daimyo* groups, to establish a coalition polity called the *bakuhan* system.

Under the rein of Tokugawa, trust was rehabilitated, and information asymmetry was alleviated through the tenacious efforts of the *bakufu* and samurai, on the one hand, and leading private intellectuals on the other. The decline in information asymmetry caused a significant reduction of transaction costs in the economy, leading to commerce-based economic growth. The seriously deteriorated trust in the Warring States period was rehabilitated by the Tokugawa *bakufu* by a purposeful policy, entailing the reestablishment of moral codes through various methods suitable for various occupational groups in the advanced division of labor. The policy brought about a drastic reduction of information asymmetry, and the recovery of trust, quite unintentionally leading to commerce-based growth through continuous decline in transaction costs in the economy.

1.2.4 Long-Term Changes in Internalized Culture

The main characteristic of culture is considered to be persistence, as is emphasized by North (1990).[22] It seems, however, that culture changes over a very long term, whenever nations or groups experience critical historical shocks to their identity or destiny. As culture changes, mental models, the behavioral and internal representation of culture at an individual level, change also. While we do not have enough knowledge about the autonomous changes of the behavioral part of mental models, we contend that changes in the internalized part of culture over a long period have special importance for the evolution of socio-economy through its effect on the behavioral part of culture. It is a fundamental power of the dynamic evolution of the socio-economic system of nations.

With regard to the Occident, Mokyr (2017) asserts that the experience during 200 years from Columbus to Newton gave rise to a radical change in social beliefs that the human lot can be improved by bettering the understanding of natural phenomena and the application of this understanding to the production process, giving rise to industry-based economic growth led by an active market for useful knowledge related to industrial technology. Habermas (1981) claims that Weber sounded an alarm bell that modernization based on capitalism have brought about a fundamental change in the internalized value system in the Occident. Under the tendency of the bureaucratization of capitalism, the traditional balanced value system that respected all the basic values equally was largely discarded, and, in tandem with the decline of religion and metaphysics, cognitive values have attained a dominant position in the mindset of individuals, excluding aesthetic and ethical values, leading to the deterioration of beliefs and values shared by social groups that have had the power of integration without coercion.

In Japan, too, there occurred a gradual change in the internalized part of culture, and hence in the mental models of the individuals, from the turmoil of the Warring States period through the Tokugawa era. The change, which took four centuries, is

[22]The definition of culture by North is not clear. We procced on the tentative understanding of his definition as transmission from generation to generation, via education and imitation, of information related to knowledge, values and other factors that influence behavior (North 1990, p. 37).

characterized by the shift of the mental models from the exclusive concerns with others nearby to the attention to the welfare of society as a whole. The change proceeded in three phases. At first, there emerged a sincere desire in society to reorganize the system of the Warring States society following the Confucian logic of the way of Heaven, which claimed that an ideal world is realized when society as well as humans follow the reason of the Heaven that embodies the truth of nature. Kanda (2010) contends that this was a unanimous longing during the final phase of the Warring States period of everyone from *daimyos* to rank and file soldiers and from the emperor to the beggars.

Probably partly reflecting the desire for the realization of the way of Heaven, the Warring States period was terminated by the one-day battle, the Sekigahara battle in the year 1600, in which almost all the major *daimyos* participated. This way of settlement was quite new; while the traditional way of assuming hegemony was by way of the time-consuming procedure of piecemeal expansion of one's territory until it covered all national land, the Sekigahara battle was a contest aimed at the establishment of the hegemony of the country as a whole all at once. In other words, while the traditional way followed the Japanese way of acquiring stepwise agreement of others nearby, the Sekigahara battle represented a once-and-for-all settlement of the disputes with the agreement of society as a whole. Instead of the slogan of stepwise integration of the whole country (*tennka-tōitsu*), the new macro-slogan of the peace of the whole country (*tennka-taihei*) was proclaimed. It was the first collective settlement of national matters in Japan, at least since the thirteenth century. Moreover, the winning Tokugawa clan did not confiscate all the territory of the loser, nor delegate its vassal to control the losers, and established the *bakuhan* system. In sum, the Tokugawa clan established a new *bakufu* on the compromise of competing powers, namely without eliminating the antagonistic power.

Finally, while the concept of the way of Heaven was denied theoretically on the ground that it assumed the passivity of humans to the principle given from the outside and neglects independent efforts to establish their own polity, the experience of the socio-economy during the Tokugawa era enhanced the consciousness of society and of national welfare substantially, although the daily life of individual was still tightly restrained by the concept of others nearby, rooted in transmigration and karma. The development of the concept of society is due to a cognitive understanding of the working of the economy. The research academy established by Osaka merchants, Kaitoku-dō, utilized imported documents on the natural sciences of the Occident in scrutinizing the worldview of Confucianism. Private intellectuals, who developed ethical codes for each occupational class, found the macro-economic effects of social division of labor. Moreover, economic development during the period gave rise to the conviction that the standardization of conduct by way of the dissemination of ethical codes brought about harmony in the economy. Individuals of the Tokugawa society, thus, were gradually emancipated from the confine of the Buddhist worldview related to transmigration and karma, consequently preparing for the acceptance of the Occidental worldview based on the notion of the public and society, which swept into Japan explosively after the Meiji Restoration.

The long-term change in the internalized part of culture occurred as a change from the narrow worldview composed of others nearby to the broader worldview composed of the public or society. This stands in clear contrast to the experience of the Occident where the change occurred from individuals tightly restrained by the dictates of God, following the concept of humans created by God, to autonomous individuals with their own cognitive, ethical and aesthetic values. Taylor (1989) describe the move as a highly gradual process starting from the study of the universe, resorting to the concept of the universe as a machine by René Descartes[23] or the possibility to remake ourselves in a rational fashion by John Locke within the confines of the law, Natural Law, laid by God (p. 171), and finally leading to the flourishment of the enlightenment movement. While the change in the internalized part of the mental model occurred in the Occident as a process of discovery of the self, the change in Japan occurred as a process of discovery of the public. It must be noted, however, that the discovery of the public in Japan did not imply the complete discarding of the concept of others nearby. Chapter 7 discusses the failure of the leaders of Meiji Japan, who tried to substitute the internalized part of culture based on others nearby with the concept of the *kokutai*, a surrogate of the Occidental concept of the public.

1.2.5 The North Theory and Tokugawa Japan

Both institutions and culture play a function of structuring society and providing social order in which the market economy works efficiently. We believe that culture has played a leading role in Japan in this regard. This assertion stands in clear contrast with North, who insists on the leading role of institutions and the subordinate and adaptive nature of cultural changes. It may be useful to conduct here a preliminary investigation into the logic of North and show how the North theorem is inapplicable to Japan. In North's framework, the institution is composed of formal institutions (regulations, laws, and constitutions), 'informal institutions' (norms of behavior, convention, and self-imposed codes of conduct related to culture), and their enforcement characteristics. Using this framework, North (1990) contends that changes in formal institutions occur mainly as a result of activities by political entrepreneurs or organizations in the face of changes in micro-level costs and the benefits of institutional restructuring. Further, it is asserted that changes in formal institutions take the initiative in the whole process of institutional evolution, and 'informal institutions' related to cultural inheritance change only adaptively after the changes in the formal institutions. While cultural evolutional theory is still in its infancy, it is contended that one salient characteristic of culture is the persistence of cultural traits in the face of changes in external conditions such as relative prices and formal

[23] It was considered that a mechanical view of the universe was the only one compatible with a God whose sovereignty was defined in terms of the endless freedom of fiat. The idea of a mechanical universe goes back to William of Occam (Taylor 1989, p. 161).

institutions.[24] It follows that the evolution of informal constraints is always gradual because of underlying, deep-seated and persistent cultural inheritance (North 1990, pp. 83–89). Moreover, North claims that the fundamental role of institutions lies in their effect to reduce uncertainty in the interaction of individuals and that this role is carried out by the working of 'informal institutions' induced by the change in formal institutions. 'Informal institutions' reduce informational asymmetry via reputation building, standardization of conduct and conventions formed out of repeated transactions, consequently reducing transaction costs and saving resources needed for information production (North 1990, pp. 27–45).[25]

For the sake of simplicity, we will confine discussion here to the cultural and institutional changes related to the Tokugawa era. Seemingly, the history of economic growth in the Tokugawa era fits, or at least does not contradict, North's theory in two respects. First, the process of economic development occurred after, or in tandem with, a drastic change in formal institutions in the form of the establishment of Tokugawa *bakufu* by political entrepreneurs. This is at least not contradictory to the theory that institution matters most in the explanation of growth. Second is the role of 'informal institutions' that reduced transaction costs. As will be discussed in detail in Chapter 6, the standardization of conduct and conventions of repeated transaction were the main mechanism of transaction cost reduction during the Tokugawa era. This seems to be not inconsistent with the theory that formal rules move first and informal rules follow, and that the latter played a crucial role in reducing uncertainty. Reckless researchers might find 'robust evidence' to support the applicability of the North theorem in the history of Tokugawa Japan.

It is important to note, however, that despite seemingly good conformity, the experience of the Tokugawa economy is crucially different from the logic of North's theorem. First, the establishment and role of formal institutions, Tokugawa *bakufu*, is due largely to the impact of changes in social beliefs. It is not a product of the decisions of political entrepreneurs based on careful cost–benefit calculations. It is true that the organization of *bakufu* was a consequence of the incremental institutional improvement of the samurai government system owing to continued efforts since the establishment of Kamakura *bakufu*. Nevertheless, the decision to establish the Tokugawa regime was caused by radical change in social beliefs during the Warring

[24]Somewhat quite differently from the assertion of North (1990), institutions in Japan before the arrival of Perry had been highly persistent and remained largely inefficient. The *ritsuryō* system established at the beginning of the eighth century as an emergency policy to meet with international tension survived until the sixteenth century, despite its apparent defects in the market economy. The establishment of the effective *bakufu* system was a lengthy process and was not completed. The *bakufu* system of the Tokugawa era, the *bakuhan* system, was a product of compromise among competing *daimyo* powers and was a significantly inefficient system, as was characterized by the system of *sankin-kōtai* (alternate attendance in Edo)—a system explained in Chapter 6. Changes in property rights had been especially slow with respect to residual control rights to lands, as is explained in Chapter 3. It took long time to implement sword-hunting from farmers (Chapter 5) and the monopoly of violence by the samurai was implemented only after the establishment of the Tokugawa *bakufu*.

[25]Dixit (2004) also emphasizes the role of repeated transaction and long-term relationship in establishing private ordering of society without relying on law.

States period; the aspiration for peace and security of society—from the emperor to beggars—motivated warring *daimyos* to cease fire and establish the Tokugawa regime as a compromise among antagonistic military powers. It might be possible that Tokugawa Ieyasu, founder of the Tokugawa *bakufu*, might have been involved in careful calculation about the costs and benefits of establishing the *bakufu*. However, it is hard to believe that mere a cost–benefit calculation of a political entrepreneur brought about the change in culture in the form of social belief. It will be argued that the establishment of the formal institution, the Tokugawa *bakufu*, occurred as a result of a radical change in the internalized part of culture. The growth of the Tokugawa economy was mainly caused by the changes in culture. The emergence of the new mentality that an effective ethical system is urgently needed for the war-addicted nation, not institutions, induced a deliberate move to a society based on a new ethical system. Quite unintendedly, the ethical development reduced the transaction costs drastically and Tokugawa growth resulted.

The second discrepancy of North's theorem from the Japanese experience is concerned with the mechanism to bring about the changes in 'informal institutions' that brought about the reduction of information asymmetry. It will also be discussed in Chapter 6 that trust, defined as a reduction of information asymmetry, was rehabilitated through tenacious and purposive efforts to reorganize the moral codes by the *bakufu* and samurai, on the one hand, and leading private intellectuals on the other. It was not a by-product of the development of formal institutions but rather a direct consequence of cultural evolution and related efforts. The efforts to develop and disseminate workable moral codes suitable for the social division of labor resulted in the standardization of conduct nationwide and ameliorated information asymmetry, leading to the rehabilitation of trust. The *ie* (house) system, which was effective in the enhancement of the trust level through repeated transaction, was also a product of cultural evolution as a device for efficient inheritance of human capital[26] accumulated through a cultural behavioral pattern, *the kyūdō* principle. The entire development of 'informal institutions' in Japan during the period is a consequence of cultural evolution and of purposive efforts to develop workable ethics, and it is difficult to explain it as a by-product of the development of formal institutions.

---

[26]It is also necessary to note the complimentary relationship between institutional developments and cultural traits. For one thing, *ie* was an informal institution that helped to promote *kyōdō* behavior by providing the succession mechanism of accumulated skills (human capital) nurtured by *kyōdō* behavior. *Ie* was effective also in providing fork theorem conditions, so that *ie* had fulfilled an important role to avoid and reduce opportunistic behavior. For another, *shokubun* regulation was a formal institution that helped the working of *kyōdō* behavior. Because people are classified into occupational groups, there occurred competition among those who belonged to the same groups. This competition retained a high degree of fairness because competitors knew each other well and were tied by ethical codes commonly held by the individuals in the same occupation, so that it was difficult to resort to unfair means to defeat competitors.

1.3 The Role of Institutions

Institutions are simply defined as socially contrived rules that constrain the behavior of individuals. This definition is similar to the definition of North (1990)—institutions as the rules of the game or the humanly devised constraints that structure human interactions.

It is our basic assertion that culture could also be the social framework that orders human interactions. We will contend that, in Japan, institutional adjustments were, by and large, ineffective in influencing socio-economic performance either in promoting economic growth or retarding socio-economic development. Let us summarize this assertion with respect to three major institutions in Japanese history: the *ritsuryō* system, feudalism and the samurai governments (the Kamakura, Muromachi and Tokugawa *bakufu*).

We will show that the role of institutions in the socio-economic history of Japan was, by and large, very weak and under the strong influence of autonomous changes in cultural factors. It is argued below, for example, that the influence of the decline of the institutions of the *ritsuryō* system on the emergence of religious reform was not significant, and the reform was, by and large, the endogenous outcome of the evolution of religion. Moreover, the drastic changes in the socio-economy were caused not by institutional factors but through radical impacts caused by autonomous changes within culture and cultural traits. This is exemplified by the decline and almost collapse of trust in the Warring States period and the rehabilitation of trust in the Tokugawa era as a result of autonomous movements within culture. What was more important was that the adjustment of institutions to the deterioration of cultural traits or the effect of institutions to ameliorate the aggravated situation was largely ineffective and quite often ended in failure. For example, it is contended that the institutional functioning of feudalism in Japan was largely ineffective under the strong influence of cultural behavioral codes.

The *Ritsuryō* System

With respect to the *ritsuryō* system, it is often asserted that the decline of this system 'caused' the collapse of Heian prosperity and, hence, the emergence of new Buddhism. The decline of aristocratic sovereignty and the privatization of production during the eleventh and twelfth centuries caused a drastic change in culture and cultural traits. Trust in society began to deteriorate. So, it is asserted that Buddhism was obliged to be engaged in the salvation of the masses, giving birth to Kamakura new Buddhism.

We doubt this conventional assertion of the causal relationship between the institutional change, the decline of the *ritsuryō* system, and the cultural phenomena, the transformation of Buddhism. It is argued that, although it is undeniable that the decline of the *ritsuryō* system triggered the change in Buddhism, both changes in the *ritsuryō* system and Buddhism had aspects programmed beforehand within themselves. It is not correct to put too much emphasis on the causal relationship between the two phenomena. Especially, it is misleading to contend that the fall of the *ritsuryō* system as an institutional change caused the cultural change of Buddhist transformation.

It is true that Kamakura new Buddhism emerged in the thirteenth century when the *ritsuryō* system began to decline. However, this does not imply that the latter was the main cause of the former. There are three reasons. Firstly, the birth of Kamakura new Buddhism owes much to the internal logic of the evolution of religion. Mahayana Buddhism, which was introduced to Japan in the sixth century and became the parent body of Kamakura new Buddhism, was a Buddhism that emerged to respond to the necessity of salvation of the masses in distress. Since the first century AD, Mahayana Buddhism developed various new doctrines and methods for this purpose. In Chapter 4, it is contended that the main doctrine introduced by Kamakura new Buddhism, the easy-practice principle, was an innovation that comprised one of the steps in the process of the evolution of Mahayana Buddhism. Moreover, the basic force that brought about the emergence of the new Buddhism was a phenomenon in the long-term evolutionary process of universal tendency, the awakening of the masses from the ancient preestablished harmony to the negation of this world that necessitated the salvation of them in the process of social and market development, as is suggested by Bellah (1964). In other words, the emergence of new Buddhism was basically a product of a predetermined shift from the religion aimed at the salvation of elites and specialized priests to a religion with a role in the salvation of the masses of layman believers, who could not afford many resources to practice.

Secondly, as will be discussed below, the *ritsuryō* system was a system introduced as an emergency policy to meet international military tension in the seventh century regarding the Korean peninsula. Since a radically sophisticated Chinese system was introduced suddenly into the significantly primitive community society of Japan, one without even the concept of private property held by families, it was destined to change and evolve after the initial establishment. It is natural to believe that the government that introduced the *ritsuryō* system was well aware of the necessity of improvement and adjustment of the system. The *ritsuryō* system continued to exist until the fifteenth century. The 'decline' of the system could be more pertinently understood as an evolution and adjustment programmed beforehand.

Thirdly, the transformation of the *ritsuryō* system is basically a phenomenon that proceeded in the continual process of market development. It is true that the acceleration of the development of the market economy occurred due to the 'decline' of the *ritsuryō* system in the sense of the privatization of landholding and the formation of private property by the aristocracy, consequently causing inequality in society, suffering of the masses and social unrest. However, it must be noted that the formation of private property was necessitated also by the development of the market economy. Although the direction of causality should be judged carefully, the real culprit was marketization, not the 'decline' of the *ritsuryō* system.

It is true that, during the thirteenth century, a drastic transformation and decline of the *ritsuryō* system due to the privatization of land occurred, and that the Kamakura new Buddhism emerged during the unprecedented turmoil and social unrest. It is easy to assert that the aggravated social order due to the decline in the *ritsuryō* system caused the necessity for the salvation of the masses in distress and to infer a causal relationship from the former to the latter, the influence of institutional changes on culture. However, it is contended below that, even if it is admitted that the former worked as a trigger for the latter, there is a profound reason to doubt the causality in the general sense.

The Feudal System

Feudalism in Japan was institutionalized by the Kamakura *bakufu*. The founder, Minamoto Yoritomo, was allowed by the imperial court in 1185 to grant official positions, *shugo* and *jitō*, to his housemen (*gokenin*). The role assigned to *shugo* and *jitō* was to maintain social security in government-owned lands (*kōryō*) and manors (*shōen*). Their roles were assigned as official position (*shiki*) designated by the imperial court and they were allowed to obtain rent income from manors. Feudalism in Japan began formally as enfeoffment of official positions (*shiki*), not land, to vassals. Partly for this reason, the samurai in Japan had a special propensity to obtain official justification for their fief control. In particular, during the Muromchi era, *daimyos* were eager to obtain official positions in the imperial court and, consequently, the right to allocate positions to them came to comprise a major source of political power for the aristocracy in charge of the administration of the imperial court.

Regarding the effectiveness of the institution of the feudal contract, it is possible to point out significant cultural impacts. It is contended that feudalism in Japan functioned in a society under the strong influence of Buddhism, in which the behavior of individuals was governed by concerns about the accumulated amount of karma (*gō*), which determines the position in transmigration in the next life. For this reason, feudal contracts were considered to be something of value of a lower dimension compared with the destiny determined in religious logic through accumulated karma. It is argued below that behavior such as self-salvation based on *en* (inter-personal relationship) that brought about the disfunction of the feudal governance system is largely related to this value system, so that the upheaval of the Warring States period was deeply rooted in culture.

In the Buddhist mind-construct of the samurai, many of whom were Zen Buddhist believers, one's relationship with others nearby and destiny in the future life is determined by the amount of karma accumulated by the inter-personal ties in past lives, so that the relationship to the ties are stronger and much more binding than master–vassal relationships, which are based on contractual relationships in the present life. The obligations of the master–vassal relationship were regarded as only temporarily binding, not related to the past nor to future lives, so that feudal loyalty could easily be disregarded in consideration of more important group ties emanating from past-life relationships and exerting influence on not only present but also future life. During the Warring States period, rebellions and treachery vis-a-vis masters as well as conflicts among vassals were daily and ubiquitous matters, giving rise to unmanageable confusion in the governance system. Moreover, conflicts among samurai were resolved by themselves with the help of others nearby, without consultation with and sanction of feudal masters.

It seems that the feudal system was not a simple contractual relationship in Japan. For one thing, the relationship with the imperial court system, the official position as well as ranking, comprised an important factor in the feudal relationship. For another, the Buddhist value system, related to the significant concerns with the amount of karma, had substantial weight in the value system of the samurai and, hence, on the value of the feudal contract. It follows that simple contract theory based on only institutional arrangements related to loyalty and land enfeoffment does not apply to the Japanese feudal system. It will be shown in Chapter 5 that imperial ranking and Buddhist value had considerably destructive influences on feudal institutions in Japan during the Warring States period.

Samurai Government; Kamakura and Muromchi bakufu

The efficiency of the *bakufu* (samurai government) institutions is closely and probably fundamentally related to conflicts between the samurai and aristocratic class, and conflicts between the two classes were deeply rooted in cultural factors, so that institutional factors related to samurai governance were not the major factor in bringing about socio-economic performance.

In the existing literature, it is implicitly assumed that the effectiveness of the samurai government, the Kamakura *bakufu*, was mainly related to the institutional mechanism. In particular, the governance system of the samurai class with respect to both vassals (*gokenin*) and other samurai powers was the focal point of analysis. We will point out that, although the importance of the governance system is undeniable, the governance issue is closely related to the relationship between two governments, the *bakufu* and the imperial court, which, in turn, was under the significant influence of cultural factors. Throughout the medieval age, *the bakufu* maintained the stance to respect the land system, the *shōen-kouryō* system (coexistence of manor and government-owned land system), that comprised the foundation of the power of the aristocracy, and shrines and temples. Both aristocrats and large temples and shrines were major owners of manors but, at the same time, pertained to the benefits of public revenue arising from publicly held lands and, more importantly, the aristocracy were the core players of the imperial government. While the two governments retained cooperative and coexisting relationships throughout the medieval age, the introduction of the institution of *shugo* and *jitō* caused the transformation of the land control system that had comprised the foundation of the economic power of the aristocracy, weakening the economic power of the aristocracy. This is because the infringement of rights to land induced strategic behavior by the aristocracy. Aristocrats began to utilize their superiority in ceremonial knowledge in the imperial court as well as the right to allocate official positions and rankings as tools to put the samurai and *bakufu* under their political control. This made conflicts over cultural matters, including hegemony in cultural development, a focal issue in the political conflicts between the aristocracy and *bakufu*.

The Kamakura *bakufu* was established at the end of twelfth century, as one section of the *ritsuryō* government in charge of military and policing roles. The imperial court retained control over all administrative matters other than military and policing activities.[27] While the *bakufu* maintained the stance to respect the *shōen-kōryō*-system, there occurred frequent land disputes between the samurai and aristocracy. This was partly caused by the culture related to the notion of the ultimate ownership of land[28]; but the main reason lay in the transformation of the agricultural production system. The agricultural production system in the Kamakura era was changing from previous large-scale extensive farming to intensive farming with settled cultivators, and the primitive village system was emerging (Gomi-Ito 2002). Under such conditions, the *jitō* felt difficulty in implementing their role that specialized in policing, so by necessity they came to be involved in general administrative matters in manors and public lands, with the consequent infringement of the rights held by the aristocracy. The *bakufu* could not resist the implicit demand by the *jitō* to establish a more efficient governance system in order to implement the role assigned to them, so that it was inevitable for the *bakufu* to tacitly approve the infringement of the landholding right of the aristocracy by the *jitō* (Yoshie 1986, p. 265). Moreover, regarding the petition of land disputes between the *jitō* and aristocrats (*honjyo-ryōke*), the *bakufu* ruled following two principles; first was the contract system[29] that specified a fixed amount of rent be given to the *honjyo-ryōke*, the manor-owning aristocracy, with all the residual income and the control right going to the *jitō*, and second the principle of dividing the rights to land as a whole half-and-half between the *jitō* and the *honjyo-ryōke* (the *shitaji-chūbun* policy).[30] Although the Kamakura *bakufu* adhered to its respect for the *shōen-kōryō* system and to the principle of mutual noninterference between the *bakufu* and the imperial court, these movements significantly damaged

[27]With respect to military and policing matters, the *bakufu* were not necessarily omnipotent. The activity was formally under the control of such sections as the *kebiishi* (judiciary and police office) in the *ritsuyō* government (Yoshie 1986, p. 267). Moreover, the policing of manors, in which *jitō* were not designated was carried out by manor-owning aristocrats (*honjyo*), and temples and shrines. After the second half of the thirteenth century, policing activity came to be implemented by the *bakufu* through the intermediation of the imperial court (Takahashi 2013).

[28]It is important to note that the infringement of the landholding right of the aristocracy by the samurai had cultural reasons that slight potentially the land-holding rights of aristocrats established on donation by land developers. In terms of non-aristocratic culture, the invasion of the rights of aristocrats, *honjyo* and *ryōke*, by *jitō* was not necessarily criminal or immoral from the viewpoint of culture during the medieval period. During the period, there remained the strong conception that the possession of land by the outsider was a temporary phenomenon, and the ultimate holding right remained with those who had originally developed (Katsumata 1979, pp. 87–118). This notion implies that the right to land donated to the aristocracy, hence the right to rents by *honjyo* and *ryōke*, could be cancelled, because aristocrats had never been engaged in land developing themselves. It could be argued that behind the violent activity of the *jitō* to invade the right of landholding was the notion that the samurai class, many of whom had been land-developing lords, were the legitimate owners of the land, or at least that the aristocrats were not the legitimate owners.

[29]This contract system was carried out by the *jitō* and the role of the *jitō* was called *ukesho* (Nagahara 1998, pp. 189–190).

[30]Ishimota (1956) claims that, owing to *shitaji-chubun*, a true feudal system based on landholding, not based on official positions approved by the imperial court (*shiki*), was 'finally established'. See Chapter 5.

the economic powerbase of aristocrats as well as the large shrines and temples.[31] Moreover, after the failure of the attempt by ex-emperor Gotoba to defeat the *bakufu* in 1221, the aristocracy lost the power to resort to military action by mobilizing the samurai, who were intimate with the imperil court (Kawai 2013).

Deprived of military power utilizing samurai groups antagonistic to the *bakufu* and economic power based on the *shōen-kōryō* system, the last resort for aristocrats to maintain influence on politics was the manipulation of official status in the imperial court, which could have influence on the legitimacy of the activities and, hence, the ultimate governing power of the samurai. To enhance the effectiveness of manipulation, aristocrats emphasized their supremacy in refinement and knowledge in cultural activities, which was indispensable for the ceremonial authority of the imperial court. The Muromachi *bakufu*, which was established after the Kamakura *bakufu* during the latter half of the fourteenth century, was captured by this strategy of the aristocrats. This was partly related to the lack of legitimacy of the founding Ashikaga clan, which was not distinguished compared with other clans as the successor of the Kamakura *bakufu*.[32] Locating the *bakufu* office in the center of Kyoto, shoguns of the Muromachi *bakufu* tried to become 'aristocratic samurai' and to obtain high official ranking in the imperial court and administrative roles in the central government of the *ritsuryō* system. This was quite different from the stance of the Kamakura *bakufu* that opened the *bakufu* office in Kamakura, 400 km away from Kyoto.

The downfall of the Kamakura *bakufu* in 1333 was the consequence of the economic weakening of vassals (*gokenin*) owing to the expenditures in the battles related to the Mongolian invasions in 1274 and 1281, and of the deterioration of their loyalty to the *bakufu* due to dissatisfaction with the policy of respecting the *shōen-kōryō* system[33] for the sake of the aristocracy, and shrines and temples. Takahashi (2013) argues that, while policy reform to convert the role of the *jitō* comprising *gokenin* from the position of mere administrator of the *shōen-kōyō* system subordinate to the aristocracy into indigenous lords independent of the aristocracy and able to engage in active and integrated ruling (*ichien-shihai*) of territory was urgently needed, such a policy was hard to implement under the reign of the Kamakura *bakufu*. It seems that the sense of cultural subordination and the sense of inferiority of the *bakufu* and the samurai to aristocrats were the major reason for this (Yoshie 1986).

During the Muromachi era, there occurred active competition regarding cultural development between the samurai and aristocrat classes. Top-ranking samurais, such as *shugo*, sought official ranking in aristocratic society and made significant efforts to obtain high evaluation regarding refinement in cultural attainments. Shogun Ashikaga

---

[31] The samurai also suffered from the situation, and the poverty of the *gokenin* (vassal) came to be a serious problem for the *bakufu*. In order to mitigate the damage, a debt cancellation order (*Einin no tokusei-rei*) was promulgated in 1297. This led to the large-scale repurchase of land by the *gokenin*, entailing upheaval and the related further insecurity of landholding (Gomi-Ito 2002).

[32] The founding Minamoto clan of the Kamakura *bakufu* was a direct heir of an emperor, while the Ashikaga clan was one of the oblique descendants of the Minamoto clan.

[33] After the end of the thirteenth century, the *bakefu* departed from the policy of non-interference and became involved in the conflict with the imperial court regarding the succession of emperorship.

Yoshimitsu devoted substantial sums to support the development of cultural activities, eagerly trying to merge samurai culture with aristocratic palace culture, and to give elegance and refinement to the former.

As a result, in the society of central government, ranking in family status, not military prowess, was the major determinant of the allocation of official positions as well as the distribution of various benefits. Whereas the samurai needed strong military power to survive during the ubiquitous warfare, the official ranking of the family was indispensable for being distinguished in terms of political power in the central government, motivating them to be engaged in the practice of cultural activities, for example, the performing arts and purchasing high-priced craft goods. A serious trade-off between the pursuit of military prowess and cultural refinement characterized the behavioral pattern of the samurai in Muromachi society. It is argued in Chapter 5 that the phenomenon of *gekokujyō* that characterizes the turmoil of the late Muromachi era was caused by the adverse selection in the hiring market of outside vassals by the *daimyos*, whose values system was fragmented into two conflicting values, military and cultural.

In sum, the effectiveness and performance of *bakufu* institutions during the Kamakura and Muromachi era were under the continual and persistent impacts of cultural factors rather than their military and administrative efficiency.

Samurai Government; Tokugawa bakufu

The contribution of institutions to the prosperous Tokugawa economy is also largely irrelevant, or at least very weak. While the aristocracy had already lost power during the Tokugawa era, the *bakufu* policy was greatly obsessed with the potential antagonism of outside (*tozama*) *daimyos*, who fought against Tokugawa in the Sekigahara battle in 1600. The *Bakufu* was continually involved in the monitoring and resorting measures to weaken the economic and military power of outside *daimyos*. *Sankin-kōtan*, the institution of assigning alternate residence in the capital city (Edo) to *daimyos*, was a typical such policy. While the institution of the *shokubun* regulation had some effect on the development of ethical rules specific to occupations, the basic motivation for the institution lay in the prevention of the secret military build-up in the rural sector by outside *daimyos*.

The *shokubun* regulation was formally introduced in the Tokugawa *bakufu*, inheriting the policy of separating the farmers and samurai (sword-hunting policy) by Toyotomi Hideyoshi. It stipulated four occupation classes: samurai, farmers, artisans and merchants. The purpose of this system lay in blocking the secret conversion of farmers into samurai soldiers. This was the urgent policy agenda for the stability of the Tokugawa regime. The demilitarization of farmers was an indispensable measure to monitor and regulate the military power of outside *daimyos*.

It will be argued below that the *shokubun* regulation had an unintended effect on economic performance through facilitating the development of ethics and standards of conduct for each occupation. To reestablish trust in society, where the social division of labor was highly developed, the classification and ranking of occupations had the unintended result of alleviating the serious information asymmetry in society. This unintended result, however, does not justify the economic institution policy of the Tokugawa *bakufu*. The institutional policies of the Tokugawa *bakufu* were strongly colored by the lack of consideration for economic efficiency. The *sankin-kōtai* system was introduced to force unnecessary fiscal expenditure to prevent the military build-up of possibly antagonistic *daimyos*. No doubt this policy imposed a severe fiscal burden on *daimyos*, probably increasing the antagonism toward the *bakufu* further. Moreover, there is much scope to doubt the rationality of policies to control the activities of merchants. For example, regulations on guild activity introduced during the 1840s from the viewpoint of disinflation are hard to justify in view of the serious disturbance to the commercial order. They could be regarded as an implicit repression policy against the merchant class.

We need to turn to the role of private and informal institutions. Informal organizations, *ie*, had a positive influence on economic growth through preventing short-sighted opportunistic behavior. Informal institutions, that is based on the joint punishment mechanism, ostracism, among merchants and farmers, had some disciplining effects in trade associations (*kabu-nakama*) and village activities. However, it is hard to believe that such informal institutions and organizations had a positive and dynamic influence to drive the engine of sustained macro-economic growth during the Tokugawa era. In this book it is contended that the dynamic growth of the Tokugawa economy owes fundamentally to the decrease in transaction costs caused by the purposive efforts to develop ethical rules suitable for the advancement of the social division of labor.

In sum, while the economic growth attained during the Tokugawa era was a largely unintended consequence of the intended efforts in the cultural development of society, the role of institutions in that growth was at least irrelevant.

Summary

In the history of Japan before the Meiji Restoration, culture took the initiative regarding changes in the development of the socio-political framework of economic activities, and institutions largely played secondary and subsidiary roles to cultural changes and even frequently failed to catch up with the changes caused by culture.

First, institutions have been largely ineffective in bringing about social order in Japan. This is typically seen in the method of ordering the socio-economy during the Tokugwa era. The powerful Tokugawa *bakufu* concentrated most of its energy on the defense of the *bakufu* system from potential attack by antagonistic outside *daimyos* and was unable to organize the collective behavior for socio-economic development. The task of establishing and maintaining the socio-economic order was largely left to the cultural power of the private sector. Standards of conduct and conventions nurtured through cultural development played effectively the role of ordering the market. The economic growth attained during the Tokugawa era was a largely unintended consequence of the intended efforts in the cultural development of society. It is hard to believe that economic institutions had substantial positive effects on Tokugawa economic growth.

Second, the inefficiency of the institutions was not a major factor related to the socio-political disorder in Japan. The inefficiency of institutions of Muromachi *bakufu* was closely and probably fundamentally related to conflicts between the samurai and aristocratic class, and conflicts between the two classes were deeply rooted in cultural factors, so that institutional factors related to samurai governance were not the major factor in bringing about socio-economic performance. The *gekokujyō* could be construed as a phenomenon of adverse selection caused by the mentality of *daimyos*, whose values system was fragmented into two conflicting values—aristocrat and samurai. The rampant moral hazards caused by relation-based politics during the Muromachi era are eloquent evidence for the proposition that hastily established institutions applied to society as a whole, without obtaining consensus, are liable to fall victim to opportunistic behavior.

Finally, the autonomous movements of culture were the dominant factor to bring about the dynamic changes in the socio-economic system of Japan. A typical example for the cultural autonomy is the relationship between the fall of the *ritsuryō* system as an institutional change and the emergence of Kamakura new Buddhism as a cultural phenomenon. It is misleading to contend a causal relationship from the former to the latter. The emergence of new Buddhism is basically a product of the programmed development of Mahayana Buddhism, following the mission assigned to it since its birth. Likewise, feudalism in medieval Japan fell into disfunction because the feudal contract between master and vassal as an institution was considered to be inferior to the cultural human relationship nurtured in the process of transmigration in Buddhism. Further, the dynamic effects of *kyūdō* behavior is an additional evidence of the autonomous influences of cultural factors on the socio-economy. *Kyūdō* behavior aggravated information asymmetry, leading to serious confusion in society during the medieval ages, whereas during the Tokugawa era, *kyūdō* behavior definitely had positive effects on the supply-side of the economy through the enhancement of the effort level of farmers and artisans.

1.4 The Plan of the Book

Chapter 2 develops the conceptual framework of this book. The concept of internalized culture and the mental models are defined and clarified in the context of a comparison of the internalized beliefs and values in the Occident and Japan. It is argued that a fundamental reason for the question why culture was important in Japan in ordering markets and shaping socio-economic incentives lies in the internalized culture in Japan. Since the belief and value systems of the Japanese, at least before the Meiji Restoration, in the deep internalized part of culture was based on concerns about others nearby—with whom individuals interact in this world as well as in the imaginary process of transmigration—differs significantly among individuals, it is costly to arrive at the sharing of mental models. On the other hand, in the Occident where the core content of the internalized part of the mental model is composed of the collective intentional concept of the public, it was less costly to use institutions in structuring and ordering markets. It follows that the comparative advantage in the technology of social building for Japan was not in institutional building but rather in cultural development. The implications of the conceptual framework are explored further in terms of the long-term flexibility of the internalized part of culture, the autonomy of culture and the causality from culture to institutions, and the emergence of the theory of institutions and culture in Tokugawa Japan.

Chapter 3 provides a macro-economic overview of the long-term growth process in Japan before the Meiji Restoration. Through an examination of the GDP series and its industrial composition, it is contended that the growth process is composed of two salient phases, before and during the Tokugawa era. The first phase is led by agricultural growth owing to technical progress supported by infrastructure investment and the second phase is led by the growth of the commerce sector. The first phase of growth was accompanied by the drastic change in the industrial structure from an agrarian economy to an economy based on the secondary and tertiary sector. The second phase is characterized by a stable industrial structure, the balanced growth of the three sectors. The mechanism of growth is investigated with respect to the three factors that comprised the major themes in the existing literature—technical progress in agriculture, the incentive effects of property rights and the role of the development of commerce. Growth before the Tokugawa era was due to agricultural technological progress against the backdrop of infrastructure investment. The balanced growth during the Tokugawa era was due to the decline in transaction costs that induced commerce-based growth, with the development of markets for products of small producers. Agricultural technology and the role of property rights were not significant as variables to explain the growth pattern of the Tokugawa era.

Chapter 4 investigates how the internalized part of culture was formed in Japan in the context of cultural history from the end of the ancient age through the beginning of the medieval age. The evolution of Japan's internalized beliefs and values is examined in the interaction of two major incidents: religious reform, the birth of Kamakura new Buddhism, related to culture, and the decline of the *ritsuryō* system, the centralized and nationalized economic system, related to the institution. It is argued that the introduction of practice simplification or the easy practice principle as a method of salvation of the masses by Japanese Buddhism, and the consequent birth of the *kyūdō* principle, occurred in the socio-economic context of the emergence of the market economy related to the decline of the *ritsuryō* system and in the theoretical context of the historical evolution of Mahayana Buddhism since its birth. The interaction with others nearby in occupational activity motivated by *kyūdō* behavior came to have additional and highly important meanings for the life of the Japanese. This is because merit transfer of qualitative transformation plays the role of converting good deeds in occupational activities motivated by *kyūdō* behavior into merits for arriving at enlightenment, emancipation from transmigration. Consequently, concerns with others nearby in the internalized belief of the Japanese mindset was intensified and came to be held widely among individuals.

Chapter 5 is devoted to the analysis of the process of the decline in trust levels in society during the medieval period and the emergence of the turmoil and misery of the Warring States period. The reasons for the decline of trust were the acceleration of the social division of labor, which enhanced informational requirements, consequently aggravating information asymmetry in society, and the defects of Buddhist ethical codes that could not provide adequate behavioral conventions and standards of conduct for the developed market economy. It is contended that, due to the heterogenization of society and aggravated informational asymmetry that brought about the deterioration of trust levels in society, the functioning of institutions in medieval Japan became increasingly inefficient and gradually unable to fulfil the social functions assigned. First was the disfunction of the political system of the *bakufu* institution. The *bakufu* institutions lost effectiveness almost completely due to the defects of relation-based politics of the central government against the backdrop of the conflicts in the value systems between aristocrats and samurai. Second, a serious deterioration of institutions occurred with respect to the feudal system. Due to the sanctification of religion-related group behavior such as self-salvation, governance based on the master–vassal relationship lost effectiveness. During the more than century-long Warring States period characterized by incessant internal wars, the aggravation of confusion due to the lowering of trust levels in society gave rise to innumerable moral hazards and adverse selections in the socio-economy.

Chapter 6 examines the process and result of the rehabilitation of trust during the Tokugawa era. It is contended that the reduction of transaction costs through the rehabilitation of trust, which had been aggravated seriously during the end of the medieval age, and the alleviation of information asymmetry in the socio-economy, was a major engine of economic growth during the Tokugawa era. The rehabilitation of trust was due mainly to the intentional efforts to improve the ethical system to accommodate the advancement in the social division of labor in the economic system. Ethics were developed and disseminated by the government and elites—such as private intellectuals and the samurai—during the Tokugawa era. Cultural development standardized the behavioral pattern significantly, and the improved forecastability of the behavior of others in the interaction, consequently reducing transaction costs significantly and giving rise to the commerce-based balanced growth of industries during the eighteenth century.

The enhanced work efforts of small producers based on the *kyūdō* principle was coordinated by the activity of merchants, leading to significant progress in the interregional division of labor. It is contended that the long-term decline of interest rates in the eighteenth century is evidence for the decline in risk premium due to information asymmetry and hence the decline of overall transaction costs.

Chapter 7 analyzes how the Japanese economy, which had experienced culture-led growth until the mid-nineteenth century, accepted and accommodated Occidental thought and institutions after the Meiji Restoration. The examination focuses on the process to adjust the mental model based on others nearby with the new value and belief system that emphasized the concept of the public. The leaders of prewar Japan experienced severe conflicts in the process and, to bridge Japanese and Occidental values, introduced three mechanisms. First was the concept of the *kokutai* (national polity) to enhance centripetality and national spirit. Second was the assignment of the role of interface between the government and the private sector to regional leaders called *meibōka* (men of repute). Third was the new form of *ie* system as a device to adjust to Occidental values and preserve the value of human capital accumulated through the period before the Meiji Restoration. Both the *meibōka* system and the new form of *ie* system played the role of mitigating the shock of the introduction of

Occidental institutions. It is controversial, however, whether the concept of *kokutai* worked effectively and realized the intention of the Meiji leaders. From the viewpoint of the model in this book, it is not easy to change cultural traditions by means of institutional devices. It is suggested that the roles of these institutional adjustments had been transitory and were destined to be revised in order to accomplish the successful fusion and coexistence of Japanese and Occidental internalized culture.

Chapter 8 examines the origin of the so-called 'collectivism of the Japanese' in the context of the mental model of the Japanese. It is claimed that collectivism of the Japanese has very little to do with the internalized culture historically nurtured in Japan, and that it is more closely related to the historical conditions after the Meiji Restoration, when the severe restrictions on the labor market were abolished under the condition of the accumulated community-specific human capital. The examination is conducted in the context of the comparative framework between England and Japan. It is shown that collectivism is related to the sharing of community-specific human capital accumulated under the condition of the absence of an efficient labor market before the dissolution of the community system. It is conjectured that the human capital in the community at the Meiji Restoration was largely composed of community-specific skills due to the under-development of the open labor market. Because community-specific skills are difficult to be transacted in the market, there occurred resistance to dissolve communities, giving rise to the stakeholder society. It must be noted that the stakeholder society born in this way has very little to do with the internalized view and values nurtured historically through deep concerns with others nearby, and is also quite different from the collective intentionality of the Occident developed under the influence of the concept of the public and humans.

Chapter 2
Mental Models and the Cost of Institutions

Why was culture important in Japan in structuring and ordering markets and shaping socio-economic incentives? A fundamental reason lies in the internalized culture in Japan. Since the belief and value system of the Japanese, at least before the Meiji Restoration, in the deep internalized part of culture was based on concerns about others nearby, with whom individuals interact in this world as well as in the imaginary process of transmigration, and others nearby differ significantly among individuals, it is costly to arrive at the sharing of mental models. It follows that the comparative advantage in the technology of social building for Japan, where the sharing of mental models is difficult and collective intentionality is low, was not in institution building but rather in cultural development.

Both institutions and culture play the role of structuring and ordering the market: institutions through providing constraints on conduct and culture through standardizing conduct. To secure the effectiveness of institutions, it is necessary to establish institutions by the participation of individuals among whom the content of mental model is shared and to minimize opportunistic behavior. In other words, any institution that fails to be established by the participation of individuals with a similar worldview is destined to be ineffective due to opportunistic behavior. Owing to the nature of the internalized belief and value system that respects small groups composed of others nearby, Japanese people were not good at collective behavior such as voluntary participation, interaction with anonymous people and sharing mental models with them. Because each group of others nearby is made up of different individuals, the worldview based on others nearby is different among individuals, so that the sharing of the mental model is costly. This explains the innate difficulty for the Japanese to order social incentives by means of institutions. Instead, the Japanese were ready to share ethical codes and standardize conduct with others nearby and establish firm informal human relationships in small groups. The relationship within a small group with others nearby extends into relationships among groups, and further results in social level sharing of ethical codes and standards of conduct. As a consequence, the ordering of incentives could be accomplished, and the standardization of economic

J. Teranishi, *Culture and Institutions in the Economic Growth of Japan*,
Studies in Economic History,
https://doi.org/10.1007/978-4-431-55627-5_2

behavior realized as a cultural equilibrium. While constraints on behavior imposed by institutions could be evaded by opportunistic behavior for profit, the standardization of conduct in a cultural equilibrium could not, although aberration might cause guilty feelings.

Following the ideas of Denzau and North (1994), Greif (2006) and Aoki (2011), we assume that individuals develop mental models to decipher and evaluate their environment, the world they experience. The novelty of our theory lies in focusing on the differences between societies with respect to the content of mental models, or on what kinds of concepts individuals utilize to explain their environment. In the Occident, individuals mainly rely on abstract concepts such as the public or humanity to explain their environment and to form their opinions about the desirable method of ordering markets and shaping incentives, while in Japan individuals rely on the concept of others nearby. The difference between the concepts causes the difference in the easiness of the sharing of mental models and, hence, in the cost of summarizing opinions about the desirable method for structuring and ordering markets and incentives.

In a nutshell, mental models are the representation of internalized culture at the individual level.[1] They are internalized beliefs and values in the mindset of individuals. The mental models of Denzau and North (1994), Greif (2006) and Aoki (2011) are concerned with and represent only internalized beliefs. We, however, consider it is more pertinent to assign mental models to represent internalized value of culture also. While, in their definitions, mental models are considered to be utilized to interpret and explain the environment, our definition is also concerned with the evaluation of the environment and with the desirability of methods of ordering markets. In other words, while they are concerned with the belief aspects of culture, our definition pertains also to the value aspects of the internalized culture. Since mental models in this book are dependent not only on the internalized beliefs of culture, but also on the internalized value of culture. mental models developed by individuals in our theory serve not only to understand but also to evaluate the environment and the desirable methods of ordering markets,

Section 2.1 develops the conceptual framework of internalized culture and mental models. Section 2.2 compares and contrasts the characteristics of the internalized beliefs and values of the Occident and Japan. Section 2.3 discusses the persistence and long-term flexibility of the mental model in Japan. The remaining two sections deal with topics that reinforce our conceptual framework. Sections 2.4 examines the model of Tabellini (2008) that deny the autonomy of cultural changes. Finally, Sect. 2.5 deals with the emergence of the theory of institutions and culture in Tokugawa Japan.

---

[1] Incidentally, culture could be represented at various levels. At the level of individuals, we consider that culture is represented by the concept of the mental models of individuals, the diversity and the sharing of which comprise the main theme of our model. At the level of social groups, culture is often represented by ideologies held by various social groups. Further, at the level of a nation, the representation of culture is frequently called a national characteristic or a national trait.

2.1 Conceptual Frameworks: Culture and Mental Models

The internalized part of Japanese culture is characterized by the emphasis on small groups composed of others nearby, in which it was easy to communicate one's own cultural stance to the socio-economy by way of trial-and-error interactions. It is possible to have mental models shared among intimate individuals and, hence, to develop ethics and basic modes of conduct. However, Japanese culture is largely inadequate to carry out strategic interaction with abstract individuals in society to arrive at the sharing of mental models. Opportunistic behavior cannot be avoided when everyone has concerns only with others nearby related with oneself and do not have concerns about the attainment of equilibrium with abstract others outside one's acquaintances. In other words, it could be quite difficult to share mental models with anonymous others, so that it would not be easy to share the image of adequate institutions that constrain the conduct of the majority of individuals of society, including abstract others.

Denzau and North (1994) emphasized the sharing of mental models in establishing institutions. Starting with the assertion that, in an economy without adequate ideologies and an institutional framework, the performance of economies and policies cannot be adequately described under the rational-choice framework of the cognitive model, they pointed out that it is necessary to take into consideration that people act in part upon the basis of their own internalized image of the world, which includes myths, dogmas, ideologies and 'half-baked' theories. Greif (2006) notes that there are two kinds of belief: internalized belief and behavioral belief (p. 36), and that internalized belief regarding the structure and details of the world we experience could directly motivate behavior at the individual level. Borrowing and expanding the idea of these two works, we adopt a model in which the culture, values and beliefs that are transmitted from generation to generation by various social groups are composed of two parts: internalized and behavioral. Mental models are representations of internalized culture at the level of individuals. Shared mental models are established as a result of the convergence of mental models through dynamic interaction between individuals. We argue that whether the comparative advantage in the technology of structuring and ordering the socio-economy lies in institution building or in cultural development is mainly related to the internalized part of culture.

2.1.1 Internalized and Behavioral Part of Culture

The internalized culture is related to the part of the culture that represents the bedrock of culture. Composed of internalized beliefs and internalized values, it offers the basis of the behavioral part of culture and is highly persistent, although it could change over the very long term.

Internalized beliefs are those regarding the structure and details of the world we experience. They reflect basic mental models that individuals develop to explain and understand the structure of their environments that are mainly composed of groups of individuals with whom the individuals are concerned. In some cultures, individuals are only concerned with concrete others nearby, while, in others, individuals behave more in consideration of abstract others, such as 'the public'. Internalized values are part of mental models that determine the basic criteria related to the choice among various rationalities regarding truth (cognition), good (ethic) and beauty (aesthetics), as well as among methods to resolve conflicts within each rationality. In other words, internalized belief is related to the evolution of the worldview held by individuals, living in a particular socio-economy, that works as the implicit background image of the maximizing and interacting behavior of groups and individuals, and the internalized value is related to the evolution of the value system as the background of the utility function in the broad sense, the functional form as well as range of variables included in the function, held by groups and individuals.

The behavioral part of culture is composed of that part of culture that controls the maximizing behavior and interaction with other individuals and groups under the constraints of the worldview and value system, determined by the internalized part of culture. In game theoretic terminology, interaction is implemented in consideration of the payoff of games and the action of other players. Behavioral belief refers to the set of actions taken by players and the behavioral value to the payoff set that specifies each player's payoff as a function of the action taken by the players.

There are two aspects to the internalized beliefs, the worldview of the internalized part of culture, one related to the structure of society and the other related to the relationship between humans and nature. Since this book is mainly concerned with the issue of institutions *vs* culture in relationship to ordering the market and coordinating incentives, analysis is mainly implemented in relationship with the worldview related to the structure of society. It is important to note that, as we discussed in Chapter 1, the worldview related to humans and nature in the Occident, in particular the anthropocentric worldview, had a significant influence on economic growth based on industrial technology. In Japan, the worldview related to nature had an influence on socio-economic stability mainly through Shintoism. The economic growth of the Tokugawa era caused by the decline in transaction costs was due mainly to the standardization of conduct and dissemination of ethical rules, so was not so much related to the worldview regarding the relationship between humans and nature.[2]

[2]It must be noted that, for the sake of simplification, we define mental models only with respect to internalized part of culture, excluding the behavioral part of culture. Since culture is composed of the behavioral and internalized parts, mental models, as the representations of culture at the level of individuals, could also be defined with respect to the behavioral part. However, the mental models of the behavioral part of culture are not directly concerned with the issue of the choice between institutions and culture as the method of ordering markets, so we define mental models narrowly, and do not touch upon the issue of the representation of the behavioral part of culture at the individual level. Greif (2006) is a pioneering work on this topic. A substantial amount of research seems to be needed in the future.

2.1.2 *On the Model of Denzau and North*

Denzau and North (1994) is a pioneering attempt to develop a model of the evolution of the internalized part of culture. Defining 'mental models'[3] as the internal representations that individual cognitive systems create to interpret the environment or interpersonal relationships, the authors analyze how a pre-modern society is modernized through the cultural learning process by use of the idea of sharing of mental models. As various 'mental models' shared subjectively in each group interact, ideology and institutions are created as a result of the convergence of the 'mental models' among groups. The authors contend that ideology and institutions are mechanisms to order interpersonal relationships in society.

Denzau and North try to explain the mechanism created by individuals to structure and order society without defining the difference between culture and institutions. They explain only that ideologies and institutions are classes of shared 'mental models'. Moreover, the Denzau and North theory of ideologies and institutions, defined as the external (to the mind) mechanisms individuals create to structure and order the environment, involves all the processes of the evolution of culture, including the change of religions, ethnic conflicts and struggles among social classes, as well as the working of political–economic institutions and societies. It is an enormous project to explain the process of change in the whole system of culture and institutions. It is true that, at the equilibrium, the 'mental models' of individuals are shared, as is claimed by the authors, but it must be noted that the sharing of 'mental models' is only a part of the necessary conditions for equilibrium in their huge model.[4]

Moreover, it seems that the sharing of 'mental models' in equilibrium seems to be possible because of the commonality among individuals of the worldview.

---

[3]It must be noted that we have added quotation marks to the term of mental model to express mental model defined by Denzau and North. Their concept of mental model is largely similar to ours, although their term is concerned only with the belief part of culture and does not touch upon the value part of culture.

[4]A similar comment applies to Aoki (2011). Following Denzau and North's theory, Aoki (2011) tries to clarify the cognitive and behavioral aspects of societal game and to explain how 'institution' is established as a social equilibrium of game-theoretic interaction among individuals. In the process of interaction among individuals, each of whom has his own mental belief based on his environment, common knowledge about the likelihood and meaning of actions is formulated as the interaction converges to an equilibrium. The 'institution' is established in its substantive form as the mutual agreeable mental belief in the equilibrium. Aoki claims that 'cultural beliefs', defined as common knowledge that is accumulated and inherited from the past, brings about the convergence to the equilibrium, comprise prior beliefs that are updated by some kind of learning process which generates observational data and concludes that 'if the agents share a cultural belief and payoff functions are mutually known up to the commonly cognizable states, then they share a stable identical behavioral belief up to the commonly cognizable states via a convergent public representation of their beliefs'. It is concluded that 'thus, a unique public representation entails a substantive form of institution'. It must be noted that defining institutions in this way is justified only when one ignores the political process determining laws and constitutions. In the case of our model, equilibrium could be attained as the sharing of opinions about the desirable form of institutions, so that actual process of establishing institutions including political decision and social interaction of individuals begins thereafter.

Although Denzau and North do not talk about the commonality of the content of the 'mental model', it seems that the almost common content of the 'metal model' is crucially important for the convergence of 'mental models' into an equilibrium. It would not be far off the mark to believe that there is an implicit assumption about the commonality of the core content in the worldview of individuals in the equilibrium of the Denzau and North model. In comparison, the mental model for the Japanese before the Meiji Restoration does not have such commonality. Mental models were composed of others nearby, which differs significantly among individuals. It follows that it is difficult to believe the sharing of the mental models in equilibrium and the convergence of mental models in general. This explains the absence of collective intentionality in Japan, and hence the difficulty in summarizing opinions about agreeable institutions as common constraints of behavior, and consequently the relative costliness of institutions as a mechanism to order the market.

It is regrettable that Denzau and North (1994) do not pay much attention to the difference between culture and institutions or ideologies and institutions. While their concept of ideologies is quite close to the culture held by social groups, they try to treat it as a primitive version of the institutions held by each group, so that there are no differences in substance between ideologies and institutions. It was already touched upon in Chapter 1 that the term 'informal institutions' to represent conventions and standards of conduct referred to in North (1990) is nothing but the product of culture. In this terminology also, North tries to neglect the difference between the two mechanisms of ordering the market and human action—institutions and culture. North may claim that both institutions as rules of games and culture as socially held beliefs and values play the same role of the structuring and ordering of the environment (the interpersonal relationships) for individuals. However, the difference between the two mechanisms is crucial once the costs of the two mechanisms are considered. In some countries the institutional mechanism is costly, and in others the cost of cultural mechanism is high. The difference in costs is based on the internalized mental model of countries, so it is not easy to change the difference. In the heyday of modernization theory when the eventual convergence with Occidental culture was forecasted by many people, the difference in the internalized culture did not seem so important, so that using the comprehensive term 'institution' to express the mechanism to order markets and human actions could to some extent be justified. However, in the context of the twenty-first century when the differences in internalized culture based on social, ethical and religious traditions among various regions and countries seems to have clear and significant influences on economic performance as well as the international coordination of policies, such a concept of 'institution' is nothing but a source of confusion.

2.2 The Mental Models in Japan and the Occident

It seems that the relative importance of culture and institutions in Japan and the Occident is closely related to the internalized and bedrock part of culture and that, in the context of long-term analysis, the beliefs and values related to religious, social and ethical traditions of the two regions are of significant relevance in this regard.

In the Occident, the mental models of individuals are composed of the concept of the public or society, while in Japan the mental model is composed of others nearby. The concept of the public is more or less the same among individuals, so that the mental models of individuals have a shared content in the Occident, whereas in Japan the membership in the concept of others nearby differs considerably among individuals, because each group of others nearby is made up of diverse individuals, so it is quite difficult to have a shared content of mental models among individuals. This explains the difference in the easiness of the sharing of mental models, and hence, in the cost of establishing institutions in Japan and the Occident. Let us explain this hypothesis by use of the concept of collective intentionality.

2.2.1 *Internalized Beliefs in Japan*

In the historical tradition of Japan, the behavior of people was governed by consideration of the images of past deeds of love and hate with others nearby during transmigration, and this comprised the major bedrock of the mental models. The effects of past deeds of interaction with others nearby is accumulated, and the accumulated amount of bad deeds, called bad karma in Buddhism, causes pains that continues for individuals unless karma is reduced by retribution. This is the core of the bedrock part of the mental model of Japan before the Meiji Restoration. For this reason, in the interaction with others, people were interested mainly in the actions of others nearby with whom they have interacted in the process of transmigration, and rarely extended their horizon of interests beyond others nearby and into a larger group of abstract individuals, including those in the concept of the public. In such a society, since group of people in the form of others nearby is specific to individual experience, the composition of others nearby differs substantially among individuals, so it is difficult to arrive at a shared mental model as a society. It follows that a sense of collective intentionality[5] is not easily nurtured.

2.2.2 *Internalized Beliefs in the Occident*

In contrast, it seems that, in the tradition of the Occident, there are strong concerns about the aggregate concept of human beings, or the public, and this comprised the bedrock of the internalized part of mental models. People respect the generalized as opposed to the limited applicability of rules and morality in the sense of Plateau (2000) and Tabelline (2008), and the extension of the circle of participation in the

[5]The term 'collective intentionality' follows Searle (2005), which contends three necessary properties of institutions: collective intentionality, assignment of functions and status function.

sense of Putnam (1993) became an important social agenda in the ordering of political systems and the market economy. The nature of the internalized part of culture seems to have played a significant role in the horizontal applicability of the institution as rules. In other words, since there is strong innate tendency to collective intentionality or the respect for the concept of the public in the Occident, mental models could be shared among abstract individuals and consequently by society as a whole. Since the mental model is shared by society, eventually institutions as rules are effective in shaping incentives and binding the conduct of constituents in society.

In the Occident, it seems that people have had, from very early times, a definite sense of collective identity as the public and a strong tendency to value collective behavior for the public. There had been a tendency to respect participation and collective movement for the public at least since the twelfth century in Italy (Putnam 1993). During the latter part of the middle age, people tried to develop institutions for an efficient trade system based on impersonal exchange such as a community responsibility system that did not rely on relationship-based interaction among individuals (Grief 2006). In France, the joint liability rule came to be established spontaneously among long-distance traders, so that medieval bills of exchange became a major form of payment and credit in the early modern period which, in turn, supported an unparalleled expansion of trade (Santarosa 2015). Since the Reformation period, following the tradition of Calvinism, the teaching that prohibits the deification of the created motivated people to behave with the concept of the public in mind, largely neglecting others nearby. This was because a close relationship with others nearby was liable to fall under suspicion for idolatry (Weber 1905).

From early modern through the modern era, collective intentionality or a behavioral tendency that emphasizes the collective welfare of the public was strengthened in the Occident, partly due to the development of modern moral philosophy, characterized by the negation of the qualitative distinction among individuals,[6] typically seen in utilitarianism. Social contract theories were the representative attempt to theorize the tendency to collective intentionality in the establishment of institutions. This tradition seems to have been inherited to the present day. In an attempt to reorganize social contract theory, Rawls (1971) contends, that through interplay among individuals, who utilize their own reason for the purpose of the public, society can find out rules (institutions) with sufficient justification and could retain autonomy as far as individuals follow the rules (Uno 1999).[7] It seems that the autonomous evolution of institutions based on collective intentionality seems to be firmly embedded in the Occidental tradition.

[6]Taylor (1989) contends that the influence of naturalism, that disregards the difference between humans who have a sense of good and other creatures who do not have, caused the tendency to deny the qualitative distinction among individuals.

[7]Uno (1999) points out that Rawls' methodology is Kantian in the sense of assuming the morality of individuals, who are regarded as objects not as instruments.

2.2.3 Why Culture, Not Institutions, in Japan?

In Japan before the Meiji Restoration, people were usually motivated to behave in relationships with others nearby, not for the public, and thereby, they relied on culture as a mechanism to order markets and developed standards of conduct and ethical codes that bind members within small groups. Among such small groups are developed standards of conduct and ethical rules related to group activities also, and the chain relationships of groups developed into macro-level standards of conduct and ethics. It was costly in Japan, which lacked the collective intentionality of individuals, to establish institutions, and a less costly way of ordering socio-economy for the Japanese was by way of cultural adjustment and cultural improvement.

We believe that the basic reason for the lack of collective intentionality in Japan lies in the cognitive worldview that is composed of others nearby. Traditionally in Japan, owing to the influence of Buddhism, others nearby in mental models include not only actual individuals they interact with in this world but also imaginal individuals[8] with whom they interacted in previous lives during the process of transmigration. Imaginal individuals are usually imagined in close relationship with actual individuals with whom they interacted. Since there did not exist any notion of the public and society of mankind in the theory of Buddhism, individuals were interested in small circles of related individuals by and large, with whom they have accumulated a sense of indebtedness (karma) in their mindset. In optimization behavior, individuals, who were eager to escape the pain of transmigration and to attain religious enlightenment, aimed for the minimization of bad karma that had been accumulated through the interaction with others nearby. Moreover, since others nearby differ considerably among individuals, it is costly to bring about the convergence of opinion among individuals. This raised serious difficulty in establishing effective institutions to bring about market and social order. This was because it took a considerable time to expand the scope of applicability of good conduct beyond the scope of others nearby and towards everyone in society in order to realize a society with efficient and fair order. Hastily established institutions applied to society as a whole, without obtaining consensus, are liable to fall victim to opportunistic behavior. The gradual establishment of standards of conduct in a small group, expecting the horizontal extension to other groups nearby, is the only method to enhance market and social order.[9] Although this takes considerable time to bring about order across the whole society, the gradual procedure to pile up piecemeal agreements through the dissemination of agreeable ethical codes and standard of conduct is effective to avoid opportunistic behavior.

---

[8] It may be worthwhile to note that behavior based on the imaginal group in the mindset is not specific to Japan. Behavior based on the imaginal community is also seen in the Occident as is emphasized by Duby (1990) with respect to medieval society and by Anderson (2006) regarding the more modern notion of national states in politics.

[9] This mechanism might remind readers of the extension of the relationship of cryptocurrency such as bit coin in modern financial society based on block chain, or the theory of holonic worldview in Casey and Luckett (2016).

In summary, when one takes the internalized beliefs of culture into consideration, others nearby, in which people are deeply interested, differs widely among individuals, so it was difficult to have a shared mental model at the individual level. In other words, because of this nature of the internalized part of culture, it is difficult to share imaged worldview of individuals beyond the confines of others nearby, so that the cost of summarizing the mental models and of realizing public representation could be very high. It follows that, in Japan, where the content of mental models was related to others nearby, institutions as rules of game are destined to lack horizontal extension of approval at the social level. Mental models were approved and shared only by a limited number of people, consequently reducing the effectiveness of rules in shaping incentives and constraining human conduct in society as a whole. This is the main reason why institutions had been ineffective to order economic behavior in Japan before the Meiji Restoration.

2.2.4 *Internalized Value in the Occident and Japan*

Not only in the internalized belief system, there seems also to be differences in the internalized value systems between the Occident and pre-Meiji Restoration Japan. In terms of the choice of social criterion for rationality among truth, good and beauty, Japan had emphasized the value related to beauty and good compared with truth. Until the end of the Tokugawa era, the Japanese had been enthusiastic about how to enhance the moral standards of society and the aesthetic virtues and devoted less effort to cognitive rationality, including understanding natural sciences.

This seems to be highly contrasting with modern Occidental experience where cognitive rationality was a leading banner for the development of society. Weber claimed that, under the modernization by way of capitalism, cognitive (truth) rationality invaded other areas of rationality related to ethical (good)and aesthetic (beauty) values and established dominance (Habermas 1981). With respect to conflicts among various standards of goods, the Japanese have been involved in conflicts among various goods ardently and positively. It seems that modern Occidental society has had a tendency to refrain from being involved in conflicts among goods and, instead, tried to seek ways to resolve the conflicts by resorting to procedural rationality (Taylor 1989).[10] While, admitting the diversity of goods, Rawls criticized existing utilitarianism on the ground that it neglects the dignity of difference among individuals, he

[10]McCloskey (2006) emphasizes the establishment of a balanced system of bourgeois virtues by the mid-nineteenth century overcoming the challenge of communism in the Occident, claiming that the twentieth century witnessed the glorious coevolution of the material and spiritual values of bourgeois capitalism. It seems however that this rosy picture of capitalistic society based on ethical values, such as love, courage, faith, justice and the like, is collapsing under the influence of the emergence of neo-liberalism and the resurgence of marketized socialist economies after the 1970s. This seems to indicate that the pursuit of material value for mankind or the public as represented by the accumulation of private wealth is still adhered to deeply as leading individual incentives of modern capitalism.

avoided being involved in conflicts among various goods and proposed the principle of justice as a permissible rule for collective action to overcome conflicts and establish social order. Uno (2015) claims that the controversy between communitarianism, that proposed the rearing of moral citizens, and Rawlsian liberalism, that emphasized freedom of choice and procedural rationality, resulted in the victory of the latter in American history.

The internalized value also has relevance in the analysis of growth patterns from the perspective of production costs *vs* transaction costs, discussed in Chapter 1. The deep involvement in cognitive rationality, motivated to seek the truth of creation of God, seems certainly to be relevant to the drastic reduction of production costs through the development of industrial technology in the Occident. Anthropocentricism in the internalized belief in the Occident had a significant influence on the pattern of growth in the Occident, because it had a synergy effect with the internalized value in cognitive rationality, as is emphasized by Mokyr (2017). It will be shown in this book that the reduction of transaction costs during Tokugawa Japan was due significantly to the (unintended) effect of deep concerns with the ethical rationality of society.

Finally, it must be added that the theory related to the evolution of the internalized part of culture and mental models is still in its infancy. This book is expected to be a small step toward the development of the theory from now on.

2.3 The Long-Term Flexibility of the Mental Models

The internalized part is a bedrock part of culture. As is emphasized by North, it is difficult for the internalized part of culture to change flexibly. The tenacity and persistence of the internalized part of the mental model should not be taken rigidly, however. It could change gradually over a very long term, probably over centuries in the historical process through social learning,[11] and significantly influence the long-term development of socio-economy. Weber deplored the change in the internalized value from the balanced pattern among cognitive, ethical and aesthetic values to the dominance of the cognitive value owing to the emergence and development of capitalism in the Occident. Denzau and North seem to believe that, not only the behavioral part of culture but the internalized part of culture, the bedrock part, will also eventually converge into a shared culture of society through the process of learning in the dynamics of mental model interaction, although we believe that the commonality of the core content of the internalized belief among individuals is a necessary condition for this.

We believe that a similar process of convergence actually occurred in Japan. Through the standardization of behavior during the Tokugawa era, people have found

[11] Denzau and North consider that both the behavioral part of culture and the internalized part of culture, the bedrock part, will eventually converge into a shared mental model of society through the process of learning in the dynamics of mental model interaction.

that, in spite of the difference among individuals in the environment related to other nearby, the reasons for the excessive avarice that gave them pain had commonality. There occurred a radical change in social belief from the Warring States period through the Tokugawa era that brought about changes in the internalized part of culture, leading to the melting phenomenon of the bedrock portion of the mental models of the Japanese. Various circumstances pertained to this change and enhanced the sense of commonality about the environment among individuals. Shintoism emphasized harmony with nature and the importance of a positive attitude to be merged with the spiritual vitality of nature. Confucianism suggested the possibility of a logic of the way of Heaven that is beyond the control of human beings. Popular ethics taught harmony brought about by the social division of labor, justifying the existence of various activities that were beyond the scope of others nearby whom individuals had met in the process of transmigration. All these cultural atmospheres, which were newly developed mainly during the Tokugawa era, nurtured a common worldview and commonality in the worldview beyond the past experiences of individuals. People were gradually emancipated from the bondage of others nearby, which is specific to individuals because of personal relationships in the past. When the impervious sense of the difference of others nearby among individuals was mitigated and overcome in this way, people came to be ready to communicate with others on the street and with a wider range of people. It did not take long for the emergence of conditions for the standardization of conduct and agreeable ethics. Both the standardization of conduct and agreeable ethics brought about trust in society.

The very long-term change in the internalized culture occurred in an irregular way. First, during the Warring States period, social conviction of the necessity to change the ethical base of society emerged under the influence of the Confucian concept of the way of Heaven. Second, this concept was thrown away through rigorous theoretical examination by researchers such as Ogyū Sorai during the Tokugawa era. Third, however, the concept of the way of Heaven survived for long especially in the mindset of the samurai class and was used to establish the integrity of political thoughts. It must be also noted that, while a persistent move to reexamine the internalized belief continued throughout the Tokugawa era at the metaphysical level, the daily lives of individuals were still rigidly tied to the restriction of a worldview based on the theory of transmigration and karma.

There is no doubt that the mitigation of the hardcore concept of others nearby, during the Tokugawa era, was one of the reasons for the smooth acceptance and introduction of Western institutions after the Meiji Restoration. Before the arrival of Perry, the Japanese had emancipated themselves from the rigid confines of the concept of others nearby based on the religious experience of transmigration.[12] However, it is worth noting that the basic characteristic of the internalized culture in the sense

[12]The range of society that was emancipated from traditional thinking is a topic worth pursuing. Matsumoto (1974) notes that the activity of Meirokusha (1873–5), established for the purpose of disseminating modern enlightenment thinking in Japan had to fight with the prevalence of the popular myth related to mountain spirits (*tengu*) and magic implemented by foxes as well as with Confucian dichotomy, such as between the reason of Heaven (*tennri*) and human avarice and reason (*ri*)and justice (*gi*).

of respect for the relationship with others nearby remained long after the Meiji Restoration. We will discuss in Chapter 7 the excessive concerns of Meiji leaders led by Ito Hirobumi about the tendency of the Japanese to be unable to understand the concept of the public, and conclude that Ito's policy to introduce the surrogate of the concept of the public by institutional device ended in a failure.

J.S. Mill (1859) deplored the tendency to neglect individuality and to allow the prevalence of mediocrity in the Occident during the period after the Reformation. He considered that behind the tendency lay the strong influence of Calvinism that asserted that the 'greatest offence of man is self-will' because 'human nature being radically corrupt, there is no redemption for anyone until human nature is killed within him' (p. 75). Owing to this theory, held even by many who do not believe themselves Calvinists, there occurred 'general tendency of things throughout the world to render mediocracy the ascendant power among mankind', so that in England 'a mass, that is to say, collective mediocrity' (p. 80) have become the virtual leaders of society, oppressing individuality and genius. Although the concern of Mill about the lack of individuality seems to be excessive, just like the concern of Itō about the lack of a sense of the public, it is worth noting that the leading thinker of Meiji Japan, Fukuzawa Yukichi, asserted that 'In the Occident, although all individuals are not necessarily very wise, they are highly good at collective mobilization of individual powers. In Japan, while there are many individuals with high intelligence and individuality, Japan does not have a mechanism for the collective cooperation of them' (Fukuzawa 1875, vol. 2, ch. 2).[13] For the Japanese it is not an easy matter to understand and make effective use of the notion of the public. Although the Japanese are considered to be good at collective action, this is often only related to collectivity as a small group composed by others nearby or collectivity as a stakeholder society in which the residual return of group-specific capital is shared, as is discussed in Chapter 8. Collective action in Japan is quite often a synonym for group action. It seems that the Japanese are still not good at organizing collective behavior related to the public and society. The harmonization of the merits of Japanese society built on close and intimate concerns with others nearby and the tendency of the insufficient devotion into public issues such as the global environmental crisis and nuclear problems is a most urgent task left for the Japanese to be tackled from now on.

2.4 On the Concept of Generalized Morality

We have argued that the internalized part of the mental model has changed gradually but radically over the long term both in the Occident and in Japan. The autonomous movement of culture should have a significant influence on economic performance through the impact on the choice of method of ordering the market system, or through the choice of technology that give rise to economy of scale. The citizenship of

[13] See further Teranishi (2014, pp. 291–295).

the theory of autonomous evolution of internalized culture is still not firmly established in economics. Tabellini (2008) is a recent pioneering contribution about the internal mental model regarding the scope of applicability of morality. His assertion of one-way causality from institutions to internalized culture, denying the autonomous evolution of the latter, is in sharp contrast with our model. It seems to represent the strong influence of collective intentionality on the institution-based development in the Occident. Let us examine his assertion more closely.

Tabellini contends a causal effect from political and economic institutions to internalized culture, and hence on current institutions. It is claimed that well-functioning institutions are observed in countries and regions where individual values are conscious with generalized (as opposed to limited) morality and were quite often ruled by non-despotic political institutions in the past. Tabellini's strategic concept, generalized and limited morality,[14] is defined in relationship to individual values and convictions about the scope of applicability of good conduct, whether towards an abstract everyone or just a narrow group which the individual identifies. Generalized morality means that individual values support a generalized applicability of good conduct to abstract every individual in society, while limited morality supports applicability to a narrow group, such as the family or clan. Tabellini contends that the internalized norm of generalized morality nurtured in non-despotic and non-hierarchical countries provides favorable conditions for well-functioning institutions through the following steps. Firstly, in countries which were freed from feudalistic arrangements, the capability of people to identify abstract individuals is nurtured, and people are instilled with confidence and respect for abstract rules, such as the rule of law, the fundamental rights of individuals, democratic procedures, and checks and balances. Secondly, individuals who practice generalized morality are more reluctant to free ride on others in economic behavior, participation in group behavior and in political activities. Thirdly, altogether, norms of generalized morality induce well-functioning institutions through motivating people to be more faithful to laws and have concerns with general social welfare.

While Tabellini (2008) is highly insightful in the sense that his concept of the scope of applicability of morality is concerned with the internalized part of culture, and his explanation of the effect of generalized morality on the emergence of modern institutions is convincing and represents a typical pattern of institutional develop in the Occident, it is regrettable that the procedure for proving the one-way causality from historical institutions (weak feudalism) to internalized culture (generalized morality) is marred by a serious sample bias in the statistical analysis.

His sample for the proof of the first proposition, causality from feudalism to limited morality or from weak feudalism to generalized morality, is confined to Occidental countries and regions or at least to countries and regions under the influence of Christianity. While we are ready to admit the constraint due to the availability of data, in a sample with similar religious and philosophical traditions, it is natural and not at all surprising that the difference in the history of 'feudalism' is statistically

[14]The origin of these concepts lies in Platteau (2000). While Platteau utilizes these concepts to characterize a broader group of societies, Tabellini focuses mainly European countries.

significant. With a broader set of samples, it is not difficult to show the invalidity of Tabellini's thesis on the causal relationship from feudalistic institutions to the scope of applicability of morality. It must be recalled that the original concept of generalized, as opposed to limited, morality in Platteau (2000) was derived through a comparison between Western countries and other developing countries, especially in Sub-Saharan Africa and north and southeast Asia. In this framework, the scope of applicability of morality has a salient meaning encompassing multifarious cultural phenomena related to property holding, the sharing of consumption, religion, the role of states, and the like. In order to show the importance of the autonomous movement of internalized culture, we will point out the Japanese experience, in which a cultural trait similar to generalized morality emerged under the institutional constraint of 'feudalism'. It will be shown that in Tokugawa Japan, which was a genuine feudalistic society in the sense of a hierarchal structure of society based on a feudal contract between master and vassals, there emerged a phenomenon of general applicability of good conduct in society.

In order to simplify our argument, we will confine our discussion to the possibility of coexistence of high levels of trust (in our definition) and 'feudalistic' regulations. It will be asked how and why a society with high levels of trust and generalized morality was established in 'feudalistic' Tokugawa Japan, where notions of the public did not exist, and individuals were interested only in the relationship with nearby neighbors. It is contended, despite a couple of differences about the definition of terms,[15] a sort of general trust or generalized morality was established in the 'feudalistic' society of Japan.

2.4.1 Chain Relationships Among Small Groups

Following the Buddhist tradition, individuals in Japan were accustomed to have been deeply concerned with others nearby, with whom they interact in this world, as well as imaginary others nearby, with whom they were acquainted in the process of

[15] As a statistical measure of generalized morality, Tabellini (2008) utilizes the concept of trust. The term 'trust' is defined with regard to the attitude to others. In a society with generalized morality, trust is applied to abstract others in the public and in society with limited morality to a small group of people identified by individuals. On the other hand, we have defined trust as the subjective probability with which an agent assesses that another agent or group of agents will perform a particular action. In terms of our definition of trust, Tabellini's concept of generalized morality seems to contain the implicit precept that individuals ought to support higher subjective probability with which abstract others follow the norm of good conduct, irrespective of the degree of feudalistic tradition. In Tabellini's definition, individuals are interested in the probability of 'good conduct' by others, while, in our definition individuals are interested in the forecastability of 'any particular performance' by others, not necessarily a performance following the norm of good conduct. Our trust is concerned with an objective description of the higher forecastability of particular actions, not a normative assertion for the broader scope of applicability of particular conduct. Moreover, there seems to be a significant difference in the institution of feudalism between the Occident and Japan and the Japanese system has undergone substantial changes over time.

transmigration. Since the Warring State period, the concept of the way of Heaven in Confucianism was introduced in Japan and supported by various strata of people, and the founder of the Tokugawa *bakufu*, Tokugawa Ieyasu, tried to utilize this concept as a guideline for public policy. As will be discussed in Chapter 5, however, the Confucian concept was unable to gain wide acceptance in Tokugawa Japan because of the neglect of the independence and positivity of people in establishing political and social order, or perhaps because of the implied passivity of individuals in the Confucian logic to the order of the Heaven and to the authority of rulers who followed way of the Heaven. It is true that, educated in the circumstance in which Confucianism was assigned as a basic training for logical thinking and as a common conceptual framework, samurai in the Tokugawa period continued to use the word 'Heaven' to justify his conduct, whenever they faced the necessity to think about the matters related to the destiny of the nation or public policy matters in general.[16] This, however, is not an assertion about political belief but must be construed as an expression of the internal autonomy of individuals (Bitō 1994). It seems that the worldview in the thinking of the Tokugawa people was not based on the Confucian concept of the public, but is more pertinently construed to be governed by the worldview of Buddhist origin that was composed of the interrelated block chain of small groups of acquaintances or others nearby.

The diffusion of the standards of conduct and ethical codes in society that established trust in the Tokugawa era was possible owing to the following cultural and institutional mechanisms. First is the role of intellectuals to develop the theoretical explanation of the socio-economic effect of the coordination among various occupations related to the social division of labor. This development was particularly salient with respect to the role of the merchant class and the inter-relationship among occupations. Ishida Baigan was a typical intellectual who taught the positive role of merchants in the social division of labor and tried to dispel their inferiority complex. Intellectual leaders, who gathered at the Kaitoku-dō research center that was established by the merchants, were energetically engaged in the investigation and dissemination of occupational ethics for merchants. Other well-known intellectuals such as Ninomiya Sontoku, who was concerned with the development of so-called popular ethics, also tried to clarify the role of the occupation of farmers in the social division of labor.

Second was the role of the *kyūdō* principle in nurturing a generalized system of respect for others. The samurai class was well-known as a faithful follower of the *kyūdō* principle nurtured by the influence of Zen, one of the sects of Kamakura new Buddhism. As a result of the pursuit of the *kyūdō* principle, the samurai class came to pursue the realization of the mindset in which they respected each other according to the level of attainment of the *kyūdō* principle. Although there was definitely a

[16]For example, the words of Saigō Takamori (1827–77) 'Do not to face with others, but face with the Heaven' is well known among the Japanese. During the turmoil after the arrival of Perry, the samurai and other high-minded patriots used to talk about their thought referring to the concept of Heaven. This, however, does not imply their faith in the Confucian theory of the rule by Heaven, but instead is quite often an expression of the internal autonomy of their mind from the turmoil of the political situations (Bitō 1994).

hierarchical ranking system of feudalism that governed administrative and political order in samurai society, human relationship was based on respect for each other regarding the attainment of the *kyūdō* principle, or in the pursuit of the norm of conduct called *bushi* (samurai)-*do* in such areas as martial skills, knowledge of literature and composition of poems, integrity and elegance of daily conduct, and the like. The scope of the applicability of the attainment of the *kyūdō* principle was horizontally extended beyond the confines of the feudal relationship of each samurai.[17] Although the bureaucratic order among samurai was determined mainly according to patrimonial family status within the restrictions of the hierarchical master–vassal relationship, the view of society held by the samurai class had horizontal extension over the whole samurai class nationwide, subjectively ordered according to the evaluation of the attainment of the *kyūdō* principle and hence to the respect held for each other. The horizontal extension of the evaluation system of *kyūdō* attainment was possible partly because the samurai had a common conceptual framework owing to their educational background related to the reading of Confucianism literature. It is important to note that the general applicability of respect for *kyūdō* behavior was realized, not by the normative idea or precept that 'good conduct' should be extended to the public or to abstract individuals, but rather endogenously born as the chain of one-to-one respect among samurai groups, like cryptocurrency's block chain theory.

It follows that the concept of the limited morality of Tabellini seems to be inapplicable in the case of Japanese samurai society, although it was a 'feudalistic' society. Despite its hierarchical structure, the samurai established a system that admitted the general applicability of conduct related to the *kyūdō* principle. It must be noted that a similar chain of evaluation of the attainment of the *kyūdō* principle was prevalent also within other occupational groups and across different occupations than the samurai class. At least, many farmers and merchants of higher than middle class tried to mimic the lifestyle of the samurai. In this way, everyone in the country was related with one another through the evaluation of the accomplishment of the norm of conduct required for the attainment of the *kyūdō* principle in his occupation—for example, *bushi-dō* in the case of the samurai, honesty in the case of merchants and diligence and reverence for nature in the case of farmers, and so on.

In summary, society in Tokugawa Japan, in which individuals, inheriting the basic worldview of Buddhist origin, has concerns only about others nearby, had horizontally extended the scope of applicability of the norms of conduct by way of respect for others, based on accomplishment in the *kyūdō* principle. The scope of applicability of good conduct was extended beyond small groups composed by others nearby. Hierarchical society is not necessarily characterized by the limited applicability of morality, although it may be different from generalized morality.

---

[17]Further, it might be worthwhile to note that Sagara contends that the samurai have attained a mental model that emphasize honor. The notion of *mujyo* (mutability) came to be construed in combination with the concept of honor within the *bushi* (samurai) society. It is also contended that the famous words in *Hagakure* that 'the essence of *bushi-dō* lies in death' has an affirmative connotation that the decision to die means not only impermanence of life but also permanence of honor. In this sense, the various behaviors caused by *bonnō*, attachment to life, must be understood as of secondary importance among the samurai.

This is because the extension of scope is not related to the value of the abstract concept of the public. It will be shown in Chapter 6 that trust established in this way in Tokugawa society played an important role in the commerce-based economic development within a 'feudalistic' society.

2.4.2 Generalizes Respect for Others

It is important to note that a society with a high level of trust was not established in Tokugawa society because of generalized morality in which trust towards abstract others was valued, but rather, because a high social level of trust in the sense of forecastability of performance of other agents was realized as an unintended result of the diffusion of ethical codes and the *kyūdō* principle. This process could be explained as follows. The prevalence of the *kyūdō* principle was considered to be beneficial for society as a whole, because a larger share of people who are aiming at enlightenment could realize a society with less avarice and hence with more tolerance. The value of the norm of conduct aimed at the *kyūdō* principle for each occupation made the high-level attainment of the *kyūdō* principle an effective measure of the reliability of individuals. Conduct based on the *kyūdō* principle became the standard of good conduct in society. Despite the absence of the notion that regards trust towards abstract others as valuable, the standardization of conduct covering various occupations resulted in the easiness of forecasting the performance of others, consequently reducing information asymmetry and enhancing the level of trust or forecastability of the performance of others in society.

It must be noted that, in the behavioral pattern of the Tokugawa Japanese, the internal evaluation of attainment in the *kyūdō* principle provided crucial motivation for engagement in *kyūdō* behavior. Since the fundamental purpose of *kyūdō* behavior lies in the attainment of enlightenment, by whom *kyūdō* behavior is implemented, the behavior of individuals in Tokugawa Japan to seek a society that was built on mutual respect was based on the longing for a harmonious society with less avarice and hence agony.

Incidentally, it must also be noted that the good conduct recommended in Tokugawa Japan mainly comprised honesty, diligence and thriftiness. Such items as trust towards others, respect of each other or tolerance have never been recommended items in the popular ethic or in ethical education.[18] Probably, it was considered that these items flowed naturally from education emphasizing the *kyūdō* principle and other good conduct.

R. Benedict, who proposed the view that Japanese society is characterized as a society with the culture of shame, whereas Western society is a culture of sin, argued that 'True shame culture rely on external sanctions for good behavior, not, as true

[18]In Confucianism, however, trust or faith to friends was recommended, along with benevolence between master and servant, justice between father and children, etiquette between husband and wife, knowledge between infant and elder.

sin culture do, on an internalized conviction of sin. Shame is a reaction to other people's criticism' (Benedict 1946, p. 223). It could be understood that this picture of Japanese culture is pretty much superficial in the following sense. A culture of shame could be construed as meaning that the behavior of the Japanese is dependent only on outside evaluation and criticism. This picture of the Japanese overlooks the internal aspects of the mindset.[19] When Benedict asserts that the Japanese seem to be sensitive only to evaluation from outside, she failed to notice that sensitiveness to the evaluation from outside comprises an integral part of mutual respect with each other. As is emphasized above, mutual respect comprised a basic building block of Japanese society in the Tokugawa era, and it is based on the evaluation on internal attainment with each other. The evaluation of others about one's attainment was considered to be possible only by those observers who have arrived at a comparable level of internal attainment. What individuals of Tokugawa Japan judged from the criticism by an observer was actually the level of internal attainment of the observer. Criticism or sanction nurtures mutual respect in this case.

It seems that the morality of the Japanese during the Tokugawa era was gradually formulated at the interface of two developments. First was the macro-organic concept of the importance of each occupation in the framework of the social division of labor. Another was the micro-internalized concept of respect for others in the process of accumulation of human capital by *kyūdō* behavior. Both social division of labor and human capital contributed to the socio-economic development of Tokugawa Japan.

2.4.3 Summary

While the assertion of Tabellini that the efficient role of institutions in European countries was due to the emancipation from feudalistic institutions that brought about a culture of generalized morality, seems to be correct, we consider that the applicability of the model outside Europe is limited. Based on this pioneering hypothesis, it seems to be necessary to develop a more general model incorporating the experience of non-Occidental countries.

We believe that, since institutions are not the only way to order the socio-economic system, it is not logically correct to deny limited morality for the reason that it is not effective in establishing institutions. While Tabellini's assertion that generalized

[19] Although it is undeniable that Benedict (1946) presents a surprisingly insightful picture of the Japanese, it is marred by many deficiencies in the understandings of Japan. One of them is too serious to overlook. While she describes in detail about another characteristic behavioral pattern of the Japanese, comparable with concerns with shame, the deep involvement in self-discipline to attain 'expertise', she did not notice at all the religious background of this behavior, and hence important relationship of the culture of shame with *kyūdō*-behavior. She seems to have read some literature on Buddhism, such as that written by Suzuki Daisetsu, but her knowledge of Buddhism is insufficient. For example, the following assertion is hard to understand. 'Even though Japan is a great Buddhist nation, ideas of transmigration and of nirvana have never been a part of the Buddhist faith of the people' (p. 237).

morality is a sufficient condition for the establishment of efficient and fair institutions is absolutely correct, it is not a necessary condition. Furthermore, it is indispensable for the creative development of humans to preserve diversity in the method of organizing society. We want to look after the possibility of society ordered and structured, not by rigid rules and laws only, but with diverse mechanisms including agreed-upon ethics and various senses of solidarity or, more generally, a mixture of institutions and diverse cultures.

2.5 Discovery of Culture and Institutions in the Thinking of the Tokugawa Era

In the following chapters, we will investigate the role of culture and institutions in the economic development of Japan from the 13th through twentieth centuries, focusing on the sustained economic growth during the Tokugawa era (1603–1868). It is interesting to note that a similar model of socio-economy from the perspective of institutions and culture was already in existence in the Tokugawa era. Focusing on the theory of Ogyū Sorai about institutions (*hōsei-setsudo*) and culture (*fūzoku*), we will trace the development of thought and argue that the importance of culture was recognized in Tokugawa thought gradually and definitely.

Intellectuals in the Tokugawa era came to discover the important role of culture as a mechanism to establish order in the socio-economy of their time. At first, there occurred the assertion of the necessity of establishing efficient institutions, but it was replaced by the discovery of the usefulness of cultural ordering through heated discussion among intellectuals and probably political leaders. It is not an exaggeration to say that the controversy related to the choice between institutions and culture was a central issue in economic thought during the Tokugawa era.

The controversy ended in the victory of culture over institutions through the 18th and nineteenth centuries. However, since it was difficult to provide a coherent and integrated theory to bridge the theory regarding institutions and culture with the theory regarding the social division of labor and the occupational *kyūdō* principle developed by popular ethic theorists, Japanese intellectuals have long been left to experience emotional turmoil. The reckless attempt of Meiji leaders to introduce the institution of *kokutai* as a surrogate for the Occidental cultural concept of the public, discussed in Chapter 7, seems to be partly rooted in this difficulty and turmoil.

It was Ogyū Sorai who first identified the issue of a choice between institutions and culture for establishing order in Tokugawa society. As is discussed in Chapter 6, Sorai was the leading thinker in the struggle with the new Confucianism. The denial of the concept of *ri* (the fundamental logic of the universe) and the related continual theory of the new Confucianism accomplished by Sorai was welcomed with enormous sympathy among intellectuals and, at the same time, aroused significant controversy in the country between sympathizers, represented by hundreds of intellectuals who organized the new Ken-en[20] school, and opponents, composed of traditional Confucians as well as the new school of thinkers, who proposed an entirely new theory of Koku-gaku based on traditional spiritual culture and the mindset of the Japanese, denying the philosophical logic of Confucians (Maruyama 1952, pp. 140–142).

The discovery by Sorai of the issue of institutions and culture, as methods of establishing ordering environments for the market economy, was accomplished in the process of theoretical examination of new Confucian theory. His inquiry started with the acceptance of the propositions about the worldview developed by Itō Jinsai. Sorai accepted and inherited Jinsai's worldview to regard the actual socio-economy as *kakubutsu* that emphasized the dynamism and variability of society (Sect. 6.2.1). Moreover Sorai expanded the *katsubutsu* concept that had been mainly concerned with the world as a physical environment of humans, *tenchi* (heaven and earth), to multifarious environments concerned with human activity, asserting not only heaven and earth but also human activities and minds are also dynamic and change in various ways. Further, he asserted that in order to give order to this dynamism of the world, some key element controllable by humans must be identified. This element was called institutions, comprising laws and regulations by the government (*hōsei-setsudo*),[21] and the rest of the dynamic world *fūzoku*, implying the whole private sector on which institutions exert power. It follows that the world (*katsubutsu*) came to be conceptualized as composed of institutions and *fūzoku*. Although Sorai did not mention it explicitly, the spiritual and mental part of human behavior, called culture in this book, is contained in the definition of *fūzoku*. For example, in his *Seidan* (literally, 'some notes on politics'), written one year before his death, he deplored the deterioration of Tokugawa society as follows. 'In these days, ancient days are far away in the past, so that old institutions are not effective. Moreover, as is just after the big civil war (Warring States era), existing institutions of the society is inheriting those established in wartime, so that *fūzoku* (culture) is not renovated. Individuals of all classes are leading their lives with too much freedom in their mentality without adequate laws and regulations' (p. 311 of reprinted version).

Incidentally, despite frequent reference to the concept of *fūzoku* in his late writings, Sosai's definition of fūzoku is not clear-cut, so that later researchers have used multifarious definitions of *fūzoku*. While Maruyama did not use the term *fūzoku* in Maruyama's theory (1952), *fūzoku* corresponds to the non-political part of the world (pp. 177–182). Fujimoto (1978) defines it as the place in which the living of individuals is carried out, comprising the mode of living, custom and common sense as well as the mentality behind the place, while Nakamura (2019) defines *fūzoku*, in terms of the properties of social dynamics, as the totality of social liquidity that exhibits irresistible dynamic power (p. 270).

Upon the acceptance and expansion of the concept of *katsubutsu*, Sorai set up two working hypotheses. One was that institutions were not exogenous rules endowed by the philosophical concept of the Heaven, but political rules contrived intentionally

[20]Named after Sorai's private school, located at Kayaba-chō, Tokyo.

[21]Sorai's definition of institution is mentioned in his *Seidan* (p. 311), reprinted in Ogyu Sorai, *Nihon-sisou-taikei*, vol. 36 (1974, Iwanami-shoten, pp. 259–446).

(*sakui-teki-ni*) by real kings (*sennō*), whom he called holy men (*seijin*), found in ancient myth in Chinese history. Another was the hypothesis that denies the variability of human nature. In new Confucianism, it was considered that there are two kinds of human mind, the *honnen* mind (orthodox mind) that was controlled by *ri* and the *kishitu* mind (natural mind) outside the control of *ri*, and it was contended that the *kishitsu* mind could be changed and controlled by the *honnen* mind. This assumption of the variability of the human mind was admitted by Jinsai. However, Jinsai claimed that it is not *ri* but humanly contrived ethics that are responsible for the variability of the mind, especially the natural mind. Sorai's second hypothesis was the assumption of the unchangeability of human mind, effectively denying both the original new Confucian theory and Jinsai's theory. He justified this assumption on the grounds that the distinction between *honnen* and *kishitsu* in the human mind is an assumption posited by Confucians for the sake of theoretical convenience, so that there is no relevance to observations about actual human behavior (Nakamura 2019, pp. 58–61).

By use of these two working hypotheses, Sorai constructed a new socio-economic model that could explain the mechanism of establishing orderly socio-economy. In this model, institutions are controlled by politicians and the influences of institutions change the state of *fūzoku*. Through the interaction of institutions and *fūzoku*, there emerges changes in the *katsubutsu*, dynamic movement of the socio-economy. It is also asserted that learning (*narai*) by individuals with respect to institutions in their daily lives plays an important role in the effective working of institutions. Fujimoto (1978) notes that learning affects the *fūzoku* by way of changes in the internalized culture of society. This is nothing but a model *a la* North of institutional changes in which institutions play a key role as the ultimate determinants of socio-economic performance, as is discussed in Chapter 1. The model is very much 'Tokugawa Japanese' also in the sense that institutions were determined by the decision and discretion (*ryōken*) of shogun, to whom *Seidan* was dedicated. At the same time, the model inherits Confucian's traditional thinking strongly in the sense that *fūzoku* was treated passively as a variable under the influence of benevolent politicians (Yoshikawa 1968)

It did not take much time for the two working hypotheses of Sorai to be critically reinvestigated, however, leading to the emergence of new versions of the model. It is worth mentioning that, in almost all the new versions, culture as a part of *fūzoku* came to play a more important role. Researchers in Koku-gaku criticized Sorai's first working hypothesis that emphasizes the Chinese tradition of policy. They denied Sorai's stance to follow the spirit of China (*karagokoro*) that inherits the political accomplishments of ancient Chinese kings, whereas they approved the idea that human characters, not the inhuman principle of *ri*, are fundamental determinants of the world. Motoori Norinaga (1730–1801), a leading Koku-gaku theorist, tried to find a way based on the Japanese spirit (*yamato-tamashii*), the ancient layer of universal value that was transmitted only in Japan, in two classic pieces of literature, *Kojiki* and *Nihon-shoki*, establishing a new version of the model in which all gods and the world were originated by two real gods in myth. The way recommended by Koku-gaku was based on the internalized born-mind, '*umaretaru mama no magokoro*', which was free not only from any Confucians and Buddhist spirits but also from all normative and philosophical values. Maruyama (1952) emphasized that this way of thought is strongly under the influence of Jinsai and Sorai who denied the hegemony of the abstract and non-human concept of *ri*.

Another version of the new model was invented by thinkers who challenged Sorai's second working hypothesis regarding the invariability of the human mind. Instead of man-made rules, institutions, the improvement of internalized values and the beliefs of humans were considered to be fundamental for the ordering of socio-economy. Intellectuals such as Ishida Baigan and Ninomiya Sontoku clarified the role of each occupation in the efficient working of the social division of labor and, in an effort to get rid of the inferiority complex of farmers and merchants and to enhance their self-confidence in their occupational activities, taught the importance of devotion in basic ethical rules such as diligence and honesty. Although their theory was described in Confucian terminology, their ideas were based on Buddhist and Shintoist thinking. Likewise, intellectuals at the private Kaitoku-dō academy tried to establish a new ethical principle for merchants and commercial activities. Under the strong influence of Occidental science and enlightenment thinking, they asserted that the human mind could be changed through the accumulation of new knowledge and investigation into the mechanism of the working of nature, not of history.

As is explained in Chapter 6, the theorists of popular ethics developed a theory to relate the occupational behavior based on the *kyōdō* principle with macro efficiency theory related to the social division of labor. However, it must be noted that they did not examine their theory in the context of institution–culture interaction.

Incidentally, it was a significant contribution in the study of Tokugawa thought that Maruyama pointed out in his 1952 work the discovery of institutions by Sorai. However, Maruyama did not notice the importance of the concept of *fūzoku* as the concept that, together with the institutions, comprised the total worldview. Maruyama concentrated the analysis of Tokugawa thought from a purely political scientific viewpoint and sought sources of political powers that could trigger political reform toward modernization. For this reason, while Maruyama clearly found the role of institutions in Sorai's conceptual framework, he classified the world into two parts, the political part of the world, which is synonymous with the place of institutions, and the remaining part simply as the non-political part of the world. By defining *fūzoku* as the non-political part of the world, he seems to have excluded all the important properties of the concept of *fūzoku*, including cultural factors. With respect to the positive role of the non-political part, he asked only how the non-political part of the world could fulfil the political role. It seems that the meaning of the efforts devoted by Tokugawa intellectuals to improve the ethical level and standard of conduct of individuals that played a significant role in the establishment of orderly society, complementing the role of institutions, was completely outside the scope of the Maruyama model. For example, Maruyama claimed that, in the logic of Motoori Norinaga, literary spirits that had once become independent from the ethical, religious and political value standard, was elevated to have political influence (Maruyama 1952, pp. 178–179).

One of the members of the Maruyama school, Matsumoto, contended that *Koku-gaku*[22] fulfilled the role to depoliticize the spirits of individuals by teaching the absolute hegemony of gods and emperors, consequently contributing to the longevity of the Tokugawa *bakufu* through enhancing obedience to feudal order in the mentality of individuals (Matsumoto 1972). In summary, the analysis by the Maruyama school of Tokugawa thought was implemented from a too narrow motivation focused on political scientific examination in order to find elements of modernization theory in Japanese history, although we would be not reluctant to respect the contribution of the school in the area of political science. It was inevitable that they failed to notice the important role of cultural factors in the dynamic evolution of the socio-economy of the Tokugawa era.

It was Yoshikawa who found that the role of institutional and political factors in Sorai theory should be understood in a comparative framework with the role of ethics or more generally culture. Yoshikawa (1973)[23] summarized the Sorai theory in three major theoretical writings on his Kobunnji-gaku and the policy recommendation to shogun Yoshimune in two points. First was the priority of politics over ethics. It is contended that Sorai considered that, with respect to the matter of the welfare of all individuals, institutions are more effective than ethics. Second was Sorai's high respect for Heaven. Sorai considered that, since the complexity of nature as *katsub-utsu* is beyond human understanding, it is best to rely on the supreme authority of Heaven for humans. Otherwise, humans were obliged to adopt a false idea such as the natural mind (*kishitu*) that could be changed by ethics, as is contended by new Confucianism. Incidentally, probably inspired by the contribution of Yoshikawa, Fujimoto (1978) finds an important relationship between institutions, *fūzoku* and learning by society, and clarified the basic structure of the Sorai model. Nakamura (2019) is a more recent contribution that examines Sorai's model in a broader conceptual framework of Sorai's thought.

As is contended in Chapter 6, culture including ethics and trust, not institutions, played an important role in socio-economic development during the Tokugawa era. The activities by intellectuals inspired by the Sorai model seem to have had significant bearings on the performance of the socio-economy. It is also asserted that the establishment of cultural ordering became a national task as a consensus of the entire society that had experienced the turmoil and hardship of the Warring State period.

However, it must be noted that economic development during the Tokugawa era was largely an unintended consequence of individual behavior. Individuals were encouraged to engage in occupational activity honestly and diligently. There is no doubt that the teaching of intellectuals about the importance of ethics and the clarification of the interrelated economic mechanism of social division labor had a significant

---

[22]Matsumoto confined the role played by Koku-gaku in this respect to the version asserted by grassroots researchers (*sōmō no Koku-gaku-sha*).

[23]Yoshikawa (1973) seems to be the most comprehensive summary of the development of Sorai theory as well as his life as a researcher. It describes vividly the process of the denial of new Confucianism and the establishment of the new Kobunji-gaku theory (*Bendō*, *Benmei* and *Gakusoku*), based on the study of the political methods of legendary Chinese saints (kings), and how policy recommendations (*Seidan* and *Taiheisaku*) at his late age were attained.

effect on behavior. *Kyūdō* behavior had revived in the Tokugawa era as a national consensus about the necessity to enhance the effort level of society. Individuals were motivated to devote enormous efforts to the accumulation of skills and hence human capital in occupational activities. Nevertheless, the alleviation of information asymmetry and the reduction in transaction costs were unintended consequences of individual activity. Individuals were never encouraged to contribute to the economic growth of the national economy nor to contribute to the welfare of society.

Chapter 3
The Process of Long-Term Growth Before the Meiji Restoration

The purpose of this chapter is to provide a macro-economic overview of the long-term growth process in Japan before the Meiji Restoration. Through an examination of GDP series and its industrial composition, it is contended that the growth process is composed of two salient phases, before and during the Tokugawa era. The reasons for growth are investigated with respect to three factors that comprise major themes in the existing literature, technical progress in agriculture, the incentive effects of property rights and the role of the development of commerce. We will argue that, while agricultural technology played a significant role, together with the effect of urbanization, during the period before the Tokugawa era, the development of commerce due to the decrease in transaction costs was a pivotal factor for growth during the Tokugawa era, and the role of property rights was not significant until the last period of the Tokugawa era.

Economic growth in pre-Meiji Restoration Japan began in the Kamakura era, from the beginning of the thirteenth century. It was composed of two phases. First was the phase of acceleration of growth until the end of the Warring States period or the beginning of the Tokugawa era. Second was another acceleration phase of growth in the Tokugawa era, from the early eighteenth century through the first half of the nineteenth century. The first phase was characterized by changes in the industrial structure from the primary to the secondary and the tertiary sector, while the second phase was characterized by the stability of the industrial structure.

The first phase of acceleration of growth after the thirteenth century was accompanied by radical change in the industrial structure. Although the primary sector showed high rates of growth until the sixteenth century, the growth of the tertiary sector and secondary sector was significantly higher, reflecting rapid urbanization and the spread of the Japanese-style urban lifestyle. The growth of the primary sector was due to various kinds of technological progress supported by infrastructure investment. In particular, the success of the two-crop system supported by the development of irrigation was most effective. There is not much evidence for the effect of property rights on agricultural growth because there did not occur much change in the system

J. Teranishi, *Culture and Institutions in the Economic Growth of Japan*,
Studies in Economic History,
https://doi.org/10.1007/978-4-431-55627-5_3

of property rights of actual cultivators during the period, although it is possible to believe that the strengthening of the autonomy of villages had some positive effects on the effort levels of individual cultivators. The growth of the two sectors was further accelerated during the Warring States period, reflecting the industrial policy aimed at the formation of local integrated economies by *sengoku* (warring state) *daimyo* and the increased military demand for manufacturing products.

With respect to the causes for the acceleration of growth during the second phase, we deny the effect of technical progress in agriculture and property rights and argue for the significant role played by changes in the commerce system and in transaction costs. It will be argued that technical progress was not a major factor that explains growth during the Tokugawa period. This is because most of the technology used in agricultural production during the period was inherited from the past, and the spread of technology was generally slow and insufficient owing to the closedness of the local *han* (*daimyo* domain) economy. In particular, the effects of new rice varieties were not significant because of the severe restrictions on the spread of new varieties by *han* governments. With respect to property rights, it will be pointed out that residual income rights had since the Kamakura era already been given to actual cultivators, and that cultivators obtained a de facto residual control right[1] only in the late eighteenth century. It follows that changes in property rights cannot explain the Tokugawa growth during most of the period, although the acquisition of the residual control right motivated cultivators to engage in various innovating activities. It is contended that the reduction of transaction costs was most responsible for Tokugawa growth through inducing active and competitive commercial activities during the eighteenth century and thereafter. Eloquent evidence to support this contention is the equality of growth rates among the three industrial sectors during the early eighteenth century through the first half of the nineteenth century. It is suggested that the decline in transaction costs in the economy owing to the overall alleviation of information asymmetry could be a sufficient condition for the phenomenon of balanced growth of the three industrial sectors.

The appendix to this chapter considers why industrial revolution *a la* the Occident did not happen in Japan.

3.1 Chronology and Macro-Economic Overview

Chronology

Let us summarize briefly the socio-political history of Japan with the help of a simple chronology given in Table 3.1. Our analysis starts with the Kamakura era when the market economy began to appear and grow, partly due to the decline of the *ritsuryō* (law and order) system, the centralized and nationalized system that had

---

[1]Property rights were authorized by the Meiji government. Following the repeal of the Eternal Prohibition of Land Alienation Act and the ordinance on Land Ticket in 1872, the Meiji government finally embarked on the reform of the land tax system and *de jure* authorization of the property rights of peasants in mid 1873.

Table 3.1 Chronology of the pre-Meiji Restoration period

Era		Sub-period		Age
Nara era	710–794			ancient
Heian era	794–1192			
Kamakura era	1192–1333			medieval
Muromachi era	1335–1573	Southern and Northern Dynasties period	1334–92	
		Warring States period	1467–1600	
Tokugawa era	1603–1867			early modern

Note Except for the Heian era, the year at the beginning of each era shows the year when the founder of the *bakufu* was designated as shogun, and the end year is the year of the termination of the shogunate. The beginning of the Heian (Nara) era is the year of the transfer of the capital to Kyoto (Nara) and the end year of the Heian era is the year of the establishment of the Kamakura *bakufu*. The Southern and Northern Dynasties period is the period of Kenmu-chūkō by emperor Godaigo and the Warring States is the period from the beginning of the Ōnin war through the year of the battle of Sekigahara

been established at the beginning of the eighth century, and when the first samurai government, the Kamakura *bakufu* (samurai government), was established at the end of the twelfth century as a section of the *ritsuryō* system in charge of military and policing roles.

The decline of the *ritsuryō* system, officially noticed at the beginning of the tenth century when government initiated the policy[2] to control privately held lands, manor (*shōen*), was already irreversible at the beginning of the Kamakura era. Roughly at the end of the thirteenth century, more than half of officially registered land in the country was manor, privately held arable land with tax[3] exemption privileges (Nagahara 1998). Starting in the eighth century from an ancient community economy, in which plural families lived together in a house and there was no patrimonial system, and hence no property inherited as family assets, private real estate came to share more than half of the national wealth in the country[4] and most of the state factories producing handicrafts were also privatized, together with the workers (artisans). Manors and factories were owned as the private properties of imperial families, aristocrats and large temples and shrines.

There naturally occurred serious conflicts regarding property, especially landholding, and the frequent armed struggles raised the role of the samurai, specialists in martial skills. The position of the samurai rose as land disputes intensified among manor owners and between *ritsuryō* officials in charge of nationally-held lands and manor owners, and the number of samurai increased as indigenous landlords, who had developed land by themselves, came to be armed in order to defend their lands.

[2]Engi-shoen-seiri-rei in 902 that tried to prevent the growth of large-scale land holding by the private sector in order to protect small farmers.

[3]Tax included compulsory labor service.

[4]There were three kinds of land: official land, manor and private land. Official records, called *Ōta-bumi*, registered only the first two categories, so that there are no data about private land.

Strengthening their power through involvement in political conflicts among imperial families and aristocrats, the samurai finally established the Kamakura *bakufu*.

The decline of the *ritsuryō* system also resulted in the emergence of the market economy. The monetarization of the agricultural products of manors and the handicrafts of privatized factories promoted the development of markets and, hence, brought about the growth of a new class, merchants. The social division of labor was accelerated further as new Buddhist sects, Kamakura new Buddhism, spread the teaching of religious training at the place of daily occupational life, instead of training in isolated temples and monasteries, was effective to attain religious salvation. The practice was called easy practice (*igyō*), compared with practice at temples, which was called hard practice (*nangyō*). The teaching of easy practice gave rise to standards of conduct, occupational *kyūdō* (truth-pursuing) behavior, which enhanced the motivation of people in occupational specializations and gave further impetus to the acceleration of the social division of labor.

Housemen of the *bakufu* (*gokenin*), who were officially appointed as *shugo* (military governors) and *jitō* (estate stewards) and assigned to take charge of policing and judicial activities in the provinces, soon came to be involved themselves in conflicts over landholding rights held by aristocrats. Assisted by informal and formal help by the *bakufu*, they rapidly increased their control over lands, with a consequent erosion of the property rights of aristocrats.

After the ruin of the Kamakura *bakufu*, the political struggles among the samurai and aristocracy (the South–North Dynasty period) resulted in victory for the samurai and the establishment of another samurai government, the Muromachi *bakufu*, by the Ashikaga clan. Successive leaders of the Muromachi *bakufu*, shoguns, were not satisfied with the position of the *bakufu* in the *ritsuryō* system as the chief of the military and policing section, and tried to obtain high ranking in the aristocracy for themselves and to control central politics. This brought about continual political and military struggles involving the *bakufu*, aristocrats and regional samurai lords, the *daimyo*, many of whom were ex-*shugo*. The property right as well as the political power of the aristocrats deteriorated further, and the disorder in central government politics gave rise to the era of nationwide internal war, the Warring States period. Repetitive and ubiquitous military struggles involving small local samurai leaders (*dogō*), indigenous lords (*kokujin*), and regional feudal lords (*daimyos*) continued for more than one and half centuries. Murders, looting and arsons were daily occurrences all over the country.

From the ruins of war emerged the third *bakufu*, the Tokugawa *bakufu*, which was established as a compromise in order to put an end to the devastation of the country. The *bakufu* was established after the one-day battle in 1600, between a *daimyo* group supporting and another *daimyo* group opposing the Tokugawa clan (the battle of Sekigahara). After the victory, the Tokugawa could no longer delegate its housemen as leaders of each *han* governed by the *daimyo*, as had been done by the appointment of *shugo* in the case of the Kamakura and Muromachi *bakufu*, and, among the 266 *han* that existed in 1698, 98 *han* were governed by indigenous *tozama* (outside) *daimyos*, most of whom had opposed, or had at least been less friendly toward, the Tokugawa in the battle of Sekigahara. The aristocracy had already lost political power

Table 3.2 Percentage share of production by industry

Year	Percentage share of production by sectors		
	Primary sector	Secondary sector	Tertiary sector
730	86.3	5.5	8.2
950	86.7	5.3	8.1
1150	86.5	5.5	8.1
1280	84.8	5.8	9.4
1450	82.2	6.8	11.0
1600	73.7	8.8	17.5
1721	62.9	10.9	26.2
1804	63.0	10.8	26.2
1846	62.7	10.9	26.3
1874	59.5	12.3	28.2

Note The primary sector is composed of agriculture, forestry and fishery. The secondary sector is composed of mining, manufacturing and construction. The tertiary sector is composed of commerce, service, and transportation, communication and public utility

completely, and the Tokugawa *bakufu* retained its political power by means of strict regulation of military build-up and resorting to various political measures to deprive the *tozama* daimyos of economic power—for example by forcing extra expenditure by the system of *sankin-kōtai* that stipulated *daimyos* live in Edo (Tokyo) for one year in every two years, and through restricting interaction with foreign countries, virtually secluding the country from foreign trade.

After the peaceful years that continued for the next two and a half centuries, Japan was obliged to open up to foreign countries and to terminate the reign of the Tokugawa *bakufu*, eventually implementing the Meiji Restoration in 1868.

Macro-Economic Overview

Let us have an overview of economic growth until the Meiji Restoration by means of a couple of GDP data, which was recently estimated and analyzed in a six-volume series published by Iwanami-shoten, Tokyo.[5] Table 3.2 shows the percentage composition of production by industry. Japan was predominantly an agrarian economy until the twelfth century. The percentage share of the primary sector in total production was as high as 86.3% in 1150. The share of the tertiary sector began to increase during the Kamakura era. The share increased from 8.1% in 1150 to 9.4% in 1280. The share went up rapidly during the Warring States period and during the early Tokugawa period toward 26.2% in 1721 in the mid-Tokugawa era. After the stability of the mid-Tokugawa era (1721–1846), the figures rose gradually again toward the end

[5]Fukao, Nakamura and Nakabayashi (2017–18) give useful information about the nature of data and method of estimation of GDP series. and Bassino, Broadway, Fukao, Gupta, Takashima (2017) examine the long-term growth of the Japanese economy based on the estimation from the viewpoint of great divergence.

of the Tokugawa era. The share of the secondary sector began to increase during the Kamakura period and went up rapidly during the Warring States period. The share rose gradually toward the end of the Tokugawa period after the stability of the mid-Tokugawa era.

Table 3.3 shows the percentage contribution to growth by sector. The contribution of the primary sector during the medieval age from 1150 to 1600 was 68.2% and of the tertiary sector was 21.6%, followed by 10.1% of the secondary sector. During the early modern age from 1600 to 1874, the percentages were 52.8%, 33.3% and 13.9%, respectively. This implies that the leading sector of growth was the primary sector during 1150–1600, and the tertiary sector, which increased its percentage contribution during 1600–1874 by 11.7% at the expense of the primary sector. The increase in contribution of the secondary sector was only 2.8%. It is important to note that the growth of the Japanese economy before the Meiji Restoration is composed of two phases. The first phase is led by agricultural growth owing to technical progress and infrastructure investment and the second phase is led by the growth of the tertiary sector. The first phase of growth, led by agriculture, was accompanied by drastic change in the industrial structure from an agrarian economy to an economy based on the secondary and tertiary sector, and the second phase, led by commerce, was characterized by a stable industrial structure, i.e. the balanced growth of three sectors. Why these two phases occurred is crucial to understand the nature of the economic growth of Japan before the Meiji Restoration.

Table 3.3 Percentage contribution to aggregate production growth by sectors (%)

	Primary sector	Secondary sector	Tertiary sector
1150–1600	68.2	10.1	21.6
1600–1874	52.8	13.9	33.3

Source Takashima (2017)

Table 3.4 Annual growth rate of population and production (%)

Year	Total production	Production by sector			Population	Per capita production
		Primary	Secondary	Tertiary		
730–950	0.10	0.11	0.08	0.10	−0.09	0.19
950–1150	0.06	0.06	0.08	0.06	0.08	−0.02
1150–1280	−0.05	−0.07	−0.01	0.07	0.01	−0.06
1280–1450	0.33	0.31	0.43	0.42	0.31	0.02
1450–1600	0.48	0.41	0.65	0.80	0.35	0.13
1600–1721	0.52	0.38	0.69	0.85	0.51	0.01
1721–1804	0.22	0.22	0.22	0.22	−0.03	0.25
1804–46	0.32	0.31	0.35	0.34	0.11	0.21
1846–74	0.69	0.50	1.10	0.94	0.08	0.41

Let us look at the growth of the three sectors more closely. Table 3.4 shows the growth rates for each sector and the total production as well as population. During the first half of the Kamakura era, roughly during 1150–1280, both the primary and secondary sectors were stagnant, with negative rates of growth, and the tertiary sector began to grow at an annual growth rate of 0.07%. It is important to note that, while the rise in the share of the tertiary sector implies the growth of commerce, services and other related industries, the rise in the share of the secondary sector in this period shown in Table 3.2 does not mean the growth of manufacturing activities. This is because the growth rate of production of the secondary sector during 1150–1280 was −0.01% (Table 3.4), so that the rise of the share merely reflects the sharp decline in the production of agriculture by −0.07% during the period.

After the latter half of the Kamakura era and toward the early Muromachi era, during 1280–1450, all three sectors began to grow. Until the period covering the Warring States period and the early Tokugawa era, growth in the three sectors accelerated, except for the primary sector during 1600–1721. The growth rate fell temporarily in the mid-eighteenth century, but started to rise again, and the growth rate of all the three sectors accelerated during the latter Tokugawa era, 1721–1874.[6]

Three of the salient features to explain shares by sector and sectoral growth rates are as follows: (1) The gradual rise of the share of the tertiary sector and the decline of the primary sector during the later Kamakura and early Muromachi era; (2) The growth of all three sectors and the rapid rise of the share of the secondary and the tertiary sectors during the Warring States period and during the early Tokugawa era; (3) The rehabilitation of the growth of the three sectors during the Tokugawa era, and the constancy of the share of the three sectors until the mid-nineteenth century.

As for feature (1), we have already touched upon the effect of marketization due to the decline of the *ritsuryō* system that brought about the sharp rise in the share of the tertiary sector. This was because the decline of the centralized system implies an increase in the market activity of commerce. Further, the growth of the tertiary sector during the period is partly related to urbanization. In fact, according to Table 3.5, the share of the urban population in the total population begun to rise in the Kamakura era. This was due largely to the opening of the *bakufu* (samurai government) in the city of Kamakura, 400 km east of Kyoto. According to Table 3.6, the population of the city of Kamakura in 1252 was between 64,000 and 101,000, and this corresponds roughly to the increase in urban population of 88,000 during 1150–1280.

Urbanization is interrelated with the development of commerce and, more broadly, the tertiary sector. It is well known that one of the founders of Kamakura new Buddhism, Shinran, referred to the activity of merchants in his *Tan-ni-shō*.[7] In Kyoto, the largest and most thriving consumption city in this period with a population of 120,000 in 1150 (Table 3.6), permanent stores that sold various crafts and other goods

---

[6]Strictly speaking, the Tokugawa era ended in the year 1868. Since there are no data during 1868–74, we use this word for convenience.

[7]Sueki (2016) claims that reference to merchants reflects the worldview of Yuien, who dictated the words of Shinran and compiled *Tan-ni-shō* (p. 265). However, it is not easy to accept his assertion, because it is difficult to understand the thoughts of Shinran unless we take account of his deep interest in the changes to the socio-economy taking place during his time. See on this point Chapter 4.

Table 3.5 Urbanization

Year	Urban population (thousand)	Total population (million)	Percentage of urban population
730	124	5.8–6.4	1.9–2.1
950	135	4.4–5.6	2.4–3.1
1150	120	5.5–6.3	1.9–2.2
1280	208	5.7–6.2	3.4–3.6
1450	259	9.6–10.5	2.5–2.7
1600	1088	17.0	6.4
1650	2822	20.7	13.6
1750	4102	30.9	13.3
1850	3875	32.3	12.0
1873	3471	33.9	10.3

Table 3.6 Population of major cities until the Warring States period

City	Population at around 1600	Population at mid-16 c.	Population at early 16 c.	Population at early middle age
Kyoto	300 (1609)	300 (1571)	130–180 (at the end of 15c.)	120 (1150)
Sakai	80 (1609)	30 (1532)		
Kamakura				64–101 (1252)
Edo	150 (1609)		60 (1600)	
Sunpu	100 (1609)			
Kasugayama	30 (1578)			
Kanazawa	50 (1600)			
Yamaguchi	80 (1600)	60 (1550)	45 (1500)	
Hakata	35 (1579)	30 (1570)		

Note Population in thousand. Figures in parenthesis are year
Source Takashima (2017)

were thriving (Kurata 1952), and bills of exchange to send money to Kyoto were already available (Imai 2015, pp. 160–161). The expansion of the city of Kamakura was accompanied by an increase in the number of merchants in the population as well as by a significant expansion of commercial and service activities.

Feature (2) is closely related to the urbanization of the economy, and, during the early Tokugawa era, additionally to the development of marine transportation. According to Table 3.5, the share of the urban population was stagnant in 1450 due to warfare in Kyoto, but it rose rapidly toward 1600 and further to 1650. This is closely related to the policy of some *sengoku* (warring states) *daimyos* to let samurai vassals leave their local fiefs and live in castle towns. The policy was needed in part to build up a trained modern military power suitable for infantry battle (Sato 1974, pp. 214–223) and partly to separate the samurai from farmers in the villages in order to prevent private battles among vassals using armed farmers as soldiers. During the sixteenth century, the population in the castle towns of the *daimyo* increased rapidly. As Table 3.6 shows, the population of Yamaguchi, the main castle town of Mori Motonari, increased from 45,000 in 1500 to 80,000 in 1600, and Edo from 60,000 in 1600 to150,000 in 1609. The castle towns of the major *daimyos*—Sunpu of Tokugawa Ieyasu, Kasugayam of Uesugi Kenshin, Kanazawa of Maeda Toshiie—came to have substantial populations at the end of the Warring State period. The population of port towns like Sakai and Hakata increased, also reflecting the development of foreign trade during the period.

The policy of gathering vassals to castle towns was also extensively implemented by the Tokugawa *bakufu*. *Daimyos*, 266 in number at the end of the seventeenth century, were ordered to destroy all castles and forts in their territory, except for one castle in which the *daimyo* lived, and to let all vassals live in the castle town. The main purpose of this policy was to prevent the building-up of military power in the rural area.

When large numbers of vassals were gathered in castle towns, they needed to buy daily necessities through merchants and markets. This was the reason for the significant rise in the share of the tertiary sector during the period. Another reason for the development of the commerce sector was the policy of *sengoku daimyos* to request payment of tax by farmers in cash (*daisen-nō*). This policy, mainly adopted by *daimyos* in eastern Japan like Go-Hōjyō and Takeda, was not necessarily successful, however, because it was not easy for farmers to sell agricultural products in exchange for good quality coins. While *daimyos* requested to receive tax in good quality coins (*erizeni-rei*) in order to use them in cross-territory trade, the coins imported from China were not necessarily of good quality, and there occurred serious resistance by farmers against the policy (Nagahara 1978).

The rise in the share of the secondary sector was mainly caused by the increased demand for iron for use in military equipment and the building of castles and forts, especially during the Warring States period. Demand for iron for the use of farming equipment was not so great during the period, because commonly used farming tools were mostly made up of wood during the period. Extensive use of iron for farming tools occurred during the Tokugawa era (Hushimi 2011). It is important to note that the economy of the Warring States period realized high growth, with annual growth rates in production at 0.48% (Table 3.4). This growth was caused mainly by military reasons. First, it was a demand-led growth related to military needs for weapons that resulted in the expansion of the secondary sector. Second, it reflected the active industrial policy undertaken by the *sengoku daimyos* to strengthen their economy for military build-up. It is true that the *sengoku daimyos* implemented various institutional reforms such as standardization of currency, and integration of weights and measures, as well as the protection of market transactions. These institutional reforms were possible because of the absolute power of the *daimyos*, backed by military strength within their territories.

Furthermore, it is necessary to touch upon the effect of the development of marine transportation during the Tokugawa era. Partly in view of the failure of *daisen-nō* by *sengoku daimyos* and partly owing to the physiocratic tendency of the Tokugawa *bakufu*, under the Tokugawa reign taxation was paid in the form of rice. This gave rise to an enormous task of transportation of rice to the rice market in Osaka and Edo for monetarization. For the *bakufu*, it was necessary to transport rice obtained from its territory in the Tohoku area, and it was necessary for *daimyos* to monetize rice for financing living costs in Edo (the *sankin-kōtai* system). To facilitate transportation, the *bakufu* developed a marine transportation system from the northern coasts of Japan to Osaka through the Seto inland sea and from Osaka to Edo through the Pacific Ocean. The population of Edo grew rapidly, reaching 1.13 million in 1718, and the consumption of the Edo population was supported by the development of commercial and transportation industries. Wholesale merchants in Osaka, Edo and Kyoto accumulated enormous wealth through the transaction of rice and financial activities related to remittance of the proceeds of rice and other staple goods of local *han* (*daimyo* domains).

In order to understand feature (3), the rehabilitation of the development of the three sectors during the Tokugawa era and the shift to balanced growth, it is necessary to note the initiative of the tertiary sector, especially merchants. The commercial activity of merchants extended from the social division of labor in local markets to the nationwide regional division of labor, which realized the efficient use of resources in the national economy. The development of marine transportation was one of the reasons for this, but the crucial factor to the development of the regional division of labor was the decrease in transaction costs in the economy. The nationwide effort to develop moral codes suitable to the deepening of the social division of labor and to standardize the norms of conduct resulted in the drastic reduction of information asymmetry, and hence nurtured trust in society. The effort by the *bakufu* to spread new Confucianism as a common cultural training of the samurai, the spread of an elementary education system, as well as the devotion by private intellectuals in the research and education of moral codes for each occupation, had been effective in bringing this about. The decline in transaction costs is collaborated by the secular reduction of risk premiums in the financial markets during the early-eighteenth to early nineteenth centuries (Chapter 6).

One of the amazing features of the growth in the Tokugawa era was the stability of the industrial structure during the mid-Tokugawa era. There was a rapid rise in the share of the secondary and tertiary sectors during the periods 1600–1721 and 1846–74, but during 1721–1846, figures for the sectoral shares are surprisingly stable (Table 3.2). The growth rate of the three sectors was 0.22% during 1721–1804 and 0.31–0.35% during 1804–46, consequently entailing the stability of the industrial share at 62.7–63.0% for the primary sector, 10.8–10.9% for the secondary sector and 26.2–26.3% for the tertiary sector during the period 1721–1846, the heydays of Tokugawa socio-economy and culture. The relative slowness of aggregate growth rates might be one of the reasons for this, but nevertheless the phenomenon is remarkable. From the same table, we can note that the shares of the secondary and tertiary sectors rose steadily during the three and half centuries from 1150 to 1600 and after the year 1846. In other words, the stability of the sectoral shares during 1721–1846 is clearly an irregular phenomenon in the whole growth process. According to the celebrated finding of Colin Clark (1957), the long-term process of industrial structural change is characterized by the secular rise of the secondary and tertiary sectors and the fall of the primary sector. The stability of the sectoral production shares for a period of more than a century is a clear aberration to the findings. Why? We believe that the reason for this phenomenon, growth with a steady industrial structure, lies in the pattern of the activity of the tertiary sector, especially the commerce sector. During the early Tokugawa era (1600–1721), the commercial sector developed rapidly owing to the drastic improvement in the marine transportation system and innovation in financial technology regarding the remittance of tax revenue. Merchants in local producing areas such as Ise and Ōmi participated in nationwide commercial activity and the so-called era of three city merchants emerged. The activity had favorable impacts on the demand for goods produced in Ōmi, Ise and other Kinki areas, typically textile products and other refined craft goods. During the late Tokugawa era (1846–74), local merchants became the new leaders and expanded their power in commerce in collaboration with the industrial policy and military build-up of the *han* (*daimyo* domain) governments. The activities had impacts on the production of special manufacturing products produced in those *han*, such as paper (various *han* in Shikoku, Chōshū), indigo (Awa), wax (Aizu, Uwajima), cotton (Himeji), silk (Hikone), raw silk (Gujyō), sugar (Kagoshima) and the like(Shinpo and Hasegawa 1988). In both periods, the secondary and tertiary sectors grew faster than the primary sector.

The period 1721–1846 is different from these two periods. It was a period of stable growth in which all three sectors grew at almost the same rate. This suggests that growth during the period was brought about by impacts that influenced the activities of the three sectors equally and was not a result of sector-specific impacts, such as industry-specific technological progress or industrial policies aimed at selective industrial promotion. We believe such an influence was related to the steady and competitive growth of commerce owing to the reduction of transaction costs in the economy. Such a growth pattern in commerce should have benefited all products in the agriculture and manufacturing sectors equally. Under the Tokugawa regime there occurred a drastic decline in transaction costs owing to the alleviation of information asymmetry in society caused by the standardization of conduct and ethical codes. Merchants competed with each other to exploit the informational opportunity available for everyone. Chapter 6 shows that there occurred a drastic reduction of risk premiums in the interest rates during the period from the early 18th to the early nineteenth centuries. The reduction in transaction costs owing to the decline in risk premiums in the economy should have been the main reason for the balanced growth of the three sectors during the period. In terms of input–output analysis, the equal decline of the input–output coefficient owing to the reduction of transaction costs and the equal increase in final demand owing to the stability of the urbanized lifestyle[8] seems to be a sufficient condition for this.

It is interesting to note that small farmers actively responded to the initiative of merchants during the period. Small farmers were motivated to participate in the supply system of commodities coordinated by wholesale merchants. Although the active response of small producers to the coordination role of merchants characterized

[8]This was established during the prosperous years during the Genroku era (1688–1704).

the whole process of growth during the Tokugawa era, the behavior of small farmers in the nineteenth century is especially worth noting. They came to be involved in the production of commodity crops needed as materials for manufacturing and even supplied the labor force to the manufacturing process coordinated by merchants. It must be noted that a change in the property rights held by small farmers was an important factor that explains their active behavior during the nineteenth century. Until the mid-Tokugawa era, farmers in Japan did not have residual control rights of lands although they had residual income right from a very early period, probably from the Kamakura era. It will be argued below, in Chapters 6 and 8, that the development of the landlord system implicitly approved by the Tokugawa *bakufu* crosscut the residual control rights held by villages, consequently transforming small farmers into de facto holders of residual control rights and hence into real owners of land, and enhancing their motivation to invest in land-specific skills and equipment and to take part in the process of economic growth initiated by merchants. We believe that the rise in the growth rate at the end of the Tokugawa era, during the period 1846–74, was caused by the compounded effects of transaction costs reduction reinforced by the enhanced incentive of small farmers owing to the change in property rights and by the active response of local merchants to the industrial policy implemented by *han* governments. In Chapter 8 the effect of the authorization of de facto ownership by the Meiji government is analyzed in the context of the collectivity of the Japanese.

In summary, the two-phase growth of the Japanese economy before the Meiji Restoration can be explained as follows. In the first phase during the period from 1150 to 1600, there occurred a drastic change in the industrial structure, from an agrarian economy to an economy based on commerce and industry. This growth was incurred by the growth of agriculture, led by technical progress supported by infrastructure investment. The growth was accompanied by the expansion and diversification of consumption represented by the progress of the social division of labor, as well as the enhanced coordination and intermediation by market mechanism. The former resulted in the higher level of processing that accompanied the development of the secondary sector and the latter was brought about the growth of merchants and the tertiary sector. Since, during the process of radical change of lifestyle, the income elasticity of demand for agricultural goods was lower than the secondary and tertiary goods and services, the growth of agriculture lagged behind the growth of the secondary and tertiary sectors. The simultaneous attainment of growth of agriculture and the decline in the share of agriculture in total output was brought about in this way.

In the second phase during 1600–1874, there occurred balanced growth of industries, led by the growth of commerce. The growth was incurred by the impact of the decline in the transaction costs in the economy. The decline of transaction costs was represented by a reduction of risk premiums owing to the alleviation of information asymmetry. Chapter 6 deliberates on the reasons for the decline of transaction costs due to the decrease in information asymmetry. Chapter 5 argues that the intensified social division of labor and the specialization of activity owing to *kyūdō* behavior caused serious information asymmetry in the socio-economy, eventually leading to the Warring States period. Chapter 6 contends that the purposive efforts by the government and elites to develop ethical codes suitable for the advancement of the social division of labor entailed the standardization of conduct and new conventions, which considerably reduced information asymmetry in the interaction of individuals. Since the benefits caused by the reduction of transaction costs were shared equally by economic sectors, balanced growth in the second phase was realized.

Incidentally, although Table 3.4 shows data on population growth and per capita production, we did not discuss the change in the macro-economic implications of population growth, but rather concentrated on total production. The reason for this lies firstly in the fact that the movement of population is governed by many factors beyond the understanding of economics and, secondly, that in order to understand the welfare implication of production growth, we believe that just focusing on per capita consumption is not sufficient. Finally, per capita production as a measure of productivity is not reliable when population changes at variable rates. For more on this point, refer to Appendix attached to this chapter.

3.2 Sources of Economic Growth

Let us examine the major candidates for the causes of economic growth in the Tokugawa economy that have been discussed until now, with respect to three major topics—the technological progress in agriculture, the changes in the commercial system and the property rights to land. Technical progress in agriculture has long been a major topic of investigation, since Japan was an agrarian economy in the sense that growth did not depend on industrial growth, as in the Occident. There has been a long tradition and an accumulation of studies on the development of commerce. However, the importance of commerce had not been confirmed until recently, when long-term series of GDP were estimated. Property rights were also for long an important topic of study, partly because ownership of territory was a major theme of the political history of Japan and partly because the development of land ownership and the consequent dissolution of peasant society was considered to be a precondition for modern economic development in the tradition of Marxian economics. Moreover, the influence of Douglas North accelerated interest in the study of property rights as an institution in recent Japan.

This book aims to throw new light on the importance of commerce-based growth, through an investigation into the cultural impacts on information and transaction costs. In the previous section, we examined the recently estimated GDP series and have shown the importance of commerce in the growth of Japan before the Meiji Restoration, especially in the Tokugawa era. This section reviews the major studies related to agricultural technology, property rights and commercial development, as an introduction to the analysis below.

In Sect. 3.2.1, it will be argued that technical progress was not a major factor that explains growth during the Tokugawa period. This is because most technology in agricultural production during the period was not particularly new—major technology had been inherited from the past. Although *han* (*daimyo* domain) government devoted efforts in developing new rice varieties, the macro-economic effect was not significant because of the tight restrictions on the spread of new varieties. In Sect. 3.2.2 on property rights, we will deny its importance for growth also. It will be pointed out that the residual income right had already been given to actual cultivators since the Kamakura era, and that actual cultivators obtained the residual control right only in the later part of the Tokugawa era. Although this motivated them to be engaged in various innovating activities, the change in property rights cannot explain Tokugawa growth during most of the period, in particular until the end of the eighteenth century. Finally, in Sect. 3.2.3, it will be suggested that the reduction of transaction costs was most responsible for Tokugawa growth, through inducing active and competitive commercial activities. This proposition is proved in Chapter 6.

3.2.1 Technical Progress and Sources of Agricultural Growth

The long-term growth of agriculture is dependent on technical progress, such as methods of cultivation, agricultural equipment and tools, and the development and spread of new varieties, as well as on the level of infrastructure and the managerial system, including labor allocation. Technical progress, infrastructure and the managerial system, in turn, are influenced by the ownership of the residual control right of land. As will be clarified shortly, actual cultivators in Japanese agriculture held the residual income right from the early times under consideration, so the income right was not an important factor to affect long-term performance of agriculture. The residual control right was at first held by manor owners, or by *shōkan*, manor officials, under their control. After the decline of the manor system and the control rights of manor owners, the control right shifted to villages and village alliances under the protection and control of *sengoku daimyo* and local samurai lords (*dogō*). Village control survived the Warring States period and was inherited by the Tokugawa *bakufu* until the late eighteenth century, when the de facto development of the landlord system weakened the control power of villages. The pattern of the long-term performance of Japanese agriculture can be roughly summarized as stagnation during Kamakura era, high growth during the Warring States period and early Tokugawa era, stagnation thereafter, and the rehabilitation of growth toward the end of the Tokugawa period.

Let us summarize the interaction between technical progress, development of infrastructure and the managerial system in the historical process of the development of agriculture.

The Kamakura Era

The growth rate of the primary sector was at 0.31%, lower than the 0.43% of the secondary sector and the 0.42% of the tertiary sector during the Kamakura period (Table 3.4). Although agriculture in the Kamakura era was damaged by climatic factors, the fall of temperature since the end of Heian era, the major reason for the low growth of agriculture seems to be the low level of technological progress and infrastructure investment.[9] The level of agricultural technology in terms of equipment and tools as well as the methods of cultivation in the Kamakura era were not so different from the levels achieved at the end of the preceding Heian era (Nishitani 2017). Almost all the equipment and tools for farming emerged before the Kamakura era. The infrastructure was also inherited from the Heian era, when reclamation was actively promoted by the large landlord developers and the temples and shrines.

The main reason for the failure of growth in agriculture in the Kamakura era was the failure of adaptation to two-crop farming, which was introduced as a potentially effective method to supplement bad rice crop harvests by the introduction of off-season crops—wheat and other minor grains (Isogai 2002). The two-crop farming spread rapidly: 13% in 1275 to 30% in 1350 (Isogai 2002, p. 160).[10] However, the introduction of the new farming did not result in an increase in total production because the rice crop declined, offsetting the increased production of off-season crops. The reasons for this lay in the fact that conditions such as the availability of adequate irrigation, improvement of fertilizing, and good labor management were difficult to achieve. Fertilizers were not well developed and collective behavior in villages was still not effectively organized. Most serious was the unavailability of adequate irrigation. For successful implementation of two-crop farming, it is necessary to solve the dilemma between the imperviousness to water needed for rice paddy fields and the high permeability to raise the productivity of wheat. It is therefore necessary to prepare an efficient irrigation system that could supply sufficient water at the time of the switch from wheat planting to rice planting. This condition was hard to be satisfied when the residual control of the right of land was in the hands of manor owners, who were only interested in the irrigation of their own manors. The behavior of manor owners, most of whom lived in Kyoto, was highly exclusive and selfish; they did build a number of artificial ponds in their own manors to store rainfalls, but were never seriously involved in the renovation and control of large

[9]The impact of the introduction of the new rice variety, *akamai*, on total production seems to be not so significant either. This is because *akamai* spread widely mainly due to its durability under harsh natural conditions, not because of its high yield.

[10]The spread was relatively more significant in western Japan: during the early Meiji era, 38.4% in western Japan and 5.4% in eastern Japan (Nishitani 2017).

rivers (Hougetsu 1943), consequently failing to prepare sufficient infrastructure for effective irrigation.[11]

The Muromachi Era and the Warring States Period

The growth of agriculture during the Muromachi era and especially during the Warring States period from 1450 to 1600 is impressive (Table 3.4). The major reason for this lies in the growth of productivity by way of two-crop farming, owing to the improvement of irrigation. As the ownership of residual control rights shifted from manor owners to samurai, who intended to govern larger areas that encompassed plural manors, large-scale irrigation by use of rivers and reclamation of alluvial plains of large rivers came to be undertaken. The dramatic improvement of irrigation resulted in productivity growth by way of two-crop farming.

The growth of agriculture was due also to large-scale reclamation implemented by the *sengoku daimyo* (Yamamura 1978). Oishi (1975) notes that among the 118 large-scale public works implemented during the period from 781 through 1867, 40 were undertaken during 1550–1650. A characteristic of the public works of this period was river conservation to prevent floods on the sedimentary basin of large rivers. The large-scale works carried out by Takeda Shingen is well known. The *sengoku daimyos* had advanced technology of public works, through their construction of fortresses and castles.

Another important reason for the growth of agriculture during this period was that the movement toward the autonomy of villages, although under the protection of indigenous samurai lords, tended to be intensified. This was due partly to the improvement of irrigation. Arable lands once highly unstable due to the changing flow of rivers were stabilized by means of the improvement of irrigation. It is claimed that this gave an incentive for cultivators, who had previously been wandering in search of better job opportunities, to settle on the same land, and the motivation to be engaged in intensive small-family farming was intensified (Nishitani 2017). The stability of arable lands enhanced to some extent the effort levels of individual cultivators, but the significant effect seems to have come from the acceleration of cooperative actions in the villages. Most waste lands in villages were transformed into arable land through the fourteenth to the fifteenth centuries (*mansaku-ka*) by way of coordination at village level. During the Warring States period, villages advanced their collective behavior further, virtually monopolizing the residual control rights of land. Villages, called *sōson*, became responsible for tax payments to indigenous samurai lords and rents to outside landlords. They also engaged in collective action regarding irrigation and other infrastructure investment in collaboration with samurai lords, and even armed themselves against looting by bandits.

These changes led to various technological improvements in agriculture. New irrigation equipment for paddy fields using human treading was invented and

[11]The absence of interest in the development of infrastructure by manor owners is emphasized in Hōgetu (1943). This could be suggested by the efforts devoted to the reclamation of lands. According to his tentative estimation, paddy field during the early Heian era amounted to 862,000 *chō*, while in the early Muromachi era they made up 946,000 *chō*. This suggests that only 83,000 *chō* was newly developed during the Heian and Kamakura eras.

spread rapidly. The methods of fertilizing and of extermination of insect pests were improved. In particular, especially in Kinki region, new crop varieties for use of materials in manufacturing, such as raw silk, hemp, indigo, madder, gromwell and perilla, were spread widely. These came to be cultivated in response to the increased production of textiles and other products demanded in the Kyoto area during the Muromachi era.

The Tokugawa Era

The Tokugawa *bakufu* (samurai government) and *daimyos* devoted significant efforts to the development of new paddy fields. Arable land expanded from 2065 thousand *chō* in 1600 to 2927 thousand *chō* in 1720 and further to 3170 thousand *chō* in 1850 (Table 3.7). This seems to explain the major part of the high growth rate of agricultural production during the early Tokugawa era.

The main effect of agricultural growth through production technology was due not to new inventions but to the spread of high technology that was already in existence in some regions, especially from regions with advanced technology to other regions. There is a plethora of evidence for the regional spread of methods of agricultural production during the Tokugawa era. Against the background of high literacy levels within the population, the publication of didactic books produced by xylography gave information about how to make and use tools, and this was most effective in promoting the spread of production technology.

Tools for ploughing, an essential tool for family farming relying on human power, are a representative example. There were a variety of hoes in every region, developed in accordance with different soil conditions, types of iron and different kinds of use. Through the spread of information about the variety of hoes, each region obtained information about hoes suitable for the region and improved region-specific hoes. *Bicchū-hoe*, most suitable for deep ploughing, was the final result of the improvement through the spread of regional technology in the late seventeenth century (Nagahara 1980, p. 178). Another example was the pumping machine. Pumping machines that enabled pumping up water by treading (*ashibumi-yōsui-ki*) was invented between the twelfth–thirteenth centuries and the fifteenth–sixteenth centuries (Nagahara 1980, p. 130). These machines became widely used during the Genroku period in the late seventeenth century, when new paddy fields were developed in alluvial plains through reclamation (Furushima 1954, pp. 320–321). Further, Smith (1959) notes that a new threshing rake (*senbakoki*) used in the harvest of rice invented in Osaka region was spread to various regions.

Most important was the spread of rice-producing technology, the selection of seeds, the management of seedbeds and the water management of paddy fields. New farming tools such as the spade and hoe suitable for small family farming were widely and readily spread. The utilization of new commercialized fertilizers such as dried sardine in Hokkaidō spread nationwide through the activity of merchants. All these technologies had been invented and improved in various regions since medieval age and during the Tokugawa era the interaction of various technologies resulted in the improvement nationwide of the technology level. An exception was the threshing rake. This was invented in the Tokugawa era to cope with the labor shortage in agriculture at the time. There are two views about the exact time—the Genroku period or the Kyōho period—but both periods belong to the Tokugawa era (Furushima 1954, p. 544).

There occurred significant imports of new commodity crops. Most imports, however, occurred before the Tokugawa era or at least in the early Tokugawa era before the self-imposed seclusion, so that the effect on agricultural production during the Tokugawa era was mainly through diffusion among the regions. For example, pumpkin was imported during the Tenshō period, watermelon during the Kan-ei period, and peanuts during the early Tokugawa era (Furushima 1954, pp. 389–392). These new crops spread widely during the Tokugawa era. Cotton seed had already been imported during the Muromachi era, but spread rapidly after 1624 in Kinki areas, when the *bakufu* licensed the opening of markets in Osaka for dried sardine (*hoshika*) used for cotton production (Furusima 1954, pp. 374–375 and p. 363).

However, while better tools are conducive to labor productivity improvement, the most effective factor for agricultural growth is not good tools that saves inputs, but new high yielding crop varieties. The spread of new varieties required the transfer of seeds between regions. Information on new varieties could not be transferred by didactic books. However, this was the most difficult task to be implemented due to regulations during the Tokugawa era. Each *han* tried hard to obtain new seeds for selective breeding. However, each *han*, competing in enhancing economic power and hence military strength, kept secret their best seeds. Nogyō-gijyutsu-kyōkai (1952) gives a vivid description of how information about new varieties was kept secret and information disclosure was prohibited by the *han* and villages. Moreover, some villages were so cautious about the outflow of seeds to other villages that they even set up inspection stations at village boundaries.[12] Inspection at the checking stations was so severe that it was difficult to bring new rice seeds out of the *han*. Hayami (1973) examined the relationship between the spread of new rice varieties and the growth of production after the Meiji Restoration, and contends that the rapid growth of Japanese agriculture was due largely to the spread of new rice varieties developed after the Meiji Restoration. The abolition of feudal restrictions on the exchange of information and free travelling and transportation enabled the active development of new rice varieties by way of the mating of seeds of various regions. New varieties and related improved methods of cultivation[13] were spread rapidly nationwide by governmental experimental stations and by the efforts of skilled researchers. Hayami also shows that the exhaustion of the spread of new varieties, identified by the catching up of the backward prefectures in eastern Japan to the advanced prefectures in western Japan, corresponds closely with the decline in macro-agricultural growth in Japan after the 1910s.

[12]Villages were also concerned with intellectual property rights. This episode reveals the pervasiveness of the residual control right held by the villages.

[13]Since the leading researchers were composed of skilled veteran farmers with deep knowledge accumulated through longtime experience, the new technology was called *rōnō* (old farmer) technology.

Table 3.7 Population, arable land, and agricultural production during the Tokugawa era

Year	Population (a)	Arable land (b)	Agricultural production (c)	b/a	c/a	c/b
1600	1,200	2,065	19,731	1.72	1.64	0.96
1720	3,128	2,927	32,034	0.94	1.02	1.09
1850	3,228	3,170	41,160	0.98	1.28	1.30

Note (a) Population in ten thousand, (b) land in thousand *chō*, and (c) production in thousand *koku*
Source Hayami-Miyamoto (1988)

Hayami's study is eloquent evidence for the detrimental effect of regulations on species improvement during the Tokugawa era. It follows that, despite the sincere efforts to promote technical progress in agriculture, as emphasized by Smith (1959) and Furushima (1946), the effect of technical progress on agricultural development was insufficient. How should we explain, then, the jump in the growth rate of the primary sector from the period during 1804–46 to the period 1846–74? A couple of factors are relevant. First is the industrial policy of the *han* during the period. In the nineteenth century, almost every *han* embarked on developmental policies to cope with fiscal deficits and at the same time to implement the military build-up especially after the arrival of Perry. The policy took the form of developing the production and marketing of regional special products through *han* enterprises. Since the materials of almost all the special products were of agricultural origin, this enhanced the demand for agricultural products. Second is the activity of merchants to coordinate the production of commercial crops, most of which were material for manufacturing. Participation in the production of manufacturing was also implemented through the coordination of the side-businesses of farmers. It is surprising that farmers responded quite actively to the incentives provided by *han* enterprises and merchants. There seems to be various reasons for this. Penetration of the market economy and intensified competition among the regions were basic factors that explain the active response of farmers. Another important factor was the sense of acquisition of the residual control right over landholding by farmers. It will be shown in the next section that owing to the de facto development of the landlord system toward the end of the Tokugawa era, farmers were emancipated from the restrictions of control rights held by villages. It seems to be reasonable to believe that this enabled farmers to choose efficient and profitable managerial systems, including the flexible allocation of family labor, and to respond actively to the incentives offered by *han* enterprises and merchants.

3.2.2 *Property Rights and the Growth of Agriculture*

Let us investigate the changing role of property rights from the Kamakura era through the Tokugawa era. The following propositions are derived. First, since the Kamakura era, the property rights of cultivators were confined to income rights and, although they had residual income rights, they did not have residual control rights. Residual income rights should have enhanced the effort levels of cultivators, but since they did not have residual control rights, their incentive to be involved in the innovative utilization of assets and in the investment in land-specific skills was not sufficient. Second, we will show that the absence of the residual control rights of cultivators continued well into the Tokugawa era, and that it was only in the late eighteenth century that cultivators came to have residual control rights over their lands. This explains why the acceleration of commercial agriculture and the emergence of small manufacturing activity by small family farmers occurred after the late eighteenth century. While this phenomenon has been explained by resorting to the active role of wholesale merchants and the industrial policy of *han* governments, our findings show that the acceleration of growth during the late Tokugawa era was also related to the changes in the incentive system of farmers at the time and was due to the active response of small farmers who came to own residual control rights on their lands.

In this section we will follows the theory of property rights of Hart (1995). Hart divides property rights into two parts—residual income rights and residual control rights. Residual income and control rights are rights difficult to write into contracts.[14] By whom these residual rights are held is of crucial importance for the productivity and growth of firms. The concept of a firm corresponds to a farm in our case, but we will use the original terminology for a while. Because the future performance of firms is uncertain, it is difficult to contract the distribution of all the firm's income. There always remains an uncertain part of income that cannot be written into contracts, which is the residual income or surplus. Those who have rights in the residual part of income, not written into contract, are motivated to devote more efforts to firm activity. Therefore, who is the owner of the right for the residual part of the income is the crucial element in the efficiency and productivity of a firm. Likewise, it is impossible to specify in contract all the uses of assets held by firms. There always remain problems as to how to specify the uses of assets at the time of contracts. Especially important are the uses of assets in innovative activities. Since innovation is concerned with something not known beforehand, it is crucially important who can decide the innovative use of assets. Another important factor of firm control is investment in firm-specific activities. Workers hesitate to invest in firm-specific skills when the return on investment is uncertain. If the particular usage of assets for which workers invested in specific skills are changed abruptly to other usages by holders of control rights, for example, the return on investment could not be recovered. This possibility, called the hold-up problem, will reduce the incentive for investment in specific skills by workers. By taking hostage relation-specific investments by workers, the owner could increase its share in the residual income rights. These rights about the use of productive assets held by a firm are called residual control rights. The ownership of residual control rights is a source of power when contracts are imperfect, because

[14]The transaction costs related to contracts are composed of the costs of considering and planning for various contingencies that may arise, the costs for contracting parties of negotiating these plans, and the costs of writing plans down in such a way that, in the event of a dispute, an outside authority—a court, say—could figure out what these plans meant (Hart 1995, p. 23).

the owner of the assets has the right to decide all usages of the assets. The ownership of a firm is complete when both residual income and control rights are held.

How was productivity enhanced by the development of the property right system in an agrarian economy, in which the main productive asset is land? The effect of the property right on the efficiency and productivity of a farm is determined by the level of efforts, innovative activity in asset management, and land-specific or crop-specific investment in skills by cultivators. Let us examine the ways in which these incentives were influenced by the allocation of residual income rights as well as residual control rights. How the rights were enforced is also an important issue to be investigated.

The efficiency and productivity of farm activity is largely dependent on what kinds of rights were held by actual cultivators. It is contended below that residual income rights were held by cultivators during most of the time under investigation, but they did not have residual control rights except for during the late Tokugawa era. The endowment of residual income rights to cultivators enhanced the effort levels of cultivators at least after the mid-Kamakura era. However, since they did not have residual control rights, their incentive to be engaged in the innovation of asset management and investment in land or crop-specific skills was not high. Only in the late eighteenth century were cultivators motivated toward innovation and investment in skills.

It follows that economic growth in Japanese agriculture occurred despite the inefficient property right system. Property rights were not an important element in the growth of the Japanese agrarian economy until the end of the eighteenth century. Residual income rights enhanced the efforts of farmers after the mid-Kamakura era and kept at the same level thereafter but did not have any significant impacts through enhancing motivation for innovation nor investment in specific skills. It follows that the growth of agriculture during the Warring States period was the result of active industrial policy, including reclamation by *sengoku daimyos*, and the acceleration of growth in agricultural production during the Tokugawa era was due largely to the growth of the commerce sector due to the alleviation of information asymmetry in commercial activity.

It is worth pointing out that the importance of the difference between residual income and control rights was first recognized in the early 1970s by Nagahara. Nagahara (1973) contended that, in the context of eleventh-century public land, although residual income rights came to be given to actual cultivators, it was not possible to believe that residual control rights were established as long-term or permanent rights of cultivating the cultivator's land (pp. 136–143).

Further, it must be noted that the concept of the property right is not concerned with the issue of the 'tragedy of commons', in the sense that, with respect to a property of which ownership is not assigned clearly, individuals do not have an incentive to work out efficient arrangements. There tends to occur freeriding, with the consequent tragedy of overuse, sometimes leading to the complete loss of the property value by way of, say, excessive grazing on common land. This issue, first emphasized by Coase (1937), and that drew the attention of many social scientists including Putnam (1993), does not seem to bear importance in the Japanese case. The main reason for this lay in the efficient use of control rights held by the manor officials or villages (*sōson*). Whenever there existed unused or undeveloped land within manors, manor officials or villagers organized collective action by farmers and realized efficient and full utilization of land resources (*mansaku-ka*) by the end of Kamakura era (Nishitani 2017).

The Kamakura Era

The land system of the Kamakura era (1192–1333) is characterized by the emergence of the samurai owner, and this caused conflicts with traditional landowners composed of the aristocracy, and temples and shrines. New and traditional landowners brought in different governance systems. In the case of land held by the aristocracy and temples and shrines, the governance system can be schematized as *honjyo—ryōke—* manor officials and *geshi* or *kumon—myōshu-hyakushō* (farmer)—*sakunin* (cultivators including small *hyakushō*), while in the case of land held by the samurai as shogun—*jitō*—manor officials and *geshi* or *kumon—myōshu-hyakushō* (farmer)—*sakunin*. In other words, while the top-level holder changed from *honjyo* and *ryōke* to *shugo* and *jitō*, the middle and lower level owner system was virtually unchanged during the Kamakura era. This system of hierarchical governance system, called the *shiki* system, has its origin in the official positions of bureaucracy. While the privilege and remuneration of the official positions were converted into private assets and came to be transacted in the private sector during the Kamakura era, its authority is considered to be traced back to bureaucracy (Nagahara 1998, p. 30).

Honjyo was the top level of aristocracy, quite often related to imperial families, who received tax and rents without any control rights. *Ryōke* in the case of land held by the aristocracy and temples and shrines, and *jitō* under *shugo* in the case of land held by the samurai, are virtually the top positions in the governance system. Both *ryoke* and *jitō* delegated the implementation of management business to manor officials. Manor officials usually carried out their business through lower-level manor officials called *geshi* or *kumon*. *Myōshu-hyakushō* (farmer) were top cultivators. They cultivated land by themselves and at the same time sub-contracted cultivation to *sakunin*. *Sakunin*, major cultivators with a sub-contracting relationship with *myōshu-hyakushō*, were composed of small *hyakushō*, who were quite often local samurai. It was usual that small *hyakushō* also sub-contracted to lower-level cultivators, called *ge-sakunin*. In other words, there were layering chains of sub-contracting within the group of *sakunin*. Those subcontracted cultivators paid rents to upper level *sakunin* or *myōshu-hyakushō*, from which taxes were payed to *ryōke-honjyo* and *jitō*.

During the Kamakura era, the *myōshu-hyakushō*[15] system was introduced in lands both held by aristocrats and temples and shrines, and by the samurai. All the land in manors, except for *isshiki-den* that is directly cultivated by the landowner (*ryōke*), was sub-contracted to influential farmers, *myōshu*, who were given the name *hyakushō* and called *hyakushō -myōshu*. The aim of *ryōke* to provide *myōshu* with

[15]The origin of the *myōshu* was the *tado-humyō* system, born after the promulgation of Engi-shoen-seiri-rei in 902, which aimed at changing the policy aim from development of new land by large-scale reclamation to the protection of small cultivating farmers. Influential and well-performing farmers called *tado* were selected and sub-contracted to manage the tax collection of state-owned land (*myō*). *Tado* in charge of *myō* were called *humyō-tado*.

privilege and remuneration was to utilize the spontaneous order of village organized by them to realize effective systems of governance of manor (Inagaki 1975, p. 197). *Myōshu-hyakushō* were in charge of monitoring of cultivation by small farmers, called small *hyakushō*, obtained rents from them, and payed tax to the *honjyo-ryōke*. During the Kamakura era, the income of *myōshu-hyakushō* increased as productivity was enhanced owing to the settlement of cultivators in lands they cultivated. The tax collected by the *honjyo-ryōke* became fixed amounts as the aristocracy lost power due to the conflicts with the *jitō*. This implies that the *myōshu-hyakushō*, who obtained rents (*jishi*) from small *hyakushō* as landowners and cultivated by themselves, became residual income earners. As can be seen from the analysis of Ōtano-shō, Tachibana, who donated his privately-held land to an aristocrat (the retired emperor Go-shirakawa) as manor and became *geshi* of the manor, left part of land to be cultivated by *myōshu-hyakushō* (Nagahara 1998, p. 108). The *myōshu-hyakushō* at this period had kept the character of actual cultivators, so that it can be said that cultivators were residual income earners from the beginning of the Kamakura era. However, this does not mean that the *myōshu* had a complete set of property rights, including residual control rights. Control rights, in the sense of the long-term and permanent right of cultivation, was not established.

The small *hyakushō*, another group of actual cultivators, paid rents to the *myōshu-hyakushō*. Rents were still not fixed during the Kamakura era, so small cultivators were not residual income earners.[16] Since many agricultural workers, including small *hyakushō*, were not completely settled and wandering about looking for good sub-contracting opportunities, their negotiation power seems to have been so weak that they could not have any kind of control power over the lands they cultivated (Nishitani-Hayashima-Nakabayashi 2017, pp. 23–24).[17]

Let us move on to the issue of control rights. Manor officials composed of various ranks (upper-level manor officials called *azukari-dokoro*, lower-level manor officials called *geshi*, *kumon* and *tadokoro*) were in charge of the practical business of manor management under the control of *ryōke* or *jitō*. Their jobs were officially granted, and the right was called the manor-management right (*shōmu-ken*). In other words, residual control rights were held by landowners, *ryōke* and *jitō*, and the practical business of monitoring and tax and rent collecting were delegated to manor officials and the *myōshu-hyakushō*. On top of this system was the imperial court that approved the establishment of manors (Nagahara 1998, p. 103); *honjyo* and shogun were ordered by the imperial court to govern manors (*bunin*) at the time of the establishment of the manors (*rikken*) in the whole system of *shiki*. In summary, the ultimate residual control right was in the hands of *ryōke* and *jitō*, and the actual control and monitoring

[16] Rents became fixed after the fourteenth century, and this custom became popular during the Muromachi era.

[17] The reason for the unsettlement of agricultural workers lay in the instability of arable lands. Owing to the low level of river control, arable land was quite unstable, and it was difficult to cultivate same lands every year. There is a dispute as to until when the instability of land and the unsettlement of workers continued. Nagahara (1968) considers that it was until the end of the Kamakura era, Inagaki (1975) until the early medieval period, and Nishitani (2017) until the fourteenth century in Kinki area and until the fifteenth century nationwide.

business was delegated to manor officials at various levels and the *myōshu-hyakushō*, so that actual cultivators such as the *myōshu-hyakushō* and small *hyakushō* did not have residual control rights in the Kamakura era. The control rights exercised by the *myōshu-hyakushō* represented the policy of *the ryōke* and *jitō*, not their own.

The manor management right (*shōmu-ken*) was composed of three kinds of rights: *kenden-ken*, monitoring the user, width and quality of lands in manors for the purpose of taxation; *kannō-ken*, monitoring the cultivation of manors by the *myōshu* and lower-class cultivators; and *kendan-ken*, the judicial and police control business in manors. The *ryōke* and *jitō* were in conflict throughout the Kamakura era with respect the *shōmu-ken*. The *jitō* was given the *kendan-ken* at the time of the establishment of the Kamakura *bakufu* and tried to expand their power to other areas of *shōmu-ken* (Nagahara 1998, p. 183). The *bakufu* protected the right of the *jitō* in two ways. First, the *bakufu* contracted tax to be paid to the *honjyo* and *ryōke*, and this led to the complete shift of control right from the *honjyo* and *ryōke* to the *jitō*. Second, the *bakufu* intervened in territory disputes between the *honjyo-ryōke* and the *jitō*, and usually resolved the dispute by halving the land between the two parties.[18] This meant a serious blow to the power of the *honjyo-ryōke*.

The fact that the *myōshu-hyakushō* as actual cultivators had residual income rights implies that the property right system was efficient during the Kamakura era. However, since they did not have residual control rights, the property right could be inefficient in this respect. Although agricultural workers, including small *hyakushō*, had neither residual income rights nor control rights, this does not necessarily mean inefficiency because many of them were not firmly settled on the particular land they cultivated. The delegation of residual income rights might have induced them to have the motivation to devote greater efforts. However, even if they were given residual control rights, these rights are not underwritten by the whole property right system, so it is doubtful whether they were motivated to commit themselves in land-specific investments or innovative use of equipment.

The Muromachi Era

After the Southern and Northern Dynasties period, the political power of the Muromachi *bakufu* increased significantly and the loss of control rights by the aristocracy and large temples and shrines became serious. In the case of land held by the aristocracy and temples and shrines, the *honjyo* and *ryōke* were forced to choose sub-contracting managers (*daikan*) in collaboration with *the shugo* and *jitō*. *Daikan* were chosen largely from the *shugo*, priests and acquaintances of the *honjyo*, and engaged in tax and rent collection. This new system, called the *ukeoi-daikan* system, however, was not effective to recover the control right of aristocracy and temples and shrines. In the case of land held by the samurai, the *jitō* grew as influential military and political powers in their domains in provinces, and successfully brought the lower-level manor official system and the *myōshu-hyakushō* under their control.

---

[18]This method of resolution was called *shitaji-chūbun*. More on this point in Chapter 5.

During the Muromachi era, the monitoring rights of manors by the *ryōke* became rarely implemented, and the amount of taxation and rents became fixed. The aristocracy and temples and shrines were converted into mere fixed manor income (*tokubun*) receivers. As the power of the *shugo* in their domain encompassing plural manors and government-owned lands (*kōryō*) strengthened, the control rights of the *kokuga* (provincial governor's offices) were also absorbed into *shugo* power. Incidentally, it must be noted that the decline of power of the aristocracy was more significant compared with that of temples and shrines because the Muromachi *bakufu* was ardent to protect the latter.

In the original *shiki* system, income rights and control rights were united because each *shiki* was delegated to fulfil particular jobs in the manor governance system and, in return for the job obligation, income rights were allotted. However, as the conflicts between the *jitō* and *ryōke* intensified, the control rights held by the *ryōke* were weakened and they were converted into mere fixed income (tax) receivers. Moreover, as the necessity to control manors more effectively increased, new jobs such as the *myōshu-hyakushō* or *daikan* in charge of manor-management rights (*shōmu-ken*) were created, and income rights were separated from control rights. Under these conditions, there emerged the market for income rights, called the market for manor income rights (*tokubun-ken*), *tokubun-ken* market, which developed rapidly from the late Kamakura era, and the new landowner class, which had only income rights, mushroomed during the Muromachi era.

In other words, the landowner system came to have a dual structure, as is emphasized in Nishitani (2004). There were already traditional landowners mainly composed of rich *myōshu-hyakushō* who had expanded land under their control through their job of monitoring manors, and who came to be called simply *myōshu*. The new landowner class, which developed through the acquisition of manor income right (*tokubun-ken*) transactions, were composed of such rich individuals as priests, merchants and financiers. They utilized manor officials in their land management and their income rights were called *saku-shiki*. Both the traditional and new landowning class were under the control of local lords, called *ryōshu*, comprising powerful samurai, later called *kokujin* (indigenous lords), and large shrines and temples. They sub-contracted farm business to the *hyakushō* or *sakunin*, manor officials under the tokubun-holders, who in turn sub-contracted with actual cultivators called *ge-sakunin*.

In the Muromachi era, it became customary to write the amount of rents on *baiken*, the document used in the transaction of manor income rights (*tokubun-ken*), while in the Kamakura era such practice did not exist (Kida 2017, pp. 181, 183). This implies that, in the Muromachi era, the newly emerged landowner class with *saku-shiki* did not have residual income rights, and actual cultivators had rights to residual income.

Nishitani (2015) claims that rents became fixed in the fourteenth century[19]; the custom to halve harvests between actual cultivators (*sakunin* or *hyakushō*) and

---

[19]Nishitani notes that the custom to halve harvests between actual cultivators (*sakunin*) and *myōshu* as landowner became fixed as a rule and this triggered to move to fix rents thereafter (Nishitani 2015, p. 688; Takashima-Fukao-Nishitani 2017, p. 4).

myosho as landowners became fixed as a rule, and this triggered the move to fix rents thereafter (Nishitani 2015, p. 688; Nishitani-Nakabayashi 2017, p. 40; Takashima-Fukao-Nishitani 2017, p. 4). Although Nishitani does not explain why fixed ratio rents were transformed into fixed amount of rents, it could be construed that when the fixed ratio continued for a while, it would become convenient to take average rents in the past as a standard rent, and this gave rise to a custom to fix the amount of rents. It will be explained shortly that this process actually occurred in the Tokugawa era. Anyway, fixed rents and taxes meant that the *sakunin* or *hyakushō* were residual income right holders. Nishitani (2006) emphasizes that the *sakunin* or *hyakushō*, actual cultivators, had a strong sense of being the owners of products (*nenmō*). As the custom of paying tax and rent in cash (*daisen-nō*) developed, the *sakunin* became free to sell the products in the markets or to borrow money using their products as collateral.[20] This practice certainly enhanced the incentives of the cultivator. However, it must be noted that the actual cultivator still did not have residual control rights, although they had residual income rights.

Whereas the development of the market for income rights, the *tokubun-ken* market, in the Muromachi era implies that residual income rights were left to actual cultivators, this did not mean that cultivators had residual control rights also. Actual cultivators could inherit their cultivation rights of land to their descendants but could not sell the land to others. Land was considered to be something borrowed from the *ryōshu* (manor owners). Moreover, it is important to know that both the development of the *tokubun-ken* market and the growth of landowners occurred within the framework of the manor system (Nishitani-Hayashima-Nakabayashi 2017). In other words, despite the changes in the mechanism of income distribution, the basic control mechanism in agricultural production was in the hands of lower-class manor officials called *kumon* or *tadokoro*, and their roles to collect taxes and rents delegated by landowners were tightly related to their role of monitoring cultivators (Gomi-Ito 2002, p. 199). All the *daikan* and *myōshu* relied on the job of these lower-class manor officials with respect to the business of practical monitoring. This implies that the actual cultivators still did not have residual control rights during the Muromachi era. It must be noted that final control rights were in the hands of the *ryōshu* and were delegated to the *daikan and myōshu*.

It is well known that, during the Muromachi era in particular, *tokusei-rei*, debt cancellation orders, were frequently promulgated and *tokusei* uprisings became rampant, so that the landowning system was thrown into confusion. The *tokusei-rei* was highly effective to cancel debt obligations and the consequent transfer of 'property rights of lands' to actual cultivators. It seems to be true that the *tokesei-rei* had the effect to stabilize social unrest and rehabilitate social order through changing asset distribution and had been built in during the Muromachi era (Nishitani-Nakabayashi 2017; Hayashima 2017). It must be noted, however, that the reason for this effectiveness lay in the fact that the manor income rights (*takubun-ken*) market and the *tokusei-rei* did not touch upon the transfer of residual control rights. This implied that

[20]They also financed various current expenses needed to carry out farm management by themselves. In this sense they tried to be independent from *ryōshu* with respect to production activities.

the transaction of manor income rights (*tokubun-ken*) and debt cancellation orders by the *tokusei-rei* did not have any significant effects on the efficiency of agricultural production. This neutrality of the *tokesei-rei* might be one of the important reasons for the surge of promulgation of *tolusei-rei* for the purpose of reestablishing social order.

In the Muromachi era, unlike the *myōshu–hyakushō* in the Kamakura era, the traditional *myōshu* class and the new landowner class came to delegate actual cultivation to the *hyakushō* or *sakunin* through the sub-contracting system. Because tax and rents were fixed, the *sakunin* and *hyakushō* had residual income rights, but they did not have residual control rights. In this sense, the property rights system was not perfectly efficient during this period.

The expansion of the landlord system owing to the development of the *tokubun-ken* market did not, per se, result in the shift of residual control rights to cultivators. Residual income rights were held by cultivators and residual control rights were in the hand of landlords, who were fixed income earners as well as holders of residual control rights delegated to lower class manor officials. For residual control rights to shift to actual cultivators, it is necessary to go through the process of shifting residual control rights to the village system, the community of actual cultivators, in which actual cultivators as holders of residual income rights participate in the decision of exercising residual control rights by villages. This process occurred during the Warring States period and the system based on village autonomy was inherited by the Tokugawa *bakufu*. The final shift of residual control rights to actual cultivators occurred through the development of the de facto landlord system during the latter part of Tokugawa era, that cut across the control power of villages.

Incidentally, in the Warring States period, villages with a high level of autonomy obtained residual control rights. As, under village autonomy, actual cultivators, individual farmers, could have some degree of freedom, it is possible to argue that residual control rights had already been in the hands of actual cultivators since the period of the Warring States. However, we believe that the power of villages was so strong and covering so many aspects of farmers' lives, the freedom of individual cultivators was not necessarily sufficiently guaranteed. However, the rise in the growth rate of agriculture during the Warring States period from 0.31% during the period 1280–1450 to 0.41% during the period 1450–1600 (Table 3.4) might be partly related to the change in the property right system in which control rights was partially held by cultivators, although the main reason lay in the active implementation of irrigation by the *sengoku-daimyo*.

The Warring States Period

Owing to the excessive promulgation of *tokusei-rei* (debt-cancelling orders) and frequent riots requesting *tokusei-rei*, landholding attained through the *tokubun-ken* (manor income right) market became extremely unstable. Merchants and financiers as well as priests began to sell their *tokubun-ken* of rents and tax toward the early Warring States period. The main purchasers were *dogō*, local samurai leaders, who were the major financiers for the *myōshu* and *hyakushō*, and recurrent troubles related to loan repayments provided them with the chance of using violence to withhold *tokubun-ken* from the *tokubun-ken* holders. The *dogō* were usually vassals of leading rulers, *ryōshu* in the region including *kokujin* (indigenous lords),[21] some of whom became *senngoku-daimyos*, and were able to protect their property rights by utilizing their own military power or with the help of groups related by regional ties or blood relationship, so-called self-salvation behavior.

Villages (*sōson*) during the Warring States period had significant autonomy. To cope with the violence of *dogō* and riots, and the weakening power of the lower-level manor officers, cultivating farmers (*sakunin*) reorganized the village system and established a system called *sōson*. The village system had the right of collective cultivation and a high degree of autonomy approved by the *ryōshu* or *sengoku daimyos*, and functioned as a body to pay taxes to them and rents to the *dogō* and other *tokubun-ken* holders, collectively. This system was called *the murauke* (village sub-contracting) system. Villages established their own law (*sō-okite*), armed for self-defense, and had police and judicial rights of their own. It is true that actual cultivators enhanced the sense of ownership of their lands during this period, but it must be noted that the tendency towards collective action motivated by village autonomy became stronger also as social insecurity increased.

Since villages had strong negotiating power with respect to tax and rents, cultivators collectively had residual income rights. Villages were also in charge of maintaining irrigation systems or the other infrastructure in the village. Villages obtained the monitoring rights previously held by the lower-level manor officials under the control of the *kokujin* or *sengoku-daimyo*. The payment of tax and rent of individual cultivators became the collective obligation of villages, and villages negotiated and contracted about details of tax and labor service obligations with the *ryōshu* and *senngoku-daimyo*. Village leaders, usually comprised of the elderly, controlled the total production of the village, taking the situation of individual cultivators into consideration (Inaba 2002, pp. 229–230). Because land in the village was controlled collectively, not individually, and since individual cultivators were under the monitoring system of villages, they were not true holders of control rights on their lands. It would be fair to say that control rights on land by cultivators was not yet established to a degree sufficient to enhance work efforts and investment in land-specific skills by individual cultivators. There should have been some room for free rider problems and conflicts among village members over the use of land, if land had not have been under the control of individual cultivators.

In other words, the purpose of establishing the system of villages (*sōson*) was to protect against the recurrent violence of the *dogō*, conflicts with neighboring villages and famines, so that the village system required constituent cultivators to subordinate to the 'will of the village' in order to overcome these crises (Nishitani 2004a, pp. 65–66). Hasegawa contends that village played a role as the life-protection devise for constituents (Hasegawa 2004, p. 11). It seems to be natural to infer that this deprived

[21]The *Kokujin* were composed mainly of previous *jitō* and had control power over the territory comparable with temples and shrines and aristocracy, while the *dogō* were composed of local samurai under the control of the *kokujin* or other higher-class rulers (Nishitani 2004)

cultivators considerably of freedom in pursuing individual economic gains, apart from gains for the village as a whole.

The Warring States period, frequently characterized as the era of *gekokujyō*, a social upheaval where those below overcame those above, was a time of social liquidity and full of chances for climbing the social ladder. It was also the era when GDP began to rise rapidly. This tempted some economists to take an optimistic and progressive view about the era. Let us examine a pioneering work, Kozo Yamamura (1978), which asserts that efforts to promote independent small farming by the *sengoku-daimyos* in their effort to realize the economic development of the territory and the weakening of the control rights of the *myōshu* and *hyakushō*, resulted in the enhancement of the negotiating power of farmers in contracting, giving rise to incentives for greater efforts in cultivation. Moreover, it is claimed that the improvement in farmers' motivation owing to the acquisition of a virtual landholder status was the main reason for the expansion of agricultural production during the Warring States period. Yamamura's hypothesis is reasonable in highlighting the phenomenon of the gradual simplification of income rights and the enhancement of the bargaining power of farmers. Income rights before the era were an extremely complicated system, classified into diverse manor income right (*tokubun-ken*), but as the governance system of each *daimyo* domain was simplified owing to political integration within each domain during the late Warring States period, it became easier for farmers to negotiate with income right holders and the bargaining power of farmers became stronger.

Consequently, to the extent that the fruits of enhanced bargaining power was shared by individual farmers, this new system should have enhanced the work efforts of farmers. However, Yamamura's revisionist view, emphasizing an image of progressive farmers, seems to be derived from an analysis void of reference to two basic characteristics of the Warring States period. First is the role of villages in the property rights system. We have argued that, while residual income rights were maintained by cultivators, so that the effort level of cultivators could be considered to stay at the same level as before, the power of villages in grasping residual control rights discouraged the initiative of individual cultivators to engage in investment, just as before. In other words, the weakening of the control rights of the *myōshu* and *hyakushō* who relied on the extant *ritsuryō* manor official system, meant that villages became the new holders of control rights, replacing the *myōshu* and *hyakushō*. It follows that the residual control rights of individual cultivators did not increase and so did nor result in the enhancement of incentives of individual cultivators for, say, investment in skills. Second was the fundamental cause of the turmoil of the Warring States period. Yamamura's analysis is carried out without touching upon why the turmoil in the Warring States period arose. In this book we will argue that the turmoil was caused by the fundamental dilemma between the sophistication of the social division of labor that began and accelerated during and after the Kamakura era, on the one hand, and the cultural conflicts between aristocratic and samurai values as well as the low level of the moral codes of Buddhism in mitigating conflicts in the interaction of individuals, on the other. This dilemma, a fundamental cultural characteristic of the era, cannot be resolved without advances in the cultural system and systemization of the social division of labor. The efforts by the *sengoku daimyos* to promote independent small farming should be analyzed in relationship to the policy of disarmament of farmers by Toyotomi Hideyoshi and the *shokubun* regulation policy of Tokugawa Ieyasu. Both leaders seemed to be aware that the serious turmoil was rooted in the dilemma, and that the promotion of independent specialized farmers was one of the necessary steps to resolve the dilemma. Yamamura's emphasis on the small farmer policy seems to be derived from a simplistic modernization theory that stresses only the efficiency of competitive independent producers.[22]

The Tokugawa Era

The Tokugawa *bakufu* adopted the collective taxation system by villages by way of sub-contracting (*murauke* system) following the practice of the Warring States period. In the Tokugawa system, villages were legal persons, responsible for collective tax payments, able to launch litigation as a village, and allowed to make contract with other villages (Takigawa 1985, vol. 2, p. 97). In principle, the rate of taxation was a fixed amount for each piece of land (*kokumori*), determined at the time of the land survey with a tax rate of 50%. Although adjustments were given by evaluating the actual harvest for a typical piece of land (*tsubogari*) in order to take account of variations in annual harvests, the procedure was costly, so that, after around the 1720s (the Kyōho period), the average harvest during the past 10 or 15 years came to be used as the standard amount of taxation. The standard amount of taxation was fixed for several years, and this method, called the *jyōmen* method, was used widely thereafter (Takigawa 1985, vol. 2, pp. 129–142). In summary, taxation during the Tokugawa era was basically a fixed amount taxation system, so that cultivators had residual income right as before during most of the era. Incidentally, it is well known that tax rates of the *han* were generally higher than that of the *bakufu,* and this fact was recently confirmed by Sawai and Tanimoto. They also show that that rates declined after the eighteenth century (Sawai and Tanimoto 2016, pp. 44–45).

The land-owning units of the Tokugawa era were villages, representing the collective rights and responsibility of constituent small family farmers, cultivators. During the early period of the Tokugawa era, the boundaries of villages were determined so as to encompass all lands related to constituents, taxpaying farmers within the territory of the villages. In this system, called *muragiri*, ownership of lands by agents outside the village boundary was not allowed. The *bakufu* tried to define a village as a perfect entity that represented the private sector against the government. Since all lands were considered to be collectively held by villages, the residual control right was held by villages. The landlord system of tenancy contract was strictly prohibited. However, as the financial relationships between farmers using land as collateral

---

[22]Recent studies inherit Yamamura's viewpoint that criticized previous studies that described the era as a period filled with chronic misery caused by warfare and famine. Pointing out that both the population and production increased during the Warring States period (Kitō 2007; Farris 2006; Takashima 2017), they emphasize the causes of growth focusing more on the role of the developmental policy of *sengoku-daimyos*.

developed, defaults by farmers were inevitable, leading to the concentration of landholdings in the hands of rich farmers. A de facto landlord system developed widely after the mid-eighteenth century, especially during the nineteenth century.

As a consequence of the development of the landlord–tenancy system, residual control rights shifted from villages to individual cultivators. This shift occurred in two respects. First was the emergence of the notion of de facto control rights. During the Tokugawa era, there was no notion that differentiated control rights from income rights, since both tax payment and coordination of production was under the control of villages. The emergence of de facto income rights as a consequence of the development of the landlord–tenancy system was construed in a way to also imply control rights.

To understand this mechanism, the difference between the landlord system in the Muromachi era and that of the Tokugawa era must be examined. During the Muromachi era, the income rights of land were concentrated in the hands of the *myōshu* or *dogō* through transactions in the *tokubun-ken* market. The *myōshu* or *dogō* delegated the role of the monitoring of actual cultivators to lower-level manor officials, so that the control right was strictly differentiated from the income right, owing to the strict restrictions of manor laws inherited from the Heian and Kamakura era. In the case of the landlord system of Tokugawa era, there were no concepts that differentiated income from control rights. The concept of separation was destroyed in the turmoil of the Warring States period, together with the effectiveness of the *shiki* system that justified the behavior of lower-level manor officials. It follows that, after the demise of the *ritsuryō* system, it was natural that de facto residual income rights held by farmers were construed to imply both residual income and control rights, which were delegated to villages during the Warring States period. This way of thinking was inherited by farmers and villagers in the Tokugawa era. The de facto residual income right of landlords, therefore, came to mean also the de facto residual control right.

The second impact of the development of the landlord–tenancy system was the infringement of the boundary of territory. Rich landowners could hold land beyond the boundary of villages, and this encroached on the *muragiri* system. This meant that landlords could have residual control rights, free from village constraints. It seems that, as this way of thinking was accepted broadly, it came to be applied to small family cultivators. Small family farmers were induced to believe that they came to have de facto residual control rights that were previously held by villages and to devote efforts in the efficient utilization of land resources by means of investment in specific skills and higher efforts.

In this way, it is considered that actual cultivators in the late Tokugawa era, who already had residual income rights, came to have residual control rights, owing to the development of landlord–tenancy system. Otherwise, it would be difficult to explain the active, innovating behavior of farmers in embarking on cultivation of new commodity crops and even manufacturing activity under the guidance of wholesale merchants after the latter half of the eighteenth century.

In summary, during the first half of the Tokugawa era, actual cultivators had residual income rights but did not have residual control rights, so that the degree of efficiency of property rights was the same as in the eras before. However, after the mid-eighteenth century, the development of landlord–tenancy system destroyed the strict power of villages over residual control rights, and small farmers came to have de facto control rights over the lands they cultivated. In other words, small farmers were freed from hold-up problem and were motivated to implement firm-specific investment with higher efforts. The efficient property right system was established at the very end of the pre-Meiji Restoration history of Japan.

Although management records for actual cultivators are not available, there are a plethora of descriptive records on their active adaptation to the securing of residual control rights. For one thing, they actively introduced commodity crops and tried to increase profits. In particular, in Kinki area near the manufacturing center of Osaka, the production of commodity crops increased rapidly. After the mid-Tokugawa era, they were involved in handicraft manufacturing as side-businesses during their spare time, but soon these side-businesses changed into the main business of all family members. There appeared farmers who did not produce rice for their own consumption and purchased from other farmers. Such a conversion of side-business into specialized business was seen in the Kinki area (Settsu, Kawachi and Izumi) among producers of cotton and rapeseed farmers, or sericulture farmers in Nagano and Yamanashi. As the regional division of labor proceeded, specialization came to be seen nationwide. Especially important was the family manufacturing system under the coordination of wholesale merchants *(tonya-sei kanai-kōgyō)*, in which farmers borrowed equipment and material and returned the final products, obtaining labor charges as residuals.Farmers also purchased equipment and material of their own, produced commodities and sold them in the market, utilizing information given by wholesalers.

Further evidence of active optimization behavior by actual cultivators is seen in their choice of managerial system with respect to the production of rice, commodity crops and handicrafts. It is well known the managerial system of farming changed from large-scale farming utilizing semi-slave labor and livestock, which was typical during the manor system, to the family farming system. There are diverse views about the timing of and reasons for the transformation to family farming, but it is important to note that farmers sought the optimal organizational form suitable for enhanced residual control rights themselves. Small family farmers in Tokugawa Japan became capitalistic firms in terms of modern economic growth.

It is interesting to note that these active adaptations to the acquisition of residual control rights in the market economy proceeded under the leadership of upper-class farmers. For example, when sericulture spread in Japan, the first movers were upper-class-farmers, and the lower-class followed the leadership by leaving hired labor status (Shinpo and Saito 1989). This underlines the fact that involvement in the market was not motivated by the need for living expenses but rather by a pursuit to expand the scale of business and for higher profit opportunities.

The Stance of the Tokugawa Bakufu to the Development of the Landlord–Tenancy System

During the early period of the Tokugawa era, the ownership of land belonged to villages, not to individual farmers. In the official records of the land survey conducted by the *bakufu*, together with the names of individual farmers, the location, boundary and width of their lands were written; but this was for the purpose of calculating the amount of taxation, and not for the purpose of confirming ownership of lands. As tax payments were the collective responsibility of each village, it was natural to believe that land ownership belonged to villages. The evidence raised quite often to collaborate this assertion was the custom of the regular reallocation of land allotment (*warichi* system). For example, in Kanazawa-*han*, the ownership or cultivation rights of all the lands in each village were reallocated by lottery every 20 years (Niwa 1989). In this system, land ownership was something floating over villages, so that there was no definite ownership for each individual (Ono 1936, p. 216). This custom was widely seen in the Kyūshū and southern Shikoku regions as well as in areas of the mainland along the Japan Sea.

It seems natural to believe that ownership of this kind tends to give rise to inefficiency, such as the 'tragedy of commons',[23] because when property is owned by everyone, it is in fact owned by no one, so no one has appropriate incentives (Stiglitz 1994, pp. 11–12). However, it must be noted also that the *warichi* system was confined to low developed areas in terms of agricultural development, and that, in advanced areas, those that faced the Pacific Ocean and the Seto Inland Sea, virtual ownership changed drastically during the Tokugawa era, especially in the Kinki region near Osaka and the Tokai region near Nagoya. The transaction of land was actively carried out and the concentration of land ownership proceeded rapidly after the mid-eighteenth century. In this process, the property rights of farmers seem to have been virtually established. This conjecture could be collaborated by the fact that, in the advanced region in terms of agricultural development, active management by innovative farmers is most saliently observed. Without a high level of property rights, such active behavior would never have occurred.

The original property right system was contrived for the political purpose of securing tax revenue. However, as the market economy penetrated deeply into agriculture, farmers were motivated to utilize land resources as efficiently as possible and this necessitated de facto adaptation by the property system, while keeping *de jure* property right unchanged. In the *bakuhan* system all the land was owned ultimately by the *bakufu*; *daimyo* obtained taxation rights from their domain and farmers cultivation rights of land collectively. This system was contrived for the political and fiscal purposes of maintaining economic and military hegemony over *daimyo* and securing tax revenue. It was not allowed for the private sector to touch upon the property system, so that not only transaction but also lending and borrowing were strictly forbidden. The statute for prohibiting the permanent selling and buying of land (Denbata eidai baibai kinshi-rei) was promulgated in 1643, and land renting was also strictly prohibited since the reign of Hideyoshi.

However, to save impoverished farmers, borrowing money from rich farmers using land as collateral, while maintaining cultivation rights on the land, was allowed. This system, however, could lead to the forfeiting of pawned lands, and, in order to avoid

---

[23]For example, excessive grazing on common land, excessive rapid drilling of common oil pools and excessive fishing in international waters.

the forfeiting of land, the *bakufu* promulgated a statute prohibiting forfeiting in 1722. At the same time the *bakufu* announced its stance to encourage the redeeming of pawned lands. However, the *bakufu* repealed the 1722 statute and withdrew its announced intention the next year. This was because the announcement was accepted by impoverished farmers as the cancellation of borrowing contracts with collateral land, and there occurred a movement to recover lands used as collateral. The repeal was accepted as a signal for the liberalization of transactions involving forfeited lands, and consequently resulted in the de facto approval of land transactions (Ishii 1976, p. 22; Nagahara 1980, p. 214). The concentration of landholding and the rise of the landowning class thus virtually started in the mid-eighteenth century and accelerated toward the end of the century, whereas the *bakufu* never changed its official stance to prohibit land transactions in order to maintain the taxation system based on collective responsibility by land-owning farmers in the villages.

Enforcement of Property Rights

For the establishment of property rights as an efficient economic institution, a protection and effective enforcement mechanism is necessary. North and Thomas (1973) argued that because of the possibility of the free rider problem, effective property rights can only be provided by the state. North (1991) claimed that the role of the state is central to the effective enforcement mechanism. In the context of early modern Europe, North contends that the blending of the voluntarist structure of enforcement of contracts in the private sector with enforcement by the state was crucial in this regard

As for the enforcement of property rights by the state, it seems to be interesting to note that the experience of the Occident does not apply to Japan because private enforcement mechanisms effectively substituted the role of the state whenever the latter was not working well, at least after the Warring states period. During the Kamakura-Muromachi era, the state was solely responsible for enforcement. In the *shiki* system, the official position to enforce control rights was remunerated by income rights. Cultivators were under the monitoring and control of *shiki*-holding officials and, at the same time, paid taxes and rents to them. In other words, control and income rights were enforced as a set by the power of the state. As income rights came to be sold on the *tokubun-ken* market separately from control rights, control rights were implemented by other agents, such as the *daikan* or *myōshu-hyakushō*, who were also assigned an official position in the *shiki* system. During the Warring States period, villages (*sōson*) became owners of control rights and were responsible for tax and rent payments, and disputes about property rights came to be settled by private battles and violence. This degradation of the enforcement system of property rights resulted in the total loss of state power in the enforcement of property rights. Consequently, the Warring States period was characterized by the private enforcement of property rights. Whenever property rights were concerned with the interests of the samurai, violence and battles—self-salvation—substituted the role of states in property right enforcement and became the major measure to resolve conflicts and disputes related to property rights.

During the Tokugawa era, the *bakufu* delegated control rights and tax payment responsibility to villages, constituents of which were cultivators with the management system of family farming. Landholding and management by way of tenancy was prohibited by the *bakufu*. After the mid-eighteenth century, the official power of the *bakufu* regarding property rights was again encroached on by private powers, as the de facto concentration of landholding through the tenancy system became prevalent. However, private enforcement systems and codes of conduct, based on moral codes, developed during the era, effectively substituting the role of the state, so that it would be safe to say that the property right system worked without state power in Japan.

It follows that with respect to the role of state in the enforcement of property rights, the role was effectively substituted by the private mechanism, so that state power was not a necessary condition for the working of property rights, both in the case of the Warring States period and the Tokugawa era. The policy of land tax reform started in 1873 by the Meiji government played the role of the only authorization of de facto property rights in the private sector.

3.2.3 Patterns of Commerce

Let us discuss the relationship between the historical patterns of commerce and their background in terms of the social division of labor, information asymmetry and trust, and transaction costs in the economy. Patterns of commerce changed from nascent local markets during the Kamakura era and long distance trade backed by the protection of privileged merchants (*toimaru*) by the *bakufu* during the Muromachi era, to thriving free trade in local autonomous markets during the Warring States period, followed by the development of the efficient regional division of labor at national level during the Tokugawa era, which was realized owing to the substantial reduction in information asymmetry in society through the standardization of conduct.

The Kamakura Era

During this period, society was moving rapidly from a homogeneous to a heterogeneous society, owing to progress in the social division of labor as well as to the emergence of new classes, such as merchants and samurai. The heterogeneity of society was intensified further by the spread of *kyūdō* behavior caused by the teaching of the Kamakura new Buddhism. People were motivated to seek specialty in occupational and artistic activities in order to obtain a sense of religious salvation.

Although privatization as a result of the decline of the *ritsuryō* system induced the development of markets, markets were still very nascent, and the progress of market transactions was slow. The development of markets started from the sale of redundant products obtained as rent revenue by manor-owning aristocrats and temples and shrines. Indigenous lords also sold redundant products at local markets. Together with the move by the *myōshu* to pay rents to manor owners in cash, these phenomena had the effect to develop market transactions (Wakita 1969).

Artisans of privatized factories who were hired by imperial families, aristocrats, and large temples and shrines, began to produce not only for the use of their employers, but also to sell at market. At the same time, these artisans traveled to local areas with special licenses issued by the imperial court and with arms for self-defense against gangs of robbers, producing temple bells or other products on demand by local customers. Due to the underdevelopment of the transport infrastructure and the dangers related to transporting products as well as transferring sale proceeds, it took time to develop an efficient system of long-distance trade, so that the travelling of manufacturers by themselves was the most efficient method for the supply of products to distant customers.

Later on, they gradually came to have their own workshops and equipment, began to be settled, and became independent suppliers after the thirteenth century (Toyoda 1952). This is the major origin of manufacturers in Japan. It must be noted these artisans, from the beginning, had highly sophisticated technology suitable for producing goods for the use of high-class customers, like aristocrats and the imperial families, although there were certainly a number of indigenous, by and large unskilled, producers for local purchasers.

The Muromachi Era

During the Muromachi era, the city of Kyoto came to have a sophisticated system of commerce in terms of the varieties of commodities owing to the luxurious consumption of manor owners living in Kyoto (Wakita 1969). Bills of exchange for transferring rents were widely used, and a wholesale and transport infrastructure was developed, accompanied by the emergence of new type of merchants, trade association merchants (*toimaru*), many of whose origin were as regional manor officials (*shōkan*).

Two long-distance trade routes were developed. First was the route that connected the metropolitan area of Kyoto and local markets and another was the route connecting distant local markets (Suzuki 2000). Remarkable was the development of inter-local market trade. Asaka (1971) and Wakita (1976) contend the importance of the development of long-distant trade connecting local markets without going through and relying on the central market in Kyoto. Many kinds of ceramic products produced in various regions were traded by use of water transportation throughout western Japan. Sasaki (1972) notes that various products specific to the regions obtained a reputation and were traded through inter-reginal markets. Metal products like hoes, plows and pots as well as swords with a reputation for good quality were actively traded. In this way, skilled producers found sufficient demand to reduce average fixed costs by the use of long distance inter-local markets.

Long-distance trade seems to have flourished in the trade of luxuries and special regional products, because the high reputation of the buyers and sellers alleviated information asymmetry and hence reduced transaction costs. Another reason for the prosperity of long distant trade was the strong monopoly power of the guild system organized by trade association merchants (*toimaru*), as emphasized by Wakita (1969). Trade associations (*za*) organized by *toimaru* merchants brought trade associations organized by producers under control, and wielded monopoly power over the whole product transaction process. The monopoly power of the *toimaru* was granted by the *bakufu*, which obtained tax revenue from trade associations. Authorization by *the bakufu* would have reduced information asymmetry considerably, although the transaction costs might have remained high due to the monopoly profits obtained by the *toimaru* merchants. With respect to the long-distance trade that connected Kyoto and the local region, the Muromachi *bakufu* and regional lords, military governors (*shugo*), extended considerable protection to the privileged city merchants and repressed local merchants in order to secure their revenue from manors. The privileged city merchants, however, lost power rapidly after the eruption of the Ōnin war in 1467 that seriously damaged the city of Kyoto.

Warring States Period

The Warring States era was one in which the dichotomy between the progress of the social division of labor and the codes of conduct based on the Buddhist ethical system was at its height. Information asymmetry between people should have been at an enormously high level, incurring high risks in their interaction between people. Moral hazards were rampant and serious adverse selections gave rise to the phenomenon of the *gekokujyō*, the turbulent convention whereby the lowly supplant the high-and-mighty. *Gekokujyō* was a product of two of the salient characteristics of society: first was the serious information asymmetry in which fraud, slander and betrayal were common standards of conduct in political scenes; and second was the premature fusion of samurai culture that emphasized action and spirituality and aristocratic culture that respected knowledge and rituality, as will be discussed in Chapter5. The disfunction of public judiciary system made the resolution of disputes related to landholding, such as the methods of irrigation and land boundaries, by way of violence and battles a common practice. Never-ending violence and battles became a ubiquitous phenomenon when people, especially the samurai, were engaged in private salvation, on the basis of *kyūdō* behavior.

Severe information asymmetry would have resulted in high transaction costs. Commercial and financial transactions were only possible within local states under the governance of the *daimyo*, who later became known as *sengoku daimyo*, or warring states *daimyo*. While *sengoku daimyos* regulated trade across the boundaries of their territory, they protected commercial activities within the territory. Local free markets thrived under the control of innovating *sengoku daimyo*, who abolished checking stations within the state, realizing free travelling, and replaced the traditional privileges of trade associations with the free participation of outside merchants. Reckless merchants in relationship with powerful *daimyos* obtained huge profits through foreign trade and risky long-distance trade. Some port cities such as Sakai obtained the status of special free cities, where merchants enjoyed a high degree of autonomy and economic growth (Table 3.6).

The Warring States period was a time for merchants, because the economy was full of information asymmetry and distrust. It was an arena for merchants with personal information networks and tight human relationships within the village (*sōson*) system. The *raku-ichi* (free market) and *raku-za* (free trade association) policy of *daimyos* such as Imagawa Yoshimoto or Oda Nobunaga was not a true free market policy, but a policy to reorganize the power structure in villages and to establish efficient regional markets. They excluded the existing monopoly system rooted in villages and replaced it with privileged merchants under their control (Sakurai 2002).

The Tokugawa Era

While commerce in the early period of the Tokugawa era was governed by ambitious merchants engaged in foreign trade or monopolistic trade of commodities of each *han* (*daimyo* domain), and each commercial town was governed by merchants who led autonomous communities based on regional ties,[24] they were replaced during the eighteenth century by the merchants of three cities (Osaka, Kyoto and Tokyo) tied functionally by occupational relationships such as trade associations (*kabu-nakama*). Owing to the reduction of information asymmetry by the standardization of conduct, inter-regional trade led commerce-based economic growth. Against the background of the delicate power struggle between the *bakufu* and merchants, the market mechanism developed as trust levels were enhanced in society. The *bakufu* tried to reduce market control by trade associations, and the merchants tried to retain their monopolistic power. Both pursued the establishment of an orderly market with fair pricing and (normal) profits so far as possible. During the nineteenth century, regional local merchants grew, replacing the monopoly power of the merchants of the three cities. With the active involvement of the *han* government in industrial policy and the growth of local merchants, the market system enjoyed a heyday and economic growth at a moderate rate continued with some inflationary tendency, although the monopolistic coalition between the *bakufu* and the merchants of the three cities was threatened.

It is important to note that, while the Warring States period and the early Tokugawa era were a time of the activity of merchants, most of the Tokugawa era was, however, a time of the growth of the market. The economic development of the Tokugawa era was commerce-based economic growth, realized by the substantial reduction of transaction costs and the consequent expansion of the market. We will show that the reduction of transaction costs occurred due to the alleviation of information asymmetry in the economy that had once threatened the whole Japanese society in the crisis of the Warring State period.

The acute sense of crisis induced the whole of society, including the imperial court and the *daimyos*, samurai, merchants and farmers, to seek the establishment of a new society based on a firm ethical code. As will be discussed in Chapter 6, the Tokugawa *bakufu* was established as a compromise among *sengoku daimyos*. The *bakufu* introduced *shokubun* regulation in order to standardize the codes of conduct for each class, samurai, farmer, artisan and merchants. The samurai class

---

[24]There were 1,678 town communities in Edo in 1765, 614 in Osaka in 1753, and it is estimated that almost 10,000 town communities existed nationwide (Miyamoto 2009). Each town was allowed a high degree of autonomy, in which *machi-toshiyori* (town leaders) were elected by voting, although self-government organizations were assigned the role of end organization of the *han*.

was expected to provide an example for the code of behavior, and they built up a new lifestyle built on training in martial arts and knowledge of the new Confucianism. Scholars in religion and philosophy developed new theories for the social order and ethical codes of conduct. A large number of elementary schools were established in towns and countrywide, and nationwide high literacy levels seem to have facilitated the spread of ethics.

These efforts resulted in the standardization of behavior that led to the enhancement of trust in society and, indirectly, a substantial reduction in transaction costs in the economy. The trust level was enhanced owing to the alleviation of information asymmetry and the enhancement of the sense of reciprocity. It will be shown in Chapter 6 that transaction costs declined sharply during the eighteenth century and this is reflected in the reduction of risk premiums in interest rates.

Triggered by the rise of Edo as a huge consumption city and the development of commodity distribution based on the newly established marine transportation system, there occurred economic development led by commerce owing to the decline in transaction costs. It was an economic development caused by the regional division of labor (Nakai 1961; Miyamoto 1988). Since farmers could not move across *han* boundaries due to the regulations that regarded villages as the basic units of tax payment, labor movement was not possible, except for movements in local employment markets within each *han*. Therefore, the *han* were induced to engage in the regional division of labor through specializing in the production of goods that utilized factors of production with which they were amply endowed. This realized the efficient allocation of resources at the macro level in the national market and the consequent economic growth. The process was nothing other than the realization at a national level of the factor–price–equalization equilibrium asserted by the Heckscher-Ohlin theorem in international trade theory.[25] Incidentally, the typical pattern of regional division of labor, especially during the eighteenth century, took the form of following form. The *han* in the local districts exported food, material for manufacturing, and low-level processed goods to Osaka, and imported high-level processed goods produced in Osaka and Kyoto as well as special products produced by other *han*. Osaka imported

[25]Let us assume an economy with two goods (rice and textile) and two regions (*han*). Good 1, say textile, is capital intensive and good 2, say rice, is labor intensive. Region A, say Osaka, is endowed with abundant capital relative to labor, and region B, say Akita, with abundant labor and scarce capital. If this country is like England with the smooth movement of the factors of production, there occurs the following adjustment. At initial equilibrium, the rental price for capital compared with the labor wage is higher in region A than region B, so that capital flows out from A to B, and labor moves from B to A. In region A, there occurs a rise in the rental price of capital and a fall of wages, while in region B, a rise in wage and a fall in the rental price of capital. In equilibrium, the factor price ratio equalizes between the two regions. If this country is Tokugawa Japan, the labor market is regulated and the regional capital flow is imperfect, while the commodity market is well-developed. Before trade, the price of good 1 is relatively lower in region A than in region B. When trade occurs between the two regions, region 1 exports good 1 and region 2 exports good 2. In region A, production of good 1 increases and in region B production of good 2 increases. In region A, the relative price of good 1 rises and the rental price of capital increases, and in region B, the relative price of good 2 rises and the wage rate increases. In equilibrium, the factor price ratio equalizes between the two regions.

food, material and special products of local *han*, produced and exported manufactured goods such as vegetable oil, sake, soy sauce, ginned cotton as well as sophisticated processed goods made by artisans in Kyoto to local *han* and Edo. Incidentally, ginned cotton sent to Edo through the Pacific Ocean route was transported to the northern Kantō and Tōhoku regions by river transportation and by land routes, and was finally processed by farmers there into cotton textiles through side-business activities (Hayashi 1992).

Appendix: Industrial Technology, Population and Growth

Economic development during the Tokugawa era was led by commerce. It was so-called Smithian growth, not Schumpeterian growth, in the terminology of Mokyr (2017). There did not occur any 'industrial revolution' that characterized Occidental growth. While Tokugawa growth is characterized by the steady increase in the total production, per capita income was stagnant during the first half and increased only during the second half of the era. The purpose of this appendix is two-fold. First, it seeks the reasons for the absence of the development of industrial technology in Japan before the Meiji Restoration. Second, it explains the reason why we believe that an increase in total production is important even if per capita income growth is stagnant.

The Needham Puzzle and Japan

It is well known that China since the Sung dynasty had highly developed industrial technology and invented a number of new instruments—such as the clock, the compass, gunpowder, paper, the blast furnace, the water-powered textile machine, and so on. Needham (1969) investigated the reason why, with such a high level of technology, an 'industrial revolution' did not occur in China. It is well known that Confucianism took a positive stance toward the utilization of nature for the material benefits of human beings. As Kaji (1990) says, since the era of Confucius, Confucianism has regarded it as an ideal to control nature and establish an artificial world in which saints live. In other words, China shared the anthropocentric cosmology of the Occident (O'Brien 2009, p. 20). Nevertheless, the Chinese did not engage in research into the secrets of nature and tried to utilize the productivity of nature for economic growth. Needham's answer to this question, the so-called Needham puzzle, lay in the absence of the development of the conception of the Law of Nature, that is, in the structure of the organic worldview, held by the Chinese that harmonious cooperation of all beings arose from the fact that they were all parts in a hierarchy of wholes forming a cosmic pattern, so that what they obeyed were the internal dictates of their own natures.[26] While in the Occident 'the conception of a natural law common to all men, and of a body of Laws of Nature common to all

[26]This is nothing but a cosmology that the new Confucianism established by Chu-tzu during the Sung era inherited from Buddhism.

non-human things, had become completely differentiated' (Needham 1969, p. 311) during the sixteenth to seventeenth century, in China, there never occurred the separation of the natural philosophy (the Laws of Nature) from ethics (the natural law). For this reason, 'the available ideas of a supreme being, though certainly present from the earliest times, became depersonalized so early and were so lacking in the ideas of creativity that they prevented the development of the conception of precisely formulated laws, ordained from the beginning, of a celestial lawgiver for non-human nature, and capable, because of his rationality, of being deciphered or re-formulated by other lesser rational beings, using method of observation, experiment, hypothesis, and mathematical reasoning' (Needham 1969, p. 328). Needham contends further that, owing to this cosmology, the Chinese had deep incredulity toward the Western paradigm of the Law of Nature as imposed by the divine lawgiver, the God.

In summary, Needham contends that the absence of a personalized supreme being, who imposed the Law of Nature on the universe, explains the lack of development in China of the scientific research that comprised the basis of Occidental industrial technology. Instead of an imposed law by the personalized supreme being, the Chinese contrived Confucian cosmology, which removed the incentive for the scientific research of nature from the Chinese. This was because the organic nature of the universe implied the absence of a mechanical structure, which was a deterrent to scientific inquiry. Moreover, the notion of the pre-determined harmony of the universe rejected any attempt by humans to decipher the mechanism.

However, the notion of an organic and pre-determined harmony of nature is not sufficient to explain the lack of scientific inquiry. This is the reason for Needham to have emphasized the depersonalization of a supreme being, by which he implied the absence of an incentive to be involved in the inquiry into the secrets of creation. In the case of the Occident, salvation was the chief motivation for people, so that inquiry into the secrets of nature is based on the motivation to contribute to the glory of the Supreme Being who has all the power over salvation. Unlike Christianity or Buddhism, Confucianism is not a religion based on the salvation of people denying the present life, as is noted in Weber (1920). With a strong affirmative stance toward the present life, no such motivation arises in the case of Confucianism, so that denial of the notion of the lawgiver in the universe does not justify the absence of motivation for scientific research. Nothing related to Confucianism hampers the Chinese from developing a high-level of useful knowledge based on their own organic view of the cosmos. It seems to be necessary to emphasize the role of incentive system in the Occident and in Christianity that induced people to be engaged in the search of nature in order to prove the greatness of the divine creator. The European conversion to Christianity, or the influence of Protestantism, seems to be a crucial factor in this regard, as is emphasized by Oakley (1961), White (1978) and O'Brien (2009). Since a supreme being is depersonalized, the Chinese did not have to contribute to the glory of the Supreme Being, so they did not feel any incentive for inquiry into the secrets of nature. The absence of the incentive system in China and in Confucianism seems to be responsible for the fact that the Chinese were not compelled to commit themselves to be involved in research into the secret of nature.[27]

This book tries to answer a similar question with respect to Japan. Why did the industrial revolution not occur in Japan? Our answer to this question is also mainly cultural. Both the cognitive frame side and the value system side of culture pertain to this. In the case of Japan, the cognitive frame of culture worked in a substantially different manner than in the Occident. In the Occident, where the omnipotent God is in charge of salvation, people are motivated to seek salvation by God through contribution to the glory of God. This could be accomplished in two ways. First is the contribution to the welfare of mankind. Owing to the doctrine that prohibits the deification of the created, people refrained from involvement with the neighbor nearby and were recommended to have concerns for mankind, the *magnum opus* of God. In economic activity, people were motivated to take part in activities that contributes toward the welfare of mankind as a whole. Weber contends that this notion resulted in utilitarian behavior that emphasized the welfare of the public or society as a whole. This worldview that induced people into active involvement in factory production could contribute to the mass consumption of mankind and, at the same time, the development of knowledge that was considered useful for the enhanced welfare of mankind. Second is the involvement in the research into nature. The turn to anthropocentricism of Christianity during the medieval era stressed the importance of a belief in God, who has designed the universe for the use of humans, by way of illustrating His wisdom through exploiting nature. It is God's will that humans take advantage of creation, so involvement in scientific research, through dissecting and interrogating nature to reveal its secrets, is helpful for exploitation (White 1978).

It seems that a basic reason for the lack of an industrial revolution in Japan lay in the absence of the anthropocentric view that induced the Westerner to be involved in the search for the secrets of nature in order to improve the material lot of mankind. In Shintoism, which evolved through an appreciation of the productivity of nature as well as an awe and respect for the violence of nature, there was no room for such a view. To search for the mechanisms of nature by way of dissecting and interrogation through experiment, was beyond the imagination from the viewpoint of Shintoism, constructed as it was on the concept of coexistence with nature.

Moreover, the cognitive frame nurtured in Japan through Buddhism differs from the Occidental one in three respects. According to the economic worldview in Japan, the world around an individual is composed of a number of neighbors, whom he knows through direct contact or from information from other neighbors. There is no abstract notion of the public or mankind. Moreover, since there was no idea of the Creator, and salvation does not come from God but from self-effort to purify and repudiate earthly desires, people had no motivation to contribute to the glory of the God. Finally, the attitude toward nature was different. In addition to the stance

[27] Mokyr (2017) presents an alternative explanation for the Needham puzzle, that the main reason for this lies in China's failure to develop effective markets for useful knowledge due to the meritocracy of the Mandarin civil service examination that repressed the cultivation of creative talents.

of Shintoism, in Buddhism all creatures, including trees and plants, are considered to have Buddha nature, so that the Buddhist tradition in Japan never gave rise to any thought of the benefits of dissecting nature. Instead, coexistence was the most pertinent stance towards nature.

The value system of culture also denied the Western-style production system. Although organizations, such as the *han* (*daimyo* domain) governments and commercial companies under the *han*, had a material motivation in its operation, the value system of individuals intensified the tendency to respect spiritual values during the Tokugawa period. The spiritual character of the samurai class is typical. During the peaceful 250 years of the Tokugawa era, the samurai were constantly prepared for the next possible civil war, so that, besides serving as bureaucrats for each *han* government, a considerable part of the daily life of the samurai was spent in training in martial arts and the cultivation of spirits. Confucianism was the basic knowledge for the samurai, but Confucianism was considered to be a technique for expression and a basic frame of concepts, so that it only had instrumental values. They aimed at polishing their mind as spiritual leaders and were typical *kyūdō* principle practitioners in Buddhism, especially in Zen. The pursuit of material happiness was strictly prohibited. Since the samurai class was the spiritual leader of society, the *kyūdō* principle influenced the whole of society, so that there was no room for material value maximization in Tokugawa Japan, except for organizations like the state enterprises of the *han*. This mental state was shared even by the merchant class. As Miyamoto (1941) claims, the purpose of the *i.e* system for merchants, for example, lay in the longevity of the family.

Industrial Technology in the Occident

Mokyr (2002, 2017) contends that the growth of technology or useful knowledge is a key factor for sustained modern economic growth in the Occident. Culture, especially religion, played a central role in the development of useful technology in the Occident until the early modern period. The activity of scientists, called cultural entrepreneurs in Mokyr (2017), such as Boyle, Bacon and Newton, were strongly motivated by religion, especially Puritanism (Merton 1938). Christianity in the late middle-age and after the 16th or seventeenth centuries emphasized an anthropocentric attitude toward nature, consequently allowing and recommending the manipulation of nature for the sake of human welfare. Boyle, a Puritan, considered that he fulfilled a holy mission by becoming 'a priest of nature' and giving thanks and praise to God, the maker of all of creation. Bacon, though not a Puritan, believed that experimental science was a Christian religious activity. While during the high age of Baconian experimental science, there was no idea of direct causality from the glorification of God to the material well-being of human kind, Merton's idea, that a growing accommodation between religious belief and scientific endeavor was of considerable significance in the rise of English industrial science, is useful in understanding the explosive development of pathbreaking scientific work on the Continent during the seventeenth century (Mokyr 2017, p. 231). White (1978) contends, further, that God has given man two sources of spiritual knowledge: The Book of Scripture and the Book of Nature. People came to believe that all natural phenomena were the embodiment of

God's deed, so they were induced to be involved in the activity seeking evidence of God in nature. Exploration of the secrets of nature resulted in the affirmative approach to the manipulation of nature. It was God's will that humans take advantage of the wisdom of his creation. Oakley (1961) depicts this tendency as the denial of the Stoic or Greek theory of the law of nature as immanent, consequently giving rise to the notion of laws of nature imposed by God upon the universe.

While the religious influence on the accumulation of useful knowledge waned during the eighteenth century, Mokyr (2017) argues that the emergence of the transnational community among eminent intellectuals in Europe, the Republic of Letters, gave rise to the development of the active transnational market for useful knowledge, realizing the sustained accumulation of scientific and technological knowledge during the Enlightenment. The political fragmentation that lasted for a long period in Europe as well as the development of printing technology and the mailing system, by getting rid of the fear for incumbent political powers to repress creative destruction, was the main reason for fermenting the competitive atmosphere toward inventing and acquiring useful knowledge.

Industrial Technology in Japan

Technological development was far less active in Tokugawa Japan. As discussed in this chapter, there occurred some improvement in the quality of agricultural tools, such as hoes and spades. The selective breeding of rice was actively carried out. Since new varieties were kept secret in each *han*, however, the spread of new breeds was very limited until the time of the Meiji Restoration, so that at the macro level agricultural technology remained stagnant. Owing to the prohibition on overseas travel and trade, the building of large-scale ships for transportation came to a halt. Technological development in shipbuilding was confined to small ships for coastal trips and river transportation. Moreover, due to the severe prohibitions and monitoring by the *bakufu* that was cautious of any military build-up by potentially antagonistic *han*, the development of military-related technology was retarded. For the defense of Edo from attack by those unfriendly *han*, the *bakufu* prohibited the building of bridges over large rivers, retarding the development of land transportation vehicles. These were the concrete practical reasons for the underdevelopment of industrial technology during the Tokugawa era.

As for the use of the international market of useful knowledge, Japan had since ancient days been an active participant. Useful knowledge about technology as well as government institutions was imported from China, especially during the Tang and Sung eras. During the Tokugawa period, however, the Japanese were not ardent in the import of useful technology. Access to the international market for useful knowledge was not prohibited, but seriously retarded in Tokugawa Japan due to the self-imposed segregation policy of the country. Foreign trade was significantly restricted during the Tokugawa period. By 1639 the government had imposed a strict ban on foreign trade and overseas travelling, limiting access to foreign goods through specific ports (mainly Nagasaki) and through the Netherlands and China.[28] The official reason for

[28]Tsushima, Matsumae and Kagoshima were designated for trade with Korea, Ezo and Ryukyu, respectively.

the policy was to shut off the influence of Christianity, but the government's real and probably more important motivation lay in the prevention of foreign trade that might enrich and strengthen the power of unfriendly feudal *han* in southwestern Japan (Acemoglu and Robinson 2012).

Although the prohibition on foreign trade was maintained throughout the rest of the Tokugawa period, it must be noted that, with respect to the inflow of advanced knowledge, Tokugawa Japan took basically an open stance. Confucianism flooded in rapidly, especially after the collapse of the Ming dynasty in 1644, in the form of the import of Chinese books and the immigration of scholars from the continent. The Tokugawa government intended to make Confucianism an ethical guideline for the samurai class in the newly established stable society. The import of Occident books translated into Chinese was permitted after 1720 in so far as they did not contain information about Christianity, and the study of Dutch-language literature came to be officially promoted after 1740. The translation and publication of Dutch literature in areas such as astronomy, medical science and Newtonian mechanics was actively carried out thereafter. It is surprising, however, that the imported 'useful knowledge' was utilized not for production purpose or industrial development but rather to cultivate a worldview and ethical development. As is reported in Najita (1987), in the Kaitoku-dō research center established by rich Osaka merchants under the authorization of the *bakufu*, the main research was concerned with the social sciences, especially philosophy and ethics. Knowledge of mechanics and astronomy imported from the Occident was mainly utilized to construct a cosmology and worldview alternative to Confucian theory and the denial of traditional occultism derived from indigenous psychic beliefs. Although knowledge of the anatomy of the human body was introduced in the late eighteenth century,[29] actual medical treatment continued to be either based on empirical experience derived from trial and error dowsing without inquiring into the causes of disease, or the principles of Yin and Yang combined with the five-element theory of the universe (Nakayama 1993).

Spiritual Value

While recognizing that the propensity for growth is not universally held by people, especially in the world outside the Occident, Jones (1988) asserts that at least a small group of members in each large society is strongly motivated to pursue a materially rich life, and this induces the economic growth of the per capita income of society. As a general statement, Jones (1988) might be right. However, it seems to be still possible to think of a society where people are more strongly motivated by spiritual values than in the Occident. This book argues that in Tokugawa Japan, culture had an important direct effect on sustained growth and that, despite the strong tendency of culture toward spiritual value, it was still possible to induce economic growth through both spiritual and material values. In Tokugawa Japan, the value system of individuals as well as of society intensified the spiritual tendency. At the individual level, people are motivated to pursue the spiritual completion of the self to realize salvation, in the

[29]The private school for the study and teaching of Occidental natural sciences started in 1838, when Ogata Kōan founded Tekijyuku.

Buddhist sense. At the level of society, it was urgent to establish a workable moral system to meet the needs of the market economy that was deepening the degree of the social division of labor. Quite differently from the Christian culture, Japan's culture based on Buddhism does not have the notion of an omnipotent God that prescribes a moral system for humans and society. The old Buddhist moral system originally inherited from India did not function effectively because it was designed for the needs of practicing in monasteries, segregated from the profane world. The revision of the obsolete moral code and to contrive a workable new moral system suitable for the social division of labor was an urgent task for society and political rulers. While individuals were strongly inclined to spiritual values, organizations, such as provincial governments, the *han*, and commercial companies under the *han*, were strongly motivated to economic growth in preparation for 'next civil war', although the war did not happen until the mid-eighteenth century. Although, owing to the delicately contrived balances of power, provincial lords, *daimyos*, could not mount an open challenge to Tokugawa until the 1860s, the building up of potential military power by the provincial government was an important undercurrent, responsible for the development of the socio-economical system during the period. In other words, while individuals became increasingly oriented toward spiritual value, the *han* pursued a material goal for political and military reasons.

It is worth emphasizing that there emerged little tendency to develop useful technology in Tokugawa Japan. There are three reasons for this. First, the individual and society were confined to the pursuit of spiritual values. Second, the building up of the power of antagonistic provincial governments had to be carried out under the severe surveillance of the ruling Tokugawa regime. The import of and investment in research into military technology and equipment was utterly impossible until the mid-1850s. Finally, the cognitive frame based on Buddhism did not fit well with the development of useful technology. In Buddhism, the world had been in existence from a very remote past era, and there was no particular supreme creator of the world. So, people had no desire to seek the reasons for the creation of nature and human beings. Moreover, since salvation in Buddhism is a personal matter of attaining enlightenment (*satori*), there is no religious reason to scrutinize the secrets of creation as happened in the case of Christian-based society. In addition, the related concept of time has some relevance in this regard. While time in Buddhism moves cyclically, in Shintoism, which has influenced the Buddhism-based thinking of the Japanese significantly, there is no beginning and ending to the world (Kato 2007). This implies that there is no progress in the sense of a desire to accumulate knowledge through time. Interpreting the assertion of Benz of the University of Marburg, White (1978) contends that in Christianity, history, far from being cyclical as it is in most religions, is unique and unilinear; it is accelerating toward a spiritual goal; there is no time to lose. Therefore, work, including manual labor, is an essential and pressing form of worship. It is asserted that 'Christianity obviously is not essential to technological dynamism. What Bentz suggests, nevertheless, is that Christianly provided, historically in Europe, a set of assumptions, a cultural climate, unusually favorable to technological advance' (p. 237).

The emphasis on the spiritual value of economic attainment in Japan during this period throw a special light on the issue of how to measure economic growth. It is customary since the time of Kuznets (1965) to evaluate the degree of economic growth by use of per capita income. This measure of growth seems to be derived from the implicit assumption that the benefits of growth lie in the realization of the pleasure and ease of life obtained through higher levels of consumption by the public. No doubt this measure of growth applies to the case of Tokugawa Japan also. However, it is important to note that the Japanese during this period came to appreciate spiritual value of production activity. A large volume of consumer durables supplied to the market in Tokugawa Japan was produced individually by small producers who enjoyed the improvement of skills and communications with consumers and were probably motivated by the *kyūdō* principle. They did not have any concerns with the mass production of standardized products. They paid significant efforts to match the beauty of the products with the beauty of nature. Consumers also participated in this process by way of figuring out new methods of utilization and finding new beauty in the products. Through this process, producers obtained spiritual values that enhanced religious confidence towards salvation. In this system, the spiritual value of production activity itself was welfare improving. If we were to take this value into consideration in the evaluation of economic growth, the volume of output, not the value of per capita income, could be an adequate measure of growth.

In summary, instead of pursuing the secretes of nature and creation, culture in Japan motivated people to devote their intellectual capacity to spiritual development at both the individual and societal level. At the individual level, people were motivated to inflate their passion in production activities. The Buddhist theory of *ekō* (transferring of merits) provided them with the rationalization for this behavior, inducing people to be involved in the production of more sophisticated commodities. Economic growth, in the sense of the expansion of total production, occurred owing to the improved incentive in production activities. Furthermore, politicians and elites were motivated to develop moral structures suitable for the deepening of the social division of labor. In response to the *shokubun* regulation (the four occupational hierarchy classes—samurai, farmer, artisan and merchants) introduced by the government, the moral standards for each class were actively discussed and improved. As new moral systems were established and spread in society, the working of the market economy was improved owing to the alleviation of information asymmetry. In other words, under the strong influence of Buddhism, the Tokugawa economy was given the impetus for growth from two cultural sources: the Weberian self-disciplinary perspective, namely, the continual improvement of individual ethic-based behavior leading to higher productivity; and the Durkheimian social-disciplinary perspective, namely, the sustained decrease in transaction costs owing to the evolution of the social ethical system. Furthermore, it must be noted that all the efforts were exerted within the confines of harmony with nature. Significant consideration was paid to avoid the abuse of the productive power of nature, and to respect the cyclical aspect of lives in nature. The excessive passion that emanated from the longing for salvation in the Buddhist sense was controlled by the orientation towards stability and harmony with nature in Shintoism. In this sense, the growth of production was carried out in close relationship with religions in Japan.

How to Measure Growth

It is customary to measure economic growth by per capita production. This practice goes back to Kuznets, who gave birth to the concept of GNP. Kuznets defined the modern economic growth (MEG) of nations as the sustained increase in per capita or per worker production, most often accompanied by an increase in population and usually by sweeping structural changes (Kuznets 1966, p. 1). Why population is included in the definition of economic growth either in the form of total population or per capita production is a delicate issue, however. Kuznets examined the adequacy of this definition from two aspects. First is the practical reason. He contends that the inclusion of population in the definition of economic growth is useful in formulating the characteristics of economic growth as actually observed in the past. More specifically, it is suitable for the purpose of formulating the characteristics of economic growth observed during the past 200 years. He claimed that, in the analysis of MEG, the consideration of population is indispensable, because the interplay between sustained rises in population and rises in production was substantial enough to incur a sustained increase in per capita product.

Kuznets's assertion could be construed from the notion of MEG, which was considered to be caused by epochal innovation characterized by the extended application of science to the use of human material welfare. Scientific development was applied to the reduction of mortality and the control of birth rate, exerting an upward pressure on population, while it had much more profound impacts on the problems of economic production, causing an unprecedented rise in the production and income of nations. Kuznets notes also that he does not believe that the combination of growth of population and per capita production is applicable to the period before modern times. It follows that we need to consider this possibility more seriously.

Kuznets is more cautious in the second aspect of his definition in terms of the normative meaning of population growth. While he emphasizes the fact of the substantial growth of the population during the process of MEG in the past 200 years, he contends that, the question whether the phenomenon was actually intended by the government or considered to be desirable by the society of nations, belongs to a different issue. Moreover, he claims that 'what may seem to be desirable today is different from what has occurred in the past and may well change the path of economic growth in the future' (Kuznets 1966, p. 20).

In summary, it is true that, in the process of MEG during the past 200 years, total production and population increased simultaneously and in a way in which the growth of production was faster than the growth of population. Kuznets claims that the experience could be exceptional and the past experience before the start of MEG as well as the future prospect could be different from this, and that it is not certain whether what happened during MEG was considered to be desirable before the age of MEG or would be in the future.

It follows that when we discuss the long-term process of economic development, the concept of per capita products presents difficult problems. If the welfare level of individuals is dependent not only on per capita consumption but also on production activity, the measurement of economic growth should take account of total production. This was what we have argued with respect to the activities of small producers during the Tokugawa era. Whether the growth of per capita income is a desirable measure could become a complicated issue in this case. This is nothing but the normative implication of per capita growth referred to by Kuznets.

Moreover, as is also suggested by Kuznets, how to measure growth poses a difficult question whenever we examine long-term economic growth. For one thing, various exogenous factors that are not necessarily related to economic growth affect per capita production. It is possible that, despite the growth of production, mortality rate could increase due to the lack of adequate medical technology, in circumstances such as the deterioration of living conditions caused by excessive urbanization. It is also possible that the birth rate could decrease owing to changes in culture regarding marriage. For another, the endogeneity issue of population complicates the meaning of per capita production further in the long-term growth. This occurred not only through the Malthusian process of an actual dearth of food production, but also through the expectation of the marginal product of labor in the future conceived in the context of the economic horizon of the population. Historically in any society, it seems that the birth rate has been affected by the possibility of marriage and controlled by various method such as infanticide and abortion. Behind such phenomenon it would be natural to believe that people's expectation of the marginal productivity of labor had important bearings. Thus, the change in population could be caused by this self-realizing expectation.

As shown in Table 3.4, there occurred a significant decrease in the rate of growth in population after the early eighteenth century in the Tokugawa era, and this caused a very high growth of per capita production. If the decrease in population growth occurred as a result of the self-realizing expectation, the growth of per capita income in the Tokugawa era poses a difficult problem in terms of the welfare of society. Together with the concern with the spiritual value of production activity discussed above, we have refrained to talk much about per capita production in this book.

Chapter 4
Religious Changes in Kamakura-Era Japan

This chapter investigates how the internalized culture, characterized by the world-view based on others nearby, was formed in Japan in the context of cultural history from the end of the ancient age through the medieval age. The evolution of the internalized beliefs and values of Japan is examined in the interactions of two major incidents: religious reform, the birth of Kamakura new Buddhism, related to culture, and the decline of the *ritsuryō* (law and order) system, the centralized and nationalized economic system, related to the institution. The decline of the centralized *ritsuryō* economic system accelerated the marketization of the economy, and religious reform implemented in tandem with the decline of the *ritsuryō* system led to the simplification of practice (*igyō-ka*) as a method of the salvation of the masses, in order to help the struggle of the people with accelerated marketization. The enormous impact of the simplification of practice was the birth of *kyūdō* (true-way pursuing) behavior in the occupational and daily life of individuals. Individuals were motivated to pursue religious attainment and merits in occupational activities.

Interaction of religious reform and decline of *ritsuryō* system is examined in two levels of causality, direct and indirect, and in the comparative context of ordering of socio-economic system by institutions and culture. It is argued that main influence of the decline of *ritsuryō* system on religious reform did not lie in the direct influence of the causality from the change in *ritsuryō* system to the rise of religious reform, but in the indirect influence of the decline in *ritsuryō* system on the choice of the method of salvation in religious reform.

The adoption of practice simplification or the easy practice principle as a method of the salvation of the masses by Japanese Buddhism, and the consequent emergence of the *kyūdō* principle, occurred in the socio-economic context of the development of the market economy related to the decline of the *ritsuryō* system and in the theoretical context of the historical evolution of Mahayana Buddhism since its birth. Buddhism, introduced to sixth-century Japan, had a mission to contribute to mass salvation as a programmed course of theoretical development of Mahayana Buddhism. The influence of the development of the market economy and the acceleration of the social

J. Teranishi, *Culture and Institutions in the Economic Growth of Japan*,
Studies in Economic History,
https://doi.org/10.1007/978-4-431-55627-5_4

division of labor induced the Buddhist circle to choose the method of salvation related to the marketization of the socio-economy. The method chosen by the newly born Buddhism sect, Kamakura new Buddhism, was practice simplification (*igyō-ka*) that enabled the masses to seek both religious salvation and economic survival in the turmoil caused by the rapidly developing market economy and by the acceleration of the social division of labor.

The reason for the effectiveness of practice simplification as a method of salvation was provided by the theoretical background of Mahayana Buddhism. Kamakura new Buddhism resorted to the concept of merit transfer (*ekō*) as the justification for the method. It was the concept of merit transfer of qualitative transformation (*naiyō-tenkan no ekō*) that allowed to utilize merit transfer (*ekō*) of good deeds in profane activities for the sake of attaining enlightenment (*satori*). In this theoretical context, the new teaching of practice simplification gave rise to the behavioral pattern of *kyūdō* behavior that provided medieval society with enormous impacts with respect to behavioral pattern and the incentive structure. Since the merit transfer of qualitative transformation enabled arriving at enlightenment by means of efforts in occupational activities, *kyūdō* (true-way pursuing) behavior sanctified the occupational life of individuals, changing their lifestyle and motivation radically. Individuals were motivated to be engaged in *kyūdō* behavior to pursue both material gains and religious salvation.

Under the impact of religious reform, the internalized part of culture of Japan underwent a radical change. The worldview characterized by close concerns with the relationship with others nearby was born in this process. In Buddhist culture from the beginning, there were deep concerns with others nearby because the fundamental state of human life in Buddhism lay in transmigration, in which individuals were destined to live in close concern with others nearby, with whom interaction *karma* (*gō*), which drive the engine of transmigration, is accumulated. Practice simplification in the religious reform of Japan that gave rise to *kyūdō* behavior substantially intensified the concerns of individuals in others nearby. This is because merit transfer of qualitative transformation played the role of converting the devotion to occupational activities motivated by *kyūdō* behavior into merits for arriving at enlightenment, emancipation from the suffering of transmigration. In the Buddhism before the religious reform in Japan, although interaction with others nearby had the effect to change the amount of *karma* and hence to affect the position within the environment of transmigration, it was impossible to be freed from the pains of transmigration by means of occupational conduct. However, the fostering of capability to understand the structure of the world through the devotion to *kyūdō* behavior in occupational activities enabled one to get out of transmigration and obtain Buddhahood. In this sense, interaction with others nearby in occupational activity motivated by *kyūdō* behavior came to have additional and highly important religious meaning for the Japanese. Consequently, concerns with others nearby in the internalized beliefs of the Japanese mindset was intensified and held widely among individuals. This is the main message of this chapter.

In summary, the internalized part of culture in Japan, characterized by the worldview based on others nearby, was born as a result of the religious reform for the purpose of the salvation of the masses. The deep and intense concerns with others nearby in the mental model of the people emanated from the method of salvation of practice simplification, adopted by the Kamakura new Buddhism on the basis of the theory of merit transfer of qualitative transformation in Mahayana Buddhism. The religious reform in Japan occurred largely as an autonomous phenomenon, programed in the evolution process of Mahayana Buddhism. It follows that the causal effect from institutions, the decline of the *ritsuryō* system, to culture, the religious reform, was only indirect; the former affected the latter only indirectly through the choice of method of salvation, so it is not correct to assert that the former *caused* the latter. Needless to say, this does not deny the important effects of the method of salvation, practice simplification, and hence, of the emergence of *kyūdō* behavior on the socio-economy. Section 4.3 of this chapter points out the radical changes in lifestyle in medieval Japan caused by the religious reform. Chapter 5 shows that *kyūdō* behavior exerted enormous impacts on the working of institutions such as the bakufu (samurai government) system and the feudalism through its effects on the degree of information asymmetry and the working of incentive systems.

Furthermore, it is contended that religious reform and the consequent emergence of *kyūdō* behavior is related to the issue of the duality of the mentality of the Japanese in the medieval period. Since *kyūdō* behavior is pursuit of sacred value in the profane present life, it had the effect of sanctification of the daily life and of enhancing the sense of affirmation of the present life, intensifying positive motivation for occupation activities. The weakening of the separation of the profane and the sacred in the thinking of people proceeded in tandem with the spread of *kyūdō* behavior, under the close interactive relationship with affirmation of this world by Shintoism. This resulted in the duality of the mental structures of medieval individuals, which was composed of the affirmative behavioral part and the negative internalized part. In other words, the duality of the mindset in the sense of negation of the present life in the internalized part of culture owing to the concept of *karma* and transmigration, and the strong and enhanced affirmation of the present life in the behavioral part owing to the *kyūdō* principle characterized the structure of the individual mindset of medieval Japan. Since *kyūdō* behavior emanated from the acute longing for salvation and the strong negation of the present life, it follows that the behavioral part of culture was under the strong influence of the internalized part of culture.

It is important to note that the crucial theory related to the impact of Kamakura new Buddhism on the internalized mental structure lay in the theory of the merit transfer of qualitative transformation. Past studies of the new Buddhism concentrated mainly on the merit transfer of directional transformation. This bias seems to be rooted in the popularity of Shinran as a leader of Buddhist innovation, who emphasized merit transfer of directional transformation of Amitabha. However, the crucial theoretical key to understanding the impact of the religious changes on the culture and socio-economy of Japan lies in the introduction of the merit transfer of qualitative transformation, not directional transformation.

4.1 Cultural and Institutional Background: Initial Conditions

The focus of this book lies in the analysis of the growth of the Japanese economy after the thirteenth century when the market economy began to develop, and the social division of labor to accelerate. To do this, it is necessary to establish the cultural and institutional situation of the socio-economy before the start of economic growth. In other words, we need to establish the initial cultural and institutional conditions before the thirteenth century. The initial conditions with respect to institutions are mainly related to the centralized and nationalized system, the *ritsuryō* system, established during the period from the mid-seventh century through the year 701–02, when the Taihō-ritsuryō, the comprehensive law of the *ritsuryō* system, was enacted, and thereafter gradually amended before declining toward the middle ages. The initial conditions for culture comprised the introduction of Buddhism in the mid-sixth century from Paekche, Korea, and its development and spread as the state religion, as well as the process of fusion with pre-existing Shinto tradition.

4.1.1 Institutional Background: The Ritsuryo *System*

The *ritsuryō* system was introduced from Tang, China, in the face of the move of the Tang and the Silla of Korea to conquer Paekche and Koguryo in Korea,[1] during the mid-seventh century, and especially in response to the defeat of the allied force of Japan and Paekche against the Tang and Silla in the naval battle off the mouth of the Kum river in 663. In order to cope with international tensions, the establishment of political integrity and the military build-up were urgently needed, and this made it inevitable to introduce a highly sophisticated socio-political system, the *ritsuryō* system, of Tang to a country that had only a primitive ancient social system. The introduction, initiated in 646 (Taika-no-kaisin), was officially completed in 701–02 by the promulgation of the Taiho-ritsuryō.

Under the *ritsuryo* system, citizens were identified by a survey implemented every six years, and local lords were converted into low-class bureaucrats, local regional officers under the control of provincial state heads (*koku-shi*) delegated from central government. The provincial state (*kuni* or *koku*) was the largest unit of local government set up under the *ritsuryō* system. A patch of arable land was allocated to every citizen, who satisfied certain conditions, such as age, until his or her death, irrespective of gender and was obliged to pay taxes (*so* and *chō*) and labor service (*yō*) to the state. To facilitate the transportation of tax revenues, a national transportation system by roads and water was developed, and a judicial and administrative system, as well as a system for the mobilization of soldiers, were established. Along with

[1] The Korean peninsula in the mid-seventh century was composed of three states, Paekche located in the southern part, Koguryo in the northern part and Silla in the central part.

general administrative offices, a special office in charge of religious services was established.

For the proper functioning of the *ritsuryō* system, literally meaning governing according to fixed criminal (*ritsu*) and administrative laws (*rei* or *ryō*), the identification of citizens to be governed and governing by means of law-based government order were necessary. These conditions, however, were not easy to be satisfied in Japan at that time. First, it was extremely difficult to identify citizens to be governed. While, in Tang, the paternal family system and the house system with fixed members comprised the basic condition of the *ritsuryō* system, in Japan, where an ancient tradition of bilateral descent was still ubiquitous, neither the members of house nor the head of house were fixed, nor did the notion of house property or inheritance exist. As clarified in Yoshida (1983), the government had a hard time to identify citizens to be governed. At first, the government reorganized the clan system and requested that a clan head for each clan be designated, and in 684 the emperor gave an official name to the head that showed also their ranking in the bureaucracy (*Yakusa-no-kabane*). However, this method was not effective because, even if the head of the clan was identified, the membership of each clan was highly fluid, and it was difficult to identify citizens in each clan. In view of the indeterminacy of members of the clans, in the legislation of 701 the government tried to use the house, not the clan, as the basic unit for the identification of citizens, and introduced the inheritance system, following the paternal line, and tried to make the house (*ie*) the basic unit to be governed (*On-i-no-sei*). It took a long time to develop the house system, however, partly because the custom for a bride to live in the house of her groom was not yet established, so that the paternal line was not easy to maintain, and mainly because there was no notion of house property to be inherited, so that the role of the house as a permanent organization to carry out inheritance was not well developed. Needless to say, if the development of private property was a necessary condition for the working of the *ritsuryō* system, the system itself, based on the principle of the nationalized holding of production factors, was destined to collapse. In other words, the utilization of the *ie* system was contradictory to the basic principles of the *ritsuryō* system. As will be typically seen by conflicts over the ownership of private lands between land developers and the provincial governor's offices, *kokuga*, the development of private property in the nationalized system of the *ritsuryō* comprised a main and continuing theme of institutional change in Japan, not only during the period before the thirteenth century but also during the whole medieval period until the end of the sixteenth century. This section will start the discussion of this topic.

The second difficulty in the functioning of the *ritsuryō* system lay in the obstacles to the application of administrative and judicial rules to implement policies. This was because citizens were largely living in ancient communities in which incantation and supernatural power had maintained substantial force. The major policies ordered by central government were implemented with the help of incantation. The criminal law specified by Taihō-ritsuryō was rarely applied in the local districts in its exact form. Yoshie (1986) claims that local lords (*dogō*), who became bureaucrats in the *ritsuryō* system, implemented the policy orders regarding administration in accordance with religious rituals, and, with respect to criminals, rarely applied formal criminal laws in their jurisdictions. Even a murder was judged by indigenous methods unless it was related to national interests (pp. 128–130). Probably for this reason, Buddhism in Japan during the period was mainly evaluated as another method of incantation. The government utilized Buddhism as a method of protecting citizens from natural and other calamities, and esoteric Buddhism (*mikkyō*) introduced during the early ninth century came to obtain significant power as the core of national religion partly because of its methodology based on incantation. This issue will be discussed in detail in the next section.

4.1.1.1 Development of Private Property

There was no private property of value to be inherited at the beginning of the *ritsuryō* system. First, residences, called *yake*, composed of a block of land and a building for the use of living space and warehouse, were for the collective use of several families, so that it was impossible to inherit residence among a family line (Yoshida 1983, p. 13). Second, while official positions given through the system, *On-i-no-sei,* could be inherited paternally, inheritance was not automatic. What was allowed to inherit was the right to inherit the title of fathers and, usually, sons were given ranking lower than that of their fathers. Unless a son showed capability suitable for the position, he could not rise to the same position as his father (Hattori 1991). For official positions to become family assets to be inherited, it was necessary for it to be accompanied by the accumulation of human capital specific to the position.

Nevertheless, the accumulation of private property began gradually and steadily. Productive farmers began to accumulate wealth through saving the surplus of products and through lending rice to the less productive. Moreover, the new policy of the government initiated in 743 to promote the development of new arable lands had considerable impact. The statute called the Konden-einen-shizai Act that allowed to hold newly cultivated land permanently gave considerable impetus to the progress of private ownership and the spread of the convention of inheriting family property. The Act had a provision to prevent unfettered expansion of private holdings through a stipulation that privately held lands, not used more than three years, would be converted into government holdings, and the provincial governors' offices diligently watched the actual state of utilization and tried to nationalize newly developed lands (Nagahara 1968, pp. 50 and 73). In this sense, landholding by the developers of lands, that expanded significantly after the mid-eighth century, was highly unstable. However, it is difficult to deny that the Act provided a basic precondition for the progress of the private holding of lands (Oguchi 2002). Those productive farmers, who had obtained land through purchase and development of large arable land by themselves, grew up as a new class after the eighth century. The so-called indigenous lord class, *zaichi-ryoshu*, came to exert considerable influence on the emergence and working of the private market economy. The deterioration of the *ritsuryō* system entered a new stage of collapse thereafter.

The move to the private property society was accelerated as the aristocracy, the ruling class of the *ritsuryō* system, began to accumulate private property by themselves. There were two major methods for their accumulation of private property. First was the development of the manor (*shōen*) system. As the development of new land increased, land became the major part of private property in the country. Since the rights to land of developers, indigenous lords, was insecure because of the risk of exploitation (nationalization) by the provincial governors' offices, indigenous lords began to donate their lands to influential agents including aristocrats and imperial families, and to large temples and shrines, while retaining some rights. This was the beginning of the manor system in Japan. Influential agents obtained mainly income rights to the return of lands, while the majority of control rights were retained by indigenous lords, who were formally hired as managers, manor officials (*shōkan*), of manors. The donation of manors increased significantly toward the eleventh and twelfth centuries. The Shōen-seiri-rei statutes, in 1069, officially admitted the donation system and the holding of manor. The proportion of income from manors in the total income of aristocrats increased, surpassing the traditional income obtained as stipends related to their official positions.

The second method for the accumulation of private property by the aristocracy was the conversion of government positions into house business. It is well known that the top positions in the government came to be monopolized by powerful families like the Fujiwara clan. As is clarified by Sato (1983), there occurred the prevalent phenomenon of the sub-contracting of government positions by specific families. Government positions that needed expertise or special knowledge came to be monopolized by specific families. Those positions that required special knowledge, such as literature, ritual ceremony, law, accounting and art, thereby became family business, and related families accumulated and inherited esoteric know-how within the family, consequently monopolizing the positions as family businesses. Moreover, during the tenth century, new government positions, *ryōge-no-kan*, were created in order to manage additional administrative jobs. This included a special office, the *kebiishi*, to the public security of Kyoto and a special section, the *kurōdo-dokoro*, to manage the emperor's household. These new offices became another source of income for aristocrats, quite likely becoming additional sources of vested interests for related families.

Teranishi (2014, ch. 5) develops a detailed history of the emergence of the house (*ie*) system out of the behavior of the aristocracy to secure official positions within the *ritsuryō* system as their private property. Yoshida (1983, p. 181) notes that the substantial move to the formation of *ie* system began after the mid-twelfth century when the paternal line inheritance system emerged owing to the spread of the custom of patrimonial marriage in which a woman is taken into her husband's family. At the same time, aristocrats began to accumulate human capital in the form of skills and knowledges specific to official positions and established a system of patrimonial transmittance to their inheritors. It is important to note that the *ie* system emerged as a mechanism to secure official positions within the government system as house businesses and grew in tandem with the accumulation of human capital among aristocrats for the cultural refinement of imperial court activities.

4.1.1.2 The Emergence of the Samurai Class

During the early days, military operations were carried out by arming ordinary citizens and government officials. This soon became ineffective, as the need emerged to battle the Ezo (northerner) and Silla of Korea, whose soldiers had a high level of skill in cavalry battles and were equipped with heavy arms. A few aristocrats became specialized as armed aristocrats in charge of the military operations and defense of Kyoto, and gradually enhanced military power through the accumulation of special skills and equipment, and through the employment of hunting tribes and semi-criminals. This was the origin of the samurai as specialist families of military skills (Sato 1974; Motoki 1994). The two samurai families that dominated the samurai class during the late twelfth century, the Heike and Genji, originated in this way, and grew up through subordinating and merging local samurai groups.

As private property was accumulated, there inevitably occurred conflicts and struggles related to the ownership of property. This was the basic precondition for the rapid growth of the samurai class. Especially important for the growth of the samurai class was the arming of indigenous lords, *zaichi-ryōshu*, who needed to protect their lands from the threat of intervention and potential nationalization by the provincial governors' offices.[2] Conflicts among indigenous lords were also responsible for the military build-up of the samurai. The intensification of the struggle related to land holding among aristocrats, and the temples and shrines, also increased the demand for military power held by the samurai, and gave momentum for the expansion of the samurai class.

Yoshie (1986) contends that, especially during the early period, the government ruled by aristocrats had been very cautious about the growth of the samurai (pp. 228 and 256). It took a long time for the samurai to establish their prestige as a class as well as to be accommodated in a society ruled by aristocrats under the authority of the emperor. Their serious concerns about family ranking (*kakaku*), comprising official positions (*kanshoku*) and ranking in the ordering of imperial courts (*ikai*), and interest in the refinement of samurai culture, comprised one of the fundamental themes of the cultural development as well as political history of Japan.

4.1.2 Cultural Background: Introduction of Buddhism

When Buddhism was introduced from the king of Paekche to the emperor Kinmei (reign 539?–571) during the mid-sixth century, there occurred a political struggle between the Soga clan that supported Buddhism and the Mononobe clan that was

---

[2]During 935–941, two large rebellions by the leaders of indigenous lords Taira Masakado and Fujiwara Sumitomo erupted, as resistance to the repression of the provincial governors' offices.

related to the clans in charge of religious rituals based on traditional Shinto.[3] The victory of the former resulted in the introduction of Buddhism by the state. It is said that the reason for the introduction had almost nothing to do with any judgement as to the internal effects on the mindset of individuals, but was concerned with the issue of which religion had the larger divine benefits and smaller divine punishments. This reflects the state of political theory at the time that was mainly concerned with incantation and supernatural power, so that the choice of religion was a serious political decision.

The introduction of Buddhism for political purposes characterized the cultural atmosphere surrounding religion in Japan. While Prince Shōtoku, Shōtoku-taishi (574–624), is well known for his deep concerns with the internal aspects of human behavior, his interests in Buddhism emanated from political concerns in the face of serious struggles and battles among the Soga clan. The aim of Emperor Shōmu (reign 729–56), who was the most ardent promoter of Buddhism in early times, did not lie in the salvation of souls but in the issue of how to prevent natural and other calamities by use of the supernatural power of Buddhism.[4] He tried to establish a state in which a Buddhist-led society, with the subordination and support of the gods in Shintoism, and a belief in the teaching of Buddhism by him and other political elites, would result in the salvation of the people (Kasahara 1977).

It must be noted also that there was an additional important reason for the introduction of Buddhism as the national religion. Buddhism was important for Japan at the time because it was a synthesis of the advanced civilizations to be learned. Buddhist temples were a symbol of the high technology of architecture, and Buddhist statues were of refined industrial craft. Buddhist priests also introduced advanced knowledge in medicine and river engineering (Kasahara 1977; Sueki 2006).

At the beginning of the ninth century, two priests, Saichō (767–822) and Kūkai (774–835), returned to Japan after their study in Tang. Saichō brought back materials and knowledge for the development of an integrated theory of Buddhism, Japanese *Tendai-shū* (en-kyō) on the basis of *Hokke-scripture*, and Kūkai *hongaku* theory and esoteric Buddhism (*mikkyō*) based on *Kegon-scripture*. Kūrai established *Shingon-shū* at the temple Kongōbu-ji in the Kōya mountains. Saichō and his successors introduced esoteric Buddhism in *Tendai-shū*[5] and deepened its own theory of *hongaku* theory on the basis of *Hokke-scripture* at the temple Enryaku-ji in the Hiei mountains.

Saichō and Kūkai completed the process of the establishment of Buddhism as a national religion aimed at *chingo-kokka* (the protection and salvation of the state), and at the same time opened the way to the socialization of Buddhism in Japan, traditionally pursued by Mahayana Buddhism. The establishment of national Buddhism conducive to the safety of the state and national welfare was what emperors, such

---

[3]The term 'Shinto' did not exist at the time of the transfer to Buddhism. It is considered that under the impact of the transfer of Buddhism, people named Shinto the beliefs in the deities of heaven and earth that were traditionally in existence.

[4]The years under the reign of Shōmu were a time when people suffered seriously from draught and famine.

[5]Saichō asked for the theory and borrowed materials related to the *mikkyō* from Kūkai. The interaction of the two priests is summarized in Ando (2019, pp. 243–280).

as Shōmu,[6] had aspired after, and this finally became realized with the introduction of *mikkyō* and *hongaku* theory. In a broader perspective, the contribution of the two priests lay in the founding of Japanese Buddhism toward socialization in the sense of salvation of the masses as well as the internalized deepening of the mental models.

4.1.2.1 *Mikkyō* (Esoteric Religion)

Mikkyō was mainly brought back by Kūkai, who studied *mikkyō* under a Tang priest who specialized in *mikkyō* but also under a couple of Indian and Kashmir priests, and became the founder of *Shingon-shū*. The method of incantation utilized in chanting *sutra* was considered to be the most effective way to pray for the prosperity of the state. The most important characteristic of *mikkyō* teaching was that it admitted *sokushin-jyōbutsu*, the attainment of Buddhahood while still alive, although it required hard training called *sanmitsu-kaji*.

While *Singon-shū* developed by Kūkai admitted and recommended training for *sokushin-jyōbutsu*, Saichō, who initiated *Tendai-shū* of Japan, was more cautious, and taught that conditions to attain *sokushin-jyōbutsu* were dependent on the capability and training performed. After the death of Saichō, his followers mitigated the conditions for *sokushin-jyōbutsu*. Along with the temple Tō-ji where Kūkai taught, Enryaku-ji of Saichō became one of the two leading temples for the study and spread of *mikkyō*. The former *mikkyō* sect was called *tō-mitsu* and the latter *tai-mitsu*. Under the strong influence of these two temples, *mikkyō* was spread widely to temples all over Japan by the end of ninth century.

The theory of *mikkyō* asserts that, since *mikkyō* is the teaching of Dainichi-buddha (Mahavairocana tathagata, Skt.), who embodied the super-human principle of universal truth, it is superior to *kenkyō* that is taught by the Buddha (Gautama Siddhartha), who was human although considered to have eternal life as one of the many buddhas. Yoshie (1986) contends that *mikkyō* obtained wide support because the method of incantation utilized by *mikkyō* played a role in substituting indigenous religious rites that comprised the backbone of ancient political systems in local communities. Rulers introduced *mikkyō* to maintain the socio-political order of communities that had maintained the ancient structure. Moreover, the method of incantation and belief in Dainichi-buddha of *mikkyō* merged with the indigenous worship of mountains and gave rise to mountaineering asceticism (*shugen-dō*) at the end of the Heian era. Ando (2019) argues that the mountaineering asceticism adopted *hongaku* theory later on and influenced the spread of the notion of the Buddhahood of plants as well as the performing arts during the Muromachi era (see Appendix 2 to this chapter).

---

[6]Shōmu built *daibutsu* in Tōdai-ji and established many Buddhist temples in the local regions (regional states) called *kokubun-ji*.

4.1.2.2 The *Hongaku* Theory

The *hongaku* theory, introduced by Kūkai and developed by Saichō and successors, aimed at getting rid of anxiety about life after death by the masses. This assertion was dependent on two propositions. First is the proposition of *shitsu-u-bushō* that claims everyone is potentially entitled to attain Buddhahood, and the second is the proposition of present-day-first (*ji-jyōjyū*), which claims that the world actually observed is the only world to be concerned with and one does not have to worry about one's situation in the future life. The first teaching gets rid of anxiety about the destiny of life, and the second theory makes positive the mindset and standard of conduct in order to live the present life. Politically, it was claimed that, under the protection of the state by the *mikkyō*, it was sufficient to live 'as it is' (*aru-ga-mama*), so that it was not necessary for rulers to have concerns about the welfare of the masses.

The theory of *shitsu-u-bushō* was energetically pursued by Saichō, who intended to develop a teaching that gave the possibility of enlightenment (*satori*) to as many people as possible. Saichō denied the traditional preconditions for successful enlightenment that set a limit on the people who were qualified to arrive at enlightenment. When Saichō returned to Japan, it was thought that, following the traditional way of thinking, there were three different methods (three-*jyō*) of practicing depending on the level of potential capability of believers determined innately, and each method (*jyō*), or possible type of enlightenment,[7] was predetermined. In a controversy involving the priest Tokuitsu of the *Hossō-shū* (one of most powerful traditional Buddhism sects), Saichō asserted that the three-way theory was contrived for the convenience of teaching and that only one level (one-*jyō*) theory was real. Saicho's idealistic thinking that everyone should aim at attaining enlightenment obtained overwhelming support in the *Tendai-shū* at Enryaku-ji, and the *hongaku* theory retained its position as the major way of thinking at *Tendai-shū* after his death through the effort of successors.

The theory of present-day-first (*ji-jyōjyū*) was contrived after the death of Saichō through tenacious theoretical struggles by followers for centuries in Enryaku-ji. According to Tamura (1973a), the structure of the final form of the theory is summarized in a document, *Sanjyūsi-ka-jyō-no-kotogaki*,[8] written around 1200–50, about 400 years after Saicho's death. Tamura explains the basic structure of the theory as follows. According to the theory of Mahayana Buddhism that is constructed on the principle of relativity (*kū*),[9] while every element in the world does not have substance, everything is considered to be existing because of the interrelationship, *engi*, among every element. Ordinary people (*bonfu*) whose eyes were covered by clouds due to earthly passions (*bonnō*) cannot understand the interrelationship. In

[7] Some are able to attain their own enlightenment, some are destined to attain not only their own but also help others to attain enlightenment and some are unable to attain enlightenment at all.

[8] Reprinted in *Tendai-hongaku-ron: Vol. 9 of Nihonshisō taikei* (Tokyo: Iwanami-shoten, 1973).

[9] *Kū* is often translated as 'void' or 'nothingness', but the *Japanese–English Buddhist Dictionary* (Daito-shuppansha, 1991) recommends the translation 'relativity'.

other words, the fact that ordinary people have not yet arrived at the level of Buddhahood implies that they cannot understand the interrelationship. Conversely, those who have attained enlightenment could have a clear understanding of the interrelationship among elements that compose the world.

In terms of the relationship between the state of enlightenment (*nehan*) on the one hand, and the issue of life-and-death on the other, Mahayana Buddhism contends that, since neither *nehan* nor life-and-death has fixed substance, and both are without their own character in *kū*, it follows that there is no difference between life-and-death in the present world and the *nehan* in the other worlds. This way of thinking in traditional Mahayana Buddhism is called by Tamura the 'equality theorem based on *kū*'.[10] The *hongaku* theory takes this way of thinking further. At first, the *hongaku* theory contends that everyone, including ordinary people, has the possibility to attain enlightenment. This is called the 'endogenous equality theorem'. Next, the *hongaku* theory goes from this universal Buddhahood theory to a higher-level proposition and asserts that, since existing things in the present world embody fundamental truth, the present world and existing people embody the eternal truth of Buddha. This way of thinking is called 'phenomenal equality theorem'. Finally, the *hongaku* theory contends that things in the present world are exactly the living image of the truth, so that there is no other truth. This thinking is called 'ontological equality theorem', in which only things in the present world are captured affirmatively.

In the 'equality theorem based on *kū*', the endogenous equality theorem and the 'phenomenal equality theorem', the world is composed of two dimensions, while in the 'ontological equality theorem' the world has only one dimension. The essence of ontological equality theorem lies in the belief that existing things in the present world are the only truth. This is nothing but the affirmation of the present world as truth, so that to live 'as it is' (*aru-ga-mama*) is the only standard of conduct recommended in this theory. In other words, this way of thinking is called *ji-jyōjyū*, the eternal existence (*jyōjyū*)of the truth of Buddha in the present world (*ji*).

In terms of the timing of attainment of Buddhahood or the issue of enlightenment in the present world or another world, the *hongaku* theory contends there is no substantial difference between the two worlds, because both are just two images of the invariable truth viewed from two different directions.

By this theory, people were emancipated from concerns about the timing of enlightenment. As far as people believed in the *hongaku* theory, they were freed from anxiety about their destiny in the next world. It is sufficient to enjoy the present world by way of living 'as it is'. Further, through a detailed examination of the teaching about the practice of the *hongaku* theory, Tamura notes that there is no need to carry out particular practice in accomplishing the *hongaku* theory; just living 'as it is' is sufficient.[11]

It is important to note the close complimentary relationship between the *mikkyō* and *hongaku* theory. If *mikkyō* has succeeded to accomplish protection of the state, and the benefits of the success are trickled down to the masses not only today but

[10] We have applied the English term 'equality theorem' to the Japanese 'sō soku-ron'.

[11] For detail, see Teranishi (2014, pp. 120–121).

also in the future, it is not necessary to introduce the *hongaku* theory because they are freed from the anxiety of their destiny in this and the next life. However, in reality it was not conceivable that effective trickle down would be implemented by rulers. As is seen by the despotism by the Fujiwara clan, rent-seeking activity was prevalent during the late Heian era, and the Buddhist circle was also involved in the activities through its symbiotic relationship with the ruling class. Without an effective mechanism for trickle down, the *hongaku* theory was indispensable even if one assumes the effectiveness of the *mikkyō* in the protection of the state. Moreover, as can be seen by the above sketch, the *hongaku* theory is an extremely idealistic theory with predetermined harmony, and such an idealistic theory is liable to be abused by rulers and the related Buddhist circle, who indulged in rent-seeking, avoiding sincere efforts at mass salvation. This is the basic reason that Hōnen, Shinran and other priests embarked on the establishment of new Buddhist sects, Kamakura new Buddhism. It will be argued below that Kamakura new Buddhism was born out of the struggle with and the denial of the *hongalu* theory. Kuroda (1975) claim that Kamakura new Buddhism was born out of the struggle with the *mikkyō* in the context of political history.[12] However, this assertion, the *kenmitsu* system theory, is denied from the viewpoint of our culture–institutions framework. Incidentally, it is sometimes argued that the *hongaku* theory remained stubbornly in place until the Tokugawa era, but even the piecemeal evidence that exists suggests its influence was substantially reduced as the influence of new Buddhism grew toward the sixteenth century.

4.1.2.3 The Syncretic Fusion of Buddhism and Shinto

In tandem with the promotion of Buddhism as the national religion, the fusion of Buddhism with traditional Shinto, or the *jingi* theory, was implemented.

In the traditional way of thinking of Buddhism, gods were treated as one of the six realms lived by living things (*ujyō*) in transmigration. During the first half of the eighth century, Buddhist priests applied this notion to the gods in Shinto, so that gods were considered to be in need of salvation out of the process of transmigration with the help of humans. For this reason, Shinto shrines were built in Buddhist temples in order to help the Shinto gods get out of transmigration. Furthermore, after the second half of the eighth century, a new theory came to be widely believed that gods were the temporary form of Buddha who came to Japan to help the enlightenment of people. This theory was called the *Honji-suijyaku* theory; *honchi* means real Buddha and *suijyaku* descending. In this way, the fusion of Buddhism and Shintoism during

[12]Sueki (1998) once criticized Kuroda, arguing that Kuroda confounded the *honngaku* theory with the *mikkyō*, so that he arrived at the mistaken conclusion that the *mikkyō* was the central theme of the existing Buddhist circle at that time. Teranishi (2014) agreed with the criticism of Sueki. We, however, do not agree in this book and contend further that the real fault of Kuroda's theory lies not in this point but in his stance to explain the emergence of Kamakura new Buddhism from the viewpoint of political history. For more on this point, see Sect. 4.2.5 below.

this period took place in a way that established the dominance of Buddhism over Shintoism (Hirai 1994).

During the middle ages, there occurred significant resistance by Shintoism with respect to the secondary role assigned to it in the syncretic fusion by the *Honji-suijyaku* theory. There emerged new theories of Shintoism, such as *Ise-Shinto* and *Yoshida-Shinto*, that took Shintoism as the higher order theory emphasizing the historical origin of the country. Partly based on nationalism enhanced by victory in the Mongolian expeditions in the late thirteenth century, new theories attained support from a wide range of classes, and the fusion between the two religions was intensified.

The priest Jien of the *Tendai-shū* at the end of the Kamakura period converted himself to Shintoism and asserted an anti-*Honji-suijyaku* theory. While in the *Honji-suijyaku* theory, Buddhas are real (*honji*) and gods in Shintoism are derivative (*suijyaku*), Jien claimed that, in term of moral principle, the honesty and cleanliness emphasized in Shintoism was real and the concept of benevolence in Buddhism was secondary and derivative (Tamura 1991, p. 217). The development of Shinto theory and the relationship with Buddhism after the Muromachi era is discussed in Chap. 5.

4.2 Religious Reform in Japan

Let us discuss why religious reform occurred in Japan. As is suggested in Ienaga (1940) and Bellah (1964), the basic backdrop for the strong influence of religions in society was the enhancement of the fundamental and inherent concept of denial of this world or longing for salvation. In the Occident, Christianity was imported from the Hebrew world in the Middle East into the Hellenism world of the Roman empire in the fourth century. Buddhism was imported from India by way of China and Korea in the sixth century to Japan, where traditionally Shinto had been the native religion. Both Christianity and Buddhism replaced the affirmative concept of the present life that had prevailed previously with the notion of denial of the present life, inducing people to seek salvation. In the Occident, Greek gods embodied the ultimate ideal of perfect and harmonious humans, which was considered to be attainable through self-centered efforts aroused by the intellectual passions and Eros of humans. This ancient Hellenistic idealism, however, was denied by the spread to Rome of Christianity established on Hebrew tradition. Under the omnipotent God of Christianity, the creator of all things in the universe, man is convicted of a basic flaw of heedlessness of God, and only a turn to complete obedience was accepted. Things in this world are of no value and should be denied simply because they are merely being created. Furthermore, at the time of the Last Judgement, those who are not relieved must fall into Hell permanently. This terrifying doctrine ultimately controled people's psychology.

The advent of Buddhism in sixth-century Japan introduced the concept of the denial of this world, as is typical from the dying words of Prince Shōtoku, Shōtoku Taishi: 'Present life is without meaning and the real meaning of life is understood only through the teaching of Buddha.' The world is a perpetually changing, impermanent and transitory (*mujyō*) place, where all phenomena are produced by causation (*engi*) and interaction with each other. Men are condemned by their basic nature of greed and anger. Greed and anger throw them into a rotary machine, in which living things (*ujyō*) are in the world of transmigration (*rinne*), incessantly suffering from repetition of birth and death that occurs through travelling six realms of existence.

Religious reform was necessitated when the existing religious system and theory could not accommodate the acute longing for salvation based on intensified negation of this world. In this regard, it must be noted also that both Christianity in the Occident and Buddhism in Japan underwent significant transformation at a specific moment in history; in the Occident there occurred reformation when society moved from the medieval into the early modern era, and in Japan, when Japanese society shifted from the ancient to the medieval age, Kamakura new Buddhism was born. In both cases, the role to be fulfilled by religion changed drastically from the salvation of the elites and through the intermediation of clergymen, to the direct salvation of the masses. And the main place where religious practice was performed shifted from isolated monasteries and temples to the ordinary life of individuals. This implies that religious reform was required not only to cope with the radical intensification of the desire for salvation but also to adjust the method of salvation suitable for the changed socio-economy. In fact, the most difficult task for religious reform was to find a new and effective method of salvation to meet the needs of the new social environment.

The Mahayana Buddhism transferred to Japan had an historical mission to expand the object of salvation from the small number of selected elites to the masses. The two priests that established national Buddhism, Saichō and Kukai, found the solution to this problem in two theories, the *mikkyō* and *hongaku* theories, and especially in the complementarity relationship between the two. However, there occurred serious difficulties to this strategy owing to the radicalness of social changes. First was the dysfunction of the trickle-down mechanism of *mikkyō*. The rent-seeking and deterioration of society was so serious and the trickle-down mechanism so dysfunctional—even the ruling class came to suffer—that it became apparent that praying for the safety of the state was not effective nor sufficient to cope with the distress of the masses. Second was the failure of the *hongaku* theory in providing a direct method for salvation of the masses. Especially serious was the excessive optimism of the teaching of living 'as it is' based on the theory of *ji-jyoujyu*. Even if the theory was coherent in terms of philosophical reasoning, it did not give any sense of salvation to individuals struggling with the emergence of the market economy. Consequently, it became urgent to find a new method of salvation to replace the predetermined harmony of *hongaku* theory and provide workable teaching suitable for the rapidly marketizing socio-economy.

4.2.1 Radical Change in Socio-Economy

Let us first have a quick look at how society changed as the decline of the ancient system and marketization proceeded, consequently necessitating a new method of salvation, and how the change caused the intensification of the sense of denial of the present world and longing for salvation.

The ancient state based on the *ritsuryō* system began to change drastically and decline in two respects: the accumulation of private property mainly due to the formation of manors (*shōen*) and the growth of the samurai class mainly as a result of domestic conflict over property ownership.

By the mid-twelfth century, half of arable land in the country was converted into manors, privately owned and controlled with various privileges such as exemptions from tax payments, the labor service obligation, and police power inspections (*huyu-hunyū-ken*). Due to the consequent fall in the tax revenues of the central government, the main source of revenue for aristocrats changed from the stipend assigned to their official ranking and administrative jobs to the revenue arising from the management of manors. Their income rights to manors were not necessarily secured, however, because of the frequent invasion of their rights by provincial governors' offices, which aimed to nationalize lands and local military powers including armed indigenous lords.

Toward the end of the Heian era, the samurai class enhanced their military power, and rapidly established their political presence through their intervention in power struggles among the imperial families and related aristocrats, and in frequent disputes and conflicts with respect to land ownership. The turmoil of recurrent civil wars during the second half of the twelfth century between the two most powerful samurai groups, the Heike and Genji, ended in victory for Minamoto Yoritomo, the head of the Genji group. Yoritomo established the Kamakura *bakufu* (samurai government) in the late twelfth century,[13] which heralded the beginning of the medieval feudal age. The uprising by ex-emperor Gotoba in 1220 (*Jyōkyū-no-hen*) to defeat the *bakufu* and reestablish aristocratic sovereignty failed and confirmed the dominant power of the samurai. From then, the samurai class became a major player in the struggle with the aristocracy over the rule of the country as well as in cultural development.

The national Buddhism established on the *mikkyō* and *hongaku* theories came to change in response to the unstable socio-economy. For one thing, it was obliged to face the issue of the salvation of the masses; while the *hongaku* theory had substantial influence as a philosophy of preestablished harmony within the Buddhist circle, it was unable to develop effective teaching to guide the lifestyle of the masses, who were in the midst of the threat of everyday life and living with the rapid marketization of the economy and socio-political changes. Negative thinking about the present life, contradicting the *hongaku* theory, was rapidly developing. The development of new religious theory and positive actions by the religious circle toward the salvation of the masses came to be urgently needed. Further, the large temples that had been in charge of the protection and salvation of the state came to be involved

[13]In 1183, Yoritomo was given a comprehensive right to the administration of northeastern Japan, and in 1185 allowed to set up the *shugo* and *jitō* over the whole country. This established the position of the Kamakura *bakufu* as one the administrative powers of the country in the areas of military and policing. The denomination of Yoritomo as shogun in 1192 completed this process.

in the conflicts regarding land ownership, partly because of the weakened financial support by the state. Probably, owing to the increased instability in society, the *mikkyō* became popular as a tool for coping with the destabilized political system and spread into temples across the whole country by the end of the tenth century. Through this process, large temples and shrines became huge economic and political powers as property owners comparable with aristocrats and, at the same time, came to be engaged in corruption and rent-seeking activities.

4.2.1.1 The Kamakura *Bakufu*: A New Institution

The Kamakura *bakufu* was established as a branch of the ritsuryō system in charge of the military and policing of the country, which comprised the defense and security of the capital city Kyoto as well as, by use of military power, the maintenance of security and policing (*kendan*) in provincial administrative states (*kuni*). A *shugo* (military governor) and *jitō* (estate steward), under the command of the *shugo*, were designated for this purpose in each provincial state and were mainly composed of housemen (*gokenin*) of Yoritomo or local lords who became housemen. The eastern and northern parts of the country were virtually long under the control of the Genji clan, so that the role of the *shugo* and *jitō* in the area was carried out by existing provincial governments and other influential lords under the control of Yoritomo.

At first, Yoritomo applied the *shugo* and *jitō* system in the regions confiscated from antagonistic powers such as Heike in the western and southern Japan, and the *bakufu* did not have right to execute *kendan* in manors in regions where the *jitō* were not appointed. Gradually, however, manor-owning aristocrats came to rely on the military power of the *bakufu*, and the appointment of the *shugo* and *jitō* expanded to most of the western provincial states of Japan. The power of the Kamakura *bakufu* became nationwide after the second part of the thirteenth century (Takahashi 2013).

4.2.1.2 Struggle Over Landholding Among Aristocrats, Samurai and Large Temples

As the manor system spread in the country, the land system of the country came to be composed of a mixture of manors and publicly-held land under the control of provincial governors' offices. The land system, the *shōen-kōryō* system, established formally by the promulgation of the Shōen-seiri-rei (the Act on rearranging manors) in 1156 was revised after the establishment of the Kamakura *bakufu* so as to incorporate the role of the *jitō* in the system in 1223. Before then, the *jitō* had been used to succeed to the various rights held by defeated antagonistic powers, but, after 1223, they obtained a fixed income per unit of land under jurisdiction. However, dissatisfied with their position of mere policing agents, the *jitō* embarked on a further fierce struggle over land ownership with manor-owing aristocrats during the late thirteenth century.[14] The behavior was intensified by the increased poverty of *bakufu* housemen due to the extra expenditure to fulfil military obligations, at the time of the Mongolian invasions during 1274–81. The Kamakura *bakufu* supported the *jitō* and other housemen by way of such measures as repressing the income and control rights of manor-owing aristocrats or giving judgements unfavorable to manor owners in land ownership disputes.[15] That the *jitō* were in trouble with manor officials (*shōkan*) all over the country is vividly reported in Nagahara (1998, pp. 174–192).

As is explained in Chap. 3, the power of aristocrats in landholding declined steadily during the process, and they became gradually mere fixed-income receivers rather than owners with control and residual income rights, especially during the Southern and Northern Dynasties period after the collapse of the Kamakura *bakufu*. In contrast, the power of the *shugo* and *jitō* grew steadily, and virtually all the provincial states escaped the control of the *ritsuryō* system, and were converted to the virtually complete control of the *shugo*, a system called the *shugo-ryōgoku* system after the Southern and Northern Dynasties period.

4.2.2 Deepened Denial of the Present Life

The decline of the *ritsuryō system* and the rise of the samurai class brought about unprecedented changes in the country. Aristocrats were deeply frightened about the crisis of the class and the state system, and the populace were panicked and frantically sought ways to avoid the misfortunes and accidents of repeated warfare. Frequent natural disasters and the spread of contagious disease as well as adverse climate conditions[16] intensified the sense of uneasiness among the masses. Furthermore, privatization and the consequent emergence of the market economy must have enhanced uncertainty in the provision of daily necessities through earning income. The restlessness of the people caused by unfamiliar market transactions, the instability of the political and social system, together with natural disaster, threatened the sustainability of society. It seems that a desperate sense of the denial of this world and a longing for religious salvation intensified among all classes of people.

[14]With respect to the land held by the large temples and shrines, it seems that the *jitō* was not involved in conflict, probably because Buddhism, especially the Zen sect, spread among the samurai rapidly.

[15]To save impoverished housemen, the *bakufu* even promulgated a debt cancelation order (tokusei-rei) in 1297.

[16]Natural calamities were rampant. The warming of the earth during the Heian era caused chronic agricultural crises due to a shortage of rainfall in summer (Iijima-Nishiyachi 2002). During the period from the eighth through eleventh centuries, earthquakes of a magnitude of more than 6.5 occurred 14 times and the eruption of volcanoes was frequent; Mount Fuji erupted seven times during the period (Yamaga 2016).

4.2.2.1 Transmigration and Enlightenment

Denial of this world with regard to Buddhism was based on the theory of transmigration. In transmigration, men are condemned due to their basic nature of greed and anger. Greed and anger throw men into a rotary machine of transmigration (*rinne*), incessantly repeating birth and death that occurs through travelling six realms of existence—hell, the world of hungry spirits, animals, *asuras* (a sort of ogre living as a warrior), men and gods. Among the six, the realms of the last two, or three including *asyura*, are called good worlds (*zen-shu*), the remaining four or three realms bad worlds (*aku-shu*). Each living things (*ujyō*) can leave the bad realm (*dō*) and move into the good realm if he leads a well-behaved life, that results in the accumulation of good *karma* and the decumulation of bad *karma*, or accepts retribution. However, crucially important here is that a living thing or man cannot escape from the state of transmigration unless he has attained enlightenment (the mental state of *satori*, Buddhahood), and gets rid of *bonnō* (earthly desire), the mental functions that disturb the mind such as greed caused by excessive desire and anger by unconquerable obsession. After the attainment of enlightenment or Buddhahood, he is able to live in *jyōdo* (the Pure Land). Attaining enlightenment is only possible in principle through understanding the impermanent and transitory (*mujyō*) structure of the world, which is considered to be the view of the world held by Buddha.

The present life of men is of no value because it is a *mujyō* world; the realm of men, the present life, is transitory and short-lived and always threatened by the shift to another worse realm. Hell, in Buddhism, is not necessarily the place to stay forever, but even if one happens to get out of hell, there always remains the possibility to go to hell again, unless he extricates himself from the state of transmigration completely. To escape from the state of transmigration, one must throw away greed and anger and understand the impermanent and transitory (*mujyō*) structure of the world.

Incidentally, the transitory nature of the structure of the world is represented by the concept of *kū* in Maharana Buddhism. The *kū* concept based on the early version of *Hannya-kyō*,[17] spread by the Indian priest Nagar Juna (circa 150–250) as the essence of the wisdom of Buddha, captures the structure of the world from the viewpoint of relativity. It claims that every existence and its constituent elements are dependent on each other. All phenomena are relative and dependent upon other phenomena. This situation could be visualized as a system of dynamic simultaneous equation systems of n-degree and n-variable in economic models. The variables representing the constituent elements are called *hō* and the relationship represented by equations is called *engi* or *en*. In this system, the initial states of the variables are not specified, mainly because Buddhism does not have the notion of the beginning of the world, so that the system is perpetually moving around without anchors, initial conditions. It is claimed the structure is understood clearly or enlightenment (*satori*) is attained only when people have accomplished assigned religious practices and got rid of their *bonnō*, or anger and greed, in the secular world from their mindset.

[17]The first version of the *Hannya-kyō* was written by the year around 0 to the year 50 AD.

4.2.2.2 Impacts of *Jyōdo-kyō*

In the above, we have discussed that, in complementary with the *mikkyō* theory that tried to protect the state from natural and other calamities by means of incantation, the *hongaku* theory provided people, frightened with negative thoughts about the present life and aspiring after salvation, with a logic that justifies living positively. The *hongaku* theory, however, was based on such a preestablished harmonious logic that it was liable to deprive the necessity of religious training from Buddhism. The training in the *hongaku* theory was mainly composed of the intensive observation of the inner structure of mind, and all kinds of conduct emanating out of *bonnō* (avarice) were affirmatively approved as an image of Buddhist truth, with the consequent denial of any kind of hard reading and deep meditation (Tamura 1991, pp. 159–202). It was natural that the *hongaku* theory came to be criticized as a theory that degraded Buddhism through the admittance of unconditional enlightenment and making little of training. Moreover, the *hongaku* theory based on predetermined harmony could not suggest any effective lesson for the people living in a rapidly changing society. The precept of living 'as it is' must have intensified the desperation of people struggling in such a condition.

The most radical criticism came from the *Jyōdo-kyō* sect,[18] the leaders of which, through their activities on the streets, had been well aware of the necessity of salvation of the masses from the actual distresses in their daily lives. Moreover, the religious circle at the end of the Heian era was full of conflict over vested interests, accompanied by violence towards citizens and among temples. Generous government support for large temples had converted them into a hotbed of corruption. Priests used temple buildings as their own living space, giving their high priestly ranking to their own children and related aristocrats, and intervening in various secular disputes through arming low-ranking priests, and the like. Furthermore, the pessimism due to the theory of the last days of Buddhism (*mappō-shisō*) that was thought to begin in the year 1052, aroused a deep sense of the denial of this world. Priests acting on the streets, without belonging to any established temples, called the *hijiri*, *shōnin*, or *shami* in the *Jyōdo-shū* sect, were obtaining ardent support from the masses.

The longing for salvation by the people was at its height during the latter days of the Heian era, partly because of the impact of the publication (woodblock printing) of the book *Ōjyō-yōshū* by Genshin (942–1017), which emphasized the dreadfulness of hell in transmigration in comparison with the happiness of the *jyōdo* (the pure land) in the *Jyōdo-shū*, rebirth which was held to come about by the mercy of Amitabha. While Gennsin's book was the first systematic presentation of the *Jyōdō-kyō*, methodically it was based on the school of the *shōdō-mon* that emphasized hard and professional training and the attainment of Buddhahood by the efforts of believers, not on the *jyōdo-mon* that admitted easy practice by the use of the concept of merit transfer (*echō*). *Shōdō-mon* admitted substituting hard training by good deeds and social contribution in daily life, such as the donation of buildings or buddha statues to

[18]From the *Jyōdo-kyō* sect was born the *Jyōdo-shū* of Hōnen (and hence *Jyōdo-shin-shū*) and the *Jishū* of Ippen.

temples, but such substitution was not possible for the poor and busy masses who were urgently seeking salvation. It was the contribution of Hōnen (1123–1212) who established the method of salvation based on the easy practice principle of the *jyōdo-mon* that could be adopted by the poor masses.

4.2.3 The Emergence of Kamakura New Buddhism

Buddhist society was obliged to respond to the intensified longing for salvation by way of replacing the optimism of the *hongaku* theory. Along with the mission and tradition of Mahayana Buddhism, the strategy was to find a new method of salvation for the sake of the masses without repeating the failure of the *hongaku* theory. It was not an easy task, however, because relaxation of conditions involved the risk of weakening and losing the religious mind based on a deep understanding of religious theory, which was essential for the attainment of enlightenment.

In this regard, the crucial dilemma related to the method for salvation common to both Christianity and Buddhism must be noted. In the case of Christianity, with its omnipotent creator God, the incentive to serve for the glory of the God needs to be stressed to enhance the religious mind of the people. The solemnity of churches and the beauty of church buildings had been indispensable in Catholicism for that purpose. In the new method of salvation without the intermediation of the church introduced by Protestantism, the selectivity of salvation through the predestination proposition was emphasized to keep the religious mind as a high level. In the case of Buddhism, which did not have such an omnipotent creator and where salvation was attained by believers themselves through spiritual enlightenment (*satori*), the balancing between the conditions for salvation and the enhancement of the religious mind was also a delicate issue. The relaxation of the salvation condition such as uniform salvation applied to everyone and the teaching of living 'as it is' introduced by the *hongaku* theory was useful to broaden the recipients of salvation. This, however, inevitably incurred the risk of weakening of religious mind of people.

The final solution found by new Buddhism sects born in the Kamakura era was to associate religious practice to occupational activities in the emerging market economy. This was nothing but a new method of attaining enlightenment, practice simplification (*igyō-ka*), in the place of occupational activities in ordinary lives. For this purpose, the new Buddhist sect resorted to the theory of merit transfer (*ekō*) of qualitative transformation inherited in Mahayana Buddhism, a theory of transformation of profane good deeds into religious merits. Hard involvement in the occupations and deep thinking about the structure of the world in the place of occupational activity were recommended as good deeds transferable into religious merits for enlightenment. Under this solution, since the method of religious salvation was related to the actual occupational life of individuals, it was expected that the masses, who were suffering most in the radical changes in society and the marketization of the economy, and who could not afford enough time and energy to implement religious practice at temples, could have a more positive attitude to the present world, with enhanced hope and conviction of salvation. The new teaching based of this method contrived by various sects of the Kamakura new Buddhism had enormous impacts on the internalized part of culture as well as on the entire socio-economy of Japan. This comprises the main theme of this chapter. Let us discuss the process of invention and the impacts of the new method, practice simplification (easy practice method), in more detail.

4.2.3.1 Honen

Kamakura new Buddhism emerged under the strong leadership of Hōnen and was developed among others by Shinran (1173–1262), the founder of the *Jyōdo-sin-shū* sect, Dōgen (1200–53), the founder of the *Sōtō-shū* (*Zen*) sect, and Nichiren (1221–82), the founder of the *Nichiren-shū* sect.[19] Honen studied *Tendai-shū* at the Enryaku-ji temple and founded *Jyōdo-shū*, based on which his disciple Shinran founded *Jyōdo-sin-shu*. Not only Shinran, but also Eeisai, Dōgen and Nichiren studied at the Enryaku-ji temple in their youth, so that *Tendai-shū* could be regarded as the parent body of Kamakura new Buddhism.

The intention of Hōnen was the salvation of large numbers of people seeking salvation, who were poor, uneducated and liable to commit serious wrongdoing. Hōnen was well aware of the necessity of hard training based on *shōdō-mon* in arriving at enlightenment in the true sense, but he proposed the easy practice method to offer salvation to the masses, seriously distressed under the rapidly changing and deteriorating socio-economic situation. Hōnen himself explained that he had disregarded *shōdō-mon* for the moment and followed the *jyōdo-mon* method as an emergency measure (*jiki-ron*).[20] Among many available methods, he chose chanting, and recommended specialization in chanting the name of Amitabha, as an effective method of attaining enlightenment by *jyōdo-mon*. He proposed the easy practice (*igyō*) of chanting the name of Amitabha 60,000 times per day in order to encourage the sharing of the benefits of mercy.

Hōnen emphasized that it was possible to get salvation without going to monasteries. This practice could be accomplished in daily life without interrupting occupational work in farming, hunting, handicraft manufacturing or other occupational activities. Hōnen's theory met severe criticism from the established Buddhist circle (so-called old Buddhism), however, on the grounds that the theory tended to admit a sloppy approach to Buddhism because it neglected encouragement of the believer's autonomous efforts to seek enlightenment. It might look contradictory for old Buddhism to criticize the easy practice principle of Hōnen, because old Buddhism itself took an irresponsible approach in the sense of recommending *hongalu* theory extensively, which did not require any training. However, it must be noted that the

[19]Other leaders were Eisai (1141–1215), the founder of *Rinzai-shū* (*Zen*) sect and Ippen (1239–89) who founded *Ji-shū* sect.

[20]See his *Sentaku-hangan-nenbutsu-shū* (reprinted as *Iwanami-bunko* (*Iwanami-shoten*), pp. 177–178).

main aim of old Buddhism was the salvation of talented and smart elite believers through assigning hard training, and the criticism from old Buddhism of Hōnen was that his theory took little consideration of hard training without taking the difference in the innate quality of believers into consideration.

The most serious critic of Hōnen from the established Buddhist circle was Myōe (1173–1232). His criticism was that the choice of the easy practice principle was liable to deprive the religious mind to pursue enlightenment (*bodai-shin*); becoming Buddha is possible only through an understanding of the structure of the interrelated elements of the world, and mere chanting of the name of Amitabha cannot realize this. The criticism of Myōe was based on the fundamental methodology of Buddhism and was persuasive. Followers of Hōnen had a hard time responding to the criticism.

4.2.3.2 Invention of New Methods of Salvation

In view of this criticism of Hōnen, the main efforts of the founders of new Buddhism were devoted to the theoretical device for prevention of the loss of the religious mind to arrive at enlightenment, while maintaining the aim to give salvation to the masses. In other words, while proposing the easy practice approach based on the theory of the merit transfer of qualitative transformation, the founders of new Buddhism made substantial efforts to invent effective 'brakes' on the possible sloppy attitudes of believers. Thus, Shinran denied the theory of enlightenment during present life, sticking to salvation after one's death, and emphasized the mindset of true belief in and subordination to Amitabha, although he recommended the simple practice of chanting the name of Amitabha. Moreover, he assigned the practicing of hard training in the life after one's death. Dōgen requested the hard training of seated meditation (*zazen*). Although he admitted salvation in the present world, he insisted that salvation is attained only in the process of hard seated meditation practice. Nichiren also negated salvation in the present life following Hōnen in order to prevent an easy attitude by believers, while he asserted the importance of the true belief in *Lotus Sutra* and recommended the easy practice of chanting a short sentence expressing and confirming faith in the *sutra*.[21]

4.2.4 The Structure of Kamakura New Buddhism

4.2.4.1 Conceptual Framework

Let us explain by use of a simplified conceptual framework why the emergence and innovation of Kamakura new Buddhism was important. In Buddhism, religious sects

[21] Among the plethora of literature on the thoughts of Kamakura new Buddhism, three chapters on the theory of Sinran (pp. 173–210), Dōgen (pp. 211–226) and Nichiren (pp. 227–265) in Ienaga (1997) are worth investigation.

and schools competed with each other with respect to the various dimensions for attainment of Buddhahood (enlightenment); either from the viewpoint of religious leaders or from the viewpoint of believers. It is convenient to summarize the characteristics of various schools and the evolution of Buddhist theory in terms of four dimensions: the target of salvation, the level of salvation, the timing of salvation and the method for attaining salvation. Each of the four dimensions has alternatives: two kinds of target, two levels of salvation, two timings, and four methods for the attainment of salvation.

In order to simplify the presentation,[22] let us deliberate on the evolution of Buddhism from early Buddhism until the emergence of Kamakura new Buddhism in Japan. The following simplified scheme is utilized:

- The target for salvation
  - priests and trainees
  - priests, trainees and laymen; more generally salvation of the masses could be targeted
- The levels of salvation (the final level is the ultimate purpose of religious faith)
  - preliminary level: move to good realm (*zen-shu*) within the state of transmigration
  - final level: extrication from the state of transmigration, arriving at the enlightened state of mind (*satori*) or attainment of Buddhahood
- The timing of salvation (to obtain Buddhahood in the present life is desirable for believers)

  during present life
  during life after death
- The method for salvation or attaining enlightenment (easiness of method increases as the method number gets larger)
  - Method 1—*Nangyō*: tough and hard training by means of study and meditation in the monastery and sometimes involving tough physical training in the mountains
  - Method 2—*Ekō* (merit transfer): utilization of good deeds and social contribution in daily life as merit for attaining enlightenment (merit transfer of qualitative transformation) or attaining enlightenment with the help of accumulated merit of other persons (merit transfer of directional transformation)[23]
  - Method 3—*Igyō*: simple and easy practice in daily life such as chanting a prayer to Buddha

[22] For more detailed explanation on Buddhist theory, see Teranishi (2014, 2018).

[23] See Kajiyama (1983) and Hiraoka (2016) for this terminology and related theoretical explanations.

- Method 4—*Hongaku* theory: new philosophy that there is no difference between this world and life after death, and every human is qualified to be provided with salvation.

Early Buddhism born in the fifth to fourth century BC in India adopted the most severe policy for salvation. The target for salvation was confined to priests. The preliminary level of salvation is attainable by method 2 but salvation of the final level is achieved only by method 1. Further, it was claimed that salvation is attained only in the life after death. To arrive at an understanding of the structure of the world or the attainment of enlightenment (*satori*), one must go through the hard and tough training process by means of intensive study and meditation in monasteries and temples for years. The training is called *nangyō*; *nan* means tough and *gyō* religious practice.

Mahayana Buddhism born after the first century AD and introduced to Japan in the sixth century has another name, big (*dai*)-vehicle (*jyō*) Buddhism that express the aim of the sect to offer salvation not only to elites but mainly to the masses.[24] In terms of the target for salvation, Mahayana Buddhism was developed with the aim to give salvation not only to priests but to laymen. There are two kinds of sect with respect to the timing of salvation. *Mikkyō* admitted attainment of enlightenment in the present life (*sokusin-jyōbutu*), whereas other sects mostly retained the principle that salvation is attained only in the life after death. While it continued to emphasize the effectiveness of *nangyō*, method 1, in order to disseminate their religion to the broader populace, it admitted utilizing method 2 for the final stage salvation. The admission of method 2 or merit transfer (*ekō*) symbolizes the major characteristic of Mahayana Buddhism that was established in order to widen the target of salvation to laymen. Not only admitting the transfer of accumulated good deeds and contributions to society into religious merits (merit transfer of quality transformation), Mahayana Buddhism allowed the transfer of accumulated merits to other persons to help their enlightenment (merit transfer of directional transformation), and the concept of the *bosatsu*, whose mission was to help the enlightenment of others, was introduced.

Let us turn to Buddhism in Japan. Until the thirteenth century at least, Buddhism in Japan was under the control of several large officially licensed temples located in the Kyoto and Nara areas, or what we call the (established) old Buddhism. These temples wielded overwhelming socio-political power in Japanese society through building up collusive and symbiotic relationships with the *ritsuryō* elites, the imperial family and aristocrats, and also with the samurai class after the thirteenth century. Their strategy for salvation was based on the differentiation of believers according to their innate quality or capability. In other words, both priests and laymen were targeted, but the method for salvation was differentiated.

We believe that the old Buddhism had a view of believers as humans composed of plural vehicles (*jō*) based on the capability of believers. For talented and smart

[24]The Buddhism that spread to southeast Asia is called small-vehicle Buddhism by Mahayana Buddhism, meaning targeting the salvation of priests and monks only.

believers, the hard training that comprised method 1 to arrive at final stage salvation was assigned, and salvation was given during the life after death of believers except in the case of the *mikkyō*. Although the criteria of the capability were relaxed over the years, established Buddhism stuck to the traditional principle of *nangyō*. With respect to less capable and 'dull' believers, however, established Buddhism adopted an extremely easy prescription of method 4, the preestablished harmony of the *hongaku* theory. This meant that for the majority of ordinary believers suffering from the hardships of radical socio-economic changes and without sufficient time and financial resources to carry out religious practice or good deeds appreciated by society, the old Buddhist circle provided philosophical relief only. In other words, it offered some slight consolation that the masses do not have to worry about how to get out of the bad world nor to escape from the painful state of transmigration because there is no difference between this and another world. As far as one accepts this theory, there is no need for religious practice.

While the old Buddhist circle is thought to have relied on the plural vehicle theory, Kamakura new Buddhism was based on the one vehicle (*jyō*) theory and adopted the *sitsu-u-busshō* theory more extensively, following the assertion of Saichō. In order to cope with the crisis of social order and deteriorated social security, the target for salvation of new Buddhism was mainly laymen or the masses in general. In terms of the method of salvation, the main characteristic of Kamakura new Buddhism was its adoption of method 3 or the emphasis on the easy practice principle (*igyō*). It is important to note that, while the new Buddhism adopted method 3, easy practice principle, this did not mean new Buddhism admitted an easy way to enlightenment. The meaning of practice simplification must be understood by taking other dimensions into consideration. With respect to the dimension of the level of salvation, the founders of new Buddhism contended repeatedly that believers should not be satisfied by the preliminary level salvation but make efforts to arrive at the final level of salvation. With respect to the timing of salvation, *Zen-shū* of Dōgen admitted the attainment of Buddhahood in the present life, but *Nichiren-shū* developed by Nichiren and *Jyōdo-shin-shū* by Shinran stuck to the realization of enlightenment after one's death in order to emphasize the difficulties of enlightenment.

Since the new Buddhism had significant concerns over the ultimate attainment of enlightenment (*satori*) by all believers, it was serious about the process of easy practice, and recommended all believers to make efforts to understand the ultimate structure of the world[25] and to arrive at the final stage of salvation. Furthermore, while method 3 was the main thrust of theory in Kamakura new Buddhism, Shinran

[25] Kuroda (1975) notes that the ultilization of the practice of chanting the name of Amitabha or a short sentence about the *Lotus Sutra* by new Buddhism is rooted in the practice of the incantation method of old Buddhism during the early Heian era. It is claimed that this tradition of incantation had developed into chanting practice by unregistered volunteer priests, *hijiri*, wandering the villages and towns, who had been trained in the *mikkyō* tradition. He claims that the *mikkyō* had proliferated into almost all the Buddhism sects in the tenth century. But it is important to note that these facts do not mean that Kamakura new Buddhism was born inheriting the tradition of the *mikkyō*. In fact, the new Buddhism was born out of the denial of the *mikkyō* tradition. All the sects of new Buddhism tried to get rid of the incantation style and took a negative stance to the symbiotic relationship with

recommended the additional utilization of method 2, merit transfer (*ekō*) in line with the directional transformation of merits, accumulated by Amitabha when he was still a trainee monk (*bosatsu*). In order to avoid the easy reliance of believers on merit transfer, however, Shinran devoted enormous efforts in his book *Kyō-gyō-shin-shō*[26] to emphasizing the importance of the pure and sincere belief (*shin*) in the arrival and salvation by Amitabha.[27] His teaching was that *shin* is nothing but the religious mind seeking after *saoti* (enlightenment), or *bodai-shin*. In this way, Shinran responded to Myōe's criticism of Hōnen. Likewise, Dōgen was cautions of the possibility of misunderstanding by believers that easy practice could lead to the easy realization of enlightenment. He taught that, although every believer can attain enlightenment owing to the theory of *sitsu-u-bushō*, the realization of attainment is conditional on hard training. On the basis of his theory of *shū-shō-ichijyo* that enlightenment is obtained not as a result of training but training itself is enlightenment, he emphasized the necessity of going through hard mental training by way of seated meditation (*shikan-daza*).

It is important to note the relationship between method 2 and method 3. Theoretically, easy practice principle (method 3) is possible because of the admission of merit transfer by use of good deeds and social contribution (method 2), an innovation introduced by Mahayana Buddhism. Since the masses targeted by the new Buddhism were not rich enough to implement merit transfer by way of the contribution of buildings and statutes to temples, they were expected to utilize good deeds and devotion in occupational activities. In other words, since the Buddhism introduced to Japan was Mahayana Buddhism, the adoption of the easy-practice principle was implemented within the framework of merit-transfer (*ekō*). It is well known that Shinran resorted to the use of merit transfer of directional transformation extensively; the merit accumulated by Amitabha, when he was a *bosatu*, was considered to be transferred to believers, and those who successfully attained Buddhahood owing to the merit transfer from Amitabha were requested to be engaged in hard training and help others through transferring their own accumulated merits in the life after death. Owing to the strong influence of Shinran and the popularity of the concept of the *bosatsu*, merit transfer of directional transfer seems to have been excessively emphasized in the study of Buddhism in Japan. However, most crucial in the development of Kamakura new Buddhism lay in the notion of merit transfer of qualitative transformation. This is because, since the easy practice principle (method 3) is possible because of the admission of merit transfer by use of social contributions and good deeds (method 2), the fundamental mechanism by which practice simplification with

the ruling aristocratic class during the Heian era and, except for *Zen-shū*, were repressed by the Kamakura *bakufu*.

[26]Reprinted in Hoshino-Ishida-Ienaga (1971).

[27]Moreover, Shinran assigned an obligation to carry out hard training after one's death in the other world and to return to the present world to help the enlightenment of others. These points were discussed in detail in Hoshino (1971).

respect to method 3 gave rise to the sanctification of profane daily activities, eventually leading to the emergence of the *kyūdō* principle, lay in the merit transfer of qualitative transformation.

Kajiyama (1976, 1983) claims that, in the theory of original Mahayana Buddhism, merit transfer of qualitative transformation is more fundamental than merit transfer of directional transformation. It is claimed that the original concept of *ekō* means the conversion of profane conduct such as *fuse* (contributions and donations), *shōjin* (devotion to occupational and other activities) and other good deeds into sacred phenomenon of attainment of enlightenment (*satori*) (Kajiyama 1983, pp. 163–176). Kajiyama calls this the conversion of profane activities into the intellectual capability to understand the world (*issai-chi he no ekō*[28]) (Kajiyama 1983, p. 174). The notion of merit transfer of qualitative transformation was discussed in *Hannya-kyō*, the first version of which was written by the year around 0 to the year 50 AD, while the merit transfer of directional transfer was developed in *Muryō-jyukyō* related to the teaching of Amitabha, written after the first century AD. Not only was the former concept born earlier than the latter, it is claimed that the notion of former merit transfer was more fundamental in theoretical contribution than the latter. This is because the merit transfer of qualitative transformation emanates from the fundamental effort to get over transmigration by way of nurturing intellectual capability to understand the structure of the world. Kajiyama (1976) asserts that this concept is fundamental because it is derived by use of the idea of *kū* (relativity). The basic concept of *kū* that, once an individual arrives at the right understanding of the world, there is no difference between life and death and between the state of mind filled with agony and the mindset of enlightenment, gave rise to the notion that the theory of relativity can be construed as the possibility of conversion of intellectual efforts in various deeds in the profane world into something sacred and beneficial for the attainment of enlightenment in the sense of cultivation of the intellectual capability of understanding the structure of the world. Since the *kū* concept as fundamental relativity of the structure of the world is the way of understanding arrived at by Buddha, it is natural to evaluate the intellectual capability nurtured in occupational activities as having the sacred value from the viewpoint of Buddha. In summary, *kyūdō* behavior based on merit transfer of qualitative transformation is important because it is based on the intellectual efforts of understanding the structure of this world, while merit transfer of directional transfer is based on belief in salvation by Amitabha. It seems to follow that, while both methods bring about enlightenment, the enlightenment by way of *kyūdō* behavior is more fundamental according to the stance of Buddhism based on the spirit of self-help.

It must be noted that *Jyōdo-shū* and *Jyōdo-shin-shū* are dependent on the double mechanism of merit transfer, merit transfer of Amitabha and of *kyūdō* behavior based on practice simplification, while other *Soto-shū* and *Nichiren-shū* are dependent on the single mechanism of *kyūdō* behavior.

---

[28]The word 'echo' can be expressed by another Japanese word '*hurimuke*'. The Sanskrit for the Japanese *echō* means 'conversion' (Kajiyama 1983, p. 169).

4.2.4.2 The Birth of New Buddhism and the Direct and Indirect Influence of the *Ritsuryō* System

It must be noted that the easy practice (*igyō*) could be regarded as an original innovation by the Japanese Buddhist circle in Mahayana Buddhism. Since the birth of Mahayana Buddhism at the end of the first century BC or at the beginning of the first century AD, it had introduced two crucial innovation to accommodate new layman believers. First was a drastic transformation in the concept of Buddha. While, in the Buddhism before Mahayana Buddhism, Buddha was Gautama Siddhartha, who obtained Buddhahood around fifth or fourth century BC under a pipa tree, Mahayana Buddhism considers that Gautama Siddhartha was not the real buddha and the real buddha obtained Buddhahood in the eternal past and was still alive now, and that there are many worlds other than this world in which buddhas called *nyorai* (Skt. Tathagata) are actively teaching.[29] It follows that believers came to be able to communicate with and learn from existing buddhas by way of meditation, and to learn from literatures other than memoirs of Gautama Siddhartha. There is no doubt that this new way of thinking was extremely encouraging for the masses seeking enlightenment. Second was the introduction of the concepts of the *bosatsu* and the *ekō* to help the enlightenment of laymen. While basic stance of Buddhism emphasizes self help, Mahayana Buddhism respects altruistic behavior also, so it introduced mutual help to assist the enlightenment of believers. The *bosatsu*, trainee monks, and the *ekō* are concepts introduced for this purpose. The role assigned to the *bosatsu* is to help the enlightenment of other believers, and they were expected to make self-sacrificing efforts without considering the enlightenment of themselves. The mechanism of *ekō* of directional transformation enabled helping the enlightenment of the masses by the use of the accumulated merits of the *bosatsu*.

It seems that these innovations were considered to be largely accomplished by the third century, judging from the fact that major scriptures containing these innovations were already completed by then. It could be considered that the religious reform in Japan in the thirteenth century that gave rise to the easy practice principle could be regarded as one of the series of innovations comprising steps in the program of Mahayana Buddhism that aimed at the salvation of the masses. As we have already described, it took four centuries to establish the new theory: from the *hongaku* theory of universal Buddhahood in the controversy between Saichō and Tokuitsu of the *Hossō-shū* in the ninth century, to the finding of the easy-practicing principle in the thirteenth century. Further, for the establishment of the easy practice principle, it was necessary to overcome the weakness of the *hongaku* theory in the sense of the possibility of losing the religious mind to pursue enlightenment (*bodai-shin*), pointed out by Myōe. It was only after the first half of the thirteenth century that the coherent theory of the easy practice was compiled in the form of such documents as *Sentaku-hongan-nenbutsu-shū* by Honen, *Kyō-gyō-shin-shō* by Shinran and *Shōhō-genzō* by Dogen. The easy practice method was not an idea that suddenly occurred in the religious circle of Japan. It was a glorious achievement of the sincere

[29]For example, Amitabha is still living in a western pure land.

theoretical struggle of Japanese Buddhism over centuries following the tradition of Mahayana Buddhism. The deep impact of the reform on the socio-economy is also worth noting. The teaching of practice simplification by Kamakura new Buddhism for mass salvation resorted to the concept of the *ekō* of qualitative transformation, and had a significant and long-lasting impact on the socio-economy of Japan by affecting the internalized part of culture.

Conventional theory about the emergence of Kamakura new Buddhism claims that the confusion in the socio-economy and the aggravation of socio-political stability caused by the decline of the *ritsuryō* system was the main reason for religious reform and the emergence of Kamakura new Buddhism. Religious reform occurred in the midst of radical confusion and the instability of political and economic system when people's longing for salvation intensified and existing theories and institutions were unable to respond to their need. In this conventional proposition, religious reform as a cultural change is explained as a direct result of institutional change, namely the decline of the *ritsuryo* system.

However, we must be cautious to argue that the change in the institutional arrangements in the socio-economy was the main cause of the emergence of religious reform. Although it is true that the longing for salvation of the people caused by the turmoil related to institutional changes enhanced the motivation for religious reform by the founders of new Buddhism and increased support for their activities, it is still possible to doubt the direct causality from the institutional change of the decline of the *ritsuryo* system to the cultural change of the emergence of new Buddhism. Firstly, the birth of Kamakura new Buddhism was due largely to the internal logic of the evolution of religion. Mahayana Buddhism, which was introduced to Japan and became the origin of Kamakura new Buddhism, was a Buddhism established for the purpose of the salvation of the masses. Secondly, as already shown, the *ritsuryo* system was a system introduced as an emergency policy to meet the international military tension regarding the Korean peninsula. Since a radically sophisticated system was introduced from China in a substantially primitive community-based society, without even the concept of family property, it was destined to evolve and adjust to the changing market system after its formal establishment, so that the 'decline' of the *ritsuryo* system is basically a phenomenon programmed in the sense of continual adjustment to the process of market development. In summary, it is true, during the thirteenth century, that a drastic change or 'decline' of the *ritsuryō* system due to the privatization of land triggered the movement to the emergence of Kamakura new Buddhism. However, this does not necessarily imply a direct causal relationship from the former to the latter.[30] Both cultural and institutional changes could be results of programmed transformation. It must be noted also that founders of new Buddhism, such as Hōnen, were privately motivated to devote their lives to the salvation of the masses suffering from the socio-economic changes, which were largely related to the institutional changes due to the 'decline' of the *ritsuryō* system. However, we

[30]In Teranishi (2014, 2018), we argued that the social turmoil related to the decline of the *ritsuryo* system was one of the causes of the emergence of Kamakura new Buddhism. However, we withdraw this proposition in this book.

must be cautious to associate individual motivation with the general logic that the institutional change of the *ritsuryō* system was a cause of cultural change, including the birth of new Buddhism.

So far, we have argued about the direct causal relationship between the emergence of new Buddhism and the decline of the *ritsuryō* system. It is contended that the direct influence of the latter on the former is confined only to the role of trigger. However, it is important to note that, with regard to indirect influence, the decline of the *ritsuryō* system had a significant impact on the religious reform by way of the choice of the method of salvation. This was because religious reform in Japan was implemented exactly at the time of the start of the market economy accompanied by the acceleration of the social division of labor. The founders of new Buddhism were motivated to resort to the concept of merit transfer of qualitative transformation and to convert occupational activities for the sake of survival in the emerging market economy as merit with sacred value. This is the reason that the method of easy practicing was introduced.

This seems to be the reason also for the emergence of *kyūdō* behavior, as a result of the new method of practice simplification. The masses were encouraged to be engaged in truth-seeking (*kyūdō* behavior) and to think about the structure of the world at their place of occupation in order to facilitate the merit transfer of qualitative transformation. In other words, the combined effect of the conception of merit transfer of qualitative transformation and the practice simplification resulted in the emergence of *kyūdō* behavior under the condition of the marketization as a result of the deterioration of the *ritsuryō* system.

It was also natural that there occurred significant indirect impacts from cultural change on the institutional changes. The nascent social division of labor came to be accelerated by *kyūdō* behavior, giving rise to various impacts on the socio-economy. It seems that the founders of new Buddhism, at least Shinran, were well aware of the possibility of socio-economic changes caused by religious reform.

4.2.4.3 Practice Simplification and the *Kyūdō* Principle

Compared with the established Buddhist circle that stuck to the traditional method 1 of *nangyō*, hard training in the monasteries, the essence of the teaching of new Buddhism was practice simplification, *igyō*, in the places of secular daily life. The target of the old Buddhism lay in the promotion of the *chingo-kokka* (religious protection of the state) and the consequent trickledown effects on society, whereas the main target of new Buddhism was the populace or general public, living miserable daily and occupational lives. Under new Buddhism, believers were encouraged to practice easy assignments, but at the same time to pursue attainment of enlightenment through sincere effort to understand the structure of the world. The working place came to be the place of religious practice, and activities related to occupation came to be regarded as instruments to be used in an effort to reach enlightenment by way of the theory of merit transfer of qualitative transformation. This attitude toward occupation was nothing but the *kyūdō*-principle; as is referred to in Chap. 1, *kyū* means seeking and *dō* means one's way of doing. The fundamental concept of merit transfer (*ekō*) in Mahayana Buddhism was applied to daily occupational lives. In other words, in the *kyūdō* principle, people tried to accumulate good deeds in occupational activity, regarding them as religious merits effective to arrive at enlightenment.

It is important to note that the timing of religious reform in Japan matters in the sense that reform was implemented in the midst of the emergence of the market economy partly under the strong influence of the decline of the *ritsuryō* system. Reform took the form of practice simplification so as to give salvation to the masses having trouble adjusting their occupational lives and living to the turmoil of marketization.

It seems reasonable to conjecture that the founders were aware of the emergence of *kyūdō* behavior under this circumstance. It is well known that Shinran referred to the role and necessity of the salvation of the merchants. In the thirteenth section of his *Tanni-shō*, where he discussed the inevitability of the retribution of bad *karma*, which was accumulated by bad deeds in the past, he referred to the similarity of the problem of bad deeds in occupational life and the sin of the killing of living things, arguing 'those engaged in commercial activity and farming are not different from those who live by catching fish in the sea and rivers and catching wild pigs and birds'. In this sentence, Shinran seems to be clearly aware of the changes in society, the emergence of new occupational activities based on the development of the social division of labor, and expressed his concerns about bad deeds committed by merchants, whose occupation has nothing to do with the deed of depriving the lives of living things. It is conjectured that Shinran carried out religious reform with clear recognition of the impacts of reform on the socio-economy. Table 3.2 shows that the GDP share of commerce of the tertiary sector rose from 8.1% before 1150 to 9.4% in 1280. Shinran lived from 1173 to 1262. Sueki (2016) conjectures that the sentence from *Tanni-shō* was written for the purpose of expressing the thoughts of Yuien, a disciple of Shinran, who wrote down the manuscript of *Tanni-shō* at Shinran's dictation. In view of Sueki's basic stance of understanding Shinran as the inquiry of bad deeds such as killing parents and sons, his conjecture is understandable. However, from the viewpoint of the relation to cultural changes, it seems to be still possible to believe that this sentence is an expression of the deep and serious concern with the socio-economic changes of Shinran. It is pointed out that Shinran referred to the role of commerce and merchants in several other places.[31] Although we do not have further evidence, this sentence seems to suggest that the reform of Kamakura new Buddhism was carried out with a clear recognition of the substantial impact on the socio-economy.

As will be discussed in detail in the next section, there is no doubt that the attitude of *kyūdō* in relation to daily occupational life caused profound changes in society. First, it shifted the place for the working of human intelligence from the isolated world of monasteries to the busy and chaotic daily occupational world. People were induced to use their intelligence to understand the structure of this world by use of

[31] Ienaga (1997, p. 192), Sueki (2016, p. 248), and Ama (2011, p. 200).

religious theory. This inevitably led to the recognition of the importance, and hence the affirmation, of ordinary lives in the present life.

Second, the new attitude changed the scenery of streets of towns and cities completely, at least after the Southern and Northern Dynasties period. There appeared a mass of new types of professional people. Before, everyone was engaged in all categories of economic activity; everyone cultivated their farmland with farming tools manufactured by themselves and sold their farm products at the market nearby. This scenery underwent drastic changes. People were motivated to be engaged in specialized activities, and within each specialized occupation they sought the truth of this world in the religious sense. Consequently, there occurred an intensification of occupational specialization and the accelerated progress of the social division of labor. People came to be socially identified and classified according to their specialty, say, merchants in specific commodities, artisans of specific handicraft goods or farmers producing specific crops. This inevitably enhanced the asymmetry of information in society. Forecasting the reaction of others became less easy than before due to the lack of information about the specialty of various occupations. This important phenomenon will be the main theme in the analysis of the next chapter.

Third, the impact of the Buddhism worldview on daily lives came to be intensified. In Buddhism culture from the beginning, people were interested in the quality of deeds, good or bad, and the accumulation of the effects of deeds (*karma*) through the process of transmigration. Because of the teaching of easy practice assignment, the people's attitude to daily life was put under the stronger concerns of not only *karma* accumulation but also of the intellectual concerns to understand the structure of the world for the purpose of attaining enlightenment. Before the religious reform, interaction with others nearby had the effect to change the amount of *karma* and hence to affect the position within the environment of transmigration, so that it was impossible to be freed from the pains of transmigration by means of good conduct. However, merit transfer of qualitative transformation enabled one to get out of transmigration and obtain Buddhahood. In this sense, interaction with others nearby in occupational activity motivated by *kyūdō* behavior came to have additional and highly important religious meaning for the Japanese. Not only because *karma* is the consequence of deeds produced through interaction with others nearby, but also because the structure of the structure needs to be sought in the interaction with others nearby in occupational activities to arrive at enlightenment, the behavior of people came to be carried out under the stronger influence of a consideration for the effects on others nearby, and they came to lead their present lives with deeper and more intense concern for others nearby. The internalized part of culture of the Japanese seems to have undergone significant changes in this process. Section 4.3 of this chapter develops a more detailed examination of the changes in the mental model.

4.2.4.4 Conflicts with and Influence on Established Buddhism

As a newly born tiny sect with an extremely radical assertion targeted at the masses, Kamakura new Buddhism met severe criticism and harsh repression by the old Buddhist circle. An official petition against Hōnen was presented to the imperial court in 1205 (*kōhuku-ji sōjyō*,[32] the petition by the Kōhuku-ji temple), two faithful followers were sentenced to death, and Honen himself and Shinran were condemned to exile in 1207.

The criticism by the established Buddhist circle was based on two points, as is asserted in Ienaga (1971, ch. 20, p. 393). First was the neglect of method 1 and the need for meditation and study, and the second was the lack of emphasis on the *ōhō-buppō-isō* theory—thc mutual dependence theory between the law of the emperor and the law of Buddhism. Both points were based on the stance of the old Buddhism that securing the safety of the state was fundamental, and the salvation of the populace would be automatically and indirectly realized by a strong state as a trickledown mechanism. The first criticism is based on a lack of understanding about the stance of Hōnen, that, although he developed the method of easy practice, he did not deny the fundamental importance of method 1 (*shōdō-mon*). He denied *shōdō-mon* only as an emergency measure. The second point was also based on misunderstanding, because the founders of Kamakura new Buddhism, including Hōnen, never denied the mutual dependence theory. We will examine this point in detail below.

The established Buddhist circle was, however, aware of the necessity of directly addressing the distress of the populace and helping them. There appeared priests who tried to develop the new easy-practice method (Satō 1987, p. 84), that was different from chanting the name of Amitabha or a short sentence about *Lotus Sutra*. Myōe, who criticized Hōnen, was typical of such people.[33] Not a few priests were engaged in such activities as collecting voluntary contributions from unknown people on the streets, financing the rebuilding of ruined temple buildings, or helping outcast people discarded by the government or those suffering abnormal diseases such as leprosy. Sato (1987), however, claims that these activities in the established Buddhist circle emanated from an intention to expand their power by means of religious influence and secure the available labor needed for the management of their manors.

---

[32]Reprinted in *Kamamura kyū-bukkyō* (pp. 31–42) edited by Kamata and Tanaka (Tokyo: Iwanami-shoten, 1971).

[33]See *Saijyarin* written by Myōe reprinted in *Kamakura kyū-bukkyō*, pp. 43–106 edited by Kamata and Tanaka (Tokyo: Iwanami-shoten, 1971).

4.2.5 Kenmitsu *System Theory in the Context of Culture and Institutions*[34]

There occurred the rapid spread of new Buddhism toward the end of the medieval age. Takeda (1971)[35] shows that, among the 6008 temples of the *Jyōdo-shū* existing at the end of seventeenth century, 15% were newly constructed or reconstructed during 1501–73 (72 years), 65% during 1573–1643 (60 years), and 10% during 1644–96 (52 years). Takeda points out also that the pattern of regional distribution of the number of temples among the 47 prefectures in the year 1941 and at the end of the seventeenth century has close resemblance. Since there is good reason to believe that the number of temples of each sect did not undergo significant changes after the eighteenth century until now, the finding of Takeda implies that the *Jyōdo-shū*, the most popular sect of the new Buddhism, developed rapidly after 1501 and most rapidly during the latter half of sixteenth and the first half of the seventeenth century.[36] Bitō (1992) asserts that it is reasonable to conjecture that the same tendency applies to the other sects of the new Buddhism.

Behind the growth of the new Buddhism lay the basic theory of the easy practicing principle born from the sincere desire of the founders to give religious salvation to the masses. We have argued that the easy practice principle was a remarkable achievement of Japanese Buddhism in the long-term theoretical development of Mahayana Buddhism. Our assertion is based on the tradition of the study of Japanese Buddhism developed by such scholars as Ienaga (1940) or Inoue (1956). They emphasized the innovative power of Kamakura new Buddhism, and the heroic role in mass salvation played by the founders of the new religions. During the thirteenth century when Kamakura new Buddhism was born, all the sects were extremely tiny groups with a handful of believers and supporters. It was argued that, although the new sects were very small, and except for Zen sects, even severely repressed by the government (*bakufu*), the impacts of the new theory were enormous and, just like a fire spreading on the wide empty plain, it exerted significant influence over the large mass of people.

Some of the later studies, however, were skeptical of this view. For example, Yamaori (1993) argues that the existing literature on religious history have overvalued the impact of new Buddhism on the populace, and that the reality of the basic characteristic of new Buddhism as the religion of a small groups of disciples and elites surrounding the founders should be noted. This assertion seems to be true with respect to the thirteenth century, since it was a new belief held among a handful of elites. Further, it is also true that it took considerable time for the new Buddhism

---

[34]Teranishi (2014) agreed with Sueki's criticism (1998) of Kuroda. In this book we do not agree and try to offer criticism from a broader stance based on a comparison of culture and institutions. See footnote 12 of this chapter.

[35]See also the explanation by Bitō (1992) on the study of Takeda.

[36]Calculating from various information in Shimada (2012), the rough number of believers, as of the year 2009, is as follows: *Jyōdo-shin-shū* 12.4 million, *Jyōdo-shū* 6.2 million, *Shingon-shū* 9.3 million and the total of the six sects of old Buddhism 0.6 million. The number of temples is *Jyōdo-shin-shū* 18,800, *Jyōdo-shū* 6900, *Sōto-shū* 14,600 and *Shingon-shū* 12,500.

to be accepted firmly in society. In terms of the number of temples and believers, a rapid dissemination happened only after the sixteenth century, as is shown by Takeda (1971) above, so that the real influence on society seems to have taken place after the Southern and Northern Dynasties period and especially during the Warring States period and the Tokugawa era.

The most powerful theoretical criticism of the Ienaga–Inoue proposition was offered by Kuroda (1975), who criticized the existing religious history as having neglected the fact that strong social, political and cultural power was retained by the established Buddhist circle or old Buddhism, from the eighth century until the end of the medieval period. While this criticism is reasonable from the viewpoint of the gradual development of new Buddhism, Kuroda's argument goes further, however, and presented an ambitious hypothesis of the emergence of Kamakura new Buddhism focusing on the political symbiotic relationship among the old Buddhists, the samurai power and aristocratic class, denying the cultural origin and impacts of new Buddhism.[37] Since Kuroda's hypothesis is based on an opposite theoretical position to this book, in the sense of emphasizing the influence of political institutional mechanisms on the development of culture and denies the endogeneity of the evolution of culture, it is necessary to give a detailed examination of it.

Kuroda's hypothesis, *kenmitsu* system theory,[38] is composed of the following four propositions. First, since the Heian era, the Buddhist circle established a symbiotic coalition with the rulers composed of the *bakufu* (samurai) and aristocracy related to the imperial court. The coalition was based on a theory, the *ōhō-buppō-isō* theory, the theory of mutual dependence between the law of the emperor and the law of Buddhism. This theory, through claiming that Buddhist law serves the state (*chingo-kokka*, religious protection of the state) by the use of the power of incantation of the *mikkyō* and that state law serves Buddhism by entitling the name of holy king, who governs the world on earth, to the emperor (*konrin-ō*), established firmly the dominance of religion over the state.

Second, it is also claimed that the group of large temples became a significant political power in the country, and the three-cornered coalition (the *kenmon* system) of aristocracy, samurai and large temples, comprised the basic political system of Japan toward the end of the middle ages. As the *ritsuryō* system declined, state subsidies to old Buddhist temples were severely reduced and then virtually terminated after the twelfth century, and this induced old Buddhist temples to survive through

[37] Kuroda's hypothesis had a significant impact on the study of the Buddhist history of Japan partly, because it was a hypothesis presented from outside the circle of Buddhist study. Sueki (1998) gives a detailed examination of the study, including other related publications, and Taira (1902) brings forth some supporting argument for the Kuroda theory. Satō (1987) is a most valuable examination of Kuroda theory from a broader perspective, including the socio-economic aspects.

[38] '*Mitsu*' means *mikkyō*, esoteric Buddhism, and '*ken*' *kengyō*, exoteric Buddhism, which was a generic name for the various sects other than the *Shingon-shu* and *Tendai-shu*. According to the explanation of the *mikkyō*, the *kengyō* was a simplified version of the teaching of Buddha so as to be helpful for the understanding of ordinary believers. The concept of the *kenmitsu* system implies that the Buddhist society of medieval Japan was characterized by the overwhelming influence of old Buddhism in which the *mikkyō* established dominance over the *kengyō*.

embarking on large-scale manor acquisitions. In fact, almost all the old Buddhist temples succeeded in reviving as huge manor holders toward the end of the medieval age.

Third, the new Buddhism that emerged in the thirteenth century criticized old Buddhism with respect to the symbiotic relationship with the ruling classes and their methodology based on the *mikkyō* (Kuroda 1975, pp. 481–482). This attitude incurred the harsh repression of new Buddhism by the Kamakura *bakufu*,[39] whose stance comprised respect for the existing system ruled by the aristocracy and old Buddhism.[40]

Fourth, in order to cope with repression by the *bakufu*, and to continue criticism of old Buddhism, the founders of Kamakura new Buddhism established a new theory that provided alternative reasons and causes (*dōri*) for the political system (Kuroda 1975, pp. 491–492). However, the power of old Buddhism was so strong that the Buddhism during the medieval period was characterized by the dominance of old Buddhism. New Buddhism shared only a subsidiary part of Buddhism and was unable to carry through its critical stance, finally compromising with the old Buddhism (Kuroda 1975, p. 479).

The assertions of Kuroda (1975) had considerable influence as a critical view on the conventional thought that emphasized the innovating cultural role of Kamakura new Buddhism. This was because his assertion was a challenge to the methodology of existing literature that studied the history of Buddhism within the paradigm of the history of ideas. Kuroda's methodology was perfectly new in approaching the issue from the structure of the political system.

However, Kuroda's analysis is marred by inconsistent logic in reasoning as well as by an insufficient understanding of the political power of old Buddhism. The most serious inconsistency in reasoning is the fourth, concluding, proposition, which is concerned with the logic that explains the mechanism by which the criticism of old Buddhism gave rise to new Buddhism as an alternative political assertion. Why did criticism of old Buddhism result in the emergence of new Buddhist political theory? It is regrettable that Kuroda does not explain this proposition to any sufficient degree. There is only one sentence that is concerned with this assertion: 'since the theory of mutual dependence of old Buddhism comprises the fundamental stance of the old Buddhism, new Buddhism whose stance lay in the advocacy of heretical doctrine and criticism of old Buddhism should express their attitude toward the ruling powers' (Kuroda 1975, p. 497). This sentence offers a clue to Kuroda's assertion that new Buddhism needed to express a political stance. It is important to note that what the new Buddhism criticized about the old Buddhism was the absence of concern for the salvation of the masses, not the symbiotic relationship with the ruling class that was established on the theory of mutual dependence. In other words, there was no

---

[39]Repression was directed at the *Jyōdo-shū* and *Nichiren-shū*. Not only Hōnen and Shinran, but Nichiren was also deported. *Zen-shū* was not repressed probably because it had many believers in the samurai class and was protected by the *bakufu*.

[40]It is noted that the Kamakura *bakufu* respected the *Shōen-kōryō* system under the aristocracy and the large temples and shrines in Chap. 1.

intention of criticizing the political *ōhō-buppō-isō* theory among the founders of new Buddhism.

Let us assume that old Buddhism at the time was characterized by two traits: the symbiotic political stance with the ruling class and the lack of a sincere attitude to the issue of mass salvation. The denial of the first trait implies the expression of an alternative political stance, while denial of the latter means devotion to the salvation of the masses. However, in this sentence, Kuroda seems to assume that only the former is a trait of the old Buddhism, and, through replacing the criticism of the latter trait with criticism of the former trait, asserts that the target of criticism was laid on the political stance of the old Buddhism. Further, it is true that the criticism on the methodology based on the incantation of the *mikkyō* was liable to give rise to the misunderstanding that it was a criticism of the symbiotic stance. However, we should note that the incantation of the *mikkyō* is not necessarily and exclusively used for the purpose of praying for *chingo-kokka* (the religious protection of the state). Moreover, while it is possible to believe that the criticism was sometimes directed to the ruling political class also, the criticism was related to the stance of the ruling class vis-à-vis Buddhism, not to the political stance.

With this misunderstanding, it is natural that Kuroda is unable to raise any concrete evidence about the political assertions of the founders of new Buddhism and has ended with an enumeration of evidence that seems to be, by and large, incorrect. What Kuroda regards as Shinran's criticism of the *bakufu* was concerned with the aberration of Buddhist law, not of political rule,[41] and what Nichiren advocated in his *Rishō-annkoku-ron* was not the establishment of an alternative political state but a country in which true Buddhist teaching is respected (*bukkokudo*). Moreover, as Kuroda admits himself, Eisai had no intention to be concerned with politics (Kuroda 1975, pp. 496–501)[42] and nor did Dōgen (Sueki 2016, p. 99).

Further, in relation with the second proposition regarding the position of the old Buddhism in the power balance of the three-cornered system (the *kenmon* system), a more careful investigation is needed. Even if one admits that old Buddhist temples shared one corner of the three-cornered system during the Heian era, the role of the temples was not concerned with the political and military after the thirteenth century. Although the large temples had made significant contributions to the study of Buddhist theory and the protection of artistic culture with the consequent acquisition of some political influence during the Muromachi era, their political role outside matters of their private interests was limited, and, needless to say, their military power was far weaker compared with the *sengoku-daimyo*. In terms of their economic

[41] Kuroda quotes the famous sentence 'shujyō shinka hō ni somuki' ('high-ranking masters and their servants violate law') in *Kyō-gyō-shin-shō* (Kuroda 1975, p. 497). The term '*hō*' (law) means the law of Buddhism, in particular, the five serious sins (*gogyaku*). The aim of Shinran's assertion lay in the necessity of the realization of the country in which the teaching and law of Buddhism is respected. Incidentally, the five sins are composed of the killing of one's father, the killing of one's mother, the killing of holy priests, the injuring of Buddha, and the destruction of a Buddhist school or organization, and the slander of Buddhist law.

[42] Eisai asserted the harmonization and cooperation between old and new Buddhism, and supported the *ōhō-buppō-isō* theory (Taga 1965).

role, their position was more or less parasitic to the ruling powers, comprising the aristocracy and samurai. This point is eloquently described in Sato (1987) with respect to the manor management. It is claimed that the mutual dependence theory (the *ōhō-buppō-isō* theory) was utilized to fortify the logic to justify the manor holding and necessary privileges. It was converted into an assertion that the purpose of the ownership of manors by the temples and shrines lay in the securing of the holy areas governed by gods and Buddhas on the profane national territory governed by the state. Following this logic, the temples and shrines obtained exemption from taxation and intervention by state police power, and wielded control over inhabitants in the manor as if they were servants of the gods and Buddhas. Furthermore, Sato claims that, although the old Buddhist circle adopted the *hongaku* theory during the Kamakura era, the introduction of the *hangaku* theory by old Buddhism did not come from the pure intention of the salvation of the populace in general, but rather aimed at satisfaction of the pecuniary motive to obtain additional believers and hence funds to reestablish burnt-down temple buildings through donation (*kanjin* activity) or at increasing the number of believers under their control as an additional labor force in the manors.

In summary, the *kenmitsu* system tried to serve the welfare of the people indirectly, by protecting the state, through a trickledown mechanism. The theory of *chingo-kokka* (the religious protection of the state) by use of the power of the incantation of the *mikkyō* aimed at this purpose. However, what founders of new Buddhism pursued was quite different from this. They chose to work on the internalized mindset directly to respond to the acute longing of salvation by the masses. The conclusion they arrived at was the salvation of the masses through the easy practice principle, enabling and encouraging the masses to learn the true teaching of the buddha. It follows that to assert that they intended to provide alternative reasons and causes (*dōri*) for the political system was completely wide off the mark.

It seems to be safe to conclude that the hypothesis set out by Kuroda (1975) about the political origin of Kamakura new Buddhism is theoretically bankrupt. It is an ambitious attempt to assert the influence of political institutions on the development of culture.[43] However, in his core logic, Kuroda replaced criticism of the lack of religious motivation (the salvation of the masses) with criticism of the political theme (the symbiotic political stance). Moreover, the logic by which Kuroda denies the effect of the cultural factor is not robust enough. He denies the influence of the motivation for religious reform based on the turmoil during the late Heian era,

[43]Sueki (2016) seems to present a statement that Shinran asserted the superiority of Buddhist law over the emperor's law and tried to work on politics (Sueki 2016, p. 201). However, while Sueki's assertion of the militant attitude of Shinran in his criticism of the *bakufu* is understandable (*tatakau nenbutu-sha*), this seems to be a serious overstatement. What Shinran had in mind was a state of the country in which the emperor and the masses lived under the protection of Buddhism, and not the political pattern of government. For example, the expressions in Wasan and the attitude of Shotoku-taishi (Sueki 2016, pp. 198–202) are concerned with the relationship of the law of Buddhism and the peace of the country, not with the relationship of political law and the peace of the country, and it is quite difficult to believe that Shinran's criticism of the *bakufu* is related to the political stance of the *bakufu* as a government.

contending that is unnatural 'to believe that the experience of phenomena such as social confusion, political corruption, pessimism related to the *mappō* theory (the theory related to the End of Buddhism) had persistent influence over more than one hundred years from the time of Hōnen and Eisai to the time of Nichiren and Ippen' (p. 489). In terms of the motivation for religious reform of the founders, however, what we must notice is not the private experiences of the founders, but the long-term mission of the school of Mahayana Buddhism regarding the salvation of the masses. As we have sketched in the history of Mahayana Buddhism above, the school had continued a theoretical investigation for the mission from the first century AD. The efforts paid by a number of priests in Japan during the four centuries from the time of Saichō to the thirteenth century must be construed from this perspective of the long-term evolution of cultural paradigms, on which the real and basic motivations of the founders of new Buddhism were based. Furthermore, another crucial reason for the failure of the Kuroda hypothesis to capture the effect of culture lay in the concept of the three-cornered coalition comprising aristocrats, large temples and samurai. Although this concept may be useful as a handy description of the political system in the medieval period, it conceals fundamental cultural conflicts due to the differences in value systems between aristocracy and samurai culture that were so crucial in the social history of Japan. We will investigate this issue more closely in the next chapter.

4.3 The Impacts of New Buddhism

Kamakura new Buddhism was born as a common faith of small groups of elites gathered around its founders. Since it was such an extremely tiny organization at first, it cannot be compared with the established and government-sponsored old Buddhism. It grew, however, to the largest religion by the beginning of the Tokugawa era, both in terms of the number of believers and temples. Furthermore, this book contends that teaching based on the easy practice (*igyō*) principle adopted by the new Buddhism had enormous impacts on the socio-economic system of Japan, at least before the Meiji Restoration. The reason why these impacts occurred could be summarized in the following four propositions. First, the *kyūdō* principle nurtured by the new Buddhist teaching had brought about radical changes in people's lifestyle. Second, it had influence on the emergence of the new artistic culture, that came to be known worldwide as Japanese-style arts. Third, the new lifestyle and the new arts were embedded in such informal institutions as the *ie* system and were inherited as human capital. Finally, the impacts of the *kyūdō* principle on the mindset of people was reinforced by the historical process that went through Hegelian dialectic steps, comprising contradictions, their solutions and final reaffirmation.

4.3.1 Radical Changes in Lifestyle and Worldview

4.3.1.1 The *Kyūdō* Principle

Buddhism is a religion of enlightenment (*satoti*) based on intellectual training. The ultimate aim of the training lies in the pursuit of the causes of agony caused by anger, obsession and earthly desires and in the attainment of the mental state of enlightenment by way of overcoming the agony. To arrive at enlightenment, one must understand the mechanism of the human mind and the structure of the world through the process of hard training involving the acquisition of wisdom, rigorous discipline, and deep meditation. The new teaching of easy practice (*igyō*) of Kamakura Buddhism changed the process of enlightenment completely. Those who had been brought up in the teaching of hard training in monasteries, however, did not abandon intellectual training. Rather, they were taught and encouraged to divert the intellectual training from studying and meditating in the monastery to the pursuit of Buddhist truth in their ordinary and occupational lives.[44]

This is because the abandonment of hard training did not imply giving up of the Buddhist way of viewing the world and lives. Ienaga (1940) contends that the continuous worldview of the ancient Japanese that enabled human beings to travel freely to and from present and future world was replaced by the image of an irreversible chain of the worlds of transmigration. Furthermore, Koizumi Yagumo (1896) asserts that Buddhism embedded the notion of *karma* and its retribution in the way of thinking of the Japanese who lived until early modern times so deeply that their feelings and actions were tinted completely with the notion of retribution for deeds done in previous lives. The practice simplification induced people to be involved in *kyūdō beh*avior to obtain the sense of enlightenment in various activities in their ordinary lives. In other words, devotion in occupational and artistic activities was regarded as a substitute for hard training in monasteries. The lifestyle of people changed gradually, but definitely after the Kamakura era. It is pointed out that during the period of the Southern and Northern Dynasties (1336–92) and the Muromchi era (1392–1573), the aim of life for people eager to attain enlightenment was either to acquire distinguished skills in some fields or to obtain sufficient fortune to be deemed a man of virtues (Matsumoto 1956; Yokoi 1975). From aristocrats to the lowly, people devoted themselves to the pursuit of skills in some occupational or artistic area in order to 'congratulate' the present life and confirm the sense of attainment of enlightenment. Through devoting themselves to these aims, people felt the opportunity of escaping from the dreadful thought of hell and came to behave as if they had an affirmative

---

[44]Yoshimoto (1981) considers that Shinran recommended to give up intellectual activity in the religious practice of Buddhism and asked 'if we do not have to engage in training and studying of scriptures, how should we use our energy and passion to improve ourselves?' (pp. 221–222). It is clear that this question is quite wide off the mark. What was recommended by Shinran was not to give up intellectual activity but rather to change the use of the intellectual ability from reading and meditating to occupational activities.

view of the present life, although their mindset was deeply tinted with the negation of this world. There emerged the mushrooming of new specialized occupations and workers in performing arts such as women of the *demimonde*, *nō* and *sarugaku* players, doctors and yin-yang diviners, and in various handicrafts such as blacksmith, makers of Japanese swords, carpenters, *fusuma* makers, or plasterers. They devoted themselves to occupational and artistic activity as *kyūdō beh*avior, pursuing the spiritual completion of skills. Those who engaged in *kyūdō* activities or *shokunō-min* (*min* means people and *shokunō* means specialized skill in occupation) were given the generic name of 'fellows of specialty' (*michi-michi-no yakara*), where *yakara* means fellows and *michi* means *dō* in the word of *kyūdō* (Amino 1984). In other words, it must be noted that the social division of labor was accelerated during the period owing to the diffusion of standards of conduct related to *kyūdō* behavior. A monumental study of the social division of labor is Amino (1980), which describe the activities of various artisans vividly and the drastic change in society during the Southern and Northern Dynasties period. Amino ascribes the change to the import of foreign (Chinese) currency during the period, which caused active economic behavior, but the import of currency was at least partly a result of the export of various handicraft goods, so the fundamental determinant should be the *kyūdō* behavior that elevated productivity and the quality of the goods.

The enormous efforts made by the retired emperor Go-Shirakawa (1127–92) devoted to training in singing *Imayō*, popular songs enjoyed during the Heian era, is vividly described in *Ryōjin-hishō*, authored and edited by the ex-emperor himself.[45] It is interesting to know that he was motivated to engage in this training to get over the process of transmigration safely and attain enlightenment after his death (Baba 2010, pp. 299–310).

The samurai were also involved in the training of martial arts to attain enlightenment following Zen thought. The *Gorin-sho* book, written by the distinguished expert in martial arts at the end of the Warring States period, Miyamoto Musashi (circa 1584–1645), describes the essence of his skills in battles, referring to Buddhist concept of relativity and contending the importance of the mindset in which doubts were waved off (Kamata 1986, pp. 31–33, 242–246). That the concept of relativity (*kū*) is related to activism in the Mahayana Buddhism in Japan was emphasized also in Umebara (1996, p. 305).

4.3.1.2 Japanese-Style Arts

The Muromachi era is well known for the emergence of so-called Japanese-style arts. In addition to the tea ceremony and flower arrangement, such arts as linked-verse, Indian ink painting, Japanese-style painting as well as Japanese-style architecture and gardening were born under the ample support of the Muromachi *bakufu* and shoguns, who tried to obtain the trust of the aristocracy and the imperial court

---

[45]The original and modern Japanese version of *Ryōujin-hishō* is given in Baba (2010) with detailed notes.

through active involvement in artistic salon society activities. Old Buddhist temples played a substantial role in this regard as providers of logistics and the spiritual backbone for artistic activities. It is our contention that the true contribution of the old Buddhist sects in the development of Japanese society during this period lay not in their economic-political power as owners of large manors, but as the supporters of the cultural development of society. Yamazaki (1990) claims that both in the tea ceremony and flower arrangement, progress in skill comprised only the intermediate aim of the arts; the final aim of art performance was in the pursuit of the moral completion of the personality and individuality (p. 66). In this way, the *kyūdō* principle became widely shared not only among aristocrats and *daimyos* but also among commoners. People devoted themselves to the pursuit of artistic skills backed by Buddhist spirits ultimately aimed at enlightenment. Many Japanese lived their lives either as specialists in occupational activities of production or as members of consumption groups to express themselves in the artistic society. Incidentally, there appeared specialists in the evaluation of the degree of progress in artistic achievements. Yoshida Kenkō (circa 1283–after 1352), famous for his essay 'Tsurezure-gusa',[46] is typical of such persons. His essay gives abundant examples of people in the city of Kyoto who had acquired distinguished skills in some specific field and were deeply respected by others. It is also well known that Zeami (circa 1363–1443) polished his creative skills in *nō* play and established *nō* as a high-level performance art in a salon presided over by shogun Asikaga Yoshimitsu (reign 1368–94) and Ashikaga Yoshimochi (reign 1394–1423). The first book authored by Zeami, *Hūshikaden*,[47] on the training and production of *nō* play, describes how he devoted enormous efforts to polish his skills in response to the criticism and appreciation in the theater attended by the shogun and his housemen.

4.3.1.3 Weakened Separation of the Profane and the Sacred

Not only the emergence of the new lifestyle based on *kyūdō* behavior, the new Buddhism brought about a drastic change in the worldview, or in the way to see this world, in the sense of weakening the separation of the profane and the sacred.

In Buddhism in general, the present life is viewed as simply negative from the viewpoint of transmigration. However, the negative view of the present life did not imply a negative and passive attitude toward the present ordinary life. This was because the profane aspects of the present life were rigorously separated from the sacred aspects in traditional Buddhist thinking, in which the pursuit of salvation was only possible by secluding oneself from ordinary life and becoming a priest. Separation of the sacred from the profane was the essential wisdom of Buddhism historically, but this wisdom was discarded in Mahayana Buddhism, and hence in Kamakura new Buddhism in Japan, in which the pursuit of the religious salvation of men on the streets in the profane world came to be the main task of Buddhism.

---

[46]See Nishio and Yasuraoka (1928).

[47]Ichimura (2011) gives an original and modern Japanese version of *Hūshikaden*.

The emergence of *kyūdō* behavior implies the sanctification of this world. Together with the influence of the *hongaku* theory, it introduced the attitude to regard the present life and life-after-death with the same Buddhist insight. In other words, the teaching to pursue Buddhist truth in the actual occupational life implied the recommendation of the attitude to see this world and the future world through the same eyeglass. New Buddhism introduced a tendency for people to look at present-day life simultaneously with future life. Since in every religion the future is regarded as sacred, this meant that this world was seen with some tint of sacredness. In this way, the rigorous separation of the sacred from the profane that characterized the traditional Buddhist stance was substantially weakened. In other words, the pursuit of sacred value in present value came to be the standard of conduct.

When the separation of the sacred from the profane is weakened in the thinking of people, the various benefits of the present life, including material gains or present-day contractual relationships, tend to lose their meaning, and this could exert a significant blow to the stability and sound workings of the actual institutional arrangements of the socio-economy. Contractual relationships such as the feudal master–vassal relationship came to be regarded as of lower value compared with *kyūdō* behavior, which was related to the status of life in the future, and self-salvation behavior in conflict resolution in line with *kyūdō* behavior came to be regarded as something of higher value. We believe that this attitude of Mahayana Buddhism intensified by Kamakura new Buddhism had important implications for the aggravation of social stability during the Warring States period.

4.3.1.4 Changes in the Internalized Beliefs: Worldview Based on Others Nearby

The easy practice principle of Kamakura new Buddhism had a radical impact on the worldview of the Japanese people in the medieval period. Individuals, who were assigned a task to arrive at enlightenment or at least to move to a good world in transmigration through *kyūdō* behavior in their daily occupational lives, came to pay closer attention to the human relationships with others nearby and, consequently, in their worldview, others nearby came to have more significance than before. Through the process of embeddedness in moral codes, conventions and standards of conduct, this impact on the worldview had a continued influence on individuals after the medieval age and even in modern times.

In every society at every time, people are interested in the relationship with others nearby. Why was the relationship with others nearby so important in Japan? There are two reasons for this; one is related to the fundamental teaching of Buddhism from the time of early Buddhism, and the other additional reason is related to the development of the new Buddhism in Japan.

Let us start with the fundamental teaching of Buddhism. In Buddhism destiny in the future world is not predetermined, by an omnipotent God for example, but is determined by the efforts of believers in this world. If a Buddhist tried hard and succeeded to understand the structure of the world in the same way as was understood by the Buddha, he would be able to attain enlightenment and live in the Pure Land (*jyōdo*) in his life after death. Since such good fortune is not easy to obtain, he lives usually in one of the six realms in transmigration and seeks a better realm in which to live. The effort in this world is measured by the stock of *karma* at the time of his death, which is a sum of accumulated amount of *karma* in the past lives and the additional amount of *karma* accumulated in this world. He can increase the stock of good (bad) *karma* by being engaged in good (bad) deeds or could decrease the stock by accepting good (bad) retribution of *karma*. *Karma* as a result of deeds caused by earthly desires (*bonnō*), such as indulgence in love or beauty, craving for life, hatred and malice and the like, is caused by interactions with others nearby.[48] This is the basic reason for a Buddhist to have a severe concern for relationships with others nearby. Relationships with others nearby are of decisive importance because they determine the lives of believers not only in this world but also in their future lives after death.

How consideration for others nearby influences the internalized belief, especially on the worldview, could be understood as a simulation in the mind models of individuals. Since the stock of *karma* is decisive in the determination of life in the next world, and the stock of *karma* could be changed only by conduct in this world, individuals are motivated to implement a simulation as to how their conduct and relationships with others nearby affect the stock of *karma*. The relationships with others nearby came to be a clue to judge the degree of progress and to evaluate the adequacy of the methods chosen to arrive at enlightenment or to evaluate the level of the stock of *karma* at the end of his life. Individuals in the medieval period of Japan lived their present lives always with an image of the Pure Land as well as of three bad worlds (*aku-shu*) in transmigration, especially hell. In this regard, it seems to be important to note that, when individuals were reborn in hell, they were believed to retain their memory of their present lives.[49] Individuals were considered to be able to think about the reasons for the accumulation of *karma* in the life before their death. With this mechanism in mind, individuals were able to implement a simulation of the lives in the hell and the effects of their interactions with others nearby on the accumulation of *karma* that might cause their rebirth in hell. This is the basic reason why the relationships with others nearby influences the internal mental models. It follows that, owing to the practice of simulation in the mind set of individuals, the

[48] Earthly desires and passions (*bonnō*) cause bad deeds and consequently the accumulation of bad *karma*, which causes suffering (pain). In Buddhism, there are eight kind of suffering: in addition to the pain caused by birth (rebirth), ageing, disease and death, the pain arising from separation from intimate persons, the pain of having hatred and malice toward others, the pain of not having things others have, and the pain arising from existence with the physical and spiritual entity. From this taxonomy, it could be understood that out of the eight pains, the latter four pains are concerned with the relationship with others nearby with whom individuals meet in the present world.

[49] Ikoma (2018) contends that, while at the time of rebirth as humans, individuals do not retain memory of their past lives, in the case of rebirth in hell (or as hungry spirits), they retain memory of the present life. This is because rebirth in hell occurs not from the placenta of their mothers (*taishō*) but as a result of a phenomenon of sudden birth as adults (*keshō*) (Ikoma 2018, pp. 3–5).

internalized belief about the structure of the world, in which individuals live, came to be mainly composed of relationship with others nearby.

An additional reason for the serious concern with others nearby for the Japanese lies in the development of Buddhism in Japan. In Japan, following the emphasis on the concept of merit transfer (*ekō*) in Mahayana Buddhism, practice in Buddhism came to be carried on in occupational lives following the *kyūdō* principle. The interaction with others nearby in occupational life came to have religious meaning, especially with respect to the possibility of enlightenment through the concept of merit transfer (*ekō*) of qualitative transformation. The possibility of enlightenment was originally a matter related to purely intellectual activities to pursue the meaning of the structure and mechanism of the world through meditation and studying. The theory of merit transfer converted the intellectual capability to understand the structure of the world nurtured through the devotion in occupational activities to be counted as religious merits. As is explained above, Kajiyama (1983) emphasizes the nature of the *ekō* of qualitative transformation as conversion of profane activities into intellectual capability to understand the world (*issai-chi he no ekō*).

While the accumulation of *karma* affects the life within transmigration through determining the realm to live, merit transfer affects the possibility of escaping from transmigration by enlightenment. It follows that in Japan after the religious reform the interaction with others nearby came to have a significant influence on the entire destiny of individual believers: the realm to live in transmigration as well as the possibility of enlightenment. In terms of the incentive for economic activity, since the arena for the behavior to seek enlightenment shifted from monasteries and temples to the shop floors of occupation activities, the economic and social activities of the Japanese after the Kamakura era came to be implemented under the stronger influence of concerns with others nearby. In addition to the profit and consumption utilities, the relationship with others nearby in the process of devotion to occupational activities came to have deep and intense effects on economic incentives in Japan after the religious reform.

It seems worthwhile to point out that the emphasis on others nearby in the internalized belief in Japan stands in clear contrast with the prohibition, with the concept of idolatry, on concern for others nearby in the teachings of Calvinism in the Occident. At the time of religious reform in the Occident, the arena for religious practice shifted from churches to daily lives. People came into direct contact with God by means of reading the bible without the intermediation of churches. At the same time, in Calvinist teaching in particular, to enhance the glory of God, intimate relationships with others nearby or contact with and interest in other creations of God, was prohibited for the reason that excessive concern about the mere creations of God was an act to degrade the glory of God the creator. 'Any emotional – that is, not rationally determined – personal one-to-one relationship easily falls under the suspicion of idolatry' and, as Baxter claimed, 'it is an irrational act and not fit for a rational creature to love any one farther than reason will allow us – It very often taketh up men's minds so as to hinder their love of the God' (Weber 1905, p. 137).

There seems to be a plethora of literature about the enormous influence of this teaching on the behavior of the Puritans through converting the basic worldview from the village community traditionally organized on customs and personal connection to the one that is based on the keen abhorrence of idolatry and the rejection of 'irrational' intimacy with others nearby. Spufford (1974) gives a vivid description of the behavior of the Puritans based on this principle in seventeenth-century England, leading to the dissolution of village communities (pp. 319–350). Collinson (1983) also describe the process of the formation of Puritan sects in English villages during the sixteenth century (pp. 1–17). Chapter 5 of Walzer (1965) describes how the Puritans disapproved of any reliance upon connections like local loyalty, kinship, familial alliance and marriage, and dissociated themselves from crucial traditional relationship including their family. 'Like the state, the family was viewed as a divine institution, established at God's preemptory command, which men entered by contract. The contract produced a society "by the good government whereof, God's glory may be advanced"' (p. 188). Weber's assertion, that the denial of relationships with others nearby resulted in adherence to the theory of utilitarianism that emphasizes the welfare of the majority or the public, because it is the most free from suspicion of idolatry,[50] seems to be worth noting in this context.

This seems to be a radical difference in the outcome of religious reform in Japan and the Occident. In Japan, people intensified the relationship and concerns with others nearby, whereas in the Occident relationship with others were restricted and people were recommended to be individualistic with each other, and to have more concern with humans as a whole, the public and other societal collectives.

Incidentally, our idea of the difference on the emphasis on others nearby and the public is related to the assertion by Abe (1995) that, while there is a strong concern about the concept of *seken*, there is no notion of society. *Seken* is a concept used traditionally by the Japanese to express the abstract group composed of others nearby. Abe contended that since *seken* is not organized by the intention and initiative of individuals, it is a given condition for individuals, and that because the main principles that govern the concept of *seken* is seniority and reciprocity, the concept of *seken* explains the insufficient respect for the dignity of individuality in Japanese society. It must be noted that Abe emphasized too much the autonomous repressive effects of *seken* and the passivity of individuals. The concept of *seken* fails to take the synergy effect with concerns with others nearby with *kyūdō* behavior into consideration. It seems to be more pertinent to use the concept of concerns with others nearby combined with *kyūdō* behavior rather the the *seken* concept. Abe's conclusion about the lack of dignity of individuality seems to be too stereotypical.

Abe's assertion reminds us of the definition of Japanese culture by Benedict (1946) as the culture of shame compared with the culture of sin in the Occident. As is discussed in Chap. 1, Benedict's definition of Japanese culture failed to take into consideration the important other side of the coin, that the concerns about shame are closely related to the strong concerns about the establishment of the

[50]The *utilitarian* version, that the economic cosmos should serve the purpose of the 'good of the many, the common good, etc' is a consequence of the idea that any other interpretation leads to (aristocratic) idolatry, or that it serves not God's glory, but the carnal 'cultural' purposes (Weber 1905, p. 183).

self that was nurtured in *kyūdō* behavior. As is typically seen in the spirit of the samurai since the medieval era, Japanese culture regards individualistic behavior with high esteem.[51] Fukuzawa Yukichi developed a highly insightful argument that the Japanese, endowed with high level of intellectuality at the individual level, is not good at collective behavior, whereas Western people are good at implementing collective and group action although they are not necessarily ranked at a high level in general in terms of intellectuality (Fukuzawa 1875, p. 115). Our argument developed so far about the difference of the internalized belief between the Japanese and the Westerner has an important bearing on the assertion of Fukuzawa. The weakness of the Japanese in collective action pointed out by Fukuzawa is deeply rooted in the worldview of the Japanese that respects the interaction of others nearby and largely disregards the contribution to the abstract concept of the public.

As we have already touched upon in Chap. 2, the difference between the emphasis on others nearby in Japan and on the public in the Occident in the internalized belief, especially with respect to the economic worldview, has significance to the difference between Japan and the Occident with respect to the method to arrange coordination among individuals and ordering the market: culture in Japan and institutions in the Occident. We believe the difference is deeply related to the cultural tradition between the two regions. Since the coordination of behavior by means of institutions is susceptible to free rider problems, the establishment of institutions must be implemented by mobilizing the participation of the majority of individuals concerned. The worldview and the propensity of Occidental individuals to emphasize the welfare of the public is highly suitable and economical for this purpose, whereas in Japan where individuals are mainly interested in others nearby it is not easy to mobilize the participation of large numbers of individuals at once. In Japan, where the internalized belief regarding the worldview is constructed by the relationship among others nearby, it is more efficient and less costly to coordinate the behavior of individuals by means of incremental diffusion of moral codes and standards of conduct.

4.3.2 Affirmation and Negation of This World

In the thinking of the Japanese before the introduction of Buddhism, Shinto doctrine composed of affirmation of the present life and the monistic and continuous worldview had been dominant. People considered that they could travel freely to and from the underground world (*yomi-no-kuni*) where souls of the dead reside, the present world on the ground (*ashihara-no-nakatsu-kuni)* and the heavenly world (*takama-ga-hara*) of gods in the sky. Present life or this world was accepted without any skepticism, and people never looked for the ideal world beyond the present world in which they lived. The advent of Buddhism destroyed this concept of continuity and prepared the way for the emergence of the negation of the present life toward the

[51] Ikegami (1995) claims that individualism in the medieval era comes about in tandem with the sense of honor.

end of the ancient age.[52] Partly owing to the spread of the End of Buddhism law (the *mappō* theory) that predicted the arrival of the age when the teachings of Buddhism were neglected, the negation of the present life became the main thought of the time toward the end of the ancient age.[53]

Ienaga (1940) contends, however, that the middle ages of Japan were characterized by the strong sense of the affirmative view of this world that coexisted with the negation of this world, claiming that the 'medieval era of Japan was an age of the concept of absolute affirmation established on the notion of absolute negation' (p. 109). It is contended that the ancient concept of affirmation of this world emphasized in Shintoism regained support by individuals after the denial by Buddhism; because of the impact of Buddhism that denied the present world, the affirmative attitude, indigenously held by individuals since the ancient age, was reconfirmed more strongly during the Muromachi era.[54]

Our analysis so far seems to support the duality proposition of Ienaga. We believe that the affirmation of this world was intensified by the evolution of two new notions related to Buddhism; the *hongaku* theory that recommended to accept this world 'as it is' and *kyūdō* behavior born by the impact of Kamakura new Buddhism. The theory of 'to live as it is', or *ji-jyōjyū*, contended by the *hongaku* theory, was interpreted as follows. That humans are living in the world of transmigration is a grave fact that one is unable deny, but nevertheless we should not be concerned with the world in the future too much. It is important to live 'now' positively on the assumption that the present world, however immutable it seems to be, represents the only eternal world. *Kyūdō* behavior, born as a result of the emergence of Kamakura new Buddhism, approved to implement religious practices at the scene of ordinary occupational activity. Since this enabled poor individuals to practice and search for enlightenment, the incentive to practice, as well as affirmative attitudes to daily life in the present life, were enhanced.

The duality of affirmation and negation during the medieval era in Japan has been widely noted by researchers. While Koizumi Yagumo (1896) and Ikoma (2018) emphasize that people lived with serious concerns with past lives in fear of the accumulation of *karma*, and Yokoi (1975, vol. 2) contends that the optimistic attitude and affirmation of the present world by the Muromachi people has an aspect of the paradoxical expression of the serious misery of life in the Warring States society,

---

[52]Umebara (1996) claims that, through quoting the notion of *gensō-ekō* of Shinran, the continuity theory continued to be alive after the advent of Buddhism. This seems to be wrong because *gensō-ekō* is possible after the completion of hard training in another world, so that it belongs to a different category from the concept of automatic and free travelling between this and another world in Shinto.

[53]In this theory, the time after the birth of Buddhism was divided into three phases: the period when the rules of Buddhism were strictly respected, the period when individuals did not seek enlightenment even if Buddhist rules were respected on the surface, and the period when the rules of Buddhism were completely neglected. It was claimed in Japan that the third period began in the year 1052.

[54]Ienaga himself explains this duality by offsetting the effect of the inevitability of the deeds of killing living things by humans, that cause the negative connotation of the present life, by means of the deed of the *sesshu-fusha* (the life of living things served for humans is respected and celebrated) (p. 98).

so that people were motivated to 'celebrate' the present life in order to overcome their misery and pray for salvation. On the other hand, Satake (1973) asserts that folk tales in the medieval age concluded with happy ends without exception. Based on this finding, he concludes that the attitude of individuals during the period was significantly influenced by the traditional affirmative attitude of the Japanese since the ancient age. Quoting the finding of Satake, Sakurai (1996) denies the influence of Buddhism on the lifestyle of ordinary people in the medieval age, and contends that the aesthetic lifestyle of aristocrats, based on the sense of mutability as is depicted in *Turezure-gusa*, was irrelevant to the actual lifestyle of ordinary people who were optimistically engaged in the pursuit of material gains (pp. 337–375).

Both assertions seem to be right. Koizume, Ikoma and Yokoi focus on the internalized part of the mental model of the medieval Japanese, while Satake and Sakurai are talking about the behavioral characteristics of the people. With respect to the behavioral part, the *kyūdō* principle and *hongaku* theory are responsible for the positive and affirmative tendency. However, behind the influence of the *hongaku* theory and *kyūdō* principle were deep and long-term concerns with *karma* and transmigration in the internalized mental attitude. In other words, the duality of the mindset in the sense of the negation of the present life in the internalized part and the affirmation of the present life in the behavioral part characterize the structure of the individual mindset of medieval Japan.

It is important to note that the duality and the dilemma of the incentive system lay behind the thinking of Yoshida Kenkō, the author of *Turezure-gusa*; individuals in medieval Japan lived their behavioral lives positively, but at the same time retained deep concerns about their past and future lives in their internal mindset. It is quite easy to focus on the behavioral part only, since it enables one to write a coherent story by use of orthodox economic theory. However, in the context of long-term historical analysis, the neglect of internalized culture is liable to give rise to a serious misunderstanding of the nature of the Japanese history.

The Kamakura era was a time when nascent economic growth started in Japan. Owing to *kyūdō* behavior, occupational specialization was enhanced, and the social division of labor was accelerated. With many kinds of specialists producing diversified products, the urban population increased, giving rise to various businesses facilitating transaction and commercial activities. Wealthy individuals also emerged mainly out of the commercial and financial activities. As a result, it is claimed that in medieval Japan the desire of the individual was either to became rich or to be distinguished in occupational and artistic activities (Matsumoto 1956; Yokoi 1975). It is interesting to note that wealth was quite often associated with virtue; rich individuals were called virtuous men (*utoku-no-hito*). In this concept also, we are inclined to detect the duality of the mindset of the medieval Japanese. It is a wishful evaluation of competitive mechanism in the market economy based on the internal part of culture, from which an observation could be derived that wealthy individuals are wealthy because of the retribution of good *karma* accumulated from previous lives as well as in this world. It is also possible to say that the affirmative tendency and positive attitude toward the market economy emerged because it is helpful for the attainment of enlightenment. From this way of reasoning, the optimistic attitude to profit maximization emphasized by Sakurai could be construed as a representation of the concept of merit transfer that promoted *kyūdō* behavior by means of the hard practice in productive activities and the good deed to others nearby in commercial transactions. The behavioral part of culture is under the strong influence of the internalized culture in medieval Japan.

4.3.3 The Ie *as the Institutionalization of* Kyūdō *Behavior*

The new lifestyle in ordinary life related to the *kyūdō* principle and the new arts that emerged under the influence of *kyūdō* behavior had a persistent influence on Japanese culture well into the period after the Meiji Restoration. The main reason for this lies in the informal institutionalization of the mechanism of succession of human capital accumulated in lifestyle and arts activity. As the skills in the new lifestyle and the new art activity are accumulated as the human capital of the people, there occurred the incentive to hand down the skills from generation to generation and to contrive special informal institutional system for the purpose. Toward the early Kamakura period, those who were engaged in handicraft occupations came to have special production facilities of their own and to organize the *ie* as a device to train disciples and pass on skills to future generations. Skills were transmitted to the most talented disciple, not to the one related by blood relationship (Wakita 1988). The founder of *nō* play, Zeami, also wrote in his *Husikaden* 'that skill needs to be transferred to the most talented disciples not to sons tied by blood relationship without talent' (Ichimua 2011, p. 80). In the same book, he wrote that the *ie* is not a building or an organization but should be defined as an entity to be continued, and the *hito* (man) is not a human being but must be defined as those embodying knowledge (p. 210).

The origin of the *ie* could be traced back to the *On-i-no-sei* in the ancient *ritsuryo* era, touched above. In the bureaucratic system of *ritsuryō*, official positions were classified by the skills needed to fulfil particular functions in the bureaucracy. Satō (1983) points out the importance of the emergence of the sub-contracting system by aristocratic clans during the ninth to tenth centuries. To monopolize profits accrued to special branches of the bureaucracy, some clans accumulated specific skills and inherited the know-how within the clans. For example, the *ie* of *hō* (law) meant a family of experts in judicial business. The official position of the police and judicial section (*kebiisi*) was assigned to a particular clan of the *hō-ka*, and the position was handed down in the same clan patrimonially. Those with ample knowledge in poetry or etiquette at the palace were assigned a special role related to education and ceremony, and this position was also monopolized by a particular clan, and hereditarily transferred from generation to generation. Clans with special skills in arithmetic obtained hereditary positions in the tax section of the Treasury. In this ancient system, the *ie* functioned as a system of inheriting official rank and position, and the skills were transmitted hereditarily as a qualifying condition for the hereditary succession of official ranks. It is important to note that the relationship of skill and position with the *ie* has been reversed in medieval society. In the ancient system, official positions were the target of succession by means of the *ie*, but in the medieval system, skill was the aim of succession utilizing the *ie* system. This shift of the emphasis to skill is a mirror image of the drastic change in lifestyle that occurred in the medieval age. Human capital accumulated through the *kyūdō* principle came to be considered to have value of its own to be inherited.

The *ie* system spread to the samurai class during the medieval age. The conventional theory about the historical emergence of the samurai class had been that the class had been formed at first among indigenous landlords. Those who had accumulated land through reclamation were thought to have come to be armed to defend their territory from invasion. However, this theory about the rise of the samurai from the landowner class came to be regarded as contradicting the actual image of the early samurai class in several respects. First was that their armaments were very heavy and powerful from the start, in contrast with the imagined stopgap armaments of landowners. Second was the prominence of their skill on the battlefield. Especially, cavalry battles with the northern Ezo tribes required a high level of skill in shooting arrows from galloping horses, and this technique is difficult for landlords to acquire without training. Third was the actual history of the rise of the samurai class from the aristocrats delegated officially to periphery territories as the '*ie* of *tsuwamono* (soldier)' or specialized military power, who had military capacity comparable with that of the provincial governors' offices (*kokuga*). For these reasons it has become the common understanding that the samurai emerged as occupational groups specialized in military skills, which was patrimonially inherited (Satō 1974; Kasaya 1999). In other words, according to recent theory on the origin of the samurai, it is incorrect to believe that landlords became samurai from the start, but rather the samurai as an occupational group became landlords gradually through their struggles with aristocrats. It must be noted that this new theory does not contradict the fact that some or a considerable part of the increase in the number of samurai thereafter was due to the arming of landowners.

Moreover, there is good reason to believe that the samurai's preference for human capital in comparison with physical capital increased during the medieval period and this accelerated the formation of the *ie* by the samurai class. During the years before the Southern and Northern Dynasties period, the samurai group was composed of highly individualistic members, who were tied by personality and led by the leaders selected according to their ability in battle. Actual battle was centered on man-to-man fighting among cavaliers. As the battle skills specific to a group were accumulated and the battle style shifted from man-to-man fighting to collective fighting involving many infantrymen after the period of the Southern and Northern Dynasties, however, the training of infantrymen with respect to martial arts and the tactics of the manipulation of troops specific to each samurai group became more important. The *ie* system came to be increasingly prevalent among the samurai class as a method to inherit human capital specific to each *ie* related to the military tactics of battle. In this way, the institutionalization of skill inheritance accumulated through *kyūdō* behavior also occurred in the samurai class.

In summary, the samurai class was born as one of *shokunō-min*, 'fellows of specialty' (*michi-michi-no yakara*) specialized in *kyūdō* behavior in military skills and the *ie* system diffused among the samurai as a method to inherit and accumulate human capital from generation to generation. It will be argued in Chaps. 5 and 6 that the *ie* system spread to the farmer and merchant classes in the Tokugawa period, and this phenomenon is also related to human capital accumulation.

4.3.4 The Dialectic Process

The influence of *kyūdō* behavior was intensified partly because it radically changed the lifestyle of people, and partly because there occurred the informal institutionalization of the accumulation and inheritance of human capital through the *ie* system. It must be noted also that the social appreciation for *kyūdō* behavior itself was intensified as a norm of occupational behavior that raised effort levels and hence the productivity of the economy. It could be argued that the rise of this positive effect on the macroeconomy was possible because the impacts of new Buddhism on the *kyūdō* principle were intensified through a sort of dialectic process.

In the following two chapters it will be argued that the socio-economic impacts of *kyūdō* behavior went through the following three stages. At first, the new belief that one needed to be involved in *kyūdō* behavior to attain the benefits of salvation occurred only in the minds of the elite disciples of the new Buddhism. There occurred substantial changes in the lifestyle and worldview among the elites and the people living in the capital city in the Kyoto area. They were involved in *kyūdō* behavior and led their lives in order to attain distinguished and specialized skills. As a result, the social division of labor progressed rapidly, and new arts and Japanese-style culture emerged in aristocratic and samurai society partly owing to the support of the large temples related to the established Buddhist circle. Moreover, these changes caused diversity and complexity in socio-economic attitudes and behavior among people as a result of occupational diversity.

Secondly, when the mindset that respected *kyūdō* behavior spread to the masses nationwide, the progress of occupational specialization and the accelerated social division of labor caused serious confusion in human relationships, partly due to aggravated information asymmetry and partly due to the absence of adequate moral codes in Buddhism, which was effective only in regulating human relationships in a homogeneous static society.

Through causing a deterioration of the trust levels of society, the complexity of human relationships and the heterogenization of society gave rise to serious social turmoil. Increased information asymmetry in the heterogenized socio-economy was typically seen in the misfunctioning of the relation-based governance system of the samurai government, the Muromachi *bakufu*. The deterioration of trust in the socio-economy was enhanced as the conflict in value systems between the aristocratic and samurai classes intensified, bringing about various moral hazards and adverse selections. Moreover, the concept of merit transfer, *ekō*, led to the aspiration for homogenous society among believers of the *Jyōdo-shin-shū* of Shinran in order to share the merit of Amitabha (the merit transfer of directional transformation), so that the sharing doctrine gave rise to the large-scale *ikki* uprisings in central Japan. Not only religious movements but also direct economic movements requesting lower tax levels and the cancelation of financial obligations (*tokusei-rei*) became prevalent. Likewise, due to the sanctification of the present life, the feudal system went into a critical situation as the samurai tended to neglect feudal contracts and seek salvation by themselves through organizing voluntary groups based on various interpersonal relationships (*en*). Turmoil and warfare during the Warring States period occurred in this way.

The main cause of confusion during the period lay in the defects in the mindset of the people caused by the inadequacy of the moral codes of Buddhism, which was unable to provide social standards of conduct suitable for the accelerated social division of labor. It seems that there emerged a sort of disappointment about the social effects of the *kyūdō* principle. Social conflict and turmoil, in the Muromachi era especially during the Warring States period, thus led to the conviction among the masses that new workable moral codes were urgently needed for the recovery of trust levels and social security.

Thirdly, out of the confusion that lasted more than a century, the social desire for new and workable moral discipline that could effectively resolve the conflicts was finally realized by the establishment of the Tokugawa *bakufu*. The radical change in social belief caused by the failure or turmoil related to Buddhism had significant positive effects on economic success in Tokugawa era. New workable moral codes were developed by the intentional efforts by the *bakufu*, the samurai and private intellectuals, giving rise to new standards of conduct suitable for the advanced social development of labor.

The alleviation of information asymmetry owing to the standardization of conduct led to a reduction of transaction costs, giving rise to economic growth led by commerce. The growth was accompanied by the enhanced effort levels and this brought about new and revised belief in *kyūdō* behavior. As the new standards of conduct were disseminated and became shared by the broad masses, the value of effort levels and *kyūdō* behavior were reevaluated. The initial Buddhism-based belief in the *kyūdō* principle at the individual level that emerged during the Kamakura era was finally converted into the social belief in the Tokugawa era, and, while the initial impacts on the socio-economy during the Kamakura era were confined to the self-conscious elites, in the final impacts during the Tokugawa era, *kyūdō* behavior became shared among the broad populace, including farmers and merchants. In summary, there occurred the social reaffirmation of *kyūdō* behavior, and the impact of new Buddhism was finally and firmly established in the Tokugawa era.

Alexis de Tocqueville pointed out a similar dialectic process at the individual level in relation to the right of free discussion and assembly in America. It is contended that the development of the human beliefs in the right of free discussion is guaranteed in the following way. Quite often, people tend to believe in a new idea quite firmly because they do not understand the real meaning of the idea. After some time, when there occurs objection or disagreement, they become skeptical about the idea. When they have overcome the skepticism, they become more convinced of the idea (Nora 2010). In Japan, historically, a similar dialectic process occurred at the level of society as a whole. Practice simplification born out of the drive for the salvation of the masses of new Buddhism brought about *kyūdō* behavior among the masses. There occurred significant skepticism about the social effects of the *kyūdō* principle, however, as society moved from a homogeneous and underdeveloped society characterized by low levels of social division of labor to a heterogeneous society with high levels of social division of labor. The method of organizing solidarity in society shifted from the mechanical one based on the recognition of similarity with each other to the organic one based on overall occupational specialization and the social division of labor, as described in Durkheim (1893). The accelerated specialization of occupational activity gave rise to significant information asymmetry in the market economy. Faced with the significant rise in distrust in society due to information asymmetry, the skepticism about *kyūdō* behavior was intensified and the distrust in society culminated in the turmoil of the Warring States period during the late fourteenth to the sixteenth century. The skepticism about *kyūdō* behavior and the turmoil in society was finally overcome in the Tokugawa era owing to the development of a new moral system suitable for the high degree of social development of labor. At this stage *kyūdō* behavior brought about significant benefits to the economy in the form of enhanced productivity.

Appendix 1: The Basic Logic of Enlightenment (*Satori*) in Buddhism

To help understand the process of the emergence of Kamakura new Buddhism from the Mahayana Buddhism that came to Japan during the sixth century, this appendix presents the basic concepts of Buddhism with respect to the logic of enlightenment.

Negation of This World

In the Occident, before the arrival of Christianity to the Roman Empire, there prevailed an affirmative view of this world based on ancient Hellenism. Christianity introduced the Hebrew concept of the negation of this world that, under the ruling of the omnipotent God, everything in this world is of no value because it is God's creation. Similarly, in Japan before the arrival of Buddhism, there was an affirmative view of this world that this world was continuous with the future world (*takamagahara*) in the sky as well as the past world under the ground (*yomi-no-kuni*), and it was possible for humans to travel between the three worlds freely, so there was no need to worry about the life after death (Ienaga 1940).

The transfer of Buddhism brought in the conception of the negation of this world, composed of the view of this world as an unstable and impermanent world of transmigration. This world is to be denied because it is mutable and transitory and because it is full of suffering (*ku*) caused by accumulated *karma*.

Transmigration and View of Humans

The souls of living things (*ujyō*) were considered to be in a state of transmigration repeating birth and death, moving through six realms, composed of hell, the world of hungry spirits, animals, *asuras*, men (humans) and gods (heaven).[55] Among the six, the first three are good realms (*zen-shu*) and the remaining three are bad realms (*aku-shu*).[56]

Humans (men), *asuras* and animals live on the surface of the earth, hungry spirits in a layer near the surface, and hell lives in the deepest layer underground. In hell, the souls of living things suffer incessantly from torture and unendurable heat or cold. In the realm of hungry things, souls experience relentless thirst and hunger. When souls were in the state of animals, there is little chance of salvation because animals are destined to have far more excessive avarice than humans. *Asuras* are a sort of ogre, who live the life of warriors. God (heaven) leads a highly comfortable life. But the god is not the creator of the world, is not omniscient or omnipotent, and is still suffering from earthly desires and lives the life of transmigration. Humans also live in comfortable conditions. In the three worlds of *aku-shu* living things are suffering so bitterly they are unable to practice Buddhist teachings, while god (heaven) live such comfortable lives they tend to lose the inclination to practice. Therefore, humans are in the best condition to practice and escape transmigration through attaining enlightenment. For those living in *aku-shu*, it is impossible to be get enlightenment (*satori*)and escape the state of transmigration, and all they could hope is to escape the realms and live a life of *zen-shu*, obtaining the chance to gain enlightenment[57] (Sakurabe 1989).

Humans are considered to have all the desires and attachments, or avarice, that give rise to various sufferings. Pain is composed of pain from birth (rebirth), growing old, disease, and death, together with the four pains—the pain of separation from a beloved, the pain of living with persons whom one hates, the pain from being unable to obtain things one seeks, and the pain that inflicts the spiritual and physical components of humans. To attain enlightenment, one need to extinguish all greed and anger as well as attachments to this world through some kind of practicing.

---

[55] Incidentally, Buddhism also has the concept of physical worlds together with the world of living things. Physical worlds are often called vessel worlds (*utsuwa-seken*) or land worlds (*kokudo-seken*), and the world of living things is called the mass world (*shūjyō-seken*) or the living creature world (*ujyō-seken*). The latter world is composed of six realms in transmigration (heaven, god, man, *shura*, animal, hell) and four states in which buddhas reside. On the other hand, there is another concept that understands the world from basic elements. This is the concept of the five elements (*goun*) world. In this concept, both the physical world and the mass world is considered to be composed of material elements (*shiki*) and four spiritual elements (reception, representation, will and cognition).

[56] Ashura could be classified as a bad realm.

[57] Ikoma (2018) argues that, in medieval Japan, there were various mechanisms to help souls to get to better worlds and alleviate agony. New type of priests, *bosatsu*, in Mahayana Buddhism, especially the *jizo-bosatsu*, always moved around the realms of transmigration and helped souls to go to better realms. The *tsuizen-kuyō*, a ceremony for the soul of the dead implemented within 49 days of the death, is effective in alleviating the effects of bad *karma* accumulated by the dead. A memorial services (*kuyō*) in honor of the dead or killed animals is also effective to help them to go to the good realms.

Since the life of humans in this world is a temporary and impermanent time between life and death repeated in the process of transmigration, life in this world is of no value and should be negated. Although, among the six realms, the latter three (*zen-shu*) were relatively comfortable worlds, those living things in the three realms are always threatened by the danger to go to the former three realms (*aku-shu*), especially to hell. Differently from the hell of Christianity, hell in Buddhism is not a place to live permanently. Even if one happens to get out of hell, however, there always exists the possibility to go to hell again, and living things are always inflicted by the fear of returning to hell.

It is important to note that, while, by way of practicing good conduct and accumulating merits, it is possible to move from the uncomfortable worlds to the relatively comfortable worlds, one can never escape the process of transmigration. To escape transmigration, one needs to attain enlightenment (*satori*). Enlightenment is possible only when one is emancipated from earthly desires(*bonnō*) and understands the true mechanism of the world through the various methods described at 4.2.3.

Graveness of Karma and Retribution

The sources of suffering (*ku*) are conduct, especially toward others. In the process of transmigration, one interacts with many others nearby, and interactions, motivated by attachment and desire, give rise to the accumulation of bad or good *karma*. Suffering that comes from accumulated *karma* is the engine that drive the machine of transmigration (Sakurabe 1989). *Karma* is the accumulated conduct caused by earthly passions through lives in transmigration vis-à-vis others.

Good or bad (evil) *karma* is accumulated over time, and part of *karma* is eliminated by accepting retribution; good *karma* (*zen-gō*) is rewarded by good retribution (*zen-ka*) and bad *karma* (*aku-gō*) by bad retribution (*aku-ka*). One's welfare level in this world is determined by the accumulated amount of *karma* in the past. The *karma* in this world together with the accumulated past *karma* that did not receive retribution determines welfare in the future. During medieval Japan, everyone considered that they were carrying the burden of accumulated *karma* (Ikoma 2018).

There are three grave principles in the nature of *karma* (Hiraoka 2016). First is the inevitability of retribution. One cannot expect a decrease of *karma* without accepting retribution. Bad *karma* does not decrease unless one suffers bad retribution and good *karma* by good retribution. Second is the rule of self-responsibility or the principle of reaping the harvest of one's own sowing (*jigō-jitoku*). One must accept retribution by the *karma* caused by his deeds; it is not possible to transfer one's *karma* to others. Third is the principle of non-cancellation. It is not possible to offset bad *karma* by good *karma*, or vice versa. Accumulated bad *karma* can only be reduced by accepting bad retribution.

These three principles were strictly maintained in the early Buddhism that prevailed until the first century BC. However, in the Mahayana Buddhism that emerged after the first century AD, the second principle was significantly mitigated by the introduction of the concept of the *ekō*. The *ekō* of direction transformation allowed to use the merits accumulated by high moral persons such as the *bosatu*[58] for the elimination of the bad *karma* of others. For example, in *Jyōdo-shin-shū*, the merits accumulated by Amitabha, when he was a young priest called *hōzō-bosatsu*, was liberally transferred to believers.

The Buddhist Concept of the World and Enlightenment (*Satori*)

The Kū Concept and Enlightenment

In Mahayana Buddhism, enlightenment is attained when one gets rid of all momentary attachment to this world and earthly passions and desires from one's mindset, and this state of mind is achieved when one understands the impermanent structure of this world, the emptiness or relativity (*kū*). The concept of the *kū* originates from the proposition that the founder of Buddhism, Buddha, did not see any fixed elements in things of this world, and was totally free from attachment. In other words, the *kū* is nothing but the essence of the wisdom of Buddha.

Buddhist Concept of the World

According to the theory of early Buddhism before the development of Mahayana Buddhism, material and spiritual elements, called the *hō*, which constitute the world (cosmos), were in existence maintaining their substance and special character from the past, in the present and through the future, so that one can recognize the things in the past and experience the retribution of *karma* emanating from deeds in the past. In the theory of Mahayana Buddhism, however, the various elements that constitute the impermanent world (cosmos) interact with each other with some causality among elements, but each of them has no substance and fixed character, so they are in a state of relativity or emptiness (*kū*). The interaction of elements called *engi*, in which x is incurred by y and y is caused by x, is a sort of simultaneous equation system that is floating without initial conditions that fix the system as an anchor. This is because there is no notion of the creation of the universe in the cosmology of Buddhism, so it is difficult to specify the initial conditions at the time of creation. The whole system is floating without an anchor and everything is related by causality with each other but does not have its own substance.

In the world of Mahayana Buddhism, one must be engaged in religious practice in repeated transmigration and attain enlightenment when one could get rids of earthly attachment, and passions and desires, just like in the world of early Buddhism. The attainment of enlightenment is possible only when one has come to understand the relative and empty nature of the world (cosmos). In other words, those who are tangled in earthly desires and accumulating *karma* cannot recognize the 'impermanent structure of the world' characterized by the concept of the *kū*. The relative and empty nature of the world of the *engi* is understood only when one has got rid of earthly desires and passions, and attachments to things in this world or reached the mindset based on the wisdom of Buddha.

---

[58] Mahayana Buddhism introduced a new type of priest, the *bosatsu*, who are specialized in helping the attainment of enlightenment by other believers.

Appendix 2: The Theory of the Coexistence of Humans with Nature

With respect to the internalized part of the mental models regarding the relationship between humans and nature, Japanese culture is said to be characterized by a strong sense of the coexistence of humans and nature. This appendix briefly traces the origin of the thought.

One of the origins of the thought lies in Buddhism. The evidence lies in the theory of the Buddhahood of plants (the *sōmoku-jyōbutsu* theory). While Hokke-kyō transferred to Japan from India by way of China contained an assertion that all living things (*ujyō*) have innate Buddhahood because they have the mind to desire enlightenment, there is no theory that asserts that things that do not have mind (*hijyō*), like plants, could become Buddha. The Japanese version of the *hongaku* theory, however, came to assert that not only living things but also plants could attain enlightenment.[59] The document, *Sanjyūshi-ka-jyō-no-kotogaki*, contends that the Buddhahood of plants is realized not because plants came to have minds, and asserts that plants have Buddhahood with its mindless state intact. This is nothing but an application of the theory of the *ji-jyojyu*. In this sense, in terms of Buddhism, it seems that the coexistence theory was born in Japan, especially through the development of the *hongaku* theory.

The sense of the coexistence of humans and nature in Japan was due not only to the *hongaku* theory but also the innate sense of the awe of the violent power of nature. Since Japan is a country with frequent natural calamities, like typhoons and earthquakes, and since the Japanese have lived on the affluence of nature as a rice-producing race in monsoon Asia, the Japanese have long had indigenous reverence for nature. Even before the transfer of rice to Japan, the Japanese had a long history, of more than 15 centuries, to live on natural products in the mountains. This nurtured both respect for and awe of the mountains and brought about mountain worship. In Shintoism, although the world is created from chaos, there is no such thing as a creator, but some eight million gods have lived in various places and some gods were considered to exist since the time of creation. Various places such as mountains and seaside, designated as the residence of gods, became objects of divine worship because the gods had played the role to keep the places safe and productive.[60] It could be argued that the reverence for nature is closely related to the lack of the notion of creation by God in Japan. McGrath (1997) points out that, in the tradition of Christianity 'nature is not divine', because nature including celestial entities is created by God, so that nature is subordinate to God, and has no intrinsic divine nature (p. 127).

---

[59] Sueki (2015) claims that the application of the *hongalu* theory to plants was due to the theoretical contribution by Tendai-priest Annen (841–?).

[60] Out of four gods who existed since the time of creation, Amaterasu-ōmi-no-kami and Kamimusubi-no-kami were considered to live in Ise-gingū and Izumo-taisha respectively in Shintoist myth. The other two, Amenominakanushi-no-kami and Takamimusubi-no-kami, have no such designated residence.

Incidentally, it must be noted that in Buddhism also there is no idea of the creator. It is considered that there are one billion physical worlds like earth. Each world is considered to be composed of four continents surrounded by seas, with high mountains called Sumeru (Skt.) in the center, and repeating cyclical change from birth, continuation, extinction and disappearance with a cycle of 1.2 billion years. The creation of the world is carried out by the accumulated power of the *karma* of various living things (Sakurabe 1989).

Umebara (1996) contends that the origin of Shinto could be traced back to the religion held by the original hunting people during the Jyōmon era (hundredth to fourth century BC), who believed in the coexistence of humans and all animals and plants as well as holding the cyclical and continuous view of the present world and the future world. It seems to be worth noting that Shintoism was strengthened by the arrival and settlement of rice cultivation during the third century BC through the third century AD. This is because Shintoism is based not only on the desire for the coexistence of humans and nature but also on the sincere awe and veneration for the violent power of nature, which was all the more deeply engrained in customary lifestyle as people faced the violent impacts of the variability of nature on the harvest and hence on human life. As is contended by Watsuji (1935), the violent power exerted by nature nurtured the receptiveness and submission that characterize the ethnic traits of Asian peoples. Rice cultivation in monsoon Asia is characterized by the seasonality of labor demand as well as receptiveness to climate changes. Moreover, the Japanese archipelago is under the perpetual threat of earthquakes and the eruption of volcanos. The newly arrived Buddhism accepted this veneration of nature through the formation of mountaineering asceticism (*Shugen-dō*) as an influential sect of Buddhism.

Chapter 5
Institutions and Trust Level During the Muromachi Era

The theme of this chapter lies in the decline in the trust level and insufficient functioning of institutions in the medieval period society. It seems that the high level of trust in ancient society, when society was homogenous and various communal ties were prevalent, declined rapidly after the thirteenth century, finally leading to the turmoil of the Warring States period during the sixteenth century. During the Muromachi era, the functioning of existing institutions, such as the *bakufu* (samurai government) system and feudalism, went into difficulty and became increasingly inefficient, gradually becoming unable to fulfil the social functions assigned.

It is asserted that the main reasons for these phenomena are cultural; one is *kyūdō* behavior brought about by Buddhist reform and another is conflicts in the value systems between the samurai and aristocracy. The *Kyūdō* principle, born as a result of the practice simplification of Buddhist reform, aggravated information asymmetry in society. This was because the *kyūdō* principle brought about an increase in the demand for information through the acceleration of occupational specification. At the same time, the behavioral pattern based on the *kyūdō* principle, in which everyone is motivated to pursue sacred value by way of the concept of merit transfer, reduced the power of existing institutional arrangements to constrain the conduct of individuals by rules related to profane values. On the other hand, cultural conflicts between two social groups, the samurai and aristocrats, had significant impacts on the process, leading to the deterioration of institutions. The *bakufu* was obliged to devote significant efforts to the competition and conflicts with the aristocracy with respect to cultural and bureaucratic leadership, and feudalism was paralyzed by the phenomenon of *gekokujyō*, social upheaval where those below overcome those above, caused by the loss of integrity of samurai spirits owing to excessive concerns with family status, an aristocratic value.

First, it is contended that *kyūdō* behavior brought about a significant decline in the level of trust through its impacts on the social division of labor, and hence on informational asymmetry. The acceleration of the social division of labor occurred in tandem with the development of the market economy. The marketization of the economy was

J. Teranishi, *Culture and Institutions in the Economic Growth of Japan*, Studies in Economic History,
https://doi.org/10.1007/978-4-431-55627-5_5

accelerated partly by the decline of the *ritsuryō* system and partly by the rapid diffusion of *kyūdō* behavior as a result of practice simplification by the religious reform in Buddhism. The privatization of production facilities gave rise to the expansion of market transactions of commodities, and producers were motivated religiously by the *kyūdō* principle to try to be distinguished as specialized producers of commodities. It seems that the social division of labor proceeded at an unprecedented pace. Since everyone tried to produce his own specialized commodities, the informational requirements of purchasers and producers increased rapidly, consequently aggravating information asymmetry in society under the nascent information-processing system.

The aggravation of information asymmetry was due also to the defect in the Buddhist ethical codes. Since the existing Buddhist ethical codes, transferred to Japan, had been basically composed of behavioral rules required for training of priests in the circumstance of quiet and isolated monasteries, the rules could not provide adequate behavioral conventions and standards of conduct for the developed market economy. Human relationships in society under the accelerated social division of labor was too complicated to be ordered and standardized by existing Buddhist ethical codes. This was another factor that decreased the forecastability of the behavior of others.

Second, it is contended that cultural conflicts in the value system between the samurai and aristocracy was responsible for the disfunction of various institutions. It is well known that the inefficiency of political institutions of the government during the Muromachi era was related to the deterioration of trust due to information asymmetry. Disfunction caused by aggravation of information asymmetry was most serious with respect to the *bakufu* institution. Governance of the central government of the Muromachi *bakufu* deteriorated seriously to a critical level, consequently bringing about the disorder of the Warring States period. Owing to the absence of leadership of shoguns in collective decision making, the Muromchi *bakufu* adopted relationship-based politics in order to cope with aggravated information asymmetry, and this invited the serious downgrading of human relationships and the proliferation of corruption, incurring various forms of moral hazard. It is contended the confusion was aggravated by the emergence of duality in the value system of samurai mentality, caused by the policy of the shoguns to merge the samurai value system with aristocratic culture. The *bakufu* institutions lost effectiveness almost completely, not only in the central government but also in local governance by the end of the fifteenth century.

It is important to note that the Buddhism-related culture also had significant influence on the efficiency of institutions through its effect on the weakening of the separation of the profane and the sacred in the mindset of individuals. Because the easy-practice principle had the effect of the sanctification of occupational activities and hence the present world, by the concept of merit transfer (*ekō*), the value of existing institutions as profane social devices was lowered in the eyes of individuals who were devoted to *kyūdō* behavior in order to attain religious merits. In other words, when the separation of the sacred from the profane is weakened in the thinking of people, the benefits of material gains and the benefits through present-day institutional relationships tend to lose importance.

The serious deterioration of institutions in this regard occurred with respect to the feudal system. Owing to the spread of *the kyūdō* principle to pursue religious merits in profane activities, the self-salvation behavior of the samurai became prevalent and private battles among samurai groups tied by religious inter-personal relationship (*en*) came to be ubiquitous, nullifying the constraints of the feudal system of master and vassals. It may be pointed out that the prevalence of the self-salvation behavior of the samurai was a reflection of the sanctification of the present world by *kyūdō* behavior. Self-salvation as *kyūdō* behavior based on religious inter-personal relationships was considered to have higher value than the profane contractual relationships of feudalism.

A substantial blow to the feudal system and the existing order of samurai society was dealt by what we call the second type of *gekokujyō*, in which, during the Warring States period characterized by incessant inner wars, higher ranking *daimyos* tended to be defeated by lower ranking *daimyos*. It is contended below that this phenomenon is related to the influence of cultural differences between the value systems of the samurai and aristocrats as well as to information asymmetry that caused adverse selection in the hiring market of vassals by *sengoku* (Warring States period) *daimyos*.

It is the main conclusion of this chapter that the institutional history of Japan before the Tokugawa era cannot be understood without reference to two basic cultural undercurrents: *kyūdō* behavior brought about by Buddhist reform and conflicts in the value systems between the samurai and aristocracy. Section 5.1 is devoted to the long-term changes in the *ritsuryō* system, and the establishment of the institutions of the *bakufu* and feudalism. Section 5.2 discusses that the deterioration in trust levels and the disfunction of institutions during the Muromachi era culminated in the phenomenon of the *gekokujyō* in the Warring States period. Section 5.3 is related to the process of cultural struggle that gave rise to Tokugawa culture.

5.1 Marketization, the Social Division of Labor and Feudalism

One of the most salient features of the development of the market economy in Japan was that marketization proceeded in tandem with the deterioration and collapse of the pre-existing centralized economy. As already discussed, Japan had a fairly developed nationalized economy since the mid-seventh century. This system, introduced from Tang, was the *ritsuryō* system, governed in accordance with the statutes (*ritsuryō* codes) and orders of central government. While all the lands as well as state enterprises were nationalized in this system, gradual privatization began in the mid-eighth century in order to utilize private incentives to develop new lands and accommodate growing populations. The privatization of lands accelerated from the tenth century when the government introduced a subcontracting system for large farmers, and through the twelfth century, the radical shift to a market economy proceeded. The privatization of state enterprises (factories of handicrafts) followed the privatization of land and was completed largely by the end of the twelfth century.

The ownership of most of the newly cultivated lands and state enterprises shifted to aristocrats, including imperial families. The sale of products from the lands and privatized enterprises accelerated the development of the market economy, accompanied by commodity production for the use of the private sector and the development of the commercial and other service sectors. The emergence of new occupations, such as merchants, artisans and transport agencies, and urbanization as a result of the progress of the social division of labor, converted the traditional homogeneous society into a heterogeneous society. The enhanced asymmetry of information between unfamiliar neighbors necessitated the adjustment of standards of conduct and conventions suitable for a new heterogeneous society. However, the establishment of standards of conduct truly suitable for the heterogenous society was not an easy matter.

Socio-political turmoil related to the decline of the *ritsuryō* system accompanied the conflicts between the aristocrat and samurai classes over land ownership, and the heterogenization of society owing to the development of the market economy brought about the demise of ancient orders and the start of the medieval age, accompanied by the establishment of a new government by the samurai, the Kamakura *bakufu*. Social unrest due to political, economic and societal changes caused by the decline of the *ritsuryō* system was amplified by frequent natural disasters, epidemic diseases, and increased internal wars.

Drastic cultural changes occurred in the religious sphere to accommodate intensified public anxiety and the acute desire for salvation by the masses. Triggered by the emergence of Kamakura new Buddhism, religious reform of the whole of Buddhism[1] in Japan gave rise to practice simplification, the easy practice principle, and this led to a drastic change in lifestyle through the proliferation of the *kyūdō* principle in daily and occupational lives. The newly born standards of conduct aiming at salvation in daily occupational life, however, intensified the motivation for specialized occupational activity and, hence, the acceleration of the social division of labor, consequently aggravating information asymmetry in society further.

Under the rein of the Muromachi *bakufu*, Buddhism spread from the aristocracy and samurai to other classes, including farmers and merchants. While a new standard of conduct was established as a result of the proliferation of *kyūdō* behavior, the consequent deepening of the social division of labor and the further specialization of individual activities aggravated information asymmetry, and gave rise to various problems related to association with unfamiliar neighbors. Trust nurtured in the traditional homogeneous community society deteriorated rapidly during the Muromachi era. A new social convention, the *gekokujyō*, those below defeat those above, threatened the collapse of the entire social order. The fundamental reason for the rise in the *gekokujy*ō was the conflict between the aristocratic value system that

---

[1] It must be noted that the old Buddhist circle also engaged in practice simplification under the influence of Kamakura new Buddhism.

respected family status and the samurai value system that emphasized competence nurtured on the battlefield and through the *kyūdō* principle.

It was the intensification of information asymmetry, brought about by the accelerated progress of the social division of labor and the religious impacts on the standards of conduct and conventions through the dissemination of the *kyūdō* principle, that aggravated the deterioration of trust and the disfunction of traditional social order, and drove society into the turmoil of the Warring States period. In this process, formal institutions were unable to catch up with the drastic changes in standards of conduct and conventions caused by cultural changes owing to religion reform.

5.1.1 Feudalism and Land Ownership

This section discusses the long-term changes in the land system beginning from the establishment of the *ritsuryo* system, which is a recurring theme of the sociopolitical history of Japan before the Tokugawa era. In Chapter 3, the land system was analyzed from the viewpoint of the changes in property rights and their implications for economic growth, focusing on the effect of the residual income and control right of land on the incentive of cultivators. In Chapter 4, the causal relationship between the decline of the *ritsuryō* system and the birth of Kamakura new Buddhism was examined in relationship to the interaction between culture and institutions. This section analyzes the rise of the samurai class and conflicts regarding land ownership with the aristocracy from the viewpoint of the institution of feudalism.

The feudalism of Japan has a salient feature as an institution that officially started from a system based on the enfeoffment of official positions from shogun to vassals, not land (fiefdom), as was the case in Occidental kingdoms. (See Chapter 8 for the case of England.) This explains why Japanese feudalism as an institution was so weak and inefficient. The feudalism of Japan was obliged to be involved in conflicts related to landholding throughout its history under the strong influence of the dual character of the government, the aristocratic government based on the imperial court system and the newly established samurai government. Partly for this reason, the samurai class developed its own culture, which was accumulated as human capital, long influencing the cultural tradition of Japan. The fragility of various institutions such as the samurai government (*bakufu*) and feudalism is rooted in the cultural effects of their origin as lower-level systems within the sovereignty of the *ritsuryo* system. The *bakafu* was born as the policing and military section of the *ritsuryō* government and feudalism began from enfeoffment by use of official positions of the *ritsuryō* administration, not enfeoffment of land. Samurai institutions were obliged to be involved in the conflicts with the aristocracy with respect to landholding and official status from its beginning. Conflicts were persistent partly due to the significant difference in value systems between the two classes. It is difficult to understand the medieval history of Japan without referring to the intense cultural conflicts between the samurai class and aristocracy. Let us examine the development of the feudalism of Japan, focusing on the changes in the landholding system.

5.1.1.1 The *Ritsuryō* Land System

The mechanism of national landholding in the *ritsuryō* system was composed of two institutions.

First was the management of state-owned land through the *handen-shūjyu* system promulgated by the edict of the Taika Reform in 646. The government allotted a patch of land to every qualified citizen in the country registered in demographic surveys carried out every six years. The government obtained tax revenue from them every year. The land had to be returned to the state after his or her death. Second was the state control of newly reclaimed land for the purpose of promoting further reclamation of land in order to accomplish economic growth or at least to accommodate the increase in population. In particular, legislation in 723 admitted that a family that had reclaimed a new arable land[2] could use it through three generations.

It was not an easy matter, however, to give incentives for new reclamation and at the same time to stick to the principle of state ownership. While the legislation of 743, touched upon in Chapter 4, of the Konden-einei-shizai Act that allowed the holding of newly cultivated land as private permanent property, was an attempt to resolve the difficult question and to complete the establishment of the *ritsuryō* system, it is considered to have finally triggered the establishment of the private holding system (Yoshida 1983; Koguchi 2002). This legislation had three important rules. First was the promotion of new reclamation by the rule to allow private permanent holding. Second was the regulation of private land holding and the prevention of the unfettered proliferation of privatization. For this purpose, the Act introduced a rule to set an upper limit on the size of landholding according to the status of the reclaimer. Third was a rule for promoting the efficient use of private lands. To this end, the Act stipulated that land, not cultivated for more than three years, was to be confiscated by the provincial governors' offices (*kokuga*) and rented to other persons, and that re-cultivators of uncultivated land were allowed to obtain the benefit of tax exemption.

The collapse of the original *ritsuryō* land system proceeded at first through the increase of privately held lands, and then through the conversion of private lands into manors (*shōen*). The increase in privately held land proceeded with the aggravation of income inequality among farmers, and the consequent downfall of poor and indebted farmers. Capable farmers obtained high income as interest revenue on loans to the poor and land rents, in addition to the income from their own farming activities. Some of them also left the land allotted by the state intentionally unused for years and obtained tax exemption benefits by re-cultivating it. Rich farmers became landlords as they expanded the land under their control through new reclamation and re-cultivation of unutilized lands. At the same time, they hired vagrant poor farmers as servants and slaves and, with this new manpower, further expanded the lands under their control.

Because provincial governors' offices were always trying to take opportunities to confiscate private lands for the purpose of extending the land under state control and to maximize tax revenue, the third rule, 'the confiscation rule', made the position of

[2] Sansei-isshin-hō. If reclamation was not new land but the repairing of existing land with broken ditches, the right to use was confined to one generation.

the reclaimer extremely unstable, as is emphasized by Nagahara (1998). Landlords who had reclaimed a large amount of land or obtained lands as collateral to defaulted lending began to rely on the aristocrats, on influential individuals related to the imperial families or on large temples and shrines. This resulted in the massive donation to them of lands by landlords as manors. At first, landlords donated their lands to aristocrats with whom they had been acquainted, and the aristocrats re-donated the lands to higher level influential families in order to secure more firmly the protection of lands from confiscation. The conversion of private land held by landlords into manors meant usually the acquisition of the privilege of tax exemption, but the revenue of landlords did not increase so much because the aristocrats and influential families obtained rent revenues, as is shown by the case study by Nagahara (1998, pp. 65–78). This implies that tax exemption was not the main reason for the proliferation of manors, but 'the confiscation rule' was the most responsible factor that caused the conversion of the land system into the manor system.

5.1.1.2 The Land System at the End of the Heian Era: The *Shōen-Kōryō* System

At the end of the Heian era, there were three kind of lands classified by the type of ownership: manor (*shōen*), state-owned land (*kōryō*) and private land. The system, the *shōen-kōryō* system, continued to exist as the institutionary basis of the land system until the end of the Muromachi *bakufu,* when the *ritsuryō* system was finally abandoned.

Manors were privately held lands with the privilege of exemption of taxes to be paid to the state. Private lands were frequently converted into manors through donation to the aristocracy and re-donation to higher ranking families in order to avoid the risk of confiscation by the provincial governors' offices. The ultimate right of ownership was held by high-ranking influential families related to imperial families and large temples and shrines called *honjyo*. *Honjyo* were re-donated the manor by aristocrats called *ryōke*, who were donated the manors directly by the original reclaimers or landlords. Landlords were appointed to official positions in manor management from the governors' offices, such as *geshi* or manor officials (*shōkan*), and became local bureaucrats in charge of the actual administrative and judicial job of manors under the instruction of the *honjyo*. The *honjyo* and *ryōke* obtained rent income called *nengu*, and the landlords obtained rent income called *jishi*. The actual cultivation was carried out by farmers or peasants called *sakushu*.

State-owned lands were lands under the control of the provincial governors' offices. Governors' offices managed the lands directly and obtained tax and other products for the use of the state. The top officers were provincial governors (*kokushi*) and their staff (*gunji*). Both were appointed by the imperial court. Towards the end of the Heian era, state-owned lands were frequently converted into private lands. Quite a few *gunji* converted their official position into patrimonial property and strengthened the control right over the state-owned land, of which they were in charge, eventually becoming landlords (*zaichi-ryōshu*). The provincial governors' offices were obliged to permit their behavior tacitly, in effect being satisfied with delegating the tax collection job to them. After the start of the reign of Shirakawa *jyōkō*[3] in 1086, a similar kind of privatization occurred on a larger scale. Quite often, the *kokushi* did not go back to Kyoto after serving the term of four years and occupied the state-owned land as virtually patrimonial territory.

Private lands were lands approved by the state but outside the direct control of provincial governors' offices. These lands were obtained through reclamation or other measures such as re-cultivation of wasteland (*kouhaichi*) and the enclosure of the small land of farmers. The large owners of private lands were landlords (*zaichi-ryōshu*). The holding of these lands needed to be approved by the provincial governors' offices; otherwise they were regarded as unused lands, confiscated and converted into state lands by the governors' offices. The threat of confiscation by the provincial governor's office resulted in the conversion of private lands into manors. The owner of private lands could obtain rent incomes called *jishi* or *kajishi* but had to pay taxes to the provincial governors' offices. Incidentally, rent incomes called *nengu, jishi* or *kajishi* were called *tokubun* (manor income) in general. In the next section we will talk about the important consequences entailed by the emergence of the market in the *tokubun* right.

There is no data about private lands, but piecemeal data, called *Ōta-bumi*, are available for 13 provinces with respect to manors and state-owned lands. The average ratio of manors, as a percentage of the sum of manors and state-owned lands, at the end of twelfth century was 61% and the medium was 72%.[4] So we can conjecture that more than half of arable land in the country, disregarding private lands, was manor at this time (Nagahara 1998, p. 86).

5.1.1.3 The Birth of Feudalism and Land

In the *shōen-kōryō* system established at the end of the Heian era, the aristocracy, the top of which comprised imperial families, or the large temples and shrines, were the ultimate owners of manors. Their income was mainly composed of two sources: income granted by official positions, the source of which was tax revenue at the imperial court and provincial governors' offices, and rent incomes from manors held as family property. The rent incomes, obtained by the aristocracy, other influential families, and the like, were a sort of residual income and, at the end of the Heian era, comprised the major part of the income of the class. After the establishment of the Kamakura *bakufu* (samurai government), the first *bakufu* of the samurai class, however, the property right of the class as *ryōke* and *honjyo* of manors was significantly encroached.

The basic governance mechanism of the *shōen-kōryō* system was the appointment of civil servants to positions called *shiki* of administrative and judicial roles of

---

[3]Emperor 1072–86. After 1086, reigned the country by the system called *insei* as ex-emperor (*Jyōkō* and after 1096 *Hōō*) during 1086–1129.

[4]The maximum was 88% and the minimum 26%.

manors and state-owned lands. The *shiki* were appointed by the provincial governors' offices (*kokuga*) and were hereditary posts allowed by the imperial court. They were endowed with the right to obtain some percentage of income (*tokubun*) out of the total products of land. Since the *shiki* were authorized by the provincial governors' offices, these roles and income rights were considered in effect to be guaranteed by imperial authority. During the Heian era, manors were governed by *shōkan* (manor official)-*shiki or gesu-shiki*, state-owned lands by *gunji-shiki* and *kokushi-shiki* and, after Minamoto Yoritomo established the Kamakura *bakufu*, two additional *shiki* related to the military role were introduced: *shugo-shiki* as the military governor of provinces, and *jitō* (estate steward)-*shiki* under the *shugo* as the actual agency to implement military and police activities and, at the same time, in charge of tax collection.

From the beginning of the Kamakura era, the *jitō* and manor-owning aristocracy class confronted each other fiercely. It is important to note that not only the Kamakura *bakufu* (1192–1333) but also the Muromachi *bakufu* (1336–1573) with the related *shugo-jitō* system was not considered to be a system replacing imperial local administration but rather as supplementary to it (Hall 1968). Just like various *shiki* in Heian era, *jitō-shiki* and *shugo-shiki* were appointed ultimately by the imperial court. Shogun Yoritomo himself was appointed by the imperial court and delegated the role to designate *shugo-shiki* and *jitō-shiki*. Both *shugo* and *jitō* were endowed with the right to obtain rent income (*tokubun*), however, so that this inevitably led to disputes and conflicts with the final owners (*ryōke* and *honjyo*) of manors who had retained the rights to residual income and control. The *shugo* and *jitō* were eager to obtain the control right of their land, and the *honjyo* and *ryōke* wanted to recover the income right allotted to the shiki of the *shugo* and *jitō*.

In the disputes, the *bakufu* took the stance to favor the *shugo* and *jitō*, most of whom were shogun's housemen (*gokenin*), and quite often ordered the final owners to acquiesce to the settlement of disputes by one of two methods, the *shitaji-chūbun* and *ukesho* systems. *Shitaji-chūbun* meant a division of the manor in dispute, on a half and half basis. In this settlement, both parties, the *shugo* and *jitō* on the one hand and the *honjyo* and *ryōke* on the other, obtained a complete set of property rights on land, comprising both income and the control right, although the size of the land was halved. In the case of settlement by the *ukesho* system, the *bakufu* ordered the *honjyo* and *ryōke* to transfer the control right to the *shugo* and *jitō* and, at the same time, recommended that contracts be made with respect to the income of the *ryōke and honjyo*. In this settlement, the *ryōke* and *honjyo* were converted into mere fixed income (*tokubun*) receivers, not control right owners nor residual income earners anymore.

These arrangements did not mean that the *jitō* were allowed to obtain permanent proprietary rights over land. Rather, their rights to lands were in principle stipulated to be cancelled after their jobs terminated.[5] However, some of the *jitō* under *shugo* began to believe themselves to be the true proprietors of the lands and tried to subdivide or grant to their vassals the lands they held. These processes weakened the power of the

[5] *Tokusei-rei* of Onin in 1297.

ryōke and *honjyo* considerably, the power of provincial governors' offices as well, while the *jitō*'s control on land utilization and farmers was substantially increased.

This was because the political title became transacted on the market. As is explained below, there occurred a rapid development of the market for *tokubun* rights, fragmenting income rights over lands, authorized by imperial power as a set of income rights and official positions of bureaucratic roles (Hashita 1975). The development of the market for the transaction of *tokubun* rights meant the market transaction of official positions and roles. It is inevitable for official positions to lose value when they are transacted on the marketplace. This was part of the reason for the collapse of the governance system in the local areas of the Muromachi *bakufu*. The collapse of the governance system implies the demise of the political rights of the *honjyo* and *ryōke*, whose power relied on the *ritsuryō* system, and the increases of the control power of the *jitō* on land and farmers.

In institutional terms, the infringement by the *jitō* and consequent sanction by the *bakufu* in the form of *shitaji-chūbun* have important institutional meaning for feudalism. At the time of the initiation of the Kamakura *bakufu*, the *bakufu* confiscated land held by antagonistic powers they defeated and redistributed it to housemen (*gokenin*) and other samurai. The redistribution, however, was not concerned with the complete set of rights related to land but only the partial right of rent (the *tokubun* right), so that, in most cases, the remining rights and the final control right was held by aristocrats. This implies that the reciprocal contract of endowment of fief and loyalty that comprised the institutional foundation of feudalism had been considerably imperfect in the initial institutional arrangement of the Kamakura *bakufu*. By way of the *shitaji-chūbun*, the housemen of the shogun (*gokenin*) and other *jitō* were finally endowed with the complete right to land although the size of the land was halved. As Nagahara (1998) claims, by the *shitaji-chūbun*, the *jitō* was able to accomplish *ichien* (perfect) control of their land. Ishimota (1956) asserts approvingly that, in this way, the feudal system as an institution was finally established in Japan (p. 179). The feudalism established by way of enfeoffment of official positions was in this way converted into one based on land enfeoffment, similar to the institution in Occidental countries (Chapter 8).

However, even if we admit the effect of the *shitaji-chūbun* and *ichien* (perfect) control on enfeoffment, the feudalism of Japan was still significantly incomplete as an institution in another dimension. Below it is argued that the imperfectness of the feudalism institution was intensified as the *kyūdō* principle born under the influence of new Buddhism gave rise to the self-salvation behavior of the samurai, neglecting the feudal rule of the master–vassal relationship. It will be shown that, quite irrespective of the method of enfeoffment, whether it was based on land or official positions, the proliferation of the self-salvation behavior among the samurai class delivered a fatal blow to the institution of feudalism.

Incidentally, it is interesting to note that the infringement of the landholding right of the aristocracy by the samurai had an important cultural and institutional meaning. In terms of culture, the invasion of the right of aristocrats, the *honjyo* and *ryōke*, by the *jitō* was not necessarily criminal nor immoral during the medieval period. During the period, there remained the strong conception that the possession of land by outsiders was a temporary phenomenon, and the ultimate holding right remained with those who had originally developed the land.[6] This notion implies that the right to land donated to the aristocracy, hence the right to rents by the *honjyo* and *ryōke*, could be cancelled, and the change of rulers (emperor as well as shogun) by inheritance (*daigawari*) was usually considered to justify the retrieval of the landholding by the original holders, called *ji-tokusei* or *ji-okoshi*. Actually, *ji-tokusei* or *ji-okoshi* that occurred frequently during the Muromachi era was implemented by this notion that was held by farmers (Katsumata 1979, pp. 87–115). Katsumata claims that the retrieval of donated land at the time of the change of ruler was a daily matter (p. 94).[7] Many high-ranking samurai in the Kamakura *bakufu* had their origin as reclaimers who, or whose ancestors, had been actively engaged in developing new land and were obliged to donate their land to the aristocracy due to the threat of nationalization by the *ritsuryō* government.[8] It follows that, from the notion stated above, the right of aristocrats to land was to a considerable extent of a temporal nature, so that it was not immoral nor criminal for the samurai to threaten the rights held by the aristocrats; or the infringement of the rights of the aristocrats was justifiable from the viewpoint of the class struggle between the samurai and aristocracy.

5.1.1.4 Demise of the Imperial Governing System

The encroachment of the right of the *ryoke* and *honjyo*, and their virtual conversion into *tokubun* receiver, continued throughout the Muromachi era, and the power of the *shugo* and *jitō* intensified. Throughout the country, the *shugo* or their relatives grew up into regional overlords and came to be called *daimyo*.[9] However, *daimyo* were still obliged to rely on the remnant power of the imperial court because their military authority over the region was legally guaranteed by the system of *shiki*, which was a combined title of income rights (*tokubun*) and the administrative and judicial role assigned by the imperial authority (Hall 1990).

To this system of *shiki*, the ultimate evidence for imperial control over the *shōen-kōryō system*, there occurred a final blow. This was emergence and rapid development of markets in the *tokubun* right. If *tokubun* is a mere right to income, there is no problem in its transaction in markets. However, since the *tokubun* right is also related to the administrative and judicial role assigned by the imperial authority, the

[6] It is conjectured that the practice of the cultivation of land was considered to be based on a contract with nature, from the viewpoint of native Shintoism, so that the right of cultivator was of sacred value.

[7] Katsumata quotes the assertion of Kikuchi (1969) that, in the usage of ancient documents, 'sale' does not mean the permanent transfer of ownership, and there remained a deep-rooted notion of the inseparability of land with its developer.

[8] Particular land, the right to which a *jitō* tried to infringe, does not necessarily coincide with land that he or his ancestor developed, and such coincidence would have been a very low probability.

[9] The origin of the *daimyo* was diverse, and there were some who rose to *daimyo* from local military power like the *kokujin* without any prior official job, but the major part of the *daimyo* came from the *shugo* or *shugo* substitutes.

market transaction in *tokubun* means the market transaction of official titles regarding administrative and judicial roles. In other words, the development of the market for *tokubun* rights, income right of land, meant the market transaction of official government positions, and there is no doubt that this led to the demise of the imperial governance mechanism (Hashita 1975). At this stage, the control mechanism of the imperial government over local society lost its power completely, and the whole of society was destined to move towards disorder, the Warring States period. While it is true that the Muromachi shoguns were authorized by the imperial power, the authority over lower level government officials was destroyed due to the development of the market for *tokunun* rights. In this situation, without the official governance system, not only rich merchants and moneylenders but also local military powers in the provinces called *dogō* (local samurai leaders) or *kokujin* (indigenous lords) became active purchasers of *tokubun* rights. Hiring *dogō* and *kokujin* as additional military power, the *daimyo* or ex-*shugo* came to be energetically involved in the extension of their territories through military conquest.

Incidentally, debt cancellation (*tokusei*) orders have been analyzed from the viewpoint of income redistribution only and the efficiency aspects have been neglected by and large in most of the existing literature. However, it seems that the *tokusei* order needs to be reexamined from the efficiency viewpoint. The *tokusei* order implies the cancelling of sales certificates of lands or certificates on credits with land as collateral between borrowers, largely farmers and villages organized by indigenous samurai leaders (*dogō*), and lenders such as *dosō*, *sakaya*,[10] and temples and shrines. The *tokusei* order in the Muromachi era was issued in response to demands following farmers riots. The first *tokusei* uprising in the Muromachi era occurred in 1428, when the shogun was changed from Ashikaga Yoshimochi to Ashikaga Yoshinori.[11] In 1441, the *bakufu* was obliged to issue an official order cancelling credits and land sales, and this was followed by the upsurge in private uprisings nationwide. Actual cultivators, who used to be wanderers looking for good working places, did not have control rights, so the *tokusei* order did not have any efficiency loss except for the impacts on income distribution related to the cancelling of credits. During the fifteenth century, however, as cultivators began to settle on lands, actual cultivators enhanced their sense of control rights (which is often called the establishment of *nomin-teki-shiki*) and their right came to be acknowledged socially (Katsumata 1979, 1996).[12] Although we believe that the control rights of actual cultivators were not

---

[10]The *dosō* and *sakaya* were major financial institutions engaged in moneylending activity and regional financial remittance.

[11]Changes of headship of the shogunate or emperorship were considered to be justified to request the cancellation of land sales, because lands were given 'lives' by developers and should be returned to the developers at the beginning of the new reign of the shogun or emperor.

[12]Certificates for land-selling by farmers came to be issued frequently (Katsumata 1979, pp. 102–107). Katsumata emphasizes that there was a deep sense of ownership of land, that ultimate ownership was held by the actual developers of lands who gave 'lives' to the lands. Katsumata claims that the *tokusei* uprising was without exception a *jiokoshi* uprising. The concept of the *jiokoshi* implies that those who developed (*okoshi*) land held ultimate rights to lands.

perfect because villages were increasingly strengthening their autonomy and collective movements (Chapter 2), this could have a serious real effect on the efficiency of agriculture with regard to the incentive of cultivators. Moreover, farmers relied heavily on the loans by the *dosō* and *sakaya* in financing outlays to purchase farming inputs, and the *tokusei* order meant the destruction of the financial mechanism (Nishitani-Nakabayashi 2017).

5.1.2 The Acceleration of the Social Division of Labor

5.1.2.1 The Dissolution of State Factories and the Development of Commerce

The collapse of the *ritsuryō* system through the privatization of land and the development of manors led to the privatization of state enterprises for handicraft production. In the *ritsuryō* system, all agricultural products and indigenous goods specific to each region, such as silk, weavings, salt, horses, processed marine products, and the like, except for the goods consumed by producers and at provincial governors' offices, were transported to the capital city Kyoto, and distributed to imperial families, aristocrats and bureaucrats,[13] as well as to large temples and shrines. Handicraft goods produced at state factories under the control of the provincial governors' offices were also transported to Kyoto and distributed to the ruling class together with products from the state factories in Kyoto. As the manor system developed, agricultural and indigenous products came to be obtained individually by each imperial family, aristocrat, and temple and shrine. This led to the privatization of handicraft goods also. The privatization of state factories was brought about, leading to the private ownership of factory equipment as well as the private hiring of skilled workers by them. The factory workers hired by imperial families were called *kugonin*, by temples *yoriudo*, and by shrines *jinin*.[14] This process is considered to have been completed roughly by the end of the twelfth century.

It is important to note that the supply of goods to markets through the proliferation of manors and the privatization of state factories gave significant impetus toward the development of the market economy. This was because the owners of manor and ex-state factories had to sell redundant goods obtained from their manors and factories in the market. As a result, the development of the market economy and the monetarization of the economy proceeded rapidly after the mid-twelfth century. Table 3.2 shows that the share of commerce and services, the tertiary sector, in GDP began to increase from 8.1 to 9.4% or more after 1150.

The market for agricultural products and manufacturing goods developed in tandem with the development of city merchants, the *toimaru* (city trade association

---

[13] At first land transportation then water transportation was used for this purpose.

[14] Some of the skilled workers became aristocratic bureaucrats (Wakita 1969; Satou 1983).

merchants),[15] by way of establishing the trade association system (*za*), under the protection of the shogun or manor-owning aristocrats, and an active bill of exchange market for the settlement of payments. The *toimaru* developed comprehensive business models related to the monetarization of rents obtained in kind. This included warehousing, financing instruments and transportation systems. When the transportation of commodities was costly, manor owners sold them at the local markets and transferred the proceeds to Kyoto by use of the bill of exchange system[16] and, at the same time, they encouraged peasants and farmers to pay rents in cash (*daisen-nō*). The market for handicraft goods developed rapidly as owners sold redundant products in the market. Workers, hired by privatized factories, were also allowed to produce goods for sale at the market by themselves. They also obtained the privilege to travel to local districts freely[17] to sell produced goods or, in the case of heavy goods such as temple bells made of cast iron, they produced them at local temples.[18] Because of the underdevelopment of the transportation system, the travelling of private factory workers was an effective way to supply handicraft goods to local districts.

Nagahara (2001) emphasized the development of the market for high-level handicraft goods such as silk textiles, refined accessories, swords, armor, and various military articles, accompanied by the accelerated progress of the diversification and division of labor (p. 207). It is contended that aristocrats, whose landholding rights were significantly infringed upon and deprived by the *jitō* and indigenous lords (*zaich-ryōshu*), retained economic power by way of enhancing their control over commercial and manufacturing activities in Kyoto. Trade associations (*za*) in Kyoto comprised a significant source of income for aristocrats before the active involvement of the Muromachi *bakufu* in the control of trade associations. Sasaki (1964), on the other hand, emphasized the progress of the social division of labor within local manors under the control of indigenous lords (p. 136). Against the background of the gradual rise in agricultural production, indigenous lords as well as the *myōshu* class actively participated in markets to sell goods obtained as rents in kind. Not only agricultural but also manufacturing goods were sold, including military equipment as well as farming tools such as spades and hoes. It is contended that new specialized manufacturers producing for local demand emerged, replacing manufacturers under

---

[15]The heyday of the *toimau* was from the end of the Kamakura era through the Muromachi era before the Warring States period. The *toimaru* had obtained huge profits by means of the monopoly power endowed by the shogun and dominated the trade association system organized by the producers. After the weakening of the Muromachi *bakufu*, the *toimaru* gradually lost the monopoly power, and declined in competition with the newly emerged regional merchants related to local *daimyos*.

[16]The bill of exchange system developed rapidly during this period as a measure to transfer the proceeds from local manors to Kyoto. Sakurai (1996) contends that bills of exchange issued by large manor owners and endorsed by bill brokers were extensively distributed and used as instruments of payment during the medieval age, when currency comprised imported Chinese currency and the economy suffered chronically from the shortage of payment instruments.

[17]They obtained certificates for free traveling issued by government offices in the name of the imperial court.

[18]They traveled collectively as a group and were armed to protect from looting by bandits.

the control of the provincial governors' offices, who were still in the primitive stage, half farmer and half manufacturer[19] (pp. 131–143).

Production of handicraft goods in local districts was promoted further by the settlement of those travelling artisans and workers in areas where materials they needed were produced. During the Warring States period, *daimyos* called *sengoku-daimyo* (Warring States period *daimyo*), many of whom had been *shugo* previously and had come to govern the local districts as their own territories without the approval of the imperial court, put provincial governors' offices under their control together with production facilities and workers, encouraging and protecting the settlement of artisans in their territories. It is important to note that the origin of the 'industrial production' of Japan lies in the state factories and workers of the *ritsuryō* system. To satisfy the needs of imperial families and aristocrats they had high level skills and motivation for *monodukuri* (craftmanship) from the beginning.

5.1.2.2 The Development of Long-Distance Commerce

Another factor related to the development of specialized manufacturing production and the intensification of the social division of labor was the role fulfilled by the development of long-distance commerce after the period of the Southern and Northern Dynasties. The *shugo* and *daimyos* were actively involved in developmental policy in their territories. Areas under their control were, however, too small to establish an autarky economy, so they were obliged to prepare facilities for transportation and distribution to enable the travelling of merchants to and from the central economy around the Kyoto area and their territories.

The inter-regional commodity market during the latter half of middle age was based on the transportation system through two kinds of trunk lines. One line connected the central market around Kyoto and local economic areas, and the other line connected various local economies directly without going through the Kyoto area (Suzuki 2000). Marine transportation under the control of the *toimaru* merchants played an important role in this respect. The specialized producers who settled and grew up in the local markets obtained sufficient demand for their products owing to the role of long-distance commerce. The more specialized the product, the broader the markets that were needed to lower the fixed cost of production and satisfy the condition of minimum production scale. The handicraft goods producers who settled in various regions in Japan after the mid-medieval period had secured sufficient demand through supplying to multiple markets in distant economies, realizing the high-level division of labor with various specialized groups beyond the level possible in local autarkic markets.

Products supplied in this way were not confined to highly luxurious goods. A typical example was the market for domestic pottery. Large vases and bowls mainly produced in the Hokuriku region have been found in the ruins of various provinces

---

[19]Manufacturers were usually provided with small patches of land (*kyūmen-den*) exempt for rent payments.

facing the Pacific Ocean, although similar products were not recorded on the list of taxation in kind in those provinces. In the ruins of the Hiroshima prefecture, pottery produced in the Kansai and Nagoya areas, in addition to Chinese pottery, has been discovered. This pottery, not necessarily luxury goods but products for daily use, were found in massive quantities. On the other hand, Sasaki (1972) contends that the amount of the nationwide distribution of luxurious craft goods demanded by the ruling class increased during the Muromachi era. Swords, cosmetics, and kettles for use at tea ceremonies are representative, and these were also major export goods from Japan to foreign countries. It is also noted that, with respect to goods for daily use, such as rice cookers, spades and hoes, high quality products from specialized areas were distributed widely and, by way of long-distance commerce, drove out products of indigenous producers.

5.1.2.3 The Rapid Development of the Social Division of Labor

We have argued that the privatization of production facilities and human capital, specialized workers and artisans, caused the accelerated development of the social division of labor in the production of high-quality products. Owing to the development of long-distance transportation, producers were able to find sufficient clients in the wealthy class of local markets, so they were able to expand production scale and reduce average fixed costs to the level sufficient to yield positive profits. This process accelerated the social division of labor, giving rise to new occupations, such as artisans and specialized handicraft producers as well as merchants in charge of long-distance trade, the *toimaru* merchants. In this way, in Japan, the decline of the *ritsuryō* system was one of the major factors for the acceleration of the social division of labor. It must be noted the *ritsuryō* system was a centralized administration and production system hastily established in order to prepare for the international military tension in east Asia. It seems possible that the transformation of the *ritsuryō* system was something foreseen from an early period, because the development of new lands to meet the needs of the increasing population could only be accomplished by way of the privatization of land holdings. However, the privatization of state enterprises might have been something beyond expectation. As the privatization of land proceeded, not only agricultural products but also handicraft goods needed in aristocratic life were inevitably supplied through the market. It is hard to confirm how much was anticipated beforehand but, anyway, the private possession of the facilities of state factories by aristocrats began and the aristocrats competed with each other to obtain the facilities. The private holding of production facilities provided the incentive for marketization, which in turn motivated market-oriented behavior by the artisans. The increase in the demand and supply of handicraft goods outside aristocratic society inevitably brought about the emergence of new occupations and 'new industries' for producing refined handicraft goods to the private sector. The emergence of merchants and transportation specialists as well as new producers and workers of handicrafts good resulted in the accelerated progress of the social division of labor. As could be confirmed by the rise of the sectorial production share shown in Table 3.2, the share of the secondary sector increased from 5.5% to 5.8 in 1280 to 6.8% in 1450. Assuming the constancy of productivity, this should have resulted in the increase in the number of producers and workers.

From the end of the Heian era through the Muromachi era, the aim of individuals who were eager to attain enlightenment was either to become distinguished in any one area or to become rich, as is emphasized by Matsumoto (1956) and Yokoi (1975). *Kyūdō* behavior to become distinguished was another factor that accelerated the social division of labor in Japan. Producers competed with each other in supplying high quality products through self-disciplining and training following the *kyūdō* principle. Many of them had their own equipment and trained apprentices in their own studios cum factories, and devoted efforts to transmit accumulated skills to the apprentices. While Amino (1984) contended that skills were transmitted through blood relationships, Wakita (1988) asserted that the production organizations, organized as *ie*, were not necessarily purely patrimonial systems but organized as a system of technology accumulation and transmission on the principle of the teacher–disciple relationship, which is not necessarily hereditary. While practically a teacher and their disciples were related through blood relationship in many cases, it is important to note that the principle was not patrimonial,[20] and successors were chosen from qualified disciples by reason of their skill or other factors. This reflects the worldview nurtured in Buddhism, in which others nearby related by the interaction in the transmigration process are of utmost importance. It is not Confucianism that emphasizes generational continuity by way of blood relationship.

Through the process, the system of the social division of labor became refined and upgraded more and more, and there emerged numerous new occupations among artisans and manufacturers. In each occupation, artisans sought ways to be distinguished in their circle. As the number of occupations increased and the interrelationship among occupations became more complicated, the homogeneous society that existed before the twelfth century was rapidly converted into a heterogeneous society during the medieval period. Moreover, since everyone stuck to his own way, discovered and developed through *kyūdō* behavior, and skills were transmitted without written documents, quite often, as closely guarded secrets among members of *ie*, the availability of open information regarding the skill and technology was significantly scarce, consequently aggravating information asymmetry in society.

We have argued that the development of industry as a result of the privatization of state factories and *kyūdō* behavior born from the new teaching of practice simplification in Buddhism accelerated the social division of labor in medieval Japan. Individuals who had been accustomed to the traditional society, where everyman made everything, should have been dazzled by the accelerated shift to a highly heterogeneous society. Information asymmetry among individuals increased at an enormous speed during the process, leading to serious conflicts in society.

---

[20] This caused serious problems in the choice of successor. For example, it is well known the founder of *nō* play, Zeami, fell into serious trouble in the choice between an adopted son and his own son, both of whom were talented.

Comparison with the experience in England will clarify how the acceleration of the social division of labor in Japan was unique. While it is customary to point out the relationship between the growth of towns, the circulation of currency and the emergence of newly skilled workers during the twelfth and fourteenth centuries in England with productivity growth through increased occupational specialization, Britnell (2001) argues that the increasing specialization characterized only a small proportion of the workforce and that the proliferation of occupational names such as 'Peter the baker' does not necessary mean the progress of the social division of labor. The basic reason for the increase in occupational names lies in the rapid increase in town dwellers as casual workers and occupational beggars, and in the necessity to identify them for the administrative purpose of the town. Occupational identifiers used by administrators did not necessarily indicate full-time occupation but to express an office or skill that most precisely distinguished them from others. It is also pointed out that those workers were not necessarily settled. Many in the rural population, cottagers and smallholders, looked for part-time employment opportunities in towns requiring no special skills and changed occupation frequently. The supposition that commercialization accompanied specialization overlooks the fluctuating and unstable availability of employment, and the insecurity of any personal attributes or skills as a foundation of livelihood.

In a nutshell, Britnell's argument indicates that the growth of towns as a result of commercialization resulted in the proliferation of diversified occupations for the purpose of part-time employment and of the diversification of sources of livelihood in England. It is not deniable that there was a similar phenomenon in Japan. The emergence and development of industry that supplied sophisticated handicraft goods to the private sector as a result of the privatization of the *ritsuryō* state factories caused the expansion of the urban sector and the consequent expansion of employment opportunities that had attracted the out-migration of the rural population. However, such characteristics as the pursuit of the quality of products from the supply side, the consequent advance in the specialization of occupations, and the formation of *ie* as a mechanism to transmit skills, seem to be something different from the case of England depicted by Britnell. In Japan, supply-side innovation certainly exerted significant influence on the quality of economic growth and of society.

5.1.3 Defects in the Moral Code of Buddhism

Practice simplification recommended by new Buddhist sects brought about enormous impacts on society in the sense of the complication of human relationships and confusion caused by the inability to deal with new social phenomena due to the insufficient development of the information system. *Kyūdō*-minded behavior, the pursuit of enlightenment (*satori*) in daily occupational life, resulted in the rapid development of occupational specification and the social division of labor. This inevitably increased the importance of interaction with nearby neighbors in people's daily lives, but the Maharana Buddhism had not built an adequate moral code to deal with this new situation, and the tragedy, not to say catastrophe, of the Warring States period emerged.

Let us explain this in more detail. Primitive Buddhism before the birth of Maharana Buddhism did not have any viewpoint based on a human society that expand spatially. The world it envisaged comprised the extension of time only. What I am today and what I will be tomorrow were the only concerns of Buddhists. As Hiraoka (2016) eloquently asserts, Maharana Buddhism, in the sense of a large vessel to accommodate a large number of believers, enlarged this scope spatially and brought in a spatial as well as temporal perspective in the thinking of Buddhists. The world came to be understood as composing of many places, in which various buddhas live until now, in addition to the earthly space where Buddha lived his life in the fifth–fourth century BC. Not only self-interest but also egalitarian considerations came to bear meaning in this worldview. The lives of Buddhists came to evolve around concerns about the level of accumulation of karma and the reasons for the changes in the accumulated stock of karma. Since karma is caused by earthly desires, struggles and negotiations related with others nearby, the notion of karma inevitably brought in the consideration of others in the sense that the existence of oneself occurs in relationship with the existence of others.[21]

The considerations about karma necessitate moral principles to be followed by believers to deal with human relationships with others. Instead of introducing concrete and detailed moral instructions to be followed, primitive Buddhism assumed that the rigorousness of the two principles of karma could provide the necessary and sufficient conditions for disciplining human relationships in society (Sakurabe 1989). It was the self-enforcing mechanism of building up the moral system that worked in the following way. The first principle was the inevitability of retribution of karma. Whether the nature of karma is good or bad, the accumulated amount of karma could not be reduced unless it was met with retribution. There is no offsetting of bad karma by good karma or vice versa. Only the absolute amount of accumulated stock of karma matters. Whatever good deed you have done, it could not be utilized to avoid the retribution of bad karma. Second was the principle of no transfer of karma to others. One's karma must be reaped by oneself, so no other person could take the consequences of one's own deeds. Theoretically, these is no doubt that these two principles could promise a perfect moral society. By insisting on the strict self-responsibility of believers for their deeds and prohibiting the offsetting of bad karma by good karma, Buddhism could bring about a highly moralistic order in human society even if it is inflicted by the complexity in human relationships. Believers, who were eager to live in better circumstances (realms) in the cycle of transmigration of souls, were forced to seek an adequate attitude in human relationships by themselves. It was expected that, in this self-enforcing mechanism of building up the moral system, the process of individual efforts would eventually give rise to an acceptable moral code, consequently establishing a highly moralistic society.

[21] A succinct explanation of the concept of karma in relationship to the concept of enlightenment (*satori*) is given in Appendix 1 of Chapter 4.

While we argued in Chapter 4 that the new teaching of practice simplification that was utilized for the purpose of self-salvation was a glorious and innovative accomplishment of Japanese Buddhism, the other side of the coin of that attainment was a tragedy for Japan; in the Mahayana Buddhism brought to Japan, the rigorousness of the karma principle had been substantially relaxed by the concept of merit transference (*ekō*). The founders of new Buddhist sects resorted to the concept extensively to facilitate the salvation of the masses. One of the side-effects of the innovative attainment was the emergence of *kyūdō* behavior, and another side-effect, which was not necessarily a responsibility of the founders of new Buddhism, was that new Buddhism overlooked the seriousness of the ineffectiveness of moral rules due to the loosening of the karma principle of Mahayana Buddhism in the new circumstances of Japan. The relaxation of the moral principle had occurred in two respects. One was the concept of merit transfer (*ekō*) of qualitative transformation that good deeds, that had effectiveness only on the choice of better realms in the transmigration process, were admitted to be effective in the attainment of enlightenment. In the theory of primitive Buddhism, the role of good deeds is confined to the addition to good karma, so that it has no effect either on the decrease of bad karma nor on the attainment of enlightenment, whereas, in Mahayana Buddhism, not only is the offsetting effect of good deeds against bad deeds admitted (Sakurabe 1989, p. 90), its role is elevated to the higher dimension of helping the enlightenment of individuals. The relaxation of the role of good karma or the good deed is a reflection of the deep concerns of Maharana Buddhism that intended to be helpful for the salvation of the masses. The qualitative transformation of karma was a readily available measure for the purpose.

Another relaxation of the principles was related to the approval of inter-personal transfer of good deeds (virtue) or good karma, namely merit transfer of directional transformation. This is nothing but the loose interpretation of the self-responsibility principle. In Mahayana Buddhism, good deeds or accumulated good karma were allowed to be transferred to the salvation of others. In other words, individuals could benefit from the good deeds accumulated by other virtuous persons without their own efforts to attain enlightenment. As already explained in Chapter 4, *Jyōdo-shin-shū* relied heavily on the relaxation of the karma principle in this sense. The teaching was established on the belief in Amitabha, who had accumulated a large amount of merit during his training days as Hōzo-bosatsu. It was taught that sincere and deep faith in Amitabha would be rewarded by the transfer of the merits of Amitabha, consequently attaining enlightenment. The rigorous self-enforcing mechanism to establish moral principles was completely discarded at this point for the sake of accomplishing the mission of the salvation of the masses.

Moreover, the moral code of Mahayana Buddhism inherited from primitive Buddhism was so simple that it was not prepared for complicated human relations. This was because primitive Buddhism assumed that the rigorous principle about karma would be sufficient eventually to bring about a moral society. Therefore, the code did not have any instructions about the attitude to be adopted toward others. Rather, it was composed only of dictates about self-disciplining that induce the right attitude in training at quiet and isolated monasteries. For example, the Eight Principles to be observed, called *Hassei-dō*, were right seeing, right thinking, right talking, right conduct, right living, right training, right praying and right intention. The ten bad conducts to be avoided were murdering, stealing, fraud, avenging, reckless speech, double-dealing, over-speech, greed, indignation and wicked view. It must be noted that there is nothing to instruct on how to smooth human relationships and avoid unnecessary conflicts with others. In other words, such instructions as honesty, trust, reliability and the like, which seem to be indispensable moral instructions in complicated human relationships, were entirely missing. It was a moral code suitable only for a homogeneous monastery society isolated from the earthly complexities of human relationships. It is true that some kind of improvement in the moral code was introduced in such codes as the *Roku-hara-mitsu*.[22] This, however, was the moral code prepared for the activity of the *bosatsu*, and not for the use of believers in their complicated daily lives.

It was right that Mahayana Buddhism devoted substantial efforts to the salvation of the masses, and relied heavily on the concept of merit transfer, but it could be argued that it should have been more cautious about the consequences of the relaxation of the rigorous principles of karma for that purpose. The relaxation of these principles, without introducing additional tight moral codes, resulted in the destruction of the self-enforcing mechanism of building up moral systems in society, and this brought about the weakness of the moral codes of Mahayana Buddhism under the focus of medieval Japan, where the interaction with others and the complexity in human relationships suddenly increased owing to the acceleration of the social division of labor and the aggravation of informational asymmetry. In other words, Japanese Buddhism should have prepared to cope with the emergence of the new society by developing a workable system of moral codes that took account of complicated human relationships. In the latter period of medieval Japan, when practice simplification or the easy practice principle introduced by the new Buddhism brought about complicated human relationships with unprecedented speed and deteriorated information asymmetry, the defect of Mahayana Buddhism with respect to its moral codes became a serious and almost fatal blow to the stability of the socio-political system by incurring the excessive sanctification of the present world.

5.2 The Collapse of Trust in the Muromachi Era and in the Warring States Period

5.2.1 *Information Asymmetry*

The serious aggravation in information asymmetry and the collapse of trust occurred in two stages. The emergence of rampant moral hazard in the central government of the Muromachi *bakufu* occurred first, and then this spread into local government

[22]Hiraoka (2016) points out that the *Roku-hara-mitsu* contained two new moral rules related to interpersonal relationship (p. 199) additional to *Hassei-dō*: *fuse* (charity and alms) and *nin-niku* (not having hatred against unjust action).

all over the country, finally leading to the phenomenon of the *gekokujyō* caused by adverse selection during the Warring States period.

At the beginning, confusion was caused by the shift to a heterogenous society due to the increased complexity of the social division of labor and the inadequacy of the existing Buddhist moral code and information-processing system. This was considered to be a manageable situation because the learning processes and an increase in accumulated information could resolve the troubles. It is possible to believe that the shoguns of the Muromachi *bakufu* thought also that they could eventually overcome the confusion through the establishment of new behavioral conventions by way of the long-term continuation of their reign. However, under the governing system of the Muromachi *bakufu*, not only did the confusion caused by information asymmetry increase, but the confusion came to encompass the fundamental discord and discrepancy in the value systems between the samurai and aristocracy. Coupled with the behavior based on Buddhist motivation by the samurai class that caused the disfunction of the feudal system, unmanageable turmoil emerged after the mid-Muromachi era, revealing fundamental defects in the existing standards of conduct and behavioral conventions.

5.2.1.1 Shift to a Heterogeneous Society

The breakdown of the *ritsuryō* system and the diffusion of the *kyūdō* principle nurtured by practice simplification brought about the accelerated progress of the social division of labor in Japanese society. The homogeneous society, in which everyone was engaged in farming, handicraft production and selling at crossroads markets, was converted into a heterogeneous society, in which farmers, artisans and merchants played roles as specialists. The ethical codes of Mahayana Buddhism built on the assumption of homogeneous and quiet monastery society were largely impotent against the complex and competitive human relationships that accompanied the changes. People were perplexed by the diversity of the conduct patterns of different occupations and competition in the market economy. The absence of information about the newly emerged specialized individuals, which gave rise to disbelief and cautiousness towards others, and which in turn encouraged the avoidance of disclosing information and dishonesty in general, aggravated the situation further. It was considered, however, that the heterogenization of the socio-economy was still manageable because the increase in the stock of information and learning by people could accommodate the discrepancy between the demand and supply of information.

Moreover, this was simply a problem in the behavioral part of culture. Old standards of conduct emphasized the importance of harmony among individuals, tacit agreement in society, and prudence and discretion in behavior, whereas the new standards required active negotiation among individuals, explicit contracts instead of tacit agreements, and competition with each other. In summary, while the asymmetry of information increased to an unprecedented level, laying down the conditions for the rise of serious moral hazards, it was still considered to be manageable by the adjustment in the behavioral part ofculture.

However, we believe that the initial informational discrepancy seems to have evolved into an unmanageable situation as the confusion changed from a simple one caused by the excess demand for information to the one related to the conflicts in the value systems in the internal mental model of individuals. This occurred through the intensification of the struggle between the value systems of the samurai and aristocracy against the backdrop of the deterioration of governance in the central government. Both the standards of conduct and the conventions of society became substantially confused after the internalized part of culture came to influence the problem caused by information asymmetry.

5.2.1.2 Aggravation Due to Conflicts in the Value Systems

The conflicts between the aristocracy and samurai in the value systems occurred in this way. The conventions that governed the old society were organized following the order of family status (*ka-kaku* or *ie-gara*). Everything, including promotion, job opportunity and income, was ranked by family status. The shoguns of the Muromachi *bakufu*, who were not so much distinguished by family status among samurai leaders, were the most enthusiastic in the leveling up of its family status. The third shogun, Ashikaga Yoshimitsu (reign 1368–94), who reigned during the most prosperous age of the Muromachi *bakufu*, was a typical example. In his strenuous pursuit of family status, Yoshimitsu approached the aristocracy so as to establish a joint governance system with them (*kōbu-gattai*), and he himself obtained the title of *dajyō-daijin* (the prime minister), which before had been given only to aristocrats. Yoshimitsu also used the name 'king' of Japan, when he negotiated with the Ming dynasty[23] and obtained the monopoly right of trade with the Ming and the right to import Ming currency.

After the beginning of the Warring States period in 1467, when the Ōnin war erupted, the convention of family status (*ka-kaku*) supremacy gradually became eroded and tended to be replaced by the convention of the supremacy of capability or competence (*kiryō*). However, it was not easy to realize and admit the shift of convention, because, in order to negate the supremacy of family status, it was necessary to separate the allocation of job and income allocation from family status. Although it was not so difficult to separate job allocation from family status, it was not easy to separate the allocation of income or fiefdom from family status. To give higher income and additional fiefdom to those with higher capability, it was necessary to find new sources of government revenue. Sakata (1969) asserts that this made inevitable the need to embark on the invasion of neighboring territories, heralding the beginning of the Warring States period. The real and most serious difficulty in replacing family status by capability lay, however, in the persistence of the convention of family status and the strategy of the aristocracy class to use family status as a political tool to cope with the samurai class. It will be shown below that the persistence of aristocratic

[23]The prosperity and gorgeous living of his age owed to the gains obtained through a monopoly of trade with the Ming and the import of Ming currency.

influence on the Muromachi *bakufu* was the fundamental reason for the occurrence of the phenomena of the *gekokujyō*, the social upheaval where those below overthrew those above.

The supremacy of family status was the other side of the coin of the supremacy of aristocratic values in the Muromachi *bakufu*. Yoshimitsu made enormous efforts to merge samurai culture with aristocratic palace culture, and to give elegance and refinement to the former. Fuji (1944) called this the establishment of ceremonial order in samurai society. It is contended that, since the samurai had been trained with the tradition of the elegance of their own everyday behavior as well as in martial arts, the new ceremonial order spread rapidly among the samurai class, especially among those of high family status and *daimyo* residing in Kyoto. For example, the family law (*kahō*) of Takeda (Kai province), one of the most distinguished *daimyo* with high family status inheriting the lineage of Emperor Seiwa, emphasized the importance of elegant behavior and attitudes toward others, including priests, women, children and the poor, as a prerequisite for the good governance of the domain. While the tradition of the samurai respected both elegance and competence, the respect for competence and capability in the aristocratic class had traditionally been relatively weak. The shift of value systems from family status to competence emphasized by Sakata (1969) meant the change in value systems from aristocratic to samurai values in general. It must be noted, however, that the aristocratic value system persisted among the high-ranking samurai, long after the weakening of the power of the Muromachi *bakufu*.

The radical changes in the culture, such as standards of conduct and social conventions, resulted in the serious discrepancy between culture and institutions. As will be discussed below, institutions such as the feudal system and the *bukufu* government could not adjust their quality in accordance with the changes in culture. The inadequacy of institutions to accommodate the changes in culture led to the collapse of trust in society during the Muromachi era, and to the tragic turmoil of the Warring States era, finally threatening the whole of society with catastrophe. It is argued below that Japan during the Warring States period barely escaped catastrophe, and succeeded to rehabilitate trust after overcoming the turmoil, owing to the establishment of a new culture adequate to overcome the asymmetry of information. This, however, was accomplished only under the reign of the Tokugawa *bakufu*. Let us trace the process of the deterioration of trust in the Muromachai *bakufu* and then examine the serious turmoil of the Warring States period.

5.2.2 The Deterioration of Trust in the Muromachi Era

The drastic transformation of the socio-economy that became apparent after the Southern and Northern Dynasties period brought about the collapse of trust in human relationships in central government, leading to a chaotic situation in the governing system in various respects. First, there occurred dysfunction of the relationship-based politics of central government due to serious information asymmetry, and this occurred in tandem with, and was accompanied by, the difficulty in establishing effective institutions, including a workable conference system (*hyōjyō*) among *daimyos*, leading to the crisis in governance at every level. As the deterioration of the political governance system proceeded, the integrity of the socio-economy was eroded further due to the unsuitability of standards of conduct and conventions with the development of the market economy and the intensification of competition.

It seems that, triggered by the deterioration of the central governing system, the confusion spread into every stratum of society, aggravating the socio-political order all over the country. The masses were obliged to seek insulation from profane obligations in safe havens called without-*en* (*muen*) places[24] (Amino 1996a)—temples that protected refugees, cities with civil autonomy, crossroads markets, and groups of performance artists. Furthermore, the confusion was aggravated by the frequent riots (*ikki*) nationwide, such as the *tokusei* riots seeking the cancellation of financial obligations and land sales contracts. Although the *tokusei* riots meant the denial of the efficiency of market competition and the development of the social division of labor, rulers were quite often obliged to take an accommodative stance to them in order to maintain social order. One of the reasons for the stance of the rulers was the neutrality of the effect of the *tokusei* order (*rei*) on the efficiency of agricultural production, as previously explained.

5.2.2.1 Relationship-Based Politics in Central Government

Ashikaga Takauji, founder of the Muromachi *bakufu*, promulgated the *Kenmu-shikimoku* in 1336, which announced that the principle of the *bakufu* administration should be based on reason and morality (*dōri*), not on the status of the governing families (*kakaku*). This reflects partly the weakness of the legitimacy of the sovereignty of the Muromachi *bakufu* governed by the Ashikaga family. The founder of the Kamakura *bakufu*, Yoritomo Minamoto, who was the legitimate leader of the Genji samurai group organized by the heir of Emperor Seiwa (reign 858–76), became the shogun through defeating another samurai group, the Heike, following ex-emperor Takakura (reign 1168–80).[25] Heike had been under severe criticism for despotism, with close connection to the Fujiwara, a leading aristocratic family. On the other hand, Takauji established the Muromachi *bakufu* in 1336 in a battle against Emperor Godaigo[26] of the Southern Dynasty and established the Northern Dynasty. The conflict between the two dynasties continued until 1392. Moreover, there were

---

[24]*En* means inter-personal relationships.

[25]Emperor Antoku, son of Emperor Takakura, was two years old in 1180 when the order to dispose of Heike was issued.

[26]The kamakura *bakfu*, in which the despotism of Tokusō was notorious, was ended in 1333 by Emperor Godaigo with the help of samurai groups, including the Nitta and Ashikaga. The government (Kenmu new government) established by Godaigo was brought down by Ashikaga in 1336, and Godaigo was obliged to establish the Southern Dynasty in Yoshino, which fought with the Northern Dynasty in Kyoto under the control of Ashikaga over the legitimacy of the national government during 1336–92.

several families that had family status at the level comparable to the Ashikaga family, so the Muromachi shoguns were obliged to pay close attention to the power balance between the other powerful lords. From the beginning of the fourteenth century to the collapse of the *bakufu* at the end of the sixteenth century, the Muromachi *bakufu* was annoyed by the incessant coups and internal wars mainly related to the choice of heirs of the *bakufu* and dominant *daimyos*, that largely reflected conflicts regarding family status.

The government system, established by Takauji following the model of the Kamakura *bakufu*, was composed of dual systems: the housekeeping (*man-dokoro*) and military (samurai *dokoro*) system of the shogun family[27] on the one hand, and the national government system on the other. The national government system was composed of two institutions: the consultative section (*hyōjyō*) and the judicial section (*hikitsuke-kata*).[28] Partly due to the frequent occurrence of internal wars, the former system of national government based on conferences among *daimyos* did not function effectively and weakened rapidly.[29] The third shogun, Yoshimitsu (1358–1408), established an autocratic system, in which every decision was made by him with the assistance of a *kanrei*, chosen from among three dominant *daimyos*: Shiba, Hosokawa and Hatakeyama. The prosperity of the *bakufu* was at its peak during the reign of Yoshimitsu, who energetically tried to raise the status of the Ashikaga family, as already noted. However, the prosperity was highly unstable since the power of the shogun was dependent on the delicate power balance of leading *daimyos*—three kanrei families and four samurai *dokoro* chief (*bettō*) families: Yamana, Isshiki, Akamatsu and Kyōgoku.

The autocratic system adopted by Yoshimitsu was soon replaced by a relationship-based political system, in which a *kanrei* and a stewardship of *man-domoro*, played dominant roles in the administration. The role of the consultative section (*hyōjyō*) in which leading *daimyos* participated, was slighted and neglected, and most policy was determined by the shogun and a *kanrei*. Instead of making decisions after meetings and conferences at the *hyōjyō*, it became customary for officers to visit the residence of the shogun or *kanrei* to obtain the direct settlement of disputes and instructions on administrative matters. Against the background of repeated internal wars, it was difficult to have regular meetings participated in by all qualified members

[27] *Man-dokoro* was in charge of the income and expenditure of the shogun family and judicial matters concerned with the fiefs of *gokenin*. The samurai *dokoro* was in charge of police and justice, mainly in Kyoto.

[28] There were three major roles for the judicial section (*hikitsuke-kata*): affairs related to endowing fiefs (*ando-sata*), disputes among fiefs (*shomu-sata*), and appointing of official positions (*kanto-sata*). The members of the *hikitsuke-kata* overlapped with those of the *hyoujyou-shu*.

[29] Satō (1963) asserted that Yoshimitsu repressed the national government system in order to integrate the dual system. Yoshida (2014), however, contends that the power of the *hikitsuke-kata* had become weakened due to the ineffectiveness of the section in the incessant internal wars. For example, the section could not decide the endowment of fiefs on the basis of the concrete evidence of achievement on the battlefield, as was customary in the Kamakura *bakufu*. This was because the shougun had endowed fiefs instantly without consulting the *hikitsuke-kata* on the battlefield, probably to raise fighting spirits.

of the consultative section (*hyōjyō*), so that quite often consulting was implemented individually.

Official positions and related material and pecuniary interests, 'wealth', were utilized as political tools and allocated in accordance with the degree of intimacy with Yoshimitsu, called *Muromachi-dono*.[30] The *daimyos* residing in Kyoto competed for political rights and material interests by way of their personal relationships with the shoguns (Yoshida 2014). It was a matter of course that corruption became rampant, and the scenery of *bakufu* politics was filled with covetousness, slander and flattery, which are either caused by or get effectiveness from information asymmetry. The fragility of the system was brought into focus when the sixth shogun, Yoshinori, was assassinated by one of the four samurai *dokoro bettō*, Akamatsu, in 1441.

The deterioration of the ethical codes and the decline of the independent and self-help spirit of the samurai that characterized the ethics of the samurai in the Kamakura era, under the reign of the Ashikaga *bakufu*, is most clearly seen in the family precept written by Sadachika Ise, who held the stewardship of the *man-domoro* from 1456 through 1473,[31] for his son. He wrote that the most important talent to be a family chief is not capability in various things but diligence and the willingness to associate with others, and that bribing by inviting to dinner and giving gifts to others is indispensable to prevent the spread of unfavorable rumors, that might ultimately invite the displeasure of the shogun (Dōbunkan henshūkyoku 1910, pp. 141–151, *Ise Sadachika kyōkun*). Having taken charge of the tutelage of the eighth shogun, Yoshimasa (reign 1449–73) in his infant days, Sadachika wielded enormous power in the *bakufu* by means of plotting and slandering. For example, he was the most ardent promoter in the unsuccessful plot to assassinate the formal successor of the Ashikaga family, Yoshimi, to replace him by the son of Yoshimasa, in cooperation with Yoshimasa's wife Hino Tomiko. This well-known scandal was a major trigger for the Ōnin war (1467–77) that heralded the beginning of the Warring States period. The deterioration of ethics in the salon culture, full of vanity, formality without substance, bribes, and relationship-based politics, and characterized by slander, plots and treachery, is also depicted in Sagara (1968).

On the other hand, relationship-based politics intensified information asymmetry, because it caused the internalization of information within concerned parties. It is important to note that the interaction of relationship-based politics and information asymmetry finally destroyed the reliability and importance of information in general through downgrading the quality of the information. It seems that, during the Warring States period, Japanese society was in a state in which information about others almost completely lost value. Takeda Shingen (1521–73), one of the most powerful *daimyos* during the Warring States period, equipped with invincible cavalry soldiers, is said to have confirmed every piece of information collected on the battlefield through asking whether it was supported by convincing and concrete evidence (Sagara 1968).

---

[30] Muromachi is the name of a town in Kyoto where the *bakufu* was installed.

[31] The Ise family was in position from the end of the fourteenth century.

5.2.2.2 The *Shugo* and *Sengoku Daimyo*

The political power of the Muromachi *bakufu* began to deteriorate after the death of Yoshimitsu in 1408, and the deterioration accelerated after the death of Yoshimasa in 1490. With respect to the central government, the deterioration was caused by the relationship-based political style. Local politics, which was basically left in the hands of local lords, *shugo*, appointed by the shogun for each province, also became dysfunctional toward the latter half of the Muromachi era. One of the reasons for this was the imperfection of the Darwinian mechanism due to the persistence of the convention of family status. While the assertion that capability, not family status, should be the guiding principle to choose leaders became stronger during the Muromachi era, the choice was always implemented without touching upon the ultimate ruling right of the top family. Just like in the shogun family, there occurred repeated coups in *shugo* fiefs, and in almost all the fiefs the control right was in the hands of conventions composed of major vassals. The notion that each fief belonged to all members of vassals came to be widely shared. However, at the same time, there was always another shared view that the ultimate representative right should be held by a member of the *shugo* family. Therefore, after a coup, the winner vassal never became the next leader of the fief and, instead, another member of the *shugo* family was given representative power (Satō 1963; Katsumata 1996). In this sense, coups and revolutions were always implemented within the confines of family status during the Muromachi era, so that the Darwinian process never worked through to realize efficient outcomes.

The *shugo*, many of whom became *sengoku daimyos* later on, competed in the arms buildup with each other by hiring *kokujin*, local indigenous lords. The intimate relationship between the *bakufu* and *shugo* during the early period of the *bakufu* established on human ties became weaker, whereas the *shugo* were always expecting the rehabilitation of the order based on the authority of the *bakufu* (Nagahara 1961, p. 512). Despite the *shugo*'s move toward independence, the *bakufu* intervened in the power struggle by sending *bakufu* housemen as executives of fiefs or by appointing other *shugo* family members or vassals to influential posts (*hōkō-shū*) in fiefs. This kind of behavior was not necessarily in accordance with the intention of fief members to establish new orders based on capability, however, so that intervention in local power struggle led to the further decline of the authority of the *bakufu* (Satō 1963, p. 30; Katsumata 1996, p. 25).

5.2.2.3 Request for Sharing and Aspiration for Homogeneity

Behind the radical changes in the culture, such as the standards of conduct and social conventions and the consequent collapse of trust during the Muromachi era, was the serious discrepancy between the moral codes inherited by Mahayana Buddhism and early Buddhism, and the accelerated progress in the social division of labor. The advance of the social division of labor was due partly to the collapse of the *ritsuryō* system and partly due to the spread of *kyūdō* behavior.

The marketization of the economy owing to the acceleration of the social division of labor resulted in the intensification of competition after economic gains. Individuals were obliged to compete for the fruits of the market economy: the acquisition of such fruit motivated individuals to participate in competition. The winners in the competition were encouraged to be engaged in further competition, whereas the losers were obliged to seek shelter from the harsh consequences of competition. Muromachi society came to be equipped with two kinds of shelters for the losers.

One of the shelters was the *muen* (without *en*) places, touched upon above, such as temples—*kakekomi* (run into) temples or *enkiri* (severance from *en*) temples, that protected refugees and the abused, cities with civil autonomy like Sakai in Izumi and Ōminato in Ise, and groups of itinerants in various performance arts. Amino (1996b) summarizes the functions of *muen* places as the disappearance of *en*-based family and master–servant relationships, emancipation from financial obligations, the absence of implication, exemption from taxation, and hiding spaces for criminals and slaves. He contends that, against the background of the spread of *muen* places, there was a move toward city society by free citizens in Japanese society during the Southern and Northern Dynasties period, in which the marketized economy run by financiers, transportation workers, artisans and merchants emerged and actively engaged in non-agricultural activities. His basic assertion lay in emphasizing the emergence of the non-agricultural economy free from tight indigenous regulations, probably led by the ideology of the supremacy of the emperor system based on agriculture (Amino 1984). Following Amino, Nakazawa (1994) presented a view of the socio-economy composed of segmented (*shikirareta*) spaces related to agriculture and governed by the *sengoku daimyo*, and smooth (*namerakana*) spaces related to non-agriculture largely governed by believers of *Ikko-shu, Jyodo-shin-shu,* aiming at an homogeneous society under the grace of Amitabha Buddha.

Both Amino and Nakazawa emphasized diversity and the free structure of the new segment of society as a counterpart to agricultural, established society regulated by the traditional powers. It is not clear, however, in what sense such a move to escape from the restriction of *en* is related to the traditional structure of society.[32] Our analysis suggests that behavior to escape from the *en*-based society emerged not from the severe restrictions of traditional agrarian society but rather because the pressure of *en* on individuals was intensified in the process of the lowering of the trust of society caused by the acceleration of the marketization of the economy. It seems to be more pertinent to consider that the pressure of *en* was intensified in the marketized lives. Because of the enhanced power of *en* under the condition of the lowered trust level, those who could not accommodate the pressure of *en* were obliged to seek *muen* places. It is too simplistic to discuss the role and emergence of *muen* places in a two-sector framework of repressive agrarian society and free

[32] While the various functions Amino raises as the burdens of *en* seem to be related to the restrictions in rural lives, it is also possible to regard them as constraints on the urban and marketized lives in the non-agricultural sector.

non-agrarian society.[33] In other words, the proliferation of *muen* places seems to be rooted in the aggravation of information asymmetry due to the acceleration of the social division of labor and the unreliability of institutions rather than the rigidity of the rural sector.

Another shelter against the market economy was related to the request for the sharing of the fruits accrued in the market economy. Uprisings such as the religious riots or the debt cancellation riots could be regarded as attempts to realize homogeneity in society by means of sharing. They represented the aspiration of the suppressed classes to negate the cruel consequences of the market economy. This, however, was anachronistic in the sense of being motivated by the desire to return to an archeological homogeneous society. The demand for rectification of the inequality caused by severe market competition was apparently incompatible with the aim of the *sengoku daimyos*, who were eager to benefit from the efficiency of the social division of labor in order to strengthen the economic power of their territories.

Moreover, the different approach of the *sengoku daimyo* toward the two kinds of riot must be noted. The *tokusei* riots were an insurrection by the people requesting the cancellation of financial debts to rich financiers, who were protected by the rulers as ample sources of fiscal revenues. The *sengoku daimyos* were ambivalent towards the *tokusei* riots: although the uprisings themselves were detrimental to the governance of their territory, the people's resistance against 'greedy' lending activity by financiers was justifiable from the viewpoint of social stability. Moreover, from the viewpoint of the residual control right, the inefficiency implications of the *tokusei* riots were not substantial, as is explained in Chapter 3.[34] However, in view of the fiscal revenue obtained from financiers, rulers are reluctant to enact harsh policies against financiers. It seems to be that the stance of the *sengoku daimyo* was more or less neutral.

On the other hand, the *ikkō* riots were an uprising of the Buddhist *Ikkō-shū* or *Jyōdo-shin-shū* sect, aiming to realize an equal and homogeneous society by way of sharing of the accumulated merit of Amitabha Buddha. Furthermore, the *ikki* people respected Amitabha Buddha as having supreme power outweighing profane rulers. Toward the end of Murimachi era, the strength of the *ikkō* riots expanded rapidly in the Hokuriku and Mikawa areas around Nagoya, mobilizing large number of believers. Starting from underdeveloped regions like mountainous and seaside areas through calling for participation of hunters, fishermen and artisans, the *Jyōdo-shin-shū* gained influence in the developed regions in the alluvial plains through the participation of farmers and merchants. They tried to establish a self-governing community tied by faith in Amitabha Buddha. The *sengoku daimyos*, however, tackled the *ikkō* riots by means of severe suppression and military crackdown without hesitation. There were two reasons for this. First, the *ikkō* sect regarded Amitabha Buddha as an

---

[33]Nishiyachi (2002) contends that the role of cities and other *muen* places needs to be treated separately.

[34]The residual control right was held by the *ryōshu* and delegated to the *daikan* and *myōshu*, so that neither cultivators nor financiers (*tokubun* right holders) had the residual control right. Therefore, the *tokusei-rei* was neutral with respect to production efficiency and had an effect on income distribution between cultivators and financiers.

omnipotent god transcending every secular power, inviting the anger and suppression of powerful leaders such as Oda Nobunaga, who was planning to be a 'king' through uniting the country. Second, they aimed at establishing a homogeneous community disregarding the consequences of market competition and the inequality caused in the developing market economy and denying any differences in occupation and hence efficiency accruing from the development of the social division of labor. This was also what could not be admitted by Oda Nobunaga, who respected the efficiency of the market economy, and energetically implemented the policy of the free market (*rakuichi-rakuza*) with free entry, the policy of promoting the market economy through abolishing the vested interests of monopolistic trade associations (*za*).

5.2.3 The Collapse of Trust and Turmoil in the Warring States Period

5.2.3.1 Self-Salvation Based on *En*

The most serious chaotic situation caused by the discord of the new behavioral conventions and existing institutions was the difficulty in establishing feudal contracts based on vassalage and enfeoffment in samurai society, consequently leading to instability in the lord–vassal relationship, the core human relationship in the feudal system.

Private battles and the exercise of military power without *bakufu* approval became ubiquitous during the latter part of the Muromachi era, especially in the Warring States period. It had been a common phenomenon during the Heian era when the judicial system was still underdeveloped, so that territorial disputes were resolved by the adversary (*tōjisha*) system, in the terminology of the annals of legislation. Territorial disputes were brought to a court in which the judges had a close relationship with either side of the parties concerned. Quite often this system resulted in private battles (*Fehde*) (Satō 2014). This situation changed drastically toward the end of the Muromachi era or during the Warring States period. Katsumata (1978, 1996) claims that the motivation of the samurai class was governed by the ethical code of self-salvation,[35] empowered by a strongly individualistic spirit. There occurred three new aspects. First, disputes resolved by means of private battle came to cover not only territorial issues but also other matters including injury, murder, default of

[35] Katsumata (1978) is translated into English by Katsumata and Collcutt, and is contained in the Princeton University Press version, as noted in the references. They use the English term 'self-redressing' for the Japanese *jiko-kyūsai*. But this term is not pertinent because *kyūsai* (salvation) based on *en* implies Buddhist salvation. It is important to note that the term *en* is neglected in the English version of the paper. The Japanese version entitled *Sengoku-hō no tenkai*, originally written by Katsumata alone, expresses the concept as '*en ni motozuku jiko-kyūsai*', which implies that the attitude to *jiko-kyūsai* conduct is based on the Buddhist notion of '*en*'. Why this substitution or misinterpretation has occurred is not clear.

financial obligations, and so on. It seems that this reflects not only the dysfunction of the central government system due to the deterioration of relationship-based governance, but also the breakdown of the administrative and judicial system at the local level due to the emergence of the market transaction of *tokubun* rights, in which judicial rights associated with bureaucratic positions were transacted together with income rights (Hashita 1975). Second, self-salvation was implemented in a group called *en* to which individual samurai belonged, namely ties such as kinship, locality, art circle, partnership in riots or in vassalage, and the like. Vassalage, in the sense of the human relationship between master and vassals, came to be conceived of as not so binding, since it was only one of many ties that bound the samurai. Third, the samurai during the period came to regard self-salvation based on *en* as the supreme behavioral code worth pursuing, consequently sharing their destiny with members in the same *en*. Supremacy in this case is based on the sanctification of behavior similar to *kyūdō* behavior.

It seems that this behavior reflects the strong influence of Buddhism and it is important to note that Buddhism revealed its highly destructive nature against social stability during the period. In the mind construct of the samurai, ties based on the *en* were the consequence of the deeds of their past lives, so that the relationship to such ties were of higher value in terms of the destiny of life under the circumstances of transmigration, and hence were stronger and much more binding than the lord–vassal relationships, which were based on only contractual relationships in the current life. Moreover, and more importantly, as discussed in Chapter 4, karma accumulated by the end of the present life determined the life in the future—whether an individual is able to get out of transmigration or in which realm in the transmigration the individual is destined to be reborn. During this period almost all the most powerful *daimyos* were ardent believers in Buddhism—Uesugi Kenshin (*Shingon-mikkyō*), Mori Motonari (*Nenbutus-shū*), and Shimazu Tadayoshi (belief in *bosatu*) among others. Kenshin blamed Takeda Shingen for lacking respect for Buddha, but Shingen himself was a most serious believer of *Tendai-mikkyō* (Sakata 1969, pp. 129–131). While the utilization of human relationships in territorial disputes in the Heian or early Muromachi era constituted so-called connections (Satō 2014) or the pursuit of material gain through the help of a 'man of influence', the behavior of self-salvation of the samurai during the Warring States period was largely based on the Buddhist concept of *en* related to the relationship in the process of transmigration.

In the context of such notions of self-salvation and of group ties, the enforcement of the feudal contract, based on reciprocity in the form of conferment of property rights in land (or official position) and the assumption of a loyalty obligation as a vassal, encountered serious difficulties. The obligations of the lord–vassal relationship were regarded as only temporarily binding, not related to past lives, so that feudal loyalty could easily be disregarded in consideration of the more important group ties emanating from relationships in past lives and the consideration of the future life. Not only rebellions and treachery but also conflicts among vassals were daily and ubiquitous matters in the *sengoku daimyo* system, and the latter, in particular, gave rise to unmanageable confusion in the governance of the *sengoku daimyo* house (*ie*). Treachery was an immoral act from the viewpoint of loyalty to masters, but it was perfectly justifiable from the viewpoint of self-salvation or loyalty to the *en*-based groups. The *sengoku daimyos* had to make enormous efforts to organize the feudalistic loyalty system with their vassals through dissolutions of the notion of *en*-based group ties. We will give a detailed account below about the laws enacted by the *sengoku daimyos*, called the *bunkoku* laws, to organize a workable and loyal vassal system under their control.

It is important to note that self-salvation based on *en* magnified the turmoil caused by information asymmetry. This was because information on *en* in prior lives, which was based on the imaginary experience of individuals, cannot be verified by concrete evidence. Moreover, while the concept of *Fehde* in Europe was mainly concerned with blood relationships, relationship based on the *en* was enlarged to the attributes of not only lineage relationship but also samurai groups, aristocrats, temples and shrines, villages, performance art groups and all other sorts of groups, so that *en* was considered to be a group related by destiny, and private battles were easily converted into battles among groups (Katsumata 1979, pp. 248–249). As a result, how a battle based on self-salvation might be expanded in line with group relationships was very difficult to forecast, so that consequent information asymmetry quite often brought trust levels in society into unmanageable confusion.

5.2.3.2 *Gekokujyō*

The nationwide turmoil and collapse of trust during the Warring States period was characterized by the conventional and hackneyed phrase, *gekokujyō*, comprising *ge* (the low), *koku* (overcome), *jyō* (the high). The *gekokujyō* is a key concept to explain the process of social transformation caused by cultural changes where the low supplanted the high-and-mighty, consequently leading to the upheaval of social and political order through the continual downward shift of the center of gravity of the power balance. There were two patterns of *gekokujyō*; one is within-family *gekokujyō* (first pattern) in which the master–vassal relationship within a ruling family (*daimyo*) was changed by the revolt of vassals, and the other was the phenomenon of between-families *gekokujyō* (second pattern) in which a low-ranked family (*daimyo*) defeated a high-ranked family (*daimyo*). It is extremely important to note the difference between and coexistence of the two patterns. This is because not only do the socio-political impacts of the phenomenon differ so much between the two patterns, but the mechanism for the occurrence of the phenomenon is quite different also. It is a crucial point to understand both patterns correctly and synthesize them in order to arrive at a proper explanation of the role of cultural change in Japanese growth. Existing studies seem to be concerned with the first pattern only.

The first pattern of *gekokujyō*, the within-family pattern, relating to the master–vassal relationship, occurred both at the level of central government, *bakufu*, and at the level of the *shugo* or *daimyo*. The simplest example of this pattern is the personal rebellion of a vassal against a master. Although this type of incident occurred frequently, most of them were caused by personal relationships and motivations, so were not related to the basic structure of society. The frequency of the incidents reflects the instability of society, but the instability of society seems to be rooted in more fundamental factors than personal hate or hostility. Much historical literature has focused, instead, on the conflicts related to inheritor struggles (Satō 1963; Katsumata 1993). These conflicts related to the characteristic governance system that came to be prevalent in the Muromachi era, where important decisions, including the choice of the heir of a family was decided by conference among the main vassals (*kashin*), not by the individual decision of the master, as was the case in the Kamakura era. The rise of confusion lay in the internal power struggle among vassals. In the case of the *bakufu*, we have already explained that, under the despotism established by Yoshimitsu, government was virtually controlled by major three *kanrei* families and four *bettō* families of samurai *dokoro*, while the official conference system of the *hyōjyō* was incapacitated. This system invited serious power struggles regarding inheritor issues after the assassination of the sixth shogun, Yoshinori, in 1429,[36] that eventually led to the Ōnin war from 1467 through 1477. The Ōnin war was the power struggle regarding the leadership of the *bakufu* between two *kanrei* families, Hosokawa Masamoto and Yamana Sozen, and was triggered by the conflict over the issue of the heirs of the Shiba and Hatakeyama families.[37] The confusion was aggravated as the conflict between the two *kanrei* was extended to a conflict between Yoshihiro, a son of the eighth shogun, Yoshimasa (reign period 1449–73), and Yoshimi, the junior brother of Yoshimasa. The war involved all the major *daimyo* residing in Kyoto and almost all the major parts of the city of Kyoto were burnt down.

Moreover, there also occurred a coup to replace the shogun by its vassal. In 1493 the *kanrei* Hosokawa Yoshimoto expelled the tenth shogun, Yoshitane, and established the new (eleventh) shogun, Yoshizumi. This coup is said to have triggered the move into the Warring States period.

It is important to note that similar conflicts occurred within *daimyo* territories nationwide. In almost all the cases, the heir issues were resolved at the conference of major vassals. Furthermore, as Katsumata (1996) contends, there is another salient feature in almost all these incidents of inheritor conflicts common to the shogun and *daimyo* families. This is that the coup or intervention by vassals rarely resulted in the supplanting of the position of the master by vassals. The consequence of coups and internal wars within families never resulted in the seizing of power by servants, but in replacing the incumbent master by another member of the same ruling family. In the case of the coup after the Ōnin war, Hosokawa established hegemony in the *bakufu*, so he could establish the 'Hosokawa *bakufu*' if he had wanted; but he did not choose to be a new shogun. Katsumata (1996) explains this by resorting to the robustness of the order based on family status (p. 17).[38] In other words, although the family status of the Ashikaga family was not sufficiently high, the *kanrei* and other

[36] Yoshinori inherited the high-handed politics of Yoshimitsu and repressed the *shugo* by military action, and this aroused serious fear among the *shugo*, leading to the unprecedented assassination of Yoshinori by Akamatsu in 1441.

[37] According to Ikegami et al. (1995), this Hatakeyama is classified as a different family (located in Kawachi) from Hatakeyama as a *kanrei*, whose main domain was Noto.

[38] Goza (2016) notes that, through the destruction and turmoil, the shogunate lost value and was not attractive for Hosokawa to inherit the position (p. 259).

related *daimyo* still stuck to the importance of family status and tried to support the continuation of the Ashikaga family.

Why did the first pattern of *gekokujyō* occur? Satō (1963) and Katsumata (1993) contend that the Confucian ideal of revolution is responsible for this. Satō (1963) claims that during the Muromachi era there occurred a widely held notion that the *shiki* (official position) of the shogun or *shugo* were not private property, but possessors were responsible for the maintenance of peace and order of the country and territories (p. 30). Katsumata (1996) ascribes the reason for the phenomena to the spread of the notion that those who cannot maintain order and peace should not rule a territory (p. 33). Both Satō and Katsumata explain that the emergence of turmoil during the Warring States period was caused by the weakening of authoritative power in society. The loss of the value of shogun status, coupled with the similar loss of the value of *shugo* status appointed by the shogun, led to the weakening of authoritative politics. The decline of the authoritative power of the shogun and *shugo* is claimed to imply the shift in value systems from family status to real capability (*kiryō*) to maintain peace and order. It must be noted, however, that, while Sato and Katsumata's theory explains the reason for the occurrence of coups by vassals and the role of the Confucian theory of revolution, it does not explain the phenomenon of the continual downward shift of the center of gravity in the power balance, that comprised the fundamental impact of *gekokujyō* on the socio-political system. This is because in the first pattern of *gekokujyō*, the coup by vassals rarely resulted in the supplanting of the position of the master by vassals, so that the level of family status did not change. In order to understand the continual change of the gravity of power balance, it is indispensable to investigate the second pattern of *gekokujyō*.

The second pattern of *gekokujyō* is concerned with conflicts between families (*daimyos*). During the Warring States period, and for more than 100 years, *daimyo* and other local lords repeatedly engaged in life-and-death battles all over the country. The second pattern of *gekokujyō* means that in the numerous battles there was a tendency for the low-ranking to defeat the high-ranking, and there occurred a reversal of the existing social order. In other words, the downward shift of the center of gravity in the power balance is the crucial characteristic of *gekokujyō*, for which a coherent explanation must be given.

The conventional understanding of the term *gekokujyō* is typically associated with the rise of Toyotomi Hideyoshi (1536/7–98), from the son of a peasant in a village near Nagoya to the powerful ruler of the whole country, the supreme minister and chancellor of an emperor (*kanpaku-dajyō-daijin*). His life is an example of the rise of the lowest ranking to the highest and was the most typical case that exemplified the continual move of the real power of society downward to individuals, the most salient feature of the second pattern of *gekokujyō*. While Hideyoshi was the most salient example of the second pattern, his case was not an exception.

Let us examine the relationship of success or failure of *daimyo* life with family status more generally. Ikegami (Y) et al. (1995) give a comprehensive list of the *shugo* during 1454–1615 as well as family history, including the family tree of 155 major *daimyos* in the Warring States period. From these data, we can obtain the following four propositions. In the following, the family is classified to belong to a high status where some member of the family had been engaged in the position of *shugo* or higher position, such as *kankei* or *bettō* of the samurai *dokoro* during the period before the beginning of the Ōnin war in 1467 after the year 1454.[39] Out of the 155 *daimyo*, 21were classified as being of high family status and 134 as low family status. The term 'ruin' of a *daimyo* means the termination of their activity as a major military power due to defeat in battle, coup, or some other reason, even if the family name (*katoku*) continued to exist thereafter; and the term 'survive' means the retention of military power after the Sekigahara battle in 1600. The name *daimyo* means family,[40] and the domain name in parentheses is a major domain governed by the family.

1. All three *kanrei* families did not survive the Warring States period. Shiba (Owari) was ruined in 1561, Hatakeyama (Noto) in 1577, and Hosakawa (Settsu) around 1592.
2. Three out of the four *bettō* of the samurai *dokoro* also did not survive. Yamana (Tajima) was ruined in 1577, and both Isshiki (Tango) and Akamatu (Harima) were ruined in 1600 after the Sekigahara war. Kyōgoku (Ōmi) barely survived but met with expropriation of territory (*kaieiki*) by the Tokugawa *bakufu*.
3. Out of 14 other high family status *daimyo* whose family members were *shugo* before the beginning of the Ōnin war, nine *daimyo* did not survive. Imagawa (Suruga) and Hatakeyama (Kawachi) were ruined in 1569, Togashi (Kaga) in 1547, Takeda (Kai) in 1582, Asai (Ōmi) in 1573, Toki (Mino) in 1525, Ōuchi (Suō) in 1555 and Kikuchi (Higo) in 1550.[41] Rokkaku (Ōmi) became a servant in charge of the daily affairs (*otogishu*) of Hideyoshi. The survivors were Uesugi (Echigo), Ogasawara (Shinano), Ōtomo (Bunngo), Sō (Tsushima) and Shimazu (Satsuma).
4. Out of the remaining 134 *daimyo* who were not *shugo* nor in higher positions before the beginning of the Ōnin war and were cited in the database of 155 family histories, 62 survived until after the Sekigahara battle and 72 were ruined. The surviving *daimyo* included the major winners of the Warring States period, such as Date (Mutsu), Tokugawa (Matsudaira),[42] (Mikawa), Oda (Owari), and Mōri (Aki). It must be noted that the family status of these four *daimyo* before the beginning of the Ōnin war was relatively low or at least not distinguished. Mōri

[39]The available list of the *shugo* does not include data before the year 1454, so that it is possible that *daimyo* families whose member had been *shugo* or of higher official position are excluded from the list of high family status group.

[40]Powerful families used to be engaged in *shugo* in plural domains. We have classified all the names of the *shugo* with the same family name as the same family unless classified separately in the family history in Ikegami et al. (1995).

[41]Shibukawa (Hizen) was also the *shugo* since before the Ōnin war for a short period, but Ikegami et al. (1995) does not give their family history.

[42]The Matsudaira family at Mikawa, who are ancestor of Matsudaira Chikauji, called themselves Tokugawa, from the eighth generation, Ieyasu.

was a small *kokujin*, Tokugawa (Matsudaira) was a *dogō*, and Oda was a high-class houseman (*jyūsin*) of the *shugo-dai* (vice-*shugo*) of the *shugo* Shiba. Date was a *jitō*, although this family was offered a position of *shugo* in 1522.[43]

These propositions show the importance of the second pattern of *gekokujyō*. There seems to be a general tendency that high family status *daimyo* with the status of *shugo* or higher were less powerful or less perseverant compared with the low family status *daimyo* in the turmoil after the beginning of the Ōnin war. While 24% (5/21) of *daimyo* whose family members were in a position of *shugo* or higher survived, the percentage of low family status *daimyo* to do so was 46% (62/134). Moreover, six out of seven leading families of the Muromachi *bakufu* (*kanrei* and *bettō* of the samurai *dokoro*) were ruined, and all the three *daimyo* who won the struggle of the Warring States period, Oda, Toyotomi and Tokugawa (Matsudaira) were out of low ranking status.

It is interesting, however, that while almost every researcher refers to the second pattern of *gekokujyō* to exposit the pervasive phenomenon of social upheaval where those below overcame those above, or to explain the turbulence where the low supplanted the high-and-mighty, no one has presented a convincing explanation about the mechanism for such occurrence. Why did those below become stronger in military power against those above? In the next section, we will try to provide the following hypothesis. We start from two conventional facts. First, it is confirmed that family status was of crucial value among the aristocratic samurai society of the Muromachi era, where the shoguns themselves made enormous efforts to merge the samurai government with the aristocratic order, *kōbu-gattai*. The value of family status tended to decline as the authority of the shogun and the *shugo* weakened due to the increase in the power of vassals against masters, as already explained by the term of the first pattern of *gekokujyō*. The value system based on family status, the typical aristocratic value system, was replaced rapidly by another value system that emphasized the capability or competence of individuals, the typical samurai value system, which was nurtured by and large through the attempt of self-salvation based on *en*. It seems that the replacement occurred less rapidly with respect to higher ranking *daimyo*, who had made significant efforts to adapt to aristocratic discipline and order to obtain the high family status. Second, it is noted that the military strength of the *sengoku daimyo* crucially depended on the scale and quality of the military power of the *kokujin* (indigenous lord), with whom the *daimyo* engaged in contract through offering benefits such as the protection of territory and salary based on the *kandaka* system. Incidentally, the *kandaka* system was a system of redistribution of rents obtained from a territory adopted by the *sengoku daimyos*, in which given proportions of the *tokubun* in the territory were redistributed to *myōshu* or other *shiki* holders, and the remaining sum was obtained by the *daimyo* and redistributed as

[43]Tanemune Date (1488–1565), who aimed for the position of the *tandai* of Ōshū, a position to govern the whole Tohoku area, declined the offer of the *shugo* of Mutsu (Shimizu 2018). Since there was no position of *shugo* in Mutsu until that time, this was an extremely kind offer, implying high respect by the *bakufu* for the military strength of Date.

kandaka among the vassals and hired *kokujin*. Those who were distributed *kandaka* were obliged to offer military and other services to the *daimyo*.[44]

On the basis of these two facts, we will contend that there occurred adverse selection in the market of hiring *kokujin* due to the serious asymmetry of information about the true capability of the *kokujin* between the *kokujin* and *daimyo*. Because of the informational asymmetry, the *daimyos* did not have any information about the competence of the *kokujin*, so were obliged to offer average benefits irrespective of competence and capability. Since data on family status was available, the *daimyos* offered benefits to the applicant *kokujin* according to family status only. For the sake of simplicity, let us assume that the family status of the applicants, the *kokujin*, is the same. High family status *daimyo*, who tended to believe that family status was most important as a quality of vassals because it nurtures discipline and order, were less generous to offer high average benefits to hire *kokujin*, whereas low family status *daimyo*, who respect competence rather than family status as the necessary quality of vassals, paid higher average benefits to applicants. A *kokujin* applicant with high competence leaves the market of high family status *daimyo* because he considers that he can obtain greater benefits from other *daimyos*, and only the *kokujin* with low competence remained in the market of the higher status *daimyo*. Consequently, the quality of the *kokujin* who applied for the high family status *daimyo* degraded in terms of competence or capability, whereas the quality of applicants for the market of the low family status *daimyo* improved owing to the application of the *kokujin* with high competence. It follows that the quality of vassals of low family status *daimyo* become higher than that of high family status *daimyo*. When high and low-ranking *daimyo* met on the battlefield, it was natural that the low-ranking *daimyo* won.

It is important to know how and why family status was respected by the *daimyos* during the Warring States period. The basic reason for the adherence of the *daimyos* to family status was that, to secure control of their territory, they needed to justify their reign by family status. The system to justify reign by the appointment to the *shugo* and *jitō* by the imperial court that existed during the period before the Warring States period did not function anymore, so that the *daimyos* had to seek symbols of family status as a second-best solution. Thus, at the time of unrest, as Katsumata (1996) contends, a coup by vassals rarely resulted in supplanting the position of the master by vassals, but rather in replacing the incumbent master with another member of the same family of the master. The family ranking of vassals was usually lower than that of the master, so this explains how the ruling class was afraid of the fall of the concept of family status and the loss of the justification for their reign. When some *sengoku daimyo* wanted to hire *kokujin* with high family status, for example relatives of ex-*shugo* or ex-*jitō*, they paid attention to the effect on their own family ranking. For example, he might have considered that hiring the relatives of ex-*shugo* as vassals symbolized that his family ranking was higher than theirs. Needless to say, the most effective way to raise family status was to acquire official ranking from the imperial courts. That the *sengoku daimyo* had eagerly tried to obtain official

[44]The *kandaka* system was replaced by the *kokudaka* system in the Tokugawa era, in which the benefits obtained in return for military and other services were paid in the form of rice.

ranking is well known. Toyotomi Hideyoshi, who finally obtained the ranking of supreme minister and chancellor to an emperor, was a typical example. The history of the methods utilized for that purpose are discussed in detail in Kaneko (1998). Toward the end of the Warring States period, the fiscal conditions of the imperial court had been so aggravated[45] that it was unable to pay the expenses to implement the ritual ceremony for endowing official rankings to the samurai and *daimyos* (Ike 1992, p. 200).

5.2.3.3 Domain Law (*Bunkoku* Law) and Sword Hunting

Changes in culture resulted in the radical development of new conventions and standards of conduct such as self-salvation based on *en* and the deterioration and virtual collapse of the trust that drove society into the unprecedented turmoil of the Warring States period. This is related to the insufficient development of institutions to accommodate changes in informal institutions caused by cultural changes. Not only the development of property rights, but also the development of other institutions, such as the judicial system to prevent self-salvation as well as the *katanagari* (sword hunting) to prevent the intensification of battles, was quite slow and could not catch up with the changes in culture and hence in informal institutions.

We have already explained the gradual process of the development of property rights in Chapter 2. In this section, we will discuss, first, the unsuccessful attempts of the *sengoku daimyo* to rehabilitate moral and social order in their domains by means of the promulgation of domain law, and then the difficulties related to the implementation of the policy of the separation of farmers and soldiers during the Warring States period. The main purpose of the promulgation of domain law lay in the establishment of societies under the rule of law in the *daimyo* domain and hence in the termination of self-salvation. The separation of farmers and soldiers was a decisive policy to put an end to the Warring States society by means of eradicating the conditions for the 'unlimited supply of soldiers' from rural society. The first policy of the domain law did not have the expected results, and the second policy of the separation of the farmers and soldiers met with serious difficulties in implementation.

Let us begin with the domain law. After the Ōnin war, the prestige of the shogun and *shugo* deteriorated seriously. Many distinguished local lords (*daimyos*) and *shugo* intensified their efforts to build integrated territories that were independent from aristocratic authority and official positions designated by the imperial court, such as shogun or *shugo*. They came to be called *sengoku* (warring state) *daimyo* and tried to strengthen their military power by incorporating indigenous lords (*kokujin*), local samurai leaders (*dogō*) and indigenous samurai (*ji*-samurai) into their vassal. Even if these indigenous military powers were accommodated into their vassal, treachery by vassals was a daily occurrence and they were quite often involved in self-salvation

[45]The aggravation of the fiscal balance of the imperial court occurred partly because lands under control became smaller due to the conversion to private manors, and partly because the taxation rights of merchants–financiers in Kyoto were withdrawn by the Muromachi *bakufu*.

Table 5.1 Major promulgation of domain law

Domain	Daimyo	Year of promulgation	Family status	Ruined (R) or survived (S)
mutsu	Date	1536	L	S
shimohusa	Yūki	1556	L	R
kai	Takeda	1547, 1554	H	R
suruga	Imagawa	1526, 1553	H	R
ōmi	Rokkaku	1567	H	R
awa	Miyoshi	1562–73	L	R
tosa	Chōsokabe	1596	L	R
suō	Ōtomo	c. 1495	H	S
higo	Sagara	1493–1555	L	S

activities based on *en*, disturbing the order among existing vassals. Moreover, the *kokujin*, many of whom were *jitō* by origin, even organized regional associations (*kokujin-ikki*)[46] to resolve conflicts by themselves without consulting the *daimyo*. For these reasons, toward the latter half of the sixteenth century the *daimyos* were motivated to promulgate laws applicable to their domain to establish authority and convert their domains into 'states'.

Table 5.1 shows the major domain laws that were enacted with the clear intention to establish judicial order in the domains, so that such documents as family lessons (*kakun*) and wills (*okibumi*) were excluded. 'S' and 'R' in the right-hand column mean the state of the *daimyo* survived (S) or were ruined (R) after the end of the Warring States period. 'H' and 'L' in the family status column mean high or low status, judged by the experience of the *shugo* by family members. In view of the scarcity of *shugo* positions compared with the number of *daimyo*, it seems that the *daimyo* of high family status were strongly motivated to promulgate domain laws during the final phase of the Warring States period, when the *daimyo* were competing to convert their domains into 'states'.

The characteristics of domain laws can be summarized as follows. First is an emphasis on the prevention of self-salvation by vassals or in the domain, common to almost all laws. The main method to prevent self-salvation was the introduction of the *kenka-ryō-seibai* article: when two quarreled, both were to be blamed and punished, or no party related to a quarrel was innocent. In addition, the rule of guilt by complicity was introduced to prohibit popular conduct based on *en*.

While some laws expressed the clear intention to establish a modern and public-minded justice system to replace the convention of self-salvation (Katsumata 1979; Shimizu 2018), it was not an easy matter. Many laws publicly announced fixed dates to hold court, but when lords were out of their castles for battle, this rule were

[46]The *kokujin-ikki* was a regional association among the *kokijin*. Members had equal rights and the association could punish members who broke decisions made by the association. The resolution of conflicts about the boundaries of territories, the utilization of water facilities, crimes, the escape of slaves (*genin* and *shojyu*), and the like were the main purpose of collective behavior.

cancelled. Sometimes, a plaintiff was required to find and bring witnesses to the court by himself. Moreover, as Ishimota (1972) contends, even in the case of Date, a mighty *daimyo* with enormous military power in the Tohoku area, the *kokujin* were reluctant to bring disputes to Date because there was a strict convention among the *kokujin* to 'consult with neighbors nearby' before bringing disputes before the lord. This means self-salvation had priority over the justice of the lord. Ishimota concludes that, despite the strong desire of Date to establish dictatorship not only in military matters but also in jurisdiction, his power was ultimately based on the support of *kokujin* power, so that even Date could not disregard the intent of the *kokujin* and their preference for self-salvation.

The second characteristic of the domain law was that it was basically drafted so as to formalize the traditional judicial conventions that prevailed in medieval society. Shimizu (2018) notes that the *kenka-ryō-seibai* was an inheritance of the indigenous convention, popular until the early sixteenth century, to settle disputes peacefully by halving things (*chūbun*). The well-known system of *chūbun* was the rule applied to territorial disputes (*shitaji-chubun*), referred in Sect. 5.1.1, between aristocratic landholders (*honjyo-ryōk*e) and new owners (*jitō)* representing the interests of the Kamakura *bakufu*. The *bakufu* adopted the policy to halve the territory under dispute between the *honjyo-ryōke* and *jito* without rigorously examining the rights of ownership, significantly damaging the landownership of the aristocracy (Nagahara 1998, pp. 189–190). The aim of the *chūbun* rule was said to lie in the idea of balancing, peculiar to those who lived in medieval Japan, that whenever it was difficult make a clear distinction between good and evil, the best way for society was to give a neutral judgement to keep the peace of mind of those concerned (Shimizu 2018).

Since the turmoil in the Warring States period is at least partly rooted in the defects of the moral codes in Mahayana Buddhism, which could not provide effective discipline to resolve disputes among heterogeneous social groups, it was inevitable that conventional rules formalized in domain laws were not effective to rectify a society in turmoil and it was extremely difficult to prohibit the convention of self-salvation. It was necessary to pursue another equilibrium system of standards of conduct based on a new set of moral codes. This was accomplished only after the establishment of the Tokugawa regime, as discussed in the next chapter.

5.2.3.4 The Separation of Farmers and Soldiers

Since it was difficult to prevent the ample supply of soldiers from the rural sector by means of the arming of farmers, the policy of the separation of farmers and soldiers was the last resort to escape the turmoil due to self-salvation and other forms of private battles among local lords.

Ikki (uprising) activity was strongly motivated by the incentive for self-salvation at the level of the individual optimizing behavior in the sense of severing every secular current tie in favor of past ties (*en*) to realize salvation. For the rulers, the demands of the uprisers could not be admitted, from the viewpoint not only of governance but also of efficiency. However, the aspiration of people to realize salvation could not be neglected. The key issue here was how to accommodate the keen aspiration of the people for religious salvation without deteriorating the efficiency of the market economy. *Shokubun* regulation, class discrimination based on occupation, was the final solution reached by the *sengoku daimyo* to resolve the dilemma. People were demarcated by main occupations: the samurai (warrior), farmer, artisan and merchant classes. The policy was gradually adopted by the major *daimyos* in the form of the separation of farmer and soldier. However, it was not an easy task to implement the policy.

At first, this policy was introduced for the purpose of depriving the power of village-level rulers, *dogō* (local samurai leaders) or *ji*-samurai (indigenous samurai). The village-level rulers had strong semi-independent power in the territories of the *sengoku daimyo*. They were usually large-scale patrimonial farmers with quite a few subordinate workers and toward the end of the Warring States period were expanding their economic power further by acquiring tenant lands. Laborers subordinated to the *dogō* or *ji*-samurai, *genin* or *shojyū*, could be mobilized as soldiers if necessary and, at the same time, the *dogō* were always strengthening their military power by means of engaging in feudal contracts with ambitious farmers who wanted to participate in samurai (warrior) society. In other words, there was a phenomenon that could be termed an 'unlimited supply of soldiers' from the pool of labor subordinated to the *dogō* or *ji*-samurai.

However, there was another side to the coin. While the *dogo* or *ji*-samurai could be a useful military reinforcement power when they were obedient to the *kokujin* or Sengoku *daimyo*, they could easily betray the lords at their own will, whenever obedience to the lords was considered to be in conflict with their core interests or *en* relationship. As a *daimyo* built up power over his domain, he adopted the policy of prohibiting feudal contracts with farmers by village-level rulers, to further enhance his control over the domain. Because such prohibition was quite often difficult to impose on such village-level rulers as the *dogō* or *ji*-samurai, it is contended by Wakita (1977) that the laws promulgated by the *daimyo*, instead, prohibited farmers to be employed as vassals of village-level leaders (pp. 206–214). In 1575, such a law was promulgated by Oda Nobunaga in in the Echizen district. This is the earliest evidence of the beginning of the separation policy between farmers and soldiers. Later on, this policy was adopted at national level as the *katanagari* policy (sword hunting, the confiscation of arms from all but the samurai) by Toyotomi Hideyoshi in 1588 after he had unified the country. Hideyoshi also promulgated a law prohibiting commercial activities by farmers in 1591, separating commerce from farming (Ando 1958). It seems that Hideyoshi saw small family farmers who specialized in agriculture as the ideal type of farmer.

As Katsumata (1996) contends, the implementation of the separation of farmers and soldiers was not possible by the *sengoku daimyos* during the Warring States period. This was because the *sengoku daimyo* were obliged to rely on the power of not only indigenous lords (*kokujin*) as military alliances but also village-level rulers like the *dogō* and *ji*-samurai. The *dogō* and *ji*-samurai had two roles: as the local military power and as large-scale farm managers. Although most *sengoku daimyo* aimed at governance without the help of the *dogō* and *ji*-samurai, their indigenous power was indispensable for the *sengoku daimyo* to bring villages under control, which had been enhancing their power with autonomous groups of armed small farmers. However, it is surprising that there scarcely occurred any significant opposition to the policy of the separation of farmers and soldiers implemented by Hideyoshi (Bitō 1992). As Yoshida (2004) pointed out, village-level rulers like the *dogō* and *ji*-samurai followed the *katanagari* policy obediently, dividing their lands among their workers, and many of them became pure farmers by themselves. There is no doubt that this phenomenon was due to the overwhelming power of Hideyoshi. It seems, however, that, toward the end of the Warring States period, people's aspiration for peace was so intensified, and the assumption of ruling power by Hideyoshi heralded the arrival of peace, so that the necessity of the self-salvation as well as self-protection behavior of the *dogō* and *ji*-samurai decreased significantly. It is well known that the behavior of self-salvation by the samurai based on *en* subsided toward the end of Warring States period.

It is important to note that this was the major mechanism for the transformation of large-scale patrimonial farming, which had remained until the end of the medieval era, into the family farming system. In other words, the transformation was triggered by the policy of the *sengoku daimyo* to strengthen their grip on their domain through weakening the military power of village-level rulers.[47] The policy to establish an agrarian society based on independent small farmers through the *katanagari* and *Taikō kenchi* (cadastral survey) implemented by Hideyoshi was the ultimate and decisive policy to accomplish the transformation. As is well known, this system was inherited as a formal institution by the Tokugawa *bakufu* by the generalized concept of the *shokubun* regulation, separating and ordering four occupations (*shokubun*)—the samurai, farmers, artisans and merchants. Under the concept of the *shokubun* regulation, agriculture based on the family labor of monogamous families, peasant farming, came to be the major type of managerial form in the agriculture of Japan thereafter, although the autonomous control power of villages over individual farmers continued to operate until about the end of the eighteenth century.

Yamamura (1978) pointed out a nascent shift to a contractual society during the Warring States period of Japan. He asserts that the farmers' possessive right to land was considerably improved,[48] so that they entered contractual relationships with the *sengoku daimyo*. This assertion seems to be right when the term 'farmer' is replaced by the term 'village', as already explained in Chapter 3. In particular, the village system, or *sōson*, the self-governing village organization that proliferated at the end of the Warring States period, had wide-range self-governing rights such as the ownership of community property (commons and properties of village shrines), police authority, and collective bargain rights with respect to tax and labor duty. Most of these self-governing rights were inherited under the reign of Hideyoshi and the Tokugawa *bakufu*. Likewise, merchants and artisans, ordered to live in castle towns during the Tokugawa period, were allowed to have a wide range of self-governing

[47] It was true that small-scale family farming already existed in the medieval age (Hasegawa 2004, p. 5).

[48] Note that Wakita (1977) is cautious of this kind of assertion.

rights collectively as town dwellers. Yoshida (1985) gives a detailed picture of town dwellers society, in which small merchants and artisans organized an autonomous system based on regional ties. Town leaders were chosen by voting, and towns were allowed to have their own administrative and judicial systems based on laws enacted by the towns.[49]

It will be argued in the next chapter that the *shokubun* regulation introduced by the Tokugawa *bakufu* brought about a homogeneous society in each occupation class, *shokubun*, and this gave the basic impetus for the pursuit of ethnic codes suitable for each of the *shokubun*, enabling the considerable reduction of transaction costs, ultimately leading to economic development based on commerce.

5.2.4 Adverse Selection and the Second Type **Gekokujyō**

So far in the existing literature, the phenomenon of the second pattern of *gekokujyō*, the between-families (*daimyo*) pattern, has been explained by circumstantial evidence, such as the revolutionary thinking or strong ambition of those below in family status. We believe that it was not thought or ambition, but the relative strength of military power held by those below against those above that was crucial for the emergence of the second pattern of *gekokujyō*. The incentive for those below to defeat those above or the general atmosphere of insurrection does not seem to be sufficient to explain the phenomenon of the second pattern *gekokujyō*. The political thinking *a la* Confucianism that justifies revolution against rulers, pointed out by Satō and Katsumata, might be a necessary condition in a broad sense, but is not a sufficient condition. So is private incentive—those below might be abused, neglected or insulted and motivated to take revenge on those above, but this does not explain the relative strength of power and outcome in battles. In sum, political thinking or the private incentive of retaliation do not explain why those below succeeded in the fight with the powerful above, and why the *gekokujyō* of the second pattern occurred as a social phenomenon in the particular historical period of Japan, giving rise to the continual downward shift of the center of gravity of the power balance.

We believe that the answer for this lies in the difference in the military power that occurred during the Warring States period, which was caused by three factors: the uneven shift of the weight in social convention from family status to capability or competence, intensified competition among the *daimyos* in recruiting local indigenous lords (*kokujin*[50]) for arms build-up, and the pervasive information asymmetry in late Muromachi society.

As already noted, the early Muromachi era was a time when family status was of utmost importance in social convention. Capability or competence did not count

[49]Miyamoto (2009) argues that this autonomy by small town-dwellers based on regional ties weakened after the eighteenth century, when large Osaka merchants came to have monopoly power and the *kabu-nakama* (trade association) system based on occupational ties was officially admitted.

[50]Another name is *kunishū*. The Chinese character *kokujin* is sometimes read as *kokunin*.

for much in the evaluation of human conduct. This convention changed drastically toward the latter half of the Muromachi era, and in the Warring States period the relative importance of family status (*kakaku*) vs capability or competence (*kiryō*) was reversed (Sakata 1969). Moreover, the degree of relative respect for capability against family status differed among *daimyos*. There were some *daimyos* such as Takeda Shingen, Asai Nagamasa and Uesugi Kenshin who had both high family status and ample capability. Generally speaking, however, it seems that a high ranking, long-established *daimyo* with social reputation tended to respect family status more than capability or competence, and a low ranking and newly established *daimyo* was liable to disregard family status and respect capability and competence more in human management.

During the Warring States period, competition among the *daimyos*[51] to hire promising vassals intensified. The vassals of the *daimyo* were composed of the *jikisann* (immediate) vassals, *fudai* (hereditary) and *ichimon* (same clan) vassals, *kokujin* vassals, and other temporal vassals, or *rōnin-shū*.[52] The core part of military power was the *kokujin*, who were indigenous feudal lords, frequently originated from the *jitō*, and could mobilize hundreds or thousands of soldiers. The domain of most of the *senngoku daimyo* was a mosaic of two kinds of territory: territory under the direct control of the *daimyo* and territory under the control of the *kokujin* (Hirayama 2018). In the case of *daimyo* Takeda (Shingen), each of the *kokujin*, called *hatamoto* in the Takeda army, was an owner of half, one or two provinces, called *kuni*. The relationship between the *kokujin* and *daimyo* was on a reciprocal contract basis (Sakata 1969, p. 58). When a *kokujin* became a member of a *daimyo* army (*hikan*), he negotiated for benefits in the form of the protection of his territory (*ando*) and salaries paid in cash (*kandaka* system), presented a written oath, and quite often provided his children or important relatives as hostages (Hirayama 2018). It is important to note that, in the contract above, the *kokujin* is chosen by the *daimyo*, but at the same time the *kokujin* had the right to choose the *daimyo*. Sakata (1969) notes that, as the acquisition of the *kokujin* became important for military build-up, competition for acquiring the *kokujin* intensified among the *daimyos* (p. 67). It is also necessary to note that there was an enormous degree of information asymmetry surrounding the contract. Information held by both the *daimyo* and *kokujin* was highly imperfect and, in particular, information about individual quality in terms of the competence of the *kokujin* had been scarce partly because treachery, illicit intercourse with enemies, and collusion were daily matters. Even if a kokujin had reputation for the victory in a battle, it may not be a proof for his competence if the victory was attained by unfair methods. Consequently, as Sugiyama (1974) points out, the quality of the military power of *daimyos* was not only highly unstable but also extremely difficult to

[51] While many of the origins of the *kokujin* was *jitō*, the major origin of the *daimyo* was *shugo*, and large *shugo* who had two, three or more provinces called *kuni* under control came to be called *taimei* during the early Muromachi era. The pronunciation of *taimei* changed to *daimyo* later on.

[52] The vassals of *kokujin* were similarly composed of three kinds of vassals: the vassal of *hudai* or of same clan member, the samurai recruited from villages (*hikan*) and the *rōnin-shū*. In this system, the second group comprised the core members in the battle.

be judged from the viewpoint of outsiders because its core part was composed of *kokujin* hired on a contract base.[53]

It is possible to argue that under these conditions there occurred adverse selection in the choice of the *kokujin*. Let us consider that a *daimyo* wants to hire *kokujin* in order to raise the military power of his vassals. Assume that there are two types of *kokujin* among the applicants of almost the same family status level[54]—competent *kokujin* who have a high probability to succeed in the implementation of military jobs assigned by the *daimyo*, and incompetent *kokujin* whose probability of success is low. While the *daimyo* knows that there are two types among the group of applicants and he may even know how the quality of the *kokujin* is affected by the benefits he offers,[55] he does not have any information about who is competent and who is incompetent, so he cannot offer different benefits for each type of *kokujin* and is obliged to offer the same average benefits to all the applicants.

Let us consider that a high-ranking *daimyo* tends to give low marks to the capability or competence of *kokujin* applicants for the job market set up by him. This is because he firmly believes that the good performance of the samurai comes mainly from disciplines and loyalty, and that both qualities are nurtured by good family status. Because the *daimyo*'s evaluation of competence or capability is low, he offers low average benefits for the newly hired. Among the two types of *kokujin* applicants, the competent *kokujin* gives up his application[56] because he considers that other *daimyo* might offer better benefits. Only incompetent *kokujin* are satisfied with the salary offered and remain in the job market. The externality of the existence of incompetent *kokujin* drives competent *kokujin* from the market.

On the other hand, a low-ranking *daimyo*, who is free from the stubborn tradition of respect for family status and has respect for capability, offers relatively high average benefits to the applicants. In this case, not only the incompetent but also the competent applicant is satisfied with the benefits level offered. It follows that, while the job market set by the high-ranking *daimyo* is filled only with incompetent applicants, the market set by the low-ranking *daimyo* includes competent applicants as well. When two *daimyo* meet on a battlefield, it is natural that the low-ranking *daimyo* defeats the high-ranking because the major determinant of the military strength of the *daimyos* is the military strength of the hired *kokujin*. The ultimate determinant of the outcome of a battle is not the *jikisann, hudai* and *ichimon* vassals, but the *kokujin* vassals, who were overwhelming in terms of the number of soldiers under control. The *gekokujyō* was actually realized as a result of information asymmetry and the difference in the degree of respect for family status as a social convention.

---

[53]See the chapter entitled *Kashindan to gunjiryōshu* in Sugiyama (1974).

[54]This is a simplifying assumption. It is possible to allow for the difference of family status among *kokujin*, but the reasoning would become cumbersome.

[55]As Stiglitz (1994) notes, in the model of the lemon in Akerlof (1970), this possibility is admitted also.

[56]Note that we are talking by use of a framework of an abstract theoretical model in economics. To give up application in the hiring market might often mean simply to become reluctant to cooperate with the *daimyo* in a particular military activity.

It is a natural result of the high level of power building up of vassals by those below compared with those above, or of the adverse selection in economic theory.

Political thought or personal revenge could be responsible as the psychological background, but do not themselves explain the phenomena of the *gekokujyō* of the second type. The value system of the samurai was composed of aristocratic values that emphasized family status and the original samurai value that respected living through self-salvation by means of competence. While the samurai had tried to develop ceremonial order with respect to attitudes in daily life and martial training in order to catch up with the ceremonial refinement of aristocrats, they devoted enormous efforts to living an honorable life to realize self-salvation, that was only possible by carrying on life through nurturing competence as samurai by way of the *kyūdō* principle. The *gekokujyō* seems to be the result of the conflict between two aspects of the value system held by samurai. Low family status samurai respected competence more than high family status samurai, probably because they had not been engaged in the development of ceremonial refinement.

In the case of the market for 'lemons (secondhand cars)' in Akerlof (1970), where a significant information asymmetry of the quality of secondhand cars exists between the secondhand car dealer and the seller of secondhand cars, the car dealer sets a lower price in consideration of the possibility of sellers of bad cars in the market, and the externality of bad car sellers drives sellers of good cars out of the market. This is the fundamental mechanism of inefficiency caused by information asymmetry. In the case of the *gekokujyō*, persistent disregard for competence or capability compared with family status in the mind construct of high family ranking *daimyo* induced them to offer a low price to *kokujin* applicants, with the consequent deterioration of the market for hiring *kokujin*. As we have mentioned, the externality of the existence of incompetent *kokujin* drove competent *kokujin* from the market. On the other hand, the market set up by lower ranking *daimyo* would thrive, causing the successful building up of stronger groups of vassals. Moreover, when high family ranking *daimyo* noticed that the competence level of newly hired *kokujin* was low, he might be induced to offer benefits lower than before in the next market he set up, with the consequent further degrading of the quality of applicants—and this process might be repeated until the market disappeared with no applicants at all. This is exactly the tragedy of adverse selection found by Akerlof.

As is skillfully summarized by Goza (2016), one of the popular accounts of the *gekokujyō* after the Ōnin war was an emphasis on the rise of mass society, composed of anonymous individuals and characterized by the absence of heroes (Nagahara 1974). This phenomenon could be explained as a shift from a society characterized by hierarchical order to one characterized by horizontal order. In our model, this could be construed as a result of simultaneous occurrence of the two patterns of *gekokujyō*. The first pattern implies the virtual loss of power of the master in feudal relationships or the emergence of the collective control by vassals excluding their master. The second pattern means the loss of the prestige of family status in the sense of the defeat of high-ranking *daimyos* by low-ranking *daimyos*. The effect of the double mechanism was sufficient to bring about a shift to a mass society 'without heroes'. Moreover, it must be noted that, in principle, the shift from hierarchical to horizontal order was destined to continue until a perfectly horizontal society was realized. However, as explained below, the process was terminated before this ultimate end was arrived at. We believe that this was because of the cruelty of the second pattern of *gekokujyō* accompanied by adverse selection and the deep sense of fear felt by every constituent of society, consequently inducing the rise of an acute desire for peace through a compromise among warring powers. In other words, the peace of the Tokugawa era was established as a compromise of antagonizing *daimyos*, so it still inherited hierarchical organizational characteristics.

It must be noted that we are not claiming adverse selection is the *only* explanation for the rise of the second pattern, the between-families (*daimyo*) pattern, *gekokujyō*. Our aim lies in pointing out the importance of the value systems and cultural factors in this phenomenon under the condition of severe information asymmetry. There is no doubt that many social and economic factors played their parts. Yoshie (1986) is a precious contribution, giving a comprehensive explanation of the phenomenon of the *gekokujyō*. Yoshie deliberated on the question of how some *shugo daimyo* were able to transform themselves into *sengoku daimyo* and others were unable to do so (pp. 412–429). Noting that during the Warring States period there emerged a tendency for local indigenous lords, including local samurai leaders (*dogō*), to seek ways to draw up feudal contracts with the *daimyo*, Yoshie contends that the success of the transformation of the *shugo* into *sengoku daimyo* was dependent on whether the *shugo* were able to build up powerful vassals through hiring indigenous local lords. It is suggested that threats to the reign of the *shugo*, such as the recurrent riots of farmers and the antagonism of commercial and industrial powers, were responsible for the failure. This theory, in effect, asserts that the ability of the *shugo* to get rid of these threats that hampered governance was the ultimate determinant for the successful transformation into *sengoku daimyo*. This theory, however, is unable to explain why the phenomenon of *gekokujyō* frightened people during the period. While the assertion that the difference in the ability of the *shugo* to get rid of threats in building up vassal power is important, this understandable explanation does not explain why everyone was so frightened. The impact of the second pattern of the *gekokujyō* was so enormous because it was a phenomenon beyond the understanding of the people living at the time. Everyone was behaving rationally, nevertheless the *gekokujyō* happened. Because the phenomenon was incomprehensible, people were frightened and induced to rely on the notion of the heavenly way of Confucianism and the like.

In contrast, we believe the process can be explained as the adverse selection in the market for hiring vassals, the difference in the success and failure in building up powerful vassals was dependent on the value system of the *daimyo*. Distinguished high family ranking *daimyo*, with respect for family status, did not so much admit the importance of the competence of the local indigenous lords (*kokujin*), while low-ranking *daimyo* considered that family status was of no importance compared to the competence of the *kokujin*. This difference in value systems was the ultimate determinant of the phenomenon. The failure of the *shugo daimyo* to transform themselves into *sengoku daimyo* was a between-family (*daimyo*) pattern, and could be regarded as a nascent version of the second pattern of the *gekokujyō*, a similar phenomenon discussed in our model in which high family status *daimyo* with low military efficiency were defeated by low family status *daimyo* with high efficiency.

The difference in value systems was common sense during these years, but no one was aware that such a factor, a matter of commonsense knowledge, was responsible for the emergence of the second pattern of the *gekokujyō*. There is no treachery, no dishonesty, nor shirking in the mechanism. In other words, this mechanism was based on perfectly rational and ethical behavior. The mechanism was obviously beyond the understanding of the people in the Warring States period, and the emergence of a phenomenon beyond imagination and understanding frightened people and moved the entire society to the aspiration for a way to escape the Warring States world. It is, however, a topic for future research to incorporate the various conditions referred by Yoshie.

5.3 Avoiding Catastrophe

During the medieval age, competitive behavior nurtured in market transactions brought about active individualism, and the specialization of occupation nurtured through the *kyūdō* principle enhanced individualism further. Individuals were motivated to be distinguished in their occupations and competed with each other. The development of commerce through the social division of labor resulted in a highly progressive and active society after the Southern and Northern Dynasties period. However, the intensification of information asymmetry due to the accelerated progress in the social division of labor, and the relation-specific politics of the Muromachi *bakufu*, brought about the serious deterioration of trust in society. There are two reasons for this. First was the closed hierarchical order of society adhered to by the aristocracy; the Muromachi *bakufu* did not care for the development of the open information system needed by the horizontal society based on commerce. Second, there was the absence of the notion of the social consequences of the development of the social division of labor; while everyone was motivated to become a specialist to seek religious truth in his occupation, he had concerns only about neighbors nearby and was indifferent about unfamiliar others. Both reasons aggravated the asymmetry of information further. The hiding of information became a basic technique to live in society; information was highly dense among groups of others nearby, while information outside the group was significantly scarce. The consequent proliferation of moral hazard substantially impaired the trust inherited from the homogeneous society.

The deterioration of trust in society was aggravated further as the information asymmetry resulted in the confusion of the hierarchical system in society through the phenomenon of the *gekokujyō*. The first pattern of the *gekokujyō* simply disregarded the hierarchical order in the struggle to obtain leadership in the shogun and *shugo* system. Influential vassals were fiercely confrontational regarding the choice of the heir to their master. Not only were there conflicts regarding the successor of dead masters, but the replacing of the incumbent master by vassals through negotiation or by the use of military measures also became customary in the Muromachi period. Vassals organized groups on the base of *en* in the past such as regional ties, blood relationships and the previous master–vassal relationship. For them, behaving based on *en* was much more important than the feudal contract with their master, since the relationship based on *en* continued not only in the present life but also in the future life. This religion-related behavioral pattern undermined the hierarchical order of society significantly.

The second pattern of the *gekokujyō* destroyed the entire social order based on tradition, status, and the existing system of official hierarchy. There occurred the continual downward shift of the center of gravity in society. This was not a phenomenon related to succession or the power struggle within a family or organization, but instead, to the destruction of the existing order among families or organizations. We have presented a model in which the basic reason for the phenomenon was adverse selection in recruiting *kokujin* as an additional military power by the *daimyos*. In the mechanism of adverse selection, there was no element of moral hazard and immoral behavior, and instead, the behavior of the *daimyos* and applicant samurai was perfectly rational. Nevertheless, the consequence was a dreadful one by which the center of the gravity of society shifted continuously downward. The second pattern seems to have put the trust of society into total collapse.

5.3.1 From Moral Hazard to Adverse Selection

During the early period of the Muromachi era, inefficiency due to information asymmetry took the form of various types of moral hazard, while during the later Muromachi era information asymmetry resulted in the adverse selection that seemed to threaten the possibility of the collapse of the whole society.

Inefficiency due to moral hazards became rampant during the early period of the era. The relationship-based politics in the Muromachi *bakufu* gave rise to a political society filled with covetousness, slander and flattery. Distrust of others increased, which in turn encouraged the avoidance of the disclosing of information and dishonesty toward others. A society with high levels of dishonesty tends to be filled with moral hazards. The hiding of information was seen at the time as essential for survival. While dishonesty, shirking and cheating are apparently immoral activities, they could be prevented in society with adequate devices such as hostage taking or collateral. The same reasoning could be applied to the phenomenon of self-salvation based on *en*. While it was difficult to forecast what kind of *en* relationship was utilized in behavior such as retaliation, it was still not entirely impossible to have an image of the formation of retaliation groups, so that it was a still manageable phenomenon. In sum, moral hazard and self-salvation based on *en* were still manageable phenomena, so that the worsening of trust due to these behaviors was not considered to be lethal for society. The impact on trust of adverse selection, however, was different.

During the latter part of the Muromachi era and during the Warring States period, information asymmetry led not only to the prevalence of moral hazards but also to the second pattern of the *gekokujyō* due to adverse selection. *Gekokujyō* due to adverse selection had unmanageable properties compared with moral hazard or self-salvation based on *en*, so that it seemed to be a dreadful phenomenon for the people of that period. In the process that gave rise to adverse selection, both the *daimyo* and *kokujin* were rational; the *daimyo* offered benefits rationally computed from their belief about the importance of competence as a quality of vassals and the *kokujin* also evaluated the benefits offered on the basis of the rational evaluation of their own competence. High family ranking *daimyo* offered low average benefits to applicants in the belief that what counts for the strength of a vassal group is the discipline and loyalty of members nurtured by good family status, and low family ranking *daimyo* offered high average benefits to applicants because they considered competence was the most decisive element that determined the quality of the vassal. Moreover, there is nothing immoral in the behavior of the *kokujin* either. The *kokujin* with high competence simply left the market because the benefits offered by the high family ranking *daimyo* were too low for his competence. Relatively incompetent *kokujin* stayed in the market because the benefits offered by the high family ranking *daimyo* were at a sufficient level judged from his own competence level.

While the moral hazard that had been ubiquitous in the early Muromachi period was an understandable phenomenon, although the immorality of those concerned should be criticized, the crucial characteristic of the second pattern (between-families) *gekokujyō* that emerged during the Warring States period lay in its incomprehensibility; perfectly normal and rational behavior consistent with morality standards gave rise to such abnormal phenomena, in which the above was defeated by the below. The incomprehensibility would have given a dreadful image of the phenomenon of the second pattern of the *gekokujyō*. A solution was available for the phenomenon of moral hazard—the enhancement of the morality level of society could reduce the moral hazard or collateral and hostage taking could be effective. Despite the high level of uncertainty and information asymmetry of self-salvation based on *en*, the mechanism was still comprehensible. With respect to adverse selection, morality is impotent as a remedy, and there seemed to be no reliable solution for the incomprehensible disease of society. For those who lived during this period, the *gekokujyō* should have been a frightening phenomenon. Moreover, the continual downward shift of the center of gravity of society should also have been a frightening sign of the collapse of the entire structure of existing society. We believe that this was the final blow to the already deteriorated trust in society. The trust in society was brought to final collapse as a result of the incomprehensible phenomenon of the second pattern of the *gekokujyō*.

The deterioration and final collapse of trust through the turmoil of the Warring States period, which continued for one and half centuries, gave rise to an aspiration in the minds of everyone in society, from the *daimyos*, samurai, farmers, and merchants to slaves, for a new society in which trust was reconstructed. There occurred a drastic change in social belief in two dimensions—one was the necessity for the improvement of institutions including the political system and another was a belief that the reform of culture related to the Buddhist circle was indispensable. In Chapter 6, we contend that in the Tokugawa era the reform of institutions was piecemeal and stopgap, and the cultural reforms and evolution in general fulfilled successfully the role of ordering socio-economy through a trial and error process. The remaining part of this chapter is a prelude for that chapter.

5.3.2 Piecemeal Reform of Institutions

What we call the piecemeal reform of institutions was implemented in three areas: (1) the establishment of a political system in the country to end warfare, (2) the building up of a system of regulating the custom of private salvation, (3) the development of an effective system to accommodate the acceleration of the social division of labor.

The first reform was concerned with the political system after the collapse of the Muromachi *bakufu* and was realized in the form of the establishment of the Tokugawa *bakufu* as the *bakuhan* system. The *bakuhan* system was a system in which a leading *daimyo*, Tokugawa, established the central government, *bakufu*, and the shogun implemented policy as a public agent (*kōgi*) over the nation, while the remaining *daimyos* were allowed to govern their domains called *han* independently, without direct intervention by the *bakufu* by way of the delegation of *bakufu* vassals as administrators. The *daimyos*, who were allowed autonomy to organize *han*, were composed of not only *shinpan* (*daimyos* of the Tokugawa clan) and *fudai* (hereditary *daimyo*) but also powerful *daimyos* who antagonized Tokugawa in the Sekigahara battle in 1600, outside (*tozama*) *daimyo*. In other words, the Tokugawa *bakufu* was established as a compromise between the *daimyos* supporting Tokugawa and the *daimyos* opposing Tokugawa. The Tokugawa clan did not dominate the antagonistic *daimyo* completely nor expropriate all their territories. Peace was attained as a coalition between the *bakufu* and *daimyos* (Hall 1991), or as a sort of elite settlement in the terminology of Jones (1988).

The second reform was also urgent. During the Warring States period, the samurai were involved in so-called self-salvation behavior in resolving territory and other kinds of disputes. It has already been noted that even Date, the supreme ruler of the Tohoku region, could not prevent this custom. One of the reasons for the prevalence of this convention was religious. The samurai preferred to settle disputes regarding territory within the circle of vassals with the help of neighbors nearby, whom they may meet in another world in the process of transmigration, confirming solidarity, and exchanging merits through fighting together in private battles. Another and more important reason lay in the deficiency of judicial system inherited from the era governed by influential aristocrats. Although this problem was difficult to resolve directly, as we have seen in the discussion of domain (*bunkoku*) law, the Tokugawa *bakufu* finally settled this through eliminating disputes regarding territories by confiscating territories from the samurai. Under the Tokugawa system all the samurai were ordered to gather in castle towns of *han* and their rights over their territories were confiscated, so that disputes over territories themselves were eradicated. In addition, the *bakufu* law strictly prohibited private battles without legitimate reasons.[57]

The third reform, the confirmation of roles in the horizontal social division of labor in society, was established as the *shokubun* regulation, a final and completed model of the policy of the separation of farmers and soldiers intended by the *sengoku daimyos*. All citizens were classified according to occupational class (*shoku*) (samurai, farmer, artisan and merchant), and their role in society (*bun*) was stipulated. In this system, information asymmetry was significantly alleviated within each *shokubun* (occupation and role) class, because society was composed of homogeneous members within each class. It must be recalled that the disfunction of trust during the medieval period had been caused by the acceleration of the social division of labor that accompanied the diversification of occupations. Furthermore, the demarcation of the occupation classes resulted in a confirmation of the role of each class in the social development of labor. The so-called popular ethic theory tried to elucidate the role of each class as well as the interdependence of classes in exploiting the fruits arising from nature and in market transactions. The *kyūdō* principle obtained its final justification in the *shokubun* regulation. Individuals were encouraged to be engaged in *kyūdō* behavior in cooperation and in competition with other members in the same class.

Since the four classes were stipulated with ranking among classes, the samurai highest and merchants lowest, it is sometimes claimed to resemble a caste system to differentiate the classes. This understanding is incorrect. The ranking of classes was introduced with the policy aim to put the merchant class below the farmer class. This policy reflects, for one thing, the intention of the *bakufu* to establish a physiocratic economy based on agricultural production and, for another, the significant cautiousness of the *bakufu* toward the power of the merchants. The *bakufu* was well aware of the power of commerce to control the wealth of the economy but, at the same time, the *bakufu* intended to repress the merchant class whose contribution to production did not seem worthwhile from the viewpoint of physiocracy. The main theme of the economic policy of the Tokugawa *bakufu* during its over two and half century reign was the control of the merchant class, and the ranking was an expression of that stance.

It seems that these piecemeal reforms were minimum amendments to institutions. The main reason for this lies in the lack of collective intentionality in society emphasized in Chapter 2. The Japanese chose to resort to solutions based on culture to cope with the unprecedented and incomprehensive outcomes that emerged during the last phase of the Warring States period.

[57] Incidentally, a similar policy of gathering vassals in castle towns was adopted by some *sengoku daimyos* toward the end of the Warring States period. The decline in the custom of self-salvation at the end of the period was due mainly to this policy.

5.3.3 Toward the Reconstruction of Moral Codes

Cultural reform started with harsh criticism of Buddhism. The ubiquitous tendency to the destructive conventions in society gradually drew attention to the deficiency of the Buddhist circle, and skepticism emerged about the teaching and policy of Buddhism. Especially notorious was the neglect of excessive self-indulgence in desire and avarice by the Buddhist circle. Since the essence of Buddhist teaching lay in the purification of minds infected by excessive earthly desires and avarice, it was possible that the rampancy of avarice provided favorable conditions for the effective propagation of Buddhism. This is because the greater the bad influence of avarice, the easier to persuade believers about the necessity to overcome it, so that, ironically, a laissez-faire approach to avarice-driven behavior could be an effective policy for promoting the Buddhist circle. Moreover, the *hongaku* theory, that everybody was qualified to attain enlightenment, was frequently accepted as a justification for the neglect of rampant avarice. As the turmoil of the Warring States period continued, the Buddhist circle was increasingly criticized for its neglect of disciplining believers.

It is important to note that that criticism was not about the Buddhist worldview or view of humanity, but the attitude of the Buddhist circle that neglected its role to prevent the harmful effects of excessive desire and avarice. The stance of the Buddhist circle, that seemed to be distorting the original meaning of the teaching for the sake of its promotion, was the real and main reason for the rise of the harsh criticism of Buddhism.

The ideal of Mahayana Buddhism to bring salvation to the masses is quite justifiable, at least from a present-day viewpoint. The practice simplification or easy practice principle that enabled the poor to obtain enlightenment (*satori*) through practicing in daily occupational life was a reasonable policy as a religion in a society filled with distressed masses. The method of salvation by means of relaxation of karma principles, however, destroyed the self-enforcing system of moral development in society. In thirteenth- and fourteenth-century Japan, where society was filled with the acute desire for salvation, the pursuit of the ideal was intensified further, and the consequent simplification of practice resulted in the rapid specialization of occupational activities and the social division of labor. The complexity in human relationships involving heterogenous others intensified at an unprecedented speed, eventually leading to the Warring States period, when political and social stability was on the verge of collapse due to the deterioration of trust.

Moreover, it must be noted that, in an attempt to bring salvation to the masses living in the profane ordinary world, Mahayana Buddhism and the Kamakura new Buddhism of Japan disregarded the basic wisdom of the separation between the sacred and the profane. In Japan at this time, people came to believe that every action in this world was related to the religious act to arrive at enlightenment, and since everyone was qualified to obtain Buddhahood, reckless behavior of whatever sort in daily life could be religiously allowed. When this kind of behavior of disregarding the separation of the sacred and the profane became prevalent, the benefits accruing in the present life, including material gain or present-day contractual relationships, tended to lose meaning, and the market economy based on costs and benefits calculations lost the basic institutional foundations to arrive at equilibrium.

It is important to note that the complementary relationship with Shintoism played a crucial role in ameliorating the shortcomings of Buddhism in this regard. The relationship between the two religions nurtured in the process of syncretic fusion, generally called *Shin-butsu-shūgō*, was converted into the division of labor between the two religions and the clear demarcation of roles in social conventions.

The theory of the *busshō* (potential Buddhahood), emphasized by Mahayana Buddhism, especially by the *hongaku* theory, was established on the assumption of continuity between the sacred and the profane. When ordinary men are qualified to obtain Buddhahood, it implies the possibility that the same human beings could continuously change from profane ordinary men to sacred buddhas through attaining enlightenment. In Shintoism, on the other hand, the sacred and the profane are strictly separated. Gods are regarded as of higher order status who bring divine protection to humans. With very rare exceptions in which the soul of the dead was deified,[58] humans were regarded as simple recipients of protection and other present-day benefits and never considered to become gods. In other words, the ranking of humans was definitely low compared with gods.

Toward the end of the Warring States period, it is possible to believe that there occurred a shift of mindset from continuity to discontinuity with respect to the relationship between the sacred and the profane. Kanda (2010) summarizes this phenomenon as the shift to a preference for the benefits endowed by Shinto gods, such as the protection of lives at the time of natural calamity or on the battlefield, the favorable natural conditions for good harvest, and safety, steadiness and peacefulness in general. The preference was expressed by prayer and the appreciation for the grace of gods at shrines, and such attitude came to be social conventions. In this mindset, humans were quite passive against the gods, and there were no arrogant elements that claimed continuity between the sacred and the profane.

The main reason for the shift of the mindset to negate the continuity between the sacred and the profane and the establishment of the complementary relationship between Buddhism and Shintoism lies in the division of labor between Buddhism and Shintoism in the conventions of society, as is emphasized by Bitō (1992). It is claimed that Buddhism came to be in charge of matters related to individuals and Shintoism to be concerned with conventions related to *ie* and local communities. The life after death was to be dealt with by Buddhism and the life during the present life by Shintoism. It seems that this demarcation reflects the enhanced consciousness of profane welfare in the present life and the roles played by *ie* and local communities therein. Bitō emphasizes that the spread of the *ie* system among farmers and merchants and of village and town communities proceeded in tandem with the rise of 'national religion' in the Tokugawa era, comprising Buddhism, Shintoism and folk religions such as mountain worship.

---

[58] Deification of humans started in the early modern period—typically seen in the deification of Ieyasu Tokugawa at Tōshō-gū or Meiji Emperor at Mejij-Jingū.

It seems that the overwhelming influence of Buddhism on the entire life of the Japanese that prevailed during the medieval period was substantially weakened in the Tokugawa era. The most radical criticism of Buddhism came from Confucians such as Fujiwara Seika (1561–1619), Hayashi Razan (1583–1657) and Kumazawa Banzan (1619–55). They claimed that Buddhism lacked a disciplining mechanism for believers, while Confucianism was equipped with a disciplining mechanism through teaching the way followed by saints, who practiced the ethics derived from the law of heaven or the motion of nature. It is interesting to note that Confucians emphasized an affinity with Shintoism, which also derived its ethical principles from the workings of nature. The so-called popular ethics taught by intellectuals such as Ishida Baigan and Ninomiya Sontoku were developed by way of the synthesis of Shintoism, Confucianism and Buddhism.[59]

During the early part of the Tokugawa era, intellectually influential *daimyos*, such as Ikeda Mitsumasa of Okayama-*han*, Tokugawa Mitsukuni of Mito-*han*, and Hoshina Masayuki of Aizu-*han*, embarked on the repression and exclusion of Buddhism in their *han*, ordering the closure of temples. However, it is important to note that the Buddhist worldview and view of humanity had been firmly embedded in the mentality of the people, and the numbers of Buddhist temples and believers increased rapidly during the sixteenth and seventeenth centuries. Partly for this reason, the Tokugawa *bakufu* adopted the policy of protecting and of utilizing Buddhism for the governing of the masses, and through organizing hierarchical relationships among temples, assigned Buddhist temples the role as the end organization of the *bakufu* in charge of registering the non-samurai population. Moreover, partly in response to the criticism of Buddhism, the founder of the Tokugawa *bakufu*, Tokugawa Ieyasu, tried to make Confucianism an official theoretical guide for government and the basis of the moral code. However, owing to criticism based on rigorous theoretical examination by intellectuals, his attempt was not realized, as is discussed in the next chapter.

[59]The Buddhist circle was more or less silent about the criticism (Asoya 1994). This attitude of Buddhism toward criticism was somewhat understandable because Mahayana Buddhism was constructed on the weakening of the disciplinary mechanism of the gravity of karma, as explained above.

Chapter 6
Cultural Foundations of Tokugawa Economic Growth

The mechanism for the economic growth of Tokugawa Japan has long been an enigma. How did sustained growth occur without relying on foreign trade and the development of industrial technology? The effect of technological progress in agriculture, the most promising candidate as an explanatory variable, had already been denied in the 1970s. Most technology utilized in Tokugawa agriculture had been inherited from past eras, and the impact of new developments such as the improvement of rice varieties were insufficient because of the lack of an effective mechanism of diffusion. Not only does technical progress fail to explain the mechanism of growth, recent analyses focusing on institutional factors have been by and large unsuccessful. Property rights had remained unchanged since the medieval ages. Although there occurred radical changes in residual control rights on land at the end of the Tokugawa era, the change cannot explain the major part of growth during the period before the nineteenth century. The relevance of such institutional factors as the role of trade associations or the development of marine transportation was at most partial.

This chapter asserts that the role of cultural factors was a major cause of the economic growth of the Tokugawa era. It is contended that the reduction of transaction costs through the rehabilitation of trust, which had been aggravated seriously at the end of the medieval ages, and the alleviation of information asymmetry in the socio-economy was a major engine of economic growth during the Tokugawa era. The rehabilitation of trust was due largely to the intentional efforts to improve the ethical system to be suitable for the advanced social division of labor in the economic system. Ethics were developed and disseminated by the government and elites such as private intellectuals and the samurai class. The diffusion of Confucianism among the samurai class, partly owing to the deliberate effort of the *bakufu*, provided the society with common conceptual framework. Leadership of samurai class to enhances the moral

This chapter is based on research supported by the Joint Usage and Research Center, Institute of Economic research, Hitotsubashi University.

J. Teranishi, *Culture and Institutions in the Economic Growth of Japan*,
Studies in Economic History,
https://doi.org/10.1007/978-4-431-55627-5_6

level of society, establishing the basic value system of society with high orientation to ethical values. The efforts of private intellectuals to develop moral principles for each occupational class derived from the examination of the social division of labor resulted in the enhancement of ethical values such as diligence and honesty.

While individuals were gradually and steadily emancipated from the mentality that was tightly governed by the disciplines and worldview of Buddhism and Shintoism, newly developed ethics came to be embedded in the common internalized belief system based on the interaction with others nearby as standardized conduct and conventions. These factors related to cultural development improved the forecastability of the behavior of others in interactions, and significantly reduced information asymmetry and hence transaction costs. The decline in transaction costs led to the commerce-based balanced growth of industries during the eighteenth century. The enhanced work efforts of small producers based on the *kyūdō* principle was coordinated by the activity of merchants, leading to significant progress in the interregional division of labor. It is contended that the long-term decline of interest rates in the eighteenth century was caused by the decline in risk premiums, reflecting reduced information asymmetry.

While the reduction of transaction costs owing to cultural changes was the main factor that drove the economic growth of Tokugawa Japan, institutions played only small roles in economic progress. As is typically seen in the frequent promulgations of decrees of mutual settlement (*Aitai-sumashi-rei*) of financial disputes, many functions were left to the coordination within the private sector, so that, while informal institutions in the private sectors such as the *ie* system and trade associations played important roles, the economic roles of government institutions were kept at a minimum. The Tokugawa economic system was characterized by the small role of the government institutions in economic and administrative areas.

Further, during the process of commerce-based economic growth, the Tokugawa *bakufu's* stance on economic policy was based on physiocracy and took an ambivalent stance toward the merchant class, sometimes repressive and sometimes symbiotic, whereas local *daimyos* were active in building up cooperative relationships with indigenous local, so-called *zaikata*, merchants. This explains the growth of the economic power of western *daimyos*, who finally defeated the *bakufu* and established the Meiji government.

6.1 Establishment of the Tokugawa *bakufu*

6.1.1 From the Toyotomi Regime to the Tokugawa bakufu

It was Toyotomi Hideyoshi (1536/7–98) who put an end to the chaos in the Warring States period, full of distrust, deception and treachery in human relations, and characterized by frequent murders, looting and warfare in everyday life. Hideyoshi was typical of the age of the *gekokujyō*. Born the son of a peasant, Hideyoshi was hired by a samurai at the age of 15. Having been hired as a lowest rank samurai (*ashigaru*) by Oda Nobunaga, Hideyoshi rapidly stepped up the ladder of promotion within samurai society, and finally became *kanpaku-dajyō-daijin* (supreme minister and chancellor to the emperor) in 1586. After the death of Oda Nobunaga (1534–82), due to the betrayal of Akechi Mitsuhide in 1582 (the Honnou-ji incident), Hideyoshi, with his overwhelming military power, accomplished the unification of the country, fragmented by the rivalry of *sengoku daimyos*, defeating Shimazu in Kyushu in 1587 and conquering Kantō in 1590. Hideyoshi, however, did not defeat Tokugawa Ieyasu militarily, but Ieyasu obeyed Hideyoshi as one of the supporting members of the Toyotomi regime in 1586. Two years after the death of Hideyoshi, Ieyasu defeated the son of Hideyoshi, Tototomi Hideyori, in the battle of Sekigahara of 1600, in which almost all *sengoku daimyos* fought in two groups—the Toyotomi group mainly composed of the *daimyos* of western Japan and the Tokugawa group mainly composed of the *daimyos* of eastern Japan. After the Sekigahara victory, Ieyasu established the Tokugawa *bakufu* in 1603. At the same time, Ieyasu eliminated the Toyotomi clan, including Toyotomi Hideyori and his son,[1] and major Toyotomi vassals through two further battles in 1614 and 1615.

After Sekigahara, Ieyasu confiscated all the domains of the seven antagonistic *daimyos* on the side of Toyotomi, valued at 4.16 million *koku*, and reduced the territories of three major *daimyos* on Toyotomi's side (Mōri, Uesugi and Satake) and Hideyori, valued at 2.26 million *koku* in total. Shimazu and Nabeshima, who fought on Toyotomi's side, were allowed to keep their domains intact (Ikegami et al. 1995, p. 575). Incidentally, at that time, total amount of *koku* in the country was about 18 million.

After the victory at Sekigahara and the further two battles that eliminated the Toyotomi clan, however, Ieyasu did not and could not dominate the major antagonistic *daimyos* nor expropriate all their possessions, including those of Shimazu, Uesugi and Mōri. Such a procedure would have thrown the country into another and endless Warring States situation. Likewise, powerful antagonistic *daimyos* did not try to resist the hegemony of Ieyasu. All the leaders were aware of the necessity to establish peace and unification as a compromise.

Tokugawa tried to weaken the power of (potentially) antagonistic outside (*tozama*) *daimyos* in favor of house (*kamon*) and hereditary (*fudai*) *daimyos* as much as possible by means of the rearrangement of *daimyo* domains. Immediately after Sekigahara, Ieyasu implemented the rearrangement of 6.42 million *koku* obtained from the Toyotomi side as part of the war settlement. This rearrangement continued through the rest of the seventeenth century. During reign of the first five shoguns until 1709, not counting the Sekigahara settlement, 200 *daimyos* was destroyed, 172 were newly created, 200 received increases in their holdings, and 280 had their domain transferred (Hall 1991). The total rearrangement amounted to 13.21 million *koku*. The transfer (*kunigae*) was implemented as a sign of favor from the shogun, usually involving an assignment to a larger domain in a strategically more important location.

[1] Hideyori committed suicide, his son was killed, and his daughter sent to a convent, so as to avoid having children.

Reduction and expropriation (*kaieki*) were applied to penalize less favored *daimyo*, quite often by resorting to the provisions of the *Buke-shohatto*[2]; the shogun could penalize them 'for failing to produce a natural heir, for making repairs on his castle without obtaining permission, for making unauthorized marriage alliance and many other seemingly minor acts that violated the code' (Hall 1991, p. 150).

Nevertheless, rearrangement was not sufficient to give dominant power to the shogunate. As of 1698, the distribution of economic power in terms of *koku*, that determined military power as will be explained shortly, was as follows. House (*kamon*) and hereditary (*fudai*) *daimyo*, 168 in number, had 9.33 million *koku*. Adding 2.61million *koku* held by bannerman (*hatamoto*), 5200 in number, and 4.21 *koku* million belonging to territory under the direct ownership of the shogun (*tenryō*), the total amount of *koku* held by insiders of the *bakufu* was 16.15 million *koku*. On the other hand, outside (*tozama*) *daimyo*, 98 in number, owned 9.83 million *koku* (Hall 1991).[3] The total possession of insider (the sum of house, hereditary, bannerman and direct ownership) was 1.64 times larger than that of outsider *daimyo*. However, if we exclude direct ownership and holding by bannerman, the size of the holding held by the *han* belonging to the Tokugawa group is comparable to the holding of outside *daimyos*. Moreover, the average *koku* amount of outsider *daimyos*, 0.10 million *koku*, was much larger than the average (0.06 million *koku*) of house and hereditary *daimyos*. In other words, the Tokugawa system was truly a coalition system as can be seen by its other name, the *bakuhan* (*bakufu* and *han*) system. Incidentally, the term *han* means political and administrative system of domains of *daimyos*, all of which were allowed autonomy under governance by *daimyos* and monitoring by the *bakufu*. In the *bakuhan* system, the *bakufu*, with the support of 168 rather small, house and hereditary *han*, confronted powerful 98 outside *han*. Incidentally, although the *bakufu* itself was an autonomous political and administrative system governed by the largest *daimyo*, the Tokugawa clan, Tokugawa is not included in the *han* because it had the additional role of monitoring other *han* and national governance.

The political structure of the Tokugawa regime, the so-called *bakuhan* system, was colored strongly as a compromise between two antagonistic groups, the *bakufu* group including house and hereditary *daimyos* and the group of *han* of outside *daimyos*. Most symbolic was the fact that the Tokugawa clan did not delegate its vassals to outside *han* as top rulers, as had been done by the Kamakura and Muromachi *bakufu*. It seems that Tokugawa was unable to do so, and the best policy for Tokugawa was to reduce the power of, and avoid the coalition among, outside *daimyos*. Both groups in the Tokugawa system were always preparing for the next civil war, although the tension lessened considerably during the eighteenth century as peace continued for more than a hundred years. The reduction in tension was especially clear with the *fudai daimyos*, who were less susceptible to the risk of confiscation of territory, with the consequent decline of loyalty to the Tokugawa clan (Bolitho 1974). However, it is

---

[2]The *buke-shohatto* was promulgated in 1615 by Ieyasu in order to regulate the behavior of *daimyo*. See Takigawa (1985) vol. 2, pp. 37–39, 71–75.

[3]Original data is given in Kanai (1962) and Totman (1967).

important to note that the basic structure of the Tokugawa system was constructed on the power balance between the two groups and that economic growth and prosperity in the Tokugawa era was built on the significant influence of that delicate balance.

Incidentally, it must be noted that the use of the term 'compromise' implies not only that the Sekigahara settlement was a compromise in the sense of postponing a decisive conclusion, but also that it was an aberration to the historically inherited method of settlement in Japan. The inherited traditional method meant gradual persuasion and getting the obedience of other *daimyos* nearby, until obtaining sovereignty in the country. The Sekigahara settlement was quite different from this tradition. Instead of stepwise integration of the whole country (*tennka-touitsu*), the Tokugawa clan proclaimed a new macro-slogan of attaining the peace of the whole country (*tennka-taihei*). It was the first collective decision of the nation in politics after the thirteenth century. As was claimed in Chapter 1, the internalized mind models of individuals of the Japanese began its long-term change around this time from exclusive concern for others nearby to the more generalized concept of the society. The term 'compromise' is used to emphasize the importance of this change[4] also.

Let us illustrate the continued tension between the Tokugawa *bakufu* and antagonistic *daimyos*, and the repression by the former of the latter. Take for instance the case of Mōri. The territory of the clan was reduced from 1.21 to 0.37 million *koku* after Sekigahara. Since the number of vassals was difficult to be reduced, this caused substantial budget deficits and a severe fall in the income level of vassals (Morishita 2012, pp. 62–76). Mōri (Chōshū)-*han*, however, continued its efforts to maintain its vassal group as a strong military organization, always ready for military emergency (Morishita 2012, pp. 197–208). Further, although Mōri-*han* tried to replenish budget revenue by adopting the state enterprise system of rice, paper, wax, indigo, salt and other products, resistance by producers and merchants hindered the smooth implementation of the policy, preventing the recovery of budget deficits, and leading to the accumulation of a heavy debt burden (Kanai 1962, p. 125). A similar situation applied to Uesugi also.[5] The total tax revenue (*koku* amount (*daka*)) was reduced from about 1.2 to about 0.3 million *koku*, and territory was shifted from Aizu to Yonezawa. Since Uesugi maintained its vassals also, the *han* budget accumulated huge debts, until Uesugi Yozan (1751–1822) succeeded in rehabilitating the budget through industrial policy and severe budget cuts. Although the territory of Shimazu (Satsuma)-*han*, another powerful antagonist at Sekigahra, was not reduced, the *bakufu* tried to weaken the economic power of Shimazu as much as possible. For example, the order issued in 1605 to prepare large stones for repairing the fence of Edo castle caused an enormous economic burden on the budget of the Shimazu-*han*. The order to repair the Kiso three rivers near the Nagoya area in 1753 imposed a heavy burden on the *han* budget, as well as the human toll, including the lives of 85 able housemen. The maintenance of the large vassal group, amounting 30–40% of

---

[4]The author is thankful to Professor Sone Yasuo of Nihon University and Professor Nakatani Takeshi of Onomichi City University for productive discussions on this point.

[5]Satake was also reduced *koku-daka* significantly but handled the situation by reducing vassals.

the *han* population, was another source of budget deficit. It is well known that, due to the severe budget deficit, Satsuma was obliged to implement a harsh policy of the exploitation of the sugar cane farmers in its newly colonized territory, *ryūkyū*. It must be also noted that the costs to fulfill the duty of *sankin-kōtai*, explained shortly, was significant for outside (*tozama*) *daimyos*, whose domains were intentionally allocated in places far away from Edo.[6] It is reasonable to believe that antagonistic feelings continued to be held by those *daimyos*, potentially throughout the Tokugawa era. It is not without reason that Mōri and Shimazu were two major forces that defeated Tokugawa in the civil war, that led to the Meiji Restoration, in the mid-nineteenth century.

Incidentally, when he succeeded the shogunate after his father's death, in an intimidation of the antagonistic powers, the third shogun Tokugawa Iemitsu (reign 1623–51) declared in front of the *daimyos* that he was ready to fight on the battlefield with anyone who intended to displace him from the shogunate. The *bakufu* was also preparing for the next civil war. A reign based on military power was the basic rule for the *bakufu* governance system (Matsumoto 1971, p. 8), and such policies as marriage with the imperial family by the daughter of the second shogun or the deification of the founder, Ieyasu, at the Toushougu shrine, complemented the policy of military threat (Hall 1991). Ogyū Sorai deplored in his later years that, even in the 1720s, there was no improvement in *bakufu* institutions, compared with military-based institutions at the beginning of the seventeenth century ('*Seidan*').[7]

6.1.2 Two Urgent Tasks for the Tokugawa bakufu

There were two urgent tasks for the Tokugawa *bakufu* that had unified Japan after the death of Toyotomi Hideyoshi. First was to establish a stable governance system over the the *daimyos* including those who had been against Tokugawa at Sekigahara. Second was to develop an ethical system effective to bring under control the turmoil in human relations in the socio-economy.

The first task was dealt with by the policy of weakening the power of potentially hostile *daimyos* by imposing additional burdens, including assignment of public works and the *sankin-kōtai*[8] (alternate attendance) arrangement. The latter, that required every *daimyo* to keep his wife and heir permanently at Edo, while the *daimyo* himself had to spend every other year there, was not a simple hostage strategy nor a

---

[6]In the case of Mōri-*han* of Chōshū in the year 1643, total fiscal revenue was 1253 *kan* (valued in silver), while total outlay in the domain including the Kyoto and Osaka offices was 1326 *kan*, and the outlay in Edo was 1260 *kan*. The deficit of 1333 *kan* roughly corresponds to the outlay in Edo. The deficit was financed by borrowing from merchants (Kanai 1962, p. 85).

[7]Reprinted in Iwanami Nihon-shisou-taikei *Ogyū-Sorai* (1973), pp. 259–446. Quotation is from p. 311.

[8]Established by Iemitsu through the promulgation of the *buke-shohatto* in 1615, and relaxed and virtually abolished after 1862.

method to secure human resources needed to run the *bakufu* bureaucracy,[9] but more it was a device to reduce the power of *daimyos* by forcing them to expend their revenues for living costs in Edo and travelling costs there (Takigawa 1985 vol. 2, pp. 87–89). In the case of Mōri (Chōshū)-*han*, the expense in cash needed for the Edo residence was 100.1% of total cash revenue (fn. 7). Moreover, it is important to note that, while the official reason for the introduction of the policy of self-imposed isolation from world trade by Ieyasu lay in the prohibition of Christianity, another more important reason was to stem the increase in budget revenue through the acquisition of trade gains by western *daimyos*. Thus, in 1609 the *bakufu* forbade the holding of large-scale ships for long-distance voyage by *daimyos* and the regulation on foreign trade was intensified further during 1633–39 (Takenaka-Sakudo 1972, p. 57).

The second task faced by the newly born Tokugawa regime was much more difficult to fulfil, and was carried out in three steps. First and of foremost importance was the introduction of the *shokubun* regulation as an ultimate form of purification of the structure of the social division of labor. Inheriting the policy of previous regimes, especially the Toyotomi, the *bakufu* adopted the policy of the separation of farmers from samurai and of samurai from farming. In administrative matters, all workers and their families were classified into four categories of occupation—samurai, farmer, artisan and merchant. Except for the samurai, all the classes were classified as in the category of commoners, in which farmers were ranked at the highest, followed by artisans, and merchants the lowest. The basic purpose of this policy lay in the removal of the social confusion in human relationships by way of adapting to and accommodating the deepening of the social division of labor.

Two additional policies complementary to the *shokubun* regulation were introduced. The *bakufu* embarked on the search for workable systems of moral codes that could bring about stability in human relationships. Starting from the examination of the logic of the way of heaven by resorting to the theory of New Confucianism, the *bakufu* ardently carried out theoretical inquiry into the new system of morality through hiring Confucians, and at the same time delegated the role of guiding the masses to the samurai. Additionally, the *bakufu* worked on the system of religion. Toward the end of the medieval ages, Buddhism, which was once religion of the aristocrats and samurai, became increasingly popular among farmers, artisans and merchants. The Tokugawa *bakufu* utilized this situation through systemizing and hierarchizing Buddhist temples in the country and incorporating them as the subordinating body in the administrative system in charge of family registration (*shūmon-ninbetsuchō*) of residents regarding population other than the samurai class.

---

[9]The *bakufu* bureaucracy was run by *kamon daimyo*, composed of relatives of the Tokugawa family and the *fudai daimyo*, usually with fiefs in local strategic districts, assisted by *hatamoto* and *gokeninn* (Takigawa 1985, vol. 2, pp. 74–75). *Hatamoto* and *gokenin* dwelled in Edo.

6.1.2.1 *Shokubun* Regulation

The *Shokubun* regulation was introduced to classify the various parts of society into four classes, in which each class was composed of homogeneous members with respect to occupation and hence in behavioral pattern, so that confusions due to the difficulty of forecasting the behavior of others was kept minimum, and at the same time it became easy to develop moral codes for each occupational groups. Among the four classes, emphasis was on the creation of the farmer class specified in agricultural activities and, in particular, not being involved in military action. However, it was the merchant class that was most seriously influenced and, as a class, merchants strenuously sought identity with a strong class consciousness.

The first priority in the introduction of the *shokubun* regulation was realized by the prohibition on the holding of arms by farmers, and was first introduced Oda Nobunaga, but implemented nationwide by Toyotomi Hideyoshi by means of the disarmament of farmers through the sword hunt decree in 1588. The disarmament of farmers was considered to be crucial to bringing about a peaceful society and terminating military conflict. This was because farmers were potential warriors during the Warring States period. A considerable number of low-class warriors were peasants by origin, as was illustrated by the case of Hideyoshi himself in his young days. Whenever farmers were equipped with weapons, the rural sector could be an unlimited source of warriors, leading endless warfare. Hideyoshi also enforced a land survey during 1582 and 1598, prohibiting farmers to participate in commercial activities, and establishing farmers as pure and independent agricultural producers cum taxpayers. Tenancy contracts were forbidden to promote independent farmers, and farmers in the same village were assigned joint responsibility to pay tax.

This policy was inherited by the Tokugawa *bakufu* in a more comprehensive form in the sense of the purification of not only farmers but also the samurai as a class. The samurai were ordered to leave their rural fiefs and live in the capital city (castle town) of each *han*.[10] Each *daimyo* and their vassals were given an annual income stipulated as a taxation right to farmers in the unit of *koku*, the size of land multiplied by the average rice productivity of a unit of land. It is important to note that the amount of *koku* meant not only income as tax revenue but also the level of armament assignment. For each *daimyo*, the *koku* amount *(daka)* meant the number of soldiers with stipulated armaments to delegate to the battlefield when the *bakufu* was involved in a war. For each vassal of the *daimyo*, the *koku* meant also the responsibility to head for the front with the stipulated number of soldiers and the specified armaments when the *daimyo* was involved in a war.

From the viewpoint of the *bakufu*, the *koku* amount of each *daimyo* represented the military power they could prepare. It is important to note here that the *koku* amount was an effective measure of military power of each *daimyo* only if farmers were disarmed and the condition of the separation of soldiers and farmers was maintained.

[10] In 1615, Ieyasu ordered the destruction of all castles and forts in *daimyo* domains, leaving only one castle as a residence for each *daimyo*. This induced *daimyo* vassals to leave local castles and agriculture and settle in castle towns as consumers and bureaucrats.

To maintain the governance of the *bakuhan* system, the *bakufu* resorted to such measures to reduce the economic power of the *daimyos* by way of assigning large-scale construction works and *sannkin-kōtai*, but at the same time it was necessary for the *bakufu* to monitor the military build-up of each *daimyo*. Without the separation of soldiers and farmers, monitoring would have been extremely difficult, so it was an indispensable policy for the *bakufu* to avoid the hidden build-up of military power by antagonistic domains. It was a costly policy in the macroeconomic sense, however, because about six per cent of the population, the samurai, was excluded from the labor force and became pure consumers, although they were assigned jobs as administrators. Yamagata Bantō, following Ogyū Sorai, pointed out that fiscal deficits and the poverty problem of the samurai class during the 1720s was caused by the excessive burden on agriculture due to the natural increase in the numbers of the samurai population who did not contribute to agricultural production. We will return to this assertion again later (Najita 1987).[11]

In a similar context, physiocracy was the indispensable policy stance for the *bakufu* not only to secure tax revenue but also to establish and maintain the *bakuhan* system in which the transparency of the military power of the *daimyo* was needed for the safety of *bakufu* hegemony. The physiocracy of the *bakufu*, however, gave rise to serious conflict with the merchant class as economic development based on commerce proceeded. The other side of physiocracy was indifference or antagonism toward the merchant class. As is argued in the last chapter (Sect. 5.3.2), it is possible to conjecture that the hidden purpose in the *shokubun* regulation of the *bakufu* lay in the control of the power of the merchant class. Through admitting trade associations (*kabu-nakama*), the *bakufu* changed the policy from alienating merchants to the policy of positive coordination after the 1720s. Nevertheless, distrust against merchants was never eliminated completely and this provided the background for the collapse of the *bakuhan* system in the mid-nineteenth century.

6.1.2.2 Unintended Economic growth Under the *Bakuhan* System

The nature of the unification and pacification attained by the Tokugawa clan as a delicate power balance between outside *daimyos* and the *bakufu* had important implications for economic growth in two respects. For one thing, there occurred a tug of war regarding the economic, and hence, military power of *daimyos* between the *bakufu* and outside *daimyos*. The *bakufu* tried to reduce the economic power of *daimyos* through forcing additional expenditures, implementing *sankin-kōtai* and financing the living costs in Edo of *daimyo* families. The order by the *bakufu* to participate in public works regarding Edo castle and other related construction works also imposed substantial burdens on the *han* budget. The *daimyo*, on the other hand, tried to increase its fiscal revenue by means of encouraging the production of staple commodities. Until the end of eighteenth century, the collection and sales of these commodities

[11]Confucian Kumazawa Banzan (1619–91) also criticized the separation between agriculture and samurai from the viewpoint of concern about the weakening of the spirit of the samurai.

was implemented by the intermediation of Osaka merchants who obtained substantial commissions and interests, so that favorable effects on the *han* budget were not significant. After the 1820s, the growth of indigenous (*zaikata*) merchants in local regions enabled the *han* to avoid the intermediation of Osaka merchants. With the help of indigenous merchants, local *han* organized state enterprises (*kokusan-kaisho*) and embarked on industrial policy. In the 1820s, cotton textile was put under the control of the state enterprise system in the Himeji *han*, followed by the Ashū, Kishū, Chōshū, Buzen-nakatsu and Hikone *han*. During the 1830 s and thereafter many new commodities such as silk, paper, wax, salt and sugar were exported directly to Edo and other areas without the help of Osaka merchants. Toward the end of the Tokugawa era, even the *bakufu* planned to start a state enterprise system (Hayashi 1967, p. 251).

For another, the settlement of the Warring States period as a compromise resulted in incessant tension in the mindset of the samurai class. The samurais were required to prepare for the expected next civil war. Because large-scale preparation for war, such as the purchase of arms from the overseas market, was certain to incur suspicion and punitive action from the *bakufu*, strengthening the samurai in terms of martial skills and spirituality was the only available means to prepare for war. The daily life of the samurai was devoted to training in martial skills and spiritual polishing up as military personnel (Nitobe 1905, ch. 10). At the same time, a considerable number of the samurai seemed to be interested in the alternative form of coalition among *han* and were inevitably led to deliberate on the desirable form of polity of the country. It was an irony that the study of Confucianism recommended by Ieyasu provided the basic concepts and guidelines for the purpose.

Furthermore, as will be discussed below, the samurai was assigned the role of leadership in constructing a new society with high levels of morality. Confucianism studied in almost all *han* came to comprise the common intellectual foundation in terms of concepts and logical reasoning for the pursuit of moral codes. The fact, that moral society was led by the samurais of all *han* nationwide, who had a common intellectual background, had an enormous impact on the spread of moral codes as well as the standardization of the behavior of the population. We will argue below that the standardization of behavior was one of the key elements that brought about the alleviation of information asymmetry. Because the alleviation of information asymmetry had reduced the transaction costs of the economy, it follows that the role of the samurais as leaders of the moral codes in society had significant side-effects on the economic growth led by commerce during the Tokugawa era.

It might be safe to say that the rapid growth of the economy was largely an unexpected and unintended result in view of the fact that the economic system formulated by Tokugawa leaders did not expect the spectacular growth of commerce in the socio-economy. It would be needless to say that the role played by the samurai in the spread of moral codes and hence in the alleviation of information asymmetry in the socio-economy was something that was utterly unintended and unanticipated. Moreover, it must be noted that the claim that the turmoil during the Warring States period was rooted in the inadequacy of ethical codes of Buddhism was shared by the majority of people in the position of leadership during the Tokugawa era. Since the basic cause of social disturbance lay in the lack of information and information asymmetry, as emphasized in the last chapter, the claim was not necessarily correct. The significant reduction of information asymmetry by the promotion and dissemination of common moral codes was also an unintended consequence for people during the Tokugawa era.

6.2 Search for Moral Code

6.2.1 Introduction of New Confucianism

In view of the confusion of human relationships during the Warring States period, Tokugawa Ieyasu encouraged the study of new Confucianism, hiring the Confucian Hayashi Razan (1583–1657) as an official adviser to the *bakufu*. It was an age when there was a strong longing for the culture of China. During the first half of the seventeenth century, substantial amounts of Chinese books were imported by way of Nagasaki,[12] and Chinese Confucians, who fled to Japan from the disturbances of the wars during the last days of the Ming dynasty, were well accepted in Japan, where the study of Confucianism was in vogue and various schools of Confucianism were competing with each other.

6.2.1.1 Ieyasu and Confucianism

There seems to be two reasons for Ieyasu to feel attracted to Confucianism. For one thing, he might have expected the immediate usefulness of Confucianism as a policy guide to rule the country. Toward the end of the Warring States period, there occurred a nationwide longing for the way of heaven (*ten-dō*) as an effective notion that could bring about new order to the country and protect people from unhappy and miserable events, replacing the existing notion of the emperor's land's or god's land that seemed to have failed to bring peace to the country and to be futile to resolve actual disasters. Ieyasu tried to shift the spiritual guideline for the samurai class from Buddhism to Confucianism, and to adopt a theory of coincidence of Confucianism and Shinto, *Shin-jyu icchi-ron*, that claimed the equality of the teaching of Amaterasu-ōminokami and the way of the Chinese saints.

Kanda (2010) summarizes the popular notion of the way of heaven at the time as follows: (1) the way of heaven determines destiny of individuals by way of grace and divine punishment, (2) there is no difference between the grace of heaven and the protection extended by Buddhism and Shintoism, (3) the grace of heaven is given only to those who respect popular ethics, (4) internal conformity with the way of heaven is more important than external behavior. Although a concrete definition and the logic

---

[12]The only port allowed to trade with European countries and China.

of the way of heaven was not clear in the popular notion, scholars of Confucianism came to associate the concept of truth or the logic of the universe (*ri*) with the notion of heaven. Razan's teacher, Fujiwara Seika (1561–1619), was an active advocator of the relationship between the logic of heaven and the *ri* concept. The official ranking given to Razan was quite high according to the salary given to him. However, there is little evidence that he was welcomed or highly esteemed, and it is uncertain how he contributed to actual policy making.[13] Incidentally, there were at least two Confucians who had exerted some influence on *bakufu* policy. Arai Hakuseki (1657–1728) is well known for his strong influence on the policy formation of the sixth shogun, Tokugawa Ienobu. However, Arai's basic policy to make the shogun the new king of Japan was too unrealistic and did not have a significant influence on the course of politics in Japan. Ogyū Sosai (1666–1728), who criticized the passivity of the political logic of new Confucianism and established a new theory (Kobunji-gaku) that emphasized the active role of policy to revitalize Tokugawa society, played the role of part-time adviser to Ienobu and the seventh shogun, Tokugawa Yoshimune.[14] Although he had an enormous impact on the development of the political and economic thought of Japan, his policy recommendations, such as the indigenization of the samurai,[15] were also unrealistic and reactionary, so that his influence on actual policy was considered to be insignificant.

Perhaps a more important reason for Ieyasu to be attracted to new Confucianism was the logic to infer the prosperity of the country from individual morality. In the logic of new Confucianism, nature and society is governed by the same universal logic of *ri*, and *ri* is also built-in the mind of humans inherently. *Ri* as an 'innate substance' in the human mind is, however, usually prevented from playing effective roles due the working of the 'acquired characteristics' of minds, called *ki*, such as selfish desire or emotional impetus.[16] To make innate *ri* work correctly, one must implement a hard study of moral rules and arrive at the completely integrated self on the basis of reason. Those who have mastered the correct morals through hard study will become holy men, qualified to teach and guide others how to behave in the right way. It follows that under the guidance of holy men, the houses of individuals will be orderly managed, regions will be ruled peacefully, and the country as a whole will prosper. In this theory, therefore, completion through the hard study of morality by individuals (*kyūri*), especially by elite individuals, is the fundamental condition for the penetration of *ri* in society as a whole, and the establishment of sound and ethical methods (*michi*) to be followed by the prosperous country. It is not difficult to conjecture that Ieyasu might be captivated by the theory of the relationship

[13]The amount given to Razan was 3000 *koku*, which was comparable with the amount of high-ranking hatamoto and much higher than the salary of other Confucians, estimated as 80 *koku*. He was not allowed to have the status of samurai and was forced for long to serve with tonsure. Watanabe (1985) argues that, although his knowledge of literature and capability in writing was appreciated, Razan did not have any influence in the policymaking of the *bakufu*.

[14]The position given to Sorai was as adviser to the secret agent of the shogun (*onmitsu-goyō*).

[15]The policy recommendation to let samurai to live in rural areas again, not in castle towns, and to engage in agricultural production.

[16]Ki causes *kishitsu* mind (natural mind) outside the control of *ri* in Chapter 2.

between individual morality and social order. This theory of Confucianism is called by Maruyama (1952) the 'continuity theory' of the three aspects of the world, i.e. the motion of nature, social order and human morality, in the sense that the same basic principle of *ri* penetrates through three aspects, so that the world is integrally governed by the unique exogenous login of heaven (*ri*).

6.2.1.2 Denial of Continuity Theory

Partly owing to the encouragement by the *bakufu*, rigorous and energetic study was conducted on the theory of new Confucianism, especially during the seventeenth and early eighteenth centuries. It is asserted by Maruyama, however, that, through study and critical evaluation, the continuity properties of Confucian theory were denied one by one, so that the theory of new Confucianism lost its integrity as a moral philosophy and political theory by mid-eighteenth century in Japan (Maruyama 1952, p. 30). Let us summarize briefly the process of the denial of continuity.[17]

The criticism of the continuity proposition between nature and the human mind, that the human mind is governed by the same principles of nature, was initiated by Yamaga Sokō (1622–85). While the new Confucianism asserted that the human mind was controlled by *ri*, the basic logic that penetrated the workings of nature, Sokō emphasized that the human mind had more dynamic aspects than was governed by the steady logic of the movements of nature, arguing that the morality of humans was not something to be attained by the study of *ri*, but should be nurtured through practicing and improvement of actual behavior. While Sokō denied the influence of *ri* on the human mind, Itō Jinsai (1627–1705) investigated critically the continuity between *ri* and the morality of society. He asserted that *ri* was nothing but the physical laws of the movement of nature and was not applicable to the way of living of humans because the world in which humans live was much more dynamic and variable (*katsubutsu*) than can be imaged by the static workings of nature, assumed in the theory of Confucianism. From this position, he pursued to build a moral theory, an alternative to the propositions of new Confucianism derived from philosophical reasoning, from a more practical reality of human society. The new moral theory, called ethical theory based on daily life (*jinrin-nichiyō no gaku*), contended that the principles of morality in society (*michi*) were not something to be derived from the logic of nature, but rather should be logically established from the viewpoint of how humans should behave (*jindō*).

Ogyū Sorai (1666–1728) further developed the critical examination of new Confucianism with respect to the proposition on political theory. Adopting the view of Jinsai about the dynamics of the world, Sorai contended that, to establish the workable order of society, the intentional working (*sakui*) of politics is indispensable. On the basis of the comprehensive study of the ancient literature of Chinese history, what

[17] We will mainly follow Maruyama (1952, pp. 22–139). However, since Maruyama's analysis of thinking in Tokugawa Japan is focused on political theory only, his explanation is biased, as is clarified in Chapter 2.

the Confucian theory regarded as the way chosen by holy men was nothing but the actual way of politics that ancient kings had contrived, so that it was claimed that social order should be designed on the basis of the policy adopted by them. With respect to the concept of *ri*, Sorai admitted the existence of *ri*, but asserted that, since there are multifarious ways to define *ri* from the viewpoint of humans, it is impossible for humans to arrive at a unique and consensus-based understanding of *ri*, in effect denying the basic logic of new Confucianism established on the unique concept of *ri* derived from nature. The criticism against moral philosophy of new Confucianism culminated in the study by Sorai, and the continuity theory based on pre-determined harmony was almost completely denied by the early eighteenth century in Tokugawa Japan (Maruyama 1952).

6.2.2 Separation of the Profane and Sacred

Although Confucianism had a pervasive influence on the samurai class and education of the masses in society, it was, however, accepted neither as a popular moral code nor a guiding principle for politics. As a popular moral code, the excessive emphasis on the worship of ancestors in the past was not in conformity with Shintoism, which put more importance on the effects arising from the renewal of generations. The social model constructed on the vertical and rank relationships did not have enough affinity with Japanese society, which attached more importance to horizontal relationships such as occupations and communities. As a principle of politics, the rigorous study by Sorai and other scholars incurred skepticism about the relevance of the legends of the Chinese kings to Japan, eventually giving rise to the development of the original theory of the Koku-gaku by Motoori Norinaga (1730–1801). However, it must be noted that Confucianism had a significant influence on the logical way and conceptual framework of thinking among the Japanese. It is true that Confucianism encountered serious criticism, but the process of active criticism itself had the effect of spreading the way of thinking of Confucianism (Watanabe 1985).

It is important to note that the most fruitful and useful development of moral philosophy in Tokugawa Japan emerged, not from Confucian theory, but from the cognition of the necessity regarding the separation of the profane from the sacred or an emphasis on present-day benefits. Through the process of the struggle with new Confucianism, it had become clear that the metaphysical inference of moral philosophy from the concept of heaven or *ri* was not easy, and this finding opened the way to approach the problem from the inverse route, i.e. not from the metaphysical but from the physical route. This seems to be one of the reasons that the separation of the profane from the sacred became to be regarded as a promising approach to resolve the confusion in society due to the ineffectiveness of Buddhist ethical codes.

Another and more important reason for why the separation of the profane from the sacred became an important key to develop workable moral codes to resolve social confusion was the recognition that the policy of Mahayana Buddhism to remove the fence that separated the profane from the sacred had brought extremely risky elements into religious practice. The intention to attain enlightenment in daily occupational life brought about the consequence that ordinary life was tinted completely with the colors of sacred values, and inherent profane colors, indispensable for sound motivation in ordinary occupational life, were abandoned or at least liable to be dismissed. As pointed out by Yanagi Muneyoshi (1889–1961), the founder of the folk-arts movement, in the world of folkcrafts, artisans are motivated to devote themselves to handicrafts production to be saved by Amitabha, and prayed that their products were saved in the same way as humans were saved (Yanagi 1942, p. 247). Needless to say, this kind of mindset could bring about an extremely dangerous situation in social conflicts, as discussed in the last two chapters. People might be involved in conflicts motivated by religious attainment, not by the rational calculation of the costs and benefits of their actions. It must be recalled that during the Warring States period, those who tried to realize self-salvation based on *en* relationships seemed to be motivated in this way.[18]

6.2.3 Shintoism and the Rise of 'National Religion'

It is important to note that the significant effects of Shintoism lay in the amelioration of the defects of Mahayana Buddhism due to the unprepared weakening of the separation of the sacred and profane and the excessive sanctification of the present world. Shintoism was an indigenous religion that emphasized present-day benefits and encouraged people to have an affirmative approach to present life. The basic logic of Shintoism is succinctly and precisely summarized in Sonoda (1994) as follows. The essence of Shintoism lies in the activating of the vital force dwelling in nature and the key practice of Shintoism of purifying (*seijyō*) aims at access to the vital force of valuable things in human life. Purifying is synonymous with the concept of wiping away of *kegare*, dirty things, in which *ke* means the miraculous power that grows the vital force of rice and *gare* (*kare*) the withering. It follows that Shintoism aims at the activation of vital forces by way of preventing the withering of the power to grow vital forces. In terms of religious practice, Shintoism carries out cerebrations and exorcism to extricate people from difficult situations, *kegare*, that might destroy

[18]Toward the end of the Warring States period, the turmoil was rooted in two cultural traits inherited from the middle ages: the tendency toward self-salvation and the tendency toward sharing, in effect denying the efficiency arising from competition. The self-salvation based on the *en* especially by the samurai class made it difficult to establish stable feudal contracts, based on reciprocity in the form of the conferment of property rights in land and the assumption of loyalty obligations as vassal. In the value system of the samurai, loyalty based on the *en* was deemed of higher value than the feudal relationship. The other trait of people's request for equality through sharing the fruits of market development was apparently detrimental to efficiency in an economy dependent on market competition, and invited deep resentment from those who had been actively contributing to the development of the market economy, such as merchants and innovating producers as well as *sengoku-daimyos* embarking on a market-based growth strategy in their territory. Both cultural traits were based on the Mahayana Buddhist tradition that emphasized transmigration and salvation through merit transfer.

vital forces, and recover the orderly situation full of *ke*. While, in Buddhism, sacred things do not exist in the present life and the present life is always captured in a negative sense, in Shintoism the guilt and *kegare* of humans were always eliminated by the power of gods through pious prayer and celebration by humans. People believed that there were eight million gods in Japan. The celebration of gods was concerned with every valuable thing and benefit in daily life, such as good harvests, high profits, protection from crisis, and the like. In sum, praying for present-day benefits and the celebration of present-day life is the essence of Shinto teaching.

The collaboration and establishment of the complementary relationship between Shintoism and Buddhism had been the basic condition for the reception of Buddhism in Japan since as early as the eighth century. The syncretic fusion of Shintoism and Buddhism (*shinbutsu-shūgō*) had been carried out energetically from both sides of Buddhism and Shintoism. The most influential and effective theory of fusion was the *honji-suijyaku* theory, which had been spread since the mid-Heian era. In this theory, buddhas were conceived as *honji*, real substance, and gods as *suijyaku*, the provisional appearance of buddhas to save the masses, as touched upon in Chapter 4. While the *honji-suijyaku* theory assumes the superiority of Buddhism over Shintoism, new theories that assert the independence and uniqueness of Shintoism were developed during the medieval age. Ise-Shintoism came to emphasize the origin of the whole nature (*konton* or *kizen*) and, from this concept, asserted the equality of the ranking among gods, buddhas and humans. Together with Shinto practices to arrive at purified states, the spiritual mindset of believers called *magokoro* (honesty and sincerity) came to be noted. Yoshida-Shintoism asserted that, from the viewpoint of the legendary origin of nature and the universe, all theories have a common origin and it is claimed that, in terms of the metaphor of a tree, Confucianism corresponds to the leaves, Buddhism to the flowers, and Shintoism to the trunk and root.

We have already discussed that Shintoism played an important role during the Warring States period, preventing society from falling into complete breakdown and catastrophe. This role of Shintoism could be construed as a warning given to the people about the possible danger incurred by the neglect of present-day values. The growth of concerns about the way of heaven pointed out by Kanda (2010) is closely related to this role of Shintoism under the influence of the syncretic fusion with Buddhism. According to Kanda, the way of heaven had the following properties: The way of heaven gives the grace and protection of the gods and Buddhas to people; To receive divine favor, one must uphold morality as his internal discipline. This seems to indicate that people at the end of Warring States period were well aware of the importance of present-day values and the necessity of morality that could guide behavior in ordinary life.

The research of some distinguished Confucians like Kumazawa Banzan (1619–91) and Yamazaki Ansai (1618–82) proceeded toward establishing Jyuka (Confucianist)-Shintoism, in which the close relationship between Shintoism and Confucianism was asserted. In particular, Ansai established new Shintoism, *Suika*-Shintoism, in which the logical structure of Shintoism was reinterpreted in the moral principles of new Confucianism. For example, applying the continuity proposition of Confucianism to Shintoism, Ansai claimed that since *ri*, the basic logic that penetrates the workings of nature, was equal to the logic of the gods, the human mind should follow the teachings of the gods in Shintoism. Itō (2012) argues that the contribution of Ansai lay in the interpretation of Shintoism as a moral theory, not as a religious theory.

The concept of 'national religion' in Bitō (1992), touched upon in the last chapter, is worth examination here. Bitō claims that, during the Tokugawa era, Buddhism and Shintoism came to comprise the national religion as a set[19] through intensifying independence with each other and at the same time the complementarity and division of labor in roles. Both Buddhism and Shintoism purified theory at an individual level, but at the societal level they intensified complementarity. Buddhism was assigned the religious matters of individuals and mainly concerned with life after death, whereas Shintoism was in charge of matters related to *ie* and villages and concerned with the present life. Funerals and ceremonies related to *bon* (all Soul's Day) was dealt with by Buddhist tradition and celebrations by festivals of villages were matters treated by Shintoism.

6.2.4 Popular Ethics

The ethical codes developed by thinkers of diverse backgrounds, such as Suzuki Shōsan (1579–1655), Ishida Baigan (1685–1744) and Ninomiya Sontoku (1787–1858), were well received by individuals and exerted a significant influence on the behavioral patterns of people during the Tokugawa era. They were written using the Confucian concept, since Confucianism was the most rigorous system of thinking and expression at the time; but ethical codes emphasized in popular ethics had almost nothing to do with Confucian teaching (Hongō 1994). Obedience to one's parents, a top item in Confucian ethical codes, was not included in the codes recommended by popular ethic thinkers and loyalty was quite often the last item touched upon.[20]

[19]Rigorously speaking, Bitō includes in the set of nationala religion folk religions practices such as nature worship including mountain worship and animism-type religion like *shugen-dō*.

[20]For example, see the comment on Ninomiya Sontoku's theory in Naramoto (1973, pp. 436–437). Morishima (1984, 2004), however, argues that the essence of Tokugawa ideology lies in Japanese style Confucianism that emphasizes feudalistic loyalty, and this 'feudalistic' ideology was inherited by the nationalistic spirit of Japanese capitalism after the Meiji Restoration and further in the corporate governance system in modern Japanese firms. However, there is persuasive criticism by Ienaga (1953) of this kind of theory, apparently constructed on the assertion of self-effacing dedication to one's masters by the samurai, contended in Watsuji (1952, ch. 5) or Maruyama (1960), that the relation of master–servant is an equilibrium in a game theoretic situation where material remuneration in the form of *go-on* is returned by the service of *hōkou*. Morishima, on the other hand, emphasizes the difference in the meaning of the concept of loyalty between Chinese feudalism that emphasizes sincerity to one's conscience and the Japanese concept that stresses self-effacing dedication to masters. This assertion also is marred by the ignorance or lack of basic scholarly investigation about such theories as Koyasu (1998), who notes that the Chinese concept had also come to emphasize self-effacing dedication after the mid-Warring States era in China

Instead, honesty, diligence and thriftiness were the three main moral codes common to popular ethics. The salient features of the codes of popular ethics were an emphasis on present-day benefits, a high appreciation for the role of the social division of labor and the necessity of the contribution to it by individuals, and the importance of the *kyūdō* principle. Let us explain this with respect to the three representative advocates above.

Suzuki Shōsan, who had been a direct vassal of Ieyasu until 42 years of age, became a Zen priest after the battle of Sekigahara. The foundation of his theory was cognition that ordinary occupational life was the place for Buddhist practice and the recommendation to attain enlightenment through contribution to society. In this sense, he was still not free from the value of the sacred, but he was the earliest person who proposed concrete codes to be followed by each occupation in the system of the social division of labor in peaceful society. He claimed that enlightenment was promised to those engaged in hard and 'brave' labor in agriculture. Honesty is most important for a merchant, and profits would be obtained automatically when he refrained from avaricious behavior, and so on.

Ishida Baigan, who had been an apprentice to merchants and started his study from Shintoism and shifted to Confucianism, taught merchants widely about his theory obtained from his own experiences as a scholar. At first, he tried to find innate *ri* in his mind following the theory of new Confucianism, but the final conclusion he came to was the importance to understand the functional value of the system of the social division of labor and to devote oneself to the assigned role in the system. This theory is summarized in his words that the ultimate aim of studying was to understand the innate substance inherently built in the minds of humans and to realize the fundamental principle of the heaven asserted in the new Confucian theory. At the same time, he emphasized that, to accomplish the aim, one must understand the *kokoro* (essence). The expression 'understanding *kokoro*', is construed by Hongō (1994) as understanding the social value of the assigned role as well as of the social division of labor given in society, through spiritual training like the *kyūdō* principle. By way of reinterpreting the concept of social class in the *shokubun* regulation, where merchants were ranked at the lowest in the assignment of social roles, Baigan tried to liberalize merchants from the contempt for them implied in Confucian thinking and in the *bakufu* regulation of the *shokubun*.

Baigan's concept of the 'essence dependent on given form (*katachi ni yoru kokoro*)' in his *Tohi-mondō* (vol. 2) is worthy of attention because it expresses his understanding of the importance of fulfilling the role in *shokubun* regulation in terms of the Confucian concept of *ri* of the heaven. He illustrates the concept by use of the insect mosquito: a mosquito bites human with his sting, while a larva of mosquito without a sting does not. What he meant was that a mosquito with a sting bites the

---

and Watanabe (1985, pp. 81–85), who contends that the difference in the conception of loyalty between China and Japan lies in the different historical role of 'saints' (successors in civil service examination) in Chinese society and the samurai in Japan. It is contended that while Chinese saints were selected as intellectual and bureaucratic leaders, the samurai in Japan grew up as military experts on the battlefields. Many of Morishima's assertions that emphasize the 'feudalistic' nature of the Japanese system seem to be based on a careless and impressionistic reasoning.

human because it follows his form of having a sting. The form of having a sting corresponds to an occupation in the system of the social division of labor and the action to bite the human is to follow the functional role assigned in the social division of labor. Just as the relationship of the role and action for a mosquito is determined by the mechanism in nature, the relationship of one's occupation and his role in the social division of labor is stipulated by the needs of society in terms of social engineering. There is nothing supernatural about the relationship, as is claimed by the new Confucian theory.

Likewise, according to Katō (1984), 'understanding *kokoro*' means that, upon the affirmation of the equality of the ri of nature and the *ri* of society (continuity theory in Maruyama's terminology), one must know the value of refraining from excessive vulgarity (*taru wo shiru*), of recognition of the assigned social role (*bun wo shiru*), and of devoting oneself into house business (*kagyō ni sei-wo-dasu*). In effect, Baigan emphasized the unification of the fundamental principle of the heaven and oneself in the sense that, to understand the value of the social system, one must follow the moral codes in society and, most importantly, internalize the value in oneself. Katō also identifies the *kyūdō* principle in the stance of Baigan to emphasize spiritual training in the place of occupation. In this sense, it seems to be not far off the mark to say that, while Baigan resorted to the concept of Confucianism in this writing, the conclusion derived is closely related to Buddhism. Baigan himself claimed that there is no difference among Shintoism, Buddhism and Confucianism in the emphasis of 'understanding *kokoro*' or the internalization of the social value of ethical codes.

Baigan tried to clarify the role of merchants in the social division of labor and emphasized the functional importance of commerce and distribution in the economy. It is well known that he claimed that the profit income obtained by merchants was synonymous with the stipend of the samurai, emphasizing the equality of the occupational classes from the viewpoint of their functional role in the economy. He taught the importance of loyalty and filial duty to realize smooth social order, but the main ethical code in his teaching lay in honesty and thriftiness. Honesty in Baigan's theory means not only avoiding making excessive profits by cheating but also following the needs of society, like postponing a request for repaying loans from those who had suffered from flood damages. Thriftiness meant not only frugality for the sake of oneself but also the efficient utilization of goods, like transferring one's claim on goods to those who need them most. The thesis developed by Baigan, aimed at developing ethical codes conducive to the development of society as a whole, and in accordance with needs arising from the development of the social division of labor, was highly appreciated not only among the merchants but also among the samurai, who had experienced severe material lives as bureaucrats in the rapidly commercializing society.

Ninomiya Sontoku grew up as the son of a bankrupt farmer and devoted his life to the rehabilitation of his house (*ie*). By way of studying by himself, he developed his own socio-economic theory on agriculture. Although he admitted the existence of the objective and physical laws of nature, he denied the theory of new Confucianism that asserted the close relationship of the law with the human mind. He had his own materialistic theory of the development of the human mind and economy, that economic development begins with the efficient utilization of the productive power of nature, and that the morality of humans began to be improved after production levels had reached a certain level. From this theory was derived his moral theory about the importance of present-day benefits. For him, an increase in production is good and the destruction of productive capacity is bad, so that the right way of leading one's daily life is to fulfil one's role in the social division of labor to contribute to the growth of production in society.

Sontoku considered that society was made up of organic and functional relationships among various occupations and asserted that agriculture was the most fundamental among occupations in the social division of labor. By this assertion, he intended to eliminate the inferiority complex of peasants and encouraged them to overcome historical mores by reforming themselves. He taught peasants that it was possible to improve their living conditions, and developed and disseminated the methods to realize the improvement. He recommended not only diligence but also thriftiness. His emphasis on thriftiness was derived from his own model of capital accumulation (the theory of *bundo* and *suijyō*) that some percentage of products should be saved for the sake of investment in the next period. Investment was concerned not only with one's own land but also with the infrastructure in villages. Sontoku's theory of saving and investment was most effective when it was applied at the regional and macro level. He became an adviser of Odawara-*han*, where he succeeded in implementing a ten-year project to rehabilitate decayed villages. Sontoku's theory acquired a high reputation, and he was asked to be economic adviser to many *han* in the Kanto area and was finally hired by the *bakufu* as a samurai.

In carrying out his job as an adviser, he persuaded the lords of the *han* to reduce budget deficits and increase surplus, and recommended to cultivate wastelands as well as to reduce the tax burden of peasants. He also developed various measures to enhance the incentive of peasants to fulfill their social roles, such as awards system for productive peasants, improving infrastructure including roads and irrigation and the repair of shrines held by villages, financial support of individual peasants through official lending, and the provision of relief rice to poverty-stricken peasants (Ōtō 2015). He claimed his theory was a mixture of Shintoism as the way of establishing a country, Confucianism as the way for improving governance of a country, and Buddhism as the way to improve human minds.

6.2.5 *Kaitoku-dō*

The economic development of the Tokugawa era based on the acceleration of the social division of labor was due to the functioning of the commercial sector and the role played by merchants. The serious economic issues during the Kyoho era (1716–36) under the reign of the eighth shogun, Yoshimune (reign 1716–45) has drawn substantial attention. The major issue was the fall of the price of rice relative to other commodity prices. Since rice comprised the main part of the fiscal revenues of the government, this had a radical impact on income distribution among classes.

The samurai class was hit most seriously and rice producers, farmers, also suffered significant damage. The debt of *han* and samurais increased, and repeated famine and riots in the rural sector fermented social unrest. Ad hoc monetary policy, by means of recoinage with the aim to raise rice prices, aggravated the confusion further.

Against this background, there occurred serious criticism and skepticism about the role of merchants and commerce. Merchants were accused of being excessively profit-oriented or 'emotional'. It was in this social atmosphere that Ishida Baigan published *Tohi-mondō* in 1736 and recommended the adequate role of merchants in the social division of labor as well as the proper ethical codes of merchants that emphasized honesty and thriftiness. It is interesting here to refer to the development of moral science at Kaitoku-dō, a semi-official research institution[21] established by influential merchants in Osaka in 1726. While Baigan's theory was concerned with practical issues related to the role of merchants in the social division of labor, the study at Kaitoku-dō focused on an examination of and emphasis on the virtue of merchants as the innate propensity of humans.

As pointed out by the insightful study of Najita (1987), a group of Confucian researchers, who got together at Kaitoku-dō, tried to develop a scientific theory of moral philosophy. Researchers at Kaitoku-dō such as Miyake Sekian (1665–1730), Tominaga Chūki (1715–46), Yamagata Banchō (1748–1821) and Kaiho Seiryō (1755–1817) intended to build up an alternative moral philosophy on the basis of social scientific methods and knowledge of the natural sciences acquired through the study of Western sciences. It was the time that the Tokugawa *bakufu* gradually changed their stance toward foreign culture, and relaxed regulation on the import of Western books and Chinese translations of Western books by way of the port city Nagasaki.

The main aim of Kaitoku-dō lay in the development of moral philosophy that supported merchants and justified their activity from the standpoint of moral principle. Najita (1987). claims that the aim of the institution lay not in the development of applied science but moral science for merchants. Kaitoku-dō members by and large admitted the criticism against the new Confucianism developed by researches Sokō, Jinsai and Sorai. Methodologically they adopted an approach that could be regarded as a sharp antithesis of the study of Sorai. First, influenced by the knowledge of the enlightenment movement in the West, they adopted a natural scientific approach instead of the historical approach of Sorai. Second, they criticized Sorai's thesis on the static human mind, strenuously emphasizing the possibility for every citizen of the development of the human mind and of acquiring higher morality.

Among the multifarious research projects, two of them regarding the market economy are worth mentioning. First is the basic stance of Kaitoku-dō toward the virtue of merchants. According to the opening-day lecture delivered by one of the founders of the institute, Miyake Sekian, in 1726, we can notice they intended to justify the virtue of the behavior of merchants by use of the notion of justice in

[21]The major founders were Miyake Setsuan and Nakai Bonnan. Kaitoku-dō obtained official approval in 1726 as an academy for tradesman. The top *bakufu* official, *Rōchū* Matsudaira Sadanobu, visited Kaitoku-dō in 1789.

competition. Quoting the understanding of Mencius about the teaching of Confucius, Sekian argued that the profit maximization behavior of merchants can be construed as the pursuit of sympathy of others (*jin*) under the constraint of justice (*gi*). The maximization of profits is not the manifestation of the avarice of emotional desire but rather it is a rational behavior dictated by the rules of justice. This is an extremely modern understanding of the market mechanism. Referring to the choice faced by Kaitoku-dō researchers about the epistemological foundation between the two alternatives, history and nature, McClousky (2006) points out the importance of the fact that 'the commercial version of temperance, justice and prudence that were admitted during the eighteenth century by some in the commercial societies of northern Europe and by at least the merchants themselves in Japan' (p. 32). Najita (1987) criticizes the conventional argument that asserts the passive and coerced role fulfilled by the merchant class at the time of the Meiji Restoration,[22] and contends that, in view of the diverse involvement of merchant thinkers in the discussion of economic policy, merchants in the late Tokugawa and early Meiji eras had a clear conceptual consciousness grounded in earlier intellectual development (p. 6). We will return to this point in the examination of the elite settlement hypothesis in the appendix to this chapter.

The second important contribution to the understanding of the market economy is the main work of Yamabata Bantō, *Yume no kawarini*. In this book, Bantō developed his own model of equilibrium about the decentralized market mechanism. First, he noted that everything in the world and every socio-economic phenomenon should be understood from the viewpoint of relativity and without resorting to the notion of central ordering. He justified his proposition asserting that, according to research into astronomy, the earth as well as human beings exist in the universe as an existence relative to the sun, quoting the heliocentric theories of Copernicus and Newton.[23] Second, Bantō claimed that the samurai should accept the proposition that things are interrelated with each other so that everything belongs to the whole. From this proposition he asserted that the social position of commerce had a close relationship with other industries, including agriculture, and that the excessiveness of the samurai population was putting an additional burden on the productive capacity on the country. He concluded that the right policy regarding rice prices lay not in monetary policy but in the excessive consumption of the samurai class, and it was necessary for the samurai to return to the rice fields and to be engaged in agriculture as they used to be.

It could be said that Bantō had a clear and modern understanding about the functioning of the decentralized market and the concept of macro-economic equilibrium that was quite close to modern economics, although references to the logic of astronomy are somewhat difficult to understand. This kind of concept of the market is not found in the theory of popular ethics, mostly developed as behavioristic rules by

---

[22] 'Demeaned as an inferior class for over two hundred years, the merchants at the end of Tokugawa era were manipulated and coerced by various contending political alignments to make, at best grudgingly, monetary contributions to causes of little concern to them' (p. 6).

[23] Bantō read Japanese translation (by Shizuki Tadao) of Dutch version of introductory text written by John Keil. See Minamoto (1984, p. 32).

economic agents. It is important to note, however, the social impacts of the activity of Kaitoku-dō were confined largely to the elite segments of merchants, and the immediate effects on the development of commerce was much more limited, compared with the effects achieved by popular ethics. Referring to the thoughts of Nakai Chikuzan and Yamagata Bantō, Najita points out that the direct influence on a generation or two later than them was limited and that the contribution of their thoughts lay only in the provision of structural basis of conceptualization. However, he concludes that, despite the lack of influence of Kaitoku-dō, 'it is undeniable that the writings of Nakai and Yamgata were not isolated and unique events but were enmeshed in a broader intellectual engagement with issues of knowledge and polity' (p. 7). It follows that the thinking of mid-eighteenth century-Japan had already matured to the extent that it was ready to expand the worldview beyond the narrow confines of others nearby, at least conceptually.

Minamoto (1984) notes that Banchō's *Yume no kawarini*' was not published but was distributed only among friends and acquaintances in the form of private transcription. Although Minamoto adds that such practice was usual with other distinguished writings at the time, the weakness of the social impact of Kaitoku-dō activity is difficult to deny. Further, Shinpo (1985) points out that Banto actually did not want his writings to be published, so it may be conjectured that the research at Kaitoku-do aimed at an elite-level deepening of the understanding of commerce, and had little intention to exercise any direct influence on popular thinking. Bantō and other members of Kaitoku-dō, such as Kusama Naokata, were leading figures in the business world; Bantō was a top manager at Masuya, one of the leading money-changers at the time, and Naotaka was also a top figure at Kōnoike, the largest money-changer with close relationships with major *han* in western Japan. Minamoto contends that Bantō, as a leading ideologue of Osaka merchant society, refrained from publicizing his theory, which might conflict with the policy of the *bakufu*.

This situation is in sharp contrast with the writings of Baigan and other popular ethic thinkers. In the case of Baigan, his theory, the Ishida-Shingaku, was spread by the Shingaku movement after his death, not only in the Kansai area but also in Kantō and other areas more widely. The writings were distributed as textbooks to a large group of followers gathered in schools built as a project of the Shingaku movement in many large regional towns. His disciples, such as Teshima Toan (1718–86), established the systematic organization of the spread of Ishida-Shingaku, in which monthly meeting were held under rigorous rules, specific writings of Baigan were designated as authorized teaching materials, and teachers were systematically trained through licensing examinations (Shibata 1971). Nakazawa Dōni (1725–1803), who studied under Toan and taught in Edo, was invited to a number of *han* residences, and had a large number of followers among the samurai. Through these movements, the thinking of Baigan and ethic codes recommended by him had enormous influence on society during the latter period of the Tokugawa era.

The thoughts of Ninomiya Sontoku were also spread widely by the help of disciples. The numbers of his followers increased as the samurais and rich farmers in fiefs, where he had helped rehabilitation, became his disciples. They helped him in collecting economic data and information, designing a financial as well as fiscal economic plan, and procuring necessary goods and funds, when Sontoku applied this theory, called *hōtoku-shihō*, to the rehabilitation policy of the regions.[24] After his death and the Meiji Restoration, private associations for disseminating and applying his theory of regional development were organized in various regions. It is also well known that the biography of his younger days was utilized by the Ministry of Education to spread ethical codes such as diligence and thriftiness at elementary schools.

6.2.6 Role of the Samurai and the Shokubun Regulation

The establishment of an ethic-based society was possible and effective partly because the samurai class cooperated and played a significant role in the project. What role should be assigned to the samurai class, deeply involved in bloody activities on the battlefields, was a serious question for the Tokugawa regime, aiming at the establishment of a peaceful society. The role assigned to the class in the *shokubun* regulation was to be engaged in the administrative task of government, the *bakufu* and *han*, and to lead the development and dissemination of ethical society. The class, constituting two million people or six per cent of the population, was ordered to leave agricultural activity, migrate to the castle city of each *han*, and fulfil the role of civil servants with an annual salary paid in cash. They were given the monopolistic right to use violence with arms and, at the same time, required to train themselves in martial arts and to acquire a basic knowledge and capability in arts such as poetry and calligraphy, as well as in the humanities, especially new Confucianism.

The role of the samurai, however, was not confined to the roles assigned in the system of *shokubun* regulation. This point was closely related to the political position of the Tokugawa regime. As we have already noted, the unity and peace attained by the Tokugawa clan had the form of a tentative political and military equilibrium, so there was the incessant possibility to reestablish a new political and military order by other powerful *han* replacing the Tokugawa clan, especially those located in western Japan. As a member of Tokugawa society, the samurai class was responsible to play the role assigned in the *shokubun* regulation, whereas as a member of a clan or *han*, the samurai must always be prepared for another military clash to rebuild the national political order based on new principles and an hegemonic structure. In the terminology of Maruyama (1960), they were constantly facing the two-sided choice between loyalty to organization and loyalty to principle. Loyalty to organization meant loyalty to each clan and to the social order of the *shokubun* regulation, while loyalty to principle implied loyalty to the principle to build up political and military order. The Tokugawa system, the so-called *bakuhan*-system, was apparently not the only possible equilibrium; there were other clans with higher lineage and legitimacy and, above all, the imperial family. From the viewpoint of cultural tradition, the

[24] A number of clansmen in the Odawara-*han* and Nakamura (Soma)-*han* became faithful and efficient followers of Sontoku (Ōtō 2015).

former role of the samurai, namely loyalty to the *shokubun* regulation, was examined in close relationship with Buddhism; how to face death and the temporality of human life was the central question, and was pursued in the framework of the *kyūdō* principle. The second problem the samurai tackled was related to new Confucianism. Although the concept of heaven and its omnipotent position in theory was gradually put under severe critical pressure by professional Confucian scholars, as already discussed, the process of the critical study of Confucianism exerted a strong influence on the thinking of the samurai class as a whole.

The samurai class was well-known as a faithful follower of the *kyūdō* principle, in the sense of pursuit of *bushi-dō*. Although less well appreciated, they were required to seek present-day ethic rules to meet *shokubun* regulation in society. Sagara (1968) contends that the moral rules of the class finally arrived at the integrity of internal conscience and attitude towards outside. This mindset is explained by use of the words of Suzuki Shōsan 'feeling shame at one's shameful mind' (*kokoro ni kokoro wo hajiru*). Sagara paraphrases this as the simultaneous pursuit of evidence as to respect for oneself and of objective evidence as to being respected by others. In other words, the samurai class came to pursue the realization of a mindset in which to feel shame about oneself was synonymous with feeling shame at others whom he respects. Through trying to realize a moral society where such mindset is shared by every individual, the samurai class established their position as the moral leaders of Tokugawa society.

Sagara (1968) contends that the Buddhist view of life and death evolved, reflecting the role of the samurai in the system of the *shokubun* regulation. The notion of *mujyō*, mutability, came to be construed in combination with the concept of honor within samurai society. The famous words in the document, *Hagakure*, that the essence of *bushi-dō* lies in death, was endowed with an affirmative connotation that the decision to die means not only the impermanence of life but also the permanence of honor. In this sense, various behaviors caused by *bonno* (earthly desires), especially attachment to life, came to be of secondary importance among the samurai.

With respect to the future course of the polity of Japan, the thinking of the samurai evolved under the strong influence of new Confucianism. The concept of heaven was the most popular clue in this respect. Although the concept lived long in the mind of the samurai during the Tokugawa era, the concept was applied to Japan in a significantly deformed, and hence highly practical, form.[25] For one thing, as discussed

[25]The essay authored by Nitobe Inazō (1862–1933) (Nitobe 1905) '*Bushi-dō* – the Soul of Japan' reveals how overwhelming was the influence of new Confucianism on the way of thinking of youngsters brought up in Tokugawa Japan. Whenever they tried to pursue the problem of how Japan should be in the future, new Confucianism was the only available source of concepts close to the notion they tried to describe as the way of thinking of the samurai. However, what Nitobe learned during his boyhood was an elementary introduction to Confucianism, which did not cover the struggle by forerunners. Therefore, while the essay is written utilizing the terminology of Confucianism, there are significant discrepancies between the content Nitobe wanted to convey to the readers and the connotation of Confucian words. For example, while the essay starts with the famous concept of *chigyō-gōitsu* (in Nitobe's interpretation 'to know and to act are one and the same') of Wan Yang Ming, a leading philosopher in new Confucianism, the concept to prioritize actions and the denial of study without action is a traditionally inherited philosophy among the

already, the notion of omnipotent heaven was theoretically attacked by scholars with respect to the continuity theory, in the sense that the principle governing nature was also applicable to human nature as well as the structure of society. Moreover, in the study of ancient literature on the concept of heaven, it was clarified that what was called the way of the saints was nothing but the historical facts of the activity of kings who had actually lived in China and was not something derived through deductive theoretical procedures. Furthermore, most crucial was the fact that Tokugawa Japan was in a transitory state, where the so-called *bakuhan* system was only a transitory equilibrium established as a compromise among military and political powers, so that historical facts about the absolute monarchy in China did not have much relevance to the situation faced by Tokugawa Japan.

Yamaga Sokō tried to develop a practical thesis about the theoretical basis of the polity and political system. His pragmatism was dependent to two propositions. First, he started from the reality of human behavior. He criticized Buddhism in the sense of the denial of *bonno* (earthly desires). According to him, human beings are existent because of avaricious feelings. If avarice is taken away from humans, they became the same thing as stone and wood. He tried to develop a political theory starting from the natural and unfettered optimization of humans. Second, he denied the omnipotent property of the Confucian concept of *ri* and considered that how humans should behave needed to be designated by concrete and realistic, not universal, logic (*jyōri*). In the realistically complicated situation that Japan was going to face, the role fulfilled by a magnificent and universal theory seemed to be limited, and if it was necessary to find out some leading concept of conduct, it must be pursued and found as a hidden logical structure in concrete and tangible phenomena, Sokō contended.

The final and crucial question, which the samurai class pursued and actually faced later on during the period after Perry, was the choice between faithfulness to the role stipulated in the *shokubun* regulation and faithfulness to the principle to be followed by the country. The theory proposed by Sokō was as follows. First, the samurai class in Tokugawa society must be faithful to the role assigned by the *shokubun* regulation. Sokō recommended that the samurai class should be a model of adequate ethic performer in society. The people of the other three classes did not have time to think about what was adequate for ethics, because they were busily engaged in their own roles of the production of material goods and services related to the living of people. Secondly, however, Sokō contended that another obligation the samurai class must fulfil lay in the pursuit of a better way of the governance of the country. The thinking of Sokō was that Japan should be a leading country comparable to China in Asia, distinguished in three virtues: courage, knowledge and benevolence (Tahara 1983).

During the peaceful years under the reign of the Tokugawa era before Perry, there was no serious contradiction between the role of the samurai in the *shokubun*

samurai since the Warring States period, so that it is not so much related to something to be inspired and taught by the theory of Wan Yang Ming. Further, his emphasis on the concept of *jin*, benevolence, seems to be too superficial. It seems that the concept of *jin* in *bushi-dō* should be construed from the viewpoint of the integrity of oneself and others as is contended in Sagara (1968).

regulation and the pursuit of the goal of the new polity for the country. The so-called Mito school stuck to the stipulation of the *shokubun* regulation and tried to be loyal to the *bakuhu* and *han*. Yoshida Shōin, however, under the strong influence of the thinking of Sokō, 'put the *bakufu* and *han* in the parenthesis', and rose up to build a new polity other than the *bakuhan* system (Sagara 1968).

6.3 Dissemination of Ethical Code and Decline in Transaction Costs

In Chapter 3, we pointed out that one of the amazing features of growth in the Tokugawa era was the stability of industrial structures during the mid-Tokugawa period, 1721–1846, especially during 1721–1804. In terms of the input–output table analysis, one of the sufficient conditions for this phenomenon were the constant or proportional changes in final demand and the proportional decline in all input–output coefficients. The former condition could be satisfied by the stabilization of lifestyle when the splendid and bubbly years in the Genroku period (1688–1704) were over, and the steady and standardized lifestyle gained popularity from the beginning of the eighteenth century. The latter condition was satisfied when all inter-industrial commercial transactions were put under the same favorable shocks. We conjectured that the steady reduction of transaction costs in the economy owing to the overall alleviation of information asymmetry was responsible for this phenomenon. This is because such an impact should have benefited all industries equally. It will be shown that under the Tokugawa regime, there occurred a drastic decline in transaction costs owing to the alleviation of information asymmetry in society caused by the standardization of conduct and ethical codes. This seems to be the main reason for the phenomenon of growth with steady industrial structures during the mid-Tokugawa era.

In this section, we present a hypothesis that the reduction in transaction costs owing to the development of ethical codes was the basic reason for commerce-based growth during Tokugawa era. At first, growth was triggered by innovation in transportation, especially marine transportation and in the settlement and remittance system between Edo and Osaka. This reduced the operational costs in commerce enormously. Then, commerce-based growth was embedded in the socio-economic system as the development and diffusion of ethical codes alleviated informational asymmetry in the economy, directly through the standardization of behavior of individuals, and indirectly through inducing institutional changes complementary with the reduction in transaction costs.

The direct effects on information asymmetry through behavioral standardization occurred as the dissemination of moral codes made the behavior of others more forecastable. As behavior under the *shokubun* regulation was standardized for each occupational group, information asymmetry was alleviated among groups such as farmers, merchants and moneylenders. Trust was fermented among them gradually.

Urban merchants used to bear high costs during the early Tokugawa era due to lack of local information. Information asymmetry was reduced drastically when information about peasants and workers held by merchants and rich farmers in the local economy came to be utilized. Indirect effects through institutional changes occurred as the dissemination of ethical codes led to the development of institutions such as the settlement system between local regions, peasant participation in the manufacturing system coordinated by wholesalers, and the *ie* system to prevent opportunistic behavior. These institutions co-evolved with the alleviation of information asymmetry, so that their development reduced information asymmetry and, at the same time, benefited from the reduction in information asymmetry.

6.3.1 Three Triggers of Initial Growth

The economic growth of the Tokugawa era was triggered by three innovations: rapid urbanization, the development of new routes for marine transportation, and the efficient new method of settlement and remittance. Urbanization occurred as a result of the policy of gathering the samurai in castle cities. The latter two innovations became necessary to supply sufficient goods to the huge consumption city of Edo and to monetize the tax revenue of the *han*, paid in kind mainly in the form of rice.

6.3.1.1 Urbanization

The first trigger of growth was the sudden urbanization of the country, the growth of the urban population, in the seventeenth century. A typical example is Edo. A local town of 6000 population in 1600 grew into a world class city with a population of 1.139 million in 1721 and remained at a similar level thereafter. Of the total population in 1721, 526,300 were merchants and artisans (*chōnin*), 525,700 were samurai, and the remaining 86,600 were priests, prostitutes and part-time immigrant workers (Takashima 2017). Likewise, the rate of urbanization rose from 6.4% in 1600 to 13.6% in 1650, as is shown in Table 3.5. This implies that a similar kind of urbanization proceeded in every castle city of the regional fiefs nationwide, to a greater or lesser degree.

Edo was a mammoth consumption city led by the vast number of vassals of the *bakufu* and other samurai dwellers related to the *sankin-kōtai* system. Whenever the price levels of goods other than rice rose, ordinances to prohibit luxury consumption were issued to the city dwellers (*chōnin*) and farmers, but there continued to prevail among samurai and city dwellers an atmosphere to live a luxurious life.

Although farmers were prohibited from eating rice in daily life and there were strict regulations on clothes, relating not only to material but also design and color, no such regulations were applied to merchants and samurai. High-ranking samurai and rich merchants enjoyed brand quality rice, wearing quality clothes with fine accessories, and were involved in theater-going and performing arts. Their daughters amused themselves in high-priced kimono with gorgeous embroidery and quality sewing.

Most of such consumption goods were transported from Kyoto in the case of delicate art crafts, and from Osaka in the case of goods for daily use. The largest textile merchant, Echigo-ya, sold at the Edo branch store colorful silk textiles produced in Kyoto by means of the newly invented technology of dyeing. Ogyū Sorai (1666–1728), a famous critic of merchants, deplored, in his *Seidan*, the spread of luxuries in the daily life of Edo citizens (Tsuji 1973).

Not only cities but also at the national level, it is known that the standard of living improved considerably. Life expectancy increased from 37.8 to 41.8 years for males and from 38.0 to 41.0 years for females, from the seventeenth to eighteenth century. A not small number of adults lived sufficiently long to become old people. The average calorific intake went up almost 1400 kilocalories by the end of the Tokugawa era (Kitō 2002). Although the intake of animal protein was not sufficient, farmers took a sufficient level of minerals from various kind of crops and vegetables. Hanley (1983) and Yasuba (1986) confirm that Japan was not far behind England in that period in terms of per capita income, life expectancy, and stature.

6.3.1.2 Marine Transportation

Land transportation was underdeveloped during the Tokugawa era, partly because of the necessity to prevent the easy movement of military forces to Edo that threatened the safety of the regime. It is well known that the construction of bridges across major rivers was forbidden for this reason. So, marine transport was the major method for the transportation of commodities. The infrastructure for marine transportation was provided by the *bakufu*,[26] which needed to transport and monetize tax paid in rice from domains under direct control in Tōhoku and southwestern Japan. Since the east coast route from Tōhoku to Edo was difficult to sail by wooden Japanese-style vessels, especially from Sendai to Chiba due to complicated tide conditions and strong winds from the northeast in winter, the western coast route from Tohoku to Osaka through the Japan Sea and the Seto inland sea was newly developed in 1672. At the same time, the existing trunk line between Edo and Osaka through the Pacific Ocean by way of the Kii peninsular was improved by the introduction of systems such as pilots and fire signals, warehouses, exemption from port taxes, and the like.

Inspired by the infrastructure investment of the *bakufu*, competition among private shipping companies intensified, giving rise to various innovations such as new types of vessels for bulky cargo transportation (*taru-kaisen*) and systems of regular voyage services, such as *higaki-kaisen*. The development of new marine transportation routes and the increase in the goods supplied from distant regions provided incentives to improve land and river transportation systems near major ports, such as inland transportation by use of the Tone river.

[26] Kawamura Zuiken, a lumber merchant good at engineering works, was ordered by the *bakufu* to develop the marine transportation system.

Incidentally, the development of these marine transportation businesses proceeded in collaboration with large wholesale merchants based in three cities—Edo, Osaka and Kyoto (the so-called three-cities merchants)—who developed the nationwide distribution system, in which they obtained necessary materials and semi-finished products from Tōhoku and other areas, sent them to Kyoto and Osaka to add finishing processing, and sold the final products to consumers in Edo and other areas. The transportation element in this process was undertaken by marine transporters such as *higaki-kaisen*. In the nineteenth century, however, local producer-merchants of region-specific products came to hire and own their own vessels, and the management of fare-based services provided by *higaki-kaisen* encountered difficulties, in tandem with the decline of the market power of the three-cities merchants.

6.3.1.3 New Method of Settlement

The third trigger, innovations in settlement and remittance between Edo and Osaka, was introduced through taking advantage of the imbalance in commodity transactions between Edo and Osaka. The first innovation was related to the necessity to remit from Osaka to Edo sales proceeds of rice collected as tax from various *bakufu* domains in southwestern Japan. During the early Tokugawa era, the money was brought to Edo in the form of cash by an overland route, but it was a highly costly and dangerous method. So the *bakufu* decided in 1690 to send the money by way of bill of exchange in the following way. The *bakufu* handed over the cash to moneychangers whose main offices were in Edo and who had branch offices in Osaka. The moneychangers bought bills receivable directed to Edo merchants from Osaka merchants, and sent the bills to the Edo main offices. The main offices converted the bills into cash and paid the proceeds to the *bakufu* treasury in Edo.

This *bakufu*-related business was gradually monopolized by Mitsui, which had to remit sales proceeds at its Tokyo branch to Osaka to get clothes for sale in Edo. Instead of remitting the money to Osaka, the *bakufu* money handled at Osaka was used, and sales proceeds at the Tokyo branch was paid to the *bakufu* treasury in Edo.

Throughout the Tokugawa era, there always existed a huge imbalance in commodity transactions between Edo and Osaka, especially until the peripheral industrial belt around Edo (the Edo-*jimawari* economy) developed in the mid-Tokugawa era. The sales of commodities to Edo by Osaka merchants was always far more than the purchase from Edo merchants, so that there were always bills receivable in Osaka.

From the early eighteenth century, this unbalanced situation came to be extensively utilized by *daimyos* who wanted to send money from their Osaka to Edo residences, and by Osaka merchants who wanted to remit sales proceeds in Edo to Osaka. The *daimyos* brought huge amount of rice obtained as tax revenue to the warehouse in Osaka and sold it on the Osaka rice market. They had to send the sales proceeds either to Edo residences of the fiefs held for *sankin-kōtai* or to their domains to finance domestic expenditure. The remittance to Edo was carried out by use of bills receivable directed to Edo.[27] A *daimyo* handed over the cash to Osaka moneychanger merchants in exchange for bills payable to *daimyos*. The moneychanger merchants bought bills receivable directed to Edo from Osaka wholesale merchants and sent the bills to Edo moneychanger merchants. Bills payable were sent to the Edo residence of the *daimyo*, and the bills receivable to Edo moneychangers. The Edo moneychanger merchants converted the bills into cash at Edo wholesale merchants, and paid the proceeds to the *daimyo*'s residence in Edo.

The commerce-based growth after the early eighteenth century was due substantially to the commodity and money flow between Edo and Osaka. After the mid-Tokugawa era, the amount of money that went through the system became even larger as the *daimyos* increased their borrowings from Osaka moneychanger merchants to finance their fiscal deficits and expenses in their Edo residences. It must be noted that since the commodity flow from Osaka to Edo was so huge, especially during the early part of the Tokugawa era, the amount of remittance by *daimyos* was not sufficient to offset the commodity flow imbalance. In other words, there always occurred the need to send cash. For example, the rise of the relative price of silver to gold in Edo at the end of the seventeenth century was caused by the shortage of silver in Edo. Since transactions in Edo were carried out in gold coin and in Osaka in silver (currency by weight), remittance to Osaka needed to be done in silver. Nakai (1961) conjectures that the rise in the silver price was caused by the need for the remittance of silver to Osaka.

Nevertheless, it is true that the availability of large sums of exchange bills of *daimyos* to send money to Edo provided the enormous opportunity to sell commodities to Edo from Osaka with low transaction costs. Within the limit set by the amount of remittance to Edo by *daimyos*, Osaka wholesale merchants were emancipated from the costly and dangerous business of transporting species overland from Edo to Osaka. It was definitely a boon to Osaka wholesale merchants to enjoy the reduction in transaction costs.

6.3.2 *Alleviation of Information Asymmetry*

The decline in transaction costs owing to innovations in marine transportation and in the method of settlement utilizing bills receivable and *daimyo* remittance triggered the growth of the early Tokugawa era. It seems that the steady growth thereafter was due to the decline in transaction costs also, but the reason was different. While risk premiums owing to serious information symmetry were the major factor that kept transaction costs high during the early Tokugawa period, despite the innovations in transportation and settlement systems, we believe that information asymmetry was alleviated and risk premiums were reduced drastically after the eighteenth century,

---

[27]Conventionally this method is considered to have been invented by Komeya Heiuemon in 1723, but Sakudō (1961) says that similar methods had been tried before him by others but a large-scale utilization of the method occurred after his invention.

causing a sustained reduction in transaction costs. There are three basic mechanisms to alleviate information asymmetry and to reduce risk premiums: (1) reduction of uncertainty about the expected action of economic agents through standardization of conduct, (2) supply of additional information by local merchants, and (3) diversification and increase in risk-bearing agents in transactions. All three mechanisms worked to reduce risk premiums during the Tokugawa era, eventually leading to sustained reduction in transaction costs.

6.3.2.1 Standardization of Conduct

We believe that in a society in which the disclosure of information is difficult to implement due to the underdevelopment of mass media or a favorable social atmosphere, the standardization of economic behavior under the influence of the dissemination of popular ethics was one of the most efficient ways that alleviated information asymmetry among economic agents and hence reduced the risk premiums felt by others, leading to the decline in transaction costs in the economy. In other words, the occupational activity of individuals followed the same behavioral rules, such as diligence, honesty and thriftiness, reciprocity in behavior tended to occur, as emphasized by thinkers like Baigan. They came to believe that other individuals also behaved in the same way as themselves—they produced goods with the same degree of diligence, priced commodities as honestly, and enjoyed life through thriftily sharing consumption goods and the blessings of nature. It would be natural to believe that this reciprocity in behavioral patterns among transacting individuals brought about the standardization of behavioral pattern in the economy.

Standardization occurred on two fronts. First, as peasants, who were in charge of part-time manufacturing, became accustomed to market transactions, they came to know the minimum level for quality standards of the products saleable in the market. This was especially true after the beginning of the sale of manufactured products at warehouses of local fiefs in Osaka. The quality management of *kura-mono* (commodities sold out from warehouses of *han*) was much stricter than private commodities, so this incentivized peasants to improve the quality of their products. Second, as merchants in local regions became richer and more powerful, the relationship between urban and local merchants became closer, and networks of merchants involving those of different regions became more comprehensive owing to network externality. In this case, it became easer for merchants to forecast the behavior of merchants in different regions, and trust among them came to be fermented.

Needless to say, from a broader perspective, for the alleviation of information asymmetry owing to standardization of behavior to occur, another necessary condition is the sharing of basic information about the economy. The background for information sharing is the development of publishing and education. Publishing using woodblock print developed during the reign of Tanuma Okitsugu (1719–88), the *Rōchū* (the highest administrator of the *bakufu*) in the latter half of eighteenth century. Woodblock artists such as Utamaro became popular, and printed books on cooking and culture, and various scientific studies were published widely. It is said that there were 800 bookshops in Edo as the end of the Tokugawa era. The number of schools (*terakoya*) began to grow during the Tanuma period, and the growth became explosive after the 1830s. According to data on 1875, there was a school for every 200 people aged 10–14. The total number of students in 13,800 schools was about 740,000, so that the number of students per school was about 60. It follows that about one-third of the population in the 10–14-years-old range attended school (Kitō 2002).

6.3.2.2 Production of Information

Another effective method to alleviate information asymmetry was the production of information or the utilization of accumulated information held by local merchants. Decisive impact on information asymmetry occurred as local merchants came to take on the role of the monitoring of local production. The initial style of commodity transaction was based on the relationship between local producers and urban merchants. Urban merchants, troubled by enormous levels of information asymmetry with local producers, used to add large margins as risk premiums in offering transaction conditions. The premium was drastically reduced as local merchants, acquainted closely with urban merchants, were involved in monitoring the activities of producers.

The process of the involvement of local merchants in monitoring production is believed to have occurred in the following three stages. First was the intermediation of transaction between urban merchants and local producers. During the early days of commercial development, local merchants were delegated the role to buy local products by urban wholesale merchants (*niuke-tonya*) and to transport them to the city. This type of merchant was called *kaitsugi* (Nakai 1961). *Kaitugi* merchants, as agents of and financed by urban merchants, gradually accumulated information on the commodities they transacted, and acquired monopsonic power and specialty in local markets. During the 1720s, *kaitsugi* trade was seen in many parts of the country: the purchase of silk produced in Gunma by Kyoto wholesale merchants with the help of *kaitsugi* merchants, the purchase of commodities such as safflower, liquor and wax produced in the Tōhoku area by Ohmi merchants with the help of local merchants, and so on. Monopsonic purchasing by local *kaitsugi* merchants lowered margins for producers, but the quality control of products improved substantially, and production and sales expanded.

Another type of merchant that appeared in the eighteenth century, and who virtually controlled the national distribution system, was a group of local merchants who grew up in local markets and entered into city markets. Those merchants, called three-cities (Osaka, Edo and Kyoto) wholesale merchants or city wholesale merchants, who had expanded business in local production areas and accumulated information about local products, opened new branch shops in cities like Edo, Kyoto and Osaka (Nakanishi 2002). The first half of the eighteenth century witnessed the active launching of new branches by this type of merchant in the cities. Especially famous were the Ise and Ōmi merchants,[28] who had expertise in supplying high quality commodities in textiles and cotton and silk fibers through efficient monitoring of local producers. During the latter half of the eighteenth century they had also branch offices in Tōhoku and other local regions, and could obtain materials of high quality by themselves and, at the same time, came to control the highly-developed manufacturing technology and artisans in Kyoto. Hayashi (1967) captures this phenomenon as the monopolistic control of the nationwide distribution system by three-cities wholesale merchants. They utilized their financial power to provide advanced payments to part-time producers in rural areas, purchased and sent the half-finished products to Kyoto, applied finishing processes by the hand of skilled artisans in Kyoto, and finally sold the final products all over the country.

The third factor was the improvement of governance and the development of the family-farmer manufacturing system under wholesaler control (*tonya-sei-kanai-kōgyō*) that occurred and became prevalent during the latter part of the eighteenth century. This pattern of relationship between merchants and producers occurred in the regions where new distinct regional products were developed. Wealthy local merchants lent materials and equipment to farmers who were ready to engage in side-businesses. Toward the turn of the century, the activity of wholesale merchants to reorganize local production systems in this way covered almost all the country and involved major commodities such as cotton textiles, silk products and the like. Hayashi (1967) notes that producers of these commodities acquired high level manufacturing technology, including finishing process, so that local wholesale merchants could sell the final products to consumers without the help of the three-cities merchants. The hegemony of the three-cities merchants began to decline radically at this stage. Landes (1969) argues that the wholesaler-controlled side-business system failed and eventually collapsed as a workable system in England due to poor governance, such as the dishonest use of raw materials and the lack of efforts by farmers. In Japan too there occurred the dishonest use of materials, but the dishonest use of materials was considered to be compensation for low wages (Hashino 2005), so was something to be resolved within rational market-based contracts, and never resulted in the collapse of the relationship between farmers and wholesalers. As will be discussed in the next section, their activity proceeded quite often in tandem with the industrial policy of the *han* aimed at developing regional-specific products. Incidentally, it is worth noting that the active participation by small farmers in the family-farmer manufacturing system under wholesaler control was possible because of the virtual attainment of residual control rights on land and the freedom of management by them after the late eighteenth century, owing to the development of the tenancy-based landlord system, as pointed out in Chapter 3.

[28]The founder of the Itōchū general trading company, Ito Chūbē, was one such Ōmi merchant.

6.3.2.3 Diversification and Increase in Risk-Bearing Agents

The Osaka wholesale merchants, the largest power among the three-cities wholesale merchants, used to sell huge numbers of commodities produced near Osaka in Edo throughout the Tokugawa era, although the production of similar products in the Edo area grew rapidly after the eighteenth century (the Edo-*jimawari* economy). During the early part of the Tokugawa era, until the mid-eighteenth century at least, the settlement of transactions of long-distance commerce was carried out under the hegemony of Osaka wholesale merchants and moneychanger merchants. The major method utilized was deferred payment, at first in cash and then by use of bills of exchange. Wholesale merchants got in contact with producers in distant regions directly. Quite often their activity was financed by moneychanger merchants in Osaka. With the help of financing by moneychanger merchants, they offered advanced payments and paid the remaining sums in cash at some designated time, such as the end of the year or after the completion of sales to retailers.[29] Since the early eighteenth century, settlement through bills of exchange instead of cash developed. In selling commodities to Edo, the Osaka wholesale merchants issued bills receivable directed to wholesale merchants in Edo. The Osaka wholesale merchants were drawers and the Edo wholesale merchants were drawees. Bills were so-called collection bills. The Osaka wholesale merchants sold the bills to Osaka moneychanger merchants, who sent the bills to Edo moneychanger merchants by use of the regular mailing service that traveled between Edo and Osaka three times per month. When the bills matured, the Edo moneychanger merchants obtained cash from the drawee merchants. In this system, the leadership in transactions was held by the Osaka wholesale merchants, who had a higher degree of freedom in deciding the timing of payment and the like, and the risk of transactions was borne by the Osaka moneychanger merchants.

Diversification and the increase in risk-bearing agents occurred in tandem with the development of the remittance and settlement system in which the hegemony held by the Osaka wholesale merchants was encroached upon, and there emerged new long-distance transactions involving agents in regions other than major cities.

The encroachment on the hegemony of Osaka was clearly seen by the development of the new settlement system between the two cities, Edo and Osaka, owing to the growth in the risk-bearing power of Edo merchants. Since around the early-nineteenth century, Edo wholesale merchants came to issue bills payable directed to Osaka wholesale merchants. Edo merchants were drawers and Osaka merchants were drawees. Bills were remittance bills. Moneychanger merchants in Edo usually bought the bills and sent them to Osaka moneychanger merchants requesting payment of the proceeds. In this system, the conditions of settlement were largely under the control of Edo wholesale merchants, and the risk of financing transactions was borne by Edo moneychanger merchants. The detailed story of this change in the settlement system during the early nineteenth century is given in Yuki (1965) with respect to sake sales from Nada in Osaka area to Edo.

---

[29]To retailers, wholesalers also applied the deferred payment system and received the proceeds after completion or at the end of the year.

Likewise, Shinpo (1967) notes similar patterns of transactions emerged in regions other than Edo from the late eighteenth to early nineteenth century. Take the case of sales of products by local producers to wholesale merchants in Osaka. Producers in local regions became issuers of remittance bills, and rich farmers in the region became financiers for producers. Rich farmers who bought the bills from local producers sent them to purchasers in Osaka and recovered the proceeds. Once there emerged risk-bearers, like rich local farmers in this case, it is likely that this kind of transaction could have occurred between any two local regions. Sakudō (1961) points out that inter-local regional bill transactions became quite popular toward the latter half of the Tokugawa era, and that this had a significant impact on the economic growth of local regions. There is no doubt that the growth of the risk-bearing capability of economic agents other than Osaka wholesale merchants decreased the risk premiums and hence transaction costs in the economy significantly.

The emergence of risk-bearers in regions other than Osaka seems to have been the result of two kinds of change in the behavior pattern of individuals. It may partly be due to the growth of rich farmers and merchants with some degree of preference for risk-taking and of the intention to contribute to the growth of their villages, but it might also be the result of the rise in trustworthiness of local producers. In other words, it is possible to conjecture that local producers became more reliable as recipients of credits because of the improvement of the quality of their products, as well as regular and diligent work efforts.

6.3.2.4 Development of ie and Trade Associations (*Kabu-Nakama*) Among Merchants

The development of moral codes in the Tokugawa era was initiated as the result of the dialectic sublation (*Aufheben*) of the confusion caused by the pursuit of the *kyūdō* (true way pursuing) principle in the profane world during the Warring States period. The birth and diffusion of the *ie* (house) system was also due to the *kyūdō* principle, because there occurred incentives to maintain the family-specific human capital accumulated by *kyūdō* behavior. Both the dissemination of moral codes and the diffusion of the *ie* system contributed to the alleviation of information asymmetry, bringing about the Tokugawa economic growth owing to the reduction of transaction costs.

As already discussed, the *ie* was at first formed in aristocratic society, and then in samurai and artisan society to transfer human capital specific to family occupation. In the Tokugawa legal system, the master and vassal relationship or feudal contracts were made between the *ie* of vassals and the *ie* of the master, not between individuals. This enhanced the importance of the *ie* system considerably. Large merchants, who grew up with the development of commerce in Tokugawa society, were mentally under the strong influence of samurai society, so they began to organize the managerial system as family businesses and to transfer the know-how and tacit knowledge to descendants in the form of family precepts. Most of the precepts transferred by merchant families emphasized the importance to fulfil the role specified by the *shokubun* regulation. At the same time, it was emphasized that the ultimate purpose of management did not lie in the maximization of profits or the accumulation of wealth per se but in the continuity of business and the longevity of family business (Miyamoto 1941). There seems to be no doubt that this attitude toward the continuation of the *ie* resulted in the respect for long-term relationships with customers and had the effect to prevent opportunistic behavior in transaction.

In addition to the *ie*, informal and privately organized institutions played important roles in reducing information asymmetry through enforcing rules and contracts. Villages (*mura*, *sōson*) were formed as a spontaneous organization for the purpose of self-government towards the end of the Warring States period. They had functions such as the ownership of village property like common land and village shrines, police power inside the villages and the right to collective bargaining regarding taxation and labor assignments with local lords. Following the convention formed under the Toyotomi regime, tax payments were formally assigned as the collective obligation of villages during the Tokugawa era. Villages had informal power to punish collectively illegal activities detrimental to the villages as a whole (*mura-hachbu*). Similar roles were fulfilled by trade associations in the urban sector. Okazaki (2005) claims that trade associations (*kabu-nakama*), organized as informal institutions and obtaining formal approval after the first half of the eighteenth century, had the function of collective punishment. Many internal codes of trade associations included articles prescribing that all coalition members should suspend trade with a person who cheated one of their own members. These punishments were applied to employees as well as to artisans too. Okazaki claims that informal institutions substituted a public system whenever the contract enforcement system was poorly enforced by the public.

6.3.3 Long-Term Reduction in Risk Premiums

We have argued that the dissemination of moral codes under the presence of the *shokubun* regulation resulted in the alleviation of information asymmetry and hence risk premiums and that the decline of transaction costs due to the decrease in risk premiums was the main cause of economic growth after the eighteenth century. Under the condition of the stable structure of demand, the reduction in transaction costs seems to have resulted in the balanced growth of the Tokugawa era. This section presents evidence of the decline of risk premiums in the macro-economy.

Let us show a rough picture of the long-term movement of risk premiums during the Tokugawa era. Panel A and B of Table 6.1 gives data on the long-term movement of interest rates. It is surprising that the average interest rate of the Kōnoike moneychangers (panel A) shows a long-term declining trend during the latter half of the seventeenth century until the early eighteenth century, and again a clearer declining trend after the mid-eighteenth century toward the end of that century. The interest rates of the Mitsui moneychanger (Osaka branch) also declined (panel B) during the eighteenth century, especially from the 1740s to the 1790s.[30] Why did this long-term decline in interest rates during the eighteenth century as well as during the latter half of the seventeenth century occur? This fact has an important implication for the nature of the market economy in Tokugawa era. To examine this phenomenon, let us take an *a la* Keynesian view on the equilibrium of the money market, that the money supply is equal to the demand for money, which is composed of transaction-purpose demand and asset-purpose demand. The demand for money for transaction purposes depends on the nominal income, and the demand for money for asset purposes depends on the return on 'securities', representing all return-yielding assets, investment and loan, in the economy. In this model, it would be reasonable to believe that the difference between the market interest rate and the rate of interest on safe assets, which is assumed to be constant at the level of the natural rate of return, is composed of two kinds of premium: risk premiums concerned with the variability in the return of 'securities' and liquidity premiums related to the risk in the settlement of transactions in commodities.

The risk premium is reduced through either the reduction of the risk aversion of asset holders (investors) or the alleviation of the risk on investment or loan.[31] It is difficult to find data on the risk premium directly, but it is possible to conjecture its movement as the difference of market interest rates and liquidity premiums. Two panels of Table 6.1 show that the market interest rate declined significantly during the Tokugawa era, so that, if it is possible to show that the liquidity premium rose or at least did not decline so much, we can conjecture that the risk premium declined

---

[30]The interest rate on *daimyo* lending by Konoike also had a declining trend until the period 1781–1800, according to Shinpo and Saito (1989). *Daimyo* lending rates were high compared with average interest rates. This seems to reflect the fact that lending to the *daimyo* was long-term or de facto long-term lending to finance structural fiscal deficits of fiefs, while average interest rates were interest rates of short-term loans to merchants and other money-changers.

[31]In terms of the standard capital asset pricing model, the risk and return of equilibrium portfolio is determined at the tangency of the utility function of investors, depending on the risk and expected return of the portfolio, and the capital market line. The capital market line is expressed as

$$\begin{aligned}\text{expected return of equilibrium portfolio} &= \text{rate of return of safe asset} + \text{market price of risk}\\ &\quad \times \text{standard deviation of the rate of return of equilibrium portfolio,}\end{aligned}$$

where

$$\begin{aligned}\text{market price of risk} &= (\text{expected return of market portfolio} - \text{rate of return of safe asset})\\ &\quad \div \text{standard deviation of market portfolio.}\end{aligned}$$

The risk premium is defined as the second term in the right-hand side of the first equation, the standard deviation of the rate of return of equilibrium portfolio multiplied by the market price of risk, so that it depends on the standard deviation of the rate of return of the equilibrium portfolio as well as characteristics of the utility function. The standard deviation of the rate of return of the equilibrium portfolio, the typical statistical measure of investment risk, represents the degree of capital market development such as reduction of uncertainty and the possibility of portfolio diversification. The characteristics of the utility function represent the preference of asset-holders, such as risk aversion and the degree of animal spirits.

significantly during the period under investigation. Assuming the constancy of risk aversion,[32] the reduction of risk premium is considered to represent the alleviation of risk on investment or loan. So, we can argue that the decline of the market interest rates in the eighteenth century was caused by the reduction of risk on investment and loan, which is related to the alleviation of information asymmetry. The alleviation of information asymmetry or the enhancement of forecastability of the behavior of others owes to the standardization of conduct through the development of moral codes as well as to the participation of local merchants who have rich information on the risk and return in the indigenous markets.

Let us show that, during the Tokugawa era, it is possible to believe that the liquidity premium in the financial market increased or at least did not decrease so much, so that it is possible to conjecture that the long-term decline in the interest rate represents the decline in risk premiums in commercial transactions. There is abundant evidence about the movement of liquidity premiums in the history of the Tokugawa economy. First, let us examine the movement of the money supply. If we neglect deposit money issued by Osaka moneychanger merchants and circulated in the Osaka area called *azukari-tegata* or *furi-tegata*,[33] the money is composed of metal coin issued by the *bakufu* and *hansatsu*, paper money issued by the *han*, convertible with species. Gold coins were used in the transactions of eastern Japan, including Edo, and silver coins in western Japan, including Osaka and Kyoto.[34] The *bakufu* issued new money in two ways. First was the production of new coins by the use of newly produced silver and gold from mines. The production of gold and silver increased most during the Warring States period and went into decline after the start of the Tokugawa *bakufu*.[35] The accumulated stock in the *bakufu* treasury decreased rapidly as the *bakufu* began to issue metal coins from the early seventeenth century (in 1601), leading to a chronic shortage in the money supply after the eighteenth century, partly owing to the export of coins abroad. The second method was the recoinage of existing silver and gold coins, which was the representative method of money supply after the eighteenth century. Whenever recoinage occurred, degraded new coins were exchanged with coins in circulation with the same nominal denomination. Not only the grade but also the design and name of coins were changed when new coins were issued. To implement the recovery of old coins smoothly, however, it was usual

---

[32]Toward the end of the Warring States era, there emerged a significant number of reckless merchants who loved risk and adventurous transactions. But such merchants decreased their influence during the eighteenth century substantially, and it is safe to assume the constancy of risk aversion in the macro-economy. The emergence of risk bearing agencies in local regions referred to above does not imply the emergence of risk-lovers, but rather an increase in the number of agents to take reasonable risk at reasonable price.

[33]*Azukari-tegata* was issued by moneychangers and circulated in the market. Moneychangers as drawers paid cash to bearers. *Furi-tegata*, called *furidashi-tegata* after the Meiji Restoration, was issued by merchants, who had deposited the balance at moneychangers, directed to moneychangers as drawees and payers.

[34]Copper coins were used for daily life in both western and eastern Japan.

[35]For example, the production of silver at the Sado-silver mine was more than 6000 *kan* in 1621, 1300 *kan* in 1643, and 860 *kan* in 1661 (Yamaguchi 1983).

Table 6.1 (Panel A) Lending rates of Kōnoike (average of the period)

Period	%	*Period*	%	*Period*	%	*Period*	%
1670–74	14.4	1710–14	6.0	1778–82	3.6	1837–40	3.1
1675–79	11.8	1715–19	6.9	1783–87	4.6	1841–45	2.5
1680–84	13.8	1720–24	5.6	1788–92	4.3	1846–50	2.4
1685–89	6.1	1725–29	7.0	1793–97	3.6	1851–52	2.5
1690–94	8.6	1730–34	7.2	1798–1802	2.1		
1695–99	11.6	1735–39	5.9	1803–07	2.2		
1700–04	8.9	1740–44	6.6	1808–12	2.3		
1705–09	5.6	1773–77	6.0	1813–16	2.2		

Source Yasuoka (1998, pp. 21–91)
Note The interest rates show the annual interest revenue divided by the lending fund. Information about how much of the lending fund is actually lent out is not available, so that denominator could include some amount of cash at hand. The figures show the average percentage of the period, and the figures during 1715–1719 lacks data for 1718, so that the figure is a four-year average. Note that there are 30 years blank between the period 1740–1744 and 1773–1777, and 20 years blank between the period 1813–1816 and 1837–1840

(Panel B) Lending rate of Mitsui (Osaka branch) (%)

Year	%	*Year*	%	*Year*	%	*Year*	%		
1728	5.3	1753		1778		1803		1828	
1729		1754	3.7	1779	2.4	1804		1829	
1730	5.1	1755		1780		1805		1830	1.7
1731		1756	4.6	1781	2.4	1806	1.4	1831	
1732	5.1	1757		1782	1.7	1807		1832	
1733		1758	3.9	1783	1.7	1808		1833	1.9
1734	4.7	1759		1784	1.7	1809		1834	
1735		1760	4.1	1785		1810		1835	
1736	5.2	1761	4.1	1786		1811		1836	1.7
1737		1762	3.9	1787	1.7	1812		1837	
1738	3.8	1763	4.0	1788		1813	2.1	1838	
1739		1764	3.9	1789		1814		1839	1.6
1740	5.4	1765	3.8	1790	1.3	1815		1840	
1741		1766	3.8	1791		1816		1842	1.7
1742	4.5	1767	4.2	1792	1.4	1817			
1743		1768		1793		1818	1.2		
1744	4.0	1769	4.2	1794	1.9	1819			
1745		1770		1795		1820			
1746	3.6	1771		1796	1.8	1821	1.5		
1747		1772	3.2	1797		1822			

(continued)

(continued)

Year	%	Year	%	Year	%	Year	%		
1748	4.8	1773		1798		1823			
1749		1774	3.0	1799	1.5	1824	2.0		
1750	3.9	1775	2.5	1800		1825			
1751		1776	2.1	1801		1826			
1752	3.6	1777	1.8	1802		1827	1.9		

Source Kagawa (1974)
Note In many years, data are available only for the latter half of the years. When both the first and the latter half of the year are available, we adopted the latter half data. With respect the following years, only data for the first half of the year are available: 1764, 1767, 1772 and 1779

that some margins (*mashibu*) were added to the nominal price by *bakufu* officials. Since recoinage usually resulted in the degrading of the quality of coins, it yielded substantial seigniorage gain for the *bakufu* treasury. This was the main method the *bakufu* adopted to increase the money supply in response to the shortage of money for transactions in the private sector as well as to finance fiscal deficits.

Recoinage was carried out by mobilizing Osaka and Edo moneychanger merchants, who, in turn, called for the collaboration of moneychanger merchants in distant local regions. It took considerable time to recover old 'good' coins from the market and exchange them with new 'bad' coins. The recoinage carried out in May 1736 (the so-called Genbun recoinage), for example, was finished by the end of 1738. Taya (1963) praises this as a highly efficient and swift accomplishment because 62% of recoinage was finished in three years (p. 290). However, what was finished at the end of 1738 was the 62% of the recoinage of the originally planned part of the project, namely the new issue of Genbun gold coin (17.425 million *ryō*) and Moji silver coin (0.525 million *ryō*) and the recovery of Kyōho gold coin (7.324 million *ryō*) and Kyōho silver coin (0.331 million *ryō*). Later on, in 1765, the *bakufu* issued a small amount of Gomonme silver coin, and from 1772, the issue of a large amount of An-ei-nishu silver coin was started and continued until 1823.[36] In Table 6.2, the money supply in 1818, is shown as 29.3 million *ryo*.[37] The figure is the result of not only recoinage during 1736–38, but also the new issue of Gomonme silver in 1765 and the new issue of An-ei-nishu silver during 1772–1817.

It is important to note that the private sector resisted the degrading of coins by means of two methods. One way was to increase the export of gold and silver.[38] During the Tokugawa era a large amount of metal coins, especially silver coins, was exported to the Netherlands and China from Nagasaki and Tsushima, and this continued until the mid-eighteenth century (Tashiro 1976). Another way was the hoarding of coins of better quality. Although data on hoarding is not available, we can assume the difference between the value of recoinage and the recovery of old

[36]Detailed information is given in Taya (1963, p. 319) and Iwahashi (1976, p. 255).

[37]*Ryo* was the unit of money, which was renamed *yen* after the Meiji Restoration.

[38]It is important to know that silver and gold were important export goods during the period.

Table 6.2 Money supply, GDP and price level

	Money supply (million ryō)	GDP (thousand koku)	Price level (silver price per 1 koku)
1695	14.0	–	49.0
1710	25.8	75.2*	65.0
1714	31.7	76.1*	162.0
1721	28.6*	77.6	70.0
1736	21.0	81.5*	53.9
1804	27.8*	93.3	54.9
1818	29.3	101.1*	57.9
1832	45.9	101.8*	73.2
1846	49.8*	106.9	88.2
1858	52.8	–	152.8

Note Money supply without an asterisk is obtained from Iwahashi (1976). The sum of gold and silver coins, and silver coins are converted into gold value at the official rate (gold 1 *ryō* = silver 60 monme). GDP without an asterisk is obtained from Takashima (2017). The price level is from Iwahashi (1981) and shows the rice price of the Hiroshima *han*

coins as a rough measure of the magnitude of hoarding. From the data in Yamaguchi (1962) it can be confirmed that, for large denomination coins, the ratio of recovery to recoinage was low. For example, 66 and 89% of Genroku-Ōban was not recovered at the time of recoinage in 1714 and 1858, respectively.[39] The estimated percentages of hoarding of koban (ichibu-kin), which comprised the main coin in circulation in 1710, rose sharply from 1818; 1.5% in 1714, 2.4% in 1736, 10.1% in 1818, 17.4% in 1842, and 19.6% in 1858. It seems that the chronic shortage of the money supply led to the belief to expect further degrading of coins in the nineteenth century, and people began to hoard larger percentages of koban. For these two reasons, it was possible that the recoinage could not sufficiently increase the money supply. During the Tokugawa period, the private sector was frequently in trouble due to the shortage of transaction balances, as is emphasized by Hayami and Miyamoto (1988).

It is possible to obtain the exact amount of gold and silver money in circulation, evaluated in gold value, at the time of recoinage,[40] as is shown in Table 6.2. The figures without an asterisk show existing coins in circulatio (Mt) at the year t of recoinage. Recoinage was implemented seven times during the Tokugawa era, which is shown in Table 6.2 by a year without an asterisk. Every coin has its own name i or j depending on the time of issue, material, shape and quality. Let us explain how the figure for the money stock in circulation at time u is obtained. t shows the year when recoinage is promulgated, s the year of previous recoinage and u the year of next

[39]Ōban was mainly used for asset accumulation, and one piece of ohban was ten-*ryō* at official price, although the market price was about seven *ryo*.

[40]The data do not include copper coins and *hansatsu*. We do not have data on copper coins. As for *hansatu*, although the number of fiefs that issued *hansatsu* is available (Table 6.3), we do not have data on the outstanding stock, except for 1842 (Yamaguchi 1966).

recoinage or the year of completion of recoinage started in year t. Recoinage at time t means the recovery of old coins issued during the period from s to t, and the issue of new coins during the period from t to u.[41] For each coin i newly issued during the period from t to u, there is data for the total amount of new issue (M_i1) and export (M_i2) during the period from *t to u*, and for other existing coins j in circulation at the year t, data on the amount in circulation at t (M_j3) and recovery during the period from t to u (M_j4) are available. It follows that the money stock in circulation at time u is obtained using the following formula[42]:

$$Mu = \sum (M_i1 - M_i2) + \sum (M_j3 - M_j4)$$

It must be noted that all the data for new issue, recovery and export are total flow amounts during the period from t to u, and yearly data during the period are not available.[43] This means that yearly data for the money stock for each year between the period from t to u cannot be obtained and must be estimated. The estimation was done by way of linear interpolation. The estimated amounts of the money stock are shown with asterisks in Table 6.2.

It seems that the money supply in gold value stayed almost stable with some fluctuation during the eighteenth century. 14.0 million *ryō* in 1695, 25.8 million in 1710, 31.7 million in 1714, 21.0 million in 1736, 29.3 million in 1818, 45.9 million in 1832. We have estimates of the GDP for the three years 1721, 1804 and 1846, during the Tokugawa era. Figures show an increasing trend. Years for which data is available for GDP are different from the year for which data on money supply is available. To make the two series comparable, the figures of GDP and money supply with asterisks are obtained by assuming a linear trend between two adjacent figures.[44] GDP grew mildly during the eighteenth century and the money supply was stable with some ups and downs. The table shows also a series of rice prices (*machi-sōba*, market price) in Hiroshima-*han*.[45] The price level rose rapidly until the early eighteenth century and stayed almost stable or gradually declined during the

---

[41]Take the case of the recoinage in 1736 (Genbun 1) called the 'Genbun recoinage'. In this case t is 1736, s is 1714 (Kyōho 1) and u is 1818 (Bunsei 1). This time, new gold coin, Genbun gold, and new silver coin, Moji silver, were issued (M_i1) and began to circulate from 1736. (The official period of circulation of both coins was from 1736 to 1828.) Old gold coin, Kyōho gold, and Kyōho silver in circulation at t were recovered (M_j3) and recoined (M_j4). At the year 1818, other coins issued before 1714, such as Genroku gold, were in circulation, although the amount was small and was not recovered, and are counted as M_j3.

[42]Exported coins were not included in the money supply, but coins hoarded or melted into bullion are included in the coins in circulation.

[43]Data on M_j3 is stock data at year t. Data on old coins, not recovered, is described as stock data at year u in Yamaguchi (1962). Since these coins were not recovered, there is no difference in the stock amount between the two years.

[44]GDP in 1600 was 41.6 million *koku* (Takashima 2017).

[45]There is also the rice price series in Osaka. The Hiroshima series is valuable because it goes back to the year 1621. The time series movement of rice prices and the general price level closely resemble each other. Detailed data is given in volume 2 (early modern) of *Nihon-Keizai no Rekishi*.

rest of period.[46] The relative stability of the money supply and the price level against the rising trend of GDP seems to indicate that the money supply lagged against the increase in nominal GDP (GDP multiplied by price), and it seems that this caused a shortage in money compared with the level of economic transactions, leading to a rise in liquidity premiums.[47]

The estimation of the money supply given with asterisks needs more explanations. When the recoinage was announced by the *bakufu*, usually some recoinage began in the same year, but, since recoinage is accompanied by the complicated process of the recovery of old coins with the help of local moneychangers, it usually took several years. It has already been noted that the new issue was possible after major part of recovering is finished.[48] Moreover, it was possible that recoinage started even before the official announcement. For example, the recoinage announced in 1695 took three years for completion, and the recoinage announced in 1710 included the issue of Kan-ei-silver that was first issued in 1706, as an emergency policy to meet the hike in the silver price in Edo. During the period between July 1706 to February 1710, Taya (1963) notes that the *bakufu* officials were involved in the delicate manipulation of margins to promote the recovery of Gennroku silver at minimum costs (Taya 1963, pp. 168–197) and to realize the expansion of the silver money supply by means of degraded coins. For these reasons, although the data on money supply at the time of the announcement (data shown without asterisks) were exact, to estimate the exact figures for other years is very difficult. Furthermore, while we have flow data for the total amount of new coinage, recovery and exports during the periods between the promulgation of recoinage and the completion for each coin, there are no annual data within the periods, so it is not possible to calculate the annual money stock. We also have information for the period on officially admitted circulation, but Yamaguchi (1662) notes that most coins were circulated after the termination of the official circulation periods. These were reasons why we have estimated the money supply for years other than those of the announcement by means of the simplest method of linear approximation. Since our aim lies in capturing the overall tendency in the excess demand for money, this simplified approach seems to be justified.

Incidentally, it is worth noting that Akashi (1989) estimated the annual money supply during the period 1725–1856 by evaluating the annual increase of the money supply using the data for the fiscal revenue of the *bakufu*. His method was based on three assumptions. First is the assumption that increase of the money supply is proportional to seigniorage gain. The second is the assumption that seigniorage gain is proportional to the transitory revenue of the *bakufu*. Transitory revenue is defined as the difference between actual revenue and the permanent part of the revenue, which

---

[46]Hayami-Miyamoto (1988) explains this movement of rice prices by two reasons. One was that the rapid increase in the rice production capacity during the seventeenth century accompanied by large-scale reclamation became effective after the turn of the century. The other was that nominal demand for rice declined due to the shortage of the money supply.

[47]There is an endogeneity problem. The shortage of the money supply could have led to the fall in nominal GDP.

[48]Because recovered coin is used as material for making new coin. Moreover, new coins might not be accepted in the economy, if there are still 'good' old coins in existence.

is derived from the third assumption, that the permanent revenue is a function of tax revenue. These assumptions are too bold, however. In particular, the first assumption is marred by the fact that the total amount of recoinage, the degree of degradation and the margin offered for recovery are a function of the fiscal deficits that necessitated the recoinage. In this sense, the relationship between seigniorage gain and the estimates of the increase in the money supply is not proportional at all, but rather is related to fiscal revenues and expenditures in a complicated structural relationship. Moreover, the percentage of seigniorage gain in transitory income changed drastically over time, depending on the fiscal deficits. The proportionality assumption, the second assumption, neglects all the economic factors behind the motivation for adopting the recoinage policy as well as changes in fiscal revenue and expenditure. In other words, the estimates Akashi (1989) obtained from the assumptions that precludes the relationship between fiscal policy and money supply cannot be utilized in the analysis of the changes in the money supply.[49]

Let us examine the movement of the money supply and nominal GDP more closely in relationship with the decline in interest rates. The yearly series of interest rates for two moneychangers in Table 6.1 shows that the decline in interest rates continued from 1730–34 to 1798–1802 for Kōnoike and from 1740 until 1790 for Mitsui. Both series went up slightly after reaching troughs and stayed around those levels until the 1840s and1850s. The movement of interest rates during the seventeenth century and early eighteenth century is irregular, but it seems safe to believe that the interest rates were sufficiently high compared with the level during the eighteenth century. Moreover, after the turn of the century, from the end of the eighteenth into the nineteenth century, the Tokugawa economy changed its macro-economic characteristics radically from a deflationary to inflationary phase, as is explained shortly. Since *hansatsu* came to be issued by many *han* in the nineteenth century, it is possible that the data on gold and silver underrepresent the money in circulation, so it seems to be pertinent to focus our examination to the eighteenth century. In terms of Table 6.2, it is not pertinent to take the year 1818 instead of 1804. Further, it must be noted that the nature of the recoinage in 1818 differed crucially from the recoinages before 1818. As is noted in Shinpo (1978, p. 62), the *bakufu* raised substantial seignories gain through exchanging degraded new coins at a par with the old coins and financed government expenditure. This was quite close to the Keynesian policy of money-financed fiscal expenditure under a managed currency system. It seems that the monetary policy of the *bakufu* changed its nature into an inflationary policy at this time. Moreover, in Table 6.2, the year 1714 was a year of exceptional peaks of rice price hikes from the viewpoint of the trend since the seventeenth century as well as in terms of cyclical fluctuations (Ōishi 1998, pp. 47–51). These considerations lead us to confine our examination of the trend in excess

[49]Moreover, the estimates of the money supply for the years 1736, 1818 and 1832 are different from the exact historical value given by Iwasaki (data used in our Table 6.2). This seems to be caused by the utilization of the average value for several years in the calculation of the base-year figures to avoid historical shocks in the Akashi estimates. This is another reason we did not used the Akashi estimates in our examination.

demand for money during the period between 1710 and 1804 or 1721 and 1804 on Table 6.2.

From 1710–1804, GDP increased by 24.1% and the price level decreased by 15.5%, so that nominal GDP increased 8.6%. The money supply changed from 25.8 million to 27.8 million, so that the growth rate is 7.8%. The increase in nominal GDP was larger than that of the money supply, so that excess demand for money was expanding during the period in this case. The money supply became scarce compared with the demand for money for transaction purposes. It could be conjectured that the liquidity premium during 1710–1804 was mildly increasing. If we take the period between 1721 and 1804 instead of 1710 and 1804, on the other hand, the money supply in 1721 was 28.6 million and the growth rate from 1721 to 1804 is minus 2.8%. During the same period, GDP increased by 20.2% and the price level decreased by 22%, so that the increase in nominal GDP was minus 1.8%, which is larger than the change of money supply. Therefore, the excess demand for money was also expanding during the period 1721–1804.

In this argument, we have estimated the money supply by linear regression in view of the fact that the change in money supply occurred gradually after recoinage started. However, since the major part of the recoinage project was finished within several years of initiation, it is possible to conduct an examination on another assumption, that the money supply changed instantaneously after the promulgation of the recoinage policy. Under this assumption, estimates of the money supply in 1721 and 1804 are 21.0 and 29.3 million *ryo*, respectively. Using this assumption, the rate of increase in the money supply during the period 1710–1814 is 15.5%, so is larger than the rate of increase in nominal GDP of 8.6%. It is conjectured that the liquidity premium decreased during the period, although not radically. If we take the period 1721–1804, on the other hand, the rate of increase in the money supply is 39.5%, which is much larger than the rate of increase in nominal GDP of minus 1.8%. This result contradicts our assertion. However, from the viewpoint of the change in the *bakufu* policy from a deflationary to an inflationary policy in the early nineteenth century, the assumption of the equality of money supply between 1804 and 1818 seems to be unrealistic. Moreover, the year 1736 corresponds with the trough in money supply due to the deflationary policy proposed by Arai Hakuseki, so the assumption that the money supply in 1721 was equal to that of 1736 is hard to justify.

Combining the above numerical examinations with the general argument that the eighteenth century was a period of money shortage, it may be not far off the mark to believe that the liquidity premium during the eighteenth century was not decreasing radically. Since the drastic decline in interest rates during the eighteenth century cannot be explained by the fall in the liquidity premium, it could be conjectured that the long-term decline in the interest rates in the eighteenth century was strongly related to the long-term decline in risk premiums in the economy. Even if we take into account the possibility of a mild rise in the liquidity premium, it is difficult to ascribe all the interest rate movements to this effect. We must conclude tentatively that the fall of risk premiums was the main reason for the decline of interest rates. We have already discussed that the alleviation of information asymmetry that caused the decline in transaction costs was the salient feature of the development of the economic system during the Tokugawa period. Empirical evidence on the decline in risk premiums seems to be an additional support for our hypothesis.

Incidentally, based on data similar to that in Table 6.1, Shinpo and Saito (1988) claim that the decline of interest rates is caused by the decline in the market power of Osaka merchants because the interest rates quoted is the data of the Osaka moneychangers.[50] It is true that both Mitsui and Konoike were originally Osaka merchants, but their activity was already nationwide, so that the interest rate series obtained from the historic records of the two Osaka merchants does not imply that the data is concerned with the local Osaka financial market.

Further, it seems worth pointing out that Shinpo and Saito have fallen into confusion because they did not clearly identify the difference between Osaka wholesale merchants and Osaka moneychanger merchants. They (1988, pp. 39–40) assert that the rise of merchants outside Osaka and their participation in trade associations (*kabu-nakama*) during the Tanuma era in the latter half of the eighteenth century is evidence of the fall of the market power of ‘Osaka merchants’ or the fall in interest rates of ‘Osaka merchants’. Their confusion is that they did not realize that the increase in the number of merchants who participated in trade associations was concerned with wholesale merchants in the area near Osaka, and the decline of interest rates they wanted to analyze was the interest rates set by the moneychanger merchants in Osaka. The fact that wholesale merchants in the districts near Osaka increased their power during the Tanuma era could be a reason for the relative decline in the market power of Osaka wholesale merchants. However, this fact has nothing to do with the fall of interest rates set by the moneychanger merchants. It might be that the moneychanger merchants enjoyed an increase in their market power vis-à-vis wholesale merchants, which increased in their number, and an increase in the interest rates on their loans to wholesale merchants.[51] In this case, the increase in the number of merchants who participated in trade associations could have brought about an increase in interest rates.

With respect to the behavior of the moneychanger merchants, Shinpo and Saito claim that the shift in the method of settlement of deferred credit from bills receivable issued by Osaka merchants to bills payable issued by Edo merchants as evidence of the weakening of the market power in the financial market of Osaka merchants. This assertion, however, neglects the fact that the shift occurred after the Kasei period (1804–30) (Yuki 1965),[52] so if the hypothesis of Shinpo and Saito is correct, the fall of interest rates of the Osaka moneychangers should have occurred in the nineteenth century, rather than in the eighteenth century.

---

[50]They use data of the average of the period. The original data is same.

[51]Shinpo raises two reasons for the expansion of *kabu-nakama* in Osaka during the Tanuma era. First, he correctly notes the raising of fiscal revenues by claiming that the forced contribution (*myoga-kin*) to the *bakufu* was the main reason for Tanuma to expand the *kabu-nakama* system in Osaka. The second reason raised by Shinpo, that there occurred the need to reorganize the order of commerce in Osaka, seems to be secondary, although this point needs further investigation.

[52]Shinpo himself asserted once in Shinpo (1968) that the shift to bills payable occurred during the nineteenth century.

Moreover, Shinpo and Saito's assertion that the fall in market power of the Osaka merchants as a whole occurred during the latter half of the eighteenth century is hard to justify from the conventional understanding of Japanese economic history. Although we admit that the market power of the Osaka merchants declined during the Tokugawa era, it is difficult to believe that the decline occurred during the eighteenth century. Hayashi (1967) contends that the period from the latter half of the seventeenth century to the latter half of the eighteenth century was the heyday of the Osaka merchants, or the three-cities merchants in her terminology, and that the fall in the market power of the Osaka merchants occurred during the nineteenth century. It follows that the decline in the market power of the Osaka merchants does not have any relevance to the decline in interest rates during the eighteenth century shown in Table 6.1.[53]

Let us examine here how the risk and liquidity premium is related to the decline in transaction costs in the context of Tokugawa Japan, in terms of a couple of examples. The impact of the fall in risk premiums seems to have occurred in the form of a decline in the costs of contract, i.e. the costs related to negotiating and writing contracts in trade and credit. Economic activities in Tokugawa Japan were carried out within the new commercial structure, as will be explained in the next section. For one thing, the participants in commerce in terms of the type of merchants and the degree of specialization were different from the past. For another, major new trade was related to long-distance transactions with unknown agents and unfamiliar commodities. This caused serious problems in information processing. The availability of open information was limited, reputation could not travel long distances, and the customs and rules of transactions differed among regions. In such a situation, the time and energy spent on the preparation of contracts would have been enormous, unless there were some regularity in the behavior of people. The standardization of behavior was the most reliable basis for making contracts. Individuals could draw up contracts in the belief that others would behave in roughly the same way as themselves and that they followed similar moral codes as themselves. Thereby, the effects of the accumulation of information and the consequent alleviation of information asymmetry owing to further information processing and risk bearing by merchants had significant effects on transaction costs in the economy.

The shortage of the currency supply seems to be the main cause of transaction costs in the economy. The inconvenience of the barter economy is well known. For a successful transaction, the double coincidence of wants is required—the commodity an agent wants to sell should be the commodity a buyer wants to buy. Whereas barter is an extreme assumption, it seems quite possible that a less extreme phenomena occurred in various parts and on various occasions in Tokugawa Japan. Let us note two episodes here. It seems that the export of silver coins during the early period should have caused a serious shortage in the transaction balance in regions in western Japan. This could be related to the data given in Table 6.3 on the number of *han* that issued

[53] Furthermore, the hypothesis of Shinpo and Saito is unable to explain the decline of interest rates of Kōnoike during the seventeenth century.

Table 6.3 Number of *han* that issued *hansatsu*

		1661–1735	*1736–71*	*1772–1817*	*1818–59*	*1860–67*
Eastern Japan	gold	3	0	1	3	2
	silver	9	8	7	17	13
	copper	1	0	1	6	11
Western Japan	gold	1	1	1	1	2
	silver	52	37	27	55	27
	copper	2	2	9	31	12

Note Obtained from Shinpo and Saito (1989). Gold, silver and copper means the unit of currency for expressing the value of *hansatsu*. The table does not include uncertain data

hansatsu.[54] *Hansatsu* was issued not only to finance fiscal deficits and emergency expenditure in the case of natural calamities but also to cope with shortages in cash for daily transactions in the *han*.[55] Shikano (1996) claims that during the nineteenth century *hansatsu* circulated widely in transactions related to expenditures in daily life. Hayami and Miyamoto (1988) conjecture that the fact that the western *han* where transactions were carried out in silver coins issued *hansatsu* from earlier times, compared with eastern *han* where gold coins were in use, is related to the shortage of silver coins due to exports.

Although the shortage in transaction balances frequently occurred most severely in the local *han*, a larger-scale shortage occurred in transactions between Edo and Osaka. Another episode is related to the rise in the relative price of silver in relation to gold during the early eighteenth century in Edo. The relative price of silver against gold, which was stable at about 9.8 during 1609–1694, went up to 11.0 during 1695–1709, to 14.0 during 1710–13, and thereafter fell to 11.5 during 1714–35 (Shinpo and Saito 1989). Nakai (1961) contends that this was caused by the shortage of silver coin in Edo at the turn of the century. Since the remittance bill was still not well developed at the time, the Edo merchants who bought Osaka commodities needed to use silver coins to pay, and the consequent increase in the demand for silver was the reason for the hike in the relative price of silver. The *bakufu* was obliged to issue silver coins, Kan-ei-silver, in 1706 and 1710, and finally resorted to the drastic degrading of silver coins in the recoinage in 1714.[56]

It is worth pointing out the drastic change in the monetary policy of the *bakufu* that occurred in the nineteenth century. During the eighteenth century, the monetary policy was basically deflationary, partly due to the shortage in gold and silver and partly because the policy paid too much attention to the quality of coins related to

[54]The issue of *hansatsu* is said to have begun in 1661 by the Fukui-*han*, but it was forbidden by the *bakufu* in 1707 and allowed again in 1730. Shikano (1996) notes that the Hukuyama-*han* already issued *hansatsu* in 1630.

[55]The number of *hansatsu*-issuing fiefs increased after 1818, reflecting the fact that many fiefs embarked on industrial policy financed by *hansatsu* during the period.

[56]Hayami-Miyamoto (1988) claims that the recoinage in 1695 was also partly related to the policy against the fall in silver coins.

the recovery rate. Because recoinage was accompanied with degrading, there always was a maximum limit to the fiscal revenue, seigniorage gain, for the *bakufu*. A high degree of degrading might lead to the loss of trust in the currency issuing right, so that it was considered to be crucial to raise the recovery rate, and this set the maximum on the seigniorage gain imposed by the exchange margin (*mashibu*) that reduced fiscal gain. Thus, during the eighteenth century, there were always severe constraints on the fiscal expenditure policy. For example, at the time of recoinage in 1736, the *bakufu* offered a high margin to promote the recovery rate, and this inevitably reduced the fiscal revenue and hence expenditure of the *bakufu*. Although the nominal money supply increased drastically from 21.0 to 29.3 million *ryo*, the impact on private expenditure of the money supply was limited because the total amount of gold and silver did not increase so much, so there was no wealth effect on consumption. The impact on aggregate demand was limited and there were no significant effects on economy activity, as is noted by Shinpo (1978, p. 57).

The situation changed radically in the nineteenth century owing to the active issue of *hansatsu* by the *han*. Although *hansatsu*-issuing *han* claimed that *hansatsu* was convertible with species, it was unthinkable to believe that all *hansatsu* was convertible into species. Otherwise, there was no fiscal merit for the *han* to issue *hansatsu*. In other words, the *hansatsu* system was effective for the economic development of the *han* because it was based on the partial reserve mechanism. It is important to note that the development of the partial reserve requirement system had a significant impact on the psychology of people. People gradually became accustomed to use an inconvertible currency and a managed currency system during the nineteenth century. The success of recoinage in 1818 was due significantly to the change in psychology of the people toward the new currency system. Newly issued money was converted into old coin at par this time despite the substantial degrading of the new coins. The exchange of new money at par was possible because people had been accustomed by this time to managed currency system owing to the issue of *hansatsu*. Economic growth with an inflationary bias during the nineteenth century, partly related to the active industrial policy by western *han*, was caused in this way.

In conclusion, it would not be far off the mark to believe that the Tokugawa economy during the eighteenth century always had a tendency to the rise of liquidity premiums due to the shortage of the money supply, caused by the decline in the output of gold and silver, the exports of metals, the difficulties of recoinage due to resistance to the degrading in the form of hoarding, and so on. It is possible to conjecture that economic growth had been severely restricted potentially by the rise in transaction costs due to the high liquidity premium. In this sense, the decrease in risk premiums through the alleviation of information asymmetry seems to have had enormous effects on economic growth by means of reducing the transaction costs of commercial activities. The long-term decline in interest rates during the eighteenth century is eloquent evidence that the latter effect, the decrease in the risk premium, offset and overwhelmed the former effect, the high liquidity premium, and realized the decline in transaction costs. As shown by Table 3.4, the balanced growth during the Tokugawa era during the period 1721–1804 or 1721–1846 seems to suggest that the overall decline in transaction costs had a close relationship with the phenomenon of the balanced growth of industries.

6.4 Economic Growth and Merchants

Commerce-based growth brought unprecedented prosperity to the country. The establishment of a morality-governed country resulted in the unintended consequence of the drastic decline in transaction costs and the consequent growth of the commerce-based economy. However, the growth of the commercial sector based on the pursuit of moral principles inevitably led to the weakening of the relative ruling power of the *bakufu*. First, since the establishment of the moral society was partly based on the *shokubun* regulation, the *bakufu* had an innate fragility in terms of the foundation of economic power: *the bakufu*'s policy was obliged to have a physiocratic orientation and to refrain from mercantilism. Under the condition of the dependence of *bakufu* revenue on rice production, the *shokubun* regulation meant the preferential treatment of agriculture and an oppressive attitude to commerce. It was inevitable that the growth of the commercial sector led to the relative weakening of the economic foundation of the *bakufu*. Second, the emphasis on moral principle was bound to nurture the conception of an alternative polity that could be a threat to the *bakufu*. At first, the *bakufu* tried to justify its ruling by resorting to new Confucianism, but this was unsuccessful, as already discussed. Through the critical study of Confucianism, it was unavoidable that there was always a search for a better system of government. In other words, under the condition of the absence of the absolute legitimacy of the *bakufu* ruling, the study of the way of heaven could always nurture a thought that might be directed to choose a polity other than the *bakuhan*-system.

6.4.1 Samurai–Merchant Relationship

Quite different from the physiocratic stance of the *bakufu* and a sort of antagonism against merchants, there occurred a coalition between elite samurais in the local *han* and the local indigenous (*zaikata*) merchants during the nineteenth century. How did merchants who aimed at material gains build a coalition with elite samurais who sought spiritual completion and found no serious value in material wellbeing?

We discussed above that the samurai class took on the role of spiritual leadership in Tokugawa society, in which the moral confusions of the Warring States period were successfully eliminated. Other classes such as farmers, artisans and merchants held the samurai in high esteem and followed their leadership, leading to the productivity growth caused by enhanced effort and collaboration. The merchant class enjoyed the benefit of the regained order in society most, owing to the establishment of trust and the alleviation of information asymmetry, consequently resulting in the reduction of transaction costs of commercial activity.

Let us discuss why there emerged a coalition between the merchants and samurai of the local *han*. For this purpose, it is necessary to note three categories of merchants, who differed in terms of the role they played in economic growth, the role played in the turmoil after the arrival of Perry and, among others, the relationship with the samurai class: Osaka moneychanger merchants, the wholesaler merchants and the local *zaikata* or *zaigo* (indigenous) merchants (Crawcour 1968).

The Osaka moneychanger merchants had a strong influence on the economy through controlling the credit system of the economy. Their major business was based on proceeds of rice and other staple products collected as tax revenues and brought to Osaka by the *daimyos* and the *bakufu*, and the related business of remittance and asset management. They also obtained profits from the underwriting of *hansatsu* and lending to thc *daimyos*.

The city wholesaler merchants, in particular the Osaka wholesale merchants, were in charge of inter-regional trade. Until the early nineteenth century, huge amounts of materials, foods, agricultural and fishery products, were imported to Osaka and processed products were exported to the nearby Kinki area and Edo. Merchants were allowed to organize trade associations and controlled the trade process.

Local indigenous merchants were late-comers. They evolved from rich farmers or local merchants in collaboration with the development of the state enterprises of *han*. They were delegated by the *han* during the latter half of the Tokugawa era the role of the sale of products and the purchase of materials for state enterprises.

6.4.2 Regional Division of Labor

Commerce-based growth occurred at first in relationship with the regional trade through Osaka, but after the early nineteenth century, the center of trade shifted to regional trade outside Osaka. Inter-regional trade through Osaka was triggered by the initial change in the political system. The establishment of a tax system paid in rice necessitated the rise of a huge rice market, mainly in Osaka, and the *sankin-kōtai* system transformed Edo into a huge consumption city. Economic growth was accelerated by innovations in marine transportation from local areas and Edo to Osaka and in the settlement and remittance system between Osaka and Edo. The city wholesale merchants, among others Osaka wholesale merchants, played a key role in the purchase of materials from local producers in various local areas, selling materials to small manufacturers in Kyoto and districts near Osaka, and the final products to Edo and other local districts. They were also major financiers of the transaction process; with respect to Kyoto manufacturers by providing them with advance payments and to local merchants with the deferred payments facility. The money for these purposes was financed by the moneychanger merchants in Osaka.

After the early nineteenth century, the market power of the city wholesale merchants, especially the Osaka wholesale merchants, began to decline rapidly. As is vividly described by Yuki (1965) with respect to the trade in sake, direct transactions between local domains without going through Osaka increased during the early nineteenth century. As a result, the Osaka wholesale merchants and city wholesale merchants in general lost power, and local indigenous (*zaikata*) merchants came to take the lead in commerce-based economic growth. There were two main reasons for this structural change. First was the technological advance of local producers of specified regional products or staple goods that made the finishing process by Kyoto artisans under the control of Osaka wholesale merchants unnecessary (Hayashi 1967). Second was the decrease in information asymmetry in the economy. The reputation and information network of Osaka wholesale merchants lost their value relatively once everyone behaved similarly according to disseminated moral codes and conventions, and one could readily forecast the responses of others.

The technological advance by local producers and their independence from the Osaka wholesale merchants during the first half of the nineteenth century has been closely studied with respect to silk weaving in Kiryū (Hayashi 1967, ch. 4). The technological advance occurred through the division of labor between sericulture and silk reeling, and then through the introduction of higher-level weaving machines and dying technology. Yarn dying technology, imported from Nishijin of Kyoto, enabled Kiryū producers to manufacture finished textiles by themselves, and this resulted in the independence of Kiryū producers from city wholesale merchants. While *kaitsugi* merchants continued to pick up finished products for the city wholesalers, a considerable amount of high-level textile, such as crape and *sa-aya*,[57] were sold directly to local consumers in the Nagoya and Tōhoku regions by indigenous (*zaikata*) merchants. A similar development was seen to some extent in the silk weaving industries in Kanazawa and Niigata. In the cotton industry also, the introduction of new weaving machines and yarn dying technology enabled the development of local production and distribution by indigenous merchants in the Saitama area. Especially radical was the development of the cotton spinning industry in the Kinki area near Osaka. Indigenous merchants organized a family-farmer manufacturing system under wholesaler control, which was equipped with high-level weaving machines and dying technology and they fought for market control with the Osaka wholesale merchants in the middle of the first half of the nineteenth century.

Incidentally, Shinpo and Hasegawa (1986) and Shinpo and Saito (1986) assert that the structural change in the pattern of the regional division of labor occurred around mid-eighteenth century, not after the early nineteenth century. However, this judgement is wrong because it is based on the assertion that the market power of the Osaka merchants declined after mid-eighteenth century, the so-called Tanuma era. The Osaka merchants, both wholesalers and moneychangers, were still leading the economic growth of the country during most of the eighteenth century. Their assertion was derived from the judgement that the decline of interest rates after the mid-eighteenth century was caused by the fall of the market power of Osaka merchants, but this judgement cannot be justified, as already explained. The decline in interest rates was caused by the decrease in information asymmetry in the whole country, and the market power of the Osaka moneychanger merchants stayed at a high level owing to the increase in the numbers of borrowers among merchants in

[57] High level silk textiles, thin and with modern designs and suitable for summer use.

the neighborhood areas of Osaka. The fact that Tanuma included these merchants in the neighborhood of Osaka in the trade association (*kabu-nakama*) system does not imply the fall in the power of wholesalers in Osaka. The main purpose of Tanuma to expand the trade association system lay in the securing of the tax base. Shinpo raises two additional reasons to support his assertion. First, when local merchants in the Kinki district brought a case about the unjust trade customs of trade associations before the Osaka *bugyō* (court), the *bugyō* (judge) took on the case. Since it was customary to leave any private disputes in trade to negotiation among the persons concerned, this action, called *Koku-so* (direct litigation to the government), was an exceptional treatment of local merchants. Secondly, the method of settlement in the trade of sake between Edo and Osaka changed from the use of bills receivable to remittance bills, reflecting the stronger bargaining power of the Edo merchants. These two incidents, however, occurred during the early part of the nineteenth century, or during the so-called *Bunka-Bunsei-ki*, not in the eighteenth century (Yuki 1965, ch. 6; Nakanishi 2002, p. 170; Shinpo and Saito 1989, p. 42).

Against the background of the technological advances in staple goods production in each local domain, as well as the production of daily life necessities consumed in local districts, the development of regional trade outside Osaka was caused by the decline in transaction costs owing to the reduction of information asymmetry. We have suggested that interest rates declined drastically toward the early nineteenth century due to the alleviation of information asymmetry. The establishment of ethical codes and the nationwide standardization of economic behavior reduced transaction costs considerably, and it became gradually possible to implement transactions without relying on the expertise and reputation of city wholesale merchants. Moreover, local *daimyos* were motivated to be involved in the economic development of their domain to cope with the fiscal deficits as well as in preparation for possible international tensions.[58] The establishment of state enterprises in local staple products were implemented with the significant assistance of local indigenous (*zaikata*) merchants. Paper (washi) in Chōshū and han in the shikoku area, wax in Aizu, Uwajima, Hukuoka and Kumamoto, indigo ball in Awa, silk in Gujyō, silk textile in Hikone, cotton in Kameoka and Himeji, tatami in Hukuyama, and sugar in Takamatsu and Kagoshima were typical staple products developed by the state enterprise system by the local *han*.

The indigenous (*zaikata*) merchants, who had been the leaders of villages and engaged in local commerce in village products, collaborated with domain samurai in the purchase of materials and the sales of products of state enterprises. In many *han*, such as Chōshū, Tosa and Tottori, the indigenous merchants succeeded in winning the competition with the Osaka wholesale merchants (Crawcour 1968) through directly transporting products to Edo by themselves. Hayashi (1967) argues that, although the strategy of these southwest *han* to get rid of the influence of the Osaka wholesale merchants was successful, it did not mean final victory over the hegemony of the city

[58]In 1818, during the Napoleonic wars, a British warship came to Nagasaki and seized a Dutch ship. This and similar incidents induced the *bakufu* in 1825 to promulgate an Act to drive off foreign ships.

wholesale merchants. This was because to sell the products transported to Edo in national markets, the network of indigenous merchants was not sufficient, and they were obliged to ask for the help of Edo wholesale merchants.

The Osaka moneychanger merchants were in a close relationship with the *bakufu* because they were in charge of *bakufu* budget administration through rice transactions, converting tax revenues in the form of rice into money.[59] The Osaka wholesale merchants were also in a symbiotic relationship with the *bakufu*, mainly through the formation of trade associations. At first, the *bakufu* had been against the formation of trade associations because of their belief in free market mechanism advocated by Oda Nobunaga. However, after the early eighteenth century (roughly the Kyōho period from 1716 to 1736), the *bakufu* changed the policy and adopted a protection policy toward Osaka wholesale merchants. The *bakufu* had been suspicious of the possibility of price control by trade associations, so the protection policy was conditional in the sense of it not being involved in the pursuit for unjustifiable profits. The protection policy was intensified under the administration of Tanuma Okitsugu (roughly 23 years after the period 1751–65) to obtain tax revenue (*myōga-kin*) from trade associations. The number of merchants who participated in trade associations was expanded, encompassing local merchants, and loan policies to merchants by the *bakufu* were introduced. Although during the Tenpō period, from 1841 to 1850, trade associations were prohibited for the purpose of disinflation, the symbiotic relationship between the Osaka moneychangers and wholesale merchants and the *bakufu* continued, right until the collapse of the *bakufu*.

The symbiotic relationship between the Osaka merchants and the *bakufu* needs to be construed carefully, however. The *bakufu* never abandoned its physiocratic view on the economy nor changed its suspicious stance toward the role of merchants. It seems that the antagonism toward the merchant class felt by the shogunate government intensified year by year. In view of Miyamoto's contention (1941) that the negative function of trade associations, such as monopolistic trading and rent-seeking, was intensified after the Bunka period (1804–18), the *bakufu*'s suspicions were not entirely groundless. It is important to note that this ambivalence between the samurai and merchants does not apply to the relationship between the local *daimyo* and local indigenous (*zaikata*) merchants. The indigenous merchants were actively and deeply involved in the industrial policy of the *han*. It was these merchants who supported the anti-shogunate movement and the civil war after 1866, by such *han* as Tosa and Chōshū (Crawcour 1968), and Satsuma as well.

Jones (1988) asserts that the elite settlement successfully avoided the tug of war between rent-seeking by the ruler and the propensity for growth. It is true that growth emerged largely in the local domains governed by *daimyos* preparing for future civil war, outside the economic activities under the control of the shogunate. However,

---

[59] Many moneychanger merchants in Osaka went bankrupt as a result of the policy to prohibit transaction in silver after the Meiji Restoration— though Mitsui, Kōnoike and some others successfully converted into modern banking. Ishii (2007) contends that this was not caused by the failure of those moneychanger merchants to adapt to the policy to establish the gold standard system, but rather because the military force of the new government intentionally destroyed their credit network to punish their collaboration with the *bakufu* in the past.

even if we admit that this movement could be called a growth propensity in Jones's sense (see the appendix to this chapter), we are not sure whether the rulers, the shogun, were rent-seekers. Most shoguns were faithful to the samurai ethical code and educated to avoid indulgence in luxury.[60] There did not occur any serious tug of war between rent-seeking and growth propensity in Japan. What determined the course of Japan toward the Meiji Restoration was the fear of invasion by Western powers, and the power of the ethical development to sacrifice loyalty to the *shokubun* regulation for the sake of loyalty to the principle to save the cultural value of the nation for the sake of the future of the country.

Incidentally, Ishii (2007) contends that many local *zaikata* merchants and Osaka wholesale merchants thrived during the turmoil after the arrival of Perry in 1853 and after the Meiji Restoration, partly owing to the prohibition on domestic trading activity by foreign merchants,[61] and some of them expanded their business in foreign trade. Many Osaka moneychanger merchants other than Mitsui and Kōnoike went bankrupt due to the antagonistic policy of the new government, but smaller moneychangers grew into banks and security companies, surviving the confusion of the Meiji Restoration.

6.4.3 Feudalism and Loyalty

Two characteristics of the feudalism of Tokugawa Japan are worth mentioning. First, the feudal contract was between the *bakufu* and the *ie* of the *daimyo* or between the *daimyo* and the *ie* of vassals, not contracts between the *bakufu* and individual *daimyo* or *daimyo* and individual vassals. The *ie* inherited by the eldest son kept the enfeoffment or right to income as a household asset. The right was patrimonial and automatically inherited as a reciprocal responsibility of loyalty, even when no service had been given in the case of the *daimyo* and some service at the domain office in the case of the *daimyo*'s vassals (Bolitho 1974). Second, the samurai either of the *daimyo* class or of their vassal class were separated from farming owing to the *shokubun* regulation. The *daimyos* were enfeoffed their domain, but the property right of land was virtually held by villages, which comprised aggregates of the *ie* of farmers. What was obtained by the *daimyos* was the right to taxation on the villages in their domain. The vassals of *daimyos* obtained income either in the form of rice or money from their master, *daimyo*.

Loyalty was basically concerned with military obligation. The administrative organization of the *bakufu* and every *daimyo* were organized in preparation for military action (Takikawa 1985, vol. 2, pp. 53–69, 85–89). Being attached to a particular post of the *bakufu* administration or of the domain office meant the obligation of

---

[60] Behind this behavior was the tradition of the Mikawa-*bushi* (samurai) out of which the Tokugawa emerged that respected humble and simple lifestyle.

[61] The treaty with the United States and the United Kingdom on foreign trade ratified in 1858 forbade the domestic activity of foreign merchants.

maintaining the assigned level of armament stipulated in the number of soldiers, guns, bows, horses and so on.

The *bakufu* had enormous power toward the *daimyo* at the time of their establishment until the middle of the seventeenth century in the sense that (1) the *bakufu* expropriated the diplomacy right from individual *daimyo*, (2) the *bakufu* could assign various services to *daimyo* including the *sankin-kōtai*, military service, construction service, and the like, (3) the *bakufu* could implement the *kunigae* and *kaieki* whenever the *daimyo* failed to obey the code of conduct stipulated in the *Buke-shohatto*. It is true that after the death of Ieyasum, Hidetada (the second shogun) and Iemitsu (the third shougun) went through hard times to establish the leadership of the *bakufu* (Hall 1991). However, the assertion of Jones that 'behind its stern exterior the regime proved surprisingly weak' (Jones 1988, p. 162) is not correct as far as the *bakufu* after the latter half of seventeenth century is concerned. The *bakufu* until the mid-seventeenth century had sufficient power to govern the country. It is important to note the reasons why the power of the *bakufu*, its relative strength, deteriorated after the eighteenth century.

The economic power of the *bakufu*, mainly based on rice agriculture became weak compared with other *daimyo*, who actively diversified the industrial structure through developing the monopolized production of local staples and became involved in foreign trade. This point is closely concerned with the relationship with the merchant class. The *bakufu* continued to protect and to be in a symbiotic relationship with Osaka wholesale merchants. The economic power of the Osaka merchants became weaker compared with local merchants as the center of gravity of production shifted from Osaka to peripheral local regions.

More importantly, the spiritual leadership of the *bakufu* gradually weakened for additional two reasons. First, the *fudai daimyo* gradually lost loyalty to the shogun and became more involved in the management of their own domain. Bolitho (1974) contends that the loyalty of the *fudai daimyo* was based on a fiction, that their loyalty to the shogun was more ardent and selfless than others by virtue of the deeds of their ancestors. Their loyalty had not been testified and refreshed on the battlefield for 200 years, since the Shimabara war in 1637–38. Their domain was automatically inherited, so that the *fudai daimyo* never felt the necessity to show gestures of loyalty to the shogun, and this invited the gradual deterioration of spirits.

Second, the samurai class were required to be involved in the pursuit of the ethical codes of society. The central issue addressed by the samurai regarding this task was the relative importance of the role of the samurai (*bun*) in the *shokubun* regulation compared with the more general principle of guiding the governance of society. The concept of the heaven inherited from Confucianism was never established as the principle to guide politics, but it continued to live on tenaciously as an idea to support the internal autonomy of individual samurai (Bitō 1994). It might be possible to argue that the samurai gradually came to recognize and emphasize their role in the country as a whole. This was especially true after the arrival of Perry. Yoshida Shōin criticized the Mito school that emphasized the ultimate value of loyalty in the lord–vassal relationship and taught the independence of the samurai in the sense of the unity with the heaven (Sagara 1968). Maruyama (1960) deliberated on the issue of loyalty to principle vs loyalty to organization. It is contended that the *bakuhan* system was maintained in the theory of the integrity of two kind of loyalty, while the Meiji Restoration was carried out on the separation of the two.

Incidentally, Ikegami (1995), in 'The taming of the samurai; honorific individualism and the making of modern Japan', claims that the individualistic behavioral patterns of the samurai developed during the medieval era, underwent significant transformation under the *bakuhan* system. The aggressive behavioral pattern of the samurai was tamed in the peaceful bureaucratic society, and the spirit of the samurai that had been characterized by individualism based on the respect for honor was gradually converted into a modern spirit characterized by loyalty to organizations and the public, suitable for the transition to modern Japan. Although this argument gives a valuable insight into the nature of Tokugawa society, it is regrettable that Ikegami's emphasis on loyalty to organizations tends to overlook another spiritual tendency of loyalty to principles related to the future vision of the country nurtured in the cultural evolution of the Tokugawa period. Moreover, Ikegami seems to fail to notice the refined individualism emphasized by Fukuzawa (1875), and the sophistication of the relationship with others by way of mutual respect asserted by Sagara (1968).

6.5 Characteristic of Culture-Led Growth of Tokugawa Japan

6.5.1 Cultural Change as a Social Movement

While the development of scientifically useful knowledge in the Occident was a phenomenon among elites comprising a small proportion of the population, in Japan the reduction of transaction costs in commerce was brought about as a result of a social movement to develop a workable system of moral codes. It is interesting to note that one of the salient features that characterizes the cultural impacts of Tokugawa growth was that changes in culture occurred as a social movement rather than an elite phenomenon. In the Occident, the cultural changes, the emergence of new beliefs and attitudes, occurred among the elites, largely confined to intellectuals, scholars, and other literate and educated minorities. In the two centuries between Columbus and Newton, European elite culture underwent radical intellectual change, giving rise to a belief that it is possible to improve material wellbeing by bettering the understanding of natural phenomena and the application of this understanding to production (Mokyr 2017). In the case of Japan, a new belief emerged in the mind construct of almost all classes, including rich and poor, and elite and non-elite, and this belief was realized as a nationwide movement to establish new moral codes to bring peace back to the country. The process was participated in not only by the Tokugawa *bakufu* but also the previously antagonistic *daimyos*. It would be not far off the mark to say that the

Tokugawa peace, as a 'compromise' between Tokugawa and its antagonistic powers, was brought about for this purpose.

To what extent people were aware that the turmoil during the Warring States period was related to the development of the market economy characterized by the social division of labor is a delicate issue. However, it is safe to assume that people did not expect any substantial direct effects of peace on the economy. It seems that, while the Occidental elites were involved in scientific research to attain material gains for humanity, in the case of Japan, growth occurred as an unintended consequence of cultural changes. When the Tokugawa *bakufu* began its effort to develop new moral codes, it is hard to believe that the relationship between the moral codes and economic growth was in their sight. They might have expected that a peaceful Japan, without the disturbances of war, might result in some sort of prosperity, but it is difficult to believe that the *bakufu* expected the continuation of commerce-based growth through the reduction of transaction costs for more than 200 years. The apathetic and ambivalent attitudes of the *bakufu* toward the merchant class is eloquent evidence for this conjecture.

In his assertion that the explosion of technological progress in the West after the eighteenth century was made possible by the direct and indirect effects of cultural changes, Mokyr (2017) contends that the elites who were engaged in research in natural science intended to produce a direct cultural effect on technological growth by changing attitudes toward the natural world. Although we are not entirely convinced by his assertion of the cultural effect on Occidental growth with respect to the magnitude of that effect, as mentioned in Chapter 1, it is interesting to note that the cultural effect on growth in the Occident was intentional.

Incidentally, Botticini and Eckstein (2005) note the following episode regarding religious change, with the economic success of the Jews. Before the eighth–ninth centuries, most Jews were farmers. With the establishment of the Muslim Empire in the eighth century, almost the entire Jewish population became urban and embarked on commercial activities. It is contended that the transition away from agriculture into crafts and trade industries was the outcome of their widespread literacy, promoted by a religious and educational reform in Judaism in the 1st and 2nd centuries, which gave them comparative advantages in urban, skilled occupations. In this case also, the effects of religious reform on the economic success of Jews in the areas of trade and commerce seem to be largely unintended.

6.5.2 Culture-Based Equilibrium and Small Government

Quite differently from the Occident, the bureaucracy in the economic system of Tokugawa society was carried out by a surprisingly small number of people. It seems that the culture-based economy was established on the internalized equilibrium of the cognitive model of individuals. Since the economic system was in equilibrium without reliance on the constraints imposed by institutions, there were less need to resolve conflicts by way of bureaucratic procedures. In the Occident, on the other hand, where institutions were established on the principle of social contract, at least from the theoretical viewpoint, there seems to have been various difficulties to be overcome in reaching equilibrium, so that the method of enforcement of the rule itself tended to be a matter to be agreed upon. The proliferation and complication of institutional devices like the parliamentary system, the judicial system, the policing system and the like, was inevitable. This seems to explain the difference in the size of government in Tokugawa Japan and the Occident.

Probably owing to the spread of moral codes nationwide, it is well known that villages in the Tokugawa era were governed with astonishingly small numbers of bureaucrats (Totman 1967). Smith (1959) ascribes this to the trust in the administrative capability of village chiefs. In towns, the administration system was also very simple and implemented by a small number of bureaucrats. Edo, with 1.129 million residents in 1718, for example, had two magistrate's office (*bugyō-sho*), a southern and northern office, in charge of the administrative and judicial business within the private sector or matters related to the three classes other than the samurai. The number of officers allocated to each office was only 25 *yoriki* and 120 *dōshin* (Takigawa 1985). Their job was complemented by town chiefs, whose number was 196 in 1715 and 264 in 1723.

To reduce the burden on the magistrate's office, judicial matters that were not serious from the viewpoint of social security, were as far as possible delegated to mutual agreement within the private sector, without the involvement of government. Decrees of mutual settlement (*Aitai-sumashi-rei*), issued in the years 1661, 1663, 1682, 1685, 1702, 1719, 1746, 1797 and 1843, were a typical method for this. The decree ordered that private troubles related to lending and credit should be left to mutual settlement by the persons concerned, while delicate and complicated issues related to the renting of land and houses, and bills of exchange, could be brought to the magistrate's office. In 1718, the number of litigations was 47,731, of which 33,037 were related to lending and credit. It is sometimes said that the implicit purpose of the decree was to lessen the debt burden of the banner-men (*hatamoto*) of the Tokugawa *bakufu*, many of whom were heavily in debt, by enabling them to bill debts. There seems to be no doubt, however, that the main purpose lay in the shortage of manpower of the magistrate's offices.

Incidentally, the roles fulfilled by private and informal institutions could be noted in this regard. Okazaki (2005) asserts that the multilateral punishing system of trade associations (*kabu-nakama*) had an important function in complementing the role of the government. Many of the agreed-upon rules of associations had articles prescribing that all members should suspend trade with any person who cheated one of their own members. This mechanism is similar to that of the traders' organizations of Maghribi merchants analyzed in Greif (2006). Okazaki claims that contract enforcement in the private sector substituted for the role of the public authority. A similar mechanism, called *mura-hachbu*, was also in existence in the villages. Likewise, Miyamoto (2009) contends that, owing to the spontaneous efforts of the trade association system (*kabu-nakama*), there occurred the development of institutions such as accounting, auditing, the measuring and inspecting system, without the help of government. Miyamoto (2009) calls this the market-enhancing function of trade associations, suggesting that trade associations played the role of decreasing transaction costs, such as contracting costs, in commercial activities.[62]

However, it is not right to overemphasize the positive role of the trade association system of the Tokugawa era in the reduction of transaction costs. One of the reasons is that the trade association system had already developed rapidly since the medieval period, especially since the Muromachi era. The Tokugawa *bakufu* had followed the policy to modernize and control trade association activity adopted by Oda Nobunaga[63] and Toyotomi Hideyoshi, and this policy was scaled up after the 1720s (Miyamoto 1938). It must be noted that the significant development of commerce in the Tokugawa era had already started in the seventeenth century. This seems to suggest that informal collaborative activities had already been in existence before the *bakufu* policy to admit and encourage trade association activities in the 1820s. There is a possibility that the policy to encourage trade associations (*kabu-nakama*) after the 1720s only had the effect of authorizing the conventions of transactions already working as underground activities. If so, the effect of trade associations cannot explain the discontinuity in commercial development that occurred in the Tokugawa era. It must be noted that we are not denying the various positive roles in improving the functions of markets by trade associations, but rather the essence of our assertion lies in the negation of the discontinuity of the roles of trade associations before and after the establishment of the Tokugawa *bakufu*. In other words, the function of the trade associations could have been at work before the Tokugawa era, so cannot explain the unprecedented growth of commerce in that era.

The second reason for skepticism about the positive influence of the trade association system is the well-known monopoly effect that restricted the production of commercial services with the aim to obtain monopoly profits. Since the age of Oda Nobunaga, policies regarding trade association activity were implemented out of concern for the monopoly profits by vested interest groups of merchants. If this effect were substantial, the level of commercial activity in terms of the production of commercial services could be reduced by the trade association system, so that trade association activity cannot explain the development of commerce in the Tokugawa era. It is highly possible that the policy of encouraging trade association behavior during the 1720s was adopted with the aim to make the collusive activity more transparent and to induce the fall of commodity prices other than rice, i.e. a rise in the relative price of rice, through the control of the monopoly behavior of trade associations (Miyamoto 1939).

These considerations about the effect of the institution of trade associations leads us to conjecture that the alleviation of information asymmetry and the decline in transaction costs that caused the unprecedented growth of commerce in the Tokugawa era

[62]Under the conditions of serious information asymmetry, the costs of contracts could be enormous. Obtaining information, negotiating with the agents of transactions, writing contracts, enforcing transactions, and renegotiation. All these activities incurred significant costs in addition to the production and transporting costs in the presence of information asymmetry.

[63]Miyamoto (1938) contends that the so-called free trade association (*rakuza*) policy of Oda Nobunaga was an attempt to transform the old trade association system to one suitable for the development of a national market economy.

were based on more fundamental factors that had not been in existence before—in other words what we have called the standardization of conduct and ethical rules owing to the intentional efforts to rebuild trust in society both by the government as well as by the private sector. While we are not reluctant to admit that the institution of trade associations could have some positive effects on the development of commerce, the overwhelming influence was the cultural development giving rise to the standardization of conduct and ethical rules. It is worth emphasizing that there was little evidence for the active participation of the *bakufu* in institutional development in economic areas. The basic policy stance of the *bakufu* was to let matters of economic affairs be settled in the private sector. Most efforts in institution building paid by the *bakufu* were related to its needs to repress the economic development of antagonistic *daimyos*, and not necessarily directly related to the development of the national economy.

Appendix: Two Existing Hypotheses on the Economic Growth of the Tokugawa Japan

In this appendix, two existing hypotheses related to the economic growth during the Tokugawa period are critically examined. First is the so-called 'industrious revolution' hypothesis, which claims that significant change in the behavioral pattern of peasants occurred owing to the changes in the endowment ratio of production factors. Second is the 'elite settlement' hypothesis, which asserts that the settlement of conflicts aiming at the welfare of society or the nation as a whole in the Tokugawa era had the effect of preventing rent-seeking by rulers, enabling the free play of innate private engines of economic growth.

Hypothesis One: Work Ethic and Family Farming

An ambitious account for the increase of per capita production was set out by Hayami (1986, 1992, 2016) and Sugiyama (2003) and claims the emergence of the mind-set of farmers after around the year 1730, resulting in various institutional and technological changes in farm sector activity. This hypothesis, broadly called 'industrious revolution',[64] contends in effect that farmers have acquired a new behavioral pattern that resulted in the pursuit of an improvement in the standard of living. It is claimed that farmers came to devote more hours in labor to raise per capita or family income by adopting labor-intensive farming methods, devoting more hours to labor, substituting human labor for livestock power, and introducing elaborate family labor allocation, including the division of labor among male and female members of family. It is even claimed that farmers were engaged in preventive family planning by way of infanticide and abortion to avoid falling into the Malthusian trap.

[64] Similar terminology is utilized by De Fries (2008) with respect to behavior to increase the labor supply for the purpose of higher consumption levels in early modern Netherlands and England.

However, this hypothesis has two crucial drawbacks. First is the lack or imperfection of empirical evidence. Hayami points out a decrease in the number of horses and cows in the Nagoya region from the 1670s to 1820, but he could not provide any data for other regions and other periods. Sugihara quotes evidence for the number of working days per year, but his data is a comparison of Japan with other Asian countries in the late nineteenth century. Sugiyama also points to other evidence for the labor allocation device, referring to the new method of cocoon rearing that enabled farmers to engage in by-employment, avoiding peak seasons of work in the rice fields. But this change occurred during the Meiji era, as noted by Sugiyama by himself.

Second, and more serious, is the lack of persuasiveness of the logic. Hayami's theory seems to be constructed on the confusion of a macro-economic historian's view on the macro land/labor ratio with respect to the *ex post* data with micro optimizing behavior in the sense of the reaction to market conditions at each historical time. His assertion is constructed on the proposition that, after the end of the great reclamation during the seventeenth century, farmers were surprised by the fact that the land/labor ratio had fallen seriously, and this led them to change their work attitude and managerial system radically. This 'surprise' theory implies that, during the period when reclamation was carried out, farmers did not adapt to the change by such methods as the improvement of their managerial system and technology, although there occurred high rates of population growth. But why? In the orthodox reasoning of economics, farmers should have continually adapted to the changing market conditions. In the expectation of an increase in the availability of land, people might have been motivated to have more family members and adjust farming technology. If it is expected that the population increase was larger than the increase in land availability (rational expectation), they would have introduced new farming based on equipment for intensive labor and the ample use of fertilizer like compost, and new farming introduced in newly cultivated land as well as existing land should have increased the amount of land in efficient unit. Even if, at the end of the great reclamation period, the land/labor ratio in the historical data is low,[65] the land/labor ratio in efficient unit should have been larger. Nagahara (1980) emphasized that land productivity definitely increased during the early Tokugawa period mainly by the development of the hoe (pp. 177–178). In other words, it is natural to believe that equilibrium is attained in efficiency unit. There is no room for 'surprise', so there is no need to change the managerial system or work ethic suddenly after the end of the great reclamation period as a response to a 'sudden' lowering of macro land/labor ratio. Hayami fell into confusion that the micro optimizing behavior of farmers was implemented following *ex post* macro-economic data.

We do not deny that there occurred an important change in the mindset of farmers or in society to be more diligent or more industrious, more honest and to lead a

---

[65] After the spur, farmers compared the macro-ratio between land and population in the years 1650 and 1730 and were surprised to find a significant drop in the land–man ratio from 1.37 (thousand *koku*/ten thousand persons) in 1650 to 0.92 in 1730. The perceived scarcity of land scared farmers, and gave a strong incentive to develop a harder and more industrious work ethos, Hayami contends.

humbler life during the Tokugawa period. This change, however, was not a consequence of the unintended outcome or 'surprise' as emphasized by Hayami. Rather, it is a consequence of deliberate and conscious social action that needs to be examined within a more careful theoretical and empirical framework. We have investigated the phenomenon within a more comprehensive framework that encompasses cultural and institutional interactions. The changes in the belief system of society that took place in the Warring States period during the fifteenth and sixteenth centuries as well as the effects of various institutional developments to accommodate the evolution of the social division of labor since the fourteenth century, are focal points in the argument.

Hayami and Sugiyama's hypothesis is related to the issue of the emergence of small family farming in Japanese history. From large-scale farming utilizing semi-slave labor and livestock, the managerial style of Japanese agriculture underwent enormous transformation at least by the end of the Tokugawa era into a system in which small family farming by the human power of family members was the dominant style of production.

Smith (1959) argues that the growth of the 'market' that characterize the agricultural and commercial development of Tokugawa Japan changed the standard of the value system that governed the economic life of peasants. As the market economy developed, 'family gain', instead of traditional lineages and the power of status, became the chief end of economic activity. The traditional standards that provided the distributive and productive system to peasants came to be ignored and were replaced by family gain that necessitated the managerial system based on family labor. On the other hand, Hayami contends that after the great reclamation period, which continued from the latter half of the Warring States period to the end of the seventeenth century, the ratio of arable land to labor declined sharply, and this enhanced farmers' motivation to increase the productivity of small land through the intensive input of labor, and they found family farming the most suitable system and diligence as the suitable virtue for the purpose.

Both Hayami and Smith's hypotheses try to explain the emergence of small family farming in the context of the Tokugawa economy after the seventeenth century, but it is regrettable they do not pay attention to the assertion that a move to the small farmer system had already been seen rather widely after the end of medieval period (Matsumoto 1956; Kuroda 1974; Toda 1967). Ishii (1979) claims that the technical changes suitable for family farming that do not need livestock as well as the institutional change that caused the decline of the manor system was the cause of the transformation of the managerial system. Araki (1953)[66] asserts that the impact of the land survey conducted by Hideyoshi to bring about a society built on independent small farmers was the main cause for the rise of the family farming system. More recently, Nishitani (2017) contends that the tendency to small family farming became clearly identified by the late medieval era and that, since large-scale farming had been needed to develop the irrigation system and to accomplish other

[66] A detailed and excellent reexamination of the Araki hypothesis is conducted by Hasegawa (2004).

improvements of land use, the change of the managerial system to family farming was a natural consequence after the completion of land development.

Although Smith's argument is only concerned with Tokugawa period, the framework is applicable to the period before the Tokugawa period. His theory could be summarized, in its core structure, as follows. The labor shortage in the rural sector as a result of urban market development made it difficult to continue large-scale farming. Together with the deterioration of the value system, owing to the growth of the market, that emphasized lineage, traditional status and employment practice, and the like,[67] this was the main reason for the conversion of the managerial system of Japanese agriculture from large-scale farming to family farming. However, from the viewpoint of international comparison, the following question seems to be unanswered. Assuming that the market development occurred not only in Japan but also in England, and that 'family gain' was an important concern in determining the behavioral pattern in both countries, why did the development of the market bring about small farming in Japan instead of the large-scale farming that occurred during the agricultural revolution before the industrial revolution in England? Smith was aware of this question, and, in Chapter 7 of his book, tried to give a tentative answer by pointing out the labor-intensive bias of technological development and an increase in labor costs in Japan. However, while the high labor cost is a convincing reason for the decline of large-scale farming, the key question was how to explain the emergence of the labor-intensive bias in technology that retarded crucially the change toward large-scale farming.

The development of technology suitable for family farming, such as labor-intensive equipment and purchased fertilizer suitable for family farming, was a long-term trend since the medieval era. Hurushima (1954) argues that the major method of ploughing had already shifted from livestock power to human power by the use of the hoe during early period of the Tokugawa era, although livestock was still utilized for the purpose of smoothing the land surface in paddy fields (*shirokaki*) (p. 302). Ishii (1976) points out that new labor-intensive technology without relying on livestock power, such as intensive utilization of land by way of the two-crop system and off-season cropping, as well as equipment like the hoe for deeper ploughing by human labor for the effective use of fertilizer like compost, had already dominated agricultural production during the last period of the medieval age before the Tokugawa era. We have already touched upon this point in Chapter 2.

It is important to note that the bias in technology noted by Smith is closely related to this point. Mainly because Smith's analysis is confined to the Tokugawa era, he considered that family farming technology was born in the late Tokugawa period. However, it is necessary to consider that the labor-intensive technology was already in existence before the Tokugawa era, although its nationwide spread occurred during the Tokugawa period, after the end of the great reclamation. Why the technology was not widely utilized before the end of the great reclamation period could be

[67]The decrease of slave or semi-slave labor such as *genin* or *shojyu* as well as *seshū-hūkōnin* (patrimonial hired labor) caused labor shortages in agriculture. Smith claims that this induced the preference for tenant farming and made the shift to family farming inevitable.

explained by the explosive growth of population, and the consequent availability of labor for large-scale farming, restricting the spread of family farming technology. The slowdown of population growth thereafter triggered the spread nationwide of family farming technology, consequently bringing about the dominance of family farming by the end of the Tokugawa era.[68] Moreover, by taking the relation-specific investment by workers as hostage, the owner could increase its share in the residual income right. Large-scale farming utilizing hired labor might not be suitable in this case. It follows that whenever relation-specific investment by workers was indispensable for increasing productivity, family farming was the most preferred managerial structure of organization. In Chapter 2 we argued that, as the residual control right of farmers was enhanced, land-specific investment tended to gain in importance. This is an additional factor that explains the acceleration to small farming toward the latter half of the Tokugawa era.

Toward the end of his book, Smith developed an impressive argument that, pointing out the immigration of rural labor to the cities in response to the pecuniary gain that caused the shortage of labor in agriculture, Japan had already prepared for economic development based on industrial technology before the arrival of Perry, in the sense of the emergence of the reserve of labor for use in industry. This proposition might be true, but one must note that another equally, or even more important, factor that prepared for the arrival of the era of industry was the emergence of active family farmers accustomed to adopt new technology, new commercial crops and new forms of management—in other words, numerous entrepreneurs in the rural sector who were ready to embark on new businesses. In view of the growth pattern after the Meiji Restoration that was dependent on innovative small and medium-sized businesses, this aspect must be emphasized more. As already discussed in Chapter 2, this was due largely to the acquisition of the residual control right by small farmers.

Hypothesis Two: Inclusive Growth Based on Elite Settlement

The political explanation set out in Jones (1988) is an interesting attempt. However, his analysis is marred with serious errors in understanding Japan, factual misunderstandings as well as serious misapprehensions as to the workings of Japanese society.

Jones claims that in Japan 'growth emerged because behind its stern exterior the absolutism of the regime was surprisingly weak' (p. 162). In other words, 'elite settlement' prevailed in the sense that the power of a ruler, who adhered to vested interests and was involved in rent-seeking, was restricted by ruling groups (Jones 1988, p. xxix).

The concept of elite settlement was borrowed from Burton and Higley (1987), which defined it as a 'broad compromise among previously warring elite factions, resulting in political stability and thus providing a necessary precondition for the

---

[68]Incidentally, the small farming technology emphasized by Hayami is not necessarily original in the Tokugawa economy, and has nothing to do with the macro-economic land/labor ratio nor with the emergence of the new work ethic. If they were acting on the land/labor ratio, they should have expected a fall in the relative price of labor. If so, they should have been motivated to expand their large-scale farming further.

sustained practice of representative democracy'. Jones applied this proposition, originally concerned with political science, to economic growth, and argued that in Japan compromise resulted in sustained economic growth, as was the case in England at the time of restoration of the monarchy in 1660 (Jones 1988, p. xxx). It is argued that, just like the case of England, in Japan central government could not get as much tax revenue as they might have hoped to indulge in luxury life by way of rent-seeking activity, but they could avoid further stalemate or debilitating conflict.

Jones considers that in the case of Japan a compromise[69] was attained between the ruling elite group comprising the former antagonistic *daimyos* and a ruler, the Tokugawa clan, and argued that, while the Tokugawa family, as is the case of rulers in general, intended to be involved in rent-seeking activity through raising the tax rate, the family's intention was not realized because of the pressure from ruling elites: 'The Tokugawa was never willing to or able to raise the rice tax above the levels set when they made a survey in the seventeenth century' (Jones 1988, p. 165). As a result, in Tokugawa era Japan, it is argued that there occurred a relatively low rate of exploitation, and consequently the market was left more free to work its productive magic, and the growth of production occurred owing to the free play of market forces.

Jones's argument is based on the following assumption that, in any economy, there always exists a tendency to improve the material welfare of society through economic growth. Jones argues that some people in every large society have tried to better their material wellbeing through saving, investing and innovating, and recurrent moves in that direction by whole societies become historically probable. Further, it is contended that, quite often, this tendency encountered serious difficulties and, historically, most societies had been trapped in a low growth equilibrium. Jones assumes that the main such difficulties were rent-seeking by the government, and this approach seems to be popular in recent literature in comparative studies from the perspective of global economic history. Acemoglu and Robinson (2012) is a representative contribution.

In sum, the Jones's model assumes that economic history is a tug of war between growth propensity and rent-seeking (p. 47) and that the low-level equilibrium due to the tug of war was avoided in Japan by elite settlement; the ruling group were strong enough to drive a hard bargain, restricting the ruler's discretion regarding his taxation power, realizing a relatively low rate of exploitation, with the consequent realization of a freer market to attain economic growth.

Before proceeding to the substantive argument, let us correct a factual misunderstanding. The tax rate of Tokugawa Japan was not determined by the ruler, the Tokugawa shogun, but was left to the discretion of each *han*; 266 *han* in the year, say, 1698. Therefore, even if the Tokugawa shogun had tried to be engaged in rent-seeking, he could not have raised taxes for that purpose. What he could do was to decide the tax rate of his territory only, which was only 25.2% of the total taxable territory of the country in that same year.

---

[69] While, with respect to Japan, Jones notes there occurred the double compromise in the sense that Tokugawa did not do away with the imperial line and did not completely dominate those *daimyos* who had been its enemies, his assertion centers on the compromise with the latter.

We believe that, with respect to Japan, the usefulness of Jones's model has severe limitations, at least in two in respects. First, although the weakness of the shogun compared with his outlook, emphasized by Bolitho (1974), on which Jones mainly relied, was true, Bolitho's assertion on this point was concerned with the situation during the nineteenth century. Bolitho emphasized that, during this period, the personal bond related to the loyalty between the hereditary *daimyo* (*fudai daimyo*) and the shogun had been significantly weakened for the following reason. The loyalty was based on the fiction that the fierce battlefield loyalty could be transmitted from father to son in the same manner as physical characteristics. However, Bolitho contends, loyalty in this sense was concerned only with obligations and not accompanied by rights, so that under the custom of the automatic inheritance of the status, the sense of loyalty of the hereditary *daimyo* was destined to deteriorate. It must be noted, however, during the seventeenth and eighteenth centuries, battlefield loyalty remained strong in the thinking of the *fudai daimyo*. As Mizubayashi (1987) asserts, during the period, the shogun had absolute power over all kinds of *daimyo* who failed to obey strict regulations, by way of the transfer of fiefs and the expropriation of territories. It must be noted that the compromise that led to the ceasefire in 1600 was not related to the military weakness of the Tokugawa, but to the change in social belief that peace and reconstruction was needed to avoid ultimate catastrophe.

Second, it must be noted that the potential of rent-seeking by the shogun was not so high in Japan, who had been brought up in the strict samurai tradition characteristic to the Mikawa samurai group. This may have some relationship with the complete downfall of the aristocracy, so that there was no need for the samurai class to compete with the aristocratic class in terms of luxurious cultural expenses. It is well known that the tax rate of the *bakufu* territory was in general substantially lower than other *daimyo* territories. This was partly because the shogun did not need to finance extra expenditure related to the obligation of *sankin-kōtai* and partly because he did not want rent-seeking activities. Recently, the long-term series of tax rates of the Kumamoto-*han* and *bakufu* territory came to be reported in Sawai-Tanimoto (2016, pp. 28–43). The data shows that from the mid-seventeenth century through the first half of the nineteenth century, the tax rate in the Kumamoto *han* was in the range of 30–50%, with a declining trend after the mid-eighteenth century, while the tax rate of the *bakufu* was in the range of 20–40% and with a similar downward trend.

Incidentally, Jones argues that, given the level of the negative effects of interest group activities or the power of the incumbent ruler on preventing innovation, the growth rate would be higher, the stronger the incentive for the material improvement or the economic wellbeing of 'some people in any society' (Jones 1988, p. 150). Who are 'some people' in Japan? If it is the local *daimyos* and vassals, an explanation based on the wish for material improvement or the ubiquitous existence of creativity does not apply. The samurai devoted their lives to attain the ideal of spiritual completion as human beings and disdained the pursuit of material wellbeing. The local *daimyos* and *han* did try to attain the economic development of their domains. However, it was not for the purpose of the material improvement of their lives, but competing for economic development in preparation for a possible future civil war, as well as international conflicts. His assertion that the samurais always accepted the situation that was economically beneficial (introduction to Japanese edition) is difficult to justify. It was the merchant class that led the economic growth of Tokugawa Japan. It follows that one needs to conduct a deeper investigation into the relationship between the merchants and samurais in regard to the establishment of elite settlements. It is regrettable Jones paid scarcely any attention to the activity of merchants in his analysis. One needs to focus on the role of merchants, who actively or cautiously sought the improvement of their material lot and built coalitions or symbiotic relationships with the samurai, as the most important potential power for economic growth.

Chapter 7
Japanese Economy and Culture After the Meiji Restoration

This chapter analyses how the Japanese economy, that had experienced culture-led growth until the mid-nineteenth century, accepted and accommodated Occidental thought and institutions after the Meiji Restoration. The examination focuses on the attempt to adjust the internal mental model based on others nearby with the new value and belief system that emphasized the concept of the public. The leaders of Meiji Japan experienced difficult conflicts in the process and, in order to bridge Japanese and Occidental values, they attempted to introduce three mechanisms. First was the concept of the *kokutai* (national polity) to enhance centripetality and national spirits. Second was the assignment to regional leaders, called *meibōka* (men of repute), the role of interface between the government and the private sector. Third was the new form of *ie* system as a device to adjust to Occidental values and preserve the value of human capital accumulated before the Meiji Restoration.

Since the ancient era, Japan has repeatedly experienced cultural interaction with foreign cultures. Buddhism that came to Japan in the sixth century had enormous impacts through introducing the concept of negation of this world and began to form the foundation of Japanese culture together with the indigenous religion, Shintoism. Confucianism, officially introduced during the Tokugawa era, was virtually denied with respect to its consistency with the value and belief system of Japan, although its conceptual framework had influenced the logical structure of the thinking of the Japanese.

After the Meiji Restoration, Japan was obliged to confront head-on Occidental culture and institutions. While Japan was invariably an enthusiastic student of Occidental technology and institutions, at least until she accomplished catch up in the post-World War II high-growth era, Japan's policy toward Occidental culture was by and large cautious. The political leaders of the Meiji, composed of low-ranking samurai of major *han* that won the civil war to overthrow the Tokugawa *bakufu*, tried to preserve the inherited culture of the Japanese as much as possible. More concretely, in terms of economic system, it was intended to stick to the traditional consumption patterns or lifestyle based on the accumulation of human capital and indigenous

J. Teranishi, *Culture and Institutions in the Economic Growth of Japan*, Studies in Economic History,
https://doi.org/10.1007/978-4-431-55627-5_7

industries, that was considered to be the basis of Japanese culture. On the other hand, they did not feel any hesitation to throw away the formal institutions inherited from the Tokugawa era. Regulations on occupational choice (the *shokubun* regulation), on regional mobility, and on transactions in labor and land were radically repealed and replaced with Occidental institutions. Advanced technology, urgently needed to cope with the international powers that, motivated by imperialism, threatened the independence of Japan, was also imported in every aspect of industrial and military areas. Moreover, the Meiji leaders introduced the new institution of the constitutional monarchy to strengthen national unity against Western powers, and at the same time, the new concept of the *kokutai* (national polity) and the role of the *meibōka* as the interface between the private sector and the government. The revised form of the *ie* system was not a tool for feudalistic contract nor for feudalistic repression but was utilized as a device to adjust the family system to Occidental values and at the same time to preserve the value of human capital accumulated during the period before the Meiji Restoration in order to maintain social stability.

It is controversial, however, whether these new concepts and institutions introduced as surrogates of Occidental cultural concepts worked effectively and realized the intention of the Meiji leaders. It seems that the introduction of the concept of the *kokutai* as a surrogate for the Occidental concept of the public ended up as an utter failure. We will argue that it failed mainly because it was an attempt to change culture, the internalized part of culture, by means of institutions, the introduction of new institutions including the Meiji constitution.

It seems that these institutional adjustments had been contrived based on bounded rationality and their roles were expected to be transitory, so that they were destined to be revised if necessary in order to accomplish the successful resolution of the conflicts and fusion between Japanese and Occidental internalized culture. After World War II, Japan abandoned the policy to preserve the cultural tradition nurtured during the period before the Meiji Restoration in order to catch up with Western mass production and mass consumption technology. It was an intentional decision necessitated by defeat in World War II and based on bounded rationality. After the 70 years of another catch-up process, Japan in the 2020s seems to be seeking to shift to another trajectory to implement the higher-level resolution of the conflict and fusion between Japanese and Occidental culture.

7.1 Cultural Attainments in the Tokugawa Era

At the end of the Tokugawa era, culture and the related informal institutions comprised a well-balanced system that played pivotal roles in the maintenance of stability and the growth of the socio-economy. They comprised two pillars of cultural traits: the trust-based society with others nearby and the stakeholder society and human capital nurtured by the *kyūdō* principle.

The completed version of culture in the Tokugawa era was a coherent and mutually complementary system in the following sense. Trust, which had desperately deteriorated toward the end of the Warring States period, was reestablished by the efforts of the Tokugawa *bakufu* and intellectuals in the private sector to develop ethical codes suitable for the development of the social division of labor. Trust was established as a chain relationship of small groups of individuals related to each other by the Buddhist notion of interrelationship in the process of transmigration. Each group was composed of concrete acquaintances largely belonging to the same occupation, not abstract individuals. The *kyūdō* principle, the individualistic version of which had been responsible for the major disturbances in the formal institutions during the Warring States period through such behavior as self-salvation and religion-related riots, was adapted to and brought in harmony with the development of the social division of labor and the accommodating stance of the present day benefits in the teaching of Shintoism. Denying the excessive sanctification of the present world in Buddhism, Shintoism converted the individualistic motivation in the *kyūdō* principle into one in harmony with not only others nearby but also with nature. The human capital accumulated through occupational *kyūdō* behavior was by and large specific to relationships in small groups of others nearby. Since the skills specific to a group lose their value when separated from the group, the human capital accumulated in this way became shared as the common property of the group. Moreover, because the amount of investment by each member in the skills specific to the group activities is difficult to be identified separately, groups tended to evolve into stakeholder societies, in which every stakeholder has some rights to residual income.

Three key concepts comprised the core in the integral structure of Tokugawa culture: trust as a chain relationship of groups of others nearby, *kyūdō* behavior in harmony with others nearby in the social division of labor, and human capital accumulation specific to groups organized by others nearby. The fusion and synergy of all these cultural traits had been synthesized into a coherent system of Tokugawa culture. Let us first take a look at the birth and development of individual traits in the system of Tokugawa culture. The discussion about the various difficulties in the fusion of this traditional culture with Occidental culture and in the introduction of Occidental institutions will be the main theme of this chapter.

7.1.1 Trust-Based Society with Others Nearby

In the Tokugawa era, the trust level was radically enhanced through the development and dissemination of moral codes, consistent with the progress of the social division of labor. The pursuit of new moral codes was carried out in various dimensions.

The central government was enthusiastic about the role of the new Confucianism. In particular, it was expected that the concept of the logic of heaven could be an effective guideline for the governance system of the *bakufu*. The study of Confucianism provided the samurai class with the basic conceptual framework of thought and a common tool of communication and sophisticated their belief and value systems. Shintoism that emphasizes present-day benefits and was compatible with the concept of heaven was reevaluated by the Confucians, and the synthesis of Confucianism and

Shintoism was energetically attempted. Buddhist temples, assigned by the *bakufu* the administrative role of the registering of the three classes other than the samurai, came to share the position of end organization of the government, and, in spite of severe criticism from Confucians, retained influence on the deep psychology and world-view of individuals. The interaction and harmonization of Buddhism, Shintoism and new Confucianism resulted in the unintended synthesis of thought regarding the pursuit of moral codes, leading to the standardization of conduct in the society. Small groups of individuals, emanating from the imaginary interaction in the process of Buddhist transmigration, were combined gradually and increasingly tightly by chain relationships. The so-called popular ethic, developed by private intellectual leaders, spread concrete moral codes such as honesty, diligence and economy, and clarified the efficiency implications of the social division of labor.

The sense of holding common moral codes reduced information asymmetry within a group organized by others nearby and, through the chain relationship of groups, enhanced the trust levels of society. The dissemination of new moral codes and the standardization of conduct had an enormous influence on the alleviation of information asymmetry in the economy, bringing about the fall of interest rates, and hence the reduction of transaction costs. Commerce-based economic growth through the coordination of small producers was realized, probably as a largely unintended consequence of the pursuit of moral codes.

7.1.2 Stakeholder Society and Human Capital

The *kyūdō* principle, born in the thirteenth century and that gave dynamism to medieval culture and society, was radically reconstrued during the Tokugawa era in the framework of the social division of labor and the market economy, rather than as a precept for the isolated individual pursuit of religious salvation. In other words, in the system of Tokugawa culture, the *kyūdō* principle was reconfirmed in its new version. In addition to seeking salvation through enlightenment at the individual level, the new *kyūdō* principle encouraged the pursuit of self-realization in the context of the social level; confirmation of one's role in society and contribution to the social division of labor.

It is worth emphasizing that the religious traits of the early *kyūdō* principle during the Kamakura era and the Southern and Northern Dynasties period were largely weakened. Rather than emphasizing devotion to one's occupation in pursuit of salvation, the new version of the *kyūdō* principle aimed at self-realization by way of confirmation of one's role in society and contribution to the social division of labor. Gradually embedded in the work ethic and entrepreneurship in society, the new version of the *kyūdō* principle and hence the new standards of conduct came to be held commonly in the minds of the Japanese of Tokugawa Japan.[1]

In a nutshell, during the Tokugawa era, the *kyūdō* principle was radically converted into the harmonization of itself with the interaction with other human beings as well as other creatures in this world, so that not only harmony and collaboration with other people nearby but also living things in nature was respected from the viewpoint of the pursuit of the true structure of the world of Buddhism. The notion of coexistence with nature or with fellow creatures was embedded in the cultural framework of the Tokugawa era. The economy of Tokugawa Japan is well-known as a coherent recycling society, reusing every redundant and residual product as a resource and minimizing the volume of waste from human activities. This concept was inherited from the worship of nature in Shintoism and converted into an ethical code under the strong influence of the concept of the universal potentiality of Buddhahood.

The harmonious *kyūdō* principle resulted in the cooperative accumulation of human capital within a group of others nearby. Moreover, the severe restriction on labor mobility during the period due to the closed *han* system and *shokubun* regulation induced individuals to resort to the utilization of group-based activities in market behavior. Individuals were motivated to be involved in investment in skills useful for the groups they belonged to, so that in this system people tended to have group-specific skills as property in the form of human capital, that could lose value outside the group.

The origin of the stakeholder society of Japan lay in the human capital accumulated in this way. While the establishment of private property rights for the sake of the proper functioning of the market system required the allotment of group property to individual constituents, the allotment required that properties be divisible without incurring much cost. As discussed in detail in the comparative framework between England and Japan in the next chapter, in a country like England, with a well-developed labor market, human capital was considered to embody mainly general skills, which were marketable, while in a country like Tokugawa Japan where the labor market was severely underdeveloped, human capital was composed of group-specific skills, which would lose most of their value outside the group. In Japan, there would be significant resistance to the division of group property. In England, the division of property did not encounter any serious difficulties, and there would be the smooth establishment of private property rights.

The division and allotment encountered serious difficulties in Japan where significant part of the property is composed of group-specific human capital, so that the

[1] Small producers pursued actively adaptation to the market through the choice of new commodities and new technology as well as the progress of the social and regional division of labor through coordination with wholesalers and through new forms of management such as efficient allocation of time in family farming. In this process, the new *kyūdō* principle was gradually embedded into the work ethic and entrepreneurship in the framework of rational maximizing behavior of small producers and farmers. The popular ethics, developed in the Tokugawa era, that emphasized self-training and self-cultivation of one's mind, opened up a small spiritual world for each occupation group and motivated individuals to seek ways to harmonize their own small worlds within the framework of the social division of labor.

group assets were held as the common property of the stakeholders. This is the main reason why society in Tokugawa Japan developed into a collection of stakeholder societies. This characteristic of Tokugawa society exerted considerable influence on the institutional development of Japan after the Meiji Restoration, especially regarding the role of the *ie* system and the village community.[2]

7.2 Cultural Strategy in the Prewar Period

Around the 1880s, the Meiji leaders who, under the leadership of Itō Hirobumi (1841–1909) and Yamagata Aritomo (1838–1922), came to have some confidence in the progress of the urgent task to construct a wealthy state with strong military power and to see a bright future course for the country. However, they faced another problem of how to maintain a society with high cultural and moral attainment in the past in tandem with the building up of the economy and military. In fact, this is the main difficulty that awaited the leaders, who were trying to establish a new country.

Tokugawa society with its high level of trust in the reliability of others and the easy availability of cooperation was a product of human relationships based on the chain relationship of small groups composed of others nearby. Although it was a harmonious and comfortable society, the maintenance of that society was not an easy matter for Japan once it embarked on the harsh circumstances of international competition. It was urgently needed to establish a society in which individuals had a broader view of society beyond others nearby in their worldview, and a competitive market economy with established private property rights.

The leaders of Meiji Japan, mainly composed of ex-samurai, were proud of the attainment of Tokugawa culture, which was established at least partly owing to the leadership of the samurai class. The political faction, called *hanbatsu* power,[3] in the early Meiji period, composed of the low-ranking samurai of major *han*, Satsuma (Shimazu-*han*) and Chōshū (Mōri-*han*),[4] that won the civil war to overthrow the Tokugawa *bakufu*, made every effort to preserve the culture. Both Itō Hirobumi and Yamagata Aritomo were low-ranking samurai of Chōshū. They felt responsibility to

---

[2]It must be noted, however, that this characteristic of group assets is concerned with group-specific human capital. With respect to non-human capital, the conditions for the development of the asset market became increasingly satisfied. Most important was the establishment of the land holding right toward the latter part of the Tokugawa era. As discussed in Chapter 2, owing to the development of the de facto landlord system, small farmers came to obtain a residual control right in the land they cultivated, which had been held by villages previously, and became the perfect owner of the land. Private ownership of land was legally authorized by the promulgation of *Chiso-kaisei-ho* in 1873 after the Meiji Restoration. It must also be noted that, not only did the nature as stakeholder society in group activity remain long afterward in Japanese society, with respect to communities such as villages, but there also remained the persistent tradition of accumulation of community-specific skills, partly owing to the *i.e* system maintained after the Meiji Restoration. This will be referred to again below.

[3]*Batsu* means clique like the term *zaibatsu*.

[4]Sometimes Tosa (Kōchi) and Hizen (Saga) were included.

maintain the two major cultural traits—a trust-based society with others nearby and a stakeholder society composed of human capital nurtured by the *kyūdō* principle. Let us discuss the issue of a trust-based society with others nearby first. The issue of human capital and a stakeholder society will be discussed in Sects. 7.2.4 and 7.2.5.

7.2.1 Society Composed of Others Nearby and the Concept of the Public

Itō, who was the first prime minister of Japan during 1885–88 and played a leading role in the promulgation of the Meiji constitution, wrote an impressive article about the high standards of morality, nurtured in samurai tradition and enforced in the everyday life of the educated. He contended that this high standard of morality was a result of 'an education which aspired to the attainment of Stoic heroism, a rustic simplicity and a self-sacrificing sprit unsurpassed in Sparta, and the aesthetic culture and intellectual refinement of Athens. Art, delicacy of sentiment, higher ideals of morality and of philosophy, as well as the highest types of valour and chivalry—all these we have tried to combine in the man as he ought to be' (Itō 1910). This article, probably written with a feeling of exaltation after the victory in the war against Russia in 1905, is an expression of the pride held by the typical ex-samurai after the Meiji Restoration.[5]

However, although the leaders were confident about the value of education and cultural traits related to the *kyūdō* principle, as well as the attainment of a society filled with trust, they seem to have been increasingly skeptical about whether and how they could inherit the concept of the society composed of others nearby. As we have discussed in Chapter 1, there certainly was a gradual and long-term change in the internalized part of culture and mental models of individuals to recognize the limitation of the traditional Buddhist worldview based on others nearby, and to seek a broader view of society during the Tokugawa era. Nevertheless, the Meiji leaders noticed that there still remained a significant distance between the Occidental notion of 'the public', or human beings as a whole, and the concept of society composed of chain relationships among groups of others nearby in Japan. In the same article, Itō confessed two deficiencies in the attainment of Tokugawa Japan. The first was the lack of 'the technical and materialistic side of modern civilization' in the sense of the underdevelopment of industrial technology. The second was the absence of 'modern ideas of public and political life'. Although Itō considered that resolving the second deficiency of Japan was mainly the task of the education of the masses of rural population, who were under the influence of the elites, it was increasingly recognized by the Meiji leaders that the issue of how to incorporate the concept of

[5] Ito was assassinated in Korea one year before the publication of the article.

the public in Japanese culture was a fundamental issue, one related to the differences in cultural traditions between the Occident and Japan.[6]

We believe that, from the viewpoint of our model based on the internalized culture, the process of constructing a political system in Japan by the Meiji leaders could be regarded as an attempt to introduce a mechanism to facilitate collective behavior as a surrogate for the concept of the public in Japan. The Meiji leaders tried to accomplish the introduction of this surrogate by two mechanisms. The first was concerned with the mechanism related to how to summarize the opinions of the private sector and mobilize them in national projects. Although this issue aroused heated discussion about the social contract theory among Meiji intellectuals, from the hindsight of a historian, we can say that it was resolved by introducing a mechanism to represent regional interests in political decision-making through mobilizing regional leaders, so-called *meibōka* (men of repute). The second mechanism was related to how to establish centripetality and 'national spirits' toward collective intentionality in the nation. This difficulty was considered to be more serious than the first, not only by Itō but also by other major leaders of Japan in charge of constructing the basic framework of the new Japan. This was because how to integrate the spirits of the nation was a task of the most urgency for Meiji Japan, given the immediate military threat of the world powers.

7.2.2 Interface with the Private Sector and the Meibōka

Let us examine the first mechanism of summarizing the opinion of the private sector related to the introduction of the concept of the public. It is convenient to begin with the issue of the rise and fall of the movement of natural rights and social contract theory introduced from the Occident.

---

[6]While Japan had made enormous efforts to introduce the concept of the public after the Meiji Restoration, it must be noted that it was not an easy matter even in the Western world, as is evidenced by the long-lasting debate over the adequacy of utilitarianism as a theory to summarize the political stance of the public or of the private sector vis-à-vis the government. The thinkers of social contract theory during the seventeenth and eighteenth centuries were not confident in the capability of the masses in arriving at an adequate solution to the issue of the initial social contract. Thus, Thomas Hobbes assumed that it was necessary for every participant to abandon natural rights to a neutral third person, and Jean Jacques Rousseau considered that initial legislation by an eminent legislator with superior intelligence was a prerequisite for the successful social contract. More recently, the controversy between the libertarians like John Rawls who denies unencumbered self and freedom for choice and communitarians like Michael Sandel who emphasizes the encumbered identity by ethnic, family-related, religious and moral obligations clearly shows the difficulties in the establishment of the concept of the public. If we believe that the self of men is established when their position about good in the moral space is established, what is good should be a central issue to be resolved by moral theory. As is contended by Taylor (1989), however, modern moral theory tried to avoid the issue about the good as much as possible and, instead, tried to emphasize procedural justifiability. Rawls' theory developed the criterion of justice by starting only with a 'thin theory of the good' (Taylor 1989, p. 89).

Acute skepticism about the adequacy of the Japanese concept of a society composed of chain relationship of groups organized by others nearby was aroused when the social contract theory, based on the concept of natural law (*tenpu-jinken-ron*), of thinkers such as Hobbes, Locke and Rousseau was introduced by the semi-official think-tank, *Meiroku-sha*, established in 1873, and by other pioneering thinkers such as Fukuzawa Yukichi, Ueki Emori, Tokutomi Sohō and Kotoku Shūsui. Against the background of their influence, the League for Establishing a National Assembly (*kokkai-kisei-dōmei*)[7] was established in 1880, and thereafter the so-called Freedom and People's Rights (*jiyū-minken*) Movement spread rapidly nationwide. According to Irokawa (1998), in Japan around this period, there were over a thousand spontaneous groups related to the movement, for the purpose of studying the theory on the rights of the people.

The main aim and demand of the movement was, through abolishing the despotic politics of members of the winning *han*, so-called *hanbatsu* politics, to assure the right of participation in political decision-making by the ruled masses and the establishment of a parliamentary system. The response was the imperial edict of 1881 for establishing the Diet and enacting the constitution in 1890. It is well documented that after the announcement of the imperial edict, the national enthusiasm for the Freedom and People's Rights Movement suddenly abated. Moreover, the feverish atmosphere to study the theory of human rights also abruptly fell away.

Why did not only the political movement itself but also the study of the theory of human rights became inactive in such a short period? There are various views about the reason for this abrupt decline in enthusiasm. Especially important was the assertion based on the Confucian background of the absorption of Occidental thought. Uete (1974) and Ishida (1976) present an explanation from the viewpoint of the fragility of the Confucian basis of education during the Tokugawa period. Since Confucianism emphasized the relationship-based rules of morality, it failed to identify the importance of independent individuality, and this resulted in the neglect of the positive and active attitude toward the social order, consequently encouraging the adaptive approach to the 'given' rules that govern not only natural phenomena but also social orders. It is concluded that, in this Confucian way of thinking, there is no room to accept the idea to construct new social order based on human rights by means of a social contract among independent individuals. This explanation seems to be dependent on the assumption that the education of the samurai by use of Confucian literature had controlled the entire thinking of the ex-samurai class and participants in the movement.[8] To disprove the explanation of Uete and Ishida, one need only

[7]The origin of this league was the Proposal to Establish a National Assembly (*minsen-giinn-seturitsu-kennpakush*) written by the vice-ministers, Taisuke Itagaki and Shinpei Etō, who proposed sending a military expedition to Korea in 1874.

[8]Miyagi (1987) criticized Uete and Ishida on the ground that Japan had a tradition of spiritualism that asserts the infinite possibility of human mind. Although she ascribes the tradition to Confucianism, referring to the influence of Confucians like Satō Issai and Yokoi Shōnan, it seems to be more pertinent to believe that the spiritualism of low-class ex-samurai and large landlords and merchants that participated in the Freedom and People's Right Movement was based on a broader cultural background including *kyūdō* behavior derived from Buddhism.

ask why, if their explanation is correct, the same samurai dared to overthrow the Tokugawa regime and establish a new government?[9] We have already discussed in detail in the previous chapters that the inapplicability of Confucianism with regard to practical political thought was already noticed by Ogyū Sorai and others.

We believe that an explanation for the abrupt falling away of the movement lay in the rise of the emergent sense of the necessity to enhance 'national spirits' in preparation for the anticipated intensification of international tension. It seems that there occurred a change in attitude toward a more positive and aggressive stance, that accompanied the introduction of the concept of *kokutai* as an artificially contrived institution to replace the traditional worldview based on others nearby. It was ambitious to work on the internalized part of culture, however. It was too difficult to accomplish, even if we admit it was implemented as a result of a decision based on bounded rationality. Let us deliberate on these points and investigate further the implication of our model of internalized culture.

As Tailor (1989) points out, the rise of social contract theory can be understood in light of the shift of the Occidental moral theory to procedural justification. Instead of defining the legitimacy of the social order by some conception of 'good society', the theory defined the legitimacy by the procedure of its inauguration (p. 86).[10] For the Japanese in the early Meiji period, however, what was most urgently needed was not the legitimacy of procedures, but the legitimacy of a society established on the sovereignty of citizens or of the answer to the question whether the sovereignty of citizens could be justified or not. While many of the advocates of the Freedom and People's Right Movement asserted the co-sovereignty of citizens and the monarch (Irokawa 1998), Nakae Chōmin asserted co-sovereignty as a preliminary step to the ultimate popular sovereignty, and Itō Hirobumi came to be confirmed in his conviction of the necessity of a constitutional monarchy system (Ida 1979). With intensified international tension during the 1880s, the national interest came to have priority over the rights of people. Moreover, as is emphasized in Barshay (2004), the government increasingly acquired confidence in the potential power of traditional institutions and cultures. As a consequence, the concerns over the hasty import of the Western system by means of a shift to popular sovereignty waned, so that during

[9]Their misunderstanding might be due to the argument developed in Maruyama (1960). Maruyama argued that, while during the Tokugawa era loyalty to principle was merged with loyalty to organizations, for the samurais who established the Meiji government, the former was separated from the latter, and loyalty to principle was more important than loyalty to organizations. In deriving this proposition, Maruyama quoted loyalty to the concept of heaven, which was a genuine Confucian concept for Maruyama or construed as a Confucian concept by the followers of Maruyama. However, as is correctly pointed out by Bitō (1994),the expression of 'to live following the concept of Heaven' during this period had already lost the rigorous Confucian meaning, and should be construed as a statement to express the simple resolution to lead one's life following one's own belief.

[10]This property of the social contract theory induced Hiroyuki Katō, one of the members of Meirokusha, to abandon the social contract theory and to shift to the evolutionary theory of H. Spenser. Tanaka (1993) condemns Katō for being unable to understand that the construction of the fiction that, in the far away past, people gathered together to draw up a social contract, was a necessary theoretical model to depict actual historical experience in England, which Hobbes and Locke witnessed.

the 1880s the government began to seek a more practical way to accommodate the interests of the private sector, not the rights of people asserted in the movement, within the confines of the constitutional monarchy system.

It must be noted that, for the Meiji leaders, the reason for the adoption of a constitutional monarchy and the denial of sovereignty of citizens was closely related to the policy of mobilizing 'national spirits' in preparation for the intensification of international tension, that accompanied the introduction of the concept of the *kokutai*. Both the *meibōka* system as a method of summarizing and mobilizing the opinion of the private sector and the enhancement of the sense of national integrity by the concept of the *kokutai* are related to the anxiety that Japanese society, based on the chain relationship of others nearby, might have an innate weakness compared with Occidental societies based on the concept of the public. Such anxiety was most strong among the Meiji leaders who were acquainted with the fortunes of China after its defeat in the Opium wars. It may not be an exaggeration to believe that the leaders of Meiji Japan tried to introduce the surrogate of the concept of the public to Japan. For that purpose, the concept of the *kokutai* was introduced from above to enhance 'national spirits' and the *meibōka* system was assigned the role to support the *kokutai* from below.

The solution to the issue of the representation of the private sector by means of mobilizing regional leaders, the so-called *meibōka* (men of repute), emerged from the intensification of conflict among regional interests and from the dissatisfaction with political power monopolized by the *hanbatsu* powers (Satsuma and Chōshū politicians), leading powers that defeated the Tokugawa regime.

Almost concomitant with the change in the stance of the central government, and as the year 1890 approached, when the Diet was promised to be opened, there emerged a significant move actively to express regional interests. A fundamental reason for this was the grave concerns about the widening of regional difference in economic development. A variety of policies and economic changes pertained to this. After around 1887, the first boom in establishing new enterprises began, centering on cotton spinning, giving rise to industrialized regions in various parts of the Japanese archipelago. There occurred intense competition for inaugurating railway services among regions around 1890. Moreover, in 1888 there erupted a political struggle between the Ministry of the Internal Affairs and the Ministry of Agriculture and Commerce about the sale of officially held forests to subsidize the municipal budget. The Minister of Finance, Matsukata Masayoshi, announced his plan to establish development banks, including regional agricultural banks, in 1890.

All these movements accompanied the participation of regional economic leaders, *meibōka* (men of repute), in collaboration with political parties, in resisting the policy by bureaucrats delegated from the central government. As is vividly described in Ariizumi (1980), Yamanashi prefecture, a leading silk-producing prefecture, entered into fierce competition with rival prefectures such as Nagano and Gunma. The *meibōka* led the political struggle against the national government in pursuit of favorable policies for the prefecture, especially inviting the railway. Driven by the fear that Yamanashi might be left behind competitors, the *meiboka* of Yamanashi resisted the policy of the prefectural governor, representing the interests of the central government, in collaboration with political parties and the *hanbatsu* power. Through this process, a nationwide informal system of interfaces between central government and the regional private sector emerged and was embedded as a bridge between the traditional concept of others nearby and the concept of the public. In the prewar system, the interface, composed of regional communities led by the *meibōka*, played an important role as intermediate organizations to mediate between regional and national interests (Teranishi 2005).

In the Occident, the difficulty about the incorporation of the concept of the public to politics lay in the diversity of value systems among individuals. On the one hand, the affirmation of the ordinary life after the religious reformation brought about a tendency to reject good of high dimension such as universal justice and universal benevolence and respect good related to the ordinary life such as diligence and honesty. Such an attitude was believed as an emancipation from repressions that prevailed before the reformation. On the other hand, the individualism that respects individual commitment enhanced the notion to regard freedom as the independence of individuals, each individual has the freedom to determine his objective by himself without external constraints. These circumstances invited the diversity of concepts of 'good' in society. To take account of the diverse concepts of 'good' and to avoid conflicts between the various concepts of 'good', procedural justification was chosen (Taylor 1989). In Japan, the diversity of the concepts of good was not a serious problem owing to the standardization of conduct during the Tokugawa era that accompanied the standardization of the value system. The political leaders after the Meiji Restoration were anxious to preserve the homogeneity of the value system and, in particular, to protect the traditional moral and social codes from the influence of socialism. The interface led by the *meibōka* was important for this purpose. While, under the system of the *meibōka* leadership, human relationships composed of the chain relationship among groups organized by others nearby are maintained, it was expected that the diversity of interests that could not be represented by the national Diet system could be absorbed by the *meibōka* system and reflected in central government politics, consequently maintaining the standardized value system in society.

The *meibōka* were wealthy merchants and landlords who became regional leaders. Many of them participated in the Freedom and People's Rights Movement during the 1870s and 1880s, and thereafter became absentee landlords, portfolio investors, or managers of commercial and industrial corporations in each region. They fulfilled three kinds of function: maintaining rural order, participating in political parties and managing local industrial activity.[11]

The *meibōka* collaborated with the government in reorganizing rural communities and were also in charge of maintaining rural order. High-ranking officials in regional governments, such as prefectural governors, were designated and dispatched by the central government, and were under the control of the Ministry of Internal

[11] It was rare that one particular *meibōka* played all three roles at the same time, though an individual might play different roles at different time.

Affairs. Under such high-ranking officials, many *meibōka* took on leadership in local governance as directors of governmental organizations, and heads of agricultural and industrial associations. Moreover, under the leadership of the *meibōka*, cultivating landlords in villages and large owner-farmers became administrators in city and town halls. And, thus, they were involved in administration and decision-making in local government and, at the same time, played the role to bridge regional interests to central government through political parties.

National political leaders regarded cities, towns, and villages led by the *meibōka* as intermediate organizations to bridge regional cum private interests and the central government policy. This could be exemplified by the management policy of the constituency system (Mitani 1995). Before 1900, a small constituency system had been used for Diet elections, with 214 one-person districts and 43 two-person districts, for a total 300 members. This system had been recommended by Yamagata Aritomo, who considered small districts suitable to represent people's demand adequately and to represent regional differences in the absence of national-level political parties. After 1900, however, constituencies were based on a large district system, reflecting the growth of national-level political parties. The system was expected to induce top-level *meibōka* at the national level to lead the maintenance of the social order, partly in preparation for war on the continent, and thus to promote the development of national-level political parties.

After victory in the war against Russia in 1905, the people's concern for national interests, which had been based on international tension, weakened, and demand for regional interests intensified. Against the rise of liberalism, *Taishō* democracy, the influence of the *meibōka* at national level on the social order was weakened and the political structure became diversified. Hara Takashi (1856–1921) was particularly concerned about the penetration of socialist ideology and sought ways to stem socialist influence and to revive the traditional role of the *meibōka* in regional governance. In his words, by introducing a small constituency system, Hara intended to expand the political value of the status of renown (*ichi-meibō*) to cope with the tendency in which the ideological symbols of socialism acquired political value. After the war against Russia, the administrative role of towns and villages increased, leading to an increase in the budget size of towns and villages accompanied by the delegation of administrative members from the central government. Hara tried to enhance the position and capability of the heads of towns and villages. By inducing the retired heads of towns and villages to participate in political parties, he aimed to establish a national political system based on renown in regional society. In other words, Hara aimed at establishing a political system in which the value system nurtured in well-managed regional society was respected in the politics related to the public. The new constituency system, with one-or-two person districts for a total of 450 diet members,[12] was promulgated in 1919, manifesting Hara's desire to make towns and villages the core political intermediate organizations based on regional economies.

[12]The total number of Diet member increased over time owing to the increase of the population and to the relaxing of the qualification of eligible voters. See Teranishi (2011, pp. 86–919) for statistical data and more detailed explanation.

7.2.3 Centripetality and 'National Spirits'

The first issue of the mechanism related to the surrogate for the concept of the public, how to summarize the opinion of the private sector, was resolved by introducing a system to represent regional interests in political decision-making by means of an interface between the central government and regions led by the *meibōka* as intermediate organizations. The second mechanism, regarding the issue of how to enhance the motivation of the nation, was considered to be more serious because the issue was related to how to raise 'national spirits' in the face of the military threat of international powers. It is argued below that the excessive concern about this issue by the Meiji leaders resulted in the introduction of the concept of the *kokutai* (national polity) as the foundation of the state, and the tendency toward the nationalism of Japan.

Behind the anxiety held by the leaders of Meiji Japan was the perception that the power of the Occidental countries was rooted to a considerable degree in the notion of the omnipotent God in Occidental cultural traditions. The omnipotent God provided Occidental states with the incentives to serve the welfare of the public or human beings, the most supreme creation by God. Thus, for the Puritan, profane asceticism was rooted in the desire to live for the sake of the glory of God. For Robert Bacon, passionate devotion to scientific research was for the purpose of enhancing the glory of God, through revealing the truth of creation. For John Locke, God's will lay in the preservation of human beings.

The chief figure for the design of the Meiji Constitution, Itō Hirobumi, emphasized the necessity to make the imperial court the spiritual and cultural foundation of Japan, claiming that, since the power of religion (Buddhism and Shintoism) was not strong enough in Japan compared with the power of Christianity in the Occident, it was necessary to make the imperial house the foundation of the state. Itō seems to have become convinced by this proposition by 1888, when he explained the draft of the constitution to a meeting of the Privy Council (Shimizu 1940, pp. 88–89; Maruyama 1961, p. 29).[13] It is important to note that the concept of the foundation of the state, the so-called *kokutai*, as a guide for the spirit of the nation was introduced by Itō regarding the difference of the position of religion in Japan in comparison with Europe. Itō deplored the lack of 'modern ideas of public and political life' among the masses or the ordinary citizens of Japan, expressed deep concern about the necessity to 'extend their vision beyond the pale of the village communities' and to lead them to 'interest themselves in the affairs of state and nation as strongly as, or even more strongly than, in the affairs of their own villages' (Itō 1910). It seems to be safe to say that Itō introduced the concept of the *kokutai* as a substitute for the notion of the public or human beings in the will of the omnipotent god in Christianity and to enhance the interest of ordinary citizens in national affairs beyond others nearby in their native community. However, it is important to note that, when Itō introduced the

[13] Around 1884, Ito did not admit the necessity to have a concept about the special foundation of the state in Japan. See the controversy between Kaneko Kentarō and Itō Hirobumi about the necessity of the *kokutai* in Japan (Hashikawa 1975).

concept of the *kokutai* as a substitute for the concept for 'public and political life', he had largely forgotten the welfare aspect of the concept, and emphasis was laid on nationalism, in the sense of enhancing the loyalty to the state and the centripetalism of the nation.[14] The concept of the *kokutai* was contrived as a fiction to enhance 'national spirits', out of the grave concerns of Itō and other Meiji leaders.

In the constitutional monarchy system of the Meiji constitution promulgated in 1889, in which the country was governed by the emperor who inherited the position from the age of myth and continued to inherit it through all eternity, the *kokutai* came to be defined as the fundamental system (*kijiku*) for the governance system of the state. At the same time, the Imperial Rescript on Education, promulgated the next year, stipulated that the *kokutai* comprised the fundamental doctrine of education, in which the emperor functioned as the moral leader of the country. Moreover, Shintoism was embedded in the governance system and was converted into so-called national Shintoism, in which the emperor was regarded as a god comparable to the position of God in Christianity

However, whether the concept of the foundation of the state, or the *kokutai*, had a persuasive influence on the thinking of Japanese citizens is not certain. We will assert that citizens, both elites and non-elites, accepted the intention of the Meiji leaders with a calm judgement and only as a guide to behavior, following the principle of bounded rationality. Moreover, it is contended that excessive concern by Itō and other leaders for the necessity to instill the notion of the public resulted in a serious defect in the Meiji constitution.

As is emphasized by White (1978, p. 236) and Mokyr (2017, p. 136), the concept of time in the culture of progress in the Occident based on Christianity was linear, extending in a straight line from the time of the beginning to the end of the world, while the concept of time in Japan was either cyclical in the Buddhist thinking or infinite with no beginning and end point in Shintoism (Kato 2016). In the Buddhist sense, it suffices to behave with horizon concern for the near future and in the sense of Shintoism it is impossible to think about the future and form a rational expectation about the whole future. It seems that the decision to shift to Occidental culture was done within a bounded rational model with limited time horizon, which was a natural concept from the religious tradition of Japan, and a serious imperfection of information and knowledge in the sense of Harbert Simon (Sent 1998). For the Japanese immediately after the Meiji Restoration, the optimal choice, given the significant uncertainly in the future of the country, was to follow the recommendation of the Meiji leaders to accept the fiction of the *kokutai*. For the Japanese after the defeat in World War II, it was optimal and rational to follow the instructions of the occupying forces and progressive intellectuals and tentatively move away from traditional culture, and not to think about the consequences into the indefinite future. Nevertheless, as North (1990) contends, culture was so persistent that 'the Japanese culture survived the US occupation after World War II' (p. 36).

[14]In the Meiji constitution, there were a couple articles that referred to the concept of the public (*kōkyō*), but most of them seemed to be related to social security, and the word related to welfare, for example article 9, is expressed as the happiness of the subject (*shinmin no kōfuku*).

7.2.3.1 The Maruyama Hypothesis

Maruyama Masao was a leading progressive advocate of Japan after World War II, who asserted that the overwhelming influence of the concept of the *kokutai* on politics, society and spirits in prewar Japan fulfilled the role to militarize Japan and led the country into imperialism.

Maruyama claimed that the political system based on the concept of the *kokutai* could be summarized as a patriarchal state, in which the emperor as a family head controlled every aspect of the functioning of the state with supreme power. It is contended that prewar Japanese society and polity can be conceived of as composed of numerous triangles with structures similar to the patriarchal state and with differing sizes: the largest is the state and the smallest is a family of a citizen. At the top, the rational bureaucratic system was at work and, at the bottom, was the irrational favoritism and patrimonial relationships of village communities. Between the top and the bottom, there occurred infinite round-trip interactions and, through the interactions, both strengthened each other. It is asserted that this system controlled Japanese society with enormous power. This was because the emperor, as the core of the state, became the omnipotent spiritual core of the nation, comparable to God in Occidental Christianity (Maruyama 1961), so that, as a consequence, the state came to be equipped with a criterion for the justification of its functioning built-in within its organization. Further, Maruyama claimed that society as the composition of numerous similar triangles with varying sizes emerged from the concept of the *kokutai* for three reasons. First is the characteristic of the Japanese cultural tradition, in which various concepts and theories are imported from abroad without adequate ordering through examination in depth. This characteristic is called the tradition of neglecting the structure of thought (*mukōzō*) or the mixed residence of spirits (*seisin no zakkyo*) in Maruyama (1961). While in Occidental society, Christianity played a role of the spiritual standard to choose and order new theories in the theoretical structure of its own, Japanese religions never tried to confront new foreign religions and revitalize themselves through the process. This tradition resulted in the attitude to judge the quality of new theories simply by the standard of similarity with existing ones (Maruyama 1961, p. 16). As a second reason, Maruyama points to the structure of the rural community in prewar Japan, in which individuality was severely repressed. In the traditional village community, there was a tendency to avoid bringing into focus the process of reaching decisions, the conflicts in interests among members. Further, the exercise of power was quite often mixed with granting benevolence. It is claimed that these characteristics of village society converted villages into end-point cells of the *kokutai* system. The third reason was the strong influence of the vertical value based on the concept of the infinity of the inheritance of the emperor position (Maruyama 1956). The notion that the emperor system was inherited from the age of myth to the future indefinitely exerted significant power on efficiency through coercing loyalty to various duties of subjects. It is asserted that the vertical axis of the inheritance of the emperor system with the infinite length that penetrates concentric circles of contemporary Japanese society, horizontally extended, dominated the functioning of contemporary Japan with an overwhelming power.

In summary, Maruyama claimed that the patriarchal and repressive emperor system based on the *kokutai* concept was accepted in prewar society because of the traditions of the mixed residence of spirits, the convention of the village community as suppressive of individuality, and the substantial influence exerted by the power emanating from the long-term history of the emperor inheritance. Maruyama's reasoning, however, is full of make-believe proof and impression manipulations, and is not logical enough. Among the three reasons he gives, the second reason invoked the criticism of many historians of mass movements. Referring to the experience of the Chichibu Commune movement in the early Meiji period, Irokawa (1970) pointed out the strong individuality and initiatives in social movements, criticizing Maruyama's assertion about the passiveness of the village community.[15] Yasumaru (1974) emphasized the fundamental progressiveness of farmers' behavior in innovating their lifestyles and rural conventions after the latter half of the Tokugawa era. If Maruyama accepted these criticisms, it would be difficult to assert the development of triangles throughout the entire rural society. Further, one of the more serious defects is that it is hard to understand that why similar triangles have been reproduced in Japanese society due to the introduction of the concept of the *kokutai*. Maruyama seems to try to ascribe it to the tradition of the mixed residence of the spirits, but he did not explain the mechanism. If he intended to claim that the conception of the *kokutai* was admitted as easily as other imported theories following the tradition of mixed residence, it contradicts his assertion of the overwhelming influence of the *kokutai* on prewar Japanese society. Why was the new theory of the *kokutai* accepted as so easily exerting such a serious impact on the lives of people? The third reason, asserting the influence of the longevity of the inheritance of the emperor tradition on the incentive structure of contemporary people, is not convincing either. Why should the length of the tradition enhance the incentive of people? His explanation that the infinity of the value is guaranteed (*tanpo sareru*) by the infinity of the length of time of the history of the emperor system is too difficult to understand.

7.2.3.2 Response of the Citizens and Behavior Based on Bounded Rationality

In order to understand how Itō and other Meiji leaders tried to instill the concept of the *kukutai*, which they contrived as a fiction, into citizens as the fundamental of the state, the hypothesis of Tsurumi (1982) is useful. Tsurumi asserted that the instillation was implemented by use of different methods for the elites and non-elites. For non-elites with an education at elementary school and in the military drafting system, the sovereignty of the emperor and the worldview based on myth related to the ancestors of the emperor were taught as truths, which must be respected unconditionally and obeyed by all citizens. For elites, with an education at school-and college-level that took Europe as a model, the fictional aspect of the concept was explicitly taught.

[15] Yasumaru (2012) points out that Maruyama considers the behavior of farmers in a social movement only as an irregular and unusual act on impulse.

Moreover, it was taught that the fiction was needed as a basis for the catch-up policy of increasing the wealth and strengthening the military power of the state through introducing advanced technological civilization. Tsurumi explains this difference in teaching about the *kokutai* as exoteric teaching to non-elite and esoteric teaching to elite, quoting the concept of *Shingon-mikkyō* of Kūkai.

Tsurumi's explanation of the method for the instillation of the *kokutai* concept seems to be highly useful in understanding the intention of the *kokutai* policy in prewar Japan. Maruyama and others, who emphasized the deficiencies and cruelty of the prewar policy, should have considered that the policy had been highly effective in converting citizens into loyal children of the emperor and driving them into the desperate war. However, it must be noted that Itō and others have introduced the concept of and education about the *kokutai* as a temporary and emergency measure to cope with the underdevelopment of the intellectual level of non-elite citizens. However, since the elite was taught the true story, it is natural to believe that the true story eventually came to be known by the non-elite. As not a few researchers such as Nakamura and Hashimoto wrote, many Japanese, at least after they had grown up, were aware that the metaphor of the emperor in myth related to Shintoism, as the equivalent to God in Christianity, was an artificial construct for nationalistic propaganda (Nakamura 2015, vol. 2, p. 131; Hashikawa 1975). Nevertheless, they considered that accepting the precept of the fiction was needed to enhance the motivation of the nation to be engaged in the policy of increasing wealth and military power. This is nothing but a decision and behavioral pattern based on bounded rationality by the people in the cultural tradition of infinitely extending or cyclically repeating time, as noted above.

However, it is important to note that Tsurumi (1982) contends that, when Japan reached an impasse in the conflict over Manchuria, and the war with China after the 1930s, the exoteric version of *kokutai* swallowed the esoteric version, and not only non-elites but also elites were trapped into the unconditional acceptance of the *kokutai* theory. This was because, after around the 1930s during the Showa era, the military began to control Japanese society with intentional politics of abusing the power of the emperor.

The author is not qualified to discuss the political mechanism of the process by which the military engaged in such arrogant behavior in politics during the prewar Showa era. However, it is well known that the power of the emperor in military affairs, or the so-called supreme command (*tōsui-ken*), was excessive, inviting the uncontrollable and incorrigible behavior of the army during the Showa era before World War II. They neglected the Diet by rejecting the appointment of a Minister for the Army, quite often inviting the disfunction of democratic decision making by the Diet. Their attitude was justified by the stipulation that the military was under the direct supreme command of the emperor and was independent from civilian control.

In this regard, it is necessary to note that the anxiety of the Meiji leaders about the absence of the concept of the public in Japanese tradition had been excessive, with the consequent conferment of too much power and sovereignty to the emperor in order to deify him. The excessiveness of the anxiety of Itō and others was two-fold. First was the lack of the correct evaluation of the sources of national power of Western states.

It must have been noted that the influence of the omnipotent God of the Occident was not only concerned with nationalism through the monotheistic nature of Christianity, but also the welfare of the public and the related impact of mass production through the voluntarism based on God's will. Even if the transformation of Shintoism to monotheism could succeed in establishing the metaphor of the emperor as a supreme being comparable to an omnipotent God, it was never effective in bringing in the notion of the public, whose welfare citizens should make efforts to enhance. It was exactly this part of Christian culture that gave birth to Schumpeterian economic growth based on innovation in industrial technology and made the Occident the leader of world civilization. Second, further evidence of the excessiveness of the anxiety of Itō and others was their insufficient appreciation of the possibility of the innate tendency to enhance nationalism without the notion of an omnipotent God. This is exactly the role fulfilled by the chain relationship among groups composed of others nearby. Until the time of World War II it was customary for many Japanese who succeeded in Tokyo in business activities went back to their native towns after their retirement. The human relationships nurtured in regional culture was much more important in prewar Japan than the enjoyment of urban life. The victory of Japan in the Russo-Japanese war was due substantially to the competition among army divisions organized by each region. Soldiers fought on the battlefield for the sake of the glory of their native regions or hometowns, as is emphasized in *Saka-no-ue-no-kumo* by Shiba Ryōtarō.

It is important to note that we are not denying the grave anxiety held by Itō about the worldview of peasants, which was narrowly confined to a small village community of others nearby. Allowing for the fact that the worldview of each peasant was confined to a narrow group of neighboring acquaintances, we still believe that the chain relationship of groups could have a sufficiently broad worldview, as pointed out in Chapter 1, by the concept of changes in the internalized part of culture. Itō and others failed to perceive this side of peasant thinking. In his study of popular ethics, Yasumaru (1974) asserted the lack of concern of the rural masses about societal or state affairs, claiming they were only interested in an extremely narrow spiritual world of the 'small community in mind' (p, 80). However, at the same time, he emphasized the active and subjective attitude to renovate oneself by means of self-training and 'polishing', despite the weakness in the sense of a narrow worldview.[16] What this book want to show is that the characteristics of the mindset of the rural peasant

[16]Incidentally, this issue is closely related to the criticism by Miyagi (1987) of Uete and Ishida referred to above (n. 7). Miyagi claimed that one of the most influential leaders of Freedom and People's Right Movement, Ueki Enari, constructed his theory about a democratic free political system with the Diet by way of combining the aspiration for a free political system, latently existent in mass society, with his political theory based on spiritualism that asserted the infinite possibility of the human mind nurtured within the Confucian concept of acting in accordance with the will of eaven (*tenjin-gōitsu*). This assertion is marred by two crucial defects. First, is already pointed out, the Confucian concept of merging with Heaven is not logically consistent with spiritualism in the sense of the infinite possibility of human mind. The second defect is that she asserts the aspiration for a free political system by the masses by referring to the study on popular ethics by Yasumaru (1974) as evidence. This is simply wrong because Yasumaru clarified that there was a lack of concern by the rural masses about the affairs of society or the state.

does not necessarily imply a weakness in nationalism in a good sense, and that Itō and others had fallen into excessive pessimism in this regard, probably providing a remote source for the disastrous consequence on the nation's fortunes during the 1940s.

From the viewpoint of our model, the attempt of the Meiji leaders to introduce the surrogate mechanism of the concept of the public was an incredibly ambitious attempt that was destined to end in failure. The attempt was nothing less than to change the internalized culture developed historically from the pre-ancient age by the management of institutions such as the constitution and the Imperial Rescript of Education. With the hindsight of a historian, they should have tried to seek a way to reconcile the conflicts between two societies more cautiously; a society based on the collective behavior of individuals motivated by the concept of the public and rely on the role of institutions vs a society based on group behavior motivated by the concerns to others nearby and rely on the role of ethics. Since this difference seems to be dependent on historically nurtured internalized culture, the resolution of conflicts by means of such methods as fusion through surrogate mechanisms seems to be difficult, and this seems to be an eternal issue to be faced by societies inheriting different cultural origins. What was needed was to have a deep understanding of and respect for other cultures in order to find higher order cooperation and fusion for mutual benefits. It was a pity that the Meiji leaders were forced by the international tensions of the time to take immediate measures for establishing surrogates.

Let us return to Maruyama. He tried to show that institutional devices have actually changed the internalized culture of individuals. Many supporters of Maruyama's theory praised his 'success' in this attempt. However, it must be noted that this 'success' was brought about by following the key assumption that the main purpose of the Meiji leaders lay in the establishment of an institutional framework of a military state controlled by the emperor system. Based on this assumption, he contended that the history of prewar Japan was evidence of the perfect working of the Meiji institutions in nurturing the culture of the military state, although the military state finally collapsed in the defeat of World War II. Following the typical view of postwar progressive intellectuals, his articles have been appreciated as the most successful analysis of the failure of prewar militarism. However, our analysis is based on the assumption that the Meiji leaders tried to establish a surrogate for the Occidental culture of the public by the institutional device of the *kokutai* (national polity). While Maruyama concluded that the Meiji institutional device of the *kokutai* achieved the aim of raising military culture in Japan, our conclusion is that the goal to establish the new culture based on the concept of the Occidental notion of the public by means of the institutional device of the *kokutai* was not achieved.

7.2.4 Stakeholder Society, Human Capital and Ie

Let us move on to the second agenda of the leaders of Meiji Japan, the stakeholder society composed of human capital nurtured by the harmony-oriented *kyūdō* principle. With the underdeveloped labor market, Tokugawa Japan was a stakeholder society with the dense accumulation of group or community-specific human capital. The building up of human capital was enhanced especially by the tendency of *kyūdō* behavior. In the dawn of modern Japan after the Meiji Restoration, how to maintain the mechanism of the accumulation of human capital and how to accommodate it within the development of the market economy and establishing modern society based on individualism posed a tough problem. A society with high social trust and cooperation, as envisaged by Putnam (1993), was expected to be built up through the active participation of individuals, reciprocity among them, and a social network that coordinated the behavior of individuals. Individuals behave so as to establish a society in which the norms of good conduct are respected in society or by abstract people generally. In Tokugawa Japan, social trust and cooperation was born and strengthened through the accumulation of group and community-specific human capital. Partly because of the constraint of the underdevelopment of the labor market, each individual engaged in *kyūdō* behavior so as to realize good conduct for the group or the community to which he belonged. The pattern of good conduct was group or community specific. The sense of sharing the results of the investment in human capital, which cannot be sold in the market, nurtured social trust and cooperation in Japanese society.

7.2.4.1 Community-Specific Human Capital

At the beginning of the Meiji era, there was a huge amount of accumulated human capital specific to communities. As discussed in detail in the next chapter, the main reason for this lay in the underdevelopment of the labor market. Because of the absence of an open labor market, the incentive for investment in general skills was weak and workers invested in firm-specific skills and recovered the costs and return of investment after the growth of the firm. In the rural villages, such investments took place in technical knowledge related to water utilization and control specific to the geographical conditions of villages, in know-how related to the production and sale of the special product of villages, in skills and knowledge related to agricultural tools specific to the local soil and climate conditions, and in knowledge about human relationships in the villages. In the commercial and handicraft-producing regions, investment was undertaken in the areas of information and human relationships nurtured by long-term transaction relationships, of information and know-how in the division of labor among producing processes in the region, of knowledge about the development of new products, and of materials and intermediate goods in the region.

In these activities, human capital specific to a community was mainly accumulated in the human capital of the house head, because cooperative activities in the region were usually organized with *ie* as units, and through activity usually participated in by house heads.

7.2.4.2 Role of *ie* and Head of *ie*

The concept of community-specific human capital, which is largely accumulated in the human capital of house (*ie*) heads, has an important bearing in understanding the role of the prewar Civil Code, promulgated in 1898. The drafters of the code were faced with a difficult problem in balancing the following three issues facing Japan as it struggled to adapt to Western culture and institutions.

(1) Accommodation of the tendency of individualism towards the nuclearization of the household in the form of the independence of the parent–children relationship and the marital relationship between husband and wife from the control of house head.
(2) Enhancing the motivation for independent activity by members other than an inheritor to be involved in business and economic activities and contribute to the growth of the national economy.
(3) Maintaining *ie* as the basic unit of regional society that supported cultural traits inherited historically; high level of social trust with others nearby and a stakeholder society composed of human capital accumulated by the harmony-oriented *kyūdō* behavior.

The first requirement was satisfied by the admitting of the marital relationship, as well as parental authority and the parent–children relationship, as independent of the rights of the house head. In the Meiji Civil Code the right of the house head was only concerned with the right to consent, so that, for example, if a family member presented a written registration to the family registration section of a public office, the section could not reject the presentation, and could not invalidate the marriage. The second requirement was also satisfied by admitting property holding by children other than an inheritor. It is important to note that there is no notion of the property of the *ie* (house) in the Civil Code. As a result, many sons other than the inheritor left the house after they had grown up, and those who succeeded in business activities could become owners of property, entirely under their own control. The biographies of the prewar period are full of such anecdotes of the accumulation of private property and the contribution to capital accumulation of the country.

It is important to note that the rights of the house head were strictly regulated in the Civil Code and were far weaker than the house head of the samurai in the Tokugawa era (Muta 1996, 1999). Most important is that there is no stipulation of inheritance of house property by inheritors, who were usually eldest sons.[17] An inheritor could inherit only two things: property held by the house head (usually his father) and various rights of the house head, including the right to consent to changes in registrations and the right to designate residence. In return, the house heads were obliged to support the family members economically (Itō and Momose 1990, pp. 72–75). This is quite different from the Tokugawa feudalism system, in which all contracts were made in a relationship between the *ie* and every right and obligation was monopolized by the house head.

[17] The assertion of Ramseyer (1996, p. 82) quoted in Hayashi and Prescott (2008) is simply incorrect.

7.2.5 *Prewar Economic Growth and Culture*

7.2.5.1 Rural Sector and the Constancy of Agricultural Employment

Many Meiji leaders considered that the culture established in the rural sector comprised the core of Japanese culture and tried to preserve the lifestyle and social order of the rural sector as much as possible: the requirement (3) above. For example, Yamagata Aritomo, who studied under Yoshida Shōin together with Itō Hirobumi in his younger days and who, with the national army he established under his control became the top leader of the country,[18] was enthusiastic in maintaining the rural order composed of *ie* and led by the *meibōka*. To accomplish the modernization of the country, the development of agriculture and indigenous industries, that comprised the main economic foundation of the *meibōka* leadership, was crucially important for securing employment opportunity and foreign exchange for the country. However, sometimes more important for Yamagata than agriculture as an industry was the stability of society and, in particular, insulation from the influence of socialist thought. For this purpose, he considered the rural foundation of society as a whole as indispensable. For example, as already touched upon, Yamagata committed to the reform of the constituency system, to make the leadership of the *meibōka* effective as a prerequisite for a sound rural community. Moreover, he was most sensitive to the development of socialist movements. Under the pressure of the agricultural cooperative, the Rice Act (*beikoku-ho*) was enacted in 1921 in order to stabilize the rice price. This Act, however, was utilized to lower the rice price by the Hara cabinet (1918–1921) of Seyūkai party and the policy was taken up by the Takahashi cabinet (1921–22). The backdrop of Seiyūkai's policy stance was Yamagata's opinion to lower rice price in order to prevent social unrest caused by socialists. The low rice price was needed to reduce the living costs of urban workers despite its damage to agriculture as an industry (Miyazaki 1980). While sacrificing agriculture, Seiyūkai, instead, tried to help rural society as much as possible, and devoted enormous efforts after 1922 to assist the rural economy by way of a bill to transfer land tax revenue of central government to local governments, although the bill was finally aborted in 1928.

One of the amazing phenomena that emerged from the effort to establish a sound rural community by the house head of *ie* and *meibōka* leadership was the constancy of the employment in agriculture through the prewar period. Table 7.1 shows that employment in agriculture during the prewar period was almost entirely stable, while total employment in the economy rose rapidly. From 1880 to 1940, total employment in the economy increased by 11.0 million, while employment in agriculture decreased by only 1.2 million and was virtually constant. This reflects the fact that, while house members other than the eldest son out-migrated villages and became hired labor in the non-agricultural sector, the eldest son, inheritor of the position and property of the house head, usually remained in the village.

---

[18]Nakamura contends that Itō was no. 1 and Yamagata no. 2 of top leaders during the Meiji era (Nakamura 2015, vol. II, p. 384).

Table 7.1 Employment in agriculture and total employment

Year	Employment in agriculture	Total employment
1880	14.7	21.9
1890	14.3	22.9
1900	14.2	24.3
1910	14.0	25.3
1920	13.9	26.9
1930	13.9	29.6
1940	13.5	32.9

Unit: million
Source Long-term Economic Statistics, vol. 2 (Tōyōkeizai-shinpōsha, Tokyo, 1988)

The discussion so far has explained that there were enough reasons for the rareness of the house heads or eldest son to leave the agriculture and their villages. They were not only the chief managers of family husbandry but also representative of each house in the cooperative activities of the village community, so had usually accumulated large amounts of human capital specific to the village. For this reason, the opportunity cost for the house head for leaving agriculture was very high. The cost was composed of property held by him, mainly land inherited from his father, and human capital, specific to the village community. While tangible property such as land could be sold at the market, community-specific knowledge and skills could not be sold in the market. Since the productivity of family-based agriculture was complemented by cooperative activities in the rural communities, the value of community-specific human capital held by the house head, internalizing external effects of cooperative activities in communities, was very high. In other words, the sum of tangible assets and community-specific human capital of a house head usually surpassed the present value of the earnings outside his village. This was the reason for the house head to stay in the village despite the out-migration of other members of the house, and hence the constancy of agricultural employment in the prewar period. The reason is closely related to the cooperative structure of the village community led by the *meibōka*.

We have already explained that the concept of the *kokutai* in the Meiji constitution and the Imperial Rescript on Education (*kyōiku choku-go*) had only limited effects of indoctrination, so that the maintenance of the *ie* system was not required by the *kokutai* concept. Moreover, there was no stipulation that prohibited out-migration of the house head in the Civil Code. Hayashi and Prescott (2008) claim, however, that feudalistic regulations retarded the shift of the labor force from agriculture to industry, caused the constancy of agricultural employment and, hence, through the insufficient supply of labor to industry from agriculture, lowered the growth rate of the prewar economy. Since the constancy of the labor force in agriculture is a rational behavior given the value of human capital plus tangible assets, and what they call feudalistic regulation is not relevant to the constancy of agricultural labor, it follows that Hayashi and Prescott's explanation on the issue of the constancy of agricultural employment and the low growth rate of the economy in prewar Japan is totally wide off the mark. Such assertions on pp. 606–608 of their work that marriage was under the strict control of the house head, that family property was monopolized by the family head and that the prewar family system is the same as the samurai family system are made without concrete evidence, but derived from the citing of secondary sources. The inadequacy of these assertions is readily confirmed by reference to such literature as Itō and Momose (1990), Muta (1996, pp. 12–18) and Tsutsui (2000).

It may be claimed that the leaders of the Meiji government tried to preserve the value of human capital embodied in the house heads of the rural sector in order to prevent out-migration of community leaders for the sake of the stability of society. *The meibōka* system as an interface between the state and the private sector was expected to play the role of enhancing the value of human capital. However, the main area of activity of the *meibōka* were non-agricultural areas including regional indigenous industries, as already touched upon, so has nothing to do with the behavior of the house heads with respect to the human capital accumulated in agriculture, although the growth of such industries might have given the incentive to out-migrate the rural sector potentially.

Incidentally, it will be explained below that the relatively low growth rate of the prewar economy was not caused by the dearth of labor supply from agriculture but mainly by the difficulty in developing heavy and chemical industries due to the low initial level of industrial technology, which was the other side of the coin of the non-Schumpeterian, commerce-based, growth during the Tokugawa era.

7.2.5.2 Consumption and Indigenous Industry

While the Meiji government devoted substantial efforts to industrial and military modernization, it did not intervene in the modernization of lifestyle, especially the consumption activity, of the people. This does not mean the reluctance of the government to modernize, but rather it was a manifestation of its *laissez faire* attitude and acceptance of modernization as a consequence of the free play of the socio-economic evolution. This stance is clearly seen in the Meiji Civil Code, which was open to individualism in family relationships and marital relations as well as individual asset holding, while stipulating the maintenance of the *ie* system by way of the inheritance of the rights and obligation of the house heads. The former factor expressed the encouragement of or the stance to welcome the modernization of lifestyle as a free play of the social dynamics, and the latter the concern about the maintenance of the basic stability of society during the process.

The modernization of consumption proceeded steadily and gradually. However, although the Western-type lifestyle was seen on the streets of large cities especially after the Taisho era, the ordinary life of most people remained traditional (Teranishi 2017a). Consumption goods were mainly supplied by indigenous industries, which also offered ample employment opportunities in the economy. Table 7.2 shows that the share of employment in indigenous industries comprised about 27.1–41.5% of the total. Further, it is worth pointing out that the new type of *kyūdō* behavior emerged in mass society during the prewar period. For example, the tea ceremony, which had

Table 7.2 Percentage composition of employment

Year	Agriculture	Non-agriculture	
		Indigenous	Modern
1881–85	70.8	27.4	1.8
1901–05	64.0	31.3	4.7
1916–20	53.3	36.1	10.6
1931–35	46.4	41.5	12.1

Note The commerce and finance sectors are included in indigenous industries
Source Nakamura (1985)

been the pleasure of the established class before the prewar period, was substantially popularized. In the Meiji era, it was adopted as an item for educating women in girls' high schools and, after the Taisho era, the tea culture witnessed an explosion in followers among the masses by way of the dissemination of knowledge through radio broadcasting and the publication of magazines. At the same time, department stores began to sell goods for the ceremony at reasonable prices and this was responded to by active purchasing by customers (Teranishi 2017a, ch. 4).

Meiji Japan was in possession of highly competitive indigenous industries such as traditional textiles, raw silk, tea and other agrarian processed goods, lacquer, processed marine products, and the like. Motivated by the opening of foreign markets and the rapid improvement of infrastructure, indigenous producers of these industries embarked on foreign trade actively all over the world. Regional chambers of commerce and overseas consulates played a crucial role in supporting their activity through information gathering and marketing activities. Indigenous industrialists were highly innovative also. For example, they became the most active users of information technologies such as the telephone and telegraphic communication, newly introduced by the government for military purposes. As Nakamura and others clarified, indigenous industries had been the leading and growing sector in Japan at least by the end of World War I (Nakamura 1985, 1997), providing employment opportunities to the growing population and obtaining foreign exchange, financing imports needed for socio-economic modernization.

The government and *zaibatsu* took full responsibility for the establishment of new modern industries. In other words, the establishment of new industries was carried out independently from existing and profitable indigenous industries and left to the free play of the new industrial leaders of the country. It could be conjectured that this division of labor between *zaibatsu* and the central government, on the one hand, and indigenous producers and local government on the other reduced the political and psychological costs significantly. In other words, indigenous producers were largely freed from involvement in the risky task of establishing new industries and specialized in maintaining employment and society. In fact, establishing new industries really was a highly risky undertaking. It was not easy for the newly transplanted modern industries to have enough growth-power and income-generating capability, partly because of the loss of tariff-setting rights at the time trade opened to Western countries. It was only after the 1920s when the cotton textile industry had sufficient international competitiveness; however, reflecting the low initial technology base, the development of heavy and chemical industries had fallen into significant difficulties, and the average competitiveness of the heavy and chemical industries was far below the international level even at the start of World War II (Teranishi 2011, ch. 4–3).

Two major characteristics of structural reform policy undertaken by the Meiji government are worth mentioning. First, the government refrained from exploitation of existing producers; it was quite reluctant to extract resources from the growing indigenous industries and to shift resources from the growing indigenous to newly established modern industries. The money required to establish the modern economy was mainly financed by land tax. Since land was the major form of asset in the economy and held widely by people outside the rural sector also, land tax was not the taxation of agricultural profits but had the nature of a taxation on wealth-holders in general. Moreover, business tax on indigenous industries was not introduced until 1896 and was kept at quite a low level throughout the prewar period. Second, the establishment of new, modern industries was carried out outside the circle of indigenous producers and through close collaboration between political leaders and *zaibatsu*. The *zaibatsu* enjoyed a high level of privileges and grew rapidly through financing by their huge retained earnings accumulation, which was possible because of various privileges and other supports extended by the government (Teranishi 2011, ch. 4–1). There is no doubt that a substantial share of the *zaibatsu*'s profits trickled down to political leaders. It is important to note that, in this framework, indigenous industrialists also enjoyed a high degree of freedom and the *meibōka* were able to retain wealth and power to lead the local rural economy

The structural reform policy of the prewar government was partly successful. It succeeded in realizing the birth of the modern economy for the first time in the non-Western world, but the economy faltered after World War I, and modern heavy and chemical industries failed to reach the leading edge on the modern technology front. The major reason for the failure of prewar structural policy after World War I lay in the exhaustion of the growth potential of indigenous industries. Many indigenous industries came under the protection policy as small and medium-sized firms after 1927. This happened partly because of the credit crunch after the financial crisis (Teranishi 2011, ch. 2–8), but mainly because the expansion of demand for products of these traditional industries reached saturation point, as was typically seen by the defeat of the silk textile industry by the new Western chemical fiber industry. Moreover, the cotton textile industry had a limitation on its demand expansion because of trade barriers due to the emergence of the block economy during the 1930s. It was a pity for Japan that the demand for the products of indigenous industries reached saturation point before heavy and chemical industries became new growing industries. In other words, the prewar Japanese economy failed after World War I because there was too little time for the heavy and chemical industries to become the new growing leading sector, replacing the predecessor, the indigenous industries. The lack of development in basic industrial technology in Japan before the Meiji Restoration might be partly responsible to this failure.

7.3 Postwar Cultural Strategy[19]

After World War II, Japan was occupied by allied forces, mainly composed of the US military, and abandoned the prewar policy to preserve the traditional lifestyle, energetically beginning to absorb Western mass-consumption culture. The consumption pattern and lifestyle were radically Westernized. There were three major reasons for this. For one, the occupation forces adopted the policy to 'educate' the Japanese by introducing their advanced culture and tried to establish Japan as a bridgehead against the communist powers in the context of the Cold War. Another reason was that so-called progressive intellectuals took the defeat and occupation as a good chance to get rid of the 'feudalistic' tendency of prewar Japan and tried hard to covert the country into an 'authentic' democratic and Westernized country. The third reason lay in the sincere introspection about the deficiency of prewar strategy that led the country to miserable defeat and occupation. There occurred deep regret about the adequacy of the policy that neglected the material, as opposed to the 'spiritual', value and the abundance related to mass production, and society as a whole decided to choose to introduce and establish a Western-style mass consumption system, consequently abandoning the *ie* system and neglecting indigenous industries (Teranishi 2017a).

In summary, Japan adopted a remarkably contrasting policy with respect to lifestyle and consumption modes after the World War II compared with the period before. The *ie* as a system to accumulate skills and knowledge related to the *kyūdō* principle and comprised of a core unit of trust among others nearby was converted into the nuclear household as a mere unit for income earning and expenditure. Likewise, indigenous industries, as places to conduct *kyūdō* behavior and nurture the aesthetic tradition to bring out products through collaboration between producers and consumers, were replaced by factory-based mass production system, contrived for the purpose of supplying large amounts of standardized consumption goods to serve the need of the masses.

It is worth noting that, while, in the prewar strategy, regions were adopted as an intermediate organization or interface between government and the private sector, industrial associations were adopted as the interface in the postwar strategy, in which the Ministry of Trade and Industry played an active role as the adjuster of government and business interests. The new interface fulfilled an important role during the high growth era, roughly from 1955 through 1980, in determining income distribution between labor and capital and controlling competitive conditions among industries, realizing the trickle down of the fruits of growth from rapidly growing industries in the heavy and chemical sector to weak and declining industries (Teranishi 2005). The activities of industrial associations weakened significantly after the end of the high growth period, however. The reason for this lies partly in the deregulation of the economy that proceeded rapidly after the 1980s but, more importantly, in the spread of Occidental ways of thinking, based on the welfare of the public and the autonomy and freedom of individuals. Neo-classical economics established hegemony in Japan

[19]See Teranishi (2017a) for more detailed discussion about the difference between the prewar and postwar strategy.

around this time, culminating in the neo-liberal economic stance of the Koizumi cabinet during 2001–06. Teranishi (2017b) presents a tentative discussion of the meaning of the neo-liberal policy of the Koizumi cabinet in comparison with the policy of the Minister of Finance Inoue Jyun-nosuke in prewar Japan during 1930–31.

However, it must be noted that this new attitude adopted after the World War II did not imply that Japan had completely abandoned the traditional *kyūdō* principle nor the worldview composed of others nearby and had permanently converted to one based on the abstract concept of the public. For example, Tsurumi (1984) notes that, although the Japanese had accepted the Western sense of justice of the at the time, they never accepted the value standard insisted on by the US government as the only universal value (p. 23). It is worth emphasizing that the decision to abandon traditional culture at the time of defeat and occupation was implemented as a decision based on bounded rationality, as described in Teranishi (2017a).

Teranishi (2017a, ch. 6) developed a preliminary argument to summarize the dynamic changes in the attitude of young Japanese to find social approval also. During the 1960s and 1970s, young Japanese, mobilized as labor for the development of modern mass-consumption industries such as consumer electrical appliances and automobiles in the city, were required to seek their positions in society in a completely different way from prewar society. Without villages and the *ie* to return to, youngsters were left to live in the nuclear family system and to find material satisfaction. Some of them fought in student riots against the economy supremacist view of society. Their resistance failed to obtain sympathy partly because of the naïve Marxist bias of their conception. During the 1980s and 1990s after the high growth era, there emerged two new types of lifestyle among young Japanese. One was a group called the *shin-jinrui* (new human race), who in the circumstance of material affluence, tried to keep their distance from homogeneous groups. They tried to resist modernity that requested homogenization, by way of indulgence in new commodities. Through being addicted to new commodities, they wanted to satisfy their need for social approval through communication by the symbolic function of consumption. Another group was called the *otaku* (indulgence group), who indulged in communication by way of electric media. Through constructing the barricade of electric appliances, they tried to find their places within their world filled with information. While surrounded by information, the *otaku* did not seek human communication.

Both the *shin-jinrui* and *otaku* sought their places within the confines of the existing frameworks of reference, but they did not try to face with internal themselves and only sought their places in commodities and information. After around 2000, there emerged a new move to find internalize oneself and seek the approval of others. They make efforts to express an ideal personality of their own (*naritai-jibun*). The new type youngsters have come to use their indulgence in commodities and information as a method to express internalized themselves. They moved away from existing brand fashions and sought their own local and original fashions. They seemed to be trying to organize their own groups that approved of each other within a small society. This might be regarded as a tentative move toward a return to the concerns of the traditional worldview composed of chain relationships of others nearby.

Chapter 8
Culture and Collective Behavior in Japan

The purpose of this chapter is to examine the origin of the so-called 'collectivism of the Japanese' in the context of the internal mental model of the Japanese. It is claimed that the collectivism of the Japanese is not directly related to the internalized culture historically nurtured in Japan, and that it is more closely related to the historical conditions after the Meiji Restoration, when the severe restrictions on the labor market were abolished under the condition of accumulated community-specific human capital. In this model, the so-called 'collectivism of the Japanese' is nothing but a stakeholder society to share the residual income within a small group. It must be noted that the stakeholder society born in this way has very little to do with the internalized view and the values nurtured historically through deep concern with others nearby, and is also quite different from the collective intentionality of the Occident developed under the influence of the concept of the public and humans.

The examination of the concept of the 'collectivism of the Japanese' as the sharing of residual income in the stakeholder society is conducted in the context of a comparative framework between England and Japan. It is shown that collectivism is related to the sharing of community-specific human capital accumulated under the condition of the absence of an efficient labor market before the dissolution of the community system. When the Meiji government repealed various feudal regulations, liberalized the labor market and authorized property rights on land, the policy aroused significant aversion to accept the dissolution of the community-based system. It is conjectured that the human capital in the community was largely composed of community-specific skills at that moment due to the underdevelopment of the open labor market. Because community-specific skills are difficult to be transacted in the

This chapter is a revised version of the following paper: J. Teranishi, 'Collectivist and individualist behavior in a comparative historical perspective: Community-specific human capital view', a paper presented at the fourth conference on *Ethnic Diversity and Economic Instability in Africa: Policies for Harmonious Development*, Oxford University, 15–17 July 2011.

J. Teranishi, *Culture and Institutions in the Economic Growth of Japan*,
Studies in Economic History,
https://doi.org/10.1007/978-4-431-55627-5_8

market, it was natural that there occurred resistance to dissolve communities so as to preserve the value of human capital as stakeholder societies.

The economic worldview nurtured through Buddhist tradition was mainly composed of a small group of acquaintances or others nearby, whereas the worldview of individuals in the Occident was more inclined to the accommodation of the generalized concept of the public and society. Seemingly, the difference seems to be responsible for the collectivity or group-orientedness of the Japanese. However, it must be noted that the deep concern with others nearby is not necessarily directly related to collective activities. It is true that serious concerns about the effect on retribution of *karma*, which is accumulated through behavioral interaction with others nearby, enhance the sense of the relatedness of individuals to others nearby; but such concerns would not necessarily cause collective behavior incorporating others nearby. An individual could be salvaged by individualistic behavior to pursue Buddhist truth by himself and seeking behavior that causes merits for a better life in the future life. In the case of the behavior of the samurai depicted by Sagara (1968), others, in the sense of respect for oneself in the eyes of others, is not necessarily related to the collective behavior with others nearby. This could be seen through the extremely individualistic behavior and mentality of the samurai despite the restrictions imposed by feudalistic society that caused loyalty to masters.

If the internalized belief system related to concerns with others nearby is not necessarily responsible for collective behavior, where does the 'collectivism of the Japanese' come from? This chapter tries to show that one of the reasons for this lies in the mechanism for sharing interests as groups. The relationship with others nearby in the Buddhist sense is not necessarily related to the sharing of interests.[1] For the rise of collective behavior, the sharing of interests in some groups is probably a sufficient condition. It will be argued below that such a sharing of interests was born by the historical experience of community-specific human capital. Since a significant human capital is considered to have been accumulated through community-specific human investment and, at least, part of this investment seems to be implemented through occupational *kyūdō* behavior, one of the main source for the collectivism of economic behavior of the Japanese seems to be related to this mechanism. It is a sharing mechanism, so that collectivity born in this way is very little to do with any other collectivity aimed at a contribution to the abstract public, although it might have significant bearings on the concept of the shareholding society.

It will be shown below that, especially after the start of growth in the Tokugawa era, human capital was accumulated by a wide variety of individuals in society. The spread of *kyūdō* behavior to farmers and merchants resulted in the accumulation of human capital in the macro-economy. Moreover, since labor mobility across classes and regions was strictly restricted in the Tokugawa era, the human capital was community-specific. Because community-specific human capital cannot be sold

[1] The false idea that sharing is an innate teaching in Buddhism was born from the concept of merit transfer of directional transformation in Jyōdo-shin-shū. However, the essential theory of Kamakura new Buddhism lies in the notion of merit transfer of qualitative transformation, as discussed in Chapter 4.

at the market, the community-specific nature of accumulated human capital had to be shared by community members after the deregulation of the labor market by the Meiji Restoration. The behavior to preserve the value of community-specific human capital resulted in the collectivity of behavior of the Japanese. In other words, it is contended that the so-called collectivism of the Japanese seen in this way is of relatively of recent origin and is not necessarily related to the historically nurtured internalized belief system composed of others nearby.

To focus on the issue of the so-called collectivism of the Japanese that is said to be distinct in international comparison, our analysis is conducted within the framework of a comparative historical analysis of Japan and England. The historical experience of England and Japan at the time of the transition from the community-based customary economy to the market economy in the sense of Hicks (1969) is compared and the impact of the establishment of property rights on the dissolution of communities is examined. The impact depends on the degree of labor market development in each economy. The establishment of private property rights means the allotment of properties, comprising human and non-human capital, among members of the community and to guarantee the rights to them legally. The allotment requires that properties are divisible without incurring much cost. In a country with a well-developed labor market, human capital is considered to embody general skills mainly, which is marketable, while in a country where the labor market is underdeveloped at the time of the establishment of property rights, human capital is composed of community-specific skills, which would lose most of their value outside the community. In the latter country, there could be significant resistance against the division of community property, and even if non-human capital is allotted among community members, some sort of social institutions would be contrived so as to maintain the value of human capital and preserve community ties. Group behavior would be more prevalent in the history of this country thereafter. In the former country, the division of property would not encounter any serious difficulties, and there would be a smooth establishment of property rights. In this chapter, it is argued that Japan corresponds to the latter and England to the former category.

Section 8.1 explains our conceptual framework. First, it confines the type of collectivist behavior focused on in this chapter to the one that seeks the intrinsic value of collectivist behavior. Second, it shows that when a country shifts from a community-based to a market-based system, there are two equilibria depending on the degree of labor market development at the time of the establishment of property rights; one equilibrium characterized by the prevalence of general skills and the smooth shift to the market economy, and another characterized by the accumulation of specific-skills and resistance to the shift to the market economy. Sections 8.2 and 8.3 examine the historical development of property rights and the labor market in Japan and England. With respect to the two countries, the two sections compare the nature of rural communities, the role of skills therein, the timing and speed of labor market development relative to the spread of property rights and, finally the process of the dissolution of communities. Section 8.4 discusses the implications of our analysis for the so-called group-oriented nature of economic behavior of the Japanese.

8.1 The Two Equilibria in the Transition to a Market Economy: A Theoretical Deliberation

8.1.1 Collectivist Behavior

Von Mises (1962) denies the existence of groups or society as independent ontological entities and asserts 'only individuals act'. Although he does not deny the 'reality of the effects brought about by the cooperation of individuals', 'collectives come into being by the thoughts and actions of individuals' and 'they disappear when the individuals adopt different way of thinking and acting' (pp. 78–79). In rejecting normative individualism as a basic position of ethics, political philosopher Gray says that 'normative individualism holds that collective goods have instrumental value only' and that 'for a normative individualist, only states of individual human lives can possess intrinsic value, with collective goods having value only in so far as they make a contribution to the good life of the individual' (Gray 1993). If we follow this definition, there are two kinds of collectivist or group behavior: (1) group behavior as an instrument to contribute to the good lives of individuals and (2) group behavior that seeks the intrinsic value of collectivist behavior that could not be reduced to the good lives of individuals. According to this taxonomy, von Mises's assertion corresponds to the denial of group behavior of type (2).

To provide an economic interpretation of the above argument, let us assume that the good life in Gray's assertion corresponds to the consumption utility obtained from present and future consumption. Consider a situation where community properties are to be distributed to community members. When all the community properties are completely allotted to members, the utility of an individual member become a function of his present income and property (the present value of his future income). In this case, group behavior is completely reducible to the individual utility of members, so that possible group behavior is only type (1). When, on the other hand, community properties are not perfectly allotted to individuals, but some of them remain to be held commonly, individual utility is affected by the commonly held portion of the community property, so group behavior come to have intrinsic value in the sense of the utility derived from common properties, the present value of common future income. Type (2) group behavior is meaningful in this case. The consumption stream of an individual is jointly determined with the consumption stream of other members of the group because of the partial commonality of future incomes.

8.1.2 Community-Specific Human Capital

In this chapter, we focus on three kinds of assets or properties: land, physical capital and human capital. Following Becker (1975), human capital is considered to be composed of specific skills, which are useful only with the current employer or which increase the productivity of the worker only in his current job, and general skills, which are useful with other employers. In other words, human capital in the form of specific skills is not marketable because it loses its productivity-enhancing effects outside the firm. While Becker is concerned with the modern firm system, so that the specific skill means the firm-specific skill, our interest is in the community system as a production unit, so that the specific skill in this chapter means the community-specific skill.

The cost of the formation of the community-specific skill is born either by the community or workers therein. Irrespective of the degree of perfectness of the outside labor market,[2] the community has the incentive to bear the costs, because trained workers cannot leave the community without losing the value of their skills even if the labor market is competitive, so that it can recoup the costs. Workers also have the incentive to bear the costs whenever the skill is properly rewarded, and the hold-up problem is avoided. They will pay the costs out of their own pockets, by borrowing from loan markets or by accepting low wages during apprenticeship.

How large is the specific human capital in a society? This could be estimated by the decrease in the wage level for workers who are obliged to leave firms against their will. Using the data of the mid-1980 s in the United States, Topel (1991) examined wage differences between the new and old jobs of workers who were permanently laid off because plants were closed or moved. He found that on average these workers earned about 14% less in their new jobs, and that the longer the worker had held his previous job, the larger the earning loss. Blair (1995), on the other hand, conjectured that the contribution of specialized human capital in American corporations in 1993 amounted to at least $226 billion or 4% of the total income generated by the corporate sector.

8.1.3 Two Equilibria in the Division of Community Properties

As is emphasized in Hicks (1969) and revealed by a number of historical experiences of Asian and European countries, the emergence of a market economy based on price mechanism means the dissolution of the community-based customary economy based on custom and command. The dissolution implies the liquidation of assets

[2]In the case of general skill, Becker (1975) asserted that when the labor market is competitive, firms are reluctant to bear the training costs. When labor market friction compresses the wage structure, and the market discounts the level of general skill, firms are motivated to bear training costs (Acemoglu and Pischke 1999).

commonly held by the community, and the distribution of the entitlement to community members. In other words, a transition to a market economy requires the establishment of private property rights (North 1980). As is emphasized in North and Thomas (1973), however, the establishment of private property rights is not an easy matter. This is because, whenever transaction costs exist, the costs of creating and enforcing property rights may exceed the benefits to any groups or individuals. Moreover, once investment in institutions or equipment is undertaken to protect the property rights from looting or other damages, it is difficult to prevent free rider problems related to the maintenance of the institutions or equipment. For these reasons, the creation of property rights has been carried out by the state in many countries. In Occident countries, property rights evolved first as owners tried to make efficient utilization of their properties, and later on it was regarded as an essential prerequisite for civil society and implemented as a major agenda of civil revolutions. In some Asian countries like Japan, property rights were created as an indispensable step in the catch-up process by the development-oriented state. In the case of colonized countries in Asia and Africa, the colonial governments led the process as part of modernization policies for the purposes of rent-extraction or effective governance. It is worth noting that the state does not necessarily establish efficient property rights. This is because the policy aim of states lies in the securing of revenues or the maximization of rents available to rulers. The development of the market economy or the pursuit of economic growth could be mere instruments for such aims. Thus, North (1980) emphasized that the property right system created by the state could quite often be inefficient with respect to resource allocation.

The argument developed by North and Thomas (1973) and North (1980), however, lacks consideration for an important issue that, in the case of the transition of a community-based to a market economy, community property needs to be divisible among community members without substantial cost. The division encounters serious difficulties when a significant part of the property is composed of community-specific human capital. For one thing, community-specific capital loses its value when it is separated from the community, so that the community property suffers serious loss in value. For another, it is difficult to allocate the entitlement to such specific capital to each individual because the imputation of investment costs for the formation of the skills is not an easy matter. For these two reasons, there tends to occur serious resistance to the dissolution of a community, especially by the possessors of large amount of community-specific human capital, who are quite often leaders of the communities.

In theory, the evolution of a market economy is usually envisaged as a gradual process, caused by an increase in productivity, the improvement of the transportation and communication systems or the globalization of the market. In that process, the labor market becomes increasingly competitive, and skills specific to particular communities tends to be replaced by general skills in order to accommodate the market mechanism. Therefore, if enough time is afforded, most of the skills might be converted into general skills and, in that case, there would be no difficulty in the division of community properties and hence the dissolution of communities. In reality, however, the degree of development of the open labor market differs substantially among economies, and hence the remaining amount of community-specific skills. For example, since looting occurs in the transportation of commodities, it is more difficult to ensure safety in transportation in commodity markets than in labor markets. Partly for this reason, labor market development started earlier in medieval England than the development of the commodity market.

The open labor market was already in existence in England in the thirteenth century in its nascent form, and the enclosure movements from the late fifteenth century onward resulted in the establishment of property rights as well as the creation of mass industrial labor. The institutional changes related to property rights, and hence the dissolution of the rural community structure proceeded in tandem with the development of the labor market. Therefore, at the time of civil revolution when private property rights on land became a nationwide agenda, England had had a sufficiently developed labor market. It is conjectured that already at that time a large part of the human capital was composed of general skills, so that the division of community assets, and hence the dissolution of the community, did not encounter so much opposition. In the early-modern history of Japan, the necessity to covert rice paid as tax into money necessitated the development of a nationwide commodity market, while labor market development was confined within local areas because of the legal segregation of occupations as well as of the regulation of labor movement by *han* government. When the Meiji government liberalized the labor market and created (or authorized) property rights on land, it is thought that the human capital in the community was largely composed of community-specific skills due to the lack of development of the open labor market, and this caused significant aversion and resistance to the dissolution of the community-based system.

It follows that there are two equilibria in the dissolution of a community economy based on custom and command, and the common property system, and the transition to a market economy based on price signal and private property rights. How much an open labor market has been developed at the time of the introduction of property rights determines the degree of penetration of individualism and collectivism in society as an organizing principle of the market economy. In an economy with a developed labor market, the share of human capital embodying general skills is large, so that the dissolution of the pre-existing community system was easy. The evolution of the market economy in this case tends to be driven by the maximization of consumption utility and the portfolio selection of assets assigned to individuals. In an economy with an underdeveloped labor market, human capital is largely composed of community-specific skills. Since the division of community properties is difficult, the behavior of individuals in the market system is influenced by consideration of the common portion of community properties even after the *de jure* establishment of property rights. The utility of individuals tends to be partly dependent on future income commonly held by community members.

Historically, the former equilibrium corresponds to the experience of the market economy in civil societies of Occidental countries like England, and the latter to that of non-Occidental countries like Japan. In the two equilibria, the meaning and scope of group behavior differ considerably. In the former equilibrium, group behavior after the establishment of the market economy is confined to those that could be reduced to the utility maximization of individuals. Collectivist activity is instrumental to individual optimization. In the latter equilibrium, there remain incentives to invest in specific skills after the transition to the market economy. People have incentives to hold human capital or future income in common. In this sense, group behavior could have its intrinsic value in addition to and apart from any instrumental value for individuals.

8.2 The Privatization of Property Rights and the Dissolution of the Community in Japan

This section examines the process of the creation of property rights and the dissolution of the rural community in Japan during the period from the establishment of the Tokugawa *bakufu* to the Meiji Restoration.

In the following, we will argue that during the process of the development of the market economy from the seventeenth century onward, the development of the labor market lagged significantly behind the commodity market, and that the Meiji Restoration established the national labor market and property right system simultaneously. For this reason, it is conjectured that there remained a significant amount of community-specific human capital, which became an obstacle to the division of community property at the time of the transition to the private property right system. This explains why the orientation toward group behavior substantially remained in Japanese society thereafter.

8.2.1 Land Holding in Rural Communities

The enfeoffment by the shogunate to the *daimyo*, and from the *daimyo* to vassals, was denominated by the amount of taxable rice, which was called *kokudaka*. The right of the *daimyos* to govern the granted land was of an 'abstract' nature (Nagahara 1980, p. 172), mainly concerned with the taxation right. It was not rare that the granted land was changed at the will of the shogunate, and the *daimyo* were obliged to move to another region (*kunigae*), as is explained in Chapter 6.

The cadastral register recorded the name of the farmer together with the width, boundary and location of the land. This was for the purpose of land tax collection and not for the confirmation of ownership. Hayami (2003) points out that because tax was imposed on each village, there was no need to confirm the holder of each plot of land, and argues that 'if one interprets the land survey implemented by Toyotomi Hideyoshi as an attempt to confirm land ownership, it would be difficult to account for the purpose of land tax reform carried out by the Meiji government'. This view is in direct opposition to the view expressed by Ishii (1966), for example, claiming that farmers were free to alienate their land as far as they fulfilled their taxpaying obligations, because the right of the lord regarding his land was confined to collect tax. Ishii's assertion holds only when all the rights regarding land are held by either farmers or lords. If we take account of the role of rural communities, the fact that the right held by the lords was limited does not necessarily mean that the remaining rights were held by individual farmers. In other words, it seems to be more pertinent to believe that the land was at least partly held by the village community. This applies not only to common land, *iriaichi*, which was indispensable for farmers' daily lives and production activities, as a source for firewood for energy and organic materials for fertilizer, but also arable lands privately held by farmers. Any lands held by a farmer had to be returned to the community unless he fulfilled his taxpaying obligations, and the transfer of the lands to his son was justified only when the son was expected to be diligently involved in cultivation (Niwa 1989). The common holding nature of land is more clearly understood through an examination of the land allotting system (*warichi-sei*), which was widespread in Kyushu, south Shikoku, and Honshu districts along the Japan Sea. For example, in the case of Kanazawa-*han*, all arable lands, excluding residential lands, were redistributed among village members every 20 years. Watanabe (1994) maintains that since there were implicit rules to confiscate the private right to land by community decision, the private rights were only indirect, and points out popular customs as additional evidence, such as the *ukemodoshi*, in which farmers were able to claim the right to their foreclosed or sold land at any time if they should return the money.

We argued in Chapter 3 that a virtual residual control right was established at least in areas with advanced agriculture, with commodity cropping and the like, after the end of the eighteenth century, so that a de facto property right was established. In this regard, it must be noted that the arguments of Hayami, Niwa and Watanabe are concerned with areas with underdeveloped agriculture other than the Kinki and Tokai areas. We will return to this issue shortly below.

8.2.2 The Development of the Commodity Market

During the Tokugawa period, commodity markets were highly developed.[3] One reason for this was the necessity for the *daimyo* to monetarize the rice and other products paid in kind as tax in order to finance the budget of the *han*. As discussed in Chapter 6, there occurred the development of marine transportation to northern Japan through the Japan Sea[4] and also of the bill of exchange system and the related growth of moneychanger merchants. This occurred because it was necessary to transport the rice to Osaka to sell it. Many of the special products of each region ware

[3]Saito (2008) doubts this point, noting that the degree of self-sufficiency was high in the daily life of farmers. However, his assertion is based on only one piece of evidence about a peasant in Nagano. Miyamoto (2008) opposes this, claiming that most special regional products were produced for the purpose of sale to nationwide markets.

[4]See Chapter 6. Because the sea lane from Siogama to Chōshi was the hardest for marine transportation, especially in winter, the sea lane on the Pacific Ocean remained underdeveloped.

monopolized by the *han* governments, which the *han* collected and transported to Osaka. From Osaka, commodities were sold all over Japan, including Edo.

From the eighteenth century onwards, there developed commodity markets for privately traded goods, reflecting productivity increase. Commodities purchased by merchants such as rice, sake, soy sauce, marine products, cotton textiles, silk products, and the like were brought to local cities, Osaka, and Edo, and then transported all over the country. In the nineteenth century, there emerged thriving local market economies in such areas as Osaka, Nagoya, and along the Seto Inland Sea. The social division of labor and the diversification of occupations were intensified, giving rise to occupations such as those that employed workers for cotton textile production, daily employment in transportation within the local regions and traders of daily life necessities.

Reflecting the development of the large-scale trade of the products paid in as tax, the commodity markets in each region were closely integrated from an early period. Even in the second half of the seventeenth century, the average correlation coefficients of the rate of changes in annual rice prices calculated for the pairs of five regions (Osaka, Hiroshima, Nagoya, Edo and Aizu) was 0.566, which was not so low compared with 0.720, the coefficient for the second half of the nineteenth century (Miyamoto 1988). The coefficient was 0.606 in the first half, and 0.641 in the second half of the eighteenth century.[5]

8.2.3 The Rise of the Labor Market

While during the Tokugawa era there did not exist freedom of occupation choice owing to the rigid *shokubun* regulation system, the Meiji government abolished this regulation and realized the equality of people of all classes. The religious census registers (*shūmon-ninbetsu-chō*) in the Tokugawa period, originating from the inquisition for suppressing Christianity, were prepared for each class. In other words, status and occupation were fixed for each household. The new Register Act, enacted after the Meiji Restoration, abolished this class-based registration system, and adopted registering based only on address (Hukushima 1967).

The Tokugawa period did not achieve any significant development of the labor market. While the labor markets developed among local cities and the surrounding villages adjusted local demand and the supply of labor locally, there was no macro-level labor market in the Tokugawa era (Saito 2006). Hayami (1988), on the other hand, emphasizes the active working of the local labor markets in the form of migrant workers between cities and villages. His evidence, however, was the data from religious census registers in Mino, which was close to the Nagoya area, with its developed

[5]These figures seem to have an increasing trend. The coefficient calculated with respect to 12 regions (five regions plus Banshū, Hukuchiyama, Bōchō, Saga, Kumamoto, Dewa and Shinshū) do not show any such trend; 0.715 in the first half of the eighteenth century, 0.664 in the second half, and 0.684 in the first half of the nineteenth century.

local market economy; so it is difficult to generalize this to the national economy. Hayami admits this and confirms that his study does not intend to claim the existence of open labor markets in general. As additional evidence for this caveat, he notes that certificates were needed to leave villages, that due to the underdevelopment of the transportation system and infrastructure, migration was physically difficult, and that migration between villages was much more difficult because of the binding nature of community relations.

It is said that the initial supply of industrial labor after the Meiji Restoration came in the form of young female workers in the cotton spinning industry and of the conversion of artisans previously involved in handicraft production (Nagahara 1980). There also occurred the massive supply of labor from the agriculture sector from the early Meiji period. According to the estimates of Minami (1970), even during 1876–80, the annual shift of labor from agriculture to non-agriculture amounted to 113,000, which was 0.67% of the existing labor force in the agricultural sector and covered 85.6% of the increase of industrial labor. There is no denying that the labor market was newly created from the Meiji era. Most of the labor force was composed of young labor other than the eldest son in the rural household (Chapter 7). As analyzed by Fei-Ranis (1964) and Minami (1970), there had been an abundant workforce with low marginal productivity, and this workforce was supplied to industry quite elastically responding to the demand for labor by the industry, the Lewisian model.

8.2.4 The Authorization of Private Property Rights and the Response of the Rural Community

In the Tokugawa *bakufu* system, land was owned ultimately and legally by the shogun. Lords were enfeoffed to collect taxes from land, and farmers obtained a cultivating right collectively at the village level in exchange for meeting tax payment obligations. In accordance with this principle, the transfer and sales of lands was strictly forbidden as was stipulated by the Eternal Prohibition of Land Alienation Act in 1643 and the Restriction on Land Division Act in 1673, which prohibited the divided succession of lands for smallholders of less than 10 *koku* for ordinary farmers and 20 *koku* for the *myōshu*. Moreover, tenancy contracts were not allowed from the time of Toyotomi Hideyoshi's land survey onward. It follows that in this system there was no room for the development of the landlord system as a principle.

The impoverishment of some farmers was inevitable in a market economy, however, so that it was allowed for them to pawn lands to rich farmers while retaining the right to cultivate the lands. Since pawning was liable to cause, and actually gave rise to, foreclosures, the *bakufu* declared in 1722 that the government would not allow foreclosures, while it encouraged redemption of lands. As discussed in Chapter 3, triggered by the confusion related to this ordinance, the transfer of landholdings among farmers and the accumulation of lands by rich farmers increased, with the consequent rise of a de facto landlord system. However, both the *bakufu* and *daimyo*, for whom the securing of the taxation system based on the village community was crucial, never officially allowed land transfer (Niwa 1989).

After the establishment of the new government by the abolition of the *han* (feudal domain) system in 1871, followed by the repeal of the Eternal Prohibition of Land Alienation Act (Denbata eidai baibai kinshi rei promulgated in 1643) and the ordinance on Land Ticket (Chiken) in 1872, the Meiji government finally embarked on the reform of the land tax system in mid 1873. Land tax was linked to the value of land, which in turn was calculated as the discounted present value of the future returns on the land, and land holders were given land tickets certifying their ownership. In this way the Meiji government established private ownership rights of land as well as the right of free alienation of land. Individual farmers, not villages, became responsible for land tax payment. The boundaries of villages were reorganized so as to be suitable for administration by the central government, not as tax payment units. As already touched upon, the government abolished class segmentation at the same time, and liberalized occupation choice. In summary, property rights were legally created simultaneously with the introduction of the free labor market, or property rights were created under the condition where no open labor markets existed previously.

This process entailed the following results. There remained a significant amount of community-specific skills in rural areas, especially embodied in the house heads of the rural families and community leaders. To avoid the loss of the value of human capital, these farmers strongly opposed the dissolution of communities. The Meiji government was in a sense ambivalent. In principle, it was intent on the introduction of an Occidental-style system based on individuality, which was the officially declared aim of the Meiji Restoration, but at the same time they were aware that family and community ties were needed to preserve the unity of society in establishing a strong state. For example, at the time of land tax reform, the right to transfer land was only granted to house heads, and when other family members wanted to sell their lands, approval by the head was needed. This rule was abolished in 1882.

The following three cases, related to the meandering process in reorganizing the local administration system by the Meiji government, show that the resistance by farmers to protect the rural community was to some extent successful, and that the value system of modernizing Japanese collectivist sentiments remained strongly thereafter. First is the preservation of the natural village system as traditional production and management units. At first, the Meiji government intended to establish an efficient system of local administration to control people directly at the individual level by local officials designated by central government. The *daiku-shōku* system, with artificial boundaries neglecting the historical formation of villages, was introduced in 1872, together with the *kukochō* system, with officially designated officers, abolishing the historical and patrimonial leaders of villages such as the *shōya* and *myōshu*. This aroused fierce resistance by prominent farmers and community leaders, and the opposition movements, merged with the Freedom and People's Rights Movement that flared up in the midst of the explosion of farmers riots to demand tax reductions, obliged the government to change its stance. The Law on Organizing the Local Administration System (Chihō-san-shin hō) promulgated in 1878 recognized the role of village communities as production and management units, and declared that, although prefectures and counties were organized from the viewpoint of local administration, towns and villages were left to be organized according to historical and natural orders.

Second was the recognition of independent budgets for self-governance and community activities. In 1884, the government revised the local tax rules in the Law on Assembly in Towns and Villages. While the aim of this law was to strengthen their grip on local administration by introducing administrative villages, revising the stance of the recognition of the natural village system in the 1878 legislation, the government respected the self-governing activities of communities, and approved a special budget item related to rural religious activities and the like, as an item separate from such usual administrative expenses as public works, sanitation, education, public offices, and so on (Ōishi 1961).

Third was the preservation of common land. After the promulgation of the Act on the Towns and Village System in 1888, the government carried out large-scale mergers of local towns and villages. The number of towns and villages decreased from 70,000 in 1888 to 14,000 in 1889 (Ono 1936, p. 342). In the process, the treatment of common land (*iriaichi*) virtually held by pre-merged communities became a controversial issue, but the controversy was settled by keeping the rights of farmers to use common land as before, thus paying respect to the history of common use of the land. Later on, the central government tried to confiscate such common lands for the purpose of the national forest policy. This again encountered fierce oppositions and rarely succeeded.

Why were farmers successful in maintaining the community identity and system vis-à-vis the centralization-oriented government? Two hypotheses have so far been set forth. First, Ōishi (1961) maintains that prominent farmers, who became absentee landlords, tried to exploit small farmers with the help of the central government. Purchasing common lands, these farmer-landlords extracted the maximum profits from tenants through allowing the utilization of common lands for their cultivation. At the same time, as virtual leaders of administrative villages, they tried to extend their business in non-agriculture over the administrative villages, which covered a wider area than the natural villages. In this model, prominent farmers-landlords and small farmers-tenants were in a conflicting relationship, and the landlords colluded with the government, which regarded the landlords' grips on peasants and the villages as politically useful for indirectly controlling the local communities.

Second is the hypothesis set forth by Ariizumi (1980) that emphasizes the cooperative endeavor by landlords and peasants to promote regional economies. In this model, prominent farmers led the local community as leaders by actively negotiating with central government for help in developing the region. It seems that their activities to obtain favors from government, such as railways, roads, and schools, could be of some benefits for their own businesses. Ariizumi, however, argues that the leaders, the *meibōka* or 'men of repute', found intrinsic value in developing their regions and quite often devoted their own assets for the purpose.

Whatever the motivation, both hypotheses emphasize that prominent farmers tried to develop regional communities through maintaining community ties. In this way, it is conjectured that the human capital accumulated by them remained productive without losing value in the market economy. Regions that succeeded in obtaining government support are thought to have developed more rapidly than other regions. Within the same region or county, the effect on economic activity of infrastructure could vary among towns and villages (Matsuzawa 2009), and this frequently triggered rivalry between towns and villages. Income inequality among counties or inequality among towns and villages were a consequence of the process. When there had existed significant inequality among regions before the introduction of government support, the extension of support towards poor regions had an equalizing effect among regions. Meiji government leaders such as Inoue Kaoru and Yamagata Aritomo were eager to utilize the resource allocation mechanism based on the *meibōka* order to stabilize and strengthen the grip on rural community. Keeping internal harmony within natural villages and the manipulating of favors at the county level were their basic strategy in this respect.

8.2.5 The Emergence of the Japanese-Style Firm System

The institutional history of Japan after the Meiji Restoration has been characterized with strong traits to emphasize the community-specific or organization-specific human capital and this culminated in the establishment of the so-called Japanese-style firm system after World War II. Let us examine the process quickly.

After the end of the World War I, the growth rate of agriculture and the related indigenous industries declined because of the stagnation of productivity growth.[6] Moreover, the government implemented a policy of lowering rice prices in order to prevent a rise in the real wages of urban factory workers. Tenancy disputes drastically increased after 1921 in both the number of cases and participants. Regional ties were no longer monolithic. The commitment of landlords to farming decreased and they converted their portfolio composition from land and related indigenous industries to investment in modern industries in large cities (Teranishi 2011). The development of the financial markets facilitated landlords to implement investment by means of financial intermediaries and financial instruments. All these factors worked to weaken the *meibōka* order.

In the modern industries, labor disputes intensified significantly after World War I, reflecting the spread of socialism among activist workers, the impact of the establishment of the Soviet Union as well as the stagnation of large manufacturing concerns in industries such as shipbuilding. It is worth noting, however, that class conflict was not established to any significant extent in Japan, despite the surge of labor disputes in the interwar period. There are several reasons for this. First, socialist movements were severely oppressed by the government, and the frequent changes in the strategy of Comintern (Communist International) caused confusion in national communist

---

[6]The basic reason for this was the end of the diffusion process of high-yielding varieties and related technologies of rice production, as is emphasized by Hayami. See Chapter 3.

party strategies. Second, Japan did not have a tradition of class conflict in agriculture in the sense of conflict between those who have production means and those who do not. Tenancy did not cause this kind of conflict, because tenant farmers were not hired labor but ‘managers’ of agricultural production firms. There did exist a small number of large-scale farms utilizing hired labor in Japan around the turn of the century, but the overwhelming portion of agricultural production was implemented by family labor.

Third, and perhaps the most important reason, was the gradual development of the Japanese-style firm system after the interwar period. Afraid that the intensification of labor disputes might endanger smooth capital accumulation, the owners and managers of large firms extended long-term employment and the seniority-based wage system toward middle managers. Because the credible promise of long-term employment prevents the hold-up problem, firm-specific skill formation started to prevail among middle-managers and, then, among white-color workers in the interwar period (Teranishi 2006). The long-term employment system and firm-specific skill formation spread among blue-color workers after World War II, as discussed in detail in Teranishi (2017a). With the consequent disappearance of differentials in the treatment between white- and blue-color workers, labor unions came to be organized for each firm irrespective of differences in occupation. In this Japanese-style firm system, workers, management and shareholders shared the value-added of a firm within a stakeholder society framework. and class conflicts disappeared. Teranishi (2005) presents a detailed explanation of the process by which the intense class conflict that flared up during the occupation period[7] after World War II was replaced by inter-industrial conflict.

With the establishment of the Japanese-style firm system and the sharing system of value-added among stakeholders, a mechanism to determine the value-added for each firm and to distribute it between labor and capital was needed. During the high-growth period after World War II, this was accomplished by inter-industry conflicts, where government intervened in the competitive conditions of industries through industrial associations and collective wage bargaining (Teranishi 2005).

The government controlled the competitive conditions of industries through various measures applied to industrial associations, such as intervention in cartel agreements, capacity and equipment adjustment in declining industries, and the manipulation of infant industry protections. The regulation of competition resulted in prices that were higher than the competitive level. When competition in almost all industries was controlled in this way, both input and output prices were at higher than competitive levels for each industry. The level of output is thus a function of the controlled prices. It follows that the value-added of each industry is controlled by the competition-preventive measures. Both input and output prices are affected by the policy-induced rents caused by regulations. If the rents included in the output prices are higher than the rents in input prices, the value-added of the industry is higher than a level determined through perfect competition, and lower if the rents are less.

[7]The occupation force, largely composed of ex-New Dealers or sympathizers of the New Dealers, was eager to promote the labor union movement in Japan.

The collective bargaining system determined the wage level for each industry. More exactly, the standard of base-up rate for each industry was determined by the bargaining that took place in spring every year. The collective bargaining system and the government intervention through industrial associations together functioned as a mechanism to determine the value-added of each industry and to distribute it between wages and profits. That is, because the system's competition preventing policies yielded policy rents, the value-added determined in this way was higher than the competitive level in industries with stricter regulations, and lower than the competitive level in industries with milder regulation.

During the high-growth era, the competition preventing regulation was stronger for declining industries such as agriculture and much milder for rapidly developing industries such as auto industries. This meant that, through this process of inter-industrial conflicts, innovation rents accrued in the auto industry were spilled over to agriculture. In summary, with the role of intermediate organizations fulfilled by industrial associations, equality of income distribution was pursued in this system.

8.3 Privatization of Property Rights and the Dissolution of Community in England

This section discusses the development of property rights, the growth of the market economy and the process of the dissolution of the rural community in England from the late medieval to early modern period. From a macroeconomic viewpoint, we will focus on three phases: the phase with abundant land and scarce labor during the eleventh and twelfth centuries, the land-scarce and labor abundance phase during the thirteenth century, and the labor scarce phase after the mid-fourteenth century. The population of England increased until the breakout of the plague around 1378, decreased during the fourteenth century until the last half of the fifteenth century, and began to grow again thereafter. In this sense, the period during the late fourteenth and fifteenth centuries with extreme labor shortage is special, but we will put the period together with the period after the sixteenth century without paying special attention to it for the sake of simplicity. Although the impacts of the plague were enormous and it is doubtful that the rural population recovered its thirteenth century peak level until the very eve of the industrial revolution in the eighteenth century,[8] trade, while diminished, did not disappear and markets, including the money market, survived during the contraction period.

In terms of wage movements, money wages were more or less constant and real wages decreased during the thirteenth century, while there was a significant increase in real wages during the fourteenth and fifteenth centuries.

Postan (1966) ascribes the fall of real wages during the thirteenth century to the population increase with land hunger, and the rise in real wages during the

[8]Needless to say, this partly reflects labor migrations from agriculture to industry.

fourteenth and fifteenth centuries to the decrease in population and labor supply.[9] The explanation by Postan seems to put too much emphasis on population movements. Part of the rise in real wages during the fourteenth and fifteenth centuries, for example, seems to be related to the increased demand for labor by the industrial sector. Postan (1966), however, denies this on the ground that textile exports did not increase and textile-producing areas such as York, Colchester and Norwich stagnated during the fifteenth century, and that the demand for labor also declined seriously with lords' demesne offsetting the possible demand increase in peasant tenant farming.

Let us summarize the main conclusions to be obtained below. The socio-economic system of medieval England, established on the manor system and rural communities, was based on community-based economic activities on open fields and common lands. During the eleventh and twelfth centuries, there emerged a primitive labor market in response to the increased demand for labor by feudal lords under the conditions of labor scarcity and land abundance. Labor employment increased substantially during the thirteenth century owing to the growth of the population. From the twelfth century onward, concomitant with the development of international trade in Europe, the commodity market based on monetary transaction also developed in England, and this gave rise to the conversion of the serf labor system into the lease tenancy system, which provided the basis for the development of the market-based transaction of land and labor. At the same time, land hunger due to population growth led to the legislation that gave *de jure* property rights to lords. The full-scale dissolution of community-based economic activity was brought about during the enclosure movement that started substantially in the second half of the fifteenth century and reached its height during the sixteenth to the first half of the eighteenth century. With the disappearance of communal agricultural practice and common lands, the de facto establishment of property rights proceeded. A massive industrial labor force was created as peasants (custom-holders) lost their tenancy rights and were evicted from villages. In this way, the decline of the manor system and the dissolution of the rural community proceeded simultaneously with the development of the labor market over three centuries. During the process it is conjectured that the human capital that was originally community-specific by and large gradually became general as people chose human capital suitable for market transactions. The dissolution of communities went on smoothly, with the consequent birth of a society based on individuality and property rights.

8.3.1 The Manor System and the Rural Community

The basic framework of the medieval England socio-economy was composed of manors and rural communities. Rural communities were formed during the Anglo-Saxon period starting from the fourth through the sixth century as various tribes

[9]The land scarcity during the thirteenth century gave rise to active reclamation and internal colonization on the one hand, and a decreased chance of land succession by young people and a consequent increase in smallholders, called cottagers and squatters, on the other hand.

migrated from the Jutland peninsular, Dean Islands and Norway, diluting the traits of old Celtic clan society and tribal bondages. The community organizations were characterized by 'community of shareholders' related to land holdings and played the role as decision-making units independent of individuals in the community (Vinogradoff 1904). The manor system was introduced after the Norman Conquest in 1066 for military, fiscal, judicial and security purposes as part of the feudal system establishment. Although rural communities were subjected to manors, the functions of communities were kept untouched by and large. In accordance with the feudal system of the infeudation of lands from the king to lords, the land rights of previous freeholders were converted into patrimonial feoffment.

Manors were composed of demesne cultivated with serf labor (labor dues) and tenured lands. The emergence of labor dues could be understood from the fact that the costs of organizing specialization and transaction through the commodity markets were high due to the insecurity of society. In other words, it was less expensive for lords to produce commodities by themselves by using serf labor than to purchase them from the markets.[10] The workforce of manors comprised villeins (serf labor) and freeholders, both of which were tenants and paid rents on leased lands. While the latter were able to return the lands to lords and leave the manor at their will, the former were unable to do so and were subject to compulsory labor service on demesnes. Both villeins and freeholders were granted rights to pass on their rights to lands to their heirs. As to the right to transfer the lands to a third person other than heirs, they were also free to do so, as long as in the case of villeins they paid entry fines to lords.

With respect to the relationship between lords and peasants, it is often claimed that peasants were legally impotent against and subordinate personally to lords. Vinogradoff (1904) criticizes this assertion, arguing that there is no stipulation in feudal law to bind peasants tightly, and that peasants stayed at particular manors because it was profitable to be engaged in villein farming even if they were subject to labor dues. North and Thomas (1971) echo this, emphasizing the contractual nature of the relationship between lords and villeins. Against this contract theory, there is a well-known counterargument by Brenner (1976), who claims that lords had to have compulsory power over peasants in order to prevent free rider problems in providing military protection for peasants, which could be considered to be public goods. In other words, lords could regulate the villeins' right of mobility through requiring that they seek permission to depart the manor and so on,[11] and hence were able to exploit villeins by raising rents. However, Brenner's argument seems to go too far in view of the fact that peasants were free to leave the manor permanently, if they wanted, and their children were not bound to stay at their birthplace. The argument by North and Thomas (1973), on the other hand, is congruent with the emphasis on the importance of the lords' military power in maintaining social security and

[10]In addition to this, transportation costs were lower for labor than commodities, and it was possible to save the monitoring costs of labor by means of manor custom laws, manor courts, and the fine system.

[11]Moreover, peasants were requested to return each year for the one or two views of frankpledge.

safety in trading. It would be fair to say that, in the contractual relationship between lords and villeins, lords had strong bargaining power over peasants based on military protection, although the power might not be so strong as could be described as a 'surplus extraction relationship' in Brenner's terminology.[12]

Rents on lands were fixed in kind or in terms of money. In addition to fixed annual rents (custom), there were rents as temporary tax (*tallage*) and key money called an entry fine paid at the time of land transfer or renewal of contracts. During the thirteenth century, rents paid in money became more popular.

The production activities in manors were carried out according to the customs of the manor and commands of the lord. The kinds of crops planted were largely stipulated by the lords and farmers cultivated open fields cooperatively. Details of cultivation, such as the timing of plowing, sowing, and reaping, were determined by the community. To reclaim and cultivate England's clay soil plains, the employment of heavy plow, *carruca* with a large ox team, usually comprising six to eight oxen, was indispensable. Keeping oxen was an essential requisite for husbandry. Moreover, the use of *carruca* represented an investment in physical capital, prohibitingly large for a single family to provide, so that peasants pooled their resources to make up a team. Managerial policy, such as the shift from a two-tier to three-tier system, was decided either by lords or by the community. Quite often communities fulfilled the role of common responsibility organization to make collective payments of tax to the lord of the manor or to the king (Vinogradoff 1904). Although it is sometimes claimed that villeins rarely produced beyond the need for their own consumption, and there was no division of labor or capital accumulation, it is also known that during the medieval period lords were intent on improvement and investment, especially reclamation, in arable farming.

The backdrop for the functioning of communities was the land system, characterized by the open field system and common lands (common use of wastelands and meadows). Under the open field system, each villein was allotted strips in the fields. The allocation was changed occasionally. The land holding of each was the sum of strips scattered around the fields, so that it was impossible to practice independent husbandry. Wastes and meadows were commonly used as pastureland for animals, including oxen for plowing, and were indispensable for peasants' lives to obtain firewood and peat. The right to use common land was rationed according to the shares in landholdings. Post-harvest stubble was also used for the common grazing of village animals. It is important to understand the reason why the strips were dispersed all over the village fields. Postan (1972) ascribes this to the logic and ethics of the common field that demanded every holder should have his share of good and bad land. It must be also noted that husbandry in manors was not necessarily subject to rigid and fixed rules and, instead, it allowed wide room for creative improvements. Especially during the fourteenth and fifteenth centuries, both lords and villagers were involved in such activities in order to adapt to the slump in open field agriculture. The substitution of wheat for rye as the principal winter crop in order to respond to the growing preference for wheaten bread, and the expanding use of legumes that

[12] Aston and Philpin (1985) give papers related to the controversy regarding Brenner's assertion.

was also caused by a shift in food preferences and resulted in soil improvement, to some extent, are typical examples.

Incidentally, Postan (1972) explains that the long and narrow form of strips in the fields also reflects the necessity of common plowing by *carruca*. The strip usually went the whole length of the field so as to reduce the frequency of the turn and the reversal of direction of plowing. The narrowness came from the fact that it was formed by a day's or half day's plow as a rule. In allotting the strips to community members, the best way was to measure in units representing the amount of land the plow could turn over in a working day.

8.3.2 The Evolution of the Labor Market

With abundant land and scarce labor during the eleventh to the thirteenth century, there occurred frequent conflicts over labor among manor lords. Villeins had the option to quit to nearby cities or manors of other lords whenever the contract term with his lord was unsatisfactory.[13] These conditions comprised the background for the emergence of a primitive labor market in the late medieval England. North and Thomas (1975) explain this as follows. There are two kinds of contract for land use: contracts with respect to labor inputs such as wage contracts or labor dues, and contracts with respect to outputs such as share-cropping or fixed rents tenancy. Let us assume that the transaction costs of contracts comprise the negotiation costs and the monitoring costs. When the commodity markets did not develop sufficiently, as was the case of eleventh- and twelfth-century England,[14] evaluating the value of products was seriously difficult due to the lack of adequate price data, so that negotiating the costs of tenancy contracts were high. On the other hand, in terms of the costs of contract monitoring and enforcing, the costs for labor-related contracts such as labor dues or wage contracts were considerable because it is usually very difficult to evaluate the amount of effort made by labor, and to verify the evaluation, while the costs for product contracts are very low, because it was sufficient to evaluate the amount, not the value, of products after the harvest. It follows that under these conditions the fact that labor dues were chosen as an equilibrium institution implies that the negotiating costs for labor dues were low compared with product-related contracts. The low negotiating costs for labor dues could only be possible with the existence of a fairly well-developed labor market.

During the thirteenth century, over-population caused by land shortage with abundant labor brought about a large mass of youngsters who could not get sufficient land,

[13]This excludes the possibility of the slavery system.

[14]There occurred criticism on North and Thomas on this point, that commodity markets had developed more than North and Thomas considered in the eleventh and twelfth centuries. North (1980) contends that underdevelopment in the period earlier than eleventh century is sufficient to prove their assertion.

and more than half the population became smallholders who could not earn enough income on their own lands. These peasants became employed labor, looking for job opportunities as workers in demesnes, villeins' hired labor or stewards. Many of them found commercial and industrial jobs as smiths, carpenters, spinners, weavers or hucksters. In some areas, hundreds of unmarried young men were sent out each year in search of employment elsewhere (Postan 1966, p. 624).

The fourteenth century witnessed the expansion of raw wool production for manufacturers in north Europe, and the fifteenth century for the newly developed textile industry in England. During the sixteenth and seventeenth centuries, the active enclosure movements for securing pastures and efficient arable farming, which will be touched upon in the next section, created a mass of landless farmers, thereby giving rise to a large-scale market for industrial workers. As a result, 60% of the population became either employed labor, out servants, cottagers or paupers in the seventeenth century (Overton 1996, p. 41). The enclosure movements brought about the mass eviction of peasants from villages; first, through the firing of the workforce for cultivation due to the conversion of arable land to pasture and, second, through making it difficult for peasants to breed their animals by grazing stubbles. The eviction of peasants and the ruination of villages occurred also by way of engrossing, where two or more farms were amalgamated into one, and superfluous farmhouses were left to fall into decay (Thirk 1967). The enclosures during the second half of the fifteenth century to the sixteenth century aimed at the conversion of arable land into pastures are called Tudor enclosure, and those from the eighteenth century onward aimed at large-scale commercial farming based on new agricultural technology are called parliamentary enclosure.

8.3.3 The Lagged Development of the Commodity Market

As mentioned in the last section, during the early and middle medieval period the costs of creating and maintaining the commodity market were considerable. The state did not recognize the necessity for developing the commodity market and, instead, was interested in raising revenues by means of granting privileges to guilds or monopolies. After the invasions by the northern tribes, the Muslims and Magyars had subsided, and peace and public order had been established, international trade in Europe, and hence the commodity markets, began to develop. In England too, in the fifteenth century after the reign of Henry II (1133–89), domestic public security improved substantially, providing favorable conditions for the development of commodity markets.

The emergence of commodity markets implied the demise of the crucial element of the manor system, labor contracts in the form of labor dues. This was because the determination of commodity prices in the market made it possible to stipulate the rental rates for lease tenancies, because it enabled the evaluation of the value of products by means of markets. The cost of negotiating contracts decreased significantly. For this reason, the tenancy contract that emerged in the twelfth century spread rapidly in the thirteenth century, and the manor system based on demesne management utilizing labor dues fell into a decline at some time during the late thirteenth century (Postan 1975).[15] In the process, farm workers in the category of villein were converted into the status either of copyholders or lease tenants. Copyholders mean those who have the legal entitlement to their lands in the form of certificates issued by manor courts among those who hold lands subject to various manor customs, called custom holders.[16] Many custom holders were later on converted into lease tenants at the request or by the coercion of lords.

Postan (1937) emphasizes the spread of the monetarization of labor dues during the twelfth century and Postan (1975) asserts that commodity market development was at its height in the thirteenth century. It must be noted, however, that the development of the commodity market was still confined to local markets for the surplus products of agriculture, and even in the sixteenth century was not nationwide (Overton 1996).[17] Moreover, there were various regulations on the markets regarding the price and quantity of trade. A fully fledged development of the commodity markets began after the sixteenth century with the improvement of the transportation system, such as roads, especially during the sixteenth to seventeenth centuries, canals in the eighteenth century and railways in the nineteenth century. The integration of local markets into a national market was completed in the nineteenth century.

8.3.4 The Privatization of Land Holding and the Dissolution of the Rural Community

The ultimate ownership of land belonged to the king under feudal law, and the law did not recognize the concept of ownership by anyone other than the king. According to the feudal enfeoffment system, lords were granted lands from the king, and peasants from lords. Between lords and peasants, there were multiple medium layers. Those who were granted land had rights to use the lands as well as to receive income, called incident (or obligation),[18] from the land. There were two ways to transfer land, by substitution or by infeudation. The former required that the land be surrendered to lords, who in turn granted the land to another, and in the latter method tenants granted

[15]Postan points out, however, that serf labor revived temporarily during the thirteenth century due to the general surge in economic activity.

[16]Lands held by villeins passed examination by the court on each occasion of surrender and alienation of landholding rights, and the new holder obtained a copy of the record at the court.

[17]Although Postan points out the development of inter-local commodity markets, his evidence seems to be confined to special local products such as tin, iron and charcoal, whose trade should not be significant in terms of quantity. Moreover, his emphasis on the regional specialization of animal husbandry does not imply the substantial inter-local trade of crops because crops could be obtained from nearby regions and the demand for crops should have been small due to low population density in animal husbandry regions.

[18]The incident was composed of the right to obtain military services, agricultural labor services, and inheritance tax, and the right to have lands granted to be surrendered, and so on.

the land to another and he became the lord of the person to whom he granted the land. The incidents remained in either case.[19]

While the enfeoffment of land was implemented individually, the cultivation of land granted to peasants was carried out collectively in accordance with community customs and they were allowed to make use of common lands, the ownership of which belonged to lords. Property rights were imperfect in the sense that it did not imply exclusive control rights. However, as the process of the so-called establishment of property rights proceeded, the common rights of farmers gradually declined over time.

The statute of Merton in 1236 and the statute of Westminster II in 1285 confirmed that freeholders had the right to have wasteland sufficient for pasturing their animals. While the right to use common lands had been tacitly approved before that time, it was formally acknowledged that freeholders' land ownership included the right to use the common lands. The lords interpreted the laws in favor of themselves, however, and claimed that their rights on land comprised the whole remaining areas after allotting the areas needed for freeholders to graze their animals (Vinogradoff 1904; Tate 1967). In other words, by these legislation the rights of lords to enclose lands at their will, provided that they left enough land for freeholder pasturing, were recognized. In this regard North and Thomas (1973) emphasize that property rights were established for freeholders and lords by these laws and by related legislation, such as the Great Charter I in 1217 and the statute *Quia emptores* in 1290. It is important to note, however, that this does not mean that lords obtained a free hand over land use or complete property rights. The right to have common land had been recognized for villeins since the old Saxon era, so that as long as demesne farming, hence the necessity for labor dues, remained, it was not possible for lords to enclose all the lands by these laws.

Our interest lies in how communal farming disappeared and how the peasants' rights in common lands were encroached on and negated as a consequence of the establishment of property rights. What is important from this viewpoint is not the *de jure* establishment of property rights as an institution, but the de facto impacts of the spread of property rights in the entire economy. We will now examine how the majority of the rural population, including villeins, came to lose their rights to common lands, with the consequent dissolution and demise of open field husbandry and rural communities. Incidentally, according to the estimation of Tawney (1912) based on a sample of 111 manors and 6203 peasants in the sixteenth century, the share of freeholders was 19.5%, and that of villeins 73.7%, the number of copyholders was 61.1% and lease tenants 12.6%.[20]

The enclosure movements beginning in the second half of the fifteenth century, substantially culminating during the period between the sixteenth and the eighteenth

---

[19]In the case of infeudation, if the person to whom land was granted from a tenant disappeared, the higher lords was apt to lose their incidents.

[20]The remaining 6.7% are classified as unknowns.

centuries,[21] brought about the conversion of land from permanent arable in subdivided common fields to permanent pasture in severalty. Enclosed land gave flexibility in farm management, offered more possibility in large-scale commercial agriculture, and raised the profitability of farm production, be it for livestock, grain or a combination of the two (Overton 1996, p. 9). At the same time, the enclosure redistributed the rights to hold and utilize lands drastically and brought about the dissolution of rural communities. The basic cause of enclosures was the decline in the relative profitability of crop production compared with animal husbandry for the following two reasons. First was the rise in wool prices owing to demand increase domestically and overseas. This is a well-known factor as was emphasized by Tawney (1912), for example. Second was the decline in the profitability of crop production due to the deterioration of soil quality. This was caused by the decrease in pasture lands for grazing animals as more pasture was put into cultivation through reclamation and new cultivation in response to land hunger. As the number of animals to be bred decreased, the supply of manure of animal origin declined, with the consequent deterioration of soil quality.

It is important to note that during the early period the development of the market economy comprised the background for the emergence of enclosures. The gradual substitution of labor dues and rent payment in kind by wage labor and money rents provided favorable ground for implementing enclosure. Owing to the development of the commodity markets and the monetarization of the economy, the feudal relationship of master and servant and compulsory labor obligations were replaced by monetary obligation, with the consequent change of the status of villeins to copyholders and lease tenants. The marketization of the feudal relationship simplified the process to convert custom holders to lease tenants, and to enclose lands by means of market-based procedures.

Moreover, with respect to parliamentary enclosure, it is worth noting that the common lands and open field system became a serious obstacle to the shift to profitable animal husbandry and the adoption of new mixed farming. Not only was it difficult to introduce the selective breeding of animals, but also the adoption of effective crop rotation utilizing turnip and clover was difficult with the system.[22] Investment in land, such as drainage, liming, and the introduction of floating meadows, was not easy when collective decision-making was required. Even if it was not impossible to adopt such methods, serious coordination failures might have arisen, reducing the effective implementation. In this sense the possibility to adopt efficient farming technology gave strong incentives for lords to carry out enclosures.[23]

---

[21] Usually the enclosure movement has been considered to be concentrated in two periods: Tudor enclosures covering the late fifteenth and the sixteenth century and parliamentary enclosures covering the eighteenth and nineteenth centuries. Recently, however, the seventeenth century is regarded as having had the fastest rate of enclosure.

[22] For example, farmers sowing tulips on their common field strips would see them eaten by other farmers' livestock (Overton 1996, p. 167).

[23] Overton notes, however, that, in addition to enclosures, engrossing of open fields was also an important factor to bring about large-scale farming (Overton 1996, p. 192).

The actual process of enclosures was diverse, but it proceeded in the following three steps in most cases: (1) the conversion of copy-holders to lease tenants, (2) the abolition of common lands by the purchase by lords, and (3) the integration of farms and the reorganization of land utilization methods. Step (1) gave rise to numerous disputes, and hence petitions, the fundamental point in dispute being whether the copies held by peasants could be legally effective in claiming rights on lands. The lords tried to promote conversion by raising entry fines, quite often leading to additional disputes whether the raise was legal, or the margin of raise adequate. The most serious issue was related to step (2). Usually, not all the common rights holders agreed with abolition, and in many cases common right holders were not necessarily land holders. With respect to Tudor enclosure especially, episodes of the injustice by lords and the use of violence to evict peasants are well known. It is said that a large number of enclosures were carried out with little regard for the interests and rights of peasants, and enclosure became the major social and political issue of the day (Tate 1967, pp. 62–73). While such writers as Gay (1903) denies the actual social importance of injustice and violence, Tawney (1912) emphasizes the conditions of the age, claiming that even a moderate change is likely to work with the most disastrous effects for those who 'tilly their grandfathers' field with grandfathers' plough' (p. 264).

From the eighteenth century onward and during the parliamentary enclosure, however, these problems were mitigated as parliament came to intervene to settle the disputes. The parliamentary law expanded the rights of lords substantially by removing common rights, which had taken the side of tenants usually in disputes with the lords before the eighteenth century. For example, it only took account of the wishes of those owning land as opposed to the common law, which took account of all those who had both ownership rights and use rights to the land. Moreover, the majority required for enclosure was calculated in terms of acres rather than the number of landowners (Overton 1996, pp. 156–158). The backdrop for this phenomenon is related to the change in public opinion, which came to put more emphasis on the promotion of efficient agriculture suitable for food supply to industrial workers instead of lenient accommodation of peasants' welfare. Partly as a result of the rapid development of enclosure, the agricultural sector in England could supply 90% of the demand for wheat in spite of the rapid increase in population—the population of England, including Ireland and Scotland, had increased from 15 million in 1801 to 27 million in 1841 (Komatsu 1953).

It is worth noting that enclosure during the eighteenth and nineteenth centuries by parliamentary law did not encounter any serious opposition from peasants.[24] This could be ascribed to that fact the enclosure process was legal and there was formal opportunity during the passage of an enclosure act for objection with a petition against the bill (Overton 1996, p. 190). Moreover, it is important to note that the

[24]Although Hammond and Hammond (1911) argue that the coercive and unfair measures taken by lords for enclosure sacrificed cottagers and squatters and aroused strong resistance by them, evidence based on the *Journals of the House of Commons* examined in Tate (1942, 1944 and 1945) does not support this assertion.

increased dependence by farmers on market transaction made it easier to resort to a market-based procedure. It is conjectured that communal agricultural practice, and the technology related to common land and embodied in peasants, were not important factors to be adhered to.

8.3.5 Summary and Reservations

So far, we have argued that the establishment of property rights proceeded in England as a gradual process from the thirteenth century onwards. The labor market that developed in the thirteenth century expanded quantitatively thereafter. *De jure* property rights were created in the same century for freeholders and lords, but the de facto realization of property rights in the economy, and hence the dissolution of communities, occurred with the enclosure movements thereafter. The movements that started substantially in the sixteenth century changed the land holding system drastically—with the consequent dissolution of the community system based on open field agriculture and common lands, creating the mass of industrial workers needed by the industrial revolution. Overton (1996) maintains that private property rights were established in England during the 300 years from c. 1550. In this way, the dissolution of the community system and the development of the labor market occurred almost in tandem and was a protracted process over a long time period from the thirteenth century onward. In such a process, it is conjectured that the human capital accumulation by the people would be largely composed of marketable general skills, so that the opposition to the dissolution of the community system was weak.

Let us add two considerations to clarify our assertion about the incentives for investment in community-specific human capital. We have argued that in England the incentive for peasants to accumulate community-specific human capital was weakened because the open labor market had developed before the establishment of property rights. In this regard, it is possible to believe that the obsolescence of community-specific human capital due to the stagnation of crop agriculture in the framework of the open field system could be another factor to weaken the incentives. The functioning of the open field system was conditioned by the availability of sufficient common land to breed animals. This is because animal breeding was an essential requirement for the system, both as the power for the plowing by *carruca* and as source of manure for preserving soil quality. The de facto establishment of property rights for lords through the enclosure of common lands meant a decrease in the pastures available for peasants, and hence the obsolescence of technology related to open field husbandry. This should certainly have reduced the incentive for the accumulation of community-specific human capital related to open field husbandry. Since this factor is independent of the development of the labor market by and large, it might be pertinent to treat this as an additional factor to weaken incentives.

We should not put too much emphasis on this factor, however. This is because the open field system was not entirely bound by rigid custom and rules and, instead, there was wide room for creative devices, as explained above. It could be argued, therefore, that until the countrywide introduction of new commercial agriculture and the substantial decline of the open field system in the seventeenth century, there remained incentives to improve existing technology and, to that extent, incentives, although weakened, for skill accumulation.

Furthermore, it could be argued that the incentives for investment in community-specific capital was weakened partly because traditional adherence to the natural community was weakened. Taylor (1989) argues that during the process of religious revolution and the enlightenment movement the clarification of the modern identity of the self and the birth of individualism resulted in an emphasis on personal commitment to the establishment of social organizations. Anglo-American Puritanism tended to strengthen the support for new communities established through personal commitments, while making light of the natural communities inherited traditionally. It is well-known that John Locke took an affirmative stance towards the enclosure movements in the seventeenth century. His justification for the privatization of landholding, that could have destructive impacts on the traditional natural community system, was that the improvement of production through the introduction of new agrarian technology was beneficial to the common good, hence was a way to come close to grace and to enhance the glory of God. Since the development of individualistic behavior was closely related to the identification of the self in modern society, this point should be more carefully examined in future study.

Finally, it is worth referring to the effect of lineage or kinship, since it is an important issue in the historical analysis of England from the viewpoint of individualist and collectivist behavior. McFarlane (1978) emphasized the absence of kinship as major evidence for individualism when he asserted that England was already individualistic in the thirteenth century. McFarlane's assertion is composed of three propositions: (1) in an agrarian society individualism means absence of 'peasants'; (2) the main characteristic of peasants lies in the collective holding of land based on kinship; and (3) the collective holding of land is synonymous with the absence of the individual right to buy, sell, lease and bequeath without reference to his kin.

Regarding the second point, Macfarlane defines 'peasants' as the extended multi-generational farm families that hold their lands collectively, a definition largely derived from east European experience, and tries to show that this type of peasant did not exist in thirteenth-century England. His proof of the non-existence of 'peasants' was dependent on a criticism of Homans (1941) on the ground that Homans does not present sufficient evidence for the existence of 'peasants' and on various circumstantial evidence about the development of the market economy.[25] In this regard, Whittle (2000) argues that the concepts of individual property and land markets were entirely compatible with a peasantry. With respect to the third point, we have confirmed that the individual right in the devolution of his land was gradually developed in the thirteenth century. French and Hoyle (2003) argue that what is important for the assertion of Macfarlane was not the legal rights but the frequency with which land was bought

[25]The existence of an active land market, the freedom of transfer by copy-holder parents to their sons, property holding by women, monetarization and social mobility, and the like are evidence.

and sold by non-familial transactions. Their examination of land transactions in an extended database seems to be incompatible with Macfarlane's presumption.

What is more important from our viewpoint is his first proposition, that the non-existence of the 'peasant' implies the individualistic nature of a society. Macfarlane claims that when property rights belong to the extended family as a whole, and the sale or inheritance of lands requires the consent of all family members, the farm is called a 'peasant', and a society without 'peasants' is regarded as individualistic. The absence of social groups based on lineage does not imply individualism in our sense, although it might be evidence for the dissolution of a clan society. In other words, there are two kinds of groups, one based on lineage and the other that emerged in post-clan society as a result of optimizing the decisions of free individuals. McFarlane is concerned with the former, while our concern is with the latter.

8.4 The Collectivism of the Japanese

We have compared the historical experience of England and Japan with respect to the development of the labor market and the establishment of property rights, and hence the process of the dissolution of the community system. In England the labor market was already in existence in the thirteenth century, and the enclosure movements from the late fifteenth century onward resulted in the establishment of property rights as well as the creation of mass industrial labor. The institutional changes related to property rights, and hence the dissolution of the rural community structure proceeded in tandem with the development of the labor market. It is conjectured that human capital had been composed of general skills, so that the division of community assets, and hence the dissolution of the community, did not encounter much opposition. In the early modern history of Japan, labor market development was confined within local areas because of the legal segregation of occupations and the restrictions on movement across feudal territories. When the Meiji government repealed various feudal regulations, liberalized the labor market and authorized property rights on land, there was significant aversion to accept the dissolution of the community-based system. It is conjectured that the human capital in the community was largely composed of community-specific skills at that moment due to the underdevelopment of the open labor market.

How much an open labor market had been developed at the time of the introduction of property rights determines the degree of penetration of individualism in society as an organizing principle of the market economy. In an economy with a developed labor market, the share of human capital embodying general skills is large, so that the dissolution of the pre-existing community system was easy. The evolution of the market economy in this case tended to be driven by the maximization of consumption utility and portfolio selection of assets assigned to individuals. In an economy with an underdeveloped labor market, a substantial part of human capital is composed of community-specific skills. Since the division of community property is difficult, the behavior of individuals in the market system is influenced by considerations of common community property even after the *de jure* establishment of property rights. The utility of individuals tends to be partly dependent on future income and consumption commonly held by community members.

Our comparison of England and Japan has shown that the former equilibrium corresponds to the experience of the market economy in the Occidental countries like England, and the latter to the experience of Japan. In the two equilibria, the meaning and scope of group behavior differ considerably. In the former equilibrium, group behavior after the establishment of the market economy is confined to what could be reduced to the utility maximization of individuals. Collectivist activity is instrumental to individual optimization. In the latter equilibrium, there remain incentives to invest in specific skills after the transition to the market economy. People have incentives to hold assets or future income in common. In this sense, group behavior has its intrinsic value in addition to and apart from the instrumental value for individuals.

As a concluding remark, we want to emphasize that the so-called collectivism in economic behavior is not directly related to the internalized part of culture of the Japanese, so that it is not necessarily an intrinsic characteristic of the Japanese. As we have argued, the internalized belief of the Japanese is historically composed of others nearby under the strong influence of Buddhism. However, deep concerns about the consequences of interaction with others nearby does not necessarily imply the collectivism of the Japanese. One can pursue religious and cultural value without organizing groups with others nearby; it is a very individualistic act at least in the case of Buddhism. We have shown that one of the frequently raised evidence for the collectivism in Japan, the sharing of collective interests, was related to the Meiji Restoration, when the private property system was established officially, and the labor market was liberalized. Individuals were motivated to share the value of community-specific human capital accumulated during the preceding Tokugawa era, and this was one of the main origins of the internationally famous 'collectivism of the Japanese'. It is true that the Meiji government emphasized the historical and traditional nature of collectivism in order to utilize the collectivist tendency of individuals for the policy of strengthening economic and military power. However, it is important to note that the 'collectivism' was based on two conditions. One condition was the large amount of accumulated human capital and the other was the imposition and repeal of the policy of restricting labor mobility. It is true that the former condition was largely a consequence of the long-term Buddhist tradition of Japan that emphasized *kyūdō* behavior in occupational lives since the Kamakura era, but the second condition was related to a very specific circumstance under the *bakuhan* system and the Meiji Restoration. Because the latter condition was brought on in a very recent historical circumstance, it is necessary to conclude that so-called 'collectivism', as the sharing system of residual income within a group, is not an intrinsic culture of the Japanese. A well-known hypothesis that emphasized collectivism in Japan contends that collective behavior is an intrinsic Japanese culture nurtured in collective labor in rice production under the condition of monsoon climate condition. Although we do not deny that there is some truth in this assertion, that this assertion is not a crucial factor is clear from the simple fact that there are many Asian rice-producing countries without any significant collectivism claimed as part of the national spirit. In other words, collective behavior in such a case is based only on instrumental, not intrinsic value.

Likewise, it is often contended or implied in influential studies on the Japanese firm system that the nature as a stakeholder society of the Japanese firm system is an innate tradition of Japanese society, historically formulated. This is wrong by and large because the stakeholder society has its origin in quite recent roots since the Meiji Restoration. The innate nature of the Japanese firm and society based on cultural history since the ancient age has very little to do with the behavior based on the sharing of residual incomes.

Finally, in the context of collectivity of the Japanese, we need to confirm that the Japanese worldview based on others nearby has both significant merit as well as serious weakness. Since the worldview nurtured historically is related to the small group of others nearby, the Japanese still seriously lacks the ability to act on the general notion of the public or mankind as a whole. This defect is clearly seen in the insufficiency of efforts in relationship with such issues as the nuclear abolition movement or global environmental protection. It seems that the lack of collective intentionality and the inactiveness of Japan in these issues is based on the self-deceptive conception of the term 'collectivism of the Japanese as a national characteristic', that has very little to do with the true collective behavior related to the notion of the public. What the Japanese are good at is group activity and not activity for the public or the humans. With respect to these issues, Japanese must learn more. Nevertheless, it must also be noted that there are important merits of the historical tradition of the group activity based on the concept of others nearby. First is the strength of individuality and the robustness of a society nurtured through the deep concerns with others nearby. The individuality of the Japanese is robust because the relationship with others nearby is based on respect for others. While the individuality of the Occident was developed largely as a one-to-one relationship with God, individuality in Japan is based on the relationship that has been nurtured through mutual respect for individual completion, and this also explains the robustness of a society that was organized as a chain relationship of small groups. The second merit of the Japanese system is that group organized as others nearby allows to be composed of diverse members. This is the basic advantage of Japanese-style group behavior. The reason for this lies in the origin of group behavior in Japan based on the image of transmigration in which individuals are incessantly interacting with different types of individuals and other creatures in nature. Moreover, since others nearby differs significantly among individuals, the Japanese have historically nurtured the ability to accommodate and harmonize diverse worldviews.

We have emphasized the robust individuality and the weak sense of the public as the intrinsic characteristics of the Japanese. It must be recalled that this exactly corresponds to the Fukuzawa's judgement in 1875, immediately after the Meiji Restoration, touched upon in Chapter 2.

References

(Japanese publication titles are translated into English by author, for the convenience of readers)
Abe K (1995) Seken toha nanika (What is 'people'). Kōdansha, Tokyo
Acemoglu D, Pischke JS (1999) The structure of wages and investment in general training. Jour Pol Econ 107(3):539–572
Acemoglu D, Johnson S, Robinson JA (2005) Institutions as the fundamental cause of Long-term growth. In: Aghion P, Durlauf S (eds) Handbook of economic growth. Elsevier, Amsterdam, pp 385–465
Acemoglu D, Robinson JA (2012) Why nations fall: the origins of power, prosperity, and poverty. Crown Business, New York
Akashi S (1989) Kinsei-kōki Keizai niokeru kahei bukka seicho: 1725–1856 (Money, prices and growth during the latter period of early modern). Keizai-kenkyū 40(1):42–51
Akerlof GA (1970) The market for 'lemons': quality uncertainty and the market mechanism. Qua Jour Econ 84(3):488–500
Alesina A, Giuliano P (2015) Culture and institutions. Jour Econ Lit 53(4):898–944
Ama T (2011) Shinran. Chikuma-shobō, Tokyo
Amino Y (1980) Nihon-chūsei no minshū-zō (Image of the masses in medieval Japan). Iwanami-shoten, Tokyo
Amino Y (1984) Nihon chūsei no hi-nōgyō-min to ten-nō (Non-farmers and the emperor in medieval Japan). Iwanami-shoten, Tokyo
Amino Y (1996a) Muen, kukai, raku (Social places out of market relationship). Heibonsha, Tokyo
Amino Y (1996b) Nihon chūsei-toshi no sekai (World of medieval society in Japan). Chikuma-shobō, Tokyo
Anderson B (1983) Imagined communities: reflection on the origin and spread of nationalism. Verso, London and New York
Ando R (2019) Rettō shukusai-ron (Festivals in the archipelago). Sakuhinsha, Tokyo
Ando S (1958) Kinsei zaikata-shōgyō no kenkyū (Study on local commercial activity in early modern period). Yoshikawa-kōbunkan, Tokyo
Aoki M (2011) Institutions as cognitive media between strategic interactions and individual beliefs. Jour Econ Be Org 79(1–2):20–34
Ariizumi S (1980) Meiji-seiji-shi no kisokatei (Fundamental process of Meiji Politics). Yoshikawa-kōbunkan, Tokyo
Asaka T (1971) Nihon kodai shukōgyō-shi no kenkyū (Study of history of ancient handcraft industry). Hōsei-daigaku-shuppankai, Tokyo
Asoya M (1994) Jyukyō to bukkyō, shintō no kōshō (Interaction of Confucianism with Buddhism and Shintoism). In: Nihon shūkyō jiten. Kōbundō, Tokyo, pp 500–503

J. Teranishi, *Culture and Institutions in the Economic Growth of Japan*, Studies in Economic History,
https://doi.org/10.1007/978-4-431-55627-5

Aston TH, Philpin CHE (1985) The Brenner Debate; agrarian class structure and economic development in pre-industrial Europe. Cambridge University Press, Cambridge

Baba M (2010) Ryōjin-hishō kudenshū (Commentary of Ryōjin-hishō). Kōdansha, Tokyo

Barshay S (2004) The social sciences in modern Japan: the Marxian and modernist traditions. University of California Press, Berkeley

Bassino J, Broadway S, Fukao K, Gupta B, Takashima M (2017) Japan and the great divergence, 1730–1874, discussion papers in economics and social history, 156, University of Oxford

Becker GS (1975) Human capital: a theoretical and empirical analysis, with special reference to education, 2nd edn. National Bureau of Economic Research, Cambridge, MA

Bellah RN (1964) Religious evolution. Amer Socio Rev 29(3):358–374

Benedict R (1946) The chrysanthemums and sword: pattern of Japanese culture. Houghton Mifflin Company, Boston

Bitō M (1992) Edo-jidai toha nanika (What was Edo period). Iwanami-shoten, Tokyo

Bitō M (1994) Ten no shisō (Conception of Heaven). In: Nihon shūkyō jiten. Kōbundō, Tokyo, pp 503–506

Blair M (1995) Ownership and control: rethinking corporate governance for the twenty-first century. The Brookings Institution, Washington, DC

Boldyrev L, Herrmann-Pillath C (2013) Hegel's 'objective spirit', extended mind, and institutional nature of economic action. Mind Soc 12(2):177–202

Bolitho H (1974) Treasure among man: *fudai* daimyo in Tokugawa Japan. Yale University Press, New Haven, CT

Botticini M, Eckstein Z (2005) Jewish occupational selection: education, restrictions, or minorities? Jour Econ Hist 65(4):1–72

Bowden PJ (1952) Movements in wool prices, 1490–1610. Yorkshire Bulletin 4:110–124

Brenner R (1976) Class structure and economic development in pre-industrial Europe. Past & Present 70:30–75

Britnell RH (2001) Specialization of work in England, 1100–1300. Econ Hist Rev 65(1):1–16

Casey MJ, Luckett O (2016) The social organism. Google Play

Coase RH (1937) The nature of the firm. Economica 4:286–405

Clark C (1957) The conditions of economic progress. Macmillan, London

Collinson P (1983) Godly people, essays on English Protestantism and Puritanism. The Hambledon Press, London

Crawcour ES (1968) Changes in Japanese commerce in the Tokugawa period. In: Hall JW, Jansen JR (eds) Studies in the institutional history of early modern Japan. Princeton University Press, Princeton, NJ, pp 180–201

Denzau AT, North DC (1994) Shared mental models: ideologies and institutions. Kyklos 47(1):3–31

De Vries J (2008) The industrious revolution: consumer behavior and the household economy, 1650 to the present. Cambridge University Press, Cambridge

Dixit AK (2004) Lawlessness and economics; alternative modes of governance. Princeton University Press, Princeton, NJ

Dōbunkan-henshūkyoku (1910) Nihon kyōiku bunko (kakun-hen) (Collection of family precepts). Dōbunkan, Tokyo

Duby G (1990) L'europe au Moyen age: art roman, art gothique. Flammarion, Paris

Durkheim E (1984) The division of labour in society/Emile Durkheim (1893); with an introduction by Lewis Coser; translated by Halls WD. Macmillan, Basingstoke

Farris WW (2006) Japan's medieval population: famine, fertility, and warfare in a transformative age. University of Hawaii Press, Honolulu

Fei JC, Ranis G (1964) Development of the labor surplus economy: theory and policy. Richard A. Irwin, Inc., Homewood, IL

French HR, Hoyle RW (2003) English individualism refuted and reasserted: the land market of Earls Colne (Essex), 1550–1750. Econ Hist Rev 56:595–622

Friedman M, Friedman R (1980) Free to choose: a personal statement. Penguin, New York

Fuji N (1944) Chūsei buke-shakai no kōzō (Structure of samurai society in medieval period). Meguro-shoten, Tokyo
Fujimoto M (1978) Sorai ni okeru seido to hūzoku (Institutions and hūzoku in Sorai). Machikaneyama-ronsō (Nihon-gaku) 12:1–18
Fukushima M (1967) Nihon-shihonshugi to ie seido (*Ie* system and Japanese capitalism). Tokyo-daigaku-shuppankai, Tokyo
Fukuzawa Y (1975) Bunmei-ron no gairyaku (Introduction on civilization). Matsuzawa H (ed), Iwanami-shoten, Tokyo
Furushima T (1954) Nihon nōgyō gijyutsu-shi (History of agricultural technology). Jicho-sha, Tokyo
Fushimi M (2011) Kinsei nōgyō-shi no kaishaku; seiryōki no kenkyū (Understanding agricultural history of early modern Japan: a study on seiryōki). Shibundō-shuppan, Tokyo
Gay EF (1903) Inclosures in England in the sixteenth century. The Quar Jour Econ 17(4):576–597
Gomi F, Ito S (2002) Tenkanki no tochi-shoyū (Landholding during the turning period). In: Watababe T, Gomi F (eds) Tochi-shoyū-shi (Shin taikei nihon-shi vol 3). Yamakawa-shuppansha, Tokyo, pp 165–203
Goza Y (2016) Ōnin no ran (Ōnin war). Chūōkōron-shinsha, Tokyo
Gray J (1993) Post-liberalism: studies in political thought. Routledge, London and New York
Greif A (1993) Contract enforceability and economic institutions in early trade: the Maghribi trader's coalition. Am Econ Rev 83(3):525–548
Greif A (1994) Cultural beliefs and the organization of society: a historical and theoretical reflection on collectivist and individualist societies. Jour Pol Econ 102(5):912–950
Greif A (2006) Institutions and the path to the modern economy; lessons from medieval trade. Cambridge University Press, New York
Guiso L, Sapienza P, Zingales L (2006) Does culture affect economic outcomes? Jour Econ Per 20(2):23–48
Guiso L, Sapienza P, Zingales L (2016) Long-term perspective. Jour Euro Econ As 14(6):1401–1436
Habermas VJ (1981) Theorie des Kommunikativen Handelns. Suhrkamp Verlag, Frankfurt am Main
Hall JW (1990) The Muromachi *bakufu*. In: Yamamura K (ed) The Cambridge history of Japan, vol 3. Medieval Japan. Cambridge University Press, Cambridge, pp 175–230
Hall JW (1991) The *bakuhan* system. In: Hall JW (ed) The Cambridge history of Japan, vol 4. Early modern Japan. Cambridge University Press, Cambridge, pp 128–182
Hammond JL, Hammond B (1911) The village labourer 1760–1832: A study in the government of England before the Reform Bill. Longmans, Green and Co., London
Hands DW (2001) Reflection without rules: economic methodology and contemporary science theory. Cambridge University Press, Cambridge
Hanley SB (1983) A high standard of living in nineteenth-century Japan: fact or fantasy? Jour Econ Hist 43(1):183–192
Hart O (1995) Firms, contracts and financial structure. Oxford University Press, Oxford
Hasegawa Y (2004) Jyoshō, kinsei tochi-shoyū shi no genzai (Introduction to the study of land-holding history). In: Chūsei kinnsei tochi-shoyū shi no saikōchiku. Aoki-shoten, Tokyo, pp 3–22
Hashikawa B (1975) Kokutai-ron no rensō, sono shūchi to ifu (Association of kokutai-ron: shyness and awe). Tenbou (Chikuma-Shobō) 201:16–35
Hashino T (2005) Toiya-sei kara kōjyō-sei he, senkanki nihon no orimono-gyō (From wholesaler-system to factory system). In: Okazaki T (ed) Seisan-soshiki no Keizai-shi. Tokyo-daigaku-shuppankai, Tokyo, pp 33–74
Hashita T (1975) Ryōshu shihai to hō (Reigning by lords and legal system). In: Iwanami- koza: nihon-rekishi vol 5 (chūsei 1). Iwanami-shoten, Tokyo, pp 169–210
Hattori S (1991) Ie seiritsu-shi no kenkyū: sosen-saishi, on-na, kodomo (Study of emergence of *ie*: religious rites of ancestors, women and children). Azekura-shobō, Tokyo
Hayami A (1973) Nihon ni okeru keizai-shakai no tennkai (Development of socio-economy in Japan). Keio-tsūsin, Tokyo

Hayami A (1988) Kinsei nōmin no chiiki-kan-idou to kaisōkan-idou (Regional and inter-class mobility of farmers in early modern Japan). In: Asao N (ed) Nihon no shakaishi, vol 6. Shakaiteki shoshūdan. Iwanami-shoten, Tokyo, pp 191–213
Hayami A (2003) Kinsei nihon no keizai-shakai (Socio-economy in early modern Japan). Reitaku-daigaku-shuppankai, Tokyo
Hayami A (2016) Japan's industrious revolution; economic and social transformations in the early modern period. Springer
Hayami A, Miyamoto M (1988) Gaisetsu 17seiki-18 seiki (During 17–18th century, an outline). In: Hayami A, Miyamoto M (eds) Nihon-keizai-shi, vol 1. Keizai shakai no seiritsu. Iwanami-shoten, Tokyo, pp 217–270
Hayami Y (1973) Nihon nōgyō no seichō-katei (Growth process of Japanese agriculture). Sōbunsha, Tokyo
Hayashi F, Prescott EC (2008) The depressive effect of agricultural institutions on the prewar Japanese economy. Jour Pol Econ 116(4):573–631
Hayashi R (1967) Edo toiya-nakama no kennkyu (A study on toiya-nakama in Edo). Ochanomizu-shobō, Tokyo
Hayashi R (1992) Nihon no kinsei vol. 5 Shounin no katsudou (Activities of merchants in early modern in Japan). Chūōkōronsha, Tokyo
Hayashima D (2017) Chusei no kinyū (Financial system in medieval period). In: Nihon-keizai no rekishi, vol 1. Iwanami-shoten, Tokyo, pp 116–142, 143–145
Hicks JR (1969) A theory of economic history. Oxford University Press, London, Oxford and New York
Hicks JR (1989) A market theory of money. Clarenden Press, Oxford University Press, Oxford
Hill C (1967) Society and puritanism in pre-revolutionary England. Secker & Warburg, London
Hirai N (1994) Shinbutsu kōsho to shintō no jiritsu (Interaction with Buddhism and independence of Shintoism). In: Nihon shūkyō jiten. Kōbundō, Tokyo, pp 60–64
Hiraoka S (2016) Gou toha nanika: koui to dōtoku no bukkyō shisō-shi (What is gō: history of thought on behavior and ethic). Chikima-shobō, Tokyo
Hirayama Y (2018) Sengoko daimyo to kunishū (Warloads and citizen). Kadokawa, Tokyo
Hōgetsu K (1943) Chūsei kangai-shi no kenkyū (Study of history of irrigation in medieval period). Yoshikwa-kōbunkan, Tokyo
Homans GC (1960) English villagers of the thirteenth century. Russell & Russell, New York
Hongō T (1994) Tsūzoku dōtoku niokeru jyukyō-teki yōso (Confucianism elements in popular ethics). In: Nihon shūkyō jiten, Kōbundō, Tokyo, pp 514–521
Hoshino (1971) Kyō-gyō-shin-shō no shisō to naiyō (Idea and content of Kyō-gyō-shin-shō). In: Hoshino M, Ishida M, Ienaga S (eds) Nihon shisō-shi taikei, vol 11. Shinran. Iwanami-shoten, Tokyo, pp 495–576
Hoshino M, Ishida M, Ienaga S (eds) (1971) Nihon shisō-shi taikei, vol 11. Shinran. Iwanami-shoten, Tokyo
Ichimura H (2011) Hūshikaden (sacred book of 'no' drama). Kōdansha gakujyutu bunko, Kōdansha, Tokyo
Ida S (1979) Minyaku-yakukai chūdan no ronri (Logic of interruption of translation of the Social Contract). Shisou (Iawanami-shoten) 641:54–83
Ienaga S (1940) Nihon no shisōshi ni okeru hitei no ronri no hattatsu (Development of the logic of negation of present life in Japan). Kōbundō, Tokyo
Ienaga S (1953) Shujyū-dōtoku no ichi-kōsatsu (On the ethical relationship between master and servant). Shigaku-zasshi 62(3):1–20
Ienaga S (1997) Inenaga saburō-shū (Collected papers of Ienaga Saburō), vol 2. Iwanimi-shoten, Tokyo
Ike T (1992) Sengoku, shokuhou-ki no choutei-seiji (Imperial court politics during Warring States period and age of Oda and Toyotomi). Hitotsubashi-daigaku kenkyū-nenpō (keizaigaku-kenkyū) 33, pp 171–253

Ikegami E (1995) The taming of the samurai class: honorific individualism and the making of modern Japan. Harvard University Press, Cambridge, MA

Ikegami Y et al (1995) Chronic sengoku-jidai (Chronic warring states period). Kōdansha, Tokyo

Ikoma T (2018) Chikushō, gaki, jigoku no chūsei bukkyō-shi (History of Buddhism in medieval japan: beasts, hungry devils and hell). Yoshikawa-kōbunkann, Tokyo

Inaba Y (1981) Nihon chusei shakai-siron (History of medieval period society of Japan). Tokyo-daigaku-shuppankai, Tokyo

Inagaki Y (1975) Chūsei no nōgyō-keiei to shūshu-keitai (Pattern of management and income distribution in medieval agriculture). In: Nihon-chūsei-shakai shiron. Tokyo-daigaku-shuppankai, Tokyo, pp 189–228

Imai M (2015) Shinran to *Tan-ni-shō* (Shinran and Tan-ni-shō). Yoshikawa-kōbunkan, Tokyo

Inoue M (1956) Nihon jyōdo-kyō seiritsu-shi no kenkyū (Establishment of Jyōdo-kyō in Japan). Yamakawa-shuppansha, Tokyo

Irokawa D (1970) Meiji no bunka (Culture of Meiji). Iwanami-shoten, Tokyo

Irokawa D (1998) Jiyū-minken-shisō (Freedom and people's rights movement). In: Iwanami tetsugaku shisō jiten. Iwanami-shoten, Tokyo, p 729

Yū Ishida (1976) Nihon kindai shisōshi ni okeru hō to seiji (Law and politics in the history of political ideas of modern Japan). Iwanami-shoten, Tokyo

Ishii K (1976) Nihon keizai-shi (History of Japanese economy). Tokyo-daigaku-shuppankai, Tokyo

Ishii K (2007) Keizai hatten to ryōgae-shō kinyū (Economic development and financing by money-changers). Yūhikaku, Tokyo

Ishii S (1966) Kenryoku to Tochi-shoyū (Political power and land-holding). Tokyo-daigaku-shuppankai, Tokyo

Ishimota T (1956) Kodai-makki seiji-shi-jyosetsu (Introduction to political history at the end of ancient era). Miraisha, Tokyo

Ishimota T (1972) Kaisetsu (Commentary). In: Ishii and others (ed) Nihon shisō-taikei, vol 21. Chūsei seiji-shakai shisō (jyō). Iwanami-shoten, Tokyo, pp 565–646

Isogai F (2002) Chūsei no nōgyō to kikō (Agriculture and climate in medieval period). Yoshikawa-kōbunkan, Tokyo

Itō H (1910) Some reminiscences of the grant of the new constitution. In: Okuma S (ed) Fifty years of new Japan. Kraus Reprint Co, London, pp 122–132

Itō S (2012) Shintō toha nanika (What is Shintoism). Chūōkōron-shinsha, Tokyo

Itō T, Momoki T (1990) Jiten Shōwa senzenn-ki no nihon: seido to jittai (Japan during the former half of Shōwa: institutions and reality). Yoshikawa-kōbunkan, Tokyo

Iwahashi M (1976) Tokugawa jidai no kahei-sūryō (Money supply in Tokugawa era). In: Sūryō-keizaishi ronshū, vol 1. Nihon Keizai no hatten. Nihonkeizai-shinbunsha, Tokyo, pp 241–260

Iwasaki M (1981) Nihon rekishi-gaku kenkyū-sousho vol 17, Kinsei ninon bukka-shi no kenkyū: kinnsei beika no kōzō to hendō (History of prices in early modern Japan: rice price). Ōhara-shinseisha, Tokyo

Jones EL (1988) Growth recurring: economic change in world history. The University of Michigan Press, Ann Arbor

Kagawa T (1974) Mitsui-ryōgaeten no keiei to chikuseki (Management and asset accumulation by money-changer Mitsui). Mitsui-bunko-ronsō 8:1–86

Kaji N (1990) Jyukyō toha nanika (What is Confucianism). Chūōkōron-shinsha, Tokyo

Kajiyama Y (1976) Han-nya-kyō, kū no sekai (Han-nya-kyō: the world of *kū*). Chūōkōron-sha, Tokyo

Kajiyama Y (1983) Satori to ekō (*Satori* and *ekō*). Kōdansha, Tokyo

Kamata S (1986) Miyamoto Musashi: gorin no sho (Commentary on *Gorin no sho*). Kōdansha, Tokyo

Kanai M (1962) Nihon-rekishi-sinsho, Hansei (Governing han). Shibundō, Tokyo

Kanda C (2010) Shūkyō de yomu sengoku-jidai (Warring states period from the viewpoint of religion). Kōdansha, Tokyo

Kaneko T (1998) Chūsei buke-seiken to seiji-chitsujyo (Samurai Government and political order in medieval period). Yoshikawa-kōbunkan, Tokyo

Kasahara K, Shimode S (1977) Bukkyō no denrai to Nara-bukkyō no keisei (Introduction of Buddhism and emergence of Nara Buddhism). In: Kasahara K (ed) Nihon shūkyō-shi. Yamakawa-shuppansha, Tokyo, pp 35–62

Kasaya K (1999) Jyoron, ie no gainen to sono hikaku-shi-teki kōsatu (Concept of *ie* in comparative historical perspective). In: Kasaya K (ed) Kuge to buke, vol 2. Ie no hikaku-bunmei-shi-teki kōsatsu. Shibunkaku-shuppan, Kyoto, pp 3–26

Katō S (1984) Edo-shisō no kanōsei to genjitsu (Possibility and reality in Edo ideas). In: Nihon no meicho, vol 18. Tominaga Chūki, Ishida Baigan. Chūōkōron, Tokyo, pp 7–50

Katō S (2007) Nihon ni okeru jikan to kūkan (Time and space in Japan). Iwanami-shoten, Tokyo

Katsumata S (1978) Sengoku-hō no tenkai (Development of legal system during Warring States period). In: Nagahara K, Hall JW, Yamamura K (eds) Sengoku-jidai:1550nen kara 1650nen no shakai-tenkan. Yoshikawa-kōbunkan, Tokyo, pp 107–125. English edition: Nagahara K, Hall JW, Yamamura K (ed) Japan before Tokugawa: political consolidation and economic growth, 1500 to 1650. Princeton University Press, Princeton, NJ

Katsumata S (1979) Sengoku-hō seiritsu-siron (Rise of legal system in the Warring States period). Tokyo-daigaku-shuppankai, Tokyo

Katsumata S (1996) Sengoku-jidai-ron (On the Warring States period). Iwanami-shoten, Tokyo

Kawai Y (2013) Jishō-jyuei no nairan to Kamakura bakufu no seiritsu (Internal war of Jishō-jyuei and establishment of Kamakura *bakufu*). In: Nihon-rekishi, vol 6. Iwanami-shoten, Tokyo, pp 61–96

Kida K (2017) Chūsei ni okeru fudosan-kakaku no kettei-kōzō (Determination of property price during the medieval period). In: Nihon-keizai no rekishi, vol 1. Iwanami-shoten, Tokyo, pp 177–196

Kikuchi Y (1969) Nihon kodai tochi-shoyū no kenkyū (Study on landholding in ancient Japan). Tokyo-daigaku-shuppankai, Tokyo

Kitō H (2002) Bunmei to shite no edo-shisutemu (Edo system as a civilization). Kōdansha, Tokyo

Kitō H (2007) Zusetsu jinkōde miru nihon-shi; jyōmon-jidai kara kin-mirai-shakai made (History of Japan from the viewpoint of population). PHP kenkyūjyo, Tokyo

Koizumi Y (Hearn L) (1896) Zensei no kan-nen (Conception of past lives). In: Koizumi Y (1951) Kokoro: nihonjin no naimen-seikatsu no anji to eikyō (trans: Hirai T). Iwanami-shoten, Tokyo, pp 216–245

Komatsu Y (1953) Eikoku shihonshugi no Ayumi (History of British capitalism). Waseda-daigaku-shuppankai, Tokyo

Koyasu N (1998) Chūkū (Loyalty and filial). In: Iwanami tetsugaku shisō Jiten, p 1074

Kurata H (1952) Shinran (Shinran: a novel). Kadokawa-shoten, Tokyo

Kuroda T (1975) Nihon chūsei no kokka to shūkyō (State and religion in medieval Japan). Iwanami-shoten, Tokyo

Kuznets S (1966) Modern economic growth. Yale University Press, New haven, CT

Landes DS (1969) The unbounded Prometheus: technological changes and industrial development in Western Europe from 1750 to the present. Cambridge University Press, Cambridge

Landes DS (2000) Culture makes almost all the difference. In: Harrison LE, Huntington SP (eds) Culture matters: how value shape human progress. Basic Books, a member of the Perseus Books Group, pp 2–28

Locke J (1690) Two treatises of government. In: The works of John Locke, a new edition corrected, vol 5. Thomas Tegg etc., London, pp 207–485

MacFarlane A (1978) The origin of English individualism. Basil Blackwell, Oxford

Maddison A (2007) Contours of the world economy, 1–2030 AD; essays in macro-economic history. Oxford University Press, London

Maruyama M (1952) Nihon seiji shisō-shi kenkyū (Study on the history of political thought in Japan). Tokyo-daigaku-shuppankai, Tokyo

Maruyama M (1956) Chō-kokka-shugi no ronri to shinri (Logic and psychology of Ultra-nationalism). In: Gendai seiji no shisō to kōdō, vol 1. Miraisha, Tokyo, pp 7–24
Maruyama M (1960) Chūsei to hangyaku (Loyalty and rebellion). In: Ito S, Odagiri H (ed) Kindai-nihon sisō-shi kōza 6 Jiga to kankyō. Chikima-shobō, Tokyo. Reprinted in Maruyama Masao chosaku-shū vol 8 1959–1960 (1996), Iwanami-shoten, Tokyo, pp 163–277
Maruyama M (1961) Nihon no shisō (Thoughts in Japan). Iwanami-shoten, Tokyo
Matsumoto S (1956) Jyoron (Introduction). In: rekishigaku-kenkyūkai, nihon-shi-kenkyūkai (ed) Nihon rekishi kōza, vol 2. kodai-chūsei, Tokyo-daigaku shuppankai, Tokyo pp 1–18
Matsumoto S (1971) Atarashii seiji-ishiki no hōga (Emergence of new political thinking). In: Hashikawa B, Matsumoto S (eds) Kindai-nihon seiji-shisō-shi. Yūhikaku, Tokyo, pp 3–32
Matsumoto S (1974) Kindai nihon no chiteki jyōkyō (Intellectual situation of modern Japan). Chūōkōronsha, Tokyo
Matsuzawa Y (2009) Meiji Chihō-jichi-taisei no kigen (Origin of local self-government in Meiji). Tokyo-daigaku-shuppankai, Tokyo
McCloskey DN (2006) The bourgeois virtues: ethic for an age of commerce. The university of Chicago Press, Chicago and London
McGrath AE (1997) Christianity: an introduction. Blackwell, Malden MA, Oxford and Carlton, Australia
Merton RK (1938) Science, technology, and society in seventeenth-century England. Howard Fertig Press, New York
Mill JS (1859) On liberty. Shields CV (ed), The liberal Arts Press, New York
Minami R (1970) Nihonkeizai no Tenkanten (Turning point in Japanese economy). Sōbunsha, Tokyo
Minamoto R (1984) Senkuteki keimou-shisou-ka Bantō to Seiryō (Pioneering thinker Bantō and Seiryō) In: Nihon no meicho, vol 23. Yamagata Bantō, Kaiho Seiryō. Chūōkōron, Tokyo, pp 5–84
Miyagi K (1987) Nihon no kindaika to jyukyō-teki shutai (Confucianism subject in the modernization of Japan). Nihonshi kenkyū 295:129–151
Miyamoto M (1938) Kabunakama no kenkyū (Study on trade association). Yūhikaku, Tokyo
Miyamoto M (1941) Kinsei shōnin-ishiki no kenkyū (Study on the mental attitude of merchants during the early modern period). Yūhikaku, Tokyo
Miyamoto M (1988) Kinsei nihon no shijyō-keiai (Market economy in early modern Japan). Yūhikaku, Tokyo
Miyamoto M (2009) Shijyō to kigyō (Market and firms). In: Miyamoto M, Kasuya M (eds) Keieishi; Edo no keiken 1600–1882. Mineruva-shobō, Kyoto, pp 49–83
Miyazaki R (1980) Taisho demokurashi-ki no nouson to seitou (2) (Villages and political parties during the period of Taisho-democracy [2]). Kokka-gakkai-zassi 93(9,10):693–750
Mizubayashi A (1987) Hōken-sei no saihen to nihon-teki shakai no kakuritsu (nihon-tsūshi 2) (Reorganization of feudal system and establishment of Japanese-style society: history of Japan vol 2). Yamakawa-shuppansha, Tokyo
Mokyr J (1999) Editor's introduction: the new economic history and the industrial revolution. In: Mokyr J (ed) The British industrial revolution; an economic perspective. Westview Press, a member of the Perseus Books Group, pp 1–127
Mokyr J (2002) The gifts of Athena: historical origins of the knowledge economy. Princeton University Press, Princeton and Oxford
Mokyr J (2017) A culture of growth: the origins of the modern economy. Princeton University Press, Princeton and Oxford
Morishima M (1984) Naze nihon wa seikou sitaka: senshin-gijyutsu to nihon-teki sinjyō (Why Japan succeeded: advanced technology and Japanese way of thinking). TBS-buritanika, Tokyo
Morishima M (2004) Naze nihon wa ikidumatta noka (Why Japan came to face impasse). Iwanami-shoten, Tokyo
Morishita T (2012) Bushi to iu mibun, jyōka-machi no kashin-dan (Status of bushi). Yoshikawa-kōbunkan, Tokyo
Motoki Y (1994) Bushi no seiritsu (Emergence of bushi). Yoshikawa-kōbunkan, Tokyo

Muta K (1996) Senryaku to siteno kazoku: kindai nihon no kokumin kokka keisei to jyosei (Family as a strategy: formation of nation state and women in modern Japan). Shinchōsha, Tokyo
Muta K (1999) Kawashima Takeyoshi, Nihon-shakai no kazōkuteki-kōsei (Review of Kawashima, *Nihon-shakai no kazōkuteki-kōsei*). In: Tsutsui K (ed) Nihon no rekishi shakai-Gaku. Iwanami-shoten, Tokyo, pp 123–133
Nagahara K (1961) Nihon hōkensei seiritsu-katei no kenkyū (Study on the process of establishment of feudal system). Iwanami-shoten, Tokyo
Nagahara K (1968) Nihon no chūsei-shakai (Medieval society in Japan). Iwanami-shoten, Tokyo
Nagahara K (1973) Nihon chūsei shakai-kōzou no kenkyū (Study on social structure in medieval Japan). Iwanami-shoten, Tokyo
Nagahara K (1974) Nihon no rekishi, vol 10. Gekokujyō no jidai (Age of *gekokujyō*). Chūōkōron-shinsha, Tokyo
Nagahara K (1978) Daimyo-ryōgoku-ka no kandaka-sei: tōgoku-daimyo wo chūsin to shite (*Kandaka* system in daimyo domains: case of Northern Japan). In: Nagahara K, Hall JW, Yamamura K (ed) Sengoku-jidai:1550nen kara 1650nen no shakai-tenkan. Yoshikawa-kōbunkan, Tokyo, pp 1–21. English edition: Japan before Tokugawa: political consolidation and economic growth, 1500 to 1650. Princeton University Press, Princeton, NJ
Nagahara K (1980) Nion-keizai-shi (Economic history of Japan). Iwanami-shoten, Tokyo
Nagahara K (1998) Shōen (Manor system). Yoshikawa- kōbunkan, Tokyo
Nagahara K (2001) Nihon no chūsei-kokka (Mevieval state in Japan). Iwanami-shoten, Tokyo
Najita T (1987) Visions of virtue in Tokugawa Japan: the Kaitokudō, the merchant academy of Osaka. University of Chicago Press, Chicago and London
Nakai N (1961) Bakuhan-shakai to shōhin-ryūtsū (*Bakuhan* society and commodity distribution). Hanawa-shobō, Tokyo
Nakamura S (2019) Sosai-gaku no shisōken (World of Sorai-gaku thoughts). Perikansha, Tokyo
Nakamura T (1985) Meiji-Taishō-ki no Keizai (Economy during Meiji Taishō period). Tokyo-daigaku-shuppankai, Tokyo
Nakamura T (ed) (1997) Nihon no Keizai-hatten to zairai-sangyō (Economic development and indigenous industry in Japan). Yamakawa-shuppansha, Tokyo
Nakamura T (2015) Meiji Taishō-shi (History of Meiji-Taisho). Hara A, Abe T (eds), Tokyo-daigaku-shuppankai, Tokyo
Nakanishi S (2002) Kinsei, kindai no shōnin (Merchants during early modern and modern period). In: Sakurai E, Nakanishi S (eds) Ryūtsū keizai-shi. Yamakawa-shuppansha, Tokyo, pp 149–198
Nakayama S (1993) Kinsei nihon no kagaku-sisō (Ideas of science in early modern Japan). Kōdansha, Tokyo
Nakazawa S (1994) Akutō-teki shikou (Way of thinking of *akutō*). Heibonsha, Tokyo
Naramoto T (1973) Ninomiya Sontoku no hito to shisō (Person and idea of Ninomiya Sontoku). In: Nihon-shisō taikei, vol 52. Ninomiya Sontoku and Ohhara Yūgaku. Iwanami-shoten, Tokyo, pp 403–441
Needham J (1969) The grand titration; science and society in east and west. Routledge, London and New York
Nishiyachi H (2002) Chūsei tochi-shoyū kenkyū no shiten (Viewpoint of the study on landholding in medieval period). In: Watababe T, Gomi F (eds) Shin-taikei nihon shi, vol 3. Tochi-shoyū shi. Yamakawa-shuppansha, Tokyo, pp 165–203
Nishio M, Yasuraoka K (1228) Tsurezure-gusa (Commentary on *Tsurezure-gusa*). Iwanami-shoten, Tokyo
Nishitani M (2004) Chūsei kōki ni okeru kakyū tochi-shoyū no tokushitsu to hensen (Characteristics and evolution of lower-level landholding during late medieval period). In: Chūsei kinnsei tochi-shoyū shi no sai-kōchiku. Aoki-shoten, Tokyo, pp 43–72
Nishitani M (2006) Nihon chūsei no shoyū-kōzō (Property ownership in medieval Japan). Hanawa-shobō, Tokyo

Nishitani M (2015) Chūsei-kōki ni okeru Yamashiro-no-kuni Kamikuse-no-sou no nōgyō-seisan-ryoku (Agricultural productivity in Yamashiro-no-kuni Kamikuse-no-sou during the late medieval period). Fukuoka-daigaku Jinbun-ronsō 47(3):679–730
Nishitani M (2017) Chūsei no nōgyō-kōzō (Structure of agriculture in Medieval era). In: Nihon-keizai no rekishi, vol 1. Iwanami-shoten, Tokyo, pp 148–177, 230–231
Nishitani M, Nakabayashi M (2017) Shotoku to shisan no bunpai (Distribution of income and assets). In: Nihon-keizai no rekishi, vol 1. Iwanami-shoten, Tokyo, pp 33–49, 54–55
Nishitani M, Hayashima D, Nakabayashi M (2017) Seifu no yakuwari (Role of government). In: Nihon-keizai no rekishi, vol 1. Iwanami-shoten, Tokyo, pp 23–33, 54–55
Nitobe I (1905) Bushido: the soul of Japan. G.P. Putman's Sons, New York
Niwa K (1989) Tochi-mondai no kigen (Origin of land problem). Heibonsha, Tokyo
Nora E (2010) Democracy in America: historical-critical edition of 'De la démocratie en Amérique' of Tocqueville A (1835, 1840) (translated from the French by Schleifer JT). Liberty Fund, Indianapolis
North DC (1980) Structure and change in economic history. Norton & Co., Inc., New York
North DC (1990) Institutions, institutional change and economic performance. Cambridge University Press, Cambridge, UK and New York
North DC (1991) Institutions. Jour Econ Per 5(1):97–112
North DC, Thomas RP (1973) The rise of the western world; a new economic history. Cambridge University Press, Cambridge, UK and New York
Nōgyō-gijyutsu-kyōkai (1952) Meiji ikō ni okeru nōgyō gijyutsu no hatten (Technical progress in agriculture after Meiji). Nōgyō-gijyutsu-kyōkai, Tokyo
Oakley F (1961) Christian theology and the Newtonian science: the rise of the concept of the laws of science. Church History 30(4):433–457
O'Brien PK (2009) The Needham question updated: a historiographical survey and elaboration. Hist and Tech 29:7–28
Oguchi M (2002) Kodai-teki tochi-shoyū no tokusitsu to gaikan (Overview of characteristics of ancient landholding). In: Watanabe T, Gomi F (eds) Tochi-shoyū shi. Yamakawa- shuppansha, Tokyo, pp 5–10
Ōishi K (1961) Nihon chihou-gyōzaisei-shi jyosetsu (Introduction to history of financing of local government). Ochanomizu-shobō, Tokyo
Ōishi S (1975) Kinsei (Early modern). In: Kitajima M (ed) Shin-taikei nihon shi, vol 3. Tochi-seido shi. Yamakawa-shuppansha, Tokyo, pp 21–194
Ōishi S (1998) Kyōho kaikaku no shōgyō seisaku (Commercial policy in Kyōho reform). Yoshikawa-kōbunkan, Tokyo
Okazaki T (2005) The role of the merchant coalition in pre-modern Japanese economic development: a historical and institutional analysis. Exp Econ His 42(2):184–201
Olson M (1965) The logic of collective action: public goods and theory of groups. Harvard University Press, Cambridge, MA and London
Ono T (1936) Nihon Sonraku-shi Jyosetsu (Village history of Japan). Iwanami-shoten, Tokyo
Ōtō O (2015) Jinbutsu-sōsho 281 Ninomiya Sontoku (Ninomiya Sontoku). Yoshikawa-kōbunkan, Tokyo
Overton M (1996) Agricultural revolution in England: the transformation of the agrarian economy 1500–1850. Cambridge University Press, Cambridge
Pinkard T (1994) Hegel's phenomenology: the sociality of reason. Cambridge University Press, New York
Plateau J (2000) Institutions, social norms, and economic development. Routlege, London and New York
Postan MM (1937) The chronology of labour service. Trans R Hist Soc, Fourth Series 20:169–193
Postan MM (1966) Medieval agrarian society in its prime: Section 7 England. In: The agrarian origin of middle ages (Cambridge economic history of Europe vol 1), Cambridge University Press, Cambridge, pp 548–632

Postan MM (1975) The medieval economy and society: an economic history of Britain in the middle ages. Weidenfeld and Nicolson, London
Putnam R (1993) Making democracy work. Princeton University Press, Princeton, NJ
Quine WVO (1995) From stimulus to science. Harvard University Press, Cambridge, MA
Ramseyer JM (1996) Odd markets in Japanese history. Cambridge University Press, New York
Rawls J (1971) A theory of justice. Harvard University Press, Cambridge, MA
Sagara T (1968) Bushi-dō (Kyudō principle of samurai). Hanawa-shobō, Tokyo
Saito O (1988) Daikaikon, jinko, shōnō-keizai (Large-scale reclamation, population and peasant economy). In: Hayami Y, Miyamoto M (eds) Nihon-keizai-shi, vol 1. Keizai shakai no seiritsu. Iwanami-shoten, Tokyo, pp 171–216
Saito O (2008) Hikaku keizai hattenron (Comparative economic development). Iwanami-shoten, Tokyo
Sakata Y (1969) Sengoku-bushi (Bushi in warring states). Fukumura-shuppan, Tokyo
Sakudō Y (1961) Nihon kahei kinyū-shi no kenkyū (Study on monetary and financial history in Japan). Miraisha, Tokyo
Sakurabe H (1989) Ningen to sekai (Humans and the world). In: Iwanami-kouza tōyō shisō, vol 10. Indo-bukkyō 3. Iwanami-shoten, Tokyo, pp 76–94
Sakurai E (1996) Chūsei no keizai-shisō (Economic thought in medieval Japan). In: Nihon chūsei no keizai-kōzō (Economic structure of medieval Japan). Iwanami-shoten, Tokyo, pp 337–376
Sakurai E (2002) Chūsei no shōhin-shijyō (Commodity market in medieval period). In: Sakurai E, Nakanishi S (eds) Shin-taikei-nihon-shi, vol 12. Ryūtsū-keizai-shi. Yamakawa-shuppansha, Tokyo, pp 199–234
Sent EM (1998) Bounded rationality. In: Davis JD, Hands DW, and Mäki U (eds) The handbook of economic methodology. Edward Elgar, Cheltenham, pp 36–40
Santarosa VA (2015) Financing long-distance trade: the joint liability rule and bills of exchange in eighteenth century France. Jour Econ His 75(3):690–719
Sasaki G (1972) Chūsei shōhin ryūtsu-shi no kenkyū (Study on the history of distribution of commodities). Hōsei-daigaku-shuppannkai, Tokyo
Sasaki G (1964) Shōen no shōgyō (Commerce in Manors). Yoshikawa-kōbunkan, Tokyo
Satake A (1973) Minwa no shisō (Idea of folklore). Heibonsha, Tokyo
Satō H (1987) Nihon chūsei no kokka to bukkyō (State and Buddhism in medieval Japan). Yoshikawa-kōbunkan, Tokyo
Satō S (1963) Muromachi bakufu ron (Muromachi *bakufu*). In: Iwanami kōza nihon-rekishi vol 7 (chūsei 3). Iwanami-shoten, Tokyo. Reprinted in Sato S (1990) Nihon chūsei-shi ronshū (Essays on medieval history of Japan). Iwanami-shoten, Tokyo, pp 1–48
Satō S (1974) Nanbokuchō no dōran (Upheaval of South-North Dynasty period). Chūōkōron-shinsha, Tokyo
Satō S (1983) Nihon no chūsei-kokka (Medieval state in Japan). Iwanami-shoten, Tokyo
Satō Y (2014) Chūsei no hō to saiban (Laws and trials in medieval period). In: Iwanami- kōza nihon-rekishi vol 7 (chūsei 2). Iwanami-shoten, Tokyo, pp 145–180
Sawai M, Tanimoto M (2016) Nihon-keizai-shi; kinsei kara gendai made (Economic history of Japan; from early modern to modern). Yūhikaku, Tokyo
Schumpeter JA (1926) Theorie der wirtschaftlichen Entwicklung: eine Untersuchung über Unternehmergewinn, Kapital, Kredit. Zins und den Konjunkturzyklus. Duncker & Humblot, München and Leipzig
Shibata M (1971) Kaisetsu: sekimon-singaku ni tsuite (Commentary on sekimon-shingaku). In: Nihon-shisō-taikei, vol 42. Sekimon-shingaku. Iwanami-shoten, Tokyo, pp 447–510
Shikano Y (1996) Itaku kenkyukara mita hansatsu no ryūtsū-jittai (Distribution of *hansatsu*: findings by contracted research). Kinyu-kenkyu (Bank of Japan) 12:153–196
Shimada H (2012) Jyōdo-shin-shū ha naze nihon de ichiban ōinoka (Why Jyōdo-shin-shū is the largest in Japan). Gentōsha, Tokyo
Shimizu K (2018) Sengoku-daimyo to bunkoku-hō (Warring states daimyo and domain-laws). Iwanami-shoten, Tokyo

Shimizu S (1949) Teikoku-kenpō seitei kaigi (Conference to establish imperial constitution). Iwanami-shoten, Tokyo
Shinpo H (1967) Tokugawa -jidai no Shōgyō-kinyū: Nigawase-kinyū wo megutte (Financing commerce during Tokugawa era: role of documentary bills). Kokumin-keizai-zassi 115(1):29–46
Shinpo H (1968) Tokugawa-jidai no nobe-kawase kinyū (Deferred payment by bill of exchange in Tokugawa era: a pattern of commercial credit). Kokumin-kezai-zasshi 117(4):1–18
Shinpo H (1978) Kinsei no bukka to Keizai-hatten (Prices and economic development in early modern period). Tōyō-keizai-shinpōsha, Tokyo
Shinpo H (1985) Kansei no bijinesu eri-to: Osaka-shōnin Kusama Naokata ni miru Edo-jidai-jinn no keiei-kankaku (Business elite in Kansei period: management sense of Kusama Naokata). PHP kenkyūjyo, Kyoto
Shinpo H, Hasegawa A (1988) Shohin seisan ryūtsu no dainamikkusu (Dynamics of production and distribution of commodities). In: Hayami A, Miyamoto M (eds) Nihon-keizai-shi, vol 1. Keizai shakai no seiritsu. Iwanami-shoten, Tokyo, pp 217–270
Shinpo H, Saito O (1989) Gaisetsu 19seiki he (Towards 19th century, an outline). In: Hayami A, Saito O (eds) Nihon-keizai-shi, vol 2. Kindai Keizai Seicho no taidou. Iwanami-shoten, Tokyo, pp 1–66
Smith TC (1959) The agrarian origins of Japan. Stanford University Press, Stanford, CA
Sonoda M (1994) Shizen, hūdo to shintō (Nature, climate and Shintoism). In: Nihon-shukyō- jiten. Kōbundo, Tokyo, pp 56–60
Spufford M (1974) Contrasting communities: English villagers in the sixteenth and seventeenth centuries. Cambridge University Press, Cambridge
Stiglitz JE (1986) Theory of competition, incentives and risk. In: Stiglitz JE, Mathewson M (eds) New development in the theory of market structure. MIT Press, Cambridge, pp 399–449
Stiglitz JE (1988) Economic organization, information, and development. In. Chenery H, Srinivasan TN (eds) Handbook of development economics, Elsevier Science Publication, Amsterdam, pp 94–160
Stiglitz J (1994) Whither capitalism? The MIT Press, Cambridge, MA, and London
Sueki F (1998) Kamakura bukkyō keisei-ron: sisōshi no tachiba kara (Formation of Kamakura Buddhism: from the viewpoint of history of ideas). Hōzōkan, Kyoto
Sueki F (2006) Nihon shūkyō-shi (History of religion in Japan). Iwanami-shoten, Tokyo
Sueki F (2015) Sōmoku-jyōbutsu no shisō: An-nen to nihonjin no sizenkan (Idea of Buddhahood of trees and plants: view of the nature of An-nen and the Japanese). Kabusikikaisha-sanga, Tokyo
Sueki F (2016) Shinran. Mineruva-shobō, Kyoto
Sueki F (2016) Shinran: shujyō-shinka hō ni somuku (Shinran: rebelling legal order). Mineruva-shobō, Kyoto
Sugiyama H (1974) Nihon no rekishi vol 11, Sengoku daimyo (Sengoku daimyo during Warring States period). Chūōkōron-shinsha, Tokyo
Suzuki A (2000) Nihon chūsei shakai no ryūtsu-kōzō (Distribution system of medium period Japan). Hazekura-shobō, Tokyo
Tabellini G (2008) Institutions and culture. Jour Euro Econ Ass 6(2–3):255–294
Tabellini G (2010) Culture and institutions: economic development in the regions of Europe. Jour Euro Econ Ass 8(4):677–716
Taga M (1965) Eisai. Yoshikawa-kōbunkan, Tokyo
Tahara S (1983) Yamaga Sokō to shidō (Yamaga Sokō and Bushi-dō). In: Nihon no meicho 12 Yamaga Sokō. Chūōkōron, Tokyo, pp 5–76
Taira M (1992) Nihon chūsei no shakai to bukkyō (Society and Buddhism in medieval Japan). Hanawa-shobō, Tokyo
Takahashi N (2013) Kamakura bakufu-ron (On Kamakura *bakufu*). In: Iwanami-koza; nihon-rekishi, vol 6. Iwanami-shoten, Tokyo, pp 97–128
Takeda C (1971) Minzoku-bukkyō to sosen-shinkō (Folk Buddhism and ancestor worship). Tokyo-daigaku-shuppankai, Tokyo

Takenaka S, Sakudō Y (1972) Zusetsu keizaigaku-taikei 7:Nihon-keizaishi (Economic history of Japan). Gakubunsha, Tokyo

Takigawa M (1985) Nihon hōsei-shi (History of legal system in Japan). Kōdansha, Tokyo

Takashima M (2017) Keizai seichō no nihon-shi; chōchōki no GDP suikei 730–1874 (Economic growth in the Japanese past; estimating GDP 730–1874). Nagoya-daigaku-shuppankai, Nagoya

Takashima M, Fukao K, Nishitani M (2017) Seichō to makuro-keizai (Growth and macro-economy). In: Nihon-keizai no rekishi, vol 1. Iwanami-shoten, Tokyo, pp 2–23, 49–52

Tamura Y (1973a) Tendai hongaku shisō gaisetsu (Outline of Tendai-*hongaku* theory). In: Tada A, Ohkubo R, Tamura Y, Asai E (eds) Tendai hongaku-ron. Iwanami-shoten, Tokyo, pp 377–548

Tamura Y (1973b) Hogakusan-chūsho Shin-nyo-kan Sanjyūshikajyō-no-kotogaki (Original texts of Tendai-*hongaku* theory). In: Tada A, Ohkubo R, Tamura Y, Asai E (eds) Tendai hongaku-ron. Iwanami-shoten, Tokyo, pp 564–568

Tamura Y (1991) Hongaku shisō-ron (A study on *hongaku* theory). Shunjyūsha, Tokyo

Tanaka H (1993) Kindai nihon to jiyū-shugi (Liberalism and modern Japan). Iwanami-shoten, Tokyo

Tashiro K (1976) Tokugawa-jidai ni okeru gin-yushutu to kahei zandaka (Silver export and money stock in Tokugawa era). In: Sūryo-keizai-shi ronshū, vol 1. Nihon Keizai no hatten. Nihonkeizai-shinbunsha, Tokyo, pp 223–240

Tate WE (1942) Members of parliament and the proceedings upon enclosure bills. Economic History Review 12(1&2):68–75

Tate WE (1944) The Commons' journals as sources of information concerning the eighteenth-century enclosure movement. Econ Jour 54(2):75–95

Tate WE (1945) Opposition to parliamentary enclosure in eighteenth-century England. Agric Hist 19(3):137–142

Tate WE (1967) The enclosure movement. Walker and Company, New York

Tawney RH (1912) The agrarian problem in the sixteenth century. Burt Franklin

Tawney RH (1926) Religion and the rise of capitalism: a historical study. John Murray, London

Tawney RH (1941) The rise of gentry, 1558–1640. The Econ His Rev 11(1):1–38

Taya H (1963) Kinsei ginza no kenkyū (A study on silver mint in early modern era). Yoshikawa-kūbunkan, Tokyo

Taylor C (1989) Source of the self; the making of the modern identity. Harvard University Press, Cambridge, MA

Teranishi J (2005) Evolution of the economic system in Japan. Edward Elgar, Cheltenham

Teranishi J (2006) Investor right in historical perspective: globalization and the future of the Japanese firm and financial system. Asian Economic Papers 5(1):36–63

Teranishi J (2011) Senzenki nihon no kinyū-shisutemu (Financial system of prewar Japan). Iwanami-shoten, Tokyo

Teranishi J (2014) Keizai kōdō to shūkyō (Religious foundation of economic behavior). Keisō-shobō, Tokyo

Teranishi J (2017a) Rekishi to shiteno taishū-shōhi-shakai: kōdoseichō toha nani datta noka? (High mass-consumption society of Japan as history: what was high-growth period?). Keiō-gijyuku-daigaku-shuppankai, Tokyo

Teranishi J (2017b) Neoliberalism and market-disciplining policy in the Koizumi reform in Japan. In: Backhouse R, Bateman BW, Nishizawa T, Plehwe D (eds) Liberalism and the welfare state: economists and arguments for the welfare state. Oxford University Press, Oxford, pp 152–170

Teranishi J (2018) Nihon-gata shihonshugi (Japanese-type capitalism). Chūōkōron-Shinsha, Tokyo

Thirk J (1967) Enclosing and engrossing. In Thirk J (ed) The agrarian history of England and Wales (vol IV) 1500–1640. Cambridge University Press, Cambridge, pp 200–255

Topel RC (1991) Specific capital, mobility, and wages: wage rise with job security. Jour Pol Econ 99(1):145–176

Totman C (1981) Japan before Perry; a short history. University of California Press, Berkeley, Los Angeles and London

Toyoda T (1952) (Zouho) chūsei nihon shōgyō-shi no kenkyū (Study of history of commerce in medieval period). Iwanami-shoten, Tokyo

Tsuji T (1973) 'Seidan' no shakai-teki haikei (Social background of 'Seidan'). In: Nihon shisō-taikei, vol 36. Ogyu Sorai. Iwanami-shoten, Tokyo, pp 741–785
Tsurumi S (1982) Senji-ki nihon no seishin-shi 1931–1945 (Mental history of war-time Japan 1931–1945). Iwanami-shoten, Tokyo
Tsurumi S (1984) Sengo nihon no taishū-bunka-shi (Mass culture in Postwar Japan). Iwanami-shoten, Tokyo
Tsutsui K (2000) Kaisetsu, Kawashima Takeyoshi: Nihon-shakai no kazokuteki-kōsei (Commentary on Kawashima's family structure of Japanese society). In: Kawashima T, Nihon-shakai no kazokuteki-kōsei. Iwanami-gendai-bunko. Iwanami-shoten, Tokyo, pp 241–249
Uete M (1974) Nihon kidai shisō no keisei (The establishment of modern thoughts in Japan). Iwanami-shoten, Tokyo
Umebara T (1996) Kyōsei to jyunkan no tetsugaku: eien wo ikiru (Philosophy of coexistence and recycling: eternal life). Shōgakkan, Tokyo
Uno S (1999) Jiyū-shugi kyōdō-tai ronsō (on the controversy between libertarian and communitarian). Chiba-daigaku hōkei-ronsō 14(2):19–49
Uno S (2015) Ro-ruzu ni okeru zen to seigi. riberaru/komyutarian ronsō saihō (Good and justice in Rawls: revisiting controversy between libertarian and communitarian). In: Ōtaki M, Uno S, Kato S (eds) Shakaikagaku ni okeru zen to seigi. Tokyo, Tokyo-daigaku shuppankai, pp 25–48
Vinogradoff Sir P (1904) The growth of the manor, 2nd edn. (1911), G. Allen & Unwin, London
Mises Von (1962) The ultimate foundation of economic science: an essay on method. D. Van Nostrand Company Inc., New York
Wakita H (1969) Nihon chūsei shōgyō-shi no kenkyū (Study on history of commerce in Japan). Ochanomizu-shobō, Tokyo
Wakita H (1976) Muromachi-ki no Keizai-hatten (Economic growth in Muromachi era). In: Iwanami- koza nihon-rekishi vol 7 (Chūsei 2). Iwanami-shoten, Tokyo, pp 51–98
Wakita H (1988) Chūsei no mibun to bungyō-sei (Social ranking and division of labor in medieval period). In: Nagahara K, Sasaki J (eds) Nihon chūsei-shi kenkyū no kiseki. Tokyo-daigaku-shuppanakai, Tokyo, pp 35–67
Wakita O (1977) Kinsei hōkensei seiritsu shiron (Establishment of feudalism in early modern Japan). Tokyo-daigaku-shuppankai, Tokyo
Walzer M (1965) The revolution of saints; a study in the origins of radical politics. Harvard University Press, Cambridge and London
Watababe H (1985) Kinsei nihon-shakai to Sō-gaku (Sung Confucianism in early modern Japanese society). Tokyo-daigaku-shuppankai, Tokyo
Watababe T (1994) Kinsei no gōnō to sonraku-kyōdō-tai (Rich farmers and rural community in early modern period). Tokyo-daigaku-shuppankai, Tokyo
Watsuji T (1935) Hūdo (climate and culture). Iwanami-shoten, Tokyo. English edition: Watsuji T (1988) Climate and culture: a philosophical study (trans: Bownas G). Greewood Pub Group, Westport, CT
Watsuji T (1952) Nihon rinri shisō-shi (History of moral theory in Japan). Iwanami-shoten, Tokyo
Weber M (1905) Die protestantische Ethik und der Geist des Kapitalismus (*Gesammelte Aufsatze zur Religionssoziologie* Bd.1 1920 SS. 17–206). English edition: Weber M (2002) The protestant ethic and the 'spirit' of capitalism and other writings (trans: Baehr P, Wells G). Penguin Books
Weber M (1920) Einleitung; Die Wirtschftsethik der Weltreligionen, Vergleichende religionssoziologische Versuche (Gesammelte Aufsa'tze zur Religionssoziologie Bd.1 1920 SS.)
White L Jr (1978) Medieval religion and technology: collected essays. University of California Press, Berkeley, Los Angeles and London
Whittle J (1998) Individualism and the family-land bond: a reassessment of land transfer patterns among the English peasantry c.1270–1580. Past and Present 160:25–63
Whittle J (2000) The development of agrarian capitalism: land and labour in Norfolk, 1440–1580. Oxford Historical Monographs. Oxford University Press, Oxford
Yamaga S (2016) Nihon-rettō no Jishin, Tsunami, hunka no rekishi (History of earthquake, Tsunami and volcano eruption in Japan). Bere-shuppan, Tokyo

Yamaguchi K (1963) Edo jidai ni okeru kinginka no zaidaka (Issued stock of gold and silver coins in Edo era). Keizaigaku-ronshū 28(4):59–80
Yamaguchi K (1966) Hansatsu-shi kenkyū jyosetsu (Introduction on the history of *hansatsu*). Keizaigaku-romnshū 31(1):1–13
Yamaguchi K (1983) Kin-ginzan no gijyutsu to shakai (Technology of gold-silver mines and society). In: Nagahara K, Yamaguchi K (eds) Kōza nihon -gijyutsu no rekisi, vol 5. Saikō to yakin. Nihon-hyōronsha, Tokyo, pp 142–176
Yamamura K (1978) Tenka-touitsu no shosan (Consequences of integration of the nation). In: Nagahara K, Hall JW, Yamamura K (eds) Sengokujidai:1550nen kara 1650nen no shakai-tenkan. Yoshikawa-kōbukan, Tokyo, pp 206–51. English edition: Japan before Tokugawa: political consolidation and economic growth, 1500 to 1650. Princeton University Press, Princeton, NJ
Yamaori T (1993) Bukkyō toha nanika (What is Buddhism?). Chūōkōron-shinsha, Tokyo
Yanagi M (1942) Kōgei-bunka (Culture of crafts). Bungei-shunjyūsha, Tokyo
Yasuba Y (1986) Standard of living in Japan before industrialization: what level did Japan begin? A comment. Jour Econ Hist 46(1):217–224
Yasumaru Y (1974) Nihon no kindaika to minshū-shisō (Modernization of Japan and thoughts of the people). Aoki-shoten, Tokyo
Yasumaru Y (2012) Gendai nihon shisō-ron: rekisi ishiki to ideorogi (Thoughts in modern Japan: historical ideas and ideology). Iwanami-shoten, Tokyo
Yasuoka S (1998) Zaibatsu keisei-shi no kenkyū (A study of formation of zaibatsu). Mineruva-shobō, Kyoto
Yokoi K (1975) Chūsei minshūno seikatsu-bunka (Culture of daily life of medieval people). Tokyo-daigaku-shuppankai, Tokyo
Yoshida K (2014) Muromachi bakufu ron (Muromachi *bakufu*) In: Iwanami-kōza nihon-rekishi vol 8 (chūsei 3). Iwanami-shoten, Tokyo, pp 1–38
Yoshida N (1985) Chōnin to machi (Townsman and towns). In: Kōza nihon-rekishi, vol 5. Tokyo-daogaku shuppankai, Tokyo, pp 151–188
Yoshida T (1983) Ritsuryō kokka to kodai no shakai (*Ritsuryō* state and ancient society). Iwanami-shoten, Tokyo
Yoshida Y (2004) Heinō-bunri to mibun (Sword hunting and status). In: Rekishi-kennkyūkai, nihonshi-kenkyūkai (ed) Nihonshi-kōza, vol 5. Kinsei no keisei. Tokyo-daigaku-shuppankai, Tokyo, pp 133–166
Yoshie A (1986) Rekishi no akebono kara dentō-shakai no seijyuku he (nihon-tsūshi 1) (From dawn to maturity of traditional society: history of Japan vol 1). Yamakawa-shuppansha, Tokyo
Yoshikawa K (1968) Zoku no rekishi (A history of *zoku*). In: Yoshikawa Koujirō zenshū, vol 2. Chikuma-shobō, Tokyo, pp 236–249
Yoshikawa K (1973) Sorai-gaku an (A study on Sorai). In. Nihon shisō taikei, vol 36. Ogyu Sorai. Iwanami-shoten, Tokyo, pp 629–740
Yoshimoto T (1981) Saigo no Shinran (Shinran). Shunjyūsha, Tokyo
Yuki M (1965) Kinsei Nada sake keizai-shi (Economic history of sake in Nada during early modern). Mineruva-shobō, Kyoto
Zak PJ, Knack S (2001) Trust and growth. Econ Jour 111:295–321

Name Index

J. Teranishi, *Culture and Institutions in the Economic Growth of Japan*, Studies in Economic History,
https://doi.org/10.1007/978-4-431-55627-5

Subject Index

J. Teranishi, *Culture and Institutions in the Economic Growth of Japan*, Studies in Economic History,
https://doi.org/10.1007/978-4-431-55627-5

The manufacturer's authorised representative in the EU is Springer Nature Customer Service Centre GmbH, Europaplatz 3, 69115 Heidelberg, Germany. If you have any concerns regarding our products, please contact ProductSafety@springernature.com

Printed and bound by CPI Group (UK) Ltd, Croydon, CR0 4YY
22/09/2026
02220985-0007